Great Lives from History

Notorious Lives

Great Lives from History

Notorious Lives

Volume 3
Philippe Pétain - Grigory Yevseyevich Zinovyev
Indexes

Editor
Carl L. Bankston III
Tulane University

SALEM PRESS

Pasadena, California   Hackensack, New Jersey

Editor in Chief: Dawn P. Dawson

Editorial Director: Christina J. Moose	*Production Editor:* Joyce I. Buchea
Acquisitions Editor: Mark Rehn	*Graphics and Design:* James Hutson
Research Supervisor: Jeffry Jensen	*Layout:* William Zimmerman
Manuscript Editors: Sarah M. Hilbert	*Photo Editor:* Cynthia Breslin Beres
Elizabeth Ferry Slocum	*Editorial Assistant:* Dana Garey

Cover photos (pictured clockwise, from top left): Richard Nixon (Dennis Brack/Landov); Lizzie Borden (The Granger Collection, New York); Saddam Hussein (Hulton Archive/Getty Images); Adolf Hitler (Hulton Archive/Getty Images); Timothy McVeigh (Jim Bourg/Reuters/Landov); Rasputin (The Granger Collection, New York)

Copyright © 2007, by Salem Press, Inc.

All rights in this book are reserved. No part of this work may be used or reproduced in any manner whatsoever or transmitted in any form or by any means, electronic or mechanical, including photocopy, recording, or any information storage and retrieval system, without written permission from the copyright owner except in the case of brief quotations embodied in critical articles and reviews or in the copying of images deemed to be freely licensed or in the public domain. For information address the publisher, Salem Press, Inc., P.O. Box 50062, Pasadena, California 91115.

∞ The paper used in these volumes conforms to the American National Standard for Permanence of Paper for Printed Library Materials, Z39.48-1992 (R1997).

Library of Congress Cataloging-in-Publication Data

Great lives from history. Notorious lives / editor, Carl L. Bankston III.
    v. cm.
Includes bibliographical references and index.
ISBN-13: 978-1-58765-320-9 (set : alk. paper)
ISBN-13: 978-1-58765-321-6 (vol. 1 : alk. paper)
ISBN-13: 978-1-58765-322-3 (vol. 2 : alk. paper)
ISBN-13: 978-1-58765-323-0 (vol. 3 : alk. paper)
1. Criminals—Biography. 2. Terrorists—Biography. 3. War criminals—Biography. 4. Dictators—Biography.
5. Political corruption.
I. Bankston, Carl L. (Carl Leon), 1952- II. Title: Notorious lives.

HV6245.G687 2007
364.1092′2—dc22
[B]

2006032935

First Printing

PRINTED IN THE UNITED STATES OF AMERICA

Contents

CONTENTS

KEY TO PRONUNCIATION

Many of the names of personages covered in *Great Lives from History: Notorious Lives* may be unfamiliar to students and general readers. For all names, guidelines to pronunciation have been provided upon first mention of the name in each essay. These guidelines do not purport to achieve the subtleties of all languages but will offer readers a rough equivalent of how English speakers may approximate the proper pronunciation.

Vowel Sounds

Symbol	Spelled (Pronounced)
a	answer (AN-suhr), laugh (laf), sample (SAM-puhl), that (that)
ah	father (FAH-thur), hospital (HAHS-pih-tuhl)
aw	awful (AW-fuhl), caught (kawt)
ay	blaze (blayz), fade (fayd), waiter (WAYT-ur), weigh (way)
eh	bed (behd), head (hehd), said (sehd)
ee	believe (bee-LEEV), cedar (SEE-dur), leader (LEED-ur), liter (LEE-tur)
ew	boot (bewt), lose (lewz)
i	buy (bi), height (hit), lie (li), surprise (sur-PRIZ)
ih	bitter (BIH-tur), pill (pihl)
o	cotton (KO-tuhn), hot (hot)
oh	below (bee-LOH), coat (koht), note (noht), wholesome (HOHL-suhm)
oo	good (good), look (look)
ow	couch (kowch), how (how)
oy	boy (boy), coin (koyn)
uh	about (uh-BOWT), butter (BUH-tuhr), enough (ee-NUHF), other (UH-thur)

Consonant Sounds

Symbol	Spelled (Pronounced)
ch	beach (beech), chimp (chihmp)
g	beg (behg), disguise (dihs-GIZ), get (geht)
j	digit (DIH-juht), edge (ehj), jet (jeht)
k	cat (kat), kitten (KIH-tuhn), hex (hehks)
s	cellar (SEHL-ur), save (sayv), scent (sehnt)
sh	champagne (sham-PAYN), issue (IH-shew), shop (shop)
ur	birth (burth), disturb (dihs-TURB), earth (urth), letter (LEH-tur)
y	useful (YEWS-fuhl), young (yuhng)
z	business (BIHZ-nehs), zest (zehst)
zh	vision (VIH-zhuhn)

COMPLETE LIST OF CONTENTS

VOLUME I

VOLUME 2

VOLUME 3

Appendixes

Indexes

List of Sidebars

Volume I

VOLUME 2

VOLUME 3

Great Lives from History

Notorious Lives

PHILIPPE PÉTAIN
Premier of Vichy France (1940-1944)

BORN: April 24, 1856; Cauchy-à-la-Tour, France
DIED: July 23, 1951; Port-Joinville, Île d'Yeu, France
ALSO KNOWN AS: Henri-Philippe Pétain (full name)
MAJOR OFFENSE: Treason
ACTIVE: 1940-1944
LOCALE: France
SENTENCE: Death and national degradation;
    commuted to life imprisonment

EARLY LIFE

Henri-Philippe Pétain (ahn-ree fih-leep pay-ta) was born to peasants in northern France. He chose the military as one of the few opportunities available for social advancement, attending Saint-Cyr Military Academy and the prestigious École Supérieur de Guerre in Paris, where he taught upon graduation in 1888. At the outbreak of World War I, he had never seen combat.

MILITARY CAREER

During the next four years, he proved himself a very able field commander whose leadership was characterized by careful planning, meticulous attention to detail, emphasis on defensive actions, and respect for the rank and file. Pétain had no use for élan, preferring prudence to fighting spirit. Under his command, the French won the crucial Battle of Verdun (1916). The French high command then appointed Pétain as the commander of all French armies in May, 1917, in order to contain a crisis of demoralization and mutiny within the ranks. Pétain's swift application of military justice toward the mutineers is seen by some historians as a foretaste of his authoritarian rule in Vichy France; others consider that the dangers of the situation fully merited the measures taken. At the end of World War I, Field Marshal Pétain emerged an unequivocal hero, applauded by the French public and respected by soldiers of all ranks.

For the next twenty years, Pétain played a minor role in public life. In 1926, he and General Francisco Franco from Spain successfully quelled a tribal uprising in Morocco. Later he served briefly as minister of war, and in 1939 he was appointed ambassador to Spain. He supported building the Maginot Line, a line of concrete fortifications and other defenses built along the French borders with Italy and Germany; it later failed utterly to protect France from a German invasion.

Pétain found much that was attractive in Italian and Spanish fascism. He loathed communism, believed that the French nation was falling prey to moral decay, had great faith in the ability of conservative Roman Catholicism to bring about moral and spiritual renewal, and was accustomed to a military style of leadership.

VICHY FRANCE

In 1940, Nazi Germany invaded France. Faced with this crisis, the premier recalled the eighty-three-year-old Pétain from Spain and asked him to assume leadership. Pétain agreed, succumbing, as one author put it, to the flattering fallacy that he was indispensable. In early July, 1940, the National Assembly suspended the Constitution of the Third Republic, handing Pétain virtual dictatorial powers. He in turn concluded a peace treaty that left the northern half of France, including Paris, under direct German occupation, while establishing a French fascist-style puppet government in the south.

Any opprobrium attached to Pétain's premiership derives from his actions between July of 1940 and November of 1942, when Nazi Germany responded to the Allied offensives in North Africa by occupying Vichy France in earnest and Pierre Laval became effective head of state. About the same time, Pétain began showing signs of senility. By the end of the war, the mental impairment was obvious.

Pétain hoped that collaboration with the Nazis would result in a moral and economic revival in France. He reversed half a century of official separation of church and state by reintroducing Catholic doctrine into the public schools. To combat the declining birth rate, considered a symptom of moral decay, he discouraged divorce and restricted women's roles outside the home. Press and radio were heavily censored. All of this was a step backward socially but did not constitute treason. Vichy France provided provisions and economic support to Germany's fighting machine; however, the only French troops involved on the Axis side were those garrisoned in colonies.

Pétain instituted a fascist domestic militia to combat the French Resistance movement. Its brutal tactics created lingering resentment. He acquiesced in, and perhaps initially approved of, repressive measures toward Jews, who were banned from most professions and had their property placed under gentile overseers, a move amounting to confiscation. Possibly these actions saved the lives of Jews who were French citizens, 75 percent of whom survived the war. Recent refugees from Germany, of whom there were many, did not fare as well.

LEGAL ACTION AND OUTCOME

In November of 1944, the Nazis evacuated Pétain to Germany in anticipation of the advancing Allied armies. He returned voluntarily to France at the end of the war. After a lengthy trial in July-August, 1945, at which much contradictory evidence was presented, the court convicted him of treason and sentenced him to death by firing squad. French president Charles de Gaulle commuted the sentence to life imprisonment, citing his advanced age and perhaps mindful that French public opinion was nearly equally divided concerning his guilt. His codefendant Laval was executed. Pétain was transferred to the military prison at Île d'Yeu in Normandy, where he died of old age in 1951. There his remains lie, despite repeated attempts by admirers of his earlier military career to transfer them to Verdun.

IMPACT

Had Philippe Pétain remained in Spain in 1940, he would best be remembered as an able general. His later career defies simple categorization. If, as he firmly believed, resistance to the Germans was doomed to failure, then his willingness to surrender early and collaborate saved the civilian population of France from carnage such as that which occurred in Poland and Russia. It can be argued, however, that collaboration with Nazi Germany was unacceptable under any circumstances. France's early acquiescence may have prolonged the war in Europe, but even that argument is debatable. Probably the best assessment is that of a tragic figure who allowed himself to be maneuvered into a situation that posterity justly condemns but was innocent of malevolent intent.

FURTHER READING

Crane, Richard Francis. "*La Croix* and the Swastika: The Ambiguity of Catholic Responses to the Fall of France." *Catholic Historical Review* 90, no. 1 (2004): 45-66. Evaluates Pétain's pro-Catholic policies as recounted through the eyes of a liberal Catholic newspaper.

Curtis, Michael. *Verdict on Vichy: Power and Prejudice in the Vichy France Regime.* New York: Arcade, 2002. Considers that the prejudice and reactionary policies of Vichy France were a product of domestic rather than external forces.

PÉTAIN'S PLAN TO REVIVE FRANCE

On August 12, 1941, Philippe Pétain delivered a policy speech with twelve proclamations concerning his "National Revolution." Among the proclamations were the following:

Authority no longer emanates from below. The only authority is that which I entrust or delegate. . . . This is what I have decided:

1. Activity of political parties and groups of political origin is suspended until further notice in the unoccupied zone. These parties may no longer hold either public or private meetings. They must cease any distribution of tracts or notices. Those that fail to conform to these decisions will be dissolved. . . .

3. The first disciplinary sanctions against State officials guilty of false declarations regarding membership in secret societies has been ordered. The names of officials have been published this morning in the *Journal Officiel*. Holders of high Masonic degrees—of which the first list has just been published—may no longer exercise any public function. . . .

5. I will double the means of police action, whose discipline and loyalty should guarantee public order.

6. A group of Commissars of Public Power is created. These high officials will be charged with studying the spirit in which the laws, decrees, orders and instructions of the central power will be carried out. They will have the mission of ferreting out and destroying obstacles which abuse the rules of administrative routine or activity of secret societies opposed to the work of National Revolution. . . .

11. I have decided to use the powers given me by Constitutional Act No. 7 to judge those responsible for our disaster. A Council of Justice is created to that effect.

12. In the application of this same Constitutional Act, all Ministers and high officials must swear an oath of fealty to me and engage themselves to carry out duties in their charge for the well-being of the State according to the rules of honor and propriety. . . .

In 1917 I put an end to mutiny. In 1940 I put an end to rout. Today I wish to save you from yourselves. . . .

Remember this: If a beaten country is divided against itself it dies. If a beaten country can unite it is reborn. *Vive la France!*

Source: "Marshal Petain's Address to the French People," *The New York Times*, August 13, 1941.

Lottman, Herbert R. *Pétain: Hero or Traitor? The Untold Story*. New York: Morrow, 1985. Explores the continuing controversies in France regarding Pétain's place in French history.

Weisberg, Richard H. *Vichy Law and the Holocaust in France*. New York: New York University Press, 1996. Explores the role of economic factors and domestic French anti-Semitism in Vichy France.

—*Martha A. Sherwood*

SEE ALSO: François Darlan; Joseph Darnand; Jacques Doriot; Francisco Franco; Pierre Laval.

PETER THE CRUEL
King of Castile and Leon (r. 1350-1369)

BORN: August, 30, 1334; Burgos, Castile (now in Spain)

DIED: March 23, 1369; Montiel, Spain

ALSO KNOWN AS: Pedro I of Castile; Pedro el Justiciero (Executor of Justice); Pedro el Cruel; Peter I of Castile

CAUSE OF NOTORIETY: Peter earned his name by inflicting severe cruelties on his enemies and his kingdom while struggling to expand Castile and defeat his half brother, Enrique of Trastámara.

ACTIVE: 1350-1369

LOCALE: Castile

EARLY LIFE

Born in Burgos in 1334, Peter the Cruel was the oldest surviving legitimate son of Alfonso XI, king of Castile, and Maria of Portugal. Alfonso, however, preferred his mistress, Leonor de Guzmán, and her children, upon whom he bestowed many gifts and privileges. Alfonso's brutal, authoritarian rule set an example for Peter to follow upon taking the throne when his father died from the plague in 1350.

ROYAL CAREER

Sixteen-year-old Peter ruled a Castile devastated by plague and beset by economic malaise. He permitted the arrest and execution of his mother's rival, Leonor de Guzmán. Her son, Enrique of Trastámara, rebelled, was defeated, and briefly reconciled himself with the king. Meanwhile, Peter took as his mistress Maria de Padilla, who exerted great influence over him. Peter agreed to cement a Franco-Castilian alliance by marrying Blanche of Bourbon in 1353. When the French did not pay her promised dowry, Peter abandoned Blanche two days after the wedding and returned to his mistress. In 1354, he annulled his marriage to Blanche (whom he had imprisoned and later murdered), married Juana de Castro, and soon discarded her.

Meanwhile, Peter confronted a rebellion of Castilian nobles, headed by Enrique of Trastámara and aided by the Aragonese. Many Castilians resented Peter's brutal despotism, but the power-hungry nobles lacked a program to unite themselves. By 1356, Peter had defeated the rebellion and pardoned his half brothers. They soon revolted again, and Peter responded savagely, killing several of his half brothers and cousins and many other men and women with callous brutality. Peter's enemies

Peter the Cruel.

accused him of being pro-Jewish and Muslim. Like most Castilian monarchs, he relied heavily on Jewish financial expertise, and Castile's bourgeoisie generally supported him against the nobility.

Chaos and violence mounted when Peter attempted to expand Castilian territory at Aragonese expense. Aragon, the French, and the papacy aided Enrique, while Peter obtained aid from the English, led by the Black Prince (Edward, Prince of Wales). This drew Spain into the Hundred Years' War (1337-1453). In 1360, Peter drove back Enrique's invasion of Castile, but his leadership lacked strategic purpose. Sometimes Peter failed to follow up military advantages, as when he withdrew during the Siege of Valencia in 1364. In the mid-1360's, Bertrand du Guesclin and free companies of French freebooters arrived to help Enrique and to seek their fortunes at Castile's expense. Suffering reverse after reverse, Peter took refuge in France with the Black Prince in 1366. His half brother claimed the throne as Enrique II. The tide turned briefly the following year, with Peter and the English winning a great victory at Nájera. However, with Peter unable to pay the English the promised subsidy, they withdrew, leaving him to his destruction. He was defeated at the Battle of Montiel in March, 1369, by Enrique, who murdered Peter on March 23.

IMPACT

The death of Peter the Cruel left the throne to the Trastámaran Enrique II. Peter incurred the enmity of the high Castilian aristocracy by disregarding their privileges and exercising brutal autocratic power. He plunged the peninsula into a long war that destroyed his reign yet also foreshadowed Castile's growing superiority over Aragon. Although Enrique alleged that Peter was psychopathic, that he loved Jews, and that his treatment of Queen Blanche was despicable, Peter's behavior was no more autocratic, immoral, or brutal than that of his predecessors or his contemporaries. However, his Trastámaran enemies won the struggle, and thus their propaganda triumphed in the war to write history.

FURTHER READING

Estow, Clara. *Pedro the Cruel of Castile, 1350-1369.* New York: E. J. Brill, 1995. One of the best English-language studies of Peter's life, including a detailed analysis of the great contemporary account of his reign written in 1394 by Pedro López de Ayala, *Corónica del Rey Don Pedro.*

Hillgarth, J. N. *The Spanish Kingdoms, 1250-1516.* Oxford, England: Clarendon Press, 1976. Besides information on Alfonso XI and Enrique II, the book contains a chapter on Peter's reign, which emphasizes his attempt to expand Castile and create an Iberian empire.

Russell, P. E. *The English Intervention in Spain and Portugal in the Time of Edward III and Richard II.* Oxford, England: Clarendon Press, 1955. The first third of the volume analyzes Peter's English alliance and how it played out militarily in Spain.

—Kendall W. Brown

SEE ALSO: Charles II; Joan the Mad.

SCOTT PETERSON
American double murderer

BORN: October 24, 1972; San Diego, California
ALSO KNOWN AS: Scott Lee Peterson (full name)
MAJOR OFFENSES: First-degree murder of his wife; second-degree murder of his unborn son
ACTIVE: December 23 or 24, 2002
LOCALE: Modesto and San Francisco Bay, California
SENTENCE: Death by lethal injection

EARLY LIFE

The only child of Jackie and Lee Peterson, Scott Lee Peterson (PEE-tuhr-suhn) was born on October 24, 1972, at Sharp Memorial Hospital in San Diego, California. He joined a household with three half siblings from his fa-

ther's first marriage and one sister from his mother's first marriage. Peterson was doted on as a child. Living in the suburbs of affluent San Diego, he was a good student, played the piano, attended Boy Scouts, and was an avid golfer and fisherman.

After failing to make the golf team at Arizona State University, Peterson attended Cuesta College in California. He worked three jobs and played on the college golf team. In 1994, he transferred to California Polytechnic State University and majored in agricultural business. Scott met a young, beautiful coed named Laci Rocha. The two soon began dating and living together and were married in 1997. After his graduation in June, 1998, they ran a successful burger restaurant called The Shack until 2000, when they moved back to Modesto. There Peterson was an agricultural salesman, while Laci taught school nearby. In the summer of 2002, the couple announced they were expecting their first child, a boy they planned to name Conner.

CRIMINAL CAREER

Laci Peterson last spoke to her mother on the telephone on December 23, 2002. Peterson claimed that his wife was alive on the morning of December 24 and was going to walk their dog when he left to go fishing on the San Francisco Bay. Neighbors later reported that they saw him loading a large tarpaulin into the bed of his truck. After returning from his fishing trip later that day, Peterson washed his clothes, ate some dinner, and took a shower. Only then did he become curious as to his wife's whereabouts, calling police at 6:00 P.M. to report her missing.

One of the most publicized missing person's searches in U.S. history soon began, with Laci's family and Peterson himself pleading for help. A $500,000 reward was offered for her safe return, and a command center was staffed around the clock. Intense media coverage began when suspicion fell on Peterson, although Laci's family initially supported their son-in-law. In January, 2003, the police announced that Peterson had been having an affair with a woman named Amber Frey at the time of Laci's disappearance. Frey was not aware that Peterson was married at the time that she began an intimate relationship with him but contacted police when she learned Laci was missing and agreed to cooperate with them. Before Laci vanished, Peterson told Frey that he had been married but that he had "lost" his wife. She later testified that Peterson had called her during a candlelight vigil for his wife on December 31 and claimed that he was on vacation in Paris, France. Peterson continued to proclaim his innocence as he sold his wife's vehicle and their home.

On April 13, 2003, the decomposed bodies of a pregnant woman and baby boy were recovered in San Francisco Bay and identified as Laci and Conner Peterson. Five days later, Peterson was arrested in La Jolla, California, near the Mexican border, for two counts of murder. His hair was bleached blond, he had grown a goatee, and he had in his possession $15,000 in cash, camping supplies, cell phones, and Viagra.

LEGAL ACTION AND OUTCOME

Because of a great deal of publicity, a change of venue was granted, and the trial began in June, 2004, near San Francisco. Prosecutors argued that Peterson murdered

Scott Peterson. (AP/Wide World Photos)

his wife and child so that he could continue to have a bachelor's life; they presented evidence of other affairs. Almost every moment of the trial was dissected in the news, with the case dominating headlines for the duration of the trial. On November 12, 2004, a jury found Peterson guilty of two counts of murder. When the verdict was read, cheers rose from the crowd lining the steps of the courthouse. After emotional testimony from Laci's family and pleas by Jackie Peterson to spare her son's life, Peterson was sentenced to death on December 12, 2004. Peterson would await execution by lethal injection at San Quentin State Prison, which overlooks the bay where his wife's and son's bodies were found. In late 2003, Laci's parents filed a wrongful death lawsuit that sought five million dollars in compensation from Peterson; it also sought to bar him from selling and profiting from his story. The case was delayed continuously and was expected to go to trial in 2006 or 2007.

IMPACT

From the beginning, Americans were riveted by the mysterious disappearance of the beautiful expectant mother with the captivating smile. The unthinkable betrayal of her philandering husband captured the public conscience

AMBER AND SCOTT: A TELEPHONE CONVERSATION

Unknown to Scott Peterson, Amber Frey, with whom he was having an affair just prior to and after the disappearance of his wife, Laci, and their unborn son, Conner, approached the police when she became suspicious of Peterson and agreed to record their telephone conversations. One key exchange took place on January 6, 2003, less than two weeks after Laci was reported missing:

PETERSON: I have . . . I have lied to you that I have been traveling. The girl I'm married to, her name is Laci.
FREY: Uh huh.
PETERSON: She disappeared just before Christmas.
FREY: Uh huh.
PETERSON: For the past two weeks, I've been in Modesto with her family and mine searching for her.
FREY: OK.
PETERSON: She just disappeared and no one knows . . .
FREY: OK, now . . .
PETERSON: Where she's been . . .
FREY: Scott?
PETERSON: And I, I can't tell you more, because I, I need you to be protected from the media. . . .
FREY: OK.
PETERSON: OK. If you even watch the news at all, while you haven't, the media has been telling everyone that I had something to do with her disappearance. So the past two weeks I've been hunted by the media. . . . And I just . . . I don't want you to be involved . . . in this, to protect yourself. I know that I've, you know, I've destroyed. And I, God I hope . . . I hope so much that . . . this doesn't hurt you. . . .
FREY: How . . . how . . . can you possibly think this would not affect me?
PETERSON: Amber, I know it does.
FREY: Sigh.
PETERSON: But I . . . I . . . I know I had . . . I have just been torn up the last two weeks wanting to, tell you and I'm so weak that I haven't. And I just . . . just hope that . . . uh . . . I had . . . to call you and tell you that.
FREY: You never . . . you never answered my question, Scott. . . . I deserve to understand an explanation of why you told me you lost your wife and this was the first holidays you'd spend without her. That was Dec. 9 you told me this and now all of a sudden your wife's missing. Are you kidding me? . . .
FREY: I'm listening.
PETERSON: I . . . I can't now. I mean you don't understand.
FREY: But . . . I don't understand why. . . . So where is she?
PETERSON: That's what we are trying to find out. We have . . . it's a nationwide search we have . . . I mean it's a half million dollar reward for information leading to her safe return . . .
FREY: So again, you never answer my question. Why did you tell me . . . it would be the first holidays without her?
PETERSON: I can't, sweetie. I can't explain any more now.
FREY: When can . . .
PETERSON: I'm so sorry you should be angry at me and God, I hope you are. I just . . .
FREY: Yeah, isn't that what you told me before, oh I wish, you know, it'd be so much easier if you'd just hate me and not want to talk to me. And of course, the person I am of course I'm gonna say, well, you know, you told me you lost your wife. You sat there in front of me and cried and broke down. I sat there and held your hand, Scott, and comforted you and you were lying to me.
PETERSON: Yeah.

and led to courtroom commentary and to numerous Web sites, films, and books. Peterson would continue to protest his innocence and received the continued support of his family. In April, 2005, Laci's family upped the amount of their civil suit for wrongful death to twenty-five million dollars. The family feared that Peterson would profit from film deals related to the case. The death of Laci and her unborn child led to the signing of the Unborn Victims of Violence Act by President George W. Bush, which recognizes fetuses who are killed as murdered persons—a controversial law given its implications for abortion rights and pro-choice advocates.

FURTHER READING

Bird, Anne. *Blood Brother: Thirty-Three Reasons My Brother Scott Peterson Is Guilty*. New York: Regan Books, 2005. Peterson's sister offers her reasons why she now believes that her once-adored half brother killed his wife and child.

Crier, Catherine. *A Deadly Game: The Untold Story of Scott Peterson*. New York: Regan Books, 2005. As a famous courtroom commentator and former judge, Crier offers details of conversations between Peterson and Frey, interviews former mistresses and detectives on the case, and colors her hard-talking dialogue with gritty and salacious facts about the notorious murder case.

Frey, Amber. *Witness for the Prosecution of Scott Peterson*. New York: Regan Books, 2005. In a first-person account, Frey offers intimate details about her six-week relationship with Peterson and shows how she helped police once she learned of Laci's disappearance. Controversy has surrounded the book's cover, with Frey placed between pictures of Laci and Scott Peterson.

Rocha, Sharon. *For Laci: A Mother's Story of Love, Loss, and Justice*. Landover, Md.: Crown Books, 2006. Laci's mother offers a warm and moving account of the life and the loss of her daughter and grandson, and explains how she deals with her grief.

—*Denise Paquette Boots*

SEE ALSO: Marie Hilley; Seventh Earl of Lucan; Jeffrey MacDonald.

MARCEL PETIOT
French serial killer

BORN: January 17, 1897; Auxerre, France
DIED: May 25, 1946; Paris, France
ALSO KNOWN AS: Monster of rue Le Sueur; Docteur Eugène; Henri Valéry; Marcel André Henri Félix Petiot (full name)
MAJOR OFFENSES: Twenty-six counts of murder
ACTIVE: 1934-1944
LOCALE: Paris
SENTENCE: Death by guillotine

EARLY LIFE

Marcel Petiot (mahr-sel peh-tyoh) was the son of Félix Petiot, an employee of the postal services of Auxerre in north-central France, and Marthe Marie Constance Joséphine Bourdon. Marcel's mother died when he was twelve years old. Intelligent but lacking discipline, Marcel received his *baccalauréat* in 1915 and served in the French infantry during World War I. He obtained a degree in general medicine from the University of Paris on December 15, 1921, and went on to practice medicine in the small municipality of Villeneuve-sur-Yonne, which was north of Auxerre.

He subsequently became involved in politics and served as mayor of Villeneuve-sur-Yonne from 1925 to 1931 but was removed from office when irregularities in his administration came to light. He and his wife, née Georgette Valentine Lablais, then moved to Paris. In retrospect, suspicions linger that Petiot may have committed several homicides between 1924 and 1930; however, charges were not filed against him during that period.

CRIMINAL CAREER

In 1934, Petiot resumed the practice of medicine in the ninth arrondissement of Paris, near the Opéra. While tending to an abundant lower- and middle-class clientele, sometimes free of charge, he also supplied prescriptions for narcotics to local drug addicts and appears to have performed illegal abortions on the side.

During the Vichy regime of World War II, he became increasingly obsessed with material wealth and devised an elaborate scheme whereby he claimed membership in an underground escape network capable of providing, for a fee, safe passage abroad. In fact, the alleged network did not exist. Instead of providing a service, he lured his victims to a secondary residence at 21 rue Le Sueur in Paris, where he took their money, murdered them, and disposed of their bodies. Many of his victims were Jews seeking to avoid arrest or deportation; others were common criminals, prostitutes, or drug addicts.

LEGAL ACTION AND OUTCOME

The German Gestapo detained Petiot for interrogation from May, 1943, to January, 1944, but ultimately released him in exchange for 100,000 French francs. Then, in March of 1944, the doctor's homicidal enterprise came to an abrupt end, when French police, alerted by solicitous neighbors, discovered remnants of his handi-work at 21 rue Le Sueur. Petiot immediately went into hiding, changed his identity, and joined the ranks of the French Resistance, albeit briefly, before he was apprehended on October 31.

Petiot stood accused of 27 counts of murder; in all, there were 135 criminal charges brought against him. His trial consisted of sixteen public hearings and lasted from March 18 until April 4, 1946. During testimony, the doctor defiantly claimed responsibility for the execution of as many as sixty-three individuals but failed to convince jurors that his victims were either agents of the Gestapo or traitors. On April 4, he was found guilty of all but one count of murder and was sentenced to death. He was executed by guillotine on May 25, 1946.

IMPACT

Convicted of twenty-six murders but perhaps guilty of more than sixty, Marcel Petiot is now recognized as one of the deadliest serial killers in European history. His trial and execution received considerable media coverage in postwar France, while drawing attention to the plight of the nation's Jewish population during the German Occupation. Questions remain concerning the exact number of Petiot's victims, the methods used to kill them, and the disappearance of some 200 million francs believed to have been extorted from them. In 1990,

French film director Christian de Chalonge revived the chilling tale of Petiot's crimes in a movie titled *Le Docteur Petiot*.

FURTHER READING

Bowles, Brett. "Screening *Les Années Noires:* Using Film to Teach the Occupation." *French Historical Studies* 25 (2002): 21-40. Includes discussion on the use of Chalonge's movie *Le Docteur Petiot* in classroom instruction.

Grombach, John V. *The Great Liquidator*. New York: Doubleday, 1980. A full, detailed study of Petiot's life and crimes. Includes historical photographs.

Iserson, Kenneth V. *Demon Doctors: Physicians as Serial Killers*. Tucson, Ariz.: Galen Press, 2002. Offers a chapter on Petiot's homicidal career, followed by a brief history of the guillotine in France.

Maeder, Thomas. *The Unspeakable Crimes of Dr. Petiot*. 1980. Reprint. London: Penguin Books, 1992. A reliable biography focused on the essential facts; contains photographs of the crime scene, of victims, and of the trial.

—*Jan Pendergrass*

SEE ALSO: Albert Fish; John Wayne Gacy; Jack the Ripper; Dennis Rader; Harold Shipman; Sweeney Todd.

SYMON PETLYURA
President of Ukraine (1918-1919)

BORN: May 10, 1879; Poltava, Ukraine, Russian Empire (now in Ukraine)
DIED: May 25, 1926; Paris, France
ALSO KNOWN AS: Simon Petliura; Symon Vasilyevich Petlyura (full name); V. Marchenko; V. Salevsky; I. Rokytny; S. Prosvitianyn
CAUSE OF NOTORIETY: Petlyura was a leader in Ukraine's unsuccessful fight for independence and seems to have played a role in mass Jewish pogroms. It is estimated that 100,000 civilian Jews were murdered during his rule.
ACTIVE: 1918-1924
LOCALE: Ukraine, Russian Empire

EARLY LIFE

Symon Petlyura (SIH-myohn pyeht-LYEW-reh) was born to parents of modest means in Poltava, Ukraine. He

received early training for the priesthood but was expelled for his preoccupation with Ukrainian nationalism. As a young adult, he worked as a journalist, first in Kiev as editor of a socialist newspaper, *Slovo* (meaning "word"), and later in St. Petersburg as editor of *Ukrainskaya Zhyzn* ("Ukrainian life"). While in Kiev, he also cofounded the Ukrainian Labor Party. In 1914, when World War I broke out, Petlyura joined the Czarist Russian Army, eventually rising to the rank of colonel. After the 1917 Russian Revolution, he served as member of the Central Rada (a de facto parliament), which, in June, 1917, proclaimed Ukraine to be an autonomous republic.

POLITICAL CAREER

In 1917, Germany occupied Ukraine and installed a short-lived puppet government. After the German withdrawal from Ukraine in 1918, Petlyura became one of five members of the new government, the Directorate of Rada. At the start of the war between Russia and Ukraine in 1918, Petlyura emerged as the leading figure within the Directorate and thus became president of Ukraine. It was during this period that many pogroms were perpetrated against Jews in Ukraine, resulting in the deaths of an estimated sixty thousand people. Pogroms are large, violent attacks that not only kill many people but also destroy homes, businesses, and cultural and religious centers.

The Russian Civil War brought the Ukrainian independence movement into conflict with the Bolsheviks, and Jews were perceived as being strongly pro-Bolshevik, which, when combined with the latent anti-Semitism among many people in Ukraine, contributed greatly to pogroms against the Jews. It is still a matter of disagreement as to how much control Petlyura had over his troops or the population and therefore as to what degree he was responsible for the pogroms.

Some historians believe that Petlyura was the architect of the pogroms and that he initiated the infamous attacks in Proskurov, in which more than fifteen hundred Jews were killed by his subordinate Semesenko in 1919. Others argue that Petlyura was not anti-Semitic and had little or no control over bandits and peasants or even some of his own troops. They say that Petlyura had actually issued orders to his army not to be involved in pogroms and had instituted capital punishment for the crime of pogromming. In this view, Petlyura's only crime was being head of state of the country where the pogroms occurred.

Petlyura's rule over Ukraine was brief: By the end of 1919, the country was dominated by the Soviets. Petlyura fled to Poland, which recognized his regime as the legal government of Ukraine. In 1920, Petlyura's remaining troops combined with Polish forces to mount an offensive against the Soviets in Ukraine. They captured a sizable portion of Ukraine's right bank but eventually had to retreat, as the Soviets successfully launched a counteroffensive. After the Peace of Riga ended the Polish-Soviet War in 1921, Ukraine was divided between Poland and Russia, the latter taking the much larger share.

In 1923, Petlyura fled from Poland, as the Soviet Union was increasingly pressuring the Polish government to extradite him. He first went to Budapest, then to Vienna and Geneva, and finally to Paris, where he settled in late 1924. It was there, on May 25, 1926, that a Ukrainian-born Jew named Sholom Schwartzbard shot Petlyura dead. Schwartzbard's parents were among fif-teen members of his family who had been murdered in the pogroms.

IMPACT

Symon Petlyura's efforts for Ukrainian nationalism and his later assassination made him a hero and martyr for many Ukrainians. However, to the great majority of Jews, he remained the man responsible for many of the most terrible pogroms and the deaths of thousands of Jews. This gap in perceptions reinforced tensions and conflicts between Ukrainians and Jews. This tension was exacerbated by the acquittal of Schwartzbard, whose attorney succeeded in justifying assassination as an appropriate act of vengeance. Different perceptions of the history of Ukraine remain a source of conflict between modern Ukrainians and Jews. For example, the fact that a street in Ukraine is named after Petlyura is an affront to the Jewish population there.

FURTHER READING

Abramson, Henry. *A Prayer for the Government: Ukrainians and Jews in Revolutionary Times, 1917-1920.* Cambridge, Mass.: Harvard University Press, 1999. Abramson analyzes the failed efforts of Jewish and Ukrainian activists to address and overcome ethnic violence between Jews and Ukrainians after the fall of the Russian Empire. He focuses especially on the conflicting views of the role of Petlyura.

Hunczak, Taras. "A Reappraisal of Semyon Petlura and Ukrainian-Jewish Relations, 1917-1921." *Jewish Social Studies* 31 (1969): 163-183. One of two articles (see Szjakowski citation) published together in one issue that take radically different sides regarding the culpability of Petlyura in the Jewish pogroms.

Palij, Michael. *The Ukrainian-Polish Defensive Alliance: An Aspect of the Ukrainian Revolution.* Edmonton, Alta.: CIUS Press, 1995. This Ukrainian American scholar provides a thorough account of this period in the history of Ukraine, with a particular emphasis on the relationship and alliance of Polish leader Jósef Piłsudski with Petlyura.

Reid, Anna. *Borderland: A Journey Through the History of Ukraine.* Boulder, Colo.: Westview Press, 2000. Reid combines interviews, her own personal experiences, and historical research to provide a readable and fairly complete history of Ukraine's controversial history.

Reshetar, John S. *Ukrainian Revolution, 1917-1920: A Study in Nationalism.* Manchester, N.H.: Ayer Company, 1972. This book provides a thorough history and analysis of the Ukrainian national movement, including Petlyura's role within it.

Szjakowski, Zosa. "Semyon Petlyura and Ukrainian-Jewish Relations, 1917-1921: A Rebuttal." *Jewish Social Studies* 31 (1969): 184-213. The second of two articles (see Hunczak citation) that debate the culpability of Petlyura in the Jewish pogroms.

—*Jerome L. Neapolitan*

SEE ALSO: Klaus Barbie; Radovan Karadžić.

PHALARIS
Greek tyrant of Acragas, Sicily (r. 570-544 B.C.E.)

BORN: c. 610-600 B.C.E.; Acragas, Sicily (now Agrigento, Sicily, Italy)
DIED: 544 B.C.E.; Acragas, Sicily
CAUSE OF NOTORIETY: Phalaris led Acragas as a despot and used cruelty to strengthen his position.
ACTIVE: 570-544 B.C.E.
LOCALE: Acragas

EARLY LIFE

The details of the early life of Phalaris (FAL-uhr-ihs) are unreliable, preserved only in statements scattered across a variety of ancient authors. He was the son of Leodamas of Rhodes and is presumed to have been born sometime around 610-600 B.C.E. Records show him living as a young man in the city of Acragas, which was founded by Greek colonists in 580 B.C.E. He started as a tax collector, and, when the people of Acragas wanted to build a temple to the god Zeus on the highest point of the new city, he offered to ensure that the job would be done by the best craftspeople, if they put him in charge of the project. His experience as a tax collector appears to have inspired trust, and he was duly commissioned.

DICTATORIAL CAREER

At some stage in the construction of the temple, Phalaris spread a rumor that materials were being stolen and was given authority to enclose the citadel with walls. Having done so, he armed the foreigners and prisoners whom he had been using for the building work with stones and axes. Phalaris then led them in an attack on the men of Acragas during a festival. Killing most of the men, he then made himself "tyrant"—from a Greek word meaning "sole ruler"—of the city. This event is usually dated to the year 570 B.C.E.

Following the pattern of other tyrants, Phalaris engaged the population in a program of construction to beautify the city, developed trade links with other towns, and established athletic and religious festivals. He is also said to have made war against neighboring cities and to

have added them to the territory of Acragas. Aristotle reports that Phalaris was at some stage appointed military commander of Himera in northern Sicily.

Phalaris's reputation as the archetypal cruel tyrant depends largely on the bronze bull made for him by Perilaus of Athens. Phalaris would supposedly put his enemies inside it, and then a fire was lit underneath, so that the enemies were roasted alive. The cries of the agonized victims were, by some mechanism, made to sound like the bellowing of a bull. This is the version told by the Roman orator Cicero. Alternative versions from other Greek writers make Perilaus the only victim, punished by Phalaris for having designed such an appalling contrivance.

In the two imaginary speeches composed by the satirist Lucian, called *Phalaris 1* and *Phalaris 2* (second century C.E.; English translation, 1684), the tyrant defends himself against charges of cruelty, claiming that he had the best interests of the people at heart and punished only conspirators who threatened his benign rule. Nonetheless, the survival of the stories of Phalaris's outrages some six hundred years after his death tends to suggest that there may have been some truth to them. It is also possible that the bull was involved in some religious ritual—the animal is important in such contexts across the Greek world—and somehow got mixed up with the "bad tyrant myths" that became commonplace.

IMPACT

After ruling Acragas for twenty-six years, Phalaris was overthrown and killed in a rebellion led by a man called Telemachus in 544. During his reign, Acragas increased in power and underwent major architectural and industrial development. Phalaris's skill in financial matters, which gave him influence over the manual classes, seems to have been the basis of his power. Whether his bad reputation is deserved or an instance of deliberate distortion by political enemies is impossible to determine with certainty.

LUCIAN ON PHALARIS

The satirist and sophist Lucian of Samosata (c. 120-c. 180 C.E.), writing some six centuries after Phalaris lived, assumed Phalaris's voice to explain the tyrant's bad repuation and present a defense. Here "Phalaris" tells his own version of the story of the bronze bull:

And now I must explain to you the origin of my present offering, and the manner in which it came into my hands. For it was by no instructions of mine that the statuary made this bull: far be it from me to aspire to the possession of such works of art! A countryman of my own, one Perilaus, an admirable artist, but a man of evil disposition, had so far mistaken my character as to think that he could win my regard by the invention of a new form of torture; the love of torture, he thought, was my ruling passion. He it was who made the bull and brought it to me. I no sooner set eyes on this beautiful and exquisite piece of workmanship, which lacked only movement and sound to complete the illusion, than I exclaimed: "Here is an offering fit for the God of Delphi: to him I must send it." "And what will you say," rejoined Perilaus, who stood by, "when you see the ingenious mechanism within it, and learn the purpose it is designed to serve?" He opened the back of the animal, and continued: "When you are minded to punish any one, shut him up in this receptacle, apply these pipes to the nostrils of the bull, and order a fire to be kindled beneath. The occupant will shriek and roar in unremitting agony; and his cries will come to you through the pipes as the tenderest, most pathetic, most melodious of bellowings. Your victim will be punished, and you will enjoy the music."

His words revolted me. I loathed the thought of such ingenious cruelty, and resolved to punish the artificer in kind. "If this is anything more than an empty boast, Perilaus," I said to him, "if your art can really produce this effect, get inside yourself, and pretend to roar; and we will see whether the pipes will make such music as you describe." He consented; and when he was inside I closed the aperture, and ordered a fire to be kindled. "Receive," I cried, "the due reward of your wondrous art: let the music-master be the first to play." Thus did his ingenuity meet with its deserts. But lest the offering should be polluted by his death, I caused him to be removed while he was yet alive, and his body to be flung dishonoured from the cliffs. The bull, after due purification, I sent as an offering to your God, with an inscription upon it, setting forth all the circumstances; the names of the donor and of the artist, the evil design of the latter, and the righteous sentence which condemned him to illustrate by his own agonized shrieks the efficacy of his musical device.

Source: The Works of Lucian of Samosata, translated by H. W. Fowler and F. G. Fowler (Oxford: The Clarendon Press, 1905).

FURTHER READING

Andrewes, Antony. *The Greek Tyrants*. New York: Harper & Row, 1963. General account of the phenomenon of Greek tyranny.

Harmon, A. M. *Lucian, of Samosata*. Vol. 1. London: W. Heinemann, 1913. Contains *Phalaris 1* and *Phalaris 2*, two rhetorical exercises that preserve both positive and negative views of the tyrant of Acragas.

Ure, P. N. *The Origin of Tyranny*. New York: Russell and Russell, 1962. Detailed survey of all the Greek tyrants, including the ancient sources on Phalaris.

—*David H. J. Larmour*

SEE ALSO: Cypselus of Corinth; Domitian; Nero; Polycrates of Samos.

KIM PHILBY
British spy for the Soviets

BORN: January 1, 1912; Ambāla, Punjab, India
DIED: May 11, 1988; Moscow, Russia
ALSO KNOWN AS: Harold Adrian Russell Philby (full name)
CAUSE OF NOTORIETY: Philby was a Soviet agent, spying from within the British Secret Intelligence Service.
ACTIVE: 1933-1963
LOCALE: London, England; Moscow, Soviet Union; Spain; Washington, D.C.; and Beirut, Lebanon

EARLY LIFE
Harold Adrian Russell Philby (FIHL-bee) was the only son and the eldest of four children born to Harry St. John Bridger Philby and Dora Johnston. At the time of his birth, his father was working for the British Indian Civil Service. However, Harry Philby was eccentric and some-

Kim Philby. (AP/Wide World Photos)

what antiestablishment, and in time he fell out with the colonial regime, though he continued to do invaluable diplomatic work in Arabia. His son, Harold, was quickly nicknamed Kim, after the character in Rudyard Kipling's 1901 novel *Kim*.

Philby was sent back to England for his education, attending Westminster School in London, eventually becoming one of the head students of the prestigious independent school. In 1930, he gained a place at Trinity College, Cambridge University, where he studied history for his first year and moved to study economics for his final two years. He graduated with second-class honors in 1933.

The real significance of his university career, however, was his growing political commitment to communism. In the heady left-wing atmosphere of the early 1930's, he joined the University Socialist Club, where he met Guy Burgess and the economics professor Maurice H. Dobb, a Marxist. By the time he left Cambridge, Philby had become a convinced communist and believed the future lay with Soviet Russia.

He visited Austria, at the time torn between right-wing and left-wing factions. The pro-Nazis soon triumphed, and Philby attempted to rescue some of his communist friends, including a Jewish woman, Alice "Litzi" Friedman. The safest way to get her out the country was for Philby to marry her, which he did. Friedman and other communists in Austria were already seeing Philby as a suitable agent.

Back in London in June, 1934, Philby began to work with Teodor Maly, a Hungarian Soviet agent and a former priest, and agreed to work for the Soviets. It was suggested that he needed to shed his left-wing image, which he did, along with Burgess, by joining the Anglo-German Friendship Society. He was then appointed as a journalist to cover the Spanish Civil War for the fascist side of General Francisco Franco. He was so successful in this venture that Franco awarded him the Red Cross of Honor in March, 1938.

ESPIONAGE CAREER
At the outbreak of World War II, Philby had received specific instructions to become a double agent. He initially could get no further than being a war correspondent, but after the 1940 Battle of Dunkirk, in which a large Allied force was cut off in northeast France by a German armored advance, Burgess managed to get

Philby recruited into the rapidly expanding British Secret Intelligence Service (SIS), also known as MI6, or Military Intelligence Section 6, which monitored overseas intelligence. Philby was attractive to the SIS because of his knowledge of fascist Spain; his father's connections also helped. Two other former Cambridge communists also managed to get themselves recruited: Donald Duart Maclean and Anthony Blunt.

From the Iberian desk, Philby was soon shifted to Section 5, the British internal-affairs counterintelligence section, where he quickly demonstrated his efficiency. By then, Germany had invaded Russia, and for a while the SIS and the Soviet intelligence agency, KGB, were fighting a common enemy. However, by 1944, British prime minister Winston Churchill, anticipating the Cold War, had seen the need to set up a separate section of the SIS in order to deal with Soviet counterintelligence. Philby received orders to get into this new section and, by political maneuvering, got himself appointed its new head.

In September, 1945, a Soviet diplomat in Turkey alerted the British foreign office that there were at least three Soviet agents working in counterespionage in London. Philby saw the file and alerted the KGB, who promptly shipped the diplomat, Constantin Volkhov, back to Moscow. Other Soviet defectors, including Walter Krivitsky and Igor Gouzenko, had given similar warnings, but still no suspicion fell on Philby. In 1946, Philby was posted to Turkey.

Then, in 1949, Philby was posted to Washington, D.C., as MI6 intelligence liaison, a crucial posting for him from which to tell the Soviets about Anglo-American intelligence activity. By 1950, however, Philby was investigated, apparently with a view to promoting him to MI6 chief. However, the review disrupted intelligence from Krivitsky and Gouzenko, and Maclean came under scrutiny. At the same time, Burgess was posted to the United States, staying with Philby and his new wife, Aileen. Philby recognized the growing suspicion of both Maclean and Burgess; Philby warned them, and they promptly fled to Russia.

Philby was recalled and grilled by MI5, the British security agency. He was asked to resign, but his name was officially cleared by British prime minister Harold Macmillan in 1955, despite the American belief that he was guilty.

At this point, Philby began a second career as a part-time agent of MI6, in Beirut, Lebanon, ostensibly working as a correspondent for *The Observer* and *The Economist*. However, in late 1961, Anatoli Golitsin, a KGB agent working in Finland, defected to the U.S. Central Intelligence Agency (CIA). When interviewed by the chief of MI5, Golitsin confirmed that "a ring of five" within British intelligence existed. In 1963, an MI5 agent was sent to Beirut to confront Philby, who, despite offers of immunity for information, would admit only to spying for the Soviets in the past. He promptly left for Russia with his third wife, Eleanor.

Philby lived out the rest of his life in Moscow, eventually honored by the KGB and the Soviet leadership. After Eleanor's death, he married Rufina Ivanova, a Polish Russian woman, in 1971. He wrote his own memoirs in 1968, titled *My Silent War,* and later consented to a number of interviews by Western journalists. He died in 1988 and was buried with full military honors by the KGB.

IMPACT

Kim Philby's tenure in Washington undoubtedly undermined the whole of the Western Cold War intelligence system for a time and caused a rift between the British and the Americans. It is also true that Philby's passing of the names of British agents and potential defectors to the Soviet Union led to a number of deaths. Philby claimed that he was not a "double" agent but had worked only for the Soviets. His cultivated secrecy deceived all those around him.

FURTHER READING

Boravik, Genrikh, and Phillip Knightley, eds. *The Philby Files: The Secret Life of Master Spy Kim Philby*. New York: Little, Brown, 1994. Boravik was a Russian journalist with access to both KGB files and interviews with Philby. He weighs one against the other in his discussion. Particularly good analysis of Philby's Beirut years.

Hamrick, S. J. *Deceiving the Deceivers: Kim Philby, Donald Maclean, and Guy Burgess*. New Haven, Conn.: Yale University Press, 2004. Based on archives of broken Soviet codes released in 1995-1996, this book suggests British intelligence was aware of the spies earlier than suspected and that Philby was used to misinform the Soviets between 1949 and 1950.

Knightley, Phillip. *Philby: K.G.B. Masterspy*. London: Andre Deutsch, 1988. Based on a lengthy series of interviews with Philby in his Moscow apartment, supplemented by further research and interviews. Biographical in nature.

Modin, Yuri, et al. *My Five Cambridge Friends: Blunt, Maclean, Philby, Burgess, and Cairncross, by Their KGB Controller*. Translated by Anthony Roberts.

New York: Farrar, Straus and Giroux, 1994. An account that unites all five stories.

Philby, Kim. *My Silent War*. New York: Grove Press, 1968. Philby's memoir.

Philby, Rufina, et al. *The Private Life of Kim Philby*. London: Warner, 2000. Memoirs of Philby from his

last wife, who shared his Moscow exile with him until his death.

—*David Barratt*

SEE ALSO: Anthony Blunt; Guy Burgess; John Cairncross; Robert Philip Hanssen; Donald Duart Maclean.

WILLIAM LUTHER PIERCE III
American physicist and neo-Nazi

BORN: September 11, 1933; Atlanta, Georgia
DIED: July 23, 2002; Hillsboro, West Virginia
ALSO KNOWN AS: Dr. William Pierce; Andrew McDonald
CAUSE OF NOTORIETY: Pierce, one of the most prominent theorists of the white nationalist movement, founded the National Alliance in 1974 and gained widespread notoriety for writing *The Turner Diaries* in 1978.
ACTIVE: 1966-2002
LOCALE: Virginia and West Virginia

EARLY LIFE

William L. Pierce (peers) III was the oldest son of William L. Pierce II and Marguerite Ferrell Pierce. When Pierce was four, his father moved his insurance business to Norfolk, Virginia. The younger Pierce attended public schools in Norfolk until his father was hit and killed by a car in 1942. His mother then moved to Montgomery, Alabama, where the family lived with a relative. Pierce attended public schools until his last two years of high school, when he enrolled at Allen Military Academy in Bryan, Texas. Following graduation from military college in 1951, Pierce attended Rice University on an academic scholarship. He graduated from Rice in 1955 with a degree in physics. He worked for a few months at Los Alamos Scientific Laboratory in New Mexico and then attended graduate school at the California Institute of Technology. There, he met his first wife, Patricia Jones, whom he married in 1957. One year later, he worked at the Jet Propulsion Lab in California. He later resumed his graduate work at the University of Colorado, where he received a master's degree and, in 1962, a doctorate in physics. During that time, he joined the ultraconservative John Birch Society. From 1962 through 1965, Pierce taught physics at Oregon State University. Then, in 1965, he took a job at Pratt and Whitney in North Haven, Connecticut.

POLITICAL CAREER

In 1966, Pierce moved to Washington, D.C. There, he met George Lincoln Rockwell, the founder of the American Nazi Party. Beginning at this point, Pierce became active in the neo-Nazi movement in the United States. First, Pierce became editor of the *National Socialist World*, a journal published by Rockwell's World Union of National Socialists. Following Rockwell's assassination in 1967, Pierce became one of the leaders of the National Socialist White People's Party (NSWPP), the successor to the American Nazi Party. In 1970, Pierce left the NSWPP and joined the National Youth Alliance, a political organization formed by Willis A. Carto that targeted right-wing college students.

In 1974, Pierce created the National Alliance after breaking with Carto. The National Alliance was originally located in Arlington, Virginia; however, in 1985, Pierce moved his operation to a farm near Mill Point, West Virginia. From 1974 until his death in 2002, Pierce was the leader of the National Alliance, editor of its magazine, *The National Vanguard,* and editor of the group's internal newsletter, *The National Alliance Bulletin*.

In 1978, Pierce published *The Turner Diaries* under the pseudonym Andrew McDonald. This novel depicted the takeover of the world by a group called the Organization, an all-white guerrilla army that systematically exterminated blacks, Jews, and race traitors. *The Turner Diaries* was widely read by white supremacists, and it has been viewed by many as the inspiration for Timothy McVeigh's 1995 bombing of the federal building in Oklahoma City, which killed 168 persons. The book is also thought to have inspired the activities of the Order, a violent organization led by Robert Jay Mathews that broke from the Aryan Nations in the early 1980's. Mathews's group robbed banks and armored cars, counterfeited money, bombed a synagogue, and murdered Denver talk show host Alan Berg. Mathews was killed in a shoot-out with Federal Bureau of Investigation (FBI) agents in December, 1984.

In 1989, Pierce (as McDonald) published a second book, titled *Hunter*. It is a novel about a man who murders interracial couples and Jews. Pierce dedicated *Hunter* to Joseph Paul Franklin, who confessed to killing as many as eighteen persons between 1977 and 1980 in an effort to start a race war.

During the 1990's, Pierce began to use the Internet as a tool for recruitment and to spread his white supremacist beliefs. He wanted to eradicate what he perceived as Jewish control over the media and the American government; he also wanted to create whites-only homelands both in Europe and in the United States. Moreover, in 1999, Pierce began to purchase white-power music labels in order to reach out to alienated racists and neo-Nazis. He first purchased Resistance Records, a Detroit company started by Canadian skinheads. Later, he bought Nordland Records, a Swedish white-power company. These labels featured heavy-metal music with lyrics attacking minorities and Jews. Pierce also began to publish *Resistance* magazine, a publication that carried articles on white-power music.

Pierce blamed the September 11, 2001, terrorist attacks in New York and Washington, D.C., on the federal government's support for Israel. In 2002, he formed the Anti-Globalization Action Network in order both to protest the Group of Eight (G8) summit in Canada and to convince young activists in the antiglobalization movement that the National Alliance shared their anticapitalist and antiestablishment ideology. Pierce also established ties with right-wing racist parties in Great Britain and Germany.

IMPACT

The National Alliance, under the leadership of William Pierce, was the largest and most active neo-Nazi organization in the United States. Unlike most white separatist leaders, Pierce was well educated and well organized. He knew how to market his organization to disaffected white youth using various publications, a weekly broadcast, and his white-power music. At its peak, the National Alliance had an estimated fifteen hundred members and more than thirty-five cells across the United States. Following Pierce's death in 2002, the National Alliance was plagued by dissension and declined in membership and influence.

FURTHER READING

Griffin, Robert S. *The Fame of a Dead Man's Deeds: An Up-Close Portrait of White Nationalist William Pierce*. Lavergne, Tenn.: Lightning Source, 2001. This work provides many details on Pierce's life, although it does not provide much critical analysis of the man and his organization.

Swain, Carol M. *The New White Nationalism in America*. New York: Cambridge University Press, 2002. This is a comprehensive work on white nationalist groups in the United States, including the National Alliance.

Williams, Mary E. *The White Separatist Movement*. San Diego: Greenhaven Press, 2002. This book looks at different white separatist movements in the United States. It includes an essay authored by Pierce.

—*William V. Moore*

SEE ALSO: Willis A. Carto; Timothy McVeigh; Robert Jay Mathews; George Lincoln Rockwell.

PONTIUS PILATE
Roman procurator of Judaea (26-36 C.E.)

BORN: c. 10 B.C.E.; Rome (now in Italy)

DIED: After 36 C.E.; probably Vienna, Gaul (now Vienne, France)

ALSO KNOWN AS: Pontius Pilatus (Latin name)

CAUSE OF NOTORIETY: According to Christian Gospel, Pilate earned the enmity of Jews for being the one who tried and condemned Jesus of Nazareth to death.

ACTIVE: Possibly April 7, 30 C.E.

LOCALE: Jerusalem, Judaea

EARLY LIFE

Nothing is known for certain concerning the early life of Pontius Pilate (PAHN-shihs PI-leht) other than he was born in Rome or its vicinity in the late first century B.C.E. The province of Judaea was not considered prestigious, so he likely had little previous government experience. According to the Gospel of Matthew, he was married, but it is not known whether he had any children.

POLITICAL CAREER

According to Jewish historian Flavius Josephus, Pilate arrived in Judaea in 26 C.E. for a ten-year rule as procurator, or governor. He ruled from the coastal city of Caesarea, where an inscription documents his position. From there, he minted small bronze coins that served to spread Roman religious culture through symbolic representations. On major religious festivals, Pilate visited the holy city of Jerusalem, where his lack of religious sensibility resulted in a series of conflicts with Jewish religious leaders. Philo of Alexandria, a first century Jewish philosopher, supports the description of Josephus, characterizing Pilate's rule as filled with violence and abusive behavior.

Among the episodes documented by these historians was the incident when Pilate sent Roman soldiers to Jerusalem with images of the caesar, which was in opposition to the Jewish laws forbidding the public display of human images. His predecessors had refrained from sending these images to Jerusalem. However, Pilate's intent is evident in his decision to dispatch the soldiers secretly at night and in his order to put down any protest with force. On a later occasion, he instructed offensive shields to be displayed in Jerusalem. Soldiers went undercover, dressing as Jewish commoners, to infiltrate crowds and attack protesters. According to the Gospel of Luke, he ordered the slaughter of Galilean pilgrims sacrificing at the temple. Archaeology confirms that Pilate built aqueducts south of Jerusalem, but Josephus notes that these were funded by money confiscated from the temple treasury. These offenses led Jewish priests and members of the family of Herod Antipas to travel to Rome as a delegation to Caesar to request Pilate's recall. At Passover in the year 36 C.E., Pilate's troops slaughtered Samaritan worshippers near their holy Mount Gerizim, resulting in further appeals to Vitellius, the Roman legate of Syria.

THE TRIAL OF JESUS

Jesus of Nazareth died in Jerusalem, possibly on April 7, 30 C.E., executed according to the Roman system of crucifixion. He was listed at death simply as "Jesus of Naza-

Pontius Pilate, seated in foreground, interviews Jesus Christ. (Library of Congress)

reth, King of the Jews." It is true that the messianic title carried both religious and political overtones and that Jesus was regularly in conflict with Jewish religious leaders, yet the Gospel of John records that Pilate retained the right of capital punishment during this period.

Neither Jesus nor Pilate spent much time in Jerusalem, but their paths met during the spring Passover celebration in the year 30. Following several days of teaching on the temple premises, demonstrating against temple money-changers, and reportedly being anointed like the messiahs of old by a woman, Jesus was arrested under the cover of night, questioned by the high priest, and brought to Pilate for trial early that Friday morning.

The four evangelists record the trial in detail, but there are differences that make reconstruction difficult. According to the Synoptic Gospels, Jesus did not defend himself; however, the Jesus in John's story engages in dialogue concerning the meaning of his kingship and about the concept of "truth." The Gospel writers, on one hand, portray Pilate as brutal, whipping Jesus and condemning him to death; on the other hand, they portray him as somewhat sympathetic, wavering and uncertain about what to do. In Luke, Pilate three times declares Jesus' innocence. In Matthew, Pilate washes his hands of Jesus' guilt after receiving a warning from his wife. In all the Gospels, Pilate offers the pardon of a prisoner but ends up releasing Barabbas rather than Jesus. In the end, Pilate has the power to release Jesus but instead condemns him to death by crucifixion.

The Roman emperor Tiberius suspended Pilate in 36 C.E. and recalled him to Rome. However, Tiberius died in March, 37 C.E., before Pilate arrived in Rome and his review was complete. The fourth century historian Eusebius included a report that Pilate committed suicide in 39 C.E., yet it is more likely that he lived out his retirement in Rome for several decades.

PILATE AND THE MULTITUDE

In the King James versions of Jesus' trial and condemnation, Pontius Pilate is clearly intimidated by the Jewish crowd and priests who attend the trial:

Matthew 27

22. Pilate saith unto them, What shall I do then with Jesus which is called Christ? They all say unto him, Let him be crucified.
23. And the governor said, why, what evil hath he done? But they cried out the more, saying, Let him be crucified.
24. When Pilate saw that he could prevail nothing, but that rather a tumult was made, he took water, and washed his hands before the multitude, saying, I am innocent of the blood of this just person: see ye to it.

Mark 15

9. But Pilate answered them, saying Will ye that I release unto you the King of the Jews?
10. For he knew that the chief priests had delivered him for envy.
11. But the chief priests moved the people, that he should rather release Barabbas unto them.
15. And so Pilate, willing to content the people, released Barabbas unto them, and delivered Jesus, when he had scourged him, to be crucified.

Luke 23

20. Pilate, therefore, willing to release Jesus, spake again to them.
21. But they cried, saying, Crucify him, crucify him.
23. And they were instant with loud voices, requiring that he might be crucified. And the voices of them and of the chief priests prevailed.
24. And Pilate gave sentence that it should be as they required.

John 19

5. Then came Jesus forth, wearing the crown of thorns, and the purple robe. And Pilate saith unto them, Behold the man.
6. When the chief priests therefore and officers saw him, they cried out, saying, Crucify him, crucify him. Pilate saith unto them, Take ye him, and crucify him for I find no fault in him.
7. The Jews answered him, We have a law, and by our law he ought to die, because he made himself the Son of God.
8. When Pilate therefore heard that saying, he was the more afraid;
15. But they cried out, Away with him, away with him, crucify him. Pilate saith unto them, shall I crucify your King. The chief priests answered, We have no king but Caesar.
16. Then delivered he him therefore unto them to be crucified.

Impact

The insertion of the phrase "suffered under Pontius Pilate" in the Apostle's Creed guaranteed that Pontius Pilate, a relatively insignificant Roman foreign officer, would be remembered every Sunday by Christians around the world, even in the modern era. At the same time, Pilate benefited from the fact that the success of

Christianity depended upon a tolerant attitude by the Roman government to second- and third-generation Christians. Thus, Christian apologists shifted the blame for Jesus' death from Pilate to the Jews. In some parts of Christianity, traditions developed that Pilate and his wife converted to Christianity.

FURTHER READING

Bond, Helen K. *Pontius Pilate in History and Interpretation*. Cambridge, England: Cambridge University Press, 1998. A thorough scholarly study in the Society for New Testament Studies' monograph series.

Brown, Raymond E. *The Death of the Messiah*. 2 vols. Garden City, N.Y.: Doubleday, 1999. Detailed exegetical study of the Gospel accounts of the death of Jesus.

Carter, Warren. *Pontius Pilate: Portraits of a Roman Governor*. Collegeville, Minn.: Liturgical Press, 2003. First chapter includes a summary of the practices of the Roman government in the eastern provinces. Additional chapters each treat the six first century literary works that speak of Pilate: Philo, Flavius Josephus, Matthew, Mark, Luke, and John.

Maier, Pail. *Pontius Pilate*. Garden City, N.Y.: Doubleday, 1968. A novel written by a respected historian.

Phillepfontallie, Jean, and Sheldon Lee Gosner. *The Coins of Pontius Pilate*. Warren Center, Pa.: Shangri-La, 2001. A survey of the symbolism and significance of coins issued by Pilate.

Wroe, Anne. *Pontius Pilate: The Biography of an Invented Man*. New York: Modern Library, 2001. A journalist studies first century Roman culture, contemporary literary reports, a few coins, one inscription, and the fourth century Acts of Pilate to reconstruct this biography.

—*Fred Strickert*

SEE ALSO: Barabbas; Herod Antipas; Herod the Great; Flavius Josephus; Judas Iscariot.

AUGUSTO PINOCHET UGARTE
Military dictator of Chile (1973-1990)

BORN: November 25, 1915; Valparaíso, Chile

ALSO KNOWN AS: The General; Augusto José Ramón Pinochet Ugarte (full name)

CAUSE OF NOTORIETY: After bombing Chile's presidential palace, Pinochet seized power, suspended the constitution, dissolved parliament, and gave the military and national police force almost unlimited power. Dissidents were arrested and jailed and frequently tortured or murdered.

ACTIVE: 1973-1990

LOCALE: Chile

EARLY LIFE

Augusto Pinochet Ugarte (aw-GEW-stoh pee-noh-CHET ew-GAHR-teh) was the oldest of three sons and three daughters of a middle-class Catholic family. He grew up in Valparaíso, the seaport of Chile's capital, Santiago. In 1933, he joined the army as an officer cadet at Chile's Military Academy. He graduated as a sublieutenant in the infantry in 1937. He married Lucía Hiriart Rodríguez in 1943, with whom he had three daughters and two sons. During most of his military career, Pinochet had postings that advanced him in rank and enabled him to teach and to write several works on military science. The army promoted him to brigadier general in 1968 and made him intendant of Tarapacá Province. He was appointed commander general of the Santiago army garrison in 1971 and chief major general of the army in early 1972. Salvador Allende, the left-leaning president of Chile, tapped Pinochet as commander in chief of the army on August 23, 1973. Allende's Marxist policies had lost the support of his political coalition, and there had been reports for months about a possible military coup. Allende thought General Pinochet would protect his presidency.

POLITICAL CAREER

Pinochet's career as a dictator began just seventeen days later: On the late morning of September 11, 1973, he ordered army tanks and air force planes to bombard La Moneda, Chile's presidential palace. Allende was in the palace at the time. According to all available evidence, facing the certain end of his presidency, Allende chose to take his own life as bombs and bullets exploded around him. Pinochet governed the country for almost seventeen years following the bombing. He appointed himself president in 1974, suspended the constitution, dissolved parliament and trade unions, and gave the military and na-

Augusto Pinochet Ugarte. (AP/Wide World Photos)

tional police force almost unlimited power. He arrested, detained, and jailed protesters without trials.

Evidence indicates that Pinochet also directed a secret police force, the National Intelligence Directorate (DINA), to track down pro-Allende Chileans both at home and abroad. DINA tapped telephones, opened mail, and kidnapped suspects. Thousands of political prisoners were murdered, jailed, tortured, brutalized, or exiled. In an effort to silence critics completely, Pinochet and his military commanders closed congress, censored the media, purged the universities, burned books, outlawed political parties, and banned labor unions.

Gradually, Pinochet allowed greater freedom of assembly, speech, and association. Political parties began to function openly again in 1987. Pinochet's government drafted a new constitution that guaranteed he would remain president until 1989. In 1990, he allowed a plebiscite asking the people whether he should rule for another eight years. He was voted out of office, and he gave up his power. Freely elected governments have ruled Chile since that time.

LEGAL ACTION AND OUTCOME

In 1990, Pinochet's elected successor, Patricio Alwin, established the National Truth and Reconciliation Commission. The commission's report, also known as the Rettig report, led to the arrest and prosecution of Pinochet's former army officers and former leaders of the secret police.

On October 17, 1998, Spanish authorities acting through Interpol had Pinochet arrested in London while he was recuperating from back surgery performed there. Spain's warrant charged Pinochet with murders stemming from the torture and killing of Spanish citizens in Chile by DINA. The warrant requested Pinochet's extradition to Spain so that he could stand trial.

Chile's constitution allowed former presidents a permanent seat in the senate, and Chile challenged Spain's extradition, arguing that Pinochet had diplomatic immunity as a Chilean senator. The case slogged through the British court system, while Pinochet was kept under house arrest. His defenders argued that he was immune from prosecution, but public opinion surged against him.

Additionally, Pinochet's arrest in London emboldened victims of his policies to file hundreds of cases against the former dictator in Chilean courts.

In April, 2004, British courts decided that Pinochet was mentally unfit to stand trial and therefore could not be extradited to Spain. The decision allowed Pinochet to go back to Chile. Pressure to arrest and indict him peaked after an interview with Pinochet that aired on television showed his fitness for trial. The interview led to a court battle. Later in 2004, the Valech report (by the agency officially named the National Commission on Political Imprisonment and Torture Report) detailed more abuses committed by Pinochet's regime.

Finally, the courts revoked his immunity and in July, 2005, placed him under house arrest for kidnapping and murder. Later in the year, the government added a charge of tax evasion based on a U.S. Senate report that alleged Pinochet maintained illegal accounts worth as much as eight million dollars in a bank in Washington, D.C. The ninety-year-old former dictator claimed his innocence in all the charges. His day in court was still pending as of late 2006.

IMPACT

Tens of thousands of Chileans are still confronting the loss of close family members torn from them by Augusto Pinochet Ugarte's secret police. Chilean artists continue to express the plight of victims in crafts, dance, paintings, and theater. Other Chileans believe that Pinochet saved their country from communism and transformed the Chilean economy into one of the strongest in Latin America. Scholars of international law cite the 1998 detention of Pinochet in London and the subsequent legal proceedings against him as an example of how international warrants and creative use of laws can bring perpetrators of crimes against humanity to justice.

FURTHER READING

Burbach, Roger. *The Pinochet Affair: State Terrorism and Global Justice*. New York: Zed Books, 2003. Describes how international law can become a tool to bring dictators to justice for state-sponsored terrorism.

Dinges, John. *The Condor Years: How Pinochet and His Allies Brought Terrorism to Three Continents*. New York: The New Press, 2004. This book documents Pinochet's alleged creation Operation Condor: an organized effort among dictators and military juntas of Latin America to capture political exiles, interrogate and torture them, and return them to their countries of origin.

U.S. Congress, Senate Committee on Homeland Security. *Money Laundering and Foreign Corruption: Enforcement and Effectiveness of the Patriot Act*. Washington, D.C.: U.S. Government Printing Office, 2004. Includes a supplemental staff report on Pinochet's illegal U.S. accounts.

—*Richard A. Crooker*

SEE ALSO: Porfirio Díaz; Leopoldo Galtieri; Eva Perón; Juan Perón; Anastasio Somoza García; Getúlio Vargas.

KONSTANTIN PETROVICH POBEDONOSTSEV
Russian imperial official, jurist, and tutor to czars Alexander III and Nicholas II

BORN: May 21, 1827; Moscow, Russia
DIED: March 23, 1907; St. Petersburg, Russia
ALSO KNOWN AS: Russian Torquemada; Gray Cardinal
CAUSE OF NOTORIETY: Pobedonostsev, an archconservative defender of Imperial Russia's status quo at the beginning of the twentieth century, became an emblem of the regime's stubborn resistance to change.
ACTIVE: 1881-1905
LOCALE: Moscow and St. Petersburg, Russia

EARLY LIFE

Born the youngest child of a large middle-class family, Konstantin Petrovich Pobedonostsev (KAHN-stan-teen PEHT-roh-vich poh-behd-uh-NOHST-sehv) combined his mother's devotion to the Orthodox Church and his father's learning throughout his life. His father, a professor of rhetoric and Russian literature at Moscow University, tutored Pobedonostsev until he was fourteen, when he entered the elite School of Jurisprudence in St. Petersburg. There, he studied foreign languages, theology, history, and law. Upon graduation, Pobedonostsev was given a clerkship in the Senate, a powerful committee that mediated policy between government ministers and the czar. Along with regular promotions, he was appointed lecturer in Russian civil law at Moscow University in 1859 and later as tutor to three heirs to the Russian throne: Nikolai (who died in 1865) and the czars Alexander III and Nicholas II.

POLITICAL CAREER

Over the next forty years, Pobedonostsev held several state positions. In 1868, Czar Alexander II appointed him senator. In 1872, he became a member of the State Council, Russia's senior ministerial committee, and in 1880 he was named procurator (lay head) of the Holy Synod, which had governed the Russian Orthodox Church since 1721. Pobedonostsev's leadership of the Holy Synod restored church affairs to the heart of imperial government.

The assassination of Alexander II in March, 1881, marked a turning point in Pobedonostsev's career, as it did in Russia's future. Prior to this tragic event, Pobedonostsev had marginal political influence. His career was that of a dutiful imperial bureaucrat advocating just enough reform to correct abuses and to strengthen the regime's hard-won place in Europe's diplomatic order. Immediately upon assuming power, Alexander III faced a critical decision: whether to allow implementation of a constitutional proposal (called the Loris-Melikov Constitution) approved by his father on the very day of his assassination. Pobedonostsev had instilled in Alexander III a vocation to defend Orthodoxy, autocracy, and Russian nationality as principles at the core of Russian identity. In Pobedonostsev's mind, civil liberties, religious toleration, and progressive family law were not to be countenanced, and he pressed the new czar to recognize that parliaments were, in his words, "the greatest lie of our time."

Pobedonostsev's suasion proved decisive. Alexander III rejected the constitution and instead issued a temporary regulation that broadened police powers. What followed was a series of measures counteracting many of the Great Reforms of the 1860's: Land reform was thwarted, institutions of local government were curtailed, higher education was restricted, government censorship increased, the empire's minorities lost autonomy, and Jews experienced yet another wave of threats and pogroms (something Pobedonostsev himself fueled by his belief that Jews represented a revolutionary Polish influence). Pobedonostsev attached increasing importance to the role of the Russian Orthodox Church at a time of "chaos and willfulness." As procurator of the Holy Synod, Pobedonostsev sought to bring about renewal both by increasing the number of clergy, monasteries, and parish schools and by revising the seminary curriculum. Between 1881 and 1905, parish schools increased tenfold and their enrollment even more. Separation of church and state and a new definition of the church's social role also occupied Pobedonostsev's contemporaries, but he affirmed that the rippling influence of parish education was the answer to Russia's problems.

His students, Alexander III and Nicholas II, were not entirely convinced. They were not puppets in his hands, nor was Pobedonostsev the unthinking reactionary some have portrayed him to be. As a conservative ideologue, he was wedded to slow, "native" development. However, in an era of explosive economic and population growth, deteriorating urban conditions, and the influence of Western liberal ideas, Pobedonostsev was a man out of his element. As the new century approached, he became wistful for a more tranquil time, for the slower, pious rhythms of the Russian village. His private philanthropy sat oddly beside a caricatured public image of a gaunt, embittered bureaucrat with his "wings unfurled over Russia," as a poet wrote.

Five unsuccessful assassination attempts confirmed that his time had passed. He resigned his seat on the Holy Synod in October, 1905, when a general strike forced the regime to make changes—though not in time or not enough to save the empire, as the coming years would prove. Pobedonostsev died of pneumonia in March, 1907.

IMPACT

Konstantin Petrovich Pobedonostsev planted a deep distrust of popular government in Russia's last two czars, and he stiffened their resolve to resist liberalization and limits on their power through constitutional reform. His determined opposition to such reforms, even as the growing, industrializing empire began to fragment along social, ethnic, and religious lines, caused many to embrace more sweeping changes and ultimately, revolution.

FURTHER READING

Byrnes, Robert F. *Pobedonostsev: His Life and Thought.* Bloomington: Indiana University Press, 1968. Re-mains the authoritative biography of Pobedonostsev, covering every aspect of his development and career with a complete bibliography of his prolific writing.

Evtuhov, Catherine, et al. *Kazan, Moscow, St. Petersburg: Multiple Faces of the Russian Empire.* Moscow: OGI, 1997. More than two dozen articles (nineteen in Russian, six in English) place Pobedonostsev in the enterprise of empire building. His imperial vision and reactions to it are highlighted.

Polunov, A. "Konstantin Petrovich Pobedonostsev: Man and Politician." *Russian Studies in History* 39 (Spring, 2001): 8-32. A modern Russian account of Pobedonostsev's life and career, translated into English. Excerpts of Pobedonostsev's writing, expressing his disillusionment with modern life, are included in this thorough, though not groundbreaking, study.

—*Scott Lingenfelter*

SEE ALSO: Nicholas I; Grigori Yefimovich Rasputin; Yakov Mikhailovich Yurovsky.

POL POT

Cambodian dictator (1975-1979)

BORN: May 19, 1925; Prek Sbauv, Kompong Thom Province, Cambodia

DIED: April 15, 1998; Dangrek Mountains, near Choam Ksant, Cambodia

ALSO KNOWN AS: Saloth Sar (birth name); Brother Number One

MAJOR OFFENSE: Massive slaughter of the Cambodian population

ACTIVE: 1975-1979

LOCALE: Cambodia

SENTENCE: Lifelong house arrest; never tried by an internationally recognized government

EARLY LIFE

Born Saloth Sar in Prek Sbauv in the province of Kompong Thom, Cambodia, Pol Pot (pohl PAWT) began his Buddhist education at the age of eight at Wat Botum Vaddei in Phnom Penh. After a year, he went to live with an older brother, an official at the royal palace, and attended a French-run school where he was an average student. He displayed some interest in music and sports, especially soccer, but was an average player. World War II and Japanese control over French Indochina had little impact on his life. In 1943, he passed the examination for the *certificat d'études primaires complementaires* on his third try.

POLITICAL CAREER

In 1946, Saloth Sar joined the Viet-dominated Indochina Communist Party. In 1951, while studying in France on a radio engineering scholarship, he joined the French Communist Party. He became involved with other Cambodian students in what was called the Paris Study Group. This group later made up much of the leadership of the Khmer Rouge. After losing his scholarship in 1953, Saloth Sar returned to Cambodia, joined the Viet Minh, and took the nom de guerre of Pol Pot, possibly an abbreviation of *Politique Potentiel*. He became disillusioned with the Viet Minh because it focused solely on Vietnam; he then joined the Kampuchean People's Revolutionary Party, which increasingly called itself the Khmer Rouge.

After the French ceded control of Indochina in 1954, the newly independent Cambodia was under the rule of King Norodom Sihanouk. Sihanouk called for elections and abdicated his throne. Upon his election as prime minister in the new Cambodian government, the former monarch began to repress the Communists. For the following seven years, Pol Pot lived in hiding, training new members of the growing Khmer Rouge. By the late 1960's, the Cambodian government was engaged in open warfare against the Communists, who received support from the People's Republic of China.

THE KILLING FIELDS

In 1975, concurrent with the conquest of South Vietnam by Communist North Vietnam, Communists seized power in Laos and Cambodia. The Khmer Rouge remained shadowy for the first year of its rule, referring to Pol Pot only as Brother Number One and not initially acknowledging that the Khmer Rouge was the Communist Party. Pol Pot was influenced by the writings of Marxist Andre Gunder Frank, who held that only rural labor created wealth and that urban society exploited the peasants. Cambodia was renamed Democratic Kampuchea, and the Khmer Rouge began a program to turn the nation into a totally agrarian and ethnically homogeneous society. Pol Pot officially assumed the title of prime minister in 1976.

As relations with Vietnam became increasingly poor, anti-Viet hysteria grew within the ranks of the Khmer Rouge, leading to massive purges of cadre and army officers, as well as the large-scale murder of ordinary peasants. Xenophobic in the extreme, the Khmer Rouge executed an estimated ten thousand Vietnamese who lived in Cambodia as well as other people influenced by Vietnamese culture.

During almost four years of rule, the Khmer Rouge executed its suspected enemies, who included intellectuals, ethnic minorities, and anyone who had traveled abroad, spoke another language, or even wore eyeglasses. Estimates of the number of people who died as a direct result of Khmer Rouge policies vary from 1.5 million to well over 2 million people. The exact number is unknowable because of the collapse of civil society under the regime. The Khmer Rouge executed up to 100,000 people directly, while the other deaths are attributable to starvation, overwork, lack of medical care, and other causes for which the Khmer Rouge was directly responsible. Hundreds of thousands left the country as refugees.

Pol Pot, flanked by fellow Khmer Rouge leaders Ieng Sary, left, and Son Sen. (AP/Wide World Photos)

The repression of Viets led to intervention by Vietnam in December, 1978. The Vietnamese Army toppled the Khmer Rouge in 1979. What remained of the Khmer Rouge fought an increasingly marginalized guerrilla war against the Vietnamese, and later Cambodian, government forces.

Following its ouster, the Khmer Rouge maintained control over a diminishing area of Cambodia, predominantly along the Thai border. For several years Pol Pot continued to be recognized as the legitimate ruler of Cambodia by the United States and the People's Republic of China. By 1996, defections had weakened the Khmer Rouge to ineffectiveness.

LEGAL ACTION AND OUTCOME

In June, 1997, Pol Pot ordered the execution of longtime Khmer Rouge loyalist Son Sen and eleven members of his family for expressing a desire to seek amnesty from the Cambodian government. Pol Pot was arrested soon afterward by Ta Mok, the Khmer Rouge military chief, who sentenced Pol Pot to lifelong house arrest for ordering the murders. In April, 1998, sweeps by the Cambodian military forced Ta Mok to move into the jungles along the Thai border. The ailing Pol Pot remained under Ta Mok's control. On April 15, 1998, Pol Pot died, probably of a heart attack. His cremation was attended by a few dozen followers.

IMPACT

Pol Pot gave his most extensive interview about six months before his death. In it, he showed little remorse and stated his belief that he had been generally correct in the methods he used to pursue his goal that Democratic Kampuchea was to be, in his own words, "a precious model for humanity" whose egalitarian ways would erase human inclinations for exploitation, including the need for money and profit-making markets.

In his 2005 biography *Pol Pot*, Philip Short contends

POL POT'S PATRIOTISM

In 1997, Nate Thayer, a reporter for the Far Eastern Economic Review, *interviewed Pol Pot, who excused his atrocities as simply the mistakes of an ardent patriotism. He told Thayer:*

First, I want to let you know that I came to join the revolution, not to kill the Cambodian people. Look at me now. Do you think . . . I am a violent person? No. So, as far as my conscience and my mission were concerned, there was no problem. This needs to be clarified. . . . My experience was the same as that of my movement. We were new and inexperienced and events kept occurring one after the other which we had to deal with. In doing that, we made mistakes as I told you. I admit it now and I admitted it in the notes I have written. Whoever wishes to blame or attack me is entitled to do so. I regret I didn't have enough experience to totally control the movement. On the other hand, with our constant struggle, this had to be done together with others in the communist world to stop Kampuchea becoming Vietnamese. For the love of the nation and the people it was the right thing to do but in the course of our actions we made mistakes.

The question remains whether Pol Pot was a scoundrel—"Patriotism," Samuel Johnson famously said, "is the last refuge of scoundrels"—or simply insane. King Norodom Sihanouk, who knew Pol Pot well, thought the latter:

Pol Pot is very charming. . . . His face, his behaviour is very polite, but he is very, very cruel. . . . Pol Pot does not believe in God but he thinks that heaven, destiny, wants him to guide Cambodia in the way he thinks it the best for Cambodia, that is to say, the worst. Pol Pot is mad, you know, like Hitler.

Elizabeth Becker, a New York Times *correspondent, formed the same opinion. She interviewed Pol Pot and later wrote in a report to the British Broadcasting Corporation:*

"We want only peace," he said, "to build up our country." . . . Except for the occasional flickering of a wrist, Pol Pot remained motionless as he laid out his worst-case scenario, bragging that he would convince the U.S., Europe and most of Asia to support him.

I left convinced he was insane.

Sources: Nate Thayer, "My Education," *Far East Economic Review*, October 30, 1997, pp. 14-20, 21. Elizabeth Becker, "Pol Pot Remembered," available at British Broadcasting Corporation Web site.

that Pol Pot and the Khmer Rouge created "a slave state, the first in modern times." The utter lack of planning and common sense caused hunger and illness to claim a huge number of lives. Pol Pot and his followers never gave up the conviction that their plan could work, charging any shortcomings not to the brutality or miscalculations by the Khmer Rouge but to the failure of the Cambodians to work or sacrifice enough. Those failures were "corrected" by extreme punishment or by death through execution, which Pol Pot believed would deter slacking. All the while, any suspicion by Pol Pot that his leadership was questioned led to murderous purges within his own ranks. Unsustainable though it was, Pol Pot's regime lasted long enough to inflict untold agony.

FURTHER READING

Becker, Elizabeth. *When the War Was Over: Cambodia and the Khmer Rouge*. New York: Public Affairs, 1986. Standard account of the Khmer Rouge from its taking power in Cambodia until after its expulsion by the Vietnamese army. Becker traces the implementation of the Khmer Rouge's economic and ethnic ideology on Cambodia.

Kiernan, Ben. *The Pol Pot Regime: Race, Power, and Genocide in Cambodia Under the Khmer Rouge, 1975-1979*. New Haven, Conn.: Yale University Press, 2002. Scholarly account of the origins, internal workings, and fall from power of the Khmer Rouge.

Short, Philip. *Pol Pot: Anatomy of a Nightmare*. New York: Henry Holt, 2005. Extensive biography of Pol Pot intertwined with a history of the Khmer Rouge written by a senior BBC correspondent. While focusing primarily on the leadership of the Khmer Rouge, Short attempts to link it to Cambodian culture and history.

—Barry M. Stentiford

SEE ALSO: Khieu Samphan; Mao Zedong; Ne Win; Ta Mok.

JONATHAN POLLARD
American spy

BORN: August 7, 1954; Galveston, Texas
ALSO KNOWN AS: Jonathan Jay Pollard (full name)
MAJOR OFFENSE: Passing classified defense documents to Israeli agents
ACTIVE: 1979-1985
LOCALE: Washington, D.C.
SENTENCE: Life in prison

EARLY LIFE

Jonathan Pollard (PAHL-uhrd) grew up in South Bend, Indiana. His father was a prominent academic and scientist. Jonathan was the only Jewish student in his school and was bullied there. He became deeply interested in the Holocaust (seventy family members on his mother's side were murdered during this period) and in the security of the state of Israel. He graduated from Stanford University and then later attended the Fletcher School of Law and Diplomacy at Tufts University. In 1979, he was hired as an intelligence research specialist with the Field Operational Intelligence Office of the U.S. Navy in Washington, D.C.

ESPIONAGE CAREER

While at the Navy Field Operational Intelligence Office, Pollard met several Israeli operatives and contracted with them to supply classified documents in exchange for a regular monthly salary. The exact nature of these documents has never been officially revealed, but Pollard later claimed that they focused on military information concerning countries hostile to Israel, information that normally should have been shared between the United States and Israel.

LEGAL ACTION AND OUTCOME

Pollard's supervisor at work became suspicious of his activities, and the Federal Bureau of Investigation (FBI) launched an investigation. This culminated in Pollard's arrest on November 21, 1985, as he left the Israeli embassy in Washington, where he and his then-wife, Anne Henderson Pollard, had unsuccessfully sought asylum. Pollard pleaded guilty on June 4, 1986, to one count of providing a foreign country with national defense data. He was sentenced to life in prison the following March 5.

Several aspects of the court proceedings remained highly controversial. One of the main aspects of controversy was the plea agreement that Pollard reached, which included the prosecutor's recommendation that the court "impose a sentence of a substantial period of incarceration and a monetary fine." Some have claimed that the life term dispensed is disproportionate to the actual damage done and far greater than the average sentence received by other convicted spies. Many of the latter worked for countries that, unlike Israel, were not allied with the United States.

While this issue could normally have been appealed, Pollard's attorneys at the time neglected to do so within the mandatory ten-day post-sentencing time limit. A later habeas corpus petition filed with the U.S. Court of Appeals was rejected on the grounds that the ten-day requirement had not been met. At issue as well at the time of sentencing was a forty-six-page memorandum from then Defense Secretary Caspar Weinberger, the full text of which was never released to the public. It was alleged to include information especially damaging to Pollard that would greatly reduce the chances of his ever receiving a parole grant.

The case remained mired in controversy. The Israeli government, which granted Pollard citizenship in 1998, requested his release numerous times. There were rumors of impending release plans, some including "swaps" for Arab terrorists held in Israeli prisons, but no conclusive outcome as of 2006.

IMPACT

The case polarized the American Jewish community. Some felt that Jonathan Pollard's sentence was disproportionate, while others maintained that such criticism would inevitably be interpreted as a reflection of disloyalty to the United States. The case undoubtedly had a strong deterring effect on those who might contemplate assisting even "friendly" nations in the acquisition of intelligence information.

FURTHER READING

Blitzer, Wolf. *Territory of Lies*. New York: Harper and Row, 1989. A thorough accounting of all aspects of Pollard's espionage and the legal aftermath.

Henderson, Bernard. *Pollard: The Spy's Story*. New York: Alpha Books, 1988. The Pollard affair from the viewpoint of his ex-wife and codefendant, Anne Henderson Pollard.

Shaw, Mark. *Miscarriage of Justice: The Jonathan Pollard Story*. St. Paul, Minn.: Paragon House, 2001. A solid analysis of the legal dimensions and ramifications of Pollard's activities, with extensive analysis of the sentence he received.

—*Eric Metchik*

SEE ALSO: Anthony Blunt; Christopher John Boyce; Guy Burgess; John Cairncross; Klaus Fuchs; Robert Philip Hanssen; Alger Hiss; Daulton Lee; Donald Duart Maclean; Kim Philby; Ethel Rosenberg; Julius Rosenberg.

POLYCRATES OF SAMOS
Greek tyrant of Samos (c. 535-522 B.C.E.)

BORN: Date and place unknown
DIED: c. 522 B.C.E.; Magnesia, Thessaly, Greece
CAUSE OF NOTORIETY: Polycrates aimed to maintain an independent Samos and to establish maritime supremacy. To these ends, he pursued an aggressive foreign policy, annexing neighboring islands and making treaties with Egypt and Cyrene.
ACTIVE: 535-522 B.C.E.
LOCALE: Samos, Aegean Sea, and west coast of Turkey

EARLY LIFE

Information about the early life of Polycrates (puh-LIHK-rah-teez) of Samos is almost nonexistent. Most likely, he was born into a prominent aristocratic family. His father, Aeaces, survived an unstable political scene in Samos. Indeed, the fact that Polycrates seized power with the help of only fifteen soldiers suggests some sort of political arrangement.

POLITICAL CAREER

Polycrates' family may have styled themselves as champions against the Persians, who dominated the coast of Asia Minor. Originally, Polycrates shared power with his brothers, but in one of his first acts of treachery, he killed one and exiled the other. Militarily, he established Samos as a naval power with more than one hundred ships. He subdued surrounding islands and warred with one of the great cities of Asia Minor, Miletus, on the mainland. He defeated a fleet from Lesbos and placed the survivors in shackles, forcing them to dig a moat around his capital. Polycrates forged a defensive alliance with Egyptian pharaoh Amasis II against the Persians but later betrayed that alliance by volunteering forty ships to aid an invasion by Persian king Cambyses III.

Polycrates utilized his power in an attempt to elevate Samos not only militarily but also culturally. He constructed a large hole in the harbor in order to provide safe anchorage for his warships. He also built a large temple to the Greek goddess Hera and hired architect Eupalinus of Megara to construct a 3,300-foot tunnel through a mountain in order to bring water into the city. Polycrates' court attracted not only experts such as Eupalinus but also famous physicians such as Democedes and poets such as Ibycus and Anacreon. The tyrant's penchant for young men is demonstrated in his pursuit of Anacreon; in a fit of anger, he was reported to have cut off the hair of a rival lover. He also established a bazaar frequented by courtesans to compete with a similar one in Sardis.

The Greek historian Herodotus used Polycrates as an example of arrogant pride. He related the story that, fearing he had been too successful, Polycrates sought the advice of Amasis about ways to avoid being humbled by divine punishment. The pharaoh advised that he should cast away a prized possession, so Polycrates threw a valuable ring into the sea. A few days later, a fisherman caught a large fish and presented it as a gift to the king. When his servants cut it open, they found the ring. Polycrates once again inquired of Amasis, who indicated that he was fated to die.

Polycrates began to meet with reversals of fortune through his own perfidy. When he betrayed Egypt, he sent ships loaded with political rivals, expecting them not to return. However, when they did, they brought troops from Sparta and Corinth and besieged the city. Polycrates managed to defeat them only after forty days.

Shortly afterward, the Persian governor Oroetes invited Polycrates to Magnesia with the promise of wealth to rebuild his fleet. The governor indicated that he had fallen out of favor with Cambyses and needed military assistance. One tradition suggests that Oroetes had been embarrassed at a dinner when rivals mocked him about the existence of Samos's power right off the coast of his dominion. Despite warnings, Polycrates went to the meeting, only to be captured and executed. Oroetes crucified the corpse.

Impact

Polycrates of Samos became one of the last of the great tyrants of early Greek history. Herodotus utilized the tyrant's fate as an example of what happens to the proud who overstep their bounds before the gods.

Further Reading

Fine, John. *The Ancient Greeks*. Cambridge, Mass.: Harvard University, 1983. A general history of the Greek world, surveying archaeological and cultural developments from the prehistoric period to the arrival of Alexander the Great.

Freeman, Charles. *The Greek Achievement*. New York: Viking, 1999. A survey of Greek history for the general reader that focuses on the classical period but recognizes the need to explore the developmental periods.

Herodotus. *The Histories*. Translated by Robin Waterfield. New York: Oxford University Press, 1998. An excellent translation of the primary source for the general reader.

Kebric, Robert. *Greek People*. Mountain View, Calif.: Mayfield, 2001. An introduction to the society of the Greeks with excellent biographical inserts to illustrate culture.

—*Todd W. Ewing*

See also: Cypselus of Corinth; Phalaris.

CHARLES PONZI
Italian American financial swindler

BORN: March 3, 1882; Lugo, Italy
DIED: January 18, 1949; Rio de Janeiro, Brazil
ALSO KNOWN AS: Carlo Pietro Giovanni Guglielmo
    Tebaldo Ponzi (birth name); Charles Ponei; Charles
    P. Bianchi; Charles Borelli; Boston Swindler
MAJOR OFFENSES: Forgery, smuggling illegal
    immigrants, and mail fraud
ACTIVE: 1919-1920
LOCALE: Boston, Massachusetts
SENTENCE: Three years' imprisonment for forgery;
    two years' imprisonment for smuggling immigrants;
    five years' imprisonment in federal case for mail
    fraud, served four years; seven years' imprisonment
    for mail fraud in state of Massachusetts case

EARLY LIFE

Little is known of the life of Charles Ponzi (PON-zee)
prior to his emigration to the United States. Born Carlo
Pietro Giovanni Guglielmo Tebaldo Ponzi in Lugo, Italy, he was reportedly a petty criminal as a youth and was
either banished to the United States by his family or deported by Italian authorities. In 1903, the diminutive
(five-foot, two-inch) Ponzi arrived in America penniless.
He taught himself English and worked a series of jobs
in various localities before serving prison sentences in
Montreal, Canada, from 1908 to 1911 for forgery and in
Atlanta, Georgia, in the mid-1910's for smuggling illegal immigrants. During this time, Ponzi honed his skills
at financial manipulation, charm, and deception; while
imprisoned in Montreal, he convinced his mother that he
was actually working at the prison as a special assistant
to the warden. In 1918, he moved to Boston, where he began concocting an elaborate investment scheme.

CRIMINAL CAREER

Ponzi promised to remit returns as high as 50 percent to
investors by purchasing international postal vouchers in
countries with weak currencies and redeeming them in
the United States at substantial profits. His first investors
were friends and associates whose confidence was assured by Ponzi's convincing demeanor and his initial
ability to pay promised returns on their investments.
Ponzi took his enterprise public in December, 1919, emphasizing his ethnicity and immigrant status in order to
project the image of a self-made man seeking to share his
success with common folk. Using his gregarious demeanor to charm civic leaders and the media, he attracted
the support of several of Boston's most prominent citizens, in turn furthering his legitimacy with the addition
of potential investors. Newspaper advertisements highlighting the success of previous investors attracted increasing numbers of new investors; Ponzi hired agents to
bring in others. In less than six months, the scheme grew
to almost unmanageable proportions, bringing in money
so rapidly that at one point Ponzi was unable to find sufficient room in his office to store it.

However, as the number of investors increased, the
funds available to pay off their investments dwindled.
The scheme ultimately collapsed in late 1920 after newspaper exposure of Ponzi's criminal past scared off potential investors and prompted many already invested in the
scheme to withdraw their money. By this time, Ponzi was
living a lavish lifestyle and had become something of a
folk hero. It is estimated that investors recovered an average of one-third of their investments after the scheme
collapsed. Many investors lost their entire savings; still
others, having borrowed money and mortgaged property
to invest, were left penniless.

Charles Ponzi. (Library of Congress)

KUDOS FOR PONZI'S SCHEME

In the introduction to his hand-typed autobiography The Rise of Mr. Ponzi *(1937), Charles Ponzi takes great delight in quoting the accolades that his scheme initially received in the press. It is small wonder that his name became synonymous with the fraud he perpetrated.*

MEET MR. PONZI, THE CHAMPION GET-RICH-QUICK WALLINGFORD OF AMERICA

"Ponzi is the guy who put the crease in Croesus," wrote Neal O'Hara for the *Boston Traveler* toward the end of July, 1920. "He is the guy that ran up millions from a two-cent stamp. If five-spots were snow flakes, Ponzi would be a three day blizzard."

You've got to hand it to his credit. He makes your money gain 50 per cent in 45 days, which is as much as the landlords do. He delivers the goods with postage stamps, which is more than Burleson does. The way Ponzi juggles the reds and the greens, he makes Post Office look like a child's game. He simply buys stamps in Europe while the rest of the boys are buying souvenir post cards. And a postage stamp is still worth two cents in spite of the service you get for it, and any yap knows that you cannot get stuck on postage stamps unless you sit on the gluey side up.

Ponzi's way is cheaper than making money with your own sextuple press. The way he's got it fixed with postage stamps, the Government does the printing for him. He stretches a dollar into a million with all his sleeves rolled up. You furnish the dollar and Ponzi tosses in the six zeros in back of it. This baby can turn decimal points into commas on almost any bank-book. The way that Ponzi has money here and in Europe goes to prove that half of the world are squirrels and the other half nuts. The only thing that's got 'em worried is that they don't know which side is furnishing the nuts.

Worried isn't the half of it. According to Miss Marguerite Mooers Marshall, a staff writer for the *New York Evening World*, Ponzi had them in a frenzy. Listen to what she said:

Whoever said that proud old New Englanders are conservative, undoubtedly made that statement before the advent of Charles Ponzi. To-day all Boston is get-rich-quick mad over him, the creator of fortunes, the modern King Midas who doubles your money in ninety days. Did I say Boston? My mistake. I should have said the entire New England, from Calais, Maine, to Lake Champlain, from the Canadian border to New Jersey.

At every corner, on the street-cars, behind the department store counters, from luxurious parlors to humble kitchens, to the very outskirts of New England, Ponzi is making more hope, more anxiety, than any conquering general of old. Mary Pickford, Sir Thomas Lipton and smuggling booze over the Canadian border aren't in it any more.

LEGAL ACTION AND OUTCOME

Ponzi pleaded guilty to federal charges of mail fraud and was sentenced to five years in prison in 1920. Released in 1924 to face state charges, he jumped bail after receiving a nine-year prison sentence; he was recaptured in 1926 and imprisoned in Massachusetts. While a fugitive, he had operated a fraudulent land scheme in Florida, jumping bail once again to avoid a one-year prison sentence. Upon his release in 1934, Ponzi, who never had become an American citizen, was deported to Italy. There, he continued to concoct a variety of investment schemes, including a purported financial partnership with the regime of Italian leader Benito Mussolini. By the end of the 1930's, Ponzi was in Brazil working for the Italian state airline, which ceased its Brazilian operations during World War II. By the war's end, Ponzi was living in abject poverty, working odd jobs and drawing from the Brazilian unemployment fund. He suffered a stroke in 1948 and died in the charity ward of a Brazilian hospital the following year.

IMPACT

Despite the ultimate failure of its inventor, the Ponzi scheme set a precedent and led to more fraudulent investment operations, often called Ponzi schemes, in subsequent decades. These schemes have proven a viable means of swindling investors by creating the illusion of success in a scheme's early stages when sufficient funds are generated to pay investors. The perpetrators of the scheme typically attempt to abscond prior to its collapse but usually fail. Criminal charges, civil action, and bankruptcy often follow. Examples of large Ponzi schemes conducted in the United States include the "airplane game," which flourished in the 1980's; the activities of the Bennett Funding Group, which defrauded investors of approximately $700 million in the early 1990's; and the activities of Scientology minister Reed Slatkin, who bilked a number of Hollywood celebrities out of millions of dollars in the late 1990's. A Ponzi scheme sanctioned by the government of Albania failed in 1997, angering the citizenry and sparking a revolt that led to the collapse of the government. A large number of Ponzi schemes were active on the Internet at the outset of the twenty-first century.

A common variant of the Ponzi scheme is the pyramid sales scheme. Sometimes called multilevel marketing (MLM), this scheme involves the payment of a fee to authorize an individual to sell products or services and recruit other individuals into the business as subordinates, who pay commissions to their recruiters for the products that they sell. These subordinates are in turn encouraged to recruit their own salespeople to pay them commissions. Pyramid schemes often survive long enough for those at the top of the pyramid to realize substantial profits and avoid legal action, while those at the bottom of the pyramid make little or no profit and often lose money from payment of fees and commissions.

FURTHER READING

Ponzi, Charles. *The Rise of Mr. Ponzi*. Reprint. Naples, Fla.: Inkwell, 2001. A reprint of Ponzi's autobiography, written after his deportation to Italy. Containing a number of unverifiable claims, it is useful primarily for its insight into the personality of its author.

Weisman, Stewart L. *Need and Greed: The True Story of the Largest Ponzi Scheme in American History*. Ithaca, N.Y.: Syracuse University Press, 1999. Insider account of the Bennett Funding Group scam from the company's general counsel.

Zuckoff, Michael. *Ponzi's Scheme: The True Story of a Financial Legend*. New York: Random House, 2005. This detailed biography of Ponzi places his infamous financial scheme in the context of American society and culture in the early twentieth century.

—*Michael H. Burchett*

SEE ALSO: John R. Brinkley; Tino De Angelis; Bernard Ebbers; Billie Sol Estes; Susanna Mildred Hill; Megan Louise Ireland; Henri Lemoine; Victor Lustig; Alexandre Stavisky; Joseph Weil.

JAMES PORTER
American priest and pedophile

BORN: January 2, 1935; Revere, Massachusetts
DIED: February 11, 2005; Boston, Massachusetts
ALSO KNOWN AS: James Robert Porter (full name)
MAJOR OFFENSES: Sodomy, indecent assault and battery on children, and unnatural and lascivious acts
ACTIVE: 1960-1974, 1986-1987
LOCALE: Massachusetts, Minnesota, Nevada, New Mexico, and Texas
SENTENCE: Six months in prison in Minnesota; eighteen to twenty years in prison in Massachusetts

EARLY LIFE

James Robert Porter (POR-tuhr) was born in a suburb of Boston. His father was a chemist for an oil company. Porter graduated from Boston College with a degree in mathematics in 1956 and attended St. Mary's Seminary in Baltimore. He was ordained a Roman Catholic priest on April 2, 1960.

CRIMINAL CAREER

Porter began his career as a priest in 1960. He later admitted that during his priesthood, he molested between fifty and one hundred girls and boys, beginning with his first assignment at St. Mary's in North Attleborough, Massachusetts. Among these victims was Frank Fitzpatrick, who grew up to be a Rhode Island private investigator; he later tracked down Porter and publicized the abuse he suffered at Porter's hands as an altar boy. When concerned parents notified Porter's superiors of the abuse, he was reassigned to another parish. This pattern of molestation, accusation, and transferal to other parishes continued for years. Throughout this period, Porter underwent electroshock therapy (which he later blamed for his loss of memory of the abuse) and spent a prolonged period at an institution designed for priests with sexual abuse problems in New Mexico.

Pronouncing himself "cured," Porter resumed his priestly duties in Minnesota in 1969. However, he was dismissed from his assigned parish in 1970 after allegations of sexual abuse; he then found employment at a Minnesota bank after he received a dispensation from the priesthood at his request. He married Verlyne Kay Bartlett in 1976, quit his job, and raised his four biological children before divorcing his wife in 1995. He later admitted to molesting his children's fifteen-year-old babysitter, and his former wife testified that she suspected that Porter had also molested their oldest son, who later

PARISHIONERS' VIEWS

James Porter's parishioners recall him with both suspicion and uneasy fondness in "Town Secret," a Boston Globe *feature story by Linda Matchan published August 29, 1993, while Porter was under indictment for large-scale abuse.*

[M]any adults were impressed with this chatty, down-to-earth curate. . . .

"I thought he was a goofy, galooping, gangly kind of guy," says Richard L. Sherman, who belonged to a Protestant church but recalls that Porter had a strong presence in the town even among non-Catholics. "He was a priest for the kids at a time when priests interested in kids were thought to be good." . . .

"He was not likable, he was lovable," says Bob Van Ness. "He was very charismatic. You could talk to him about anything. He was accessible. He was everything every kid wanted to be, but he was an adult, in a position of power and respect." . . .

But it wasn't long before a darker side of Porter's personality emerged. He had a hair-trigger temper that could erupt on the sports field. He developed a habit of hugging girls and asking boys for back rubs. The friendly punches on boys' arms got rougher and hurt. The playful wrestling became aggressive and more physical. Some of the older boys called him "the horn," a reference to the priest's apparent horniness.

abused his own three-year-old brother before dying of a drug overdose at age twenty-three.

LEGAL ACTION AND OUTCOME

In December of 1992, Porter served four months of a six-month sentence for sexual assault on a minor in Minnesota. On December 6, 1993, Porter pleaded guilty to forty-one indictments of sexual assault on twenty-eight children under the age of sixteen in southeastern Massachusetts. He was sentenced to eighteen to twenty years in a maximum-security prison. More than five dozen victims then dropped their lawsuits in exchange for a cash settlement of more than five million dollars by the diocese of Fall River, Massachusetts. Porter finished serving his sentence in January, 2004, but continued to be in-

carcerated until a civil commitment hearing concerning his sexual dangerousness could be completed. He was still awaiting this hearing at the time of his death in 2005.

IMPACT

Father James Porter was the first priest to serve time in the Catholic Church sex abuse scandal of the 1990's. According to John Daignault, a Harvard University psychologist, Porter's victims formed "the largest single group of victims of one perpetrator, in a position of authority, in psychology's history." Hundreds of victims stepped forward as a result of this case, and the settlements that were awarded by the Catholic Church in this case and other cases precipitated a financial crisis in many Catholic dioceses both in the Boston area and in other major cities within the United States.

FURTHER READING

The Boston Globe. Betrayal: The Crisis in the Catholic Church. Boston, Mass.: Little, Brown, 2002. In methodical detail, reporters from *The Boston Globe* assemble their chronicles of the investigation of the sex abuse story in the Archdiocese of Boston in 2001-2002. The book recounts the graphic stories of the victims, the official cover-up, and the reaction of Boston Catholics to the scandal.

Jenkins, Philip. *Pedophiles and Priests: Anatomy of a Contemporary Crisis.* New York: Oxford University Press, 1996. Jenkins traces the most prominent cases of pedophile priests since the early 1980's, offering an objective look at the extent of the problem, the effects of the media's coverage, the financial repercussions on the Church's assets, and a psychological examination of repressed or recovered memory.

Plante, Thomas G., ed. *Sin Against the Innocents: Sexual Abuse by Priests and the Role of the Catholic Church.* Westport, Conn.: Praeger, 2004. A compilation of essays on the sex abuse scandal in the Church from authorities representing a variety of perspectives, including psychologists, a Vatican correspondent, and a former director of a facility that offered treatment to clergy involved in sexual abuse.

—*Mara Kelly-Zukowski*

SEE ALSO: Gilbert Gauthe.

ADAM CLAYTON POWELL, JR.
American politician

BORN: November 29, 1908; New Haven, Connecticut
DIED: April 4, 1972; Miami, Florida
CAUSE OF NOTORIETY: Though controversial for his flamboyant lifestyle and strong support of civil rights, Powell became notorious when the House of Representatives voted to deny him his congressional seat after the 1966 elections.
ACTIVE: 1944-1970
LOCALE: Harlem, New York, and Washington, D.C.

EARLY LIFE
Adam Clayton Powell (POW-ehl), Jr., was the son of one of Harlem's most influential ministers, Adam Clayton Powell, Sr., pastor of the Abyssinian Baptist Church. In spite of his privileged upbringing, Powell struggled academically at both City College of New York and Colgate University, where he alienated his peers by attempting to pass as white. After graduation, he returned to Harlem as a business manager, then associate pastor, at Abyssinian.

As his father grew closer to retirement, Powell developed a reputation across Harlem for developing ministries aimed at elevating the plight of Harlem's poor. Though many in the church harbored concerns about Powell's raw ambition and well-publicized forays with showgirls, his charismatic personality made him popular with his own generation, and in 1937, he was chosen to be the new pastor of Abyssinian.

Adam Clayton Powell, Jr. (AP/Wide World Photos)

POLITICAL CAREER
As pastor of Harlem's largest and most respected African American congregation, Powell became one of the borough's most visible figures. He fought for antilynching laws, campaigned for jobs, and picketed businesses that discriminated against African Americans. In 1940, with the encouragement of well-heeled supporters and strong backing from labor and the Democratic Party, he won a seat on the New York City Council. He continued working for civil rights in his new post but soon tired of the bureaucratic demands of the job.

In 1943, a new congressional district was established in Harlem and Powell decided to run for the seat. His campaign attracted broad support, including celebrities such as Langston Hughes and Lionel Hampton, and in 1944, he was elected the first African American Congress member from the Northeast. Though he was often abrasive and confrontational in his political dealings in Washington, he eventually ascended to the chairmanship of the House Committee on Education and Labor and played a significant role in legislation dealing with social justice.

His flamboyant and extravagant lifestyle, his wont for nepotism, and his questionable financial dealings kept Powell embroiled in scandal throughout his career. He placed his wife on his office payroll, took kickbacks from his aides, and used public funds to pay for vacations. In the early 1950's, several of his aides were convicted of tax evasion, and Powell himself was later indicted on the same charge. A decade later, he lost a well-publicized libel suit and, when he refused to pay the judgment, the House of Representatives voted in 1967 to deny him his seat. He won reelection in 1968, and the Supreme Court ordered him reinstated; however, with his power diluted and his reputation destroyed, he was defeated in the 1970 elections.

IMPACT
In an era when the struggle for civil rights was beginning to bear fruit, Powell's financial misdeeds and fast living made him an embarrassment to the cause for which he had fought during much of his life. Furthermore, Powell was not averse

to using his political power to cover up personal problems or to slandering opponents when politically expedient. When Martin Luther King, Jr., attempted to organize a protest at the 1956 Republican Convention, Powell, who was supporting Dwight D. Eisenhower's candidacy in an attempt to secure political favors, threatened to spread a rumor that King was having a homosexual affair with Bayard Rustin, another prominent civil rights activist.

In spite of the scandals, Powell is celebrated by many as a major figure in the Civil Rights movement. As one of only two African Americans in Congress at the time, Powell was instrumental in raising awareness of racial issues among politicians in Washington. He denounced President Harry S. Truman's wife, Bess, for her membership in a racially discriminatory organization and demanded service in Washington establishments that excluded African Americans. He criticized Congress for its inaction on lynching and condemned the poll taxes being used across the South to discourage African American voters. Most important, he repeatedly proposed a bill, known as the Powell Amendment, designed to deny federal funding to any agency practicing racial discrimination.

His impact extended beyond racial matters. As chair of the House Committee on Education and Labor, he was instrumental in the passage of much of the era's most progressive social legislation, including the creation of Medicare, Medicaid, and the minimum wage. President Lyndon Johnson considered Powell the primary architect of the Great Society, Johnson's landmark antipoverty program.

Powell's legacy continued to be celebrated among the citizens of New York and his constituents in Harlem. Adam Clayton Powell, Jr. Boulevard runs through the center of Harlem. In 1983, the state of New York renamed its Harlem offices the Adam Clayton Powell, Jr. State Office Building, and in 2005, worked with the Adam Clayton Powell, Jr. Memorial Committee to erect a bronze statue of Powell in front of the building.

FURTHER READING

Hamilton, Charles V. *Adam Clayton Powell, Jr.: The Political Biography of an American Dilemma*. New York: Atheneum, 1991. A well-researched and detailed exploration of how the confrontational Powell used his race and the microscope of partisan politics to challenge America's democratic ideals.

Haygood, Wil. *King of the Cats: The Life and Times of Adam Clayton Powell, Jr.* New York: Houghton Mifflin, 1993. An intimate examination of Powell's personal life and the astute and sometimes heavy-handed manner in which he used his political power in the pursuit of both personal privilege and social justice.

Powell, Adam Clayton, Jr. *Adam by Adam: The Autobiography of Adam Clayton Powell, Jr.* New York: Dial Press, 1971. A frank and revealing look at Powell's rise and fall and the flamboyant lifestyle he lived among Washington insiders, from Powell's own perspective late in life.

Ransby, Barbara. *Ella Baker and the Black Freedom Movement: A Radical Democratic Vision*. Chapel Hill: University of North Carolina Press, 2003. A biography of one of the Civil Rights movement's most influential, though little-known, figures, including Baker's distrust of Powell and several revealing incidents in their relationship.

Tate, Katherine. *Black Faces in the Mirror: African Americans and Their Representatives in the U.S. Congress*. Princeton, N.J.: Princeton University Press, 2002. A scholarly examination of the relationships between African American representatives and their African American constituencies, and the effect of those relationships on the legislative actions of the representatives.

—*Devon Boan*

SEE ALSO: Oakes Ames; Wilbur Mills.

LEWIS POWELL
Confederate conspirator in Abraham Lincoln's assassination

BORN: April 22, 1844; Randolph County, Alabama
DIED: July 7, 1865; Washington, D.C.
ALSO KNOWN AS: Lewis Paine; Lewis Payne; Lewis Thornton Powell (full name)
MAJOR OFFENSES: Attempted murder of Secretary of State William Seward; accomplice in assassination of President Abraham Lincoln
DATE: April 14, 1865
LOCALE: Mainly Washington, D.C., and surrounding area
SENTENCE: Death by hanging

EARLY LIFE

Lewis Powell (POW-uhl), the son of a Baptist preacher and gentleman farmer, was the youngest of nine children. He was probably educated by his parents at home. At the age of twelve, he was kicked by a mule while playing at home. The accident resulted in a broken jaw and a missing molar, causing the left side of his jaw to be more prominent than the right—a fact that later was important for his identification.

When Powell was fifteen, the family moved from their Georgia home to a small plantation near Live Oak, Florida, where he supervised the plantation for the following two years. In 1861, almost as soon as he learned of the outbreak of the Civil War, he volunteered to fight for the Confederacy. Accepted as a private in the infantry on May 30, 1861, the tall and handsome seventeen-year-old adolescent would never again see any of his family members.

ESPIONAGE CAREER

In 1863, Powell was wounded and taken prisoner in the Battle of Gettysburg. Transferred to the U.S. Army hospital at Baltimore, he escaped with the help of an admiring volunteer nurse, Margaret Branson. He then served with distinction in John Mosby's Rangers, which was an elite unit of the Virginia cavalry. In January, 1865, Powell left the Rangers to work with the Confederate Secret Service. When signing an oath of allegiance to the Union, he used the alias Lewis Paine. Moving to Baltimore, Powell lived at Branson's boardinghouse, which was home to several persons working in Confederate espionage. While there, he gained the

reputation of having a violent temper, especially after he assaulted an African American maid for not promptly cleaning his room.

John Surratt, a Confederate sympathizer in Maryland, introduced Powell to actor John Wilkes Booth, who recruited him to participate in a plot to kidnap President Abraham Lincoln. Booth apparently thought that Powell's physical strength and ability to use firearms would help in the venture. On March 17, 1865, Booth and his followers were prepared to capture Lincoln as the president was en route to visit a nearby hospital. The plan failed because of Lincoln's last-minute decision to cancel the visit.

Soon thereafter, Booth decided that a better scheme was to assassinate the president and other Union officials in order to produce chaos in the government. On April 14, after Booth learned that Lincoln would be attending

Lewis Powell, in overcoat. (Library of Congress)

Ford's Theatre, the conspirators held their last meeting. Powell agreed to kill Secretary of State William Seward at about the same time that Booth would kill the president. Fellow conspirator David Herold agreed to accompany Powell on the mission. Soon after 10:00 P.M., the two men arrived at the Seward home. Powell, armed with a revolver and a bowie knife, gained entrance by claiming that he was delivering medicine from the doctor. In the house, Powell brutally struck Seward's son and then rushed into Seward's room, where he slashed and stabbed the secretary numerous times before being restrained by another son and a bodyguard. Thinking that Seward was dead, Powell ran out of the house. Herold had already fled, and Powell escaped alone on his horse.

LEGAL ACTION AND OUTCOME

Having made no plans for an escape, Powell hid in a wooded area for three days. Cold and hungry, he sought refuge in Mary Surratt's boarding home. Unfortunately for him, military policemen at that moment were investigating the home, and a resident identified Powell as one of Booth's associates. The officers noticed the blood still on Powell's clothing. Soon thereafter, eyewitnesses from the Seward home identified Powell as the attacker. He neither acknowledged nor denied his guilt.

Because President Andrew Johnson and Secretary of War Edwin Stanton viewed Lincoln's assassination as an act of war, they decided to try the conspirators by a military commission. Powell's lawyer, William Doster, unsuccessfully attempted to mitigate his client's guilt by arguing that war experiences had resulted in partial insanity. Found guilty after a seven-week trial, Powell and three other codefendants were hanged on July 7, 1865. The remaining four defendants received prison sentences. Powell's body would be disinterred and buried several times, and his skull mysteriously appeared at the Smithsonian Museum in 2002.

IMPACT

At the end of the Civil War, many who had been allied with or fought for the South saw the Union victory, and the Lincoln administration at its head, as enemies of their way of life. Lewis Powell and Booth were among the more radical of these Confederate sympathizers. Powell's impact on history would have been much greater if Seward had not survived. During his trial and execution, Powell attracted considerable attention because of his handsome appearance and his stoic, detached demeanor. Some observers at the time thought that he was either mentally deficient or suffering from a psychiatric disorder. Those writers who believed in an undiscovered political conspiracy focused much of their attention on Powell, in large part because he often appeared to act irrationally. Most historians, however, have concluded that evidence of his guilt is beyond any reasonable doubt.

FURTHER READING

Hanchett, William. *The Lincoln Murder Conspiracies.* Urbana: University of Illinois Press, 1983. A good historical summary followed by excellent analyses of the many books and theories about the assassination.

Ownsbey, Betty. *Alias "Paine": Lewis Thorton Powell, the Mystery Man of the Lincoln Conspiracy.* Jefferson, N.C.: McFarland, 1993. A scholarly and sympathetic attempt to understand Powell's personality and motivation.

Shelton, Vaughan. *Mask for Treason: The Lincoln Murder Trial.* Harrisburg, Pa.: Stackpole Books, 1965. Although the book contains many interesting facts, Shelton's speculations are usually not based on good evidence or sound logic, especially his theory that Paine and Powell were two different men.

Steers, Edward, Jr. *Blood on the Moon: The Assassination of Abraham Lincoln.* Lexington: University Press of Kentucky, 2001. Steers's work is considered the finest account of the assassination written to date.

Swanson, James, and Daniel Weinberg. *Lincoln's Assassins: Their Trial and Execution.* Santa Fe, N.Mex.: Arena, 2001. A concise account that is very interesting and readable, with many excellent photographs and other illustrations.

—Thomas Tandy Lewis

SEE ALSO: John Wilkes Booth; Mary Surratt.

MIGUEL PRIMO DE RIVERA
General and dictator of Spain (1923-1930)

BORN: January 8, 1870; Jerez de la Frontera, Cádiz, Spain

DIED: March 16, 1930; Paris, France

ALSO KNOWN AS: Miguel Primo de Rivera y Orbaneja (full name); Marquis of Estella

CAUSE OF NOTORIETY: Primo de Rivera's dictatorship helped discredit the Spanish constitutional monarchy and contributed to the onset of the Spanish Civil War.

ACTIVE: 1923-1930

LOCALE: Spain

EARLY LIFE

Born in 1870 to an aristocratic family from southern Spain, Miguel Primo de Rivera y Orbaneja (mee-GEHL PREE-moh day ree-VIHR-ah ee ohr-bahn-EH-hah) graduated in 1888 from the Military General Academy in Toledo. His uncle Fernando, the first marquis of Estella and a distinguished military officer, inspired Primo de Rivera's career. When Fernando died in 1921, the nephew inherited his uncle's title. Gregarious, charismatic, and philandering, Primo de Rivera served with distinction throughout the Spanish empire and in 1911 was promoted to brigadier general. Meanwhile Primo de Rivera married Casilda Sáenz de Heredia y Suárez de Argudín in 1902, and they had six children, including José Antonio, founder of the Spanish Falange Party, and Pilar, active in both the Falange government and that of General Francisco Franco.

As Spain lurched from one political crisis to the next, Primo de Rivera became convinced that his nation's political system had failed. He was perturbed with Spain's loss to the United States in the Spanish-American War (1898) and the insurgency that threatened his nation's hold on Morocco. Equally frustrating was the breakdown of order within Spain, which was beset by poverty, unemployment, strikes, and leftist labor agitation. The constitutional monarchy seemed incapable of solving any of the problems. In 1921, the Moroccans inflicted a major defeat on the Spanish army, and some politicians accused the military of corruption and incompetence.

POLITICAL CAREER

Exasperated by the accusations and the political mess, the military overthrew the parliamentary government on September 23, 1923, and made Primo de Rivera dictator. King Alfonso XIII named him prime minister, tying the monarchy's fortunes to the dictatorship. Many Spaniards supported the dictatorship because of the political and social turmoil, although the Left opposed it. Primo de Rivera considered himself a Spanish patriot who would briefly govern Spain to right the economic and political ills caused by the politicians. He suppressed Catalan and Basque separatists and, in alliance with the French, dealt the Moroccans a crushing defeat in 1927. Under the guidance of economic minister José Calvo Sotelo, the regime built infrastructure to modernize Spain and provide public employment. The Primo de Rivera government mediated disputes between labor and management, which helped the workers. For a time, Primo de Rivera's dictatorship enjoyed broad popular support.

Nonetheless, it was a dictatorship, even if a mild one. It depended on the acquiescence of the Roman Catholic Church and the military, whose power and interests he could not challenge. Spain needed agrarian reform, but the Church and the elite prevented it. Primo de Rivera lacked a civilian constituency to whom he could turn over political power, although in 1924, he organized the Patriotic Union, a political movement that failed to generate popular enthusiasm. In 1926, he held a plebiscite to demonstrate support for his government, and the following year he convened an advisory National Assembly. It created a new constitution in 1929, to be approved by plebiscite the following year.

In 1929, however, the seeds of the dictatorship germinated. Spaniards tired of Primo de Rivera and his regime. Intellectuals resented his suppression of civil rights. Massive public spending caused rapid inflation. The post-World War I economic boom ended, and the Great Depression of the 1930's was on the horizon. When the king and military turned against Primo de Rivera, he resigned on January 26, 1930, and went into exile in Paris. He died of complications from diabetes on March 16.

IMPACT

A populist dictator, Miguel Primo de Rivera saw himself as a patriot, but despite his good intentions, his regime contributed to Spain's downward spiral into civil war, which occurred between 1936 and 1939. Discredited by his support for Primo de Rivera, the king abdicated in 1931. A republic replaced the monarchy, but it could not deal with the political factionalism, which the Depression intensified. The civil war gave birth to Franco's far more brutal fascist dictatorship.

FURTHER READING

Ben-Ami, Shlomo. *Fascism from Above: The Dictatorship of Primo de Rivera in Spain, 1923-1930.* New York: Oxford University Press, 1983. Compares Primo de Rivera's dictatorship to contemporary European regimes and, despite the book's title, argues that Primo de Rivera fell in part because his movement was not fascist.

Carr, Raymond. *Spain, 1808-1975.* Oxford, England: Clarendon Press, 1982. A detailed and insightful survey with a substantial section devoted to Primo de Rivera's dictatorship and its consequences for Spain.

Rial, James H. *Revolution from Above: The Primo de Rivera Dictatorship in Spain, 1923-1930.* Fairfax, Va.: George Mason University Press, 1986. A clearly organized but traditional account that emphasizes Primo de Rivera's personal failings as the reason for his regime's demise.

—*Kendall W. Brown*

SEE ALSO: Francisco Franco.

GAVRILO PRINCIP
Bosnian Serb nationalist terrorist

BORN: July 25, 1894; Obljaj, Bosnia, Austro-Hungarian Empire
DIED: April 28, 1918; Theresienstadt Prison, Austria
MAJOR OFFENSES: Assassination of Archduke Franz Ferdinand of Austria and his wife, Countess Sophie von Chotkovato
ACTIVE: June 28, 1914
LOCALE: Sarajevo, Bosnia
SENTENCE: Twenty years' imprisonment

EARLY LIFE

Gavrilo Princip (GAHV-ri-loh PREHN-tseep), a Serbian national, was born in Bosnia, which was under the rule of the Austro-Hungarian Empire although still de jure part of the Ottoman Empire. He was one of nine children born to Petar and Maria Nana Mičič. As a child Gavrilo contracted tuberculosis, which would eventually lead to his death. He attended school at Grahovo, the local center. An excellent student, he went to the Bosnian capital, Sarajevo, to pursue studies at the military academy but changed to the merchant's school. Princip also enjoyed medieval Serbian history and its romantic folklore.

CRIMINAL AND POLITICAL CAREER

In 1908, Austria-Hungary formally annexed Bosnia. Serbs in both Bosnia and the neighboring kingdom of Serbia reacted furiously, believing that the annexation thwarted their goal for union. Princip joined the illegal Serbian nationalist organization Mlada Bosna (Young Bosnia), and the school authorities expelled him from school. Mlada Bosna forged a secret alliance with the Serbian group in Belgrade known as Unification or Death (Ujedinjenje ili Smrt), popularly called the Black Hand. Serbia was fresh from victories in the Balkan Wars; the press openly proclaimed that the next conquests would be in Bosnia against Vienna. Unification or Death supplied Young Bosnia with money and weapons to commit terrorist acts against the Austrians.

The plan that Young Bosnia hatched was the assassination of the Austrian archduke Franz Ferdinand, whose children were in line for the throne. Franz Ferdinand was a particularly ideal and opportune target. He appeared to favor the Triune program, which would give Slavs equal rights in the empire, making the union of Bosnia and Serbia even more difficult. Furthermore, the archduke and his wife, Sophia, were planning a goodwill tour of Sarajevo for June 28, 1914. This was a double insult, as June 28 was the reputed date of the legendary Battle of Kosovo Field in 1389—a major event in Serbian folk mythology.

Because the route of the procession was well publicized, the assassins knew exactly where to station themselves. The archduke was to travel up Appel Quay, along the river to the city hall, for a ceremony. Assassins with bombs and guns were ready along the route. An assassin threw a bomb at the archduke's car, but the driver avoided it, and it damaged the following car, injuring some of the riders. After the ceremony the archduke insisted on going to the hospital to see the injured. When the driver erroneously began to turn off Appel Quay, he was told to go straight. As the driver was backing up, Princip, who had lost his nerve after the failure of the first attempt but was now precisely at that corner, seized the opportunity. He jumped on the running board of the archduke's car and fired several shots into Franz Ferdinand and his pregnant wife, fatally wounding them both. The police quickly grabbed Princip and hustled him off to jail.

UNIFICATION OR DEATH: THE BLACK HAND

In May of 1911, radical Serbian nationals joined to form the constitution of the terrorist organization Ujedinjenje ili Smrt (Unification or Death) commonly known as the Black Hand. It was this organization to which Princip, along with co-conspirators Nedjelko Cabrinovic and Trifko Grabez, belonged and which sponsored the assassination of Archduke Franz Ferdinand. Its constitution appears in part below:

ARTICLE 1. For the purpose of realising the national ideals—the Unification of Serbdom—an organization is hereby created, whose members may be any Serbian irrespective of sex, religion, place of birth, as well as anybody else who will sincerely serve this idea.

ARTICLE 2. The organisation gives priority to the revolutionary struggle rather than relies on cultural striving, therefore its institution is an absolutely secret one for wider circles.

ARTICLE 3. The organization bears the name: "Ujedinjenje ili Smrt."

ARTICLE 4. In order to carry into effect its task the organization will do the following things:

   (1) Following the character of its raison d'être it will exercise its influence over all the official factors in Serbia—which is the Piemont of Serbdom—as also over all the strata of the State and over the entire social life in it:

   (2) It will carry out a revolutionary organisation in all the territories where Serbians are living:

   (3) Beyond the frontiers, it will fight with all means against all enemies of this idea:

   (4) It will maintain friendly relations with all the States, nations, organisations, and individual persons who sympathise with Serbia and the Serbian race:

   (5) It will give every assistance to those nations and organisations who are fighting for their own national liberation and unification. . . .

ARTICLE 35. On entering into the organisation the joining member must pronounce the following oath of allegiance:

I (the Christian name and surname of the joining member), by entering into the organisation "Unification or Death," do hereby swear by the Sun which shineth upon me, by the Earth which feedeth me, by God, by the blood of my forefathers, by my honour and by my life, that from this moment onward and until my death, I shall faithfully serve the task of this organisation and that I shall at all times be prepared to bear for it any sacrifice. I further swear by God, by my honour and by my life, that I shall unconditionally carry into effect all its orders and commands. I further swear by my God, by my honour and by my life, that I shall keep within myself all the secrets of this organisation and carry them with me into my grave. May God and my comrades in this organisation be my judges if at any time I should wittingly fail or break this oath!

Source: Henri Pozzi, *Black Hand over Europe* (London: Francis J. Mott, 1935).

LEGAL ACTION AND OUTCOME

Princip was tried and, because he was a minor, he was sentenced to twenty years in prison at Theresienstadt, the maximum sentence permitted under Austrian law. While there, he lost his arm to tuberculosis and later died in 1918.

IMPACT

The consequences of Gavrilo Princip's act were the events of the following five weeks, which led to the outbreak of World War I. While Princip is remembered as the perpetrator of one of the key turning points of world history, it is doubtful that the failure of the assassination attempt would have prevented war among the great powers. The war's underlying causes most likely would have brought about the conflagration sooner or later. However, as the igniting event, the assassination has been the topic of much discussion.

Why was the route so publicized when the anti-Austrian propaganda and activity of Serbia and the Serbs was so prevalent? Was the driver of the archduke's car complicit in the plot? Were some officials in the Austro-Hungarian Empire willing to sacrifice the heir to the throne for an excuse to go to war against Serbia? What was Germany's role in the events? Did it push Vienna to make harsh demands on Belgrade in order to bring about a war that Germany believed would be short and victorious, or give Vienna a "blank check," simply stating that it would back up any decision the Austrians made? Did Serbia refuse to give in to Austrian demands because it knew Russia and France would stand behind it?

In any case, the assassination brought about the war, which indeed ended the Austro-Hungarian Empire and created an enlarged Serbia—Yugoslavia, including Bosnia.

A museum dedicated to Mlada Bosna was opened

on the corner where the assassination took place, and Princip's footprints were carved in the sidewalk in front to memorialize the assassin. In 1991 Bosnia, which was established as an autonomous republic within Yugoslavia, declared its independence, and a bloody civil war among the Serbs, Croats, and Bosnians erupted. According to the 1995 Dayton Accords, the republic was divided among the three ethnic groups. A group of Serbian nationalists opposed to the accords formed a secret organization called Gavrilo Princip, which threatened Serbian officials in the republic.

FURTHER READING

Cassels, Lavender. *The Archduke and the Assassin: The Road to Sarajevo*. New York: Stein and Day, 1985. A standard academic monograph which covers the life of Princip and the events of June 28, 1914. Extensive bibliography.

Dolph Owings, W. A., ed. *The Sarajevo Trial*. Chapel Hill, N.C.: Documentary, 1984. A collection of documents about Princip's trial, including an account by the assassin himself. Notes by the editor.

Fromkin, David. *Europe's Last Summer: Who Started the Great War in 1914?* New York: Knopf, 2004. This account of the origins of World War I challenges the view that it was an unfortunate series of accidents and lays the blame on the intentions of Berlin.

Ross, Stewart. *Assassination in Sarajevo: The Trigger for World War I.* Chicago: Heinemann Library, 2001. Designed for middle-school students, this book explains the events of June 28, 1914, with maps and illustrations, detailing how the assassination led to World War I.

—*Frederick B. Chary*

SEE ALSO: John Bellingham; Sante Jeronimo Caserio; Leon Czolgosz; Giuseppe Fieschi; Charles Julius Guiteau; Richard Lawrence; Eligiusz Niewiadomski.

JOSEPH PROFACI
Mafia boss

BORN: October 2, 1897; Villabate, Palermo Province, Sicily, Italy

DIED: June 7, 1962; New York, New York

ALSO KNOWN AS: Olive Oil King; Joe Profaci

CAUSE OF NOTORIETY: Profaci's various illegal enterprises included labor rackets, gambling, loan-sharking, extortion, and drug trafficking.

ACTIVE: 1920's-1960's

LOCALE: New York

EARLY LIFE

Born in Palermo, Italy, in 1897, Joseph Profaci (proh-FAH-chee) was part of a wave of Sicilian Mafiosi who immigrated to New York during the 1920's. With already-established ties to several criminal organizations and legitimate businesses, Profaci required little mentoring upon his arrival. He quickly moved up the ranks of organized crime in New York and earned a reputation as one of the most hated mob bosses in the history of the American Mafia.

CRIMINAL CAREER

Throughout his three-decade reign as boss of the Profaci crime family, Profaci maintained a close alliance with fellow mob boss Joseph Bonanno. With the backing of the Bonanno crime family, Profaci's leadership went unchallenged for a large part of his criminal career. Like other Mafiosi, Profaci made extra income and was able to protect his illegal enterprises by involving himself in legitimate business. For a time, he was one of the United States' largest importers of olive oil, an honor that earned him the nickname the Olive Oil King. While he was successful in his legitimate business ventures, most of Profaci's wealth came from traditional Mafia enterprises of extortion and protection rackets.

Despite being a faithful churchgoer and a large contributor to church charities, Profaci gained the reputation of being a tyrant within his own crime family. In keeping with Old World traditions, he demanded monthly dues from all of his men. These dues were supposed to be held in a "slush fund" to take care of legal fees and support the families of Mafia "soldiers" when they were imprisoned. Most of the money, however, ended up in Profaci's pockets. Profaci also demanded a large share of his soldiers' illegal profits, which led to a great deal of resentment and hostility within the family.

LEGAL ACTION AND OUTCOME

In 1959, Profaci ordered the murder of a numbers operator who had stopped paying tributes. Joseph "Joe Jelly"

863

Gioiello, a member of a Profaci crew headed by the notorious Gallo brothers, carried out the hit. Brothers Larry, Albert, and Joey Gallo expected to receive a large share of the deceased operator's gambling business, but to their dismay, Profaci distributed most of the business among his friends and family. This event sparked a family war that pitted Profaci and his associates against the Gallo brothers and several other defectors.

Other New York City bosses, with the exception of Profaci's longtime ally Bonanno, eagerly anticipated the family's self-destruction. However, the bloody war never did reach a conclusion. In 1961, the Gallo faction suffered a major loss when Joe Gallo was sent to prison for extortion. In 1962, Profaci died of cancer, leaving the family under the control of his brother-in-law Joseph Magliocco. Magliocco died of natural causes in 1963 and was replaced by Joseph Colombo, Sr., who in 1964 arranged a truce with the Gallo faction.

IMPACT

The Profaci crime family (known today as the Colombo crime family) was one of five Italian American syndicates to emerge from the Castellammarese War, which pitted mob boss Salvatore Maranzano and his Old World followers against Joe Masseria, whose followers included both Sicilian and non-Sicilian Mafiosi. While the Maranzano group would emerge victorious, Salvatore's Old World style and traditions irritated the more Americanized gangsters who were moving up the ranks of organized crime in New York at this time. Before Maranzano's assassination in 1931, he appointed Joseph Profaci head of his own family.

During his three-decade reign as boss, Profaci carried on the Old World traditions of the original Sicilian Mafia. While remembered by some as a greedy, iron-fisted dictator, Profaci saw himself as a traditionalist. His death marked the end of an era in the American Mafia. The Profaci/Colombo family would remain one of the most powerful organized crime groups in New York, involved in a wide array of crimes, including narcotics trafficking, gambling, loan-sharking, cigarette smuggling, pornography, and counterfeiting.

FURTHER READING

Abadinsky, Howard. *Organized Crime*. 7th ed. Belmont, Calif.: Wadsworth/Thomson Learning, 2003. Provides a detailed analysis of organized crime in New York and Chicago and examines several emerging international groups.

Bonanno, Bill. *Bound by Honor: A Mafioso's Story*. New York: St. Martin's Press, 1999. Bonanno dispels several myths about the American Mafia and provides rare insights into several New York crime families.

Bonanno, Rosalie, and Beverly Donofrio. *Mafia Marriage*. New York: St. Martin's Paperbacks, 2003. Rosalie Bonanno's intimate account of life inside the Mafia offers shocking details about two infamous New York crime families.

—James C. Roberts and Thomas E. Baker

SEE ALSO: Joe Colombo; Joe Gallo; Salvatore Maranzano; Joe Masseria.

PUYI
Last emperor of China (r. 1908-1924) and emperor of Manchukuo (r. 1932-1945)

BORN: February 7, 1906; Beijing, China
DIED: October 17, 1967; Beijing, China
ALSO KNOWN AS: Pu Yi; P'u-i (Wade-Giles); Aisin Gioro; Henry Puyi; Xuantong (Pinyin reign name); Kangde (of Manchukuo); Hsüan-t'ung (Wade-Giles reign name)
MAJOR OFFENSE: War crimes, specifically collaboration with the Japanese
ACTIVE: 1932-1945
LOCALE: China, primarily Beijing, Tianjin, Mukden (Shenyang), and the Soviet Union
SENTENCE: Detained without trial for nine years; then pardoned

EARLY LIFE

From his birth in 1906, Puyi (pew-ee) was groomed for imperial office. His father, Zaifeng, the second Prince Chun, was half brother of the reigning Guangxu emperor, and his mother, Youlan, Princess Chun, was a Manchu lady whose father was an imperial general. When Puyi was only two, his uncle the Guangxu emperor died, and on December 2, 1908, Puyi was enthroned as the Xuantong emperor. His father became his regent.

IMPERIAL CAREER

The Chinese Revolution led to Puyi's abdication on February 12, 1912. China became a war-torn republic, but

Puyi was permitted to stay in Beijing's imperial Forbidden City. After he captured Beijing, the warlord Zhang Xun restored Puyi as emperor on July 1, 1917, but widespread Chinese opposition caused Puyi's second abdication on July 12. In 1922, one year after the suicide of his mother, Puyi married his wife, Wan Rong, and his concubine Wen Xiu. On November 5, 1924, another warlord, Feng Yuxiang, expelled Puyi and his family from the Forbidden City. Puyi escaped to the Japanese concession in Tianjin, where he soon came under Japanese influence.

After the Japanese conquered Manchuria from the Chinese in 1931, they looked to Puyi to legitimize their occupation. As a Manchu, Puyi seemed an ideal candidate to set up a puppet government. The Japanese army offered Puyi the rule of Manchuria as a country independent of China. In November, 1932, Puyi agreed and was taken to Manchuria.

Despite his wishes to use Manchuria for his restoration as emperor of China, the Japanese merely allowed Puyi to become president of the new state of Manchukuo on March 9, 1932. Only Japan, Germany, and Italy recognized Manchukuo, with the League of Nations opposing its creation.

Puyi served the Japanese propaganda that promoted the creation of a modernized, independent Manchuria while, in effect, turning the country into a Japanese industrial and agricultural base in what was formerly northeast China. Puyi allowed his Japanese advisers to run the government in his name.

For his loyalty, the Japanese rewarded Puyi with imperial honors. On March 1, 1934, he became the Kangde emperor of Manchukuo. In 1935, Puyi visited Japan and paid homage to Japanese emperor Hirohito (r. 1929-1989). He refused, however, to marry a Japanese, taking the Manchu teenager Tan Yuling as his third wife in 1937, his concubine having divorced him in 1931.

When Japan invaded China in 1937, Puyi's Manchukuo was ordered to support the Japanese war effort. Puyi allowed the resources of Manchukuo to go to the Japanese fighting the Chinese. On his second visit to Japan, in 1940, Puyi accepted emperor Hirohito's ancestors as his own.

As Japan entered World War II against the Western Allies, Puyi let Japan turn Manchukuo into a tightly policed military support center. The Manchu were forced to labor hard for the Japanese war effort, and rations continued to be reduced. With his first wife an opium addict and

Puyi, Emperor of Manchukuo.

Tan Yuling dying in 1942, perhaps poisoned by the Japanese, Puyi married a Han Chinese, the high school student Li Yuqin. He also allegedly pursued a palace boy. As the tide of war turned against Japan, Puyi participated in honoring kamikaze pilots departing from Manchukuo. On August 9, 1945, the Soviet Union declared war on Japan and attacked Manchukuo. When Japan surrendered on August 15, Puyi abdicated as emperor of Manchukuo.

LEGAL ACTION AND OUTCOME

On August 18, while he was stopping over at Shenyang on his attempted escape flight to Japan, Soviet paratroopers who had just arrived arrested Puyi in the airport terminal. Taken as a prisoner of war to the Soviet Union, Puyi was housed rather well. In 1946, he was flown to Tokyo to testify against his former advisers, now accused Japanese war criminals. After mainland China became Communist in 1949, the Soviets handed over Puyi to China in 1950.

In China, Puyi was detained without trial in Fushun

War Criminal Prison in Manchuria. He was treated as a criminal, forced to do labor and to undergo re-education. He began writing a confessional autobiography indicating his reform. Imprisoned for nine years, Puyi was pardoned on the suggestion of Mao Zedong and released on December 4, 1959.

After his release, Puyi worked for a year in the Beijing Botanical Gardens before becoming a historian in 1961. Divorced since 1956, he married his last wife, nurse Li Shuxian, in 1962. He was appointed to a party committee and published his autobiography in 1964. Just as Puyi was beginning to be harassed at the outbreak of the Cultural Revolution in 1966, he died of kidney cancer on October 17, 1967.

IMPACT

Puyi was too young actually to reign as the last emperor of China. His decision to ally himself with the Japanese turned him into a notorious anti-Chinese collaborator. However, as an ethnic Manchu, his dislike of the Han Chinese, his former subjects, was fueled by memories of his expulsion from the Forbidden City in 1924, during which three bombs were dropped on the palace, and the defilement of his imperial ancestors' tombs by the troops of a republican warlord in 1928.

Whatever good Puyi intended to do for his people as emperor of Manchukuo was ruined when he let the resource-rich empire to be run as a virtual Japanese colony. Puyi allowed the Japanese to oppress his people and freely use his country as a military base. When released from jail, Puyi became a symbol of the success of Communist re-education.

FURTHER READING

Bertolucci, Bernardo, director. *The Last Emperor*. 1987. Historical film chronicling Puyi's life fairly accurately, shot in part on location in Beijing's Forbidden City. Contains newsreels of his rule as emperor of Manchukuo.

Pu Yi, Aisin-Gioro. *From Emperor to Citizen*. Translated by W. J. F. Jenner. 1964-1965. Reprint. Beijing, China: Foreign Languages Press, 2002. Confessional autobiography of Puyi, which he started to write in Chinese prison.

Spence, Jonathan. *The Search for Modern China*. Reprint of rev. ed. New York: W. W. Norton, 2001. Puts Puyi in the context of twentieth century Chinese history and covers his deposition, his years with the Japanese, his arrest by the Soviets, his release from prison, and his death.

—*R. C. Lutz*

SEE ALSO: Yoshiko Kawashima; Mao Zedong; Yuan Shikai.

MUAMMAR AL-QADDAFI
Libyan head of state and commander in chief of the armed forces

BORN: 1942; near Surt, Libya

ALSO KNOWN AS: Muammar Abu Minyar al-Qaddafi (full name); Mu'ammar al-Qaddafi; Muammar al-Gaddafi; Moammar al-Qadhafi

CAUSE OF NOTORIETY: Qaddafi allegedly aided and abetted international terrorism and revolutions, as well as political assassinations.

ACTIVE: 1970's-1980's

LOCALE: Munich, Berlin, Athens, Rome, Scotland, and elsewhere

EARLY LIFE

Born in a shepherd family some twenty miles south of the coastal town of Surt (also known as Sirte), Muammar al-Qaddafi (MOO-ahm-mahr ahl kah-DAH-fee) was the only son of Mohammed Abdul Salam bin Hamed bin Mohammed and Aisha Qaddafi. He belonged to the small al-Qaddafa tribe, predominantly of Arabized Berber stock.

Muammar al-Qaddafi. (AP/Wide World Photos)

Sensitive to the value of education, Qaddafi's parents started young Qaddafi on a cycle that was to see him in a Qur'ānic elementary school at Surt, a secondary school at Sebhā in the Fezzan region where his family had moved, at another secondary school at Misrātah, and at the University of Libya in Benghazi to study history. However, Qaddafi was not a particularly good student at any institution.

His initial political activism took the form of supporting general, anticolonial movements. In 1963, he entered the Royal Libyan Military Academy in Benghazi, where he was joined by some of his earlier schoolmates. Following graduation in 1965, Qaddafi attended a military school in Beaconsfield, England, for training in advanced military communications. Upon his return, he was assigned to the Libyan army's signal corps in 1966.

POLITICAL CAREER

While still a cadet, Qaddafi had formed the secret Unionist Free Officers Movement in emulation of his icon, Egypt's Colonel Gamal Abdel Nasser, with the avowed objective of assuming power. After several delays, Qaddafi and his fellow officers overthrew the regime of the sickly and aging King Idris I in a nearly bloodless coup on September 1, 1969. Thus, at age twenty-seven Qaddafi, soon promoted to colonel, became the leader of the world's fourth largest oil producer. Qaddafi chaired a Revolutionary Command Council, which initially functioned as the new regime's executive branch.

The regime was popular in its early years as it undertook serious efforts to redistribute the country's large landholdings, spread the growing oil revenues among the masses, and fiercely uphold the country's independence. After taking over the remaining United States and British military bases in Libya in 1970, Qaddafi nationalized Italian and Jewish property, embarked on more radical measures at home and abroad, and, eventually, nationalized all foreign oil companies. Domestically, in 1973, Qaddafi introduced a series of workers' committees and congresses at all levels of the state in order to implement his economic and social theories. These theories were highlighted in *The Green Book* (1976-1978), which roughly spelled out in three slim volumes Qaddafi's philosophy of the revolution. The treatise covered Arab nationalism and anti-imperialism, an unorthodox form of pan-Islamism, as well as complete egalitarianism.

COLONEL QADDAFI ADVISES THE WEST

Although many world leaders continued to distrust him into the twenty-first century, Muammar al-Qaddafi began normalizing relations with Europe and the United States. On his Web site, in fact, he seems to want to protect the West from the dangers of radical Islam:

The plans of Islamist Turks in Europe and obviously behind them the Islamic grass roots is to revive Albania as an Islamic state, as well as Bosnia. Therefore, infidel Europe, as they believe, will be for the first time before the pressure of the new European Islamic front, behind which is the entire Muslim world, one which will force Europe into embracing Islam or pay poll tax, this is provided for in the Quran as a duty. Such information could be surprising or amusing to some, but for Muslims it is a message from God that has to be realized.

The future from now on is for Islamic parties in Turkey and for supporters of Ben Laden. Subscription to any Islamic party, particularly if they are newly formed in Turkey, is surprising. In few years time, several millions, including one million women, joined one of the Islamic parties in Turkey. Ben Laden, the Mullahs and the Loya Jirgah (Grand Assembly) will be happy and indeed gainers if Turkey joins the European Union.

Furthermore, Turkey will drag with it to Europe a set of problems and indeed explosive ones, such as the Kurdish problem, sectarian conflict, and a potential war over the Tigris and Euphrates, membership of the Organization of Islamic Conference, Islamic D8, and Turkey's roots in the Islamic Central Asian states. . . .

It was possible for me not to toll this alarm bell and not to uncover this horrifying map. However, due to my responsibility to the stability of the world in the first place and peace in the Mediterranean, which the Arabs possess its southern coast—of which Libya occupies two-thousand kilometers of this southern coast, since there is no coast in the south without Libya—all this makes it incumbent upon me to speak out to the world about what I see as far as this strategic issue is concerned, which will have serious reflections that will touch my country, its region and then shake the entire world, before it is too late and before a decision is taken that will have serious consequences.

Source: AlGathafi Speaks, www.algathafi.org.

Most notoriously, Qaddafi was identified as the instigator or financier of international terrorism and the exporter of revolution. Many believed him to have held significant roles in the massacre of Israeli athletes at the 1972 Munich Olympics, the killing and injuring of U.S. military personnel at a West Berlin discotheque in 1986, and the blowing up of Pan American Flight 103 over Lockerbie, Scotland, in 1988; each of these acts involved serious loss of life in the air or on the ground. However, in 1986, the Reagan administration in Washington, D.C., retaliated against Qaddafi with Operation El Dorado Canyon: It bombed military targets in Tripoli and Benghazi. Collateral damage involved private and foreign property, and Qaddafi's adopted infant daughter, Hanna, was killed.

Qaddafi's subversive activities included his material support for such revolutionary groups as the Irish Republic Army, the Palestine Liberation Organization, the Soviet-based Red Army brigades, and other "liberation fronts." Moreover, in 1973, Libyan forces seized the uranium rich Aozou Strip in Chad (a slice of land bordering Libya) but eventually bowed to a World Court ruling and withdrew in 1994.

Following the collapse of his Soviet sponsors at the end of the Cold War in 1991, Qaddafi became much more compliant with international pressures, including those from the West. Thus, by 1999, he agreed to hand over to a court in the Netherlands the two Libyan agents who had been accused of planting the explosives aboard Pan American Flight 103. By 2003, he also paid the ordered compensation to the flight's victims. Furthermore, he agreed to terminate his weapons of mass destruction program and opened his facilities to international inspection. His return to acceptance by the West (although not so much by America) climaxed in the lifting of sanctions against Libya and the visit of British prime minister Tony Blair to Qaddafi, who, in 2004, characteristically received the head of state in his desert tent.

Not all Libyans agreed with Qaddafi. By 1975, a number of army officers were charged with trying to overthrow the regime; a public execution of twenty-two of them was held in 1977. Thereafter, the government engaged in a program of political assassination of Libyan dissidents, who were characterized as "stray dogs." In the meantime, the mercurial Qaddafi fell out with a number of foreign leaders, such as Egyptian president Anwar el-Sadat, for having signed the Camp David peace accords with Israel, anathema to Qaddafi, in 1979. Conversely, at various times Qaddafi courted Egypt, Syria, Tunisia, Chad, and Morocco in the interest of pan-Arab unity of which Qaddafi hoped to be champion, like his hero Nasser.

IMPACT

Muammar al-Qaddafi, the consummate revolutionary and leader of the world's onetime "rogue" state, did not ultimately change the world; rather, the world changed him. By 2001, Qaddafi was expressing sympathy for the victims of the September 11 terrorist attacks against the United States and publicly hoped for more foreign investments in Libya. In May, 2006, the administration of U.S. president George W. Bush removed Libya from its list of terrorist nations and planned to renew normal diplomatic and commercial relations. Some surmise that perhaps highly fluctuating oil prices had a sobering effect on Qaddafi's revolutionary sensibilities or that he may have discovered the great difficulty in forging Arab unity—an issue about which he professed great disappointment. Of lasting importance has been his Great Man-Made River Project and his significant progress in raising his country's living standards.

FURTHER READING

Arnold, Guy. *The Maverick State: Gaddafi and the New World Order.* New York: Cassell, 1996. Assesses Qaddafi's disproportionate ability to make waves in the world thanks to his unpredictability and his oil-generated resources.

Christman, Henry M., ed. *Qaddafi's "Green Book": An Unauthorized Edition.* Buffalo, N.Y.: Prometheus Books, 1988. An introduction and translated text of Qaddafi's philosophy of the revolution.

Stanik, Joseph T. *El Dorado Canyon: Reagan's Undeclared War with Qaddafi.* Annapolis, Md.: Naval Institute Press, 2003. Details the American air attack of April, 1986, on Libya, as well as other retaliatory strikes meant to punish Qaddafi for his role in international terrorism.

Tanter, Raymond. *Rogue Regimes: Terrorism and Proliferation.* New York: St. Martin's Press, 1998. Highlights Qaddafi's state-sponsored terrorism and his attempts to build weapons of mass destruction.

Vandewalle, Dirk, ed. *Qadhafi's Libya, 1969-1994.* New York: St. Martin's Press, 1995. Includes a series of essays detailing the Libyan leader's revolution and its consequences.

—*Peter B. Heller*

SEE ALSO: Sani Abacha; Abu Nidal; Idi Amin; Samuel K. Doe; Saddam Hussein; Ayatollah Khomeini; Haile Mengistu Mariam; Muhammad Siad Barre; Charles Taylor.

WILLIAM CLARKE QUANTRILL
Confederate partisan leader during the American Civil War

BORN: July 31, 1837; Canal Dover (now Dover), Ohio
DIED: June 6, 1865; Louisville, Kentucky
ALSO KNOWN AS: Charley Hart; Charles William Quantrill
CAUSE OF NOTORIETY: As the leader of the most active of the pro-Confederate irregular forces operating along the Kansas-Missouri borderlands, Quantrill received international notice as the perpetrator of one of the Civil War's most horrific atrocities, the sack of Lawrence, Kansas.
ACTIVE: August 21, 1863
LOCALE: Missouri, Kansas, and Kentucky

EARLY LIFE

William Clarke Quantrill (KAN-trihl) was the eldest child of Thomas Henry Quantrill, a tin fashioner turned school principal, and his wife, Caroline Cornelia Clarke. His father having died when William was seventeen, the younger Quantrill tried to make his way by teaching school, hunting, and doing odd jobs in Ohio, Indiana, and Illinois. Suspected of committing murder in Mendota, Illinois, he briefly returned home, then made his way west as far as Utah before arriving in Kansas Territory to take part in the border wars between antislavery and proslavery forces. Gaining an unsavory reputation as a con artist, rustler, and, again, homicide suspect, Quantrill, under the assumed name of Charley Hart, first sided with antislavery "Jayhawkers." In 1860 he betrayed three companions and henceforth identified himself with the proslavery and, later, Confederate cause.

MILITARY CAREER

Joining Confederate forces at the outbreak of the Civil War (though never apparently as part of a regular unit), Quantrill was present at the Confederate victory at Wilson's Creek, Missouri, on August 10, 1861. However, organized warfare was not to his liking, and he became part of the impromptu, irregular bands that emerged

The sack of Lawrence, Kansas. (Library of Congress)

along the frontiers of Missouri, Arkansas, Kansas, and the Indian Territory (Oklahoma), and which, while proclaiming their support for either side, usually had their own agenda. Quantrill's marksmanship and ruthlessness had made him a local hero in Blue Springs, Missouri, and he joined the partisans there, operating under the command of Andrew Walker. In December, 1861, upon Walker's resignation, Quantrill became the undisputed leader.

Quantrill's Raiders became the most audacious and effective of the partisan guerrilla forces along the Missouri border, terrorizing and quite often murdering prisoners in cold blood. Quantrill's forces were instrumental in capturing Independence, Missouri, August 10-11, 1862. Four days later, General Thomas C. Hindman fully authorized Quantrill's unit. Quantrill was thus elected to his only known commission, as captain in the Confederate forces, though he would claim the title of colonel by war's end.

In 1863, he met and married Sarah Catherine King; they apparently had no children. On August 21, 1863, having eluded the defensive cordon erected at the Kansas border by General Thomas Ewing, Jr., Quantrill de-

scended with 450 men on the town of Lawrence, Kansas, pillaged and torched most of the buildings, and shot down some 200 men, most of whom were unarmed. Others died in the flames. The sack of Lawrence was Quantrill's most controversial action but was followed on October 6, 1863, by the ambush of the ceremonial escort for Major General James G. Blunt at Baxter Springs, Kansas. About ninety of Blunt's men were shot after surrendering, and fewer than ten of the command (including Blunt himself) were able to escape death.

Retreating to Texas for the winter of 1863-1864, Quantrill's men proved so unruly and disruptive, and revelations of the full nature of Quantrill's atrocities so disgusted Confederate authorities, that the guerrilla chief was arrested by General Henry McCulloch on March 30, 1864, but almost immediately escaped. In 1864, Quantrill's band broke apart; a group under William "Bloody Bill" Anderson defected, and in the summer of 1864 Quantrill himself was deposed from the leadership by George Todd. Before the year was done, both Todd and Anderson were slain, and Quantrill's activities were relegated to occasional, minor raids. At some time in November-December, 1864, Quantrill hatched a plan to move his operations to Kentucky, ostensibly to get as far as Virginia, but the surrender at Appomattox seemed to eliminate that option. Quantrill's band was finally tracked down by Edwin Terrell's pro-Union partisans at Taylorsville, Kentucky, on May 10, 1865. During a brief skirmish, Quantrill was shot in the spine; he later died of his wound in the Louisville military prison hospital.

IMPACT

As the leading pro-Confederate guerrilla during most of the conflict, William Clarke Quantrill occupied Union troops that might have otherwise been used elsewhere; thus Quantrill probably much prolonged the fighting in the war's Western theater. The atrocities he perpetrated, however, were widely condemned even by pro-Confederates and bequeathed to the region within which he operated a lasting legacy of horror and revulsion. The relentless fashion, moreover, in which the Raiders conducted their campaigns spilled over into the postwar period when outlawed bands and vigilante groups carried on old feuds, attempted to avenge past grudges, and continued to unsettle the Missouri-Kansas frontier for years to come. The desperado gang led by Frank and Jesse James, and Cole and Jim Younger—all of whom had served under Quantrill—proved to be the most successful and was not disbanded until the 1880's.

FURTHER READING

Goodrich, Thomas. *Black Flag: Guerrilla Warfare on the Western Border, 1861-1865*. Bloomington: Indiana University Press, 1995. Places Quantrill in the overall context of the fighting on the fringes of the Confederacy. Includes detailed campaign maps.

Leslie, Edward E. *The Devil Knows How to Ride: The True Story of William Clarke Quantrill and His Confederate Raiders*. New York: Da Capo Press, 1998. This account, one of the most balanced on the subject, skillfully places the Quantrill phenomenon within the context of its era and region, fitting it into the overall pattern of atrocity and retaliation practiced by both sides.

Martin, Jane A., and Jeremy Ross, eds. *Spies, Scouts, and Raiders: Irregular Operations*. Alexandria, Va.: Time-Life Books, 1985. Fourteen pages are devoted to the details of the story of Quantrill's Raiders and the offshoot bands of George Todd and "Bloody Bill" Anderson.

Nichols, Bruce. *Guerrilla Warfare in Civil War Missouri, 1862*. Jefferson, N.C.: McFarland, 2004. Quantrill plays a significant role in this "slice" of the war in the West.

Schultz, Duane. *Quantrill's War: The Life and Times of William Clarke Quantrill, 1837-1865*. New York: St. Martin's Press, 1996. Detailed and highly readable account which nonetheless relies too much on anecdotal material and makes Quantrill more one-dimensional than he actually was.

—*Raymond Pierre Hylton*

SEE ALSO: Jesse James; Henry Wirz; Cole Younger.

JOHN QUELCH
English pirate

BORN: c. 1665; London, England
DIED: June 30, 1704; Boston, Massachusetts
MAJOR OFFENSES: Robbery and murder
ACTIVE: August, 1703-February 17, 1704
LOCALE: Marblehead, Massachusetts, and the Atlantic Ocean near Brazil
SENTENCE: Death by hanging

EARLY LIFE

A contemporary account chronicling the 1704 proceedings against John Quelch (jon kwehlch) includes the only known information regarding his early life, noting that Quelch's mother was in London at the time of his birth, approximately thirty-eight years prior to when Massachusetts authorities sentenced him.

At some point, Quelch traveled to the New England colonies, where he probably engaged in seafaring activities, as sources referred to Quelch having navigation expertise which resulted in his later being designated to lead a pirate crew. He may have worked as a privateer, acquiring insight and practice in the seizure and plundering of vessels.

CRIMINAL CAREER

During July, 1703, Massachusetts governor Joseph Dudley contracted with Boston businessmen for privateering services of their brigantine, *Charles*, to secure French trading ships based near Newfoundland and Acadia (modern Nova Scotia). By August, a crew, including Quelch, had prepared the *Charles* to embark from the harbor at Marblehead, northeast of Boston.

In letters, Captain Daniel Plowman warned the vessel's owners that he distrusted the crew and that those businessmen should choose another captain. Crew members prevented owners from boarding the ship to consult Plowman. Departing on August 4, Plowman soon became sick and stayed in his cabin, which several members of the crew prevented him from leaving. After Plowman died on August 6, the mutineers designated Quelch as their captain. Some crew members, including slaves, asked to return to port but were refused.

Quelch and his men reached South American waters by fall, 1703. Interested in acquiring gold, Quelch focused on pursuing trade ships near Brazil. His crew first attacked a Portuguese fishing vessel on November 15, 1703, stealing its contents, including fish and salt. They continued assaulting crafts from that country through February 17, 1704, seizing eight additional vessels and a cargo of gold, silk, and other valuables. His crew sank at least one ship and wounded and killed Portuguese crewmen.

LEGAL ACTION AND OUTCOME

Heading north, Quelch reached Marblehead in May, 1704, and told his men to disperse. Late in that month, the *Boston News-Letter* reported that the *Charles* had docked. After reading the news concerning their ship, the owners asked authorities to apprehend and charge the mutineers. Lieutenant-Governor Thomas Povey distributed a proclamation authorizing the arrest of the pirates and confiscation of stolen cargoes. Militia captured and jailed Quelch on May 25. Authorities emphasized that he had violated Article XVIII, which diplomats from England and Portugal included in the Treaty of May 16, 1703, defining piracy during peacetime between those countries.

Officials held a trial for Quelch on June 19, 1704, before the Court of Admiralty at Boston's courthouse. Quelch heard several of his crew testify against him. He claimed he had not known about that treaty, asserting that he had thought privateering Portuguese vessels was legal. Judges ruled Quelch and five associates guilty, sentencing them to death. After Quelch spoke about being falsely accused and the risks of wealth, officials hanged him and his crew members on June 30, 1704.

IMPACT

John Quelch's trial was an early application of royal piracy laws in the colonies. His piracy emboldened some Massachusetts officials to profit from his gains. Soon after Quelch's arrest, legal authorities secured cargo he had robbed, kept some items, and disbursed portions to associates and the royal treasury. Portugal and traders were not reimbursed for their stolen goods.

In late June, 1704, the *Boston News-Letter* printed a distinctive broadsheet describing Quelch's trial, in addition to regular issues. Many scholars considered circulation of that independent issue devoted to trial news the earliest special edition of a newspaper in the North American colonies. Readers in Quelch's birthplace received copies of the trial edition specially shipped to England.

FURTHER READING

Dow, George F., and John H. Edmonds. *The Pirates of the New England Coast, 1630-1730.* Introduction by Ernest H. Pentecost. Glorieta, N.Mex.: Rio Grande Press, 1993. Appendixes include the text of Quelch's speech prior to his execution and Plowman's privateering commission and instructions.

Pennell, C. R., ed. *Bandits at Sea: A Pirates Reader.* New York: New York University Press, 2001. Considers legal implications when judges exonerated slaves Quelch had seized on captured ships and forced into piracy.

Seitz, Don C. *Under the Black Flag: Exploits of the Most Notorious Pirates.* Mineola, N.Y.: Dover, 2002. Devotes a chapter to Quelch's piracy and trial, placing his crimes in the context of colonial thievery.

—*Elizabeth D. Schafer*

SEE ALSO: Samuel Bellamy; Charlotte de Berry; Stede Bonnet; Anne Bonny; William Dampier; William Kidd; Sir Henry Morgan; Grace O'Malley; John Rackham; Mary Read; Bartholomew Roberts; Edward Teach.

VIDKUN QUISLING
Norwegian fascist leader (1933-1945)

BORN: July 18, 1887; Fyresdal, Norway
DIED: October 24, 1945; Oslo, Norway
ALSO KNOWN AS: Vidkun Abraham Lauritz Jonssøn
  Quisling (full name)
MAJOR OFFENSE: High treason against the kingdom
  of Norway
ACTIVE: 1940-1945
LOCALE: Norway, mainly Oslo
SENTENCE: Death by firing squad

EARLY LIFE

Vidkun Quisling (VIHD-kewn KWIHS-lihng) was the son of Jon Lauritz Quisling, a Lutheran minister and genealogist, and Anna Karoline Bang, both of whom were tied to respected families in the Telemark region of southern Norway. The family had three sons, Vidkun, Jorgen, and Arne, and one daughter, Esther. Vidkun was a talented and energetic student who received high marks as a war academy cadet, excelling in mathematics. He served in the Norwegian military between 1918 and 1921, where he achieved the rank of major. In his early career he served as a military attaché in Petrograd, Russia (1918-1919), and Helsinki, Finland (1919-1921), and as a relief worker in Russia with the famed Norwegian explorer Fridtjof Nansen.

Quisling was made a commander of the Order of the British Empire for his humanitarian work in Russia, the Ukraine, and the Caucasus region. From 1931 to 1933 he was defense minister in the Karlstad government, led by the Agrarian Party. While defense minister, Quisling exposed the Labor Party's plan to set up a Bolshevik regime in Norway which would have been backed by Russia. He was forced to resign as defense minister, however, after setting his office ablaze in imitation of the Reichstag fire.

In 1933, on Norway's Constitution Day, May 17, Quisling and Johan Hjort organized the Norwegian fascist party, known as the National Unity Party or Nasjonal Samling. The party was anticommunist, strongly nationalistic, and based on the Nazi principles of governance. A golden Saint Olav's cross on a red background was adopted as the party's primary symbol. As the party developed an extremist pro-German and anti-Semitic stance, it lost support from its early agrarian power base as well as that of the Lutheran state church.

CRIMINAL CAREER

Quisling was a fascist politician and traitor who admired Adolf Hitler's so-called new order and aided the Nazi conquest and occupation of Norway in World War II. On the day German forces invaded Norway, April 9, 1940, Quisling declared a coup d'état in a news broadcast, announcing his creation of an ad hoc government. His announcement coincided with the flight of King Haakon VII and the Norwegian government out of the country. All political parties were banned except for Quisling's fascist National Unity Party, which undertook intelli-

Vidkun Quisling. (AP/Wide World Photos)

gence efforts similar to the Nazi Schutzstaffel (SS) to detect and arrest persons active in the Norwegian underground.

Quisling appointed himself head of government, but this government collapsed after five days, and Josef Terboven was installed as Reichskommissar, Hitler's highest-ranking authority in Norway. A thirteen-man commission, largely Quisling's followers, was established to handle most of the details of governance. Quisling was appointed minister president in 1942 and assumed power on February 1, 1943, in a calculated move by Hitler and Terboven to diffuse Norwegian public resentment against the Nazis by placing a Norwegian in a prominent post. Quisling was never popular within his party, however, and also had a difficult association with Hitler and other Nazi masters. He managed to hold power until he was arrested on May 9, 1945, at Gimle, a mansion on Bygdøy in Oslo.

LEGAL ACTION AND OUTCOME

Quisling was charged with and convicted of high treason and executed by firing squad along with two other National Unity Party members on the grounds of Akershus Fortress on October 24, 1945. The exiled Norwegian government had reinstated capital punishment in order to execute those convicted in the postwar trials, a controversial issue in a country that had not used the death penalty for many years. Quisling's Russian wife, Maria Vasilijevna Pasetskjnikova, was not charged with crimes of any kind and lived out her life in Oslo, dying in 1980. The Quislings had no children.

IMPACT

When Vidkun Quisling appointed himself the fascist leader of Norway, it was the first time in history that a coup was announced in a public news broadcast. Quisling's collaboration with Hitler facilitated the Nazi occupation of Norway for five tense and difficult years. The

---

FROM UNIVERISM TO UNIVERSISM

Although Vidkun Quisling was a man of action—a soldier and politician—he saw himself first of all as a philosopher and political prophet. He formulated his own philosophy as early as 1917, a combination of Norwegian nationalism, primitive Christianity, and spirituality. Called Univerism, it called upon people to become responsible for their own freedom and salvation by discovering these for themselves. They were to do so by meditating upon truth, worshiping God, and participating in society.

In fact, this third element, societal activism, moved Quisling to found the Nasjonal Samling (NS). He insisted that the NS had nothing to do with the German Nazi Party, Nationalsozialistische Deutsche Arbeiterpartei (NSDAP). He once claimed that his philosophy inspired Adolf Hitler to create his own ideology, a claim that apparently annoyed Hitler.

As leader of the NS, Quisling kept himself apart from confrontations, debates, and discussions as much he could. He preferred to inform others of his thinking in writing. This had an unfortunate consequence for the NS. The absence of strong, involved leadership opened the party to power struggles among rivals and reduced its efficacy. Historians have blamed this infighting for NS's disastrous showing in the 1936 elections.

Quisling's long-range plan was to found a World Univerism League, an organization combining philosophy, religion, and party. He hoped it would replace the League of Nations as the venue for international cooperation. It is difficult to believe that, had the Nazis prevailed in World War II, Hitler would have permitted such an organization. In any event, Quisling's idealism came to an abrupt end in 1945.

Univerism, however, did not die. By the twenty-first century, it received new impetus via the Internet. Also called Universism, the relation of the modern form to Quisling's philosophy is tenuous at best, but the basic idea is the same: personal search for verity. According to the Universist Foundation, its adherents are people who search for meaning, believe that no source outside themselves has ultimate authority and constantly re-evaluate their beliefs, consider moral judgments to depend solely on those directly involved, value institutions only so far as they help people in their search for meaning, and have faith that full human potential can be achieved. The new Universists, however, do not put the same emphasis upon political and societal activism as did Quisling.

Norwegian resistance movement was well organized and strong, however, and hindered the Nazis on many fronts, making it virtually impossible for them to win broad support among the Norwegian people. Quisling had visited Hitler in Germany as early as 1939, warning him of Joseph Stalin's plans for aggression, but Hitler did not like him and dismissed him as a man of little use to the Nazi effort.

Like Brutus and Benedict Arnold, the Quisling name became synonymous with "traitor," especially one who aids a foreign invader. The British press coined the term shortly after the Nazi invasion, and the BBC broadcast it around the world. Quisling authored several books, including *Russland og vi* (1931; *Russia and Ourselves*, 1931); his writings were strongly anticommunist and fueled a growing suspicion and fear of communist ideology. The Quisling mansion on Bygdøy, now called Villa Grande, has been converted to a museum in remembrance of Holocaust victims.

FURTHER READING

Barth, Else M. *A Nazi Interior: Quisling's Hidden Philosophy*. New York: Peter Lang, 2004. An in-depth analysis of Quisling's thinking, which had roots in Christian fundamentalism and Universalism and was greatly influenced by his admiration of Hitler's new order.

Dahl, Hans Fredrik. *Quisling: A Study in Treachery*. New York: Cambridge University Press, 1999. Tells the story of Quisling's treason with particular emphasis on the roots of his philosophy, his internal struggles, and tensions within his National Unity Party.

Høidal, Oddvar K. *Quisling: A Study in Treason*. Oslo: Norwegian University Press, 1989. A comprehensive biography of Quisling and his role as a collaborator in the Nazi occupation of Norway.

—*Ann M. Legreid*

SEE ALSO: Joseph Darnand; Adolf Hitler; Pierre Laval; Philippe Pétain.

PUNIŠA RAČIĆ
Serbian nationalist politician

BORN: Date unknown; Berane, Montenegro
DIED: 1945; Serbia
MAJOR OFFENSE: Assassination of Yugoslav assembly member Stjepan Radić
ACTIVE: June 20, 1928
LOCALE: Parliament building, Belgrade, Kingdom of Serbs, Croats, and Slovenes (Yugoslavia)
SENTENCE: Twenty years of house arrest to be served in Požarevac, Serbia

EARLY LIFE
Puniša Račić (POO-nee-shah RAH-cheech) was a Montenegrin from the town of Berane. It is impossible to understand his political goals without examining the relationship of his nationality with the rest of Yugoslavia. Serbia dominated Yugoslavia, which was officially called the Kingdom of Serbs, Croats, and Slovenes for more than a decade after its founding in 1918; the new state had been assembled, reflecting a variety of local and great power interests, from territory from the former Habsburg and Ottoman Empires, as well as from the independent Serbian and Montenegrin monarchies. In addition to Serbs, Croats, and Slovenes, the country contained significant numbers of other nationalities. Montenegrins and Serbs are closely related peoples in terms of language, culture, history, and religion; some consider them to be first cousins, and others consider them the same people with two different names. Montenegro had also given up its independence and its royal family to merge with Serbia in 1918, further evidence of the way in which key sectors of its society were fully committed to Serbia at the time.

Interwar, or royal, Yugoslavia had many problems. Throughout the 1920's, fiery debates raged about the 1921 Vidovdan Constitution, which established the Kingdom of Serbs, Croats, and Slovenes as a unitary state. The strongest opposition to the Karađorđević royal family—led at the time by King Alexander I—and the Radical Party emerged in Croatia. There, the Croatian Peasant Party (HSS), led by Stjepan Radić, alternated between boycotting the government and participating in it. Radić was a fiery and mercurial figure who sought international assistance from various sources to curb Serbian power; in the late 1920's, he even formed an alliance with the opposition.

POLITICAL CAREER
At the time of Račić's political activity, a party called the Radicals predominated in both Montenegro and Serbia;

Račić was a member of this party and also had connections to nationalist paramilitary organizations. On June 20, 1928, Račić, who had been elected to the Yugoslav assembly, or Skupština, the year before, pulled out a revolver in the middle of a heated political and personal exchange during a parliamentary session in Belgrade and began firing. He killed two members of the Croatian Peasant Party, including Radić's nephew; he wounded two other people; and he fatally wounded Radić, who died on August 8. Račić fled the building but was later arrested and sentenced to house arrest in a nearby city.

Questions about Račić's motives remain. He was close to the Serbian king and court, so some have speculated, though it is not proven, that he was acting under orders to kill Radić. Some wonder if he did so to provide an excuse for the king to shut down the democratic system; others wonder if it was his goal simply to remove Belgrade's strongest opponent. Some radical Croats even believed that the killing of the three parliamentarians was proof of the regime's intention to kill off the Croats as a people.

IMPACT
Račić's act of assassination was significant in two ways. First, it punctuated the end of the Kingdom of Serbs, Croats, and Slovenes by paving the way for King Alexander to form a royal dictatorship, abrogate the constitution, and thoroughly reorganize the country's ethno-territorial units to perpetuate Serb rule. A more moderate leader named Vlatko Maček replaced Radić at the helm of the HSS, which remained strong but did not regain power until 1939. Second, the assassination reflected the turbulent nature of politics in the kingdom throughout the 1920's. The level of mistrust between parties and nationalities had grown incredibly high, and conspiracy theories and actual plots and personal altercations in Parliament abounded. Amid the postassassination despair, the Croatian fascist organization known as the Ustaše was founded. The violence of the Ustaše and related groups would claim the life of King Alexander in 1934 and, aided by the Axis Powers after 1941, of hundreds of thousands of Yugoslavs.

Račić was found during World War II by a military unit of the Partisans. Led by the communist Tito, the Partisans were the most effective resistance force in the Balkans and set up a new postwar Yugoslav state. The Partisans executed Račić as a terrorist of the old regime, and they then set about rehabilitating the idea of "brotherhood and unity" among the South Slavic peoples.

FURTHER READING

Banac, Ivo. *The National Question in Yugoslavia: Origin, History, Politics.* Ithaca, N.Y.: Cornell University Press, 1984. The magisterial work on the development of competing nationalist ideologies among the South Slavs, especially Serbs and Croats.

Biondich, Mark. *Stjepan Radić, the Croat Peasant Party, and the Politics of Mass Mobilization, 1904-1928.* Toronto, Ont.: University of Toronto Press, 2000. This political biography of Račić's most famous victim explores the chaotic nature of interwar politics in Yugoslavia.

Cox, John K. *The History of Serbia.* Westport, Conn.: Greenwood Press, 2002. This history of Serbia places the actions of Račić in long-range historical perspective by tracing the growth of the conflict between Serbs and Croats.

Kulundžić, Zvonimir. *Atentat na Stjepana Radića.* Zagreb: Stvarnost, 1967. This exhaustive study is the main historical work in Serbo-Croatian on the assassinations carried out by Račić.

Pavelić, Ante. "Adventures II: Ten Years of Struggle in the Homeland, 1918-1929." Translation available online at http://www.pavelicpapers.com/documents/pavelic/ap0047.html. These self-serving memoirs by the founder of Croatia's fascist movement (the Ustaše) are not reliable as history, but they do impart the tension, animosity, and paranoia that gripped Yugoslavia before and after Račić's deed.

—*John K. Cox*

SEE ALSO: Radovan Karadžić; Slobodan Milošević; Ante Pavelić; Tito

JOHN RACKHAM
Caribbean pirate

BORN: Date and place unknown
DIED: November 17, 1720; St. Jago de la Vega, Jamaica
ALSO KNOWN AS: Jack Rackham; Calico Jack
MAJOR OFFENSES: Piracy, robberies, and felonies on the high seas
ACTIVE: Early eighteenth century
LOCALE: Jamaica and throughout the Caribbean
SENTENCE: Death by hanging

EARLY LIFE

Almost nothing is known about the early life of John Rackham (RAK-am), including information about where and when he was born and raised. He first appears in the historical records around 1718 as quartermaster on an English vessel commanded by Captain Charles Vane. When Vane refused to attack a well-armed French vessel, Rackham was chosen leader by the crew; he took over the ship and succeeded in defeating and looting the French vessel. Rackham then turned the crew to piracy. He became known as Calico Jack because of the colorful clothing he wore. Rackham later decided to take the offer of the King's Pardon and settled in New Providence. There, he met and became infatuated with a married woman, Anne Bonny.

CRIMINAL CAREER

Rackham and Bonny then assembled a crew, with Bonny disguised as a man, and entered into a career of pirating. Another woman, Mary Read, also disguised herself as a man and was a member of Rackham's crew. First Bonny and then Rackham eventually found out that Read was a woman, and together they carried out a number of raids and attacked and looted ships throughout the area.

LEGAL ACTION AND OUTCOME

In late October, 1720, while Rackham and the crew were supposedly drunk, pirate hunter Jonathan Barnet attacked and captured them. A trial was held at St. Jago de la Vega, Jamaica, and although the group of pirates pleaded innocent, all were found guilty. Rackham and his crew—with the exception of the two women, who were pregnant and had their sentences stayed—were hanged on November 17. As a warning to others against committing acts of piracy, Rackham's body was put in a cage and hanged from a gibbet.

IMPACT

John Rackham was known primarily for his association with the two most famous women pirates, Anne Bonny and Mary Read. Several contemporary works, whose ac-

John Rackham.

them or attended the trial. One work, a pamphlet titled *The Tryals of Captain John Rackham and Other Pirates* (c. 1717), was submitted to the British Public Records. Another, *A General History of the Robberies and Murders of the Most Notorious Pirates, from Their First Rise and Settlement in the Island of Providence to the Present Year*, was published in 1724 by an author calling himself Captain Charles Johnson, although he was believed to have been author Daniel Defoe. Whatever the truth may have been, the two female crew members and the tales of their exploits, as well as the infamous trial, guaranteed Calico Jack Rackham's place as a legendary figure among the pirates of the Caribbean.

FURTHER READING

Botting, Douglas. *The Pirates*. Alexandria, Va.: Time-Life Books, 1978. An illustrated collection describing the men and women, ships, and life and times of the great age of piracy. Includes bibliography and sections on Bonny, Read, and Rackham. Notes that Defoe, in his accounts, was totally obsessed with Bonny.

Cordingly, David. *Under the Black Flag: The Romance and the Reality of Life Among the Pirates*. New York: Random House, 1995. Contains notes on historical sources, trial transcripts, and records. Notes that Rackham's targets were relatively small vessels and that he was less bloodthirsty than many of the other pirates of the time.

Defoe, Daniel. *A General History of the Pyrates*. 1724. Reprint. Edited by Manuel Schonhorn. Mineola, N.Y.: Dover, 1999. A classic work on pirates, including information on Calico Jack Rackham, based on both historical records and unsubstantiated information.

—*Martha Oehmke Loustaunau*

SEE ALSO: Anne Bonny; Mary Read.

counts cannot be verified, were published and described the lives of Bonny and Read. It is thought that they might have been interviewed for their life stories, or that some of the information may have come from those who knew

Dennis Rader
American serial killer

Born: March 9, 1945; Wichita, Kansas
Also known as: BTK Killer; BTK Strangler; Dennis Lynn Rader (full name)
Major offenses: Murder and attempted murder
Active: 1974-1991
Locale: Wichita, Kansas
Sentence: Ten consecutive life sentences

Early Life
From all accounts, Dennis Rader (RAY-dur) had a normal childhood, though some have reported his early bullying and abuse of animals (often an indicator of future violence). Rader attended Wichita State University and went on to join the Air Force, in which he served from 1965 until 1969, when he was discharged. In 1974 Rader began working for ADT Security Services.

Criminal Career
Rader would work for ADT until 1989. He also worked for the U.S. Census Bureau in 1989, collecting information at residences. In the 1970's, he married and had two children. When not working, Rader volunteered his time with a local Boy Scout troop and was active in his church. He later was employed as a compliance officer in Park City, Kansas. Through his various employments, Rader easily could have gained trust and access to people's homes and personal information.

Rader's murders began in 1974. His first victims were four members of the Otero family. Joseph and Julie Otero were found dead, tied up and suffocated. Two of their five children, their daughter Josephine and son Joey, were also found dead in the house. Other murders soon followed.

Approximately nine months after the Otero murders, an anonymous phone call was placed to the Wichita *Eagle*, giving directions to a textbook in the public library. Inside the book a letter was found claiming credit for the Otero murders and promising more. Because the letter contained details that had not been released by the police, its authenticity was not questioned. This exchange began an extended correspondence between Rader and the police or media. The killer was dubbed BTK, for "Bind, Torture, Kill," which was often the signature Rader used when communicating with law enforcement authorities or media.

Rader killed at least ten people and attempted to murder at least six more during his criminal career. Like some other serial killers, he enjoyed writing and phoning the press or law enforcement authorities. He reported his murders and enjoyed taunting police, using this outlet to terrify Wichita residents already fearful of an unknown serial killer in their neighborhood. Rader tended to wait for his selected victims in their homes. After the victims arrived, they would be bound, sometimes partially clothed, tortured, then strangled. Often, items were missing from the crime scenes, indicating that the killer was taking souvenirs of his crimes with him, possibly to relive the incidents at a later date. Although semen was found at some of the crime scenes, autopsies revealed that the victims had not been sexually assaulted.

As quickly as the murders had begun in 1974, they seemed to stop in 1979. The BTK case became cold through the 1980's with no new murders, tips, or leads. Then, in 2004, the investigation was reopened after a letter sent to the Wichita *Eagle* claimed responsibility for a 1986 murder. After other correspondence from BTK was traced and investigated, Rader was arrested on February 26, 2005.

Legal Action and Outcome
After being arrested and tried for the BTK murders, Rader was sentenced to a minimum of 175 years in prison without the possibility of parole. The sentence was the toughest one the judge could impose for Rader's crimes because Kansas allowed no death penalty at the time the crimes were committed.

Impact
Dennis Rader provides one of several examples of how a seemingly "normal" individual can lead a double life. Like serial murderers Ted Bundy and John Wayne Gacy, Rader did not appear to be the cold-blooded killer he eventually turned out to be. He appeared to be a normal middle-class husband and father. He worked in a "normal" job and was active in church and community affairs. Secretly, however, he held fantasies of torture and murder and acted upon them, killing at least ten people in Wichita and terrorizing the community by taunting the press and police. His eventual arrest shocked those who knew him, victims' families, and others within the community.

Before Rader's notoriety, many had believed that serial murderers stop killing only when they are jailed or otherwise incapacitated, move away, or die. Rader, who proved that sometimes serial killers "lie dormant," had stopped killing in the late 1970's and had seemed to disappear. When the thirtieth anniversary of his first murders drew near and a new book about the killings was ready for publication, he resurfaced to recapture the publicity he had received as BTK, which ultimately led to his arrest. His narcissistic and perverted need for attention and control speaks not only to the personality disorders of such sociopaths but also to Americans' obsession with fame and notoriety, which may help explain Rader's wanting to be heard from once again as BTK, even though it resulted in his undoing.

FURTHER READING

Beattie, Robert. *Nightmare in Wichita: The Hunt for the BTK Strangler.* New York: New American Library, 2005. Discusses the search for the BTK Strangler when he was still terrorizing Wichita. The author provides an update of the case following Rader's arrest.

Singular, Stephen. *Unholy Messenger: The Life and Crimes of the BTK Serial Killer.* New York: Simon & Schuster, 2006. The author uses Rader's confessions to the BTK crimes to discuss the killer's life and criminal career. In addition, the author discusses the hunt for BTK while his crimes were still unsolved.

Smith, C. *The BTK Murders: Inside the Bind Torture Kill Case That Terrified America's Heartland.* New York: St. Martin's Press, 2006. This book discusses the investigation into the BTK murders and the eventual capture of Dennis Rader. In addition, the author discusses evidence against Rader and Rader's confessions.

—*Jenephyr James*

SEE ALSO: Joe Ball; David Berkowitz; Kenneth Bianchi; Ted Bundy; Angelo Buono, Jr.; Andrei Chikatilo; Andrew Cunanan; Jeffrey Dahmer; Albert DeSalvo; John Wayne Gacy; Leonard Lake; Charles Ng; Richard Speck; Aileen Carol Wuornos.

GILLES DE RAIS
Marshal of France and serial killer

BORN: September or October, 1404; Champtocé, France

DIED: October 26, 1440; Nantes, France

ALSO KNOWN AS: Baron de Raiz; Baron de Retz; Baron de Rays; Gilles de Laval; Bluebeard (in legend)

MAJOR OFFENSES: Rape, murder, and sorcery

ACTIVE: c. 1431-1440

LOCALE: Brittany, France

SENTENCE: Execution by hanging and burning

EARLY LIFE

Gilles de Rais (jzheel deh ray) was born into fifteenth century French nobility; in fact, at that time, he inherited the largest fortune in France. He served in the French military during the second half of the Hundred Years' War, beginning his military career at sixteen. He is most famous for fighting alongside Joan of Arc, eventually receiving the title marshal of France in honor of his service. After Joan of Arc was captured and killed, Rais retired from military service to his family's castle in Brittany as a baron. It is this point at which his reputation changes drastically from valorous war hero to one of history's most notorious criminal fiends.

Gilles de Rais.

TRIAL OF A FIFTEENTH CENTURY SERIAL KILLER

The Reverend Sabine Baring-Gould (1834-1924) was a cleric, folklorist, novelist, and author of more than five hundred works, including the lyrics to the hymn "Onward, Christian Soldiers." In his Book of Were-Wolves, *he devotes three chapters to Gilles de Rais (also known as Gilles de Laval or the maréchal de Retz), in a fictional account of the trial:*

On the 24th October the trial of the Maréchal de Retz was resumed. The prisoner entered in a Carmelite habit, knelt and prayed in silence before the examination began. Then he ran his eye over the court, and the sight of the rack, windlass, and cords made a slight shudder run through him. . . .

"My lord! relieve yourself of the burden of your crimes by acknowledging them at once," said [Pierre de] l'Hospital [president of Brittany and chief prosecutor] earnestly.

"Messires!" said the prisoner, after a moment's silence: "it is quite true that I have robbed mothers of their little ones; and that I have killed their children, or caused them to be killed, either by cutting their throats with daggers or knives, or by chopping off their heads with cleavers; or else I have had their skulls broken by hammers or sticks; sometimes I had their limbs hewn off one after another; at other times I have ripped them open, that I might examine their entrails and hearts; I have occasionally strangled them or put them to a slow death; and when the children were dead I had their bodies burned and reduced to ashes."

"When did you begin your execrable practices?" asked Pierre de l'Hospital, staggered by the frankness of these horrible avowals: "the evil one must have possessed you."

"It came to me from myself,—no doubt at the instigation of the devil: but still these acts of cruelty afforded me incomparable delight. The desire to commit these atrocities came upon me eight years ago. I left court to go to Chantoncé, that I might claim the property of my grandfather, deceased. In the library of the castle I found a Latin book—Suetonius, I believe—full of accounts of the cruelties of the Roman Emperors. I read the charming history of Tiberius, Caracalla, and other Caesars, and the pleasure they took in watching the agonies of tortured children. Thereupon I resolved to imitate and surpass these same Caesars, and that very night I began to do so. For some while I confided my secret to no one, but afterwards I communicated it to my cousin, Gilles de Sillé, then to Master Roger de Briqueville, next in succession to Henriet, Pontou, Rossignol, and Robin." He then confirmed all the accounts given by his two servants. He confessed to about one hundred and twenty murders in a single year.

"An average of eight hundred in less than seven years!" exclaimed Pierre de l'Hospital, with a cry of pain: "Ah! messire, you were possessed!"

Source: Sabine Baring-Gould, *The Book of Were-Wolves: Being an Account of a Terrible Superstition* (London: Smith, Elder, 1865).

CRIMINAL CAREER

Readers must consider Rais's postwar activities with suspicion, as Rais and his accomplices confessed under torture. Some scholars believe that other noblemen, envious of Rais's lands, fabricated the charges against him. Whatever the truth may be, Rais was accused of sorcery (a capital crime in fifteenth century France) but is better known for the atrocities he is said to have committed against between 140 and 800 peasant children, mostly boys—the precise number is impossible to determine. Accusations against Rais included the torture, mutilation, rape, and murder of these children in the most gruesome of circumstances. Some accounts link the murder of children with Rais's attempts at alchemy and making a pact with the devil. Other authorities view Rais as a sexual sadist who found more satisfaction in horrific acts of torture and mutilation, as well as necrophilia, than in rape itself. Authorities finally arrested Rais in 1440.

LEGAL ACTION AND OUTCOME

Rais's trial was conducted by both secular and ecclesiastic courts on charges of murder, sodomy, and heresy. Testimony from the parents of missing children as well as that of Rais's accomplices helped convict Rais. However, he and his accomplices confessed voluntarily to murder and sorcery (the worse of the two crimes, given that the victims were peasant children), a move which spared him court-ordered torture. Instead, Rais was sentenced to die by hanging and burning, which occurred on October 26, 1440.

IMPACT

Gilles de Rais, though possibly one of the world's most prolific serial killers, has had more influence on historians and criminologists than on popular culture. He remains fascinating for the vast scope, sheer audacity, and ghastly monstrosity of his crimes, all of which have eclipsed his service to wartime France. He is the source of the legend of Bluebeard and may have influenced Bram Stoker's 1897 novel *Dracula*. Many consider him a precursor to the modern-day serial killer.

FURTHER READING

Hickey, Eric W. *Serial Murders and Their Victims*. 2d ed. Albany, N.Y.: Wadsworth, 1997. A disturbing account of Rais's activities that links him with early Eastern European vampire myths. Hickey numbers Rais's victims at eight hundred, which would make him one of history's most prolific serial murderers.

Holmes, Robert M., and Stephen T. Holmes, eds. *Contemporary Perspectives on Serial Murder*. Thousand Oaks, Calif.: Sage, 1998. Researchers here again

place Rais's victim toll at eight hundred children and emphasize the fact that serial murder is not a uniquely American phenomenon, as some people tend to think.

Schechter, Harold. *The Serial Killer Files*. New York: Ballantine Books, 2003. Schechter gives Rais the benefit of the doubt, numbering his victims at 140 and including the possibility that Rais may have been framed by land-hungry nobility. However, even Schechter recognizes the monstrous sadism of Rais's acts, his objective to torment his child victims as viciously as possible for his sexual satisfaction. Illustrations are included.

—*Charles Avinger*

SEE ALSO: Elizabeth Báthory; Henri Désiré Landru.

THENMULI RAJARATNAM
Assassin and suicide bomber

BORN: 1974?; Sri Lanka
DIED: May 21, 1991; Sriperumbudur, India
ALSO KNOWN AS: Dhanu
MAJOR OFFENSES: Assassination and suicide bombing
ACTIVE: May 21, 1991
LOCALE: Sriperumbudur, India

EARLY LIFE

Thenmuli Rajaratnam (thehn-MOO-lee rah-jah-RAHT-nahm) was born in Sri Lanka in the midst of ethnic conflict between the majority Sinhalese and minority Sri Lankan Tamils. Tamils are descendants of the inhabitants of the Indian region Tamilakam, which includes present-day Indian states Tamil Nadu and Kerala as well as Sri Lanka. Civil war between Sinhalese and the Tamils, who resented official and unofficial governmental preference for Sinhalese, broke out in 1983 after a long series of discriminatory acts against the Tamils, including removing the citizenship of more than one million Tamils in 1950, the passage of the "Sinhala Only Act" in 1956, and the massacre of three thousand Tamils in 1983.

A Tamil, Rajaratnam grew up in a country torn by strife. In 1987, after the failure of an armistice, Indian governor Rajiv Gandhi sent troops into Sri Lanka to intervene, leading to the deaths of more than one thousand of those troops. Some accounts maintain that Rajaratnam

was raped by members of these troops, but this remains unconfirmed.

Motivated by patriotism as well as revenge, as a teen Rajaratnam joined the Liberation Tigers of Tamil Eelam (the LTTE or Tamil Tigers), a military organization attempting to establish an independent Tamil state called Tamil Eelam in northeastern Sri Lanka. The Tigers trained her in their resistance movement and eventually prepared her for the assassination that would also take her life.

CRIMINAL CAREER

At the age of seventeen, Rajaratnam learned that Gandhi would be campaigning in Tamil Nadu for upcoming parliamentary elections. When last in power in 1987, Gandhi had sent Indian troops into Sri Lanka to enforce a peace accord; the Tamil Tigers feared that he would do so again.

Upon discovering that Gandhi would be addressing a public meeting in Sriperumbudur (also known as Tamil Nadu), the Tigers dispatched Rajaratnam to assassinate him. Rajaratnam was prepared with a belt bomb that held the explosive material on her lower back. A detonator switch was in front, where she could reach it easily. The bomb was a research department explosive (RDX), which held about ten thousand 2-millimeter steel bars. Rajaratnam approached Gandhi, placed a celebratory sandalwood garland around his neck, and activated the bomb as she stooped to touch his feet.

It is believed Gandhi knew what was happening and tried to stop her, because his face bore the majority of the impact of the blast. With her act, which killed thirteen bystanders as well, Rajaratnam became one of the most famous women suicide bombers of all time.

LEGAL ACTION AND OUTCOME

While conducting a lengthy inquiry into the failure of Gandhi's security, the government searched for Rajaratnam's co-conspirators. After seven years, in 1998, twenty-six people were convicted and imprisoned for having planned and aided the assassination attempt.

IMPACT

Thenmuli Rajaratnam's assassination of Rajiv Ghandi caused popular support for the Tamil Tigers to wane. The group that gained the most from Rajaratnam's act was, in fact, an opposing group, the All-India Anna Dravida Munnetra Kazhagam (AIADMK) Party, led by Jayalalitha Jayaraman, which gained substantially at the polls as a result of public anger. The Tamil Tigers continued committing assassinations and other acts of violence throughout the following years until it finally agreed to a cease-fire brokered by Norway in 2001.

FURTHER READING

Kaarthikeyan, D. R., and Radhavinod Raju. *Triumph of Truth: The Rajiv Gandhi Assassination—The Investigation.* Chicago: New Dawn Press, 2004. Written by two of the investigators responsible for tracking down Rajaratnam's co-conspirators, this account details both the events leading up to the assassination and its aftermath.

Richardson, John. *Paradise Poisoned: Learning About Conflict, Terrorism, and Development from Sri Lankha's Civil Wars.* Kandav, Sri Lanka: The International Center for Ethnic Studies, 2005. This study of violence in Sri Lanka provides an overview of the multiple conflicts that have been waged in it across the past century.

Somasundaram, Daya. *Scarred Minds: The Psychological Impact of War on Sri Lankan Tamils.* Thousand Oaks, Calif.: Sage, 1998. Beyond providing a succinct account of the history of war in Sri Lanka, the author analyzes the impact of the ongoing struggle on the psyche of the country's inhabitants.

—*Cat Rambo*

SEE ALSO: Nathuram Vinayak Godse; Beant Singh; Satwant Singh.

ILICH RAMÍREZ SÁNCHEZ
Venezuelan terrorist

BORN: October 12, 1949; Caracas, Venezuela
ALSO KNOWN AS: Carlos the Jackal
MAJOR OFFENSES: Terrorism, bombings, and skyjacking
ACTIVE: 1973-1983
LOCALE: England, France, and the Middle East
SENTENCE: Life imprisonment

EARLY LIFE

Ilich Ramírez Sánchez (IHL-yich rah-MEER-ehz SAN-chehz) was named by his father, José Altagracia Ramírez Navas, a wealthy Venezuelan Communist leader, after the founder of the Soviet Communist Party. Navas, a staunch Marxist, insisted that his three sons' names reflect the identity of his idol, Vladimir Ilich Lenin.

Ilich's parents divorced in 1958 because of his father's numerous extramarital affairs. His mother traveled between Jamaica and Mexico for several years before moving back to Caracas. The constant upheaval disorganized Ilich's adolescence. In addition, he was the target of teasing from peers about his weight. Ilich consoled himself by telling others that one day the rest of the world would come to know his deeds and greatness.

Ilich's father sent his son to the best communist schools to instill Marxist/Leninist political philosophy in the young man, including Moscow's Patrice Lumumba University. His education had helped engender an emerging terrorist. Ilich's next destination was a guerrilla training camp in Jordan run by the Popular Front for the Liberation of Palestine (PFLP). It was there that he gained the nickname Carlos, reportedly given to him by Palestine Liberation Organization official Bassam Abu Sharif. The press would later christen Carlos "the Jackal" when a copy of Frederick Forsyth's book *The Day of the Jackal* (1971) was found in his belongings, although it did not actually belong to him.

TERRORIST CAREER

From an investigative perspective, law enforcement authorities found it difficult to link Ramírez to specific

CARLOS THE JACKAL AND ISLAM

In 2002, Carlos the Jackal told the London-based Arabic newspaper Al-Hayat *of his response to the attacks on the United States during September 11, 2001:*

I followed the news of the attack from the beginning without stopping. I cannot describe the great feeling of satisfaction.

What is more, he claimed to have been aware of the initial planning:

I attended an exciting meeting of cadres from anti-imperialist groups of different ideologies. In an informal, unofficial way the need was agreed to respond with bombings in the United States.

He expressed nothing but praise for al-Qaeda leader Osama Bin Laden. Asked what message he would send to Bin Laden, he replied:

I would begin with brotherly greetings, then I would encourage him to continue the struggle and safeguard his life, because he has become a symbol of the jihad. I hope that he is still living, and if he has not been martyred he will undoubtedly play a decisive role.

Like many terrorists, Carlos the Jackal views the United States as the great enemy but, curiously, not its people:

[In the U.S.] people are really great and do not deserve the hatred of the whole world. Nevertheless, every lover of justice hates the American imperialists, the worst tyrants in the history of humanity.

In 2003, Carlos the Jackal published Revolutionary Islam *(Éditions du Rocher), written from his jail cell. In it, he proclaims his conversion to Islam and again expresses his support of Osama Bin Laden and jihad. In fact, he calls upon "all guerrilla, terrorist, and other revolutionary groups throughout the world, regardless of their religious or ideological beliefs" to join with Islamist terrorists in attacks on the United States:*

Only a coalition of Marxists and Islamists can destroy the U.S. . . . terrorism is the cleanest and most efficient form of warfare . . . part of the landscape of your rotting democracies.

Ramírez's later participation in terrorist acts included two failed grenade bombings of El Al jets at Orly Airport in France in 1975. Later that year, he and five others invaded a meeting of the Organization of Petroleum Exporting Countries (OPEC) in Vienna and took more than sixty hostages, all of whom they later released. Ramírez was subsequently expelled from the PFLP for failing to execute two of the senior oil ministers of Middle Eastern states.

He was blamed for other attacks for which it is now clear he bore no responsibility, such as the attack on Israeli athletes at the 1972 Olympics in Munich and the hijacking of Air France flight 193 to Entebbe in 1976. Ramírez, nonetheless, was a suspect in several bombings involving numerous casualties in France in 1982 and 1983. He was allegedly involved in the planning and execution of several attacks against Israel in the mid-1980's.

Carlos the Jackal was seen in the roles of hedonistic playboy and, alternately, dedicated communist terrorist. Ramírez became an almost mystical terrorist and media personality during the 1980's. However, he disappeared from the scene near the end of the decade. Some media representatives described him as a ruthless terrorist and professional mercenary, while others portrayed him as a psychotic and incompetent criminal. Numerous disguises, false identities, and passports facilitated Ramírez's image as an elusive master terrorist.

crimes. The most useful cases in that regard concerned the assassination of two unarmed French counterintelligence agents and a 1973 attempt on the life of Joseph Edward Sieff. In one of Ramírez's early botched terrorist attacks for the PFLP, he attempted the assassination of British businessman Sieff in 1973. The Jewish millionaire was the owner of the Marks & Spencer department store chain. Ramirez shot his victim in the face; Sieff survived the foiled execution because the weapon malfunctioned.

LEGAL ACTION AND OUTCOME

Originally, French courts tried Ilich Ramírez Sánchez in absentia for the 1975 deaths of two Paris policemen and a PFLP guerrilla who had turned Israeli spy. In 1994, Ramírez's terrorist career ended when he was apprehended in Sudan. He had been sedated for a liposuction procedure when French law enforcement authorities entered the operating room and arrested him. Ramírez was tried and sentenced to life imprisonment at the maximum security wing of France's Le Santé prison on December 23, 1997.

IMPACT

As of 2006, Ilich Ramírez Sánchez resided in a French prison; Carlos the Jackal or inmate Ramírez had become detainee 872686/X. In 2003, his book, *L'Islam révolutionnaire*, a collection of his writings, was published in Monaco. In the book he states his support for the 2001 terrorist attacks on the United States. Several fictional characters have been based on Ramírez, including a character in Tom Clancy's novel *Rainbow Six* (1998).

FURTHER READING

Follain, John. *Jackal: Finally, the Complete Story of the Legendary Terrorist Carlos the Jackal.* New York: Arcade, 1998. A biographical account of Ramírez's terrorist and revolutionary career. The analysis includes a portrait of Carlos the Jackal's private life.

Waugh, Billy, with Tim Keown. *Hunting the Jackal: A Special Forces and CIA Ground Soldier's Fifty-Year Career Hunting America's Enemies.* New York: William Morrow, 2004. An autobiographical account of the author's experiences, with specifics on the tracking of Carlos the Jackal. Also reviews other special operations missions.

Yallop, David. *Tracking the Jackal: The Search for the World's Most Wanted Man.* New York: Random House, 1993. A biographical account of Carlos the Jackal's life and mystique and an almost sympathetic account of Ramírez's crimes.

—*Thomas E. Baker and James C. Roberts*

SEE ALSO: Abu Nidal; Mohammed Atta al-Sayed; Osama Bin Laden; Baruch Goldstein; Khalid Shaikh Mohammed; Muammar al-Qaddafi; Abu Musab al-Zarqawi; Ayman al-Zawahiri.

GRIGORI YEFIMOVICH RASPUTIN
Russian mystic

BORN: c. 1870; Pokrovskoye, Siberia, Russia
DIED: December 30, 1916; Petrograd (now St. Petersburg), Russia
ALSO KNOWN AS: Grigori Yefimovich Novykh (birth name); Grigory Yefymovich Rasputin; Grigory Efimovich Rasputin
CAUSE OF NOTORIETY: Because Czar Nicholas II and Empress Alexandra believed that Rasputin was able to alleviate the medical problems of their son, Rasputin attained considerable power in late imperial Russia.
ACTIVE: 1906-1916
LOCALE: Russia, especially St. Petersburg (Petrograd)

EARLY LIFE

There is much uncertainty about the first thirty years of the life of Grigori Yefimovich Rasputin (greh-GOH-ree yah-FEH-mo-vich rahs-PYEW-tehn). He was raised in a small village in western Siberia, and his father was a moderately prosperous and literate peasant who had a reputation for stealing and drinking too much vodka. As a young man, Rasputin followed his father's example. At about the age of nineteen, he married Praskovia Dubrovina, a tolerant wife who learned to accept his constant womanizing and long absences. The couple had five children.

Sometime after his marriage, Rasputin visited the

Grigori Yefimovich Rasputin.

RASPUTIN FORESEES HIS ASSASSINATION

According to his secretary, Aaron Simonovich, Rasputin wrote the following letter on December 7, 1916, nearly three weeks before he was murdered. Some historians speculate Simonovich himself faked the letter. Even so, Rasputin did not have to be a clairvoyant to recognize that he was in trouble. He had powerful enemies, enemies who had sworn to end his influence over the czarina. Strangely, Rasputin seems to have been more worried about a threat from Russian peasants than the dangers posed by his more obvious enemies, the nobility. Perhaps he was thinking of the Bolsheviks.

I write and leave behind me this letter at St. Petersburg. I feel that I shall leave life before January first. I wish to make known to the Russian people, to Papa, to the Russian Mother and to the children, to the land of Russia, what they must understand. If I am killed by common assassins, and especially by my brothers the Russian peasants, you, Tsar of Russia, have nothing to fear, remain on your throne and govern, and you, Russian Tsar, will have nothing to fear for your children, they will reign for hundreds of years in Russia. But if I am murdered by boyars, nobles, and if they shed my blood, their hands will remain soiled with my blood, for twenty-five years they will not wash their hands from my blood. They will leave Russia. Brothers will kill brothers, and they will kill each other and hate each other, and for twenty-five years there will be no nobles in the country. Tsar of the land of Russia, if you hear the sound of the bell which will tell you that Grigory has been killed, you must know this: if it was your relations who have wrought my death then no one of your family, that is to say, none of your children or relations will remain alive for more than two years. They will be killed by the Russian people . . . I shall be killed. I am no longer among the living. Pray, pray, be strong, think of your blessed family.

Source: Greg King, *The Murder of Rasputin: The Truth About Prince Felix Youssoupov and the Mad Monk Who Helped Bring Down the Romanovs* (New York: Arrow, 1996).

pilgrimages to Mount Athos, Kiev, and Jerusalem. After he moved to Kazan in 1902, his charismatic personality, magnetic eyes, and pious discourse impressed important clergymen and laymen. His admirers called him a *staretz* (an elder of high spirituality), and many people came to believe that he possessed special powers for healing and precognition.

POLITICAL CAREER

Visiting St. Petersburg for the first time in 1903, Rasputin attracted a number of influential supporters, including relatives and friends of Czar Nicholas II and his wife, Alexandra. On a second visit in 1906, he was granted an audience with the royal couple. Following a religious discussion, Rasputin blessed their hemophiliac son, Alexis, with a Siberian relic, which appeared to make the young czarevitch feel better. Then, while visiting the home of Prime Minister Piotr Stolypin, Rasputin prayed over Stolypin's injured daughter, who soon recovered.

During the following ten years Rasputin successfully alleviated Alexis's bleeding numerous times. Historian Robert Massie suggests that Rasputin's success probably came primarily from his ability to use hypnotic suggestion to relax the boy. Whatever the explanation, Nicholas and Alexandra expressed great confidence in the mystical powers of "our friend." Increasingly, however, there were widespread rumors about his sexual escapades and drinking parties.

When the czar was informed of Rasputin's scandalous life, he initially dismissed the *strannik* from court. The pious and superstitious czarina, however, exercised great influence over her relatively weak husband, and she convinced him that the scandals were unfounded. Rasputin returned to his unofficial position of court healer. Because the czarevitch's genetic illness was kept secret from the public, many Russians assumed that Rasputin was having a romantic relationship with the czarina, a rumor that further tarnished the image of the royal family.

With the outbreak of World War I, Rasputin's influence increased, especially after the czar decided to take

Verkhoture Monastery, where he experienced an intense religious conversion. Markary, a mystical hermit, became his mentor. Rasputin was influenced by the Khlysty sect, whose members practiced intense prayer and sometimes self-flagellation. He also embraced some of the doctrines of the Skopsty, a renegade sect noted for teaching that sinful acts, particularly sexual ones, followed by sincere repentance, were the surest means for obtaining salvation.

Relying on intuitive inspiration, Rasputin had contempt for book learning and never pursed any systematic training in theology. Following his conversion, he experienced religious visions and periods of ecstasy. With the encouragement of Markary, he resolved to become a *strannik* (wandering pilgrim), and he made a series of

personal command of the army at the front. In his absence, Prime Minister Boris Sturmer usually deferred to the czarina in making appointments and decisions about public policy. The czarina looked to the advice of Rasputin. In view of Alexandra's German background, it is not surprising that rumors spread about her and the "mad monk" being in the pay of the Germans.

The dashing Prince Felix Yusupov and other members of the royal court decided that the only way to eliminate Rasputin's baneful influence was to arrange for his murder. Yusupov therefore invited Rasputin to dine at his home on the evening of December 29, 1916. When Yusupov served his guest cyanide-laced cakes and wine, the poison had no effect. In panic, Yusupov shot Rasputin with a pistol, but the monk managed to escape to the courtyard, where accomplices beat him and again shot him. The assassins then threw his body into a hole in the Neva River. When his corpse was discovered three days later, the lungs were full of water, indicating that Rasputin had died by drowning.

While the elite of Petrograd welcomed Rasputin's demise, Nicholas and Alexandra were furious. The two main conspirators were discovered, and, because they were relatives of the czar, they were eventually sent into exile. In the countryside, where Rasputin was viewed as a "man of the people," many peasants were infuriated to learn that the main assassins, because of their royal status, were not appropriately punished.

IMPACT

Because of the contempt and vilification heaped upon Rasputin, his negative impact on Russian history has probably been exaggerated. Although Rasputin added to the unpopularity of the royal family, particularly during the war, some historians have argued that he actually served as a buffer, displacing some of the anger toward Nicholas and Alexandra onto himself. After Rasputin's death, of course, that buffer no longer existed. His assassination clearly did not solve any of the fundamental problems of the imperial regime. Even though Rasputin's influence was not the most important reason for the downfall of the imperial government, the fact that such a bizarre individual could gain political power demonstrated the dismal condition of absolutist institutions under the last czar.

FURTHER READING

De Jonge, Alex. *The Life and Times of Grigorii Rasputin.* New York: Coward, 1982. An interesting and readable narrative but not as scholarly or dependable as Fuhrmann's work.

Fuhrmann, Joseph T. *Rasputin: A Life.* New York: Praeger, 1990. A scholarly and well-documented biography of Rasputin.

Massie, Robert K. *Nicholas and Alexandra.* 1967. Reprint. New York: Black Dog & Levanthal, 2005. This well-written classic in popular history presents a compelling and generally dependable portrait of Rasputin and his influence.

Radzinsky, Edvard. *The Rasputin File.* New York: Doubleday, 2000. Detailed descriptions based on a government investigation of 1917, with testimony only from people who actually knew Rasputin.

Rasputin, Maria. *Rasputin: The Man Behind the Myth.* Englewood Cliffs, N.J.: Prentice Hall, 1977. A devoted daughter's attempt to refute the many allegations leveled against Rasputin.

Youssoupoff, Felix. *Lost Splendor: The Amazing Memoirs of the Man Who Killed Rasputin.* Translated by Ann Green and Nicolas Katkoff. 1953. Reprint. Chappaqua, N.Y.: Turtle Point Press, 2003. A new edition of the memoir, giving a firsthand account by the man responsible for the assassination.

—*Thomas Tandy Lewis*

SEE ALSO: Felix Yusupov.

FRANÇOIS RAVAILLAC
French assassin

BORN: 1578; Touvre, near Angoulême, France
DIED: May 27, 1610; Paris, France
ALSO KNOWN AS: Judas
MAJOR OFFENSES: High treason and regicide
ACTIVE: May 14, 1610
LOCALE: Paris, France
SENTENCE: Tortured, drawn, and quartered using four
  horses

EARLY LIFE
François Ravaillac (fran-swah rah-vi-yahk) was born in 1578 in Touvre, near Angoulême, France, the grandson

of a respected legal officer in the local judiciary. François's father, Jean Ravaillac, was nevertheless a delinquent who lived off beggary and charity. He beat his wife and probably his sons and ultimately abandoned them. François Ravaillac never married. He sided with his mother after his parents' legal separation and shared her deep religious faith. A social outcast, Ravaillac earned a meager living working at low-level court jobs and by tutoring students. Before 1608 he joined the religious order of the Feuillants but was dismissed after only six weeks. Not long thereafter he was imprisoned for debt.

CRIMINAL CAREER
By 1609, the religiously devout Ravaillac began to consider himself a prophet and savior. He traveled to Paris, ostensibly to see Henry IV and beseech him to force the Huguenots in France (French Protestants) to return to the Catholic faith. His attempts to speak with the king were thwarted, however, and Ravaillac grew increasingly frustrated. By 1610, as Henry prepared for war in the Netherlands, Ravaillac came to believe that the king intended to declare war on the pope. At this point, the delusional man felt he needed to defend the pope by committing regicide. In the spring of 1610 he set out for Paris, and on Friday, May 14, he trailed the king's carriage through the streets of Paris. When the coach stopped on the crowded rue de la Ferronnerie, Ravaillac jumped up on the wheel and stabbed Henry three times. The king was rushed to the Louvre but was pronounced dead on arrival.

LEGAL ACTION AND OUTCOME
After killing Henry IV, Ravaillac did not attempt to run away and was immediately taken into custody. Held in the Conciergerie, he was repeatedly interrogated and tortured over the following thirteen days but claimed no part in any conspiracy and swore he had acted alone. The Paris Parlement found Ravaillac guilty of high treason and regicide on May 27, 1610, and immediately carried out his sentence of public torture and execution. While the crowds cursed the hated assassin, Ravaillac's executioners submerged his arm in burning sulfur,

Henry IV contemplates his future marriage in this engraving. (Library of Congress) tore his flesh with hot pincers, and poured molten lead into his wounds. He was then drawn and quartered by four horses in an agonizing death that took more than ninety minutes to complete. Finally, his body parts were burned and his ashes thrown to the wind.

IMPACT

Henry IV's sudden death put an end to the war in the Netherlands. It also accelerated the demise of Huguenot privilege in France. Henry's queen, the very Catholic Marie de Médicis, oversaw the new government of the boy king, Louis XIII, and a quick exclusion of Protestants ensued. France grew increasingly intolerant of its Huguenot population over the course of the seventeenth century until the famous revocation of the Edict of Nantes in 1685 ended the limited religious liberty Huguenots had enjoyed under Henry IV. Finally, Henry's assassination ensured his godlike status in the annals of French history, much as President John F. Kennedy's assassination elevated his status in American myth. Indeed, some historians argue that if Henry had lived, the war in the Netherlands might have brought negative consequences to his otherwise successful and well-remembered reign.

FURTHER READING

Mousnier, Roland. *The Assassination of Henry IV.* Translated by Joan Spencer. New York: Scribner, 1973. The translated version of Mousnier's classic remains an outstanding source in English on the history of Ravaillac.

Orr, Gregory, director. *The Day They Died.* New York: Gregory Orr Productions and A&E Television Networks, 2002. The video focuses on famous deaths in history and includes a segment on the trial and execution of François Ravaillac.

Walker, Anita W., and Edmund H. Dickerman. "Mind of an Assassin: Ravaillac and the Murder of Henry IV of France." *Canadian Journal of History* 30, no. 2 (August, 1995): 201-229. A psychological and sociological analysis of Ravaillac and his motives. The assassin's abusive background and marginalization within French society are determined to have been the forces that drove him to regicide.

—*Annette Finley-Croswhite*

SEE ALSO: John Bellingham; Jacques Clément; John Felton; Balthasar Gérard.

JAMES EARL RAY
American assassin of Dr. Martin Luther King, Jr.

BORN: March 10, 1928; Alton, Illinois
DIED: April 23, 1998; Nashville, Tennessee
ALSO KNOWN AS: Eric S. Galt; Ramon Sneyd
MAJOR OFFENSE: First-degree murder
ACTIVE: April 4, 1968
LOCALE: Memphis, Tennessee
SENTENCE: Ninety-nine years' imprisonment

EARLY LIFE

James Earl Ray, the son of George Ellis and Lucille Ray, was the oldest of seven siblings. The Ray family was poor and moved often because of Ellis's frequent legal problems. James had very little supervision, and by the age of fourteen he was spending most of his time in the local brothel. Like most men during World War II, Ray served in the military. He left the army with a general discharge in December, 1949. Ray soon served his first jail term in California for a burglary charge. Following this period, Ray would be in and out of prison, living the life of a failed petty criminal.

CRIMINAL CAREER

Ray was charged with and convicted of a bevy of crimes in his lifetime, including armed robbery, burglary, forgery, unauthorized use of a motor vehicle, and escaping from prison. Nevertheless, Ray would be merely a statistic in the National Bureau of Prisons' archives were it not for the events of April 4, 1968. On that night, civil rights leader Dr. Martin Luther King, Jr., was gunned down while standing on the balcony of the Lorraine Hotel in Memphis, Tennessee. King was shot one time and died later in a Memphis hospital. Almost one year earlier, on April 23, 1967, Ray had escaped from the Missouri State Prison.

LEGAL ACTION AND OUTCOME

On April 19, the Federal Bureau of Investigation (FBI) announced that Ray was the primary suspect in the assassination of King. Ray, a man of little means and less education, managed to elude the authorities for two months while traveling from Atlanta to Canada, Portugal, and

London under the names Ramon Sneyd and Eric S. Galt. Finally, on June 8, 1968, immigration authorities in London took Ray into custody as he attempted to board a plane for Brussels, Belgium. When Ray protested the extradition to the United States, the British authorities were presented with the evidence. Ray was extradited to the United States and returned to Memphis, Tennessee.

A few days after his return, Ray's legal advisers released the following statement:

RAY AND CONSPIRACY

Although James Earl Ray confessed to assassinating Dr. Martin Luther King, Jr., after he went to prison he recanted. Ray insisted that he was innocent and had been used as a patsy by the real killer or killers. Three lines of conspiracy theories sprang from Ray's change of heart and from the basic assumption that he was too inept to be the culprit.

- The first conspiracy has Ray simply as a lookout for the real killer. This killer was hired, as was Ray, by a mysterious man named Raoul. It was Raoul who arranged for Ray's escape to Canada and then to England, where he was arrested. Amateur investigators have identified at least two candidate Raouls; both have been exonerated. The motivation for Ray or Raoul's supposed actions remains murky.

- The second line of conspiracy thinking comprehends a variety of roles played by the U.S. government. It especially draws from the famous antipathy between Dr. King and the Federal Bureau of Investigation (FBI), especially its director, J. Edgar Hoover. Ray, the argument runs, was a fall guy. The real assassin was from the Green Berets, the Central Intelligence Agency (CIA), or the Mafia. The government had Dr. King killed out of fear that he would support the anti-Vietnam War movement.

- The third type of conspiracy theory revolves around racism and anticommunism. White supremacists, racists acting alone, or militant anticommunists killed Dr. King outright or arranged and financed the assassination.

While none of these theories has established itself as correct, many Americans subscribe to one. Dr. King's son Dexter King and widow Coretta Scott King both stated publicly their belief that Ray was innocent and vowed to find the real killer. One of Dr. King's closest advisers, Hosea Williams, said of Ray, "I think he was set up. I want to see him before he dies and I want to tell him, 'Don't feel too bad. They used you. A lot of people gave their life for Martin Luther King, but they took your life from you.'" Andrew Young, who witnessed the assassination, held similar views, and the Reverend Jesse Jackson, also a witness, wrote in the introduction to Ray's 1997 autobiography, *Who Killed Martin Luther King Jr.?*, "I have always believed that the government was part of a conspiracy, either directly or indirectly, to assassinate Dr. Martin Luther King, Jr."

Source: James Earl Ray, *Who Killed Martin Luther King Jr.? The True Story by the Alleged Assassin* (New York: Marlowe and Company, 1997).

From August, 1967, when he met Raoul in Montreal, down to King's death, he moved at Raoul's direction. . . . He delivered the rifle to Raoul, and then from about 4:30 to nearly 6 he sat downstairs in Jim's Grill drinking beer, waiting for Raoul. He says it was Raoul who fired the shot, and ran down the stairs, and threw down the rifle, zipper bag, and jumped in the Mustang where Ray was waiting, and the two drove off together.

Raoul, according to Ray, was the mastermind behind the assassination. After investigating Ray's story, his legal counsel advised him to plead guilty to the charges in order to avoid the death penalty. Ray fired his initial counsel; however, his new counsel advised him to do the same. In an issued statement, Ray said that he "fired a shot from the second floor bathroom of the rooming house and fatally wounded Dr. Martin Luther King who was standing on the balcony of the Lorraine Motel."

On May 10, 1969, Ray pleaded guilty to the assassination of King. However, Ray added to the judge that he "was not saying there had been no conspiracy, because there had been." Ray was sentenced to ninety-nine years in prison for the first-degree murder of King.

Ray later recanted his admission of guilt and claimed that it was his brother and Raoul who carried out the assassination. He spent the remainder of his years attempting to prove his innocence. On June 10, 1977, Ray escaped from Brushy Mountain State Prison but was soon recaptured.

On August 16, 1978, Ray testified before the House Select Committee on Assassinations. The committee concluded that the evidence pointed to Ray as the killer but that it was also likely that a white-supremacist group in St. Louis was involved. The group reportedly had a fifty-thousand-dollar bounty for the killing of King and may have had the connections and finances necessary for Ray's escape.

IMPACT

The impact of the assassination of Martin Luther King, Jr., on American society was immeasurable. The nation's cities, simmering with racial tension at the time, exploded in violence. Immediately following King's assassination, there were riots in more than one hundred American cities. Perhaps more than at any time since the American Civil War one hundred years earlier, the nation seem on the brink of being torn apart.

While the riots would eventually die down, the controversy of the assassination did not. Decades later, a solid majority of Americans believed that King was assassinated as a result of a conspiracy (poll numbers range between 60 percent and 80 percent). Like the conspiracy theories surrounding the assassinations of President John F. Kennedy in 1963 and Senator Robert F. Kennedy in 1968, such conspiracies are likely never to be proven or disproven.

In death as in life, Dr. King has become an icon of the ongoing struggle against racism in the United States. His principle of nonviolent resistance and a steadfast stand against racial prejudice continues in his name, and a holiday dedicated to his memory is observed annually in January within the United States.

FURTHER READING

Posner, Gerald. *Killing the Dream: James Earl Ray and the Assassination of Martin Luther King, Jr.* New York: Random House, 1998. Posner brings forth new evidence to assess the case against Ray.

Ray, James Earl. *Who Killed Martin Luther King, Jr.? The True Story by the Alleged Assassin.* New York: Marlowe, 1992. Ray's own version of the crime.

U.S. Congress. House. Select Committee on Assassinations. *Compilation of the Statements of James Earl Ray.* Washington, D.C.: U.S. Government Printing Office, 2001. Details the information uncovered during the 1978 investigations of Ray.

—*Ted Shields*

SEE ALSO: Lee Harvey Oswald; Jack Ruby; Sirhan Sirhan.

MARY READ
British pirate

BORN: c. 1685; possibly London, England
DIED: April 28, 1721; St. Jago de la Vega, Jamaica
ALSO KNOWN AS: Mary Reade; Bloody Mary
MAJOR OFFENSES: Piracy and assault and theft on the high seas
ACTIVE: Early 1700's-1720
LOCALE: Jamaica and throughout the Caribbean
SENTENCE: Death by hanging, stayed when she revealed that she was pregnant

EARLY LIFE

Few facts can be verified regarding the early life of Mary Read (reed), based primarily on an account published by Captain Charles Johnson, said to have been Daniel Defoe, in 1724. She was thought to have been born in London to the wife of a sea captain around 1685. Her mother evidently dressed her and raised her as a boy, as Mary apparently was illegitimate, and a male baby, the son of the sea captain, had died. Mary was passed off as the son, and the captain's mother helped support the family for a time after the captain was lost at sea. Read worked as a footboy for a time in a wealthy household but finally ran away to sea. She then joined the British military, where she was cited for valor and bravery in Flanders. While in the military, Mary met and fell in love with a fellow soldier, whom she ultimately married. Exiting from the military, they purchased and operated an inn named The Three Horseshoes.

After the death of her husband, Mary, again disguised as a man, boarded a ship bound for the West Indies. One story is that her ship was attacked by pirate Calico Jack Rackham, and she became a member of his crew. She was later said to have fallen in love with another pirate in the crew and married him.

CRIMINAL CAREER

Embarking on a life of piracy, Mary met Anne Bonny, another woman disguised as a man, who was Rackham's lover. The two women ultimately discovered their mutual gender, and Rackham was also informed. They continued to fight as pirates of Rackham's crew, wreaking havoc throughout the Caribbean Sea and conducting raids and looting ships until their capture by pirate hunter Captain Jonathan Barnet in late October, 1720. They were all charged with acts of piracy, felonies, and robberies. All pleaded innocent.

LEGAL ACTION AND OUTCOME

Calico Jack Rackham and his crew, including Read and Bonny, were found guilty. All were sentenced to hang, but the sentences of Read and Bonny were stayed because of their claims of pregnancy. Read was taken by a fever while in prison in St. Jago de la Vega and died there before giving birth.

IMPACT

Mary Read, along with her cohort Anne Bonny, became a figure of legend as a notorious woman pirate. Her exploits were famous at a time when women had very few options and no rights. While such behavior was considered scandalous, she showed that women could engage in the exploits of men and could live as they chose. Several historical works, the complete veracity of which it is impossible to determine, were later distributed, which described Read and Bonny as notorious criminals and succeeded in making them legends of the Great Age of Piracy in the Caribbean.

FURTHER READING

Botting, Douglas. *The Pirates.* Alexandria, Va.: Time-Life Books, 1978. An illustrated collection describing the time of piracy, the men and women, the ships, and the life and times of the Great Age of Piracy. Contains a bibliography and sections on Mary Read and Anne Bonny, among other infamous characters of the time.

Cordingly, David. *Under the Black Flag: The Romance and the Reality of Life Among the Pirates.* New York: Random House, 1995. Well-documented account of pirates and their lives, which addresses questions of how women could have lived in such conditions disguised as men, how they could have survived the rigorous and dangerous conditions, and whether it was unusual for women to become pirates.

Defoe, Daniel. *A General History of the Pyrates.* 1724. Reprint. Edited by Manuel Schonhorn. Mineola, N.Y.: Dover, 1999. Updated and corrected reprint of Defoe's classic work on pirates.

—Martha Oehmke Loustaunau

SEE ALSO: Anne Bonny; John Rackham.

MADAME RESTELL
American abortionist, midwife, and contraception provider

BORN: May 6, 1812; Painswick, Gloucestershire, England

DIED: April 1, 1878; New York, New York

ALSO KNOWN AS: Ann Trow (birth name); Ann Sommers; Anna Caroline Lohman; Ann Summer

MAJOR OFFENSE: Procuring a miscarriage

ACTIVE: 1839-1878

LOCALE: New York, New York

SENTENCE: One year in prison in Blackwell's Island Penitentiary, New York

EARLY LIFE

Madame Restell (reh-STEHL) was born Ann Trow, the daughter of a farm laborer in Gloucestershire, England. At fifteen, she married Henry Sommers, the village tailor. They emigrated to Manhattan in 1831. Sommers died of typhoid fever within two years of their arrival. His widow married Charles Lohman, a printer for the New York *Herald*, in 1836.

CRIMINAL CAREER

About three years after her marriage, Ann Lohman placed newspaper advertisements as "Madame Restell,

female physician and professor of midwifery" and claimed that her pills promised cures for the "stop-page of menses." She opened a discreet office on Greenwich Street, where she sold abortifacients, provided abortions, and ran a de facto adoption agency and midwifery practice. Her clients ranged from the desperately poor to the highest echelons of Manhattan society, and Restell grew infamously wealthy.

In the 1840's, aborting a "quick fetus" (one that a woman feels moving) in New York State was a crime of second-degree manslaughter. Attempting an abortion at any time during pregnancy was considered a misdemeanor. Restell was not the only abortionist to advertise in newspapers, and the police usually turned a blind eye to what was a fairly common practice. Eventually, because of pressure from outspoken antiabortion crusaders, the district attorney pressured Maria Bodine, one of Restell's abortion clients, to sign a complaint against Restell and had the abortionist arrested.

LEGAL ACTION AND OUTCOME

The case went to trial on October 25, 1847. The district attorney brought five counts of manslaughter—four for

Madame Restell.

an abortion on a quick fetus and one on a fetus not quick—against Restell. Because the time line of Bodine's pregnancy was unclear, Restell was convicted only on the lesser charge—procuring a miscarriage—and served a one-year sentence in the women's prison on Blackwell's Island.

After her release, Restell moved her business to Chambers Street. With her brother, Joseph Trow, she and her husband began selling abortifacients through the mail to points beyond New York. After the American Civil War (1861-1865), the Lohmans built a grand mansion on the corner of Fifth Avenue and Fifty-second Street, but Charles died shortly after its completion. Madame Restell continued to see patients in her new home office.

In the 1870's, Restell's activities caught the attention of Anthony Comstock, a Christian reformer driven to eradicate New York of "vice," which, in his definition, included abortifacients. In February, 1878, Comstock

fabricated a story about his wife's unwanted pregnancy, and Restell sold him some pills. The sale was enough cause for police to arrest Restell. Her trial was set for April 1, 1878, but she committed suicide that morning, climbing into a tub of water and cutting her throat.

IMPACT

Although it was well known that abortions were widely performed by doctors or abortionists advertising in print media throughout New York, abortion rights foes lobbied successfully in curtailing its legality. In 1845, New York legislators passed laws stiffening penalties for performing abortions. Women who sought abortions could be punished for a misdemeanor. In 1870, abortion was made a felony. In 1873, the Comstock Act criminalized the distribution of obscene materials through the mail, including contraceptives. In her day, Madame Restell's notoriety brought these issues to the forefront of society's consciousness, and she continued to appear as an icon even in modern literature, such as Marge Piercy's 2005 novel, *Sex Wars*, which uses real-life characters.

FURTHER READING

Horowitz, Helen Lefkowitz. *Rereading Sex: Battles over Sexual Knowledge and Suppression in Nineteenth Century America*. New York: Vintage, 2003. An examination of nineteenth century sexual practices, including the influences of religion and the media. Horowitz discusses Restell's place in this cultural history.

Reagan, Leslie J. *When Abortion Was a Crime: Women, Medicine, and Law in the United States, 1867-1973*. Berkeley: University of California Press, 1998. A history of abortion rights and those who practiced abortion in the United States prior to its legalization by *Roe v. Wade*.

Srebnick, Amy Gilman. *The Mysterious Death of Mary Rogers: Sex and Culture in Nineteenth Century New York*. New York: Oxford University Press, 1997. Srebnick lays out the mystery of Mary Rogers's murder, possibly from a botched abortion, and her tenuous link to Restell, while also tracking Victorian sexuality and the press.

—Olivia Boler

SEE ALSO: Anthony Comstock.

JOACHIM VON RIBBENTROP
Foreign minister of Nazi Germany, 1938-1945

BORN: April 30, 1893; Wesel, Germany
DIED: October 16, 1946; Nuremberg, Germany
ALSO KNOWN AS: Ulrich Friedrich Willy Joachim Ribbentrop (full name); Joachim Ribbentrop
MAJOR OFFENSES: Conspiring to wage aggressive war, waging aggressive war, war crimes, and crimes against humanity
ACTIVE: January, 1938-May, 1945
LOCALE: Germany
SENTENCE: Death by hanging

EARLY LIFE
Joachim von Ribbentrop (YOH-ah-kheem fahn RIHB-ihn-trohp) was born to a German army officer and his wife in Wesel on April 30, 1893. As a child he was well

Joachim von Ribbentrop.

traveled, attending school in Switzerland and visiting France and Britain before World War I. In 1911, he worked briefly in London for a German importer, moving soon to Canada, where he worked on the Canadian-Pacific Railway, and the United States, where he worked as a journalist in Boston and New York. The war brought him back to Germany in 1914, and he joined the 125th Hussars, winning an Iron Cross. A serious wound landed him in the hospital, and eventually he joined the Ministry of War and then the German peace delegation that signed the Treaty of Versailles in 1919. He left the army after the peace and became a champagne salesman for a French firm in the Rhineland. He also married into the wine business in 1920; he and his wife made quite a fortune in the midst of the continental depression.

As a businessman, Ribbentrop tended to steer clear of politics but joined the Nazi Party on the eve of Adolf Hitler's rise to power. Hitler took a liking to him and appointed him his adviser for foreign affairs. Ribbentrop created a small fiefdom within the Nazi empire and soon had several hundred people under his direction. In 1934, Hitler appointed him Delegate for Disarmament Questions; in 1935, ambassador-at-large; and between August 11, 1936, and February 4, 1938, as Germany's ambassador to Britain. Ribbentrop riled his English hosts with his habitual Nazi salutes and liberal use of swastikas in decorating. In the reordering of the German hierarchy in February, 1938, Ribbentrop replaced Foreign Minister Konstantin von Neurath. As Hitler's foreign minister, Ribbentrop helped lay the diplomatic groundwork for the German successes in the early stages of World War II.

NAZI CAREER
After the war, the International Military Tribunal indicted Ribbentrop on all four general counts: conspiring to wage aggressive war, waging aggressive war, war crimes, and crimes against humanity. With regard to the waging of aggressive war, Ribbentrop's activities clearly displayed his key roles in the absorption of Austria (the Anschluss) and the Czechoslovak Sudetenland in 1938 and 1939. He worked closely with pro-German groups in both countries and knew that his guarantees to the French and British of no further German territorial demands were a sham. He continued to mislead the French and British in the months before the invasion of Poland, conspiring with Hitler to keep them in the dark and carrying out negotiations with the Soviet foreign minister

Vyacheslav Molotov for the division of Poland. Ribbentrop knew of Hitler's plans against Norway, Belgium, the Netherlands, Denmark, and France well in advance of their enactment, and when the Germans turned west in the spring of 1940, Ribbentrop defended the aggression against world outrage. He also participated in the negotiations with the fascist Italian government over the Axis invasion of the Balkans in 1941 and with the Japanese over the German invasion of the Soviet Union. In general, he was the architect of Hitler's extraordinarily belligerent foreign policy.

Regarding Ribbentrop's indictment for war crimes, or breaches in the commonly accepted rules of the conduct of war, the Tribunal cited his presence at key meetings at which the Nazi leadership agreed to the brutal treatment of captured Allied combatants. They also attributed to him the guilt of all of his underlings who ran the Nazi-occupied states of Europe. Guilt for the atrocities and general brutality of Nazi military occupation was placed squarely on his shoulders. Here is also where the court found the justification for indicting him of crimes against humanity. As Germany's chief diplomat, Ribbentrop helped force compliance with Hitler's "final solution" of the "Jewish problem" from Axis allies and puppet states, on several occasions insisting on speedy mass deportations. He was also present at meetings at which specific policies for the destruction of European Jewry were discussed and planned. After Hitler's suicide, Admiral Karl Dönitz, his successor, dismissed Ribbentrop as a prelude to opening negotiations for surrender.

LEGAL ACTION AND OUTCOME

Ribbentrop was captured by the Allies and placed on trial before the International Military Tribunal in Nuremberg. He was found guilty on all of the tribunal's four counts. He tried to defend himself by attributing all of the impetus to Hitler and distancing himself from his allegiance to him. The court, however, found that Ribbentrop was an active and very sympathetic participant in planning and carrying out the Reich's monstrous policies and that Ribbentrop was loyal to the end. On October 16, 1946, he was the first of the Nazi war criminals to be hanged in Nuremberg.

IMPACT

The damage inflicted on the world by the Nazi policies and warmaking, in which Joachim von Ribbentrop conspired, is beyond any accounting. The importance of his appearance before the international court was highly significant in that the victorious Allies modeled for the world a radical intolerance of the kind of bellicose diplomacy practiced by Ribbentrop and his foreign office.

FURTHER READING

Bloch, Michael. *Ribbentrop*. London: Abacus, 2003. Very well-documented study of the man and his influence in Hitler's government.

Ribbentrop, Joachim von. *Documents on the Events Preceding the Outbreak of the War*. Honolulu: University Press of the Pacific, 2004. Originally complied by Ribbentrop and the German Foreign Office in the midst of World War II as a response to anti-Nazi propaganda and defense of Nazi belligerence.

Vizulis, Izidors. *The Molotov-Ribbentrop Pact of 1939*. New York: Praeger, 1990. A careful study of the agreement that opened the way for Nazi conquest of western Poland and the opening of World War II.

Weitz, John. *Hitler's Diplomat: Joachim von Ribbentrop*. London: Weidenfeld and Nicolson, 1992. More biographical than analytical in its treatment of Ribbentrop's roles in laying groundwork for the Nazi hegemony in Europe.

—*Joseph P. Byrne*

SEE ALSO: Karl Dönitz; Adolf Hitler; Vyacheslav Mikhailovich Molotov.

RICHARD III
King of England (r. 1483-1485)

BORN: October 2, 1452; Fotheringhay Castle, Northamptonshire, England

DIED: August 22, 1485; Bosworth Field, Leicestershire, England

ALSO KNOWN AS: Richard Plantagenet; Richard, duke of Gloucester

CAUSE OF NOTORIETY: Despite his attempt to restore order and dynastic stability during the Wars of the Roses, Richard III became the victim of character assassination by Tudor propagandists and became known as a tyrant king.

ACTIVE: 1483-1485

LOCALE: England

EARLY LIFE

Richard Plantagenet (plan-TA-jeh-neht), the future Richard III, was the youngest surviving child of Richard, duke of York, and Cecily, the daughter of Ralph Neville. Because his father was a claimant to the throne occupied by Henry VI of the House of Lancaster, Richard was embroiled from infancy in bitter power struggles. His was the era of the Wars of the Roses, a civil war fought between members of the House of York and the House of Lancaster over entitlement to the throne. Richard was seven when the Yorkists were routed at Ludford in 1459, and his mother threw herself on the king's mercy.

When the Yorkists turned the tables at Northampton, Richard of York was designated as Henry's heir; Cecily and her three youngest children—George, Margaret, and Richard—returned to London. When the compromise failed and their father was killed at Wakefield, Richard and George were sent to Burgundy for their safety. The young men were initially an embarrassment to the duke of Burgundy, but their status changed when their eldest brother won the Battle of Towton and seized the throne, becoming Edward IV. George was created duke of Clarence and, at age nine, Richard became the duke of Gloucester. Richard was placed in the household of his mother's kinswoman, Richard Neville, earl of Warwick. He remained there until he was adjudged to have come of age at sixteen, when he went to court.

ROYAL CAREER

Richard remained steadfastly loyal to Edward IV, unlike the earl of Warwick or his brother, the duke of Clarence; their opposition devolved into open conflict in June, 1469. Richard was appointed constable of England and given substantial estates in Wales, which he left to supervise in November. He returned to London in July, 1470, to help Edward IV recover from another rebellion. Clarence and Warwick then mounted a French-supported invasion in September, forcing Edward IV and Richard to flee; they regrouped in The Hague and mounted their own Burgundian-supported invasion in January, 1471. Warwick was defeated at Barnet on April 14, and Edward IV and Richard defeated the main Lancastrian army at Tewkesbury on May 4. What part Richard played in the first battle is unrecorded, but he led the vanguard in the second one.

Edward IV gave Richard the confiscated Neville estates in the north of England, and Richard married Warwick's second daughter, Anne. Her older sister Isabel was, however, married to the duke of Clarence, who immediately pressed his own claim to the estates. Edward IV was pressured into dividing them but eventually lost patience with Clarence and, under the charge of treason, sent his unruly brother to a private execution on February 18, 1478. Richard fought for Edward IV in France and also took an army to Scotland to support the

Richard III. (Library of Congress)

duke of Albany against James III; he had to retreat when Albany capitulated in advance of his arrival.

Richard was still in the north when Edward IV died on April 4, 1483. Preparations were made to crown the elder of Edward IV's sons, also called Edward, who was twelve. Richard hurried to London, taking young Edward into custody en route and arresting the boy's uncle, Earl Rivers. He arrived in London on May 4 as de facto Lord Protector. He found the royal household in dire financial straits, and although he paid off its immediate debts, he was never able to put the kingdom's financial affairs in order, a root cause of his eventual downfall.

On June 13, 1483, Edward IV's former chamberlain, Lord Hastings, was abruptly seized and executed, and several other councilors arrested. Richard took charge of his nephews, Edward V and Richard, duke of York. Edward V soon took up residence in the Tower of London, where he was joined by his brother Richard in mid-June. The older Richard postponed Edward V's coronation, and on June 22, Ralph Shaw preached a sermon at St. Paul's Cross, alleging that both young princes were illegitimate, because Edward IV was already married when he wed the boys' mother. (Richard's first intention had been to claim that it was Edward IV who was illegitimate—a contention that modern historians have substantiated—but he apparently thought better of it.) Richard, duke of Gloucester was crowned king on June 25.

On August 29, while Richard was away from London, an attempt was made to seize the two princes from the Tower. They were probably murdered shortly thereafter, as they were never seen again, although their exact fate remained a mystery for centuries. Opposition to Richard was henceforth focused on Henry Tudor (who became King Henry VII in 1485), whose support grew as Richard's faded, most significantly when the duke of Buckingham deserted him, although Buckingham's rebellion was swiftly crushed.

THE WARS OF THE ROSES

After the death of England's triumphant warrior king Henry V in 1422, his infant son became Henry VI and succeeded to the throne. Pietistic and weak-minded, Henry VI proved to be a disaster as a monarch, the worst since the Plantagenet line began with William the Conqueror in 1066, according to most historians. He suffered a nervous breakdown in 1453, and the Council of England, weary of his ineptitude, created a protectorship for England under Richard, duke of York, or Richard III. Richard became de facto ruler. When Henry VI recovered a year later, his family, the Lancastrians, had the protectorship terminated.

Richard of York and his followers, however, knew their position was precarious under the resurgent Lancastrians. Richard's decision to fight the restoration of the king started the Wars of the Roses—so called by later writers because Lancaster took as a symbol the red rose, while York took the white rose. Hostilities began when Richard led an army against the king's forces at St. Albans in 1455. Fifteen more battles, and many skirmishes, occurred at intervals during four phases of conflict: from the first battle until Edward IV (Richard of York's son) became king in 1461 and defeated the Lancastrians at the Battle of Towton; from the rebellion of Edward's former backer, the earl of Warwick, until Warwick's defeat in battle in 1471, along with the Lancastrians again; from the coronation of Richard III until invasion from France by the exiled Henry Tudor and the Battle of Bosworth in 1485, in which Richard III was killed and the Yorkists defeated; and finally, the opposition following the coronation of Henry VII until the Battle of Stokes in 1487. Even then, however, the Yorkists posed a threat until 1499, when their last strong leader, Perkin of Warbeck, was captured and executed.

The war embroiled the nobility in general, but all ranks suffered casualties. Among the highest nobility to die in battle or be executed after capture were the dukes of Somerset, Buckingham, York, and Norfolk; the earls of Northumberland, Dorset, Shrewsbury, Salisbury, Rutland, Devon, Wiltshire, Warwick, and Lincoln; the marquess of Montagu; and Edward, Prince of Wales.

More than the Yorkist cause died with Richard III. Civilization was changing, and to many historians he was the last of the medieval kings of England. Henry VII, a canny administrator and financier, was the first of the Renaissance kings.

Richard's wife died in 1485, amid rumors that he had already promised to marry Elizabeth Woodville in order to secure firmer links with the family of Edward IV's wife. Henry Tudor landed at Milford Haven on August 7, 1485; Richard's forces met his near Market Bosworth on August 22. No reliable record of the battle survives, but it seems that Richard led a direct attack on Henry's position and was then overwhelmed by forces mustered by William Stanley, who changed sides at the last moment.

IMPACT

Henry Tudor's entitlement to the throne was weak, so he bolstered it with a sustained flood of propaganda that represented Richard as a treacherous, murderous tyrant.

Henry's descendants carried that program forward with increasing ingenuity, sponsoring Sir Thomas Moore's scathing *History of King Richard III* (1543) and William Shakespeare's vicious account in *Richard III* (pr. c. 1592-1593, revised 1623). Although one of Henry VII's lickspittles, William Burton of York, referred to King Richard as a "crocheback" in 1491, there is no evidence that he was physically deformed, and his military record speaks against this notion. It was undoubtedly Edward IV who licensed the executions of Henry VI and the duke of Clarence, and there is no evidence that King Richard's wife was murdered. He probably did order the execution of the princes in the Tower of London, but it was a political move typical of the era. Although the Renaissance had begun in Italy, England was still in the dire grip of the age of chivalry—which is to say, that of self-seeking, back-stabbing baronial bombast, when wise men always got their retaliation in first.

FURTHER READING

Cheetham, Anthony. *The Life and Times of Richard III*. London: Weidenfeld and Nicolson, 1992. A popular account produced by a highly educated writer.

Horrox, Rosemary. *Richard III: A Study in Service*. Cambridge, England: Cambridge University Press, 1989.

A balanced account that makes a determined attempt to set straight the historical record of who murdered whom, insofar as that task is possible.

Kendall, Paul, ed. *Richard III: The Great Debate*. London: Allen and Unwin, 1955. An anthology useful for its representation of the spectrum of debate relating to the precise degree of Richard's villainy, including attempts to absolve him of responsibility for the murder of the two princes.

Legge, Alfred O. *The Unpopular King: The Life and Times of Richard III*. 2 vols. London: Ward and Downey, 1885. A significant and not entirely successful attempt to set the historical record straight in the wake of the overwhelming effect that Tudor propaganda had exerted on historical accounts of Richard for three centuries.

Ross, Charles. *Richard III*. London: Eyre Methuen, 1981. A brief but well-executed summary of Richard's life and the subsequent controversies brought forth by Tudor allegations of extreme perfidy.

—*Brian Stableford*

SEE ALSO: Alexander VI; Clement VII; Joan the Mad; King John; Leo X.

JOHNNY RINGO
American gunfighter and outlaw

BORN: May 3, 1850; Green's Fork, Indiana

DIED: July 12 or 13, 1882; Sulphur Springs Valley, Arizona

ALSO KNOWN AS: John Peters Ringo (full name); John Ringgold; Jack Ringold

CAUSE OF NOTORIETY: Ringo was a legendary outlaw who took part in several murders, but he avoided prosecution.

ACTIVE: December, 1874-March, 1882

LOCALE: Central Texas, southwestern New Mexico, and southeastern Arizona

EARLY LIFE

John Peters Ringo (RIHN-goh) was the oldest of five children born to Martin and Mary Peters Ringo. When Johnny was six, the family moved to Gallatin, Missouri. In 1864, they journeyed to San Jose, California. While traveling through Wyoming, Johnny's father was killed when his shotgun accidentally discharged as he stepped

out of his wagon. Continuing their trip, the Ringo family arrived in San Jose in late October. Ringo lived with his family and worked as a farmer in San Jose until about 1870, when he moved to Texas.

OUTLAW CAREER

Ringo was issued his first criminal indictment on April 14, 1875, for disturbing the peace in Burnet, Texas; he was arrested on an indictment for disturbing the peace in December. After posting bond, he was released. Soon thereafter, he participated in a feud between German settlers and Texas cattlemen over cattle ownership in the Mason County (or Hoodoo) War in central Texas. As part of the conflict, Ringo and a friend killed well-known gambler James Cheyney on September 25, 1875. In March, 1876, Ringo and Scott Cooley were tried and convicted for threatening the lives of Burnet County law officers. Friends broke them out of the Travis County jail in Austin in May, 1876. Ringo was recaptured on October 31, 1876, and jailed again in Austin. While in jail, Ringo was indicted for the murder of Cheyney and remained in jail until early 1878. When witnesses would not testify, he was freed on May 15, 1878. In 1879, Ringo moved to Tombstone, Arizona, and worked on a ranch. He was arrested for wounding Louis Hancock in a gunfight in Safford, Arizona, on December 14, 1879.

When Ringo did not appear before a grand jury in March, 1880, for the shooting of Hancock, a warrant was issued for his arrest. To avoid being jailed, he traveled to New Mexico and Texas. In New Mexico, he reportedly participated in the robbery of a Mexican mule train on August 1, 1881.

After close friends of Ringo were killed by Wyatt Earp, Earp's brothers, and Doc Holliday in the famous gunfight at the O.K. Corral in Tombstone, Arizona, on October 26, 1881, Ringo became a fierce enemy of Earp and Holliday. He challenged them to a gunfight on January 17, 1882, but Tombstone law officers stopped it.

When Morgan Earp was murdered on March 17, 1882, some believed that Ringo was involved. It was never proven. Ringo was found dead near Turkey Creek on July 13, 1882, most likely as a result of a self-inflicted gunshot wound, although some speculate that Wyatt Earp or Holliday may have been involved.

IMPACT

During the Mason County War, Johnny Ringo developed a reputation for being the fastest gun alive. In Tombstone, Arizona, he became the chief antagonist of Wyatt Earp and Doc Holliday. Ringo became known as one of the most dangerous outlaws in the Southwest. The death of Ringo was enshrouded with mystery and controversy; it is one of the most debated deaths in the history of the Old West. After his death, he was romanticized by many writers as one of the deadliest, most feared gunfighters of the era. During the late 1950's and early 1960's, he was portrayed as a popular Western character in numerous television Westerns and in motion pictures.

FURTHER READING

Burrows, Jack. *John Ringo: The Gunfighter Who Never Was*. Tucson: University of Arizona Press, 1987. Explores the life of Ringo, confirming some legends about his encounters with Wyatt Earp and Doc Holliday.

Gatto, Steve. *Johnny Ringo*. Lansing, Mich.: Protar House, 2002. Using primary sources, Gatto renders what is probably the most accurate account of the early life of Ringo.

McCord, Jason. *Johnny Ringo: Unknown Destiny*. San Ramon, Calif.: Falcon Books, 2002. An excellent account of Ringo's participation in the Mason County War and of his confrontations with Wyatt Earp and Doc Holliday in Tombstone, Arizona.

—*Alvin K. Benson*

SEE ALSO: Curly Bill Brocius; Wyatt Earp; Doc Holliday.

EFRAÍN RÍOS MONTT
Guatemalan dictator (1982-1983)

BORN: June 16, 1926; Huehuetenango, Guatemala
CAUSE OF NOTORIETY: During Ríos Montt's regime of just over sixteen months, thousands of indigenous men, women, and children were kidnapped, tortured, killed, or displaced.
ACTIVE: March 23, 1982-August 8, 1983
LOCALE: Guatemala, particularly the Ixil Triangle, in the northwest

EARLY LIFE

Born to a Catholic family but with a Protestant grandmother, Efraín Ríos Montt (ehf-rah-EEN REE-ohs mohnt) joined the army and studied at the Polytechnic School in Guatemala City. He received specialized training in counterinsurgency warfare from the United States'

School of the Americas in Panama, graduating in 1950 as a cadet. He participated in a minor way in the 1954 overthrow of the democratically elected President Jacobo Arbenz Gúzman, which was sponsored by the U.S. Central Intelligence Agency (CIA). Ríos Montt rose through the ranks, becoming a general in 1970. In 1973 he left his liaison post at the embassy in Washington, D.C., to run in the Guatemalan presidential elections of 1974. He denounced the results, claiming that fraud had prevented him from being elected. He was sent to Spain as a military attaché to the embassy in Madrid until 1977. In 1978 he left the Catholic faith and joined the Church of the Word, a branch of the Pentecostal sect Gospel Outreach. He became a spokesman for the church.

POLITICAL CAREER

On March 23, 1982, the army interrupted Ríos Montt's Bible class to tell him they had just overthrown the government of Fernando Romeo Lucas García and would like him to assume the presidency of the new military junta. Because of the brutality of the deposed Lucas regime, most sectors of the population were hopeful. Ríos Montt began his term with a "beans and guns" campaign, promising beans to feed the hungry and guns to kill the guerrillas. Ríos Montt saw his military campaign as a kind of "holy war" against "communist" ideas. The killing, however, soon became widespread and generalized. It has been estimated that more than ten thousand Guatemalans, primarily indigenous, were killed, and at least one hundred thousand made homeless in just the first five months of his dictatorship. In the United States, the Ron-

Efraín Ríos Montt. (AP/Wide World Photos)

ald Reagan administration supported Ríos Montt, in part because of his deep anticommunism, and reinstituted the military aid.

Ríos Montt's government was overthrown on August 8, 1983. In 1989 he formed a new political party, the FRG, or Guatemalan Republican Front. He attempted to run for president as the FRG candidate, but the constitution prohibited participants in military coups from participation. He was an FRG deputy from 1990 to 2004, and elected president of congress in 1994. In 2003 he again tried to run for president, forcing a court decision to allow his candidacy. In order to run he had to step down from congress after fourteen years there.

LEGAL ACTION AND OUTCOME

Lawsuits have been filed in Guatemala and Spain against Ríos Montt. Along with several others, he is accused of genocide and crimes against humanity, charges related to the destruction of Mayan communities, their mass murder, and their displacement into inadequate living conditions.

GUATEMALAN CONSTITUTION

Overthrown on August 8, 1983, Ríos Montt formed the Guatemalan Republican Front (FRG) in 1989 and ran for the presidency then and again in 2003. On July 24 and 25 of that year, FRG radicals fomented riots in the streets of Guatemala City, attacking journalists and terrorizing other citizens in support of Ríos Montt's presidential bid. The riots kicked off a period of violence exceeded only by the civil war, which had ended in 1996: Thousands of people were murdered, shot, raped, tortured, kidnapped, and subjected to other atrocities. Tens of thousands were the victims of FRG violence for minor offenses.

Ríos Montt said this of Black Thursday and its aftermath: "El Jueves Negro lo miro con respeto, por el movimiento popular." ("I respect Black Thursday because it is a popular movement.")

In early July, 2006, Judge Santiago Pedraz of the Spanish National Court issued warrants for the arrest of Ríos Montt and another former dictator, General Oscar Humberto Mejia Victores, on charges of genocide, torture, terrorism, and illegal detention in connection with the civil war. Ríos Montt insisted that the army had "followed orders and the law" and accused the judge of forgetting that

> there was a war in Guatemala, a guerrilla war in which terrorists destroyed bridges, schools, electric plants and other buildings of the people. . . . There were some officials who committed abuses . . . the army was not a squad of assassins. . . . It was men who acted and reacted in defense of the interests of the nation and the people. . . . [My term formed] a bridge between a black past and a hopeful tomorrow, given that the guerrillas and international terrorism were defeated in Guatemala.

Source: Ríos Montt quoted in *The Miami Herald*, July 13, 2006.

IMPACT

Efraín Ríos Montt remains an extremely controversial figure. President Bill Clinton apologized for U.S. support of Ríos Montt's violent and repressive government. Human rights groups continue to press the legal case against him. Urban, ladino (non-Indian) Guatemalans sometimes recall the halcyon days under Ríos Montt when urban life was orderly. The view of indigenous Guatemalans, however, is unambiguous: Ríos Montt was a brutal dictator responsible for the torture and death of anyone who contested, or might have contested, his authority.

FURTHER READING

Ball, Patrick, Paul Kobrak, and Herbert F. Spirer. *State Violence in Guatemala, 1960-1996: A Quantitative Reflection.* Washington, D.C.: American Association for the Advancement of Science, 1999. Uses statistics along with narrative to detail the history of disappearances and murders over more than four decades.

Montejo, Victor. *Voices from Exile: Violence and Survival in Modern Maya History.* Norman: University of Oklahoma Press, 1999. Written by a native Maya forced into exile by the massacres of the Ríos Montt regime. Examines the impact of armed conflict on the indigenous community, with special focus on Ríos Montt.

Recovery of Historical Memory Project. *Guatemala: Never Again!* Maryknoll, N.Y.: Orbis Books, 1999. An abridged translation of the four volumes sponsored by the Human Rights Office of the Archdiocese of Guatemala. Provides good historical background and a separate chapter on the Ríos Montt government.

Stoll, David. "Evangelical, Guerrillas, and the Army: The Ixil Triangle Under Ríos Montt." Chapter 4 in *Harvest of Violence: The Maya Indians and the Guatemalan Crisis,* edited by Robert M. Carmack. Norman: University of Oklahoma Press, 1988. Discusses the role of evangelical Christians during Ríos Montt's regime and questions whether he truly controlled the army that put him in power.

—Linda Ledford-Miller

SEE ALSO: Fidel Castro; François Duvalier; Jean-Claude Duvalier; Leopoldo Galtieri; Ferdinand Marcos; Augusto Pinochet Ugarte; Miguel Primo de Rivera; Anastasio Somoza García; Rafael Trujillo; Getúlio Vargas.

GEORGE RIVAS

American career criminal and leader of the Texas 7 prison escapees

BORN: May 6, 1970; El Paso, Texas

MAJOR OFFENSES: Aggravated kidnapping with a deadly weapon, aggravated robbery with a deadly weapon, burglary of a habitation, escape from the Texas Department of Criminal Justice, and capital murder

ACTIVE: May 25, 1993-December 24, 2000

LOCALE: El Paso, Kenedy, and Irving, Texas

SENTENCE: Eighteen life sentences, death sentence for murder of police officer Aubrey Hawkins

EARLY LIFE

After his parents divorced when George Rivas (REE-vahs) was six, he was raised by his grandparents in El Paso, Texas. While in high school, Rivas dreamed of becoming a police officer. One year after graduating from Ysleta High School, however, he committed his first robbery and burglary. With no prior criminal record, Rivas was sentenced to ten years' probation. Meanwhile, he enrolled as a general studies major at the University of Texas, El Paso. Rivas, then a college student with two children, dropped out of school after three semesters.

CRIMINAL CAREER

During the following decade, Rivas would commit a string of robberies. In addition to committing three robberies in October of 1992, and two more in May of 1993 in El Paso, Rivas was suspected of robbing stores in other parts of Texas, in Oklahoma, and in New Mexico. After his arrest for the robbery of a Toys "R" Us store, Rivas was sentenced to eighteen terms of life in prison, seventeen of them consecutive. After four years of incarceration by the Texas Department of Criminal Justice (TDCJ), he developed a plan to escape.

As ringleader for the Texas 7 (Rivas, Joseph Garcia, Randy Halprin, Larry Harper, Patrick Murphy, Jr., Donald Newbury, and Michael Rodriguez), Rivas escaped with six fellow inmates from the John Connally Unit near Kenedy, Texas, on December 13, 2000. Known as a "model prisoner," he had been granted work detail in the maintenance area of the prison, which allowed him special privileges and the ability to carry off the biggest prison break in Texas history. Rivas and the other prisoners overpowered guards, stole their weapons, and drove a maintenance truck through the back gate of the prison.

After their escape, the group decided to rob an Oshman's sporting goods store on Christmas Eve, 2000. Twenty-nine-year-old Aubrey Hawkins had been a police officer for merely fourteen months before the group shot him dead at the scene. Hawkins's police cruiser was found with more than twenty bullet holes; the officer had been dragged from his car and shot several times in the back and head. His head was run over three times by the escapees before they fled the scene.

Rivas and the others continued at large for five weeks. Law enforcement officials finally caught up with them in Colorado, where, posing as Bible-reading Christian missionaries, the group was staying in a trailer park. On January 23, 2001, the national manhunt to capture Rivas ended, and during the next two days the rest of the now-infamous Texas 7 were captured.

LEGAL ACTION AND OUTCOME
Rivas was tried and convicted of capital murder and sentenced to die (a penalty he requested) by lethal injection. He and two other Texas 7 members, Rodriguez and Newbury, were incarcerated on death row in Texas.

IMPACT
Experts and prison officials agree that modifications in prison security would have prevented the escape of the Texas 7. Since their jailbreak, increased attention has been given to prison security issues such as locks, keys, building design, alarm systems, lighting, perimeter security, and regular supervision. Currently available technologies such as digital facial recognition and remote-view video recorders may decrease the likelihood of future prison escapes.

FURTHER READING
Culp, Richard, and Elizabeth Bracco. "Examining Prison Escapes and the Routine Activities Theory." *Corrections Compendium* 30, no. 3 (2005): 1-9. In an era of increasing prison populations and prison security, the authors discuss how and why escapes occur when they do.

King, Gary C. *The Texas 7: A True Story of Murder and a Daring Escape.* New York: St. Martin's Press, 2001. An account of the events leading up to and following Rivas's prison escape and subsequent crimes and the pursuit that ultimately led to his capture.
                                                —*Patricia K. Hendrickson*

SEE ALSO: Jules Bonnot; Jacques Mesrine; Assata Olugbala Shakur; Jonathan Wild.

ROB ROY
Scottish outlaw

BORN: Baptized March 7, 1671; Glengyle, Scotland
DIED: December 28, 1734; Balquhidder, Perthshire, Scotland
ALSO KNOWN AS: Red Robert; Raibert Ruadh; Robert Roy MacGregor (birth name); Robert Campbell
MAJOR OFFENSES: Fraud, treason, banditry, cattle rustling, and debt
ACTIVE: 1712-1726
LOCALE: Scottish Highlands
SENTENCE: Death for cattle rustling; pardoned in 1727

EARLY LIFE
Rob Roy (rawb roy) was born the third son of Donald Glas MacGregor of Glengyle, Scotland. Though his father technically did not own the family's land, his influence as well as his hereditary tenantship led to his using the customary title "of." Rob Roy's father was the chief of the MacGregor clan living in the area. Rob Roy inherited his red hair from his mother, Margaret Campbell, which resulted in his Gaelic name of Raibert Ruadh (*ruadh* meaning "red"). It is likely that while growing up Rob Roy had some education in the nearby Lowlands, for he was able to write in English. It would have been necessary for him to speak English in order to deal with the Lowlands traders.

During the first Jacobite rebellion in 1689, Rob Roy and his father fought in support of the Stuart king, James, at the successful Battle of Killiecrankie. Once the rebellion was put down, however, the name MacGregor was outlawed, and Rob Roy's father was taken prisoner. Rob Roy subsequently took on his mother's name of Campbell. He then drove cattle in the area of Crieff and was so successful in his business that he was able to purchase the lairdship of Inversnaid. He married his cousin, Mary

"Rob Roy's Grave"

The English Romantic poet William Wordsworth composed this tribute to the legendary Rob Roy, preceded by a comment: "The history of Rob Roy is sufficiently known; his grave is near the head of Loch Ketterine, in one of those small pinfold-like Burial-grounds, of neglected and desolate appearance, which the traveller meets with in the Highlands of Scotland."

A FAMOUS man is Robin Hood,
The English ballad-singer's joy!
And Scotland has a thief as good,
An outlaw of as daring mood;
She has her brave ROB ROY!
Then clear the weeds from off his Grave,
And let us chant a passing stave,
In honour of that Hero brave!

Heaven gave Rob Roy a dauntless heart
And wondrous length and strength of arm:
Nor craved he more to quell his foes,
Or keep his friends from harm.

Yet was Rob Roy as wise as brave;
Forgive me if the phrase be strong;—
A Poet worthy of Rob Roy
Must scorn a timid song.

Say, then, that he was 'wise' as brave;
As wise in thought as bold in deed:
For in the principles of things
He sought his moral creed.

Said generous Rob, "What need of books?
Burn all the statutes and their shelves:
They stir us up against our kind;
And worse, against ourselves.

"We have a passion—make a law,
Too false to guide us or control!
And for the law itself we fight
In bitterness of soul.

"And, puzzled, blinded thus, we lose
Distinctions that are plain and few:
These find I graven on my heart:
That tells me what to do.

"The creatures see of flood and field,
And those that travel on the wind!
With them no strife can last; they live
In peace, and peace of mind.

"For why?—because the good old rule
Sufficeth them, the simple plan,
That they should take, who have the power,
And they should keep who can.

"A lesson that is quickly learned,
A signal this which all can see!

Thus nothing here provokes the strong
To wanton cruelty.

"All freakishness of mind is checked;
He tamed, who foolishly aspires;
While to the measure of his might
Each fashions his desires.

"All kinds, and creatures, stand and fall
By strength of prowess or of wit:
'Tis God's appointment who must sway,
And who is to submit.

"Since, then, the rule of right is plain,
And longest life is but a day;
To have my ends, maintain my rights,
I'll take the shortest way."

And thus among these rocks he lived,
Through summer heat and winter snow:
The Eagle, he was lord above,
And Rob was lord below.

So was it—*would*, at least, have been
But through untowardness of fate;
For Polity was then too strong—
He came an age too late;

Or shall we say an age too soon?
For, were the bold Man living *now*,
How might he flourish in his pride,
With buds on every bough!

Then rents and factors, rights of chase,
Sheriffs, and lairds and their domains,
Would all have seemed but paltry things,
Not worth a moment's pains.

Rob Roy had never lingered here,
To these few meagre Vales confined;
But thought how wide the world, the times
How fairly to his mind!

And to his Sword he would have said,
Do Thou my sovereign will enact
From land to land through half the earth!
Judge thou of law and fact!

"'Tis fit that we should do our part,
Becoming, that mankind should learn
That we are not to be surpassed
In fatherly concern.

(continued)

"ROB ROY'S GRAVE" — *(continued)*

"Of old things all are over old,
Of good things none are good enough:—
We'll show that we can help to frame
A world of other stuff.

"I, too, will have my kings that take
From me the sign of life and death:
Kingdoms shall shift about, like clouds,
Obedient to my breath."

And, if the word had been fulfilled,
As 'might' have been, then, thought of joy!
France would have had her present Boast,
And we our own Rob Roy!

Oh! say not so; compare them not;
I would not wrong thee, Champion brave!
Would wrong thee nowhere; least of all
Here standing by thy grave.

For Thou, although with some wild thoughts,
Wild Chieftain of a savage Clan!

Hadst this to boast of; thou didst love
The *liberty* of man.

And, had it been thy lot to live
With us who now behold the light,
Thou would'st have nobly stirred thyself,
And battled for the Right.

For thou wert still the poor man's stay,
The poor man's heart, the poor man's hand;
And all the oppressed, who wanted strength,
Had thine at their command.

Bear witness many a pensive sigh
Of thoughtful Herdsman when he strays
Alone upon Loch Veol's heights,
And by Loch Lomond's braes!

And, far and near, through vale and hill,
Are faces that attest the same;
The proud heart flashing through the eyes,
At sound of ROB ROY's name.

Source: William Wordsworth, "Rob Roy's Grave," from *Memorials of a Tour in Scotland* in *Poetical Works*, edited by Thomas Hutchinson (Oxford, England: University Press, 1904).

Helen MacGregor of Comar, in January, 1693. Rob Roy and Mary had four sons: Ranald, Robin Oig, James Mor, and Coll.

Rob Roy appears to have entered into a formal business relationship with the duke of Montrose, from whom he borrowed money against future cattle trading earnings. In 1712, Rob Roy's head drover disappeared with one thousand pounds of the money that Rob Roy had borrowed, a substantial sum. Rob Roy went in unsuccessful search of the drover; upon his return, he found himself and his family evicted from their lands in partial payment of the debt. He then entered into a long-term struggle with the duke, from whom he stole cattle.

CRIMINAL CAREER

As early as 1709, Rob Roy owed money to various creditors, for he needed constantly to borrow money to buy more cattle. Rob Roy prepared for his eventual discrediture by signing over his properties to friends, hoping that the lands thereby would not be taken. The duke of Montrose was nonetheless able to confiscate most of Rob Roy's land; he then publicized Rob Roy's credit problems and urged all soldiers and magistrates to capture him. Therefore, what would normally have been only a matter of settling with each debtor turned Rob Roy into a fugitive who could not negotiate his way out of his debts.

In 1712, Rob Roy turned to thievery. His thievery against the duke is neither surprising nor out of line with the activities of many other Highlanders who resented the Lowlanders' encroachment and seizure of the lands they had occupied over many generations. The rugged terrain of the region lent itself particularly well to cattle rustling, and thus Rob Roy began stealing cattle from the duke. He even once kidnapped the duke's factor (agent). Rob Roy, however, soon began to rustle cattle from other local landowners who refused to pay blackmail (money paid for the protection of cattle against thieves). Rob Roy's activities eventually earned him an alliance with the duke of Argyll, who was quarreling with the duke of Montrose.

Rob Roy played to both sides in the Jacobite rebellion of 1715. He was chosen to raise the MacGregors in Aberdeenshire, and he helped guide the Jacobite army from Perth to Stirling in November. At the Battle of Sheriffmuir, a smaller army led by the duke of Argyll succeeded in stopping the Jacobite advance. Although Rob Roy played no part in this battle, at the end of the unsuccessful rebellion he was wanted for high treason for his aid to the Jacobites. It is claimed that he was captured but managed to escape multiple times.

LEGAL ACTION AND OUTCOME

Rob Roy was captured once for cattle rustling and sentenced to death, but his friends helped him to escape before his execution could take place. Rob Roy eventually received an official pardon from the king for his earlier charge of high treason.

IMPACT

The legend of Rob Roy has been retold many times and in many forms, starting with *The Highland Rogue* (1723), sometimes attributed to Daniel Defoe and written just a few years before Rob Roy's pardon of 1727, which was granted in response to public pressure. Sir Walter Scott memorialized him in *Rob Roy* in 1817, and William Wordsworth wrote a number of poems highlighting his activities. There are multiple films about his exploits, and he is affectionately known to this day as the "Scottish Robin Hood." However, much of what is written and shown on screen about Roy is quite false.

FURTHER READING

Murray, W. H. *Rob Roy MacGregor: His Life and Times.* Edinburgh: Canongate Books, 1998. Examines Rob Roy's life and attempts to dispel the myths associated with him.

National Archives of Scotland. *The Real Rob Roy: A Guide to the Sources in the Scottish Record Office.* Edinburgh: Author, 1999. This is mainly for the researcher wishing to learn more about Rob Roy through records kept in Scotland.

Stevenson, David. *The Hunt for Rob Roy: The Man and the Myths.* Edinburgh: John Donald, 2004. This comprehensive book by a noted Scottish historian challenges standard views of Rob Roy's role in the Jacobite uprising, accusing him of being a traitor.

—*Michael W. Cheek and Dennis W. Cheek*

SEE ALSO: Johnnie Armstrong; Robin Hood.

BARTHOLOMEW ROBERTS
Welsh pirate

BORN: May 17, 1682; Casnewydd-Bach, Pembrokeshire, Wales
DIED: February 10, 1722; off Cape Lopez, Gabon
ALSO KNOWN AS: Black Bart; Great Pirate Roberts; John Robert (birth name)
CAUSE OF NOTORIETY: Capturing more than 450 vessels during his relatively short career, Roberts became one of the most successful marauders in the history of piracy.
ACTIVE: 1719-1722
LOCALE: Both sides of the Atlantic Ocean

EARLY LIFE

Bartholomew Roberts (bar-THAWL-oh-mew RAW-buhrts) was a stunning man with a dark complexion and was known for his elegant style of dress. His sailing life began in the merchant service. In 1719, he signed on as second mate on the slave ship *Princess.* Captain Howell Davis, a well-known Welsh pirate, captured the *Princess,* and Roberts decided to sign on as a pirate with Davis at the relatively old age of thirty-six.

PIRATING CAREER

Six weeks after taking over the *Princess,* Davis was killed in a surprise attack at a Portuguese settlement on Prince's Island in the Guinea Gulf. Roberts's skills and courage had impressed the crew of the *Princess,* and they voted him as the ship's new captain.

Roberts's first act as captain was an act of revenge toward the Portuguese settlement for ambushing and killing Captain Davis. Roberts destroyed the settlement and then set sail across the Atlantic Ocean toward Brazil.

At the Bay of All Saints in East Bahia, Brazil, Roberts spotted forty-two Portuguese ships anchored in the port and loaded with goods to be shipped to Lisbon, Portugal. Robert boarded one of the ships and took the ship's captain as hostage. Through interrogation of the Portuguese man, Captain Roberts learned which of the merchant ships was carrying the most prized cargo. He forced his hostage to hail that ship's captain, and before the merchant ship could take defensive action, Roberts boarded it and claimed its cargo. Two guard ships that were charged to protect the merchant ships were unaware that pirates had ransacked the ship. Roberts safely sailed away with a load of sugar, gold coins, and tobacco before the guard ships could respond. One of the treasures aboard the Portuguese merchant ship was a large diamond-studded, gold cross designed for the king of Portugal. Roberts took the cross and wore it on a massive gold chain around his neck throughout his life.

In the summer of 1720, Roberts and his crew sailed from the Caribbean north to Newfoundland. At Trepassey Bay, Roberts, who had developed a reputation as being fearless, added to his infamy by attacking—with a single ten-gun sloop and a crew of sixty men—twenty-two ships lying at anchor. Approximately twelve hundred sailors were aboard the twenty-two ships, but they chose to abandon their ships rather than take their chances with Black Bart. Roberts next came across a large group of French ships not far from the harbor. He successfully attacked and destroyed the flotilla, keeping one large brigantine to carry his booty. He later armed the brigantine with more guns, named it the *Royal Fortune*, and made it his flagship.

Roberts's reputation grew, as did his coffers. In fact, Roberts became such a good pirate that by 1721, there was very little left to plunder. Roberts captured more than four hundred ships in less than four years as a pirate. However, he also became known for his harsh treatment of those he captured. Roberts felt he needed to teach the governors of Martinique and Barbados a lesson for making attempts to capture him, and he treated especially harshly any seamen from those islands whom he encountered. He was known to whip these sailors almost to death; he used others for target practice. However, Roberts was also well known for his fairness to his own crew and for his Shipboard Articles, which gave the crew the ability to vote on issues, equal access to food, and a standard percentage of the booty according to their rank on the boat.

In 1722, the commander of the *Swallow*, Captain Chaloner Ogle, who had been trying for six months to capture Roberts and his crew, finally brought Roberts's pirating career to an end. Ogle took Roberts and his hungover crew by surprise, and Roberts was killed. Roberts's crew threw him overboard, in his fancy dress and diamond-studded cross, just as he had instructed them to do upon his death.

Members of Roberts's crew who were captured were tried at Cape Coast Castle in Ghana in April, 1722. It was the largest trial for piracy ever held. Of the 264 pirates captured, some died in jail and a few, who pleaded that they had been forced into piracy by Roberts, were let go. However, most were found guilty and hanged. Eighteen of the pirates were coated with tar, put in metal encasements, and left hanging near the harbor as a warning to all that piracy would no longer be tolerated.

IMPACT

Bartholomew Roberts's ability to plunder so effectively took a financial toll on merchant traffic between countries on both sides of the Atlantic. In order to crack down on piracy, the Piracy Act was expanded in 1721, and officials who had cooperated with pirates became replaced by men who would uphold the laws and arrest pirates. The perceived romanticism of pirate life also began to fade as the general public became aware of the brutality with which Roberts and other pirates treated their captors.

FURTHER READING

Cordingly, David. *Under the Black Flag: The Romance and the Reality of Life Among the Pirates.* Orlando, Fla.: Harvest Books, 1997. Provides a colorful history of Roberts's exploits, his shear genius as a pirate, the ships he commanded, and his cruelty to those he captured.

_____, ed. *Pirates: Terror on the High Seas, from the Caribbean to the South China Sea.* Atlanta, Ga.: Turner, 1996. An excellent resource on the lives, ships, and playgrounds of most of the major pirates. It provides lively descriptions of Robert's career, how he outfitted his ships, and his effect on history.

Konstam, Angus. *The Pirate Ship, 1660-1730.* London: Osprey, 2003. Discusses the different ships that Roberts used during his career, how he traded up to better ships, and how he outfitted ships he captured to be more efficient and better armed.

—*Toby Stewart*

SEE ALSO: Samuel Bellamy; Charlotte de Berry; Stede Bonnet; Anne Bonny; Cheng I Sao; William Dampier; William Kidd; Sir Henry Morgan; Grace O'Malley; John Quelch; John Rackham; Mary Read; Edward Teach.

ROBESPIERRE
French revolutionary

BORN: May 6, 1758; Arras, France
DIED: July 28, 1794; Paris, France
ALSO KNOWN AS: Maximilien François-Marie-Isidore de Robespierre (full name); the Incorruptible
CAUSE OF NOTORIETY: As leader of the dictatorial Committee of Public Safety, Robespierre ruthlessly sent his political enemies to the guillotine during the Reign of Terror.
ACTIVE: 1793-1794
LOCALE: Paris, France

EARLY LIFE

Maximilien Robespierre (raw-behs-pyehr), the eldest child of a brewer's daughter and a barrister, studied at Louis-le-Grand, the most prestigious school in Old Regime France, where he excelled in classics. As a provincial lawyer, Robespierre used Enlightenment ideas to argue cases, appealing, for instance, to the scientific authority of Benjamin Franklin in 1782 to defend a client's use of a lightning rod. Robespierre was influenced by the philosophy of Jean-Jacques Rousseau, especially the unfortunate formulation that the general will was not necessarily determined by the majority. Accordingly, the people's will could be represented in the ideas of certain individuals before the body politic recognized its own intent. From Montesquieu, he derived the notion that a republic was sustained only by the virtue of its citizens, and during the Reign of Terror, this belief justified a fanatical persecution of anyone suspected of not living up to the highest standards of patriotic responsibility.

POLITICAL CAREER

With the calling of the Estates-General in 1789, Robespierre was elected as a deputy from Artois to the Third Estate. In the National Constituent Assembly, formed when the Third broke with the clerical and noble estates to write a constitution, his most notable achievement was to propose (1791) that members of the assembly could not be reelected to the newly constituted Legislative Assembly. He became active in the Jacobin Club, which pushed for radical measures such as the abolition of nobility, and he was elected as public prosecutor of the criminal tribunal of Paris.

On June 20-21, 1791, King Louis XVI attempted unsuccessfully to flee the French Revolution but then appeared to accept his reduced status as a constitutional monarch. The king appointed a Girondin ministry that

was eager to spread revolutionary ideals by declaring war against the Prussians and Austrians. Robespierre opposed the Girondins because he feared their belligerency might lead to a military dictatorship. Defeats on the frontier at the hands of royalist troops under the duke of Brunswick led to a storming of the Tuileries (August 10, 1792), where the royal family had been confined, and in September, to a massacre of imprisoned priests, nobles, and others by sansculottes (radical republicans) fearing that an invasion of Paris would release counterrevolutionaries. Although a member of the Commune (the municipal government), Robespierre did not instigate these massacres, usually attributed to agitation by Jean-Paul Marat and Georges Danton. With the fall of the monarchy, a new national assembly, known as the Convention, was called by Robespierre to draw up the legal basis for a republic, proclaimed on September 22.

THE REIGN OF TERROR

The trial and execution of the king (December-January, 1793) were skillfully prosecuted by Robespierre to incriminate the Girondins, but with radicalization of the

Robespierre. (Library of Congress)

TERROR AS PUBLIC POLICY

In "On the Moral and Political Principles of Domestic Policy," *a speech delivered on February 5, 1794, Robespierre proposed that government must combine virtue with terror in order to preserve the nation against internal and external enemies:*

From all this let us deduce a great truth: the characteristic of popular government is confidence in the people and severity towards itself. . . . This great purity of the French revolution's basis, the very sublimity of its objective, is precisely what causes both our strength and our weakness. Our strength, because it gives to us truth's ascendancy over imposture, and the rights of the public interest over private interests; our weakness, because it rallies all vicious men against us, all those who in their hearts contemplated despoiling the people and all those who intend to let it be despoiled with impunity, both those who have rejected freedom as a personal calamity and those who have embraced the revolution as a career and the Republic as prey. . . . Without, all the tyrants encircle you; within, all tyranny's friends conspire; they will conspire until hope is wrested from crime. We must smother the internal and external enemies of the Republic or perish with it; now in this situation, the first maxim of your policy ought to be to lead the people by reason and the people's enemies by terror. If the spring of popular government in time of peace is virtue, the springs of popular government in revolution are at once *virtue and terror:* virtue, without which terror is fatal; terror, without which virtue is powerless. Terror is nothing other than justice, prompt, severe, inflexible; it is therefore an emanation of virtue; it is not so much a special principle as it is a consequence of the general principle of democracy applied to our country's most urgent needs.

It has been said that terror is the principle of despotic government. Does your government therefore resemble despotism? Yes, as the sword that gleams in the hands of the heroes of liberty resembles that with which the henchmen of tyranny are armed. Let the despot govern by terror his brutalized subjects; he is right, as a despot. Subdue by terror the enemies of liberty, and you will be right, as founders of the Republic.

Revolution, England, Holland, and Spain joined the war against France. Food riots in Paris and counterrevolutionary revolts in the western department of the Vendée and in the southern city of Lyons, along with the war, necessitated the creation of a "Revolutionary Government." A dictatorship of the Committee of General Security and the Committee of Public Safety was established to fight against internal and external enemies. Despite his libertarian and republican ideals, Robespierre pushed measures that restricted freedom of expression and accelerated the guillotining of enemies of the republic, such as the Law of Suspects (September, 1793), designed to bring possible traitors before the Revolutionary Tribunal.

To eliminate political enemies, the Girondins were purged from the Convention and executed, along with Marie-Antoinette, in October. Robespierre then turned against the Hébertists, who were destabilizing the Revolution by demanding greater revolutionary extremes, and they were executed in March, 1794. Although the foreign threat had been largely stopped and internal rebellions repressed, Robespierre's ideological paranoia led him to see counterrevolutionary conspiracies everywhere. He demanded that his former friends and allies, the Dantonists, who were advocating an end to the Terror, be brought before the tribunal, and they were executed on April 5. From June 10 to July 27, 1794, a period known as the Great Terror, 1,376 victims died on the guillotine.

THERMIDORIAN REACTION

During the spring of 1794, Robespierre organized and took a prominent position in a Festival of the Supreme Being, meant to be a civic cult celebrating the moral principles underlying love of nation. His public authority was weakened by these religious ceremonies because they made him look ridiculous in the light of earlier de-Christianization campaigns. At the same time, other radical members of the Committee of General Security and the Convention feared that Robespierre would turn against them, notably Joseph Fouché and Collot d'Herbois, who were responsible for atrocities committed in the repression of the counterrevolution in the provinces. On July 27 (Thermidor 9 in the revolutionary calendar), a coup was launched against Robespierre and his allies, including his young protégé Louis-Antoine Saint-Just, and they were swiftly executed the following day.

Many historians attribute Robespierre's ferocity to his prickly and inflexible character, but some see him as virtuous and steadfast in the face of internal rebellion and foreign invasion. Although between eighteen thousand and forty thousand people died on the guillotine from June, 1793 to July, 1794, when Robespierre's power was at a peak, such bloodshed could not have been carried out without agreement from other members of the Revolutionary Government or without the support of popular uprisings in Paris.

IMPACT

Marxist historians describe Robespierre as the avant-garde of the bourgeoisie, but his revolutionary philosophy and methods are more characteristic of modern leftist revolutionaries, particularly notions that a vanguard minority can represent the entirety of the people and that revolutionary fervor must be maintained by constant struggle against counterrevolutionaries, real or imagined. While Robespierre is often seen, as he saw himself, as embodying the French Revolution, unlike other revolutionary figures, no statue of him can be found in Paris.

FURTHER READING

Hardman, John. *Robespierre*. New York: Addison Wesley Longman, 1999. A political biography in the series Profiles in Power.

Haydon, Colin, and William Doyle, eds. *Robespierre*.

Cambridge, England: Cambridge University Press, 1999. Essays on Robespierre's political and religious ideas, his relationship with the press and sansculottes, and his legacy in historiography, literature, theater, and modern political movements.

Jordan, David P. *The Revolutionary Career of Maximilien Robespierre*. New York: Free Press, 1985. An objective but sympathetic intellectual biography.

Thompson, J. M. *Robespierre*. 1935. Reprint. New York: Blackwell, 1988. The classic life, a comprehensive and balanced biography.

—*Bland Addison*

SEE ALSO: Fidel Castro; Porfirio Díaz; Felix Dzerzhinsky; Vladimir Ilich Lenin; Jean-Paul Marat; Marie-Antoinette; Symon Petlyura; Joseph Stalin.

ROBIN HOOD
Medieval English thief

FLOURISHED: Thirteenth century?; Yorkshire or Nottinghamshire, England

ALSO KNOWN AS: Robert le Favre; William Robehod; Robert Hod; Robert Hood; Robyn Hode; Robert, earl of Huntington; Robyn of Locksley

CAUSE OF NOTORIETY: The legendary Robin Hood was both famous and infamous for waylaying rich travelers and robbing them, as the stories go, to give to the poor.

ACTIVE: Thirteenth century

LOCALE: Barnsdale, Sherwood Forest, and Nottingham, England

EARLY LIFE

Robin Hood (RAW-bihn hood) is generally regarded as a legendary, fictional character. Nevertheless, attempts to identify a historic figure reveal that court records of the thirteenth century cite a number of candidates, such as the fugitive Robert Hood, from whom the sheriff of Yorkshire seized suspect goods in 1230. Further, the aliases "Robehod" and "Little John" appear in legal records as early as 1262, suggesting that the names were already well known and simply adopted by various criminals.

In surviving literature, the thirteenth century Robin Hood was a yeoman, or free person, as opposed to a feudal serf. He may have worked as a servant, as a trades-man, or as the owner of a small piece of land. His choice of a life of crime and revenge against authorities may have resulted from the loss of his land, unfair treatment, or financial deprivation. The earliest unquestionable reference to the figure comes from William Langland's *The Vision of William, Concerning Piers the Plowman* (c. 1362-1393; commonly known as *Piers Plowman*), in which a slothful priest asserts that although he has difficulty reciting the Lord's Prayer, he does well with "Robyn Hood" rhymes.

OUTLAW CAREER

The basic story of Robin Hood is that he and his companion Little John, along with a small group of friends, formed an outlaw gang. They moved about frequently, residing in Barnsdale and Sherwood Forests, poaching deer, fighting with swords or staffs, participating in archery contests, harassing monks, outfoxing the corrupt sheriff of Nottingham, and stealing money. Robin and his men resisted the authorities in both playful and serious ways. In one example, he unselfishly gave money to a knight whose lands were to have been confiscated by a greedy abbot. When the knight repaid the debt and retained his lands, the abbot's plan was ruined. Robin then stole and kept twice the original amount of the loan from another abbey official as a repayment.

By the sixteenth century the rustic yeoman had taken

Robin Hood, as interpreted by Frederick Warde in his play Runnymede. (Library of Congress)

on a new identity as Robert, earl of Huntington—reputedly an unfairly deposed twelfth century nobleman and defender of the true King Richard against the pretender king, John (John Lackland, king of England). This noble Robin, as he was still familiarly known, was said to have been generous to the poor.

IMPACT

The popularity of the mythic Robin Hood with the medieval people of England may be accounted for by the violence of the age and the corrupt administration of the law under which they suffered. In a land marked by deep social and economic divisions between the classes, this legendary hero stood firm against injustices perpetrated by the wealthy; thus, his popularity repeatedly peaked in times of increased oppression.

Robin Hood became the subject of ballads, games, poems, plays, novels, and eventually films—a favored hero for more than seven centuries. Perhaps because no definitive version of the life of Robin Hood has emerged, writers have felt free to adapt the legend to reflect the sociopolitical and historical concerns of their own times. In film, Robin Hood has frequently appeared as an action hero, a role in keeping with his reputation as the bold outlaw of medieval days.

FURTHER READING

Dobson, R. B., and J. Taylor. *Rymes of Robyn Hood: An Introduction to the English Outlaw*. Pittsburgh: University of Pittsburgh Press, 1976. Collection of the earliest Robin Hood ballads, plays, and outlaw songs. Introductory material preceding each selection surveys the evolution and literary development of the legend.

Knight, Stephen. *Robin Hood: A Mythic Biography*. Ithaca, N.Y.: Cornell University Press, 2003. Chronicles the adaptations of the Robin Hood legend over time in view of the historical and sociopolitical forces at work.

_____, ed. *Robin Hood: An Anthology of Scholarship and Criticism*. Rochester, N.Y.: D. S. Brewer, 1999. A collection of previously published scholarly journal articles exploring the historical, literary, political, and social issues relevant to understanding the legend of Robin Hood.

Pollard, A. J. *Imagining Robin Hood*. New York: Routledge, 2004. A historical exploration of the ways in which the Robin Hood legend reveals the distrust and cynicism of the English people in regard to authority.

Singman, Jeffrey L. *Robin Hood: The Shaping of a Legend*. Westport, Conn.: Greenwood Press, 1998. Focuses on the development of the legend from its origins through the seventeenth century, with maps and an appendix locating and dating Robin Hood games.

—*Margaret A. Dodson*

SEE ALSO: William H. Bonney; Jules Bonnot; Cartouche; Butch Cassidy; Phoolan Devi; Salvatore Giuliano; Jesse James; King John.

GEORGE LINCOLN ROCKWELL
Founder of the American Nazi Party

BORN: March 9, 1918; Bloomington, Illinois
DIED: August 25, 1967; Arlington, Virginia
CAUSE OF NOTORIETY: Rockwell started the first Nazi political party in the United States after World War II.
ACTIVE: 1959-1967
LOCALE: United States

EARLY LIFE

George Lincoln Rockwell (ROK-wehl) was the oldest of the three children of George Lovejoy Rockwell and Claire Schade. His parents were vaudeville performers who divorced when he was six years old. Rockwell lived with his mother in Illinois but would visit his father in the summer at his Southport, Maine, home. His father was an egomaniac who never showed affection for his children. Rockwell was subject also to verbal abuse and beatings by his aunt. While growing up, Rockwell was gregarious and frequently the center of attention in his social circles, but beneath the surface he had developed a fragile self-image because of his father's constant belittling and his aunt's physical and psychological abuse.

In the fall of 1938, Rockwell entered Brown University, where he became a cartoonist for campus publications. Many of his cartoons and writings were censored because they were so far out of the mainstream. In 1941, Rockwell left Brown and enlisted in the aviation cadet program of the U.S. Navy. During World War II, he saw action in both the Atlantic and Pacific theaters. In April, 1943, he married Judith Aultman. They had three daughters before their marriage ended in divorce in 1953.

In 1950, Rockwell, who was operating his own advertising firm in Portland, Maine, was recalled to active duty when the Korean War began. He was stationed at the naval air base in Coronado, California. There Rockwell was introduced to National Socialism.

POLITICAL CAREER

In 1952, Rockwell became involved in a political campaign in support of General Douglas MacArthur for the Republican presidential nomination. He attended a speech by Gerald L. K. Smith, a Nazi sympathizer and director of the Christian Nationalist Crusade. At Smith's urging, Rockwell read Adolf Hitler's *Mein Kampf* (1925-1927; English translation, 1933). From this work Rockwell concluded that only National Socialism could save white people from degradation and racial degeneration.

Rockwell continued to study Nazi literature throughout his naval career. In October, 1953, he married his second wife, Thora Hallgrimsson, whom he had met while stationed in Iceland. They honeymooned in the Bavarian Alps, where Rockwell visited Hitler's retreat at Berchtesgaden.

Following his discharge from the Navy in 1954, Rockwell met Harold N. Arrowsmith, an entrepreneur who shared Rockwell's anti-Semitic views. In 1958 Rockwell entered into an anti-Jewish publishing partnership with Arrowsmith. They named their operation the National Committee to Free America from Jewish Domination and set up headquarters in Arlington, Virginia. Arrowsmith supplied the money, and Rockwell printed and distributed the literature. The partnership had ended by August, 1958, but Rockwell continued to produce anti-Semitic literature and move in neo-Nazi circles. His second wife left him and moved to Iceland with their four children. Eventually Rockwell decided that the only way he could gain public recognition of his commitment to National Socialism was to adopt the name "Nazi." In October, 1959, George Lincoln Rockwell started the American Nazi Party with headquarters in Arlington.

Rockwell attracted media attention for his new party through a variety of techniques. He began by holding weekly rallies in Washington, D.C. His men would wear storm trooper uniforms, and Rockwell would make speeches in which he attacked Jews and blacks. In 1961, Rockwell sent a group of Nazis in a Volkswagen bus covered with hate signs on a route through the South that the desegregationist Freedom Riders had taken. Where Otto Preminger's film *Exodus* (1960), about the founding of the state of Israel, was showing in theaters, storm troopers would picket. Such activities frequently resulted in violent confrontations, which led to increased media coverage for the party.

Rockwell capitalized on his notoriety by speaking on college campuses. The speaking fees he received were a major source of income for the party. The party also raised money through the sale of its magazine, *The Storm Trooper*, Nazi literature, books, records, tapes, photographs, and films. The targets of the literature and speeches were Jews and African Americans. Jews were the greatest threat, Rockwell believed, because of the control they exercised over key components of Ameri-

ALEX HALEY INTERVIEWS THE AMERICAN FÜHRER

In 1966, Alex Haley, the African American author of Roots *(1976), went to the American Nazi Party compound to interview George Lincoln Rockwell. Their conversation was later published in the April, 1966, issue of* Playboy *magazine. After a long denunciation of blacks, Rockwell turned to his favorite theme, anti-Semitism:*

HALEY: In judging Negroes "inferior" to whites, you said a while ago that you made this appraisal on the basis of "performance." Do you find Jews inferior for the same reason?

ROCKWELL: I've never accused the Jews of being incapable of performing. As a matter of fact, I think there's a good chance they're superior to everybody else in terms of actual mental capabilities. I think the average Jew is probably sharper intellectually than the average gentile, because for years and years he's had to live by his wits. Consequently, there has evolved a race of Jews who are more agile mentally than the rest of us.

HALEY: In what way do you consider Jews inferior, then?

ROCKWELL: Spiritually. I believe that a human being, in order to be a successful person, in addition to performing—inventing a rocket or something—has got to have something he believes in, some thing more than his own survival, some thing that's a little bigger than himself. The Jews don't. They've even got a rabbi now who admits he's an atheist, Rabbi Sherwin Wine of Birmingham, Michigan.

HALEY: Perhaps you didn't know that the current Church movement toward disbelief in God originated among the Protestant clergy. In any case, Rabbi Wine's convictions are a minority voice and could not in any way be said to represent those of the Jewish faith in general. Most Jews continue to believe in God, as set down in the Torah.

ROCKWELL: Jews talk a lot about God. But actually their god, just like Marx said, is money. Cash! This is where the Jews fail—in their lack of idealism. Most of them are strictly materialists at heart. Wherever the Jews have gone, they've moved into a friendly, unsuspecting country and promptly started to glut on its people and resources. They think they're engaging in business, but actually what they're doing is eating the country up alive. And when people begin to resent their viciousness and greed, and either kick the Jews out or kill them, they always scream "Persecution!" That's not persecution. It's self-defense.

On August 25, 1967, Rockwell was shot in front of a Laundromat in Arlington, Virginia. His assassin was John Patler, a former editor of *The Storm Trooper* magazine. Patler had been expelled from the party for creating dissension between dark-haired and blond Nazis. Rockwell was denied burial at several cemeteries, including Arlington National Cemetery. Eventually his body was cremated. While Rockwell's death marked the end of the American Nazi Party, it resulted in the splintering of the movement and the creation of new neo-Nazi movements in the United States and a new generation of leaders.

IMPACT

George Lincoln Rockwell was the seminal force behind the development of National Socialism in America in the post-World War II era. He is also seen as the originator of the Holocaust denial movement, which claims that Jews invented the myth of the Holocaust to justify the founding of the state of Israel.

Numerous neo-Nazi leaders and movements in the United States were originally associated with the American Nazi Party or its successor, the National Socialist White People's Party. Of these, the best known are William Luther Pierce, founder of the National Alliance, and David Duke, Ku Klux Klan leader and founder of the National Association for the Advancement of White People and the European-American Unity and Rights Organization.

can society. He said that blacks were dangerous because they were prone to violence. Together, they were seen as promoting race-mixing. Rockwell's "solution" was to exterminate Jews and to send Americans of African descent "back" to Africa.

Despite the publicity it received, the American Nazi Party did not attract many supporters. The party had a few hundred followers in Dallas, Los Angeles, the San Francisco Bay area, Chicago, Illinois, Boston, and Virginia. Generally, the members were in their twenties, many came from broken homes, and they were prone to violence.

FURTHER READING

Rockwell, George Lincoln. *This Time the World*. New York: Pariament House, 1963. Rockwell's statement of his views.

Schmaltz, William H. *Hate: George Lincoln Rockwell and the American Nazi Party*. Washington, D.C.: Brassey's, 1999. A thorough history and analysis of Rockwell. The author's research materials include the FBI files on Rockwell.

Simonelli, Frederick J. *American Fuehrer: George Lincoln Rockwell and the American Nazi Party*. Urbana: University of Illinois Press, 1999. Draws from a variety of resources, collections, and interviews. Gives an excellent scholarly analysis of Rockwell.

—*William V. Moore*

See also: Richard Girnt Butler; Willis A. Carto; Frank Collin; David Duke; Matthew F. Hale; Jean-Marie Le Pen; Robert Jay Mathews; Tom Metzger; William Luther Pierce III; William Joseph Simmons; Gerald L. K. Smith; J. B. Stoner; Randy Weaver.

Ethel Rosenberg
American spy

Born: September 28, 1915; New York, New York
Died: June 19, 1953; Sing Sing Prison, Ossining, New York
Also known as: Ethel Greenglass (birth name)
Major offense: Conspiracy to commit espionage, under U.S. Espionage Act of 1917
Active: c. 1942-1950
Locale: New York, New York
Sentence: Death by electrocution

Early Life

Ethel Rosenberg (EHTH-ehl ROH-zihn-burg) was born Ethel Greenglass on September 28, 1915, in New York City, the daughter of Barnet and Tessie Greenglass. She graduated from Public School 22 at age eleven and entered Seward Park High School, where she appeared in school plays. Ethel was determined to attend college and become a famous actress or singer. Her father encouraged her, but her mother thwarted Ethel's theatrical ambitions. At thirteen, Ethel developed ricketic curvature of the spine, from which she never fully recovered. She was petite, five feet tall, weighing about one hundred pounds. She wore her hair straight back, and a tense expression detracted from the beauty of her face.

Ethel completed a stenographic course in a settlement house when she was sixteen and then went to work at National New York Shipping and Packing Company. She continued to pursue her theatrical interests by joining the Clark House Players, an amateur group, and she became its star. In an amateur contest at Loew's Delancey Theater she won second prize with her rendition of "Ciribiribin," a Hasidic ode to God. This led to her appearance on Major Bowes's talent scout competition, which gained her publicity and additional roles.

Ethel saved enough money from her seven-dollars-a-week wage to take singing lessons at a Carnegie Hall studio. She sought to join the Schola Cantorum, a professional choir directed by Hugh Ross. After she learned to sight-read music, she was accepted by the choir. A setback to her musical career came a year later when Ethel was unable to join the choir on tour because she could not leave her job.

Ethel and Julius Rosenberg. (Library of Congress)

ESPIONAGE CAREER

In the 1930's, at the height of the Great Depression, Ethel became a strident radical. In 1932, she was among one thousand applicants lined up for a job at a box factory. The mob grew violent, and the fire department turned water hoses on them. Ethel was knocked down but unhurt. She dwelt angrily upon perceived injustices of employers and government failure to deal with economic crises. Listening to radical demagogues preaching anarchy and socialism on street corners, Ethel was inspired to join the Young Communist League. At the league she had a new stage and audience among her fellow Communist activists, and she found the enthusiasm with which they received her speeches empowering.

In 1935, Ethel led a strike of 150 women that shut down the New York National Shipping Company. When the company hired substitutes, Ethel led the women to attack delivery truck drivers, block the streets with their bodies, and slash cartons of clothing with razor blades. After two weeks, fifteen thousand garment workers had joined the strike. The employer capitulated, agreeing to shortened work hours and raised wages. However, Ethel and ten of her lieutenants were soon fired. By the time the National Labor Relations Board restored their jobs, Ethel was working at Bell Textile Company.

In 1936, the International Seamen's Union invited Ethel to sing at a fund-raising party on New Year's Eve. There she met Julius Rosenberg, another radical Communist. The two were married in 1939, after Julius graduated from New York City College. The births of their sons in 1943 and 1947 did not diminish the extent of Ethel's activities on behalf of the Communist Party.

In 1943, Ethel and Julius suddenly ceased their open support of the Communist Party, and their subscription to the *Daily Worker* was canceled. They had become covert spies for the Soviet Union. In 1944, after Ethel's brother, David Greenglass, was assigned to the Manhattan Project in New Mexico, the secret U.S. program to develop an atomic bomb, Ethel helped recruit David to obtain atomic secrets for the Soviets. In 1945, after Julius was dismissed from the U.S. Army Signal Corps because of Communist Party activities, Ethel became so ill that she spent four months in bed. Ethel and Julius engaged in espionage five more years.

LEGAL ACTION AND OUTCOME

The Federal Bureau of Investigation arrested Julius Rosenberg on July 17, 1950, and Ethel Rosenberg on August 11. On January 31, 1951, both were indicted on charges of conspiracy to commit espionage. At the trial, March 6-28, 1951, David Greenglass and his wife testified that Ethel had typed up David's notes on atomic secrets for delivery to the Soviets and was a participant in the espionage network. Ethel's demeanor and frequent use of Fifth Amendment rights in refusing to answer questions probably harmed her defense. She was found guilty March 29, 1951, and on April 5, 1951, Judge Irving Kaufman sentenced her to death by electrocution.

Appeals to the U.S. Second Circuit Court of Appeals were denied on February 25, 1952, and June 11, 1953. The U.S. Supreme Court refused certiorari on October 13, 1952, denied a stay of execution on June 13, 1953, and six days later vacated a stay granted by Justice William O. Douglas. On June 19, 1953, Ethel Rosenberg was executed by electrocution at New York's Sing Sing Prison.

IMPACT

Ethel Rosenberg's role as a spy and the death penalty remained part of the national debate for years. The Rosenbergs' lawyers continued their defense through the press, as Ethel's two sons worked to clear the family name. Robert, the younger son, spent his life trying to prove his mother innocent and agitating against the death penalty. Supporting media blamed Senator Joseph McCarthy's Red Scare investigations and a latent anti-Semitism for the lack of public sympathy for Ethel Rosenberg. In the 1990's, when the Soviet Union was dismantled, newly released intelligence documents confirmed the Rosenbergs' involvement in espionage.

FURTHER READING

Meeropol, Robert. *An Execution in the Family: One Son's Journey.* New York: St. Martin's Press, 2003. The Rosenbergs' younger son writes about the trial and execution of his parents.

Nizer, Louis. *The Implosion Conspiracy.* Garden City, N.Y.: Doubleday, 1973. Details espionage activities and proceedings in the trial of Ethel and Julius Rosenberg.

Radosh, Ronald, and Joyce Milton. *The Rosenberg File: A Search for the Truth.* New York: Holt, Rinehart & Winston, 1983. Examines impact of the trial on family, lawyers, and American public.

—*Marguerite R. Plummer*

SEE ALSO: Joseph McCarthy; Julius Rosenberg.

JULIUS ROSENBERG
American Communist spy

BORN: May 12, 1918; New York, New York
DIED: June 19, 1953; Sing Sing Prison, Ossining, New York
ALSO KNOWN AS: Julie Rosenberg
MAJOR OFFENSES: Conspiracy to commit espionage, under U.S. Espionage Act of 1917
ACTIVE: c. 1942-1950
LOCALE: New York and New Mexico
SENTENCE: Death by electrocution

EARLY LIFE

Born on May 12, 1918, in New York City, Julius Rosenberg (JOOL-ee-uhs ROH-zihn-burg) was the son of Polish immigrants Harry and Sophie Rosenberg. Julius attended Public School 88 and the Downtown Talmud Torah, where he excelled in Hebrew studies. He graduated from Seward Park High School in 1934, at the height of the Great Depression. His passion had become radical politics. He entered City College of New York (CCNY), majoring in electrical engineering—a degree favored by political radicals because it entitled them to membership in the Federation of Architects, Engineers, Chemists and Technicians (FAECT), a militant pro-Communist union. Julius, called Julie by classmates, joined the Steinmetz Club and CCNY's Young Communist League (YCL); he spent much of his time attending political meetings, organizing demonstrations, and distributing leaflets. It was through YCL demonstrations during a labor dispute in 1936 that Julius met Ethel Greenglass, whom he married in the summer of 1939. Their first home was a shared apartment in Brooklyn. The Rosenbergs had two sons.

ESPIONAGE CAREER

After graduating from CCNY in 1939, Julius subsisted for a year on freelance work. In 1940, he was hired as a civilian employee of the U.S. Army Signal Corps. Following the Japanese attack on Pearl Harbor on December 7, 1941, and U.S. entry into World War II, Rosenberg was promoted to engineer inspector for the corps. As inspector, he traveled throughout New York and New Jersey examining electronics parts made by private industries under contracts with the Army Signal Corps. The higher salary plus travel compensation allowed the Rosenbergs to move into a new apartment on New York's lower East Side.

In 1943, the twenty-five-year-old Julius and his twenty-eight-year-old wife left the YCL to become active members in the Communist Party. Julius was named chairman of Branch 16B of the Communist Party's Industrial Division. Because the Soviet Union and the United States were allies in World War II, Rosenberg accepted without question Communist leader Earl Browder's assertion that party membership was perfectly compatible with U.S. patriotism. Rosenberg held that the United States should not have a monopoly on the atomic bomb.

Later that year, Julius's overt activities with the Communist Party stopped, and his subscription to the *Daily Worker* was canceled. Supporters suggested that Julius was forced to resign party membership to save his job with the Signal Corps. Several Communist Party members, however, indicated that if the party canceled his membership and *Daily Worker* subscription, it was a sure sign that Rosenberg had become a spy. In fact, Julius Rosenberg had begun meeting with Soviet spymaster Alexander Feklisov, who later revealed that Rosenberg provided the Soviets with information on American electronic weaponry—radar, sonar, and the heat-seeking proximity fuse.

In November, 1944, Rosenberg recruited his brother-in-law, David Greenglass, as a spy for the Soviets. Greenglass, a YCL activist, had been inducted into the Army and in July, 1944, was assigned to the Manhattan Project, the U.S. program to develop an atomic bomb, at the New Mexico testing grounds for atomic weapons. In January, 1945, Rosenberg arranged a meeting where Greenglass passed notes and sketches of the A-bomb's high-explosive lens to fellow spy Harry Gold. Early in 1945, Rosenberg was dismissed from the Signal Corps because his membership in the Communist Party had been discovered. He then opened a machine shop, which failed in 1947.

LEGAL ACTION AND OUTCOME

The Federal Bureau of Investigation arrested Rosenberg on July 17, 1950. Ethel Rosenberg was arrested on August 11. On January 31, 1951, both Rosenbergs were indicted by a grand jury for conspiracy to commit espionage under the Espionage Act of 1917. The trial was held March 6-28, 1951. Co-conspirators Gold, Greenglass, and Morton Sobell testified to the Rosenbergs' espionage activities. On March 29, 1951, the jury returned a verdict of guilty, and on April 5, 1951, Judge Irving Kaufman sentenced Julius to death in the electric chair.

An appeal to the U.S. Second Circuit Court of Appeals was denied February 25, 1952. The U.S. Supreme Court refused certiorari on October 13, 1952. A new appeal based on new evidence was denied by the Court of Appeals on June 13, 1953, one week before the date of execution. On June 17, Supreme Court justice William O. Douglas granted a stay, which was vacated by the full Court on June 19, 1953, just hours before Julius and Ethel Rosenberg died in the electric chair at Sing Sing Prison.

IMPACT

A national debate about the Rosenbergs' guilt and the severe penalty raged in the news media for years, and communist sympathizers have waged protests for years. The Rosenbergs' sons maintained their parents' innocence and worked unceasingly for years trying to clear the family name. Many sympathizers in the media blamed Senator Joseph McCarthy's intense investigation of Communists in the United States for fostering hatred and making false accusations against Communists working in the government and on defense projects. Soviet spymaster Feklisov, however, stated that Julius Rosenberg was a Soviet spy, and in 1990, Soviet Premier Nikita S. Khrushchev's memoirs confirmed that Rosenberg helped the Soviet Union obtain the A-bomb. The decoded Venona cables released by the Central Intelligence Agency and the National Security Agency also confirmed the Rosenbergs' espionage activities.

FURTHER READING

Feklisov, Alexander, Sergei Kostin, and Ronald Radosh. *The Man Behind the Rosenbergs.* New York: Enigma Books, 2004. Narrative of KGB agent Alexander Feklisov, detailing his recruitment and handling of Rosenberg as a Soviet spy, 1943-1946.

Meeropol, Robert. *An Execution in the Family: One Son's Journey.* New York: St. Martin's Press, 2003. Memoir of Rosenberg's younger son about the ordeal of the trial and execution of his parents.

Nizer, Louis. *The Implosion Conspiracy.* Garden City,

THE ROSENBERGS' SENTENCE

Judge Irving R. Kaufman handed down the following statement in the Rosenberg case on April 5, 1951:

Citizens of this country who betray their fellow-countrymen can be under none of the delusions about the benignity of Soviet power that they might have been prior to World War II. The nature of Russian terrorism is now self-evident. . . .

I consider your crime worse than murder. . . . I believe your conduct in putting into the hands of the Russians the A-bomb years before our best scientists predicted Russia would perfect the bomb has already caused, in my opinion, the Communist aggression in Korea, with the resultant casualties exceeding 50,000 and who knows but that millions more of innocent people may pay the price of your treason. Indeed, by your betrayal you undoubtedly have altered the course of history to the disadvantage of our country.

No one can say that we do not live in a constant state of tension. We have evidence of your treachery all around us every day—for the civilian defense activities throughout the nation are aimed at preparing us for an atom bomb attack. Nor can it be said in mitigation of the offense that the power which set the conspiracy in motion and profited from it was not openly hostile to the United States at the time of the conspiracy. If this was your excuse the error of your ways in setting yourselves above our properly constituted authorities and the decision of those authorities not to share the information with Russia must now be obvious. . . .

In the light of this, I can only conclude that the defendants entered into this most serious conspiracy against their country with full realization of its implications. . . .

The statute of which the defendants at the bar stand convicted is clear. I have previously stated my view that the verdict of guilty was amply justified by the evidence. In the light of the circumstances, I feel that I must pass such sentence upon the principals in this diabolical conspiracy to destroy a God-fearing nation, which will demonstrate with finality that this nation's security must remain inviolate; that traffic in military secrets, whether promoted by slavish devotion to a foreign ideology or by a desire for monetary gains must cease. . . .

N.Y.: Doubleday, 1973. Gives details of the espionage activities as well as the legal proceedings during the prosecution of Julius and Ethel Rosenberg.

Radosh, Ronald, and Joyce Milton. *The Rosenberg File: A Search for the Truth.* New York: Holt, Rinehart and Winston, 1983. Examines the impact of the trial on the family, the lawyers, and the American public.

—*Marguerite R. Plummer*

SEE ALSO: Anthony Blunt; Christopher John Boyce; Guy Burgess; John Cairncross; Klaus Fuchs; Robert Philip Hanssen; Alger Hiss; Daulton Lee; Joseph McCarthy; Donald MacLean; Kim Philby; Jonathan Pollard; Ethel Rosenberg.

ARNOLD ROTHSTEIN
American organized crime leader

BORN: January 17, 1882; New York, New York
DIED: November 6, 1928; New York, New York
ALSO KNOWN AS: The Brain; Big Bankroll; A.R.;
  Man Uptown
CAUSE OF NOTORIETY: Rothstein, one of the early
  kingpins of organized crime, engaged in gambling,
  loan-sharking, drug dealing, and labor racketeering.
  He reputedly played a role in the fixed 1919 World
  Series.
ACTIVE: 1900-1928
LOCALE: New York and Saratoga Springs, New York

EARLY LIFE

Arnold Rothstein (ROTH-steen) was the second of four
children born to Abraham and Esther Rothstein. Young
Rothstein rebelled against his father's Orthodox Jewish
values and by most accounts had an unhappy childhood.
He frequently expressed genuine hatred of his brother
Harry. While Rothstein had little interest in school and
was held back two grades, he was gifted in mathematics.
After dropping out of high school at the age of sixteen,
his expertise in billiards offered him a modest income.
Rothstein then frequented craps games, where he again
achieved some success. It was at these games that he began making more money through loans to other gamblers.

In an attempt to please his father, Arnold became a
traveling salesman (selling hats and other head wear) and
worked in his father's factory. He stayed away from
vices for a time. However, his next job—as a cigar salesman—brought him back to frequenting poolrooms and
gambling houses. Rothstein's gambling lifestyle, in addition to the fact that he married Carolyn Green, a practicing Roman Catholic, led to a lifelong estrangement
from his father.

GANGSTER CAREER

After living frugally and saving his money, Rothstein left
cigar sales to attempt a life as a professional gambler and
took bets on various sporting events and elections. While
he rarely lived in an ostentatious manner, he was known
for carrying a significant bankroll in public, which added
to his reputation as "big time." Rothstein used political
connections to act as a go-between for New York's Tammany Hall politicians and various perpetrators of vice
throughout the city. He was able to provide "protection"
from police raids. These relationships with politicians

and police served Rothstein well, making it possible for
him to launch a series of criminal enterprises throughout
his career.

Rothstein started his own gambling house and rapidly
gained substantial notoriety. One notable case was that
of Percival Hill, the president of the American Tobacco
Company, who reportedly lost $250,000 to Rothstein.
Rothstein was versatile with his business model. When a
public crackdown on political corruption led to raids on
gambling houses, Rothstein developed "floating" crap
games, which would take place on short notice in various locations around the city. This sense of organization distanced him from the small-time gambling operators.

Because floating craps games are subject to being
robbed, Rothstein was frequently on guard and armed.
One evening, out of concern that his game was being
robbed, Rothstein fired three bullets through a doorway
at uninvited individuals who were trying to make their
way into the room. Instead of robbers, the shots actually
hit one police inspector and two detectives. Rothstein instantly disappeared, and all the other gamblers claimed
that Rothstein was never present at the scene. While none
of the police officers was seriously injured, Rothstein's
legend grew. Nobody testified against him, and his case
was dismissed.

Rothstein was heavily diversified in nightclubs,
gambling houses, racehorses, bootlegging, smuggling,
drugs, and various scams that developed in response to
the Harrison Narcotics Tax Act and Prohibition. These
various operations employed numerous individuals,
many of whom would later become notorious organized
crime figures themselves. Rothstein also bankrolled
legitimate ventures such as Broadway shows and the
high-profile antiques importer Vantines. Rothstein's unofficial office was a table at Lindy's Restaurant in Times
Square.

While Rothstein is frequently referred to as the man
who fixed the 1919 World Series, his actual role in the series is questioned. It was certainly not his largest bet, and
he clearly was not directly contacting players for the fix.
While he was questioned by authorities about his role, he
was never indicted.

Rothstein died on November 6, 1928, from complications related to a November 4 gunshot wound. Though
he died approximately thirty-six hours after he was shot,
he never spoke a word about who the perpetrator was.

George McManus was arrested for fatally shooting Rothstein over a bad debt, but he was acquitted after prosecutorial witnesses revised their stories at the trial.

A number of other mysteries will always be associated with Rothstein. He managed his enterprises with little black books using symbols that were understood only by him. His holdings were so diversified that nobody truly knew what he had at the time of his death.

IMPACT

The myths about Arnold Rothstein were perpetuated through popular entertainment. He was the model for the character Nathan Detroit in the musical *Guys and Dolls* (pr. 1950) and the character Meyer Wolfsheim in F. Scott Fitzgerald's *The Great Gatsby* (1925). Modern historians focus on Rothstein's incredible ability to organize a structure of diversified criminal enterprises, which in turn led to many multibillion-dollar organized crime enterprises, including the modern drug trade. His operations assisted the development of numerous organized crime figures, such as Meyer Lansky, Dutch Schultz, and Lucky Luciano.

FURTHER READING

Clarke, Donald H. *In the Reign of Rothstein*. New York: Grosset and Dunlap, 1929. Published shortly after Rothstein's death. Clarke offers a contemporary account that glamorizes Rothstein's life and his dealings with high-profile individuals.

Katcher, Leo. *The Big Bankroll: The Life and Times of Arnold Rothstein*. Reprint. New York: Da Capo Press, 1994. Originally published in 1959, this account by veteran news reporter Leo Katcher covers the perception, myths, and realities of Rothstein.

Pietrusza, David. *Rothstein: The Life, Times, and Murder of the Criminal Genius Who Fixed the 1919 World Series*. New York: Carroll and Graf, 2003. While this book goes into great detail to describe the complex development of Rothstein's diversified criminal empire and life as a gambler, Pietrusza also notes that Rothstein should be credited as the organizer of the modern drug smuggling trade.

—*John C. Kilburn, Jr.*

SEE ALSO: Legs Diamond; Shoeless Joe Jackson; Meyer Lansky; Lucky Luciano; Dutch Schultz.

DARLIE ROUTIER
American murderer

BORN: January 4, 1970; Altoona, Pennsylvania
ALSO KNOWN AS: Darlie Lynn Peck (birth name); Darlie Lynn Routier (full name)
MAJOR OFFENSE: Capital murder
ACTIVE: June 6, 1996
LOCALE: Rowlett, Texas
SENTENCE: Death by lethal injection

EARLY LIFE

Darlie Routier (ROO-tee-ay) had an unremarkable childhood, despite the divorce of her parents when she was seven years old. When her mother remarried, Darlie, her mother, and her stepfather relocated to Lubbock, Texas. While in high school, she met her future husband, Darin Routier, and they were married in August, 1988. Their first son, Devon, was born in 1989, and their second child, Damon, was born in 1991. Darin Routier had a successful computer-related business, and the Routiers moved to an affluent neighborhood in Rowlett, Texas. There they enjoyed an extravagant lifestyle, characterized by their purchases of expensive automobiles, boats, clothing, and jewelry.

After several years, Darin Routier's business began to falter. Darin and Darlie were also experiencing marital problems, and there were rumors of extramarital affairs. Darlie Routier was described by neighbors to have been obsessed with her appearance and allegedly had little patience with her children. Despite this, she gave birth to a third son, Drake, in 1995. After the pregnancy, Routier experienced postpartum depression and began taking diet pills in order to lose her pregnancy weight. She also began to have suicidal ideations.

CRIMINAL CAREER

On June 6, 1996, emergency services in Dallas received a call from Darlie Routier. She was screaming that she and two of her sons had been stabbed. When police arrived, Routier told them of an intruder, dressed in dark clothes and a baseball cap, who had broken into her home and stabbed her and her two sons before fleeing through the garage while her husband and infant son slept upstairs.

In fact, Routier concocted this story; she had actually stabbed Devon and Damon before inflicting her own injuries on herself. She staged a crime scene to make it appear that an intruder had entered their home. The boys were brutally killed by stabbing, but Routier suffered only superficial wounds. Her motive was said to be an insurance scam, an attempt to salvage what was left of her affluent lifestyle.

LEGAL ACTION AND OUTCOME
On June 18, 1996, Routier was arrested and charged with capital murder for the deaths of her two sons, Damon and Devon. She was indicted by a Dallas County, Texas, grand jury on two counts of capital murder, and a gag order was imposed on all individuals involved in the case. Her trial was then moved out of Dallas County because of the pretrial publicity the case received. On February 1, 1997, a jury found Routier guilty of the stabbing death of her son Damon, and she was subsequently sentenced to death by lethal injection. After a series of appeals, her conviction and sentence were upheld by the Texas Court of Criminal Appeals in May, 2003.

IMPACT
Darlie Routier's crimes, conviction, and sentencing have been the subject of numerous books. Many of these works have discussed the problems associated with her trial, such as the discrepancies and flaws in the transcripts of her trial proceedings, the unprecedented assignment of an independent court reporter to review the transcripts and cassette tapes of the trial, and a series of unanswered questions about DNA evidence found at the crime scene. Routier alleged that police failed to investigate other leads and focused solely on her.

FURTHER READING
Brown, Christopher Wayne. *Media Tried, Justice Denied: Behind the Truth and Lies of the Darlie Lynn Routier Murder Case.* Lewisville, Tex.: Ad Vice Marketing, 1999. Contains many pages of color crime scene photographs, the first that were made available to the public.

Davis, Barbara. *Precious Angels: A True Story of Two Slain Children and a Mother Convicted of Murder.* New York: Onyx, 1999. This account of Routier's trial, written while her case was under appeal, takes the viewpoint that Routier was indeed guilty of the murders of her sons.

Davis, Don. *Hush Little Babies: The True Story of a Mother Who Murdered Her Own Children.* New York: St. Martin's Press, 1997. Account of the Routier children's murders and the subsequent trial of their mother.

Springer, Patricia. *Flesh and Blood.* New York: Pinnacle, 1997. Contains a detailed account of the events that occurred on the night of the murders, an explanation of the investigation, and an extremely detailed description of the trial.

—Carly M. Hilinski

SEE ALSO: Diane Downs; Magda Goebbels; Susan Smith; Andrea Yates.

JACK RUBY
American businessman

BORN: March 25, 1911; Chicago, Illinois
DIED: January 3, 1967; Dallas, Texas
ALSO KNOWN AS: Jacob Leon Rubenstein (birth name)
MAJOR OFFENSE: Murder of Lee Harvey Oswald
ACTIVE: November 24, 1963
LOCALE: Dallas, Texas
SENTENCE: Death, reversed on appeal

EARLY LIFE
Jack L. Rubenstein was born to Polish Jewish immigrant parents in Chicago in 1911. Growing up in a large, working-class family, Rubenstein was a rebellious, troubled youth who occasionally lived in foster homes be-

cause of his juvenile delinquency. As a teenager, Rubenstein was attracted to organized crime and began running errands for gamblers and gangsters. In 1939, he was implicated but later exonerated in the murder of a labor union official. Rubenstein was drafted into the U.S. Army Air Corps in 1943 and discharged in 1946.

CRIMINAL CAREER
In 1947, Rubenstein and his brothers moved to Dallas, Texas, in order to operate a mail-order business and help their sister to manage a nightclub. Concerned that they might lose business because of anti-Semitism, the Rubenstein brothers soon changed their surname to

Jack Ruby shoots Lee Harvey Oswald, center, in a Dallas police station. (Library of Congress)

known strippers, Ruby was frustrated by his failure to make the Carousel a financial success with a sophisticated clientele. People close to Ruby later noted how angry and agitated he was by the assassination of President John F. Kennedy in Dallas on November 22, 1963. After Lee Harvey Oswald was arrested for the murders of Kennedy and a Dallas police officer, Ruby went to the Dallas police headquarters on November 24. As police led Oswald to a waiting car for transfer to a jail, Ruby confronted Oswald and fatally shot him.

LEGAL ACTION AND OUTCOME
The Dallas police immediately arrested Ruby, who was charged with murder. Melvin Belli, a nationally prominent defense attorney, represented Ruby without charge. Belli tried but failed to get Ruby acquitted on the grounds of insanity. Ruby was convicted of murder on March 14, 1964, and sentenced to death. Ruby remained in jail while his lawyers appealed his conviction and sentence. In November, 1966, Ruby's lawyers succeeded in having his conviction and death sentence reversed and in securing a change of venue to Wichita Falls, Texas, for a new trial to be held in February, 1967.

Suffering from lung cancer, Ruby was admitted to Parkland Hospital in Dallas for pneumonia on December 9, 1966, and died there on January 3, 1967, from a blood clot.

IMPACT
Following Jack Ruby's arrest for shooting Oswald, many conflicting perceptions of Ruby's motives for killing Oswald have arisen. Conspiracy theorists, especially those who believe that organized crime planned and implemented Kennedy's assassination, often claim that Ruby was a Mafia hit man who was told to kill Oswald in order to silence him. They emphasize Ruby's connections to organized crime, especially to powerful gangsters who felt angered by President Kennedy's failure to overthrow Castro in 1961, and Attorney General Robert F. Kennedy's aggressive prosecution of gangsters and his 1959 trip to Cuba. Scholars of President Kennedy's assassination who support the Warren Commission's

Ruby. Ruby successively managed several dance halls, nightclubs, and strip clubs in the Dallas area. In 1959, he traveled to Cuba to visit Lewis McWillie, a Dallas gambler who was imprisoned by Fidel Castro. McWillie was later linked to nationally known gangsters, such as Santo Trafficante, Jr., and Carlos Marcello, who lost major investments in Cuba because of Castro's revolution and resented the Kennedy administration's crackdown on organized crime.

As the owner and manager of the Carousel strip club from 1960 to 1963, Ruby ingratiated himself with the Dallas police by providing them with free liquor and entertainment at the Carousel and delivering free sandwiches to Dallas police headquarters. He was well known to the police and his employees for his quick temper, eccentric behavior, and tendency toward violence, especially against unruly customers. Ruby often carried a concealed handgun, presumably for maintaining security at the Carousel and protecting large sums of money. Despite his publicity gimmicks and efforts to hire well-

conclusion that Lee Harvey Oswald acted alone dismiss the idea that Ruby was a Mafia hit man. They claim that Ruby, like Oswald, was a mentally unstable person who acted impulsively when he committed this murder. For evidence, they cite Ruby's comments immediately after his arrest. Ruby asserted that he wanted to prove that Jews were brave, retaliate on behalf of the reputation of Dallas, do the police a favor, and spare Jacqueline Kennedy the agony of testifying at Oswald's trial. Ruby later claimed, however, that he killed Oswald impulsively without a motive.

After his March, 1964, conviction, Ruby repeatedly asked the Warren Commission to interview him. When Chief Justice Earl Warren and other commission members came to Dallas to interview Ruby in June, 1964, Ruby asked Warren to relocate his confinement to Washington, D.C., because he feared he would be killed in his Dallas jail cell, apparently as part of a conspiracy to take over the American government. In March, 1965, he stated in a televised interview that no one would ever know the "true facts" about his motives and that people with "an ulterior motive" would never allow these true facts to be revealed to the world. Ruby's contradictory, changing statements about his motives for killing Oswald and whether there was a conspiracy to kill Kennedy intensified and prolonged the conspiracy controversy. A widely accepted and definitive explanation of Ruby's motive for killing Oswald may never be determined.

FURTHER READING

Belli, Melvin M. *Dallas Justice: The Real Story of Jack Ruby and His Trial.* New York: McKay Press, 1964. An account of Ruby's trial by his leading defense attorney.

Kantor, Seth. *The Ruby Cover-Up.* New York: Kensington, 1978. An investigation that criticizes the findings of the Warren Commission and claims that Ruby was part of a conspiracy to kill and silence Oswald.

Posner, Gerald L. *Case Closed: Lee Harvey Oswald and the Assassination of JFK.* New York: Random House, 1993. An updated defense of the Warren Commission's conclusions that rejects the idea that Ruby was part of a conspiracy.

Wills, Garry, and Ovid Demaris. *Jack Ruby.* New York: New American Library, 1967. A detailed biography of Ruby, especially his life in Dallas.

—*Sean J. Savage*

SEE ALSO: Lee Harvey Oswald.

ERIC RUDOLPH
American terrorist

BORN: September 19, 1966; Merritt Island, Florida
ALSO KNOWN AS: Eric Robert Rudolph (full name); Bob Rudolph; Robert Randolph; Bob Randolph; Jerry Wilson; Olympic Park Bomber
MAJOR OFFENSES: Bombing, murder, and robbery
ACTIVE: July 27, 1996-May 31, 2003
LOCALE: Atlanta, Georgia; Birmingham, Alabama; and western North Carolina
SENTENCE: Four life sentences without parole plus 120 years in prison

EARLY LIFE
Eric Rudolph (EH-rihk REW-dahlf) grew up in Florida. After his father, Robert Rudolph, died of melanoma in 1981, Eric moved with his mother, Pat Rudolph, to western North Carolina. There Eric explored the Nantahala National Forest. He also met a neighbor, Tom Branham, who discussed his antigovernment views with Rudolph.

Rudolph attended school in Nantahala. One school paper he submitted declared that the Holocaust—the Nazi murder of six million Jews during World War II—had never occurred. After ninth grade Rudolph quit school and studied at home to earn a general equivalency diploma. He also worked at various carpentry jobs.

In November, 1994, Rudolph accompanied his mother to Schell City, Missouri, where they attended the Church of Israel, led by Christian Identity minister Dan Gayman. During 1985 Rudolph attended Western Carolina University for two semesters. He next enlisted in the U.S. Army in August, 1987, and underwent basic training at Fort Benning, Georgia. Rudolph was then assigned to Fort Campbell, Kentucky, to serve in the 101st Airborne Division. By January, 1989, military officials had discharged Rudolph for insubordination. Rudolph returned to North Carolina and bought his mother's house. There he grew and sold marijuana. By May, 1996, he had sold his home and was renting nearby property. He began identifying himself with false names.

CRIMINAL CAREER

During the 1996 Summer Olympics, after midnight on July 27, emergency operators in the Atlanta area received two anonymous phone calls warning that a bomb was planted in the Centennial Olympic Park, where musical performers entertained Olympics fans. At 1:20 A.M., a pipe bomb exploded, killing Alice Hawthorne and wounding approximately one hundred people, including Hawthorne's daughter Fallon Stubbs.

On January 16, 1997, Rudolph detonated two bombs at Northside Family Planning Services in Atlanta, hurting seven people. He targeted Atlanta's Otherside Lounge, a gay bar, on February 21, 1997, injuring four people in an initial bombing. Authorities located and disabled another bomb before it exploded.

On January 29, 1998, at 7:33 A.M., Rudolph bombed the New Woman, All Women Healthcare Clinic in Birmingham, Alabama. The explosion killed policeman Robert Sanderson and seriously wounded nurse Emily Lyons. Having heard the explosion, Jermaine Hughes, a student at the nearby University of Alabama, Birmingham, campus, noticed a suspicious-looking man leaving the area. Hughes followed the man and called an operator, describing the truck the suspect drove and giving its North Carolina license plate number. Law enforcement agencies used that information to identify Rudolph as the bombing suspect. They searched his mobile home on January 30. Rudolph was not found, but by February 8, hunters near Murphy, North Carolina, had discovered his truck. Six days later, a federal warrant charged Rudolph with the Birmingham bombing.

LEGAL ACTION AND OUTCOME

On May 5, 1998, the Federal Bureau of Investigation (FBI) designated Rudolph one of its ten most wanted fugitives, offering a one-million-dollar reward for information resulting in his arrest. Rudolph eluded searchers over the following five years. In letters he later wrote to his mother, he described how he survived by stealing garden produce and restaurant refuse. A store owner, George Nordmann, reported that Rudolph had asked to purchase sustenance on July 7, 1998. Nordmann refused Rudolph, who nevertheless took Nordmann's truck and food, leaving five hundred dollars in cash. Law enforcement personnel located Nordmann's truck, though not Rudolph, in the Nantahala National Forest. Government and private searchers used dogs, helicopters, and infra-

red and heat detectors to search for the suspect, but in vain.

By October 14, 1998, authorities had officially charged Rudolph with bombings at all three Atlanta sites. That fall, FBI director Louis Freeh visited the Andrews, North Carolina, headquarters of the investigation, stating that his agents would remain in the region until they located Rudolph. During the following year, agents investigated break-ins possibly attributable to Rudolph, who remained elusive. Many frustrated searchers believed he had died. The Andrews headquarters finally closed in June, 2000. Federal grand juries indicted Rudolph on November 15, 2000.

Then, on May 31, 2003, Murphy policeman Jeff Postell arrested Rudolph in a grocery store parking lot. Rudolph told Postell, who was unaware whom he had captured, that his name was Jerry Wilson but later, at the jail, admitted that he was Eric Rudolph. On June 3, 2003, Rudolph pleaded not guilty for the Birmingham clinic bombing.

Rudolph had stockpiled 250 pounds of dynamite in North Carolina. Federal prosecutors offered Rudolph life sentences instead of the death penalty if he would reveal the explosives' location. On April 8, 2005, Rudolph accepted that deal. He pleaded guilty on April 13. Rudolf refused media interviews but issued an eleven-page statement detailing, among other things, his anti-abortion rights views.

At his July 18, 2005, sentencing hearing, Rudolph listened to Birmingham bombing victims' statements before the judge sentenced him to two life sentences without the possibility of parole. In Atlanta on August 22, 2005, Rudolph heard victims and apologized for the Olympic Park bombing but not others. The judge gave Rudolph four life sentences without parole plus 120 years. He was then transferred to a subterranean, high-security Colorado prison.

IMPACT

The U.S. government invested approximately thirty million dollars searching for Eric Rudolph, the most expensive and intensive domestic search for a fugitive to date. Many people in Rudolph's community embraced his cause, believing that his taking violent actions in the name of his beliefs was morally correct. Some people profited by creating and selling Rudolph merchandise. Because the fugitive Rudolph was celebrated throughout western North Carolina, law enforcement officials were constantly unsure if locals were helping them or Rudolph.

Few books or movies have featured Rudolph. Emily Lyons self-published a book telling how the bombing affected her life, including color images of her injuries. After Rudolph was apprehended, the USA television network announced plans to film the story. Rudolph's mother stated she would write a book. Rudolph himself posted prose on anti-abortion-rights Web sites.

FURTHER READING

Freeh, Louis J., with Howard Means. *My FBI: Bringing Down the Mafia, Investigating Bill Clinton, and Fighting the War on Terror*. New York: St. Martin's Press, 2005. Emphasizes the FBI's perseverance in finding Rudolph and how that agency's searches pressured Rudolph to scavenge and alter his behavior, resulting in his capture.

Schuster, Henry, with Charles Stone. *Hunting Eric Rudolph*. New York: Berkley Books, 2005. A CNN producer assigned to Rudolph coverage and a Georgia Bureau of Investigation Anti-Terrorist Unit director offer in-depth information. Photographs of evidence and wanted posters supplement the text, which concludes before Rudolph was sentenced.

Walls, Kathleen. *Man Hunt: The Eric Rudolph Story*. Saint Augustine, Fla.: Global Authors, 2003. North Carolina writer provides local information unavailable in other books. Includes photographs of sites relevant to the Rudolph case.

—*Elizabeth D. Schafer*

SEE ALSO: Theodore Kaczynski; Timothy McVeigh; Terry Nichols.

NICOLA SACCO
Italian anarchist

BORN: April 22, 1891; Torremaggiore, Italy
DIED: August 23, 1927; Boston, Massachusetts
ALSO KNOWN AS: Ferdinando Sacco (full name)
MAJOR OFFENSES: Robbery and murder
ACTIVE: April 15, 1920
LOCALE: South Braintree, Massachusetts
SENTENCE: Death by electrocution; posthumously pardoned

EARLY LIFE
Nicola Sacco (NEE-coh-lah SAH-coh) was born in Torremaggiore, Italy, in 1891. Though his father was a merchant, Sacco received only the basic formal education common in the Italy of his day. At age sixteen Sacco emigrated to the United States with a brother and settled in Massachusetts. Because Sacco had little formal education and no marketable skills, only menial jobs were open to him. He began work at an Italian American-owned company and was soon promoted to laborer. As was common in the construction industry, employees were laid off in winter. Thus forced to seek other employment, Sacco began doing textile work.

After his brother returned to Italy, Sacco learned the shoemaking trade. He went to work at a shoe manufacturing company. In 1912, as a skilled and employed tradesman, he married Rosina Zambelli. One year later their son, Dante, was born. Their daughter, Ines, was born in 1920.

ANARCHIC CAREER
In 1912, Sacco began to associate with anarchists because he sympathized with their demands for equality for all. Convinced of the need for a radical solution to the perceived inherent injustice of capitalist society, Sacco regularly attended anarchist meetings and also began writing for a well-known anarchist newspaper.

After the United States entered World War I on the side of Italy, Sacco could not support a conflict he considered unjust. He and his new friend Bartolomeo Vanzetti went to Mexico until they could return to Massachusetts unthreatened by con-

scription. Little did they know that after the war had ended, a different form of injustice would take their lives.

Defendants in the most celebrated political trial in history, Sacco and Vanzetti were accused of the April 15, 1920, South Braintree murders of F. A. Parmenter, a paymaster of a shoe factory, and Alessandro Berardelli, the company's payroll guard.

LEGAL ACTION AND OUTCOME
On the evening of May 5, 1920, Sacco and Vanzetti were arrested. By the end of the month they found themselves in the Massachusetts Superior Court standing trial before Judge Webster Thayer. On July 14, both defendants were found guilty of murder. Later, they would be sentenced to death. Because of such factors as openly displayed bias against the defendants by Judge Thayer, a jury that seemed chosen expressly to convict, false eyewitness testimony, and a strong cultural bias against the defendants' radical political beliefs and ethnicity, the conviction of Sacco and Vanzetti was protested throughout the United States, Europe, and Latin America. Newspaper editorials throughout the world denounced the unfairness of the trial, and government authorities received thousands of protest letters.

Bartolomeo Vanzetti, left, and Nicola Sacco.

In 1925, another man, a local gang member, confessed his guilt and admitted that neither Sacco nor Vanzetti had been involved in the murders. After the Massachusetts courts refused to reopen the case, Governor Alvan T. Fuller responded to the tremendous mass protests and newspaper criticisms by creating an investigatory committee chaired by the president of Harvard University, A. Lawrence Lowell. When the governor's refusal to grant clemency was supported by the committee, renewed demonstrations and mass protests broke out across the United States, and from Mexico City to Paris. Although evidence pointed to the guilt of a local gang and to the unfairness of the trial, Sacco and Vanzetti, maintaining their innocence to the end, were executed on August 23, 1927. Massachusetts governor Michael Dukakis formally cleared the two men in 1977.

IMPACT

The criminal case against Nicola Sacco and Bartolomeo Vanzetti is a historical milestone. This case underscored the last days of a significant American anarchist movement. Though the two defendants underwent a criminal prosecution, at trial were two anarchists who had American antiradicalism and xenophobia working against them. Thus, the trial marked the impact of the anti-anarchist, anticommunist, xenophobic hysteria of the early twentieth century. The conviction and execution of the two Italian immigrants moved many to question openly the fairness of an American political and judicial system that would allow a political crucifixion of two foreign-born anarchists.

Many American intellectuals, such as John Dos Passos, attacked the trial as an assault on American freedoms and proof of a dual system of justice based on class distinctions and ethnicity. Protests from judicial community leaders, such as Harvard law professor and future Supreme Court justice Felix Frankfurter, assailed the unfairness of the trial, the bias of the judge and jury, the weakness of the evidence, the unprofessional conduct of police, and the near-perjury of prosecution witnesses.

The Sacco and Vanzetti trial is still hotly debated. Most accounts declare the men's innocence and point to xenophobic, anti-Italian and antiradical prejudice. While some studies hold that the guilty verdict may have been valid, no works have definitively determined the culpability of either defendant. The only certainty is that both Sacco and Vanzetti suffered for their ethnicity and political beliefs. The sole definitive conclusion is that the anarchist cause to which both were so impassionedly dedicated suffered a death much more silent than theirs.

FURTHER READING

Avrich, Paul. *Sacco and Vanzetti: The Anarchist Background*. Princeton, N.J.: Princeton University Press, 1991. Through research of anarchist sources, Avrich gives a definitive assessment of the case and of the anarchist movement.

Binelli, Mark. *Sacco and Vanzetti Must Die!* Normal, Ill.: Dalkey Archive Press, 2006. Presents an intriguing review of the controversy surrounding the case.

Frankfurter, Felix. *The Case of Sacco and Vanzetti: A Critical Analysis for Lawyers and Laymen*. Boston: Little, Brown, 1927. In a still indispensable work, Frankfurter does much to reveal the trial's unfairness.

Topp, Michael. *The Sacco and Vanzetti Case: A Brief History with Documents*. New York: Macmillan, 2005. Offers a summary of the varied views and documents concerning the Sacco and Vanzetti case.

Vanzetti, Bartolomeo. *Background to the Plymouth Trial*. Chelsea, Mass.: Road to Freedom Press, 1927. This important monograph presents an intriguing and personal review of the case and the cause.

—*Pietro Lorenzini*

SEE ALSO: Bartolomeo Vanzetti.

MARQUIS DE SADE
French libertine author

BORN: June 2, 1740; Paris, France
DIED: December 2, 1814; Charenton, near Paris, France
ALSO KNOWN AS: Donatien Alphonse François de Sade (full name); D. A. F. Sade; Comte de Sade; Louis Sade
MAJOR OFFENSES: Pornography, sodomy, corruption of minors, and sacrilege
ACTIVE: 1763-1801
LOCALE: Paris, Marseille, Arcueil, and La Coste, France
SENTENCE: Imprisoned at various times for a total of twenty-nine years; sentenced to death at one point but then granted a reprieve by the king

EARLY LIFE
Donatien Alphonse François de Sade, commonly known as the Marquis de Sade (mar-kee duh sahd), belonged to the upper echelon of French aristocracy. His father, a diplomat under King Louis XV of France, was descended from a long line of Provençal nobility; his mother was a lady-in-waiting to a princess of Condé. At the age of ten, Sade entered the Parisian Collège Louis-le-Grand, academy of choice for the nation's future elite. Then, four years later, he began training as an officer in the king's light cavalry. He received a taste of combat

Marquis de Sade.

during the Seven Years' War (1756-1763) and in 1759 was promoted to the rank of captain, only to be demobilized at the war's end. On May 17, 1763, he married, upon his father's insistence, Renée-Pelagie Cordier de Montreuil, the daughter of a wealthy Parisian magistrate.

LIBERTINE CAREER
Five months into his marriage, Sade's curious erotic practices occasioned the first in a series of public scandals associated with his name. On October 18, 1763, he invited an unemployed fan maker and prostitute named Jeanne Testard to spend the night with him in one of several recreational cottages he had been renting in Paris. She denounced him to a police commissioner the following day for having indulged in various forms of extravagant sexual behavior, including masturbation with a crucifix, algolagnia, and incitement to sodomy. As a nobleman, Sade managed to avoid public trial but was nonetheless imprisoned for about two weeks in the royal dungeon at Vincennes.

A second incident occurred when, on April 3, 1768, he escorted Rose Keller, a thirty-six-year-old widow, to a cottage in the remote Parisian suburb of Arcueil for an evening of debauchery during which he flogged her with a cat-o'-nine-tails, leaving visible wounds. When the affair came under official investigation, the marquis and his family silenced the plaintiff by paying her four hundred francs, but they were unable to quell the expression of public outrage that ensued. The marquis's sexual transgressions became the talk of prominent salons in the French capital, while critical accounts of the incident appeared in popular gazettes and broadsheets.

LEGAL ACTION AND OUTCOME
As a result of his misconduct, Sade spent between six and seven months in the custody of various royal prisons, in part for his own protection. Less than four years later, he was again in similar straits. On the afternoon of July 27, 1772, during a trip to the southern port of Marseille, he and a male servant joined four prostitutes in a libidinous orgy replete with barbed whips, carminative aphrodisiacs, and degrading voyeurism. When a fifth prostitute, who received a visit from the marquis later that evening, fell dangerously ill from an excessive dose of the marquis's aphrodisiac, the authorities intervened. The marquis, refusing to submit to public trial, was sentenced to death in absentia by a local court for attempted poisoning

and sodomy. Arrested on December 8 and detained for several months at Fort Miolans in Savoy, he escaped to the safety of his estate at La Coste, Provence, where he remained for several years.

His stay at La Coste was plagued by new scandals such as the little girls episode of December, 1774-January, 1775 (the corruption of five teenage girls attached to his household) and the pregnancy of his chambermaid a few months later. He was seized by royal decree during a trip to Paris on February 13, 1777, and, with the exception of one short-lived escape to La Coste, remained a prisoner in various locations until his official release on April 12, 1790. During those twelve years of confinement he wrote for later publication some of the most shocking works of erotic literature yet known to the world, including *Les 120 Journées de Sodome* (1904 and 1931-1935; *The 120 Days of Sodom*, 1954), *La Philosophie dans le boudoir* (1795; *Philosophy in the Bedroom*, 1965), and *Justine* (1791; English translation 1889).

The marquis's past reputation and the scandalous nature of his published work led to his renewed arrest on March 6, 1801. After two brief incarcerations, he was transferred to an asylum for the insane at Charenton, where he spent the remainder of his life. During that time, he produced plays for his fellow inmates and wrote three noteworthy historical novels: *La Marquise de Gange* (pb. 1813; the marquise of Gange), *Adélaïde de Brunswick* (wr. 1812, pb. 1966; *Adelaide of Brunswick*, 1954), and *Histoire secrète d'Isabelle de Bavière* (wr. 1813, pb. 1953; the secret history of Isabella of Bavaria).

IMPACT

As a controversial historical figure and a writer, the Marquis de Sade occupies a prominent place in literature, art, cinema, philosophy, and modern culture in general. Rediscovered in the early twentieth century, his writings were embraced by André Breton and members of the Surrealist movement as a testament to the author's struggle against censorship and his revolt against the hypoc-

---

DE SADE'S GOLDEN RULE

In Dialogue Between a Priest and a Dying Man *(wr. 1782, pb. 1927), the characters debate about God, the afterlife, and sin. The dying man, voicing de Sade's own views, concludes:*

Let the evil deed be proscribed by law, let justice smite the criminal, that will be deterrent enough; but if by misfortune we do commit it even so, let's not cry over spilled milk; remorse is inefficacious, since it does not stay us from crime, futile since it does not repair it, therefore it is absurd to beat one's breast, more absurd still to dread being punished in another world if we have been lucky to escape it in this. God forbid that this be construed as encouragement to crime, no, we should avoid it as much as we can, but one must learn to shun it through reason and not through false fears which lead to naught and whose effects are so quickly overcome in any moderately steadfast soul. Reason, sir—yes, our reason alone should warn us that harm done our fellows can never bring happiness to us; and our heart, that contributing to their felicity is the greatest joy Nature has accorded us on earth; the entirety of human morals is contained in this one phrase: *Render others as happy as one desires oneself to be*, and never inflict more pain upon them than one would like to receive at their hands. There you are, my friend, those are the only principles we should observe, and you need neither god nor religion to appreciate and subscribe to them, you need only have a good heart. But I feel my strength ebbing away; preacher, put away your prejudices, unbend, be a man, be human, without fear and without hope forget your gods and your religions too: they are none of them good for anything but to set man at odds with man, and the mere name of these horrors has caused greater loss of life on earth than all other wars and all other plagues combined. Renounce the idea of another world; there is none, but do not renounce the pleasure of being happy and of making for happiness in this. Nature offers you no other way of doubling your existence, of extending it.

Source: Marquis de Sade, *"Justine," "Philosophy in the Bedroom," and Other Writings* (New York: Grove Press, 1965).

---

risy of conventional morality. Such an appraisal stood in stark contrast to his portrayal as a sexual misfit in the annals of clinical psychology. The marquis and his work gained iconic currency through depictions by Man Ray, René Magritte, and Clovis Trouille and provided material for numerous plays and films from Luis Buñuel's *L'Âge d'or* (1930) to productions by Peter Weiss, Pier Paolo Pasolini, Yukio Mishima, and Doug Wright. Major editions of the marquis's collected works published in French between 1966 and 1998 have provided significant impetus to Sadean scholarship, leading to the organization of international colloquia in England (1997) and the United States (2003). The word "sadism," referring to a delight in cruelty, is taken from Sade's notorious name.

FURTHER READING

Bongie, Laurence L. *Sade: A Biographical Essay.* Chicago: University of Chicago Press, 1998. Challenges attempts to rehabilitate Sade as a champion of human liberties.

Du Plessix Gray, Francine. *At Home with the Marquis de Sade.* New York: Simon & Schuster, 1998. A balanced, well-documented biography; offers insight into the social and legal norms of eighteenth and early nineteenth century France.

Philipps, John. *The Marquis de Sade: A Very Short Introduction.* New York: Oxford University Press, 2005. Seeks to dispel the myth of Sade's demoniac character; includes discussion of his major works and their significance in the postmodern world.

—*Jan Pendergrass*

SEE ALSO: Cartouche; Charlotte Corday; Claude Duval; Henri Désiré Landru; Jean-Paul Marat; Marie-Antoinette; Gilles de Rais; Robespierre; Eugène François Vidocq.

ANTÓNIO DE OLIVEIRA SALAZAR
Dictator of Portugal (1932-1968)

BORN: April 28, 1889; Vimiero, near Santa Comba Dão, Beira Alta Province, Portugal

DIED: July 27, 1970; Lisbon, Portugal

CAUSE OF NOTORIETY: Presiding over Europe's last colonial empire, Salazar was determined to keep control of Portugal's African colonies at any cost.

ACTIVE: 1932-1968

LOCALE: Portugal, mostly Lisbon

EARLY LIFE

Born in 1889, António de Oliveira Salazar (ahn-TOH-nee-oh thay oh-lee-VEHR-ah SAL-ah-zahr) was a law graduate of the University of Coimbra, where he eventually became a professor of political economy. His intellectual and administrative powers were such that the army summoned him to a ministerial post after the military coup of 1926. As a young man, Salazar established a monastic lifestyle—he was unmarried, ascetic, and extremely hardworking. These traits would characterize him for his entire life.

POLITICAL CAREER

Dictator during the twentieth century's most turbulent decades, Salazar is the leading figure in modern Portuguese history. Unlike his most steadfast ally, Spain's Francisco Franco, who took power as a general, Salazar came from an academic and intellectual background. His early successes in stabilizing Portugal's economy reflected a technocratic approach to economic questions that he applied throughout his career. However, the final years of his regime were taken up almost completely with military issues.

Salazar's dictatorship is unique in that he did not seize power by political or military means—he acquired it through administrative expertise. In 1926, the Portuguese army under General Antonio Carmona overthrew the tumultuous Republic of Portugal. Because of his reputation in political economics, Salazar was installed as finance minister of the new militarily controlled government, but he resigned when he found his range of action curtailed. In 1928, he was reinstated as finance minister and, with the Portuguese economy in chaos, obtained almost total power over the nation's finances.

On the strength of his immediate stabilization of government finances, he was appointed in 1932 as prime minister and president of the Council of Ministers and given dictatorial powers under Portugal's constitution of 1933. For the following four decades, Salazar's National Union (União Nacional) Party would dominate Portugal. Salazar filled his ministry with Portugal's leading economic technocrats.

The new constitution implemented Salazar's authoritarian vision of a New State (Estada Novo). Salazar pursued a vision of "corporatism," seeking harmony in industrial relations through tight regulations of labor and employers. His corporatism explicitly drew on Catholic social teaching and papal encyclicals, although some historians see a greater influence in the fascist movement of Benito Mussolini, whom Salazar is known to have admired. In his authoritarian New State, Salazar repressed dissent and criticism. Elections and legislative bodies were found unnecessary, and the political police force (PIDE) watched over all activities. Salazar formed the Portuguese youth into militaristic organizations and fervently supported the Nationalist revolt and government of Francoist Spain.

The post-World War II era saw some political liberalization in Portugal as it joined the North Atlantic Treaty Organization in 1949 and the United Nations in 1955. An amnesty was granted for political prisoners, and censorship was relaxed. In the 1950's and 1960's Portugal also shared in the dynamic economic growth of the Iberian Peninsula.

DECOLONIZATION

The final years of Salazar's dictatorship were dominated by the question of the African possessions Portugal had colonized since the era of Vasco da Gama in the fifteenth century. In the early 1960's, wars of liberation broke out in Angola, Mozambique, and Portuguese Guinea. Salazar's New State had incorporated the idea that Portugal and its colonies were interdependent entities, as reflected in the Colonial Act of 1930. Portugal's anachronistic and futile wars to retain its colonies not only revealed the worst aspects of Salazar's dictatorship but also contributed to the misery of those African nations, which continues to this day. Although Salazar held power until becoming disabled in 1968, his New State was dismantled in 1974, four years after his death in 1970.

IMPACT

António de Oliveira Salazar was one of the longest-reigning dictators of the twentieth century. Although Portugal was repressive, its people were spared the mass killings that engulfed much of Europe during the bloody 1930's and 1940's. Salazar's PIDE secret police organization was feared, but Portugal's law did not allow the death penalty. Although Salazar was Franco's most fervent ally, and six thousand Portuguese soldiers died on the Nationalist side during the Spanish Civil War, Salazar's true impact on foreign affairs lay in Africa. Under Salazar, the Portuguese colonies suffered years of warfare, when other European countries had since granted independence to their colonies. The unhappy material conditions of today's Angola and Mozambique must be attributed, at least in part, to Salazar's vain military efforts to retain his colonies as well as to the vicious Marxist regimes that sought power upon Portugal's retreat.

FURTHER READING

Gilbert, Martin. *1933-1951*. Vol. 2 in *A History of the Twentieth Century*. New York: William Morrow, 1999. In this comprehensive history of the World War II era, Salazar emerges as Franco's greatest ally in Franco's war against the Spanish Republic.

Howard, Michael, and Wm. Roger Louis. *The Oxford History of the Twentieth Century*. New York: Oxford University Press, 2002. Louis's chapter "The European Colonial Empires" briefly assesses Salazar's purported role as modernizer of Portugal's African colonies, the last to be retained by a European power.

Lewis, Paul. "Salazar's Ministerial Elite, 1932-1968." *The Journal of Politics* 40, no. 3 (August, 1978): 622-647. Scholarly monograph on Salazar's use of technocratic ministers as the basis of his dictatorial power.

Pinto, Antonio Costa. *Salazar's Dictatorship and European Fascism: Problems of Interpretation*. New York: Columbia University Press, 1996. Situating Salazar's dictatorship in the fascist movements of twentieth century Europe, Pinto classifies Salazar's dictatorship with authoritarian dictatorships such as that of Engelbert Dollfuss of pre-Nazi Austria rather than the murderous regimes of Benito Mussolini and Adolf Hitler.

—Howard Bromberg

SEE ALSO: Francisco Franco; Benito Mussolini.

YOLANDA SALDÍVAR
Latina murderer

BORN: September 19, 1960; San Antonio, Texas
MAJOR OFFENSE: Murder of Tejano singer Selena Quintanilla-Perez
ACTIVE: March 30, 1995
LOCALE: Corpus Cristi, Texas
SENTENCE: Life in prison

EARLY LIFE
Born in San Antonio, Texas, Yolanda Saldívar (sahl-DEE-vahr) was the youngest of seven children born to retired restaurateur Frank Saldívar. Considered a good student, Saldívar began her career in the medical profession as a licensed dental assistant. After several years in

Yolanda Saldívar, right, with Selena. (AP/Wide World Photos)

this occupation in Texas, Yolanda attended night school to complete her degree in nursing.

CRIMINAL CAREER
Saldívar became interested in Selena's music and in 1991 asked if she could organize a fan club. She was hired as the president of the Selena Fan Club and put in control of the club's finances and membership. Yolanda and Selena became close friends and the fan club became a moneymaking avenue for the singer. In 1994, Selena branched out from the music business and bought several salon boutiques; she assigned management of these businesses to Saldívar.

In February, 1995, trouble started with the Selena Fan Club. People complained that they had not received the fan packets for which they had paid. The Quintanilla family confronted Saldívar. Money also started to turn up missing from one of Selena's bank accounts. On March 12, 1995, Selena fired Saldívar. Although she was fired, Saldívar continued to work because there were papers missing and the business was preparing to file taxes. On March 30, Selena went to where Saldívar was staying in Corpus Cristi, at a Days Inn motel, in order to get some missing paperwork. After this meeting, Selena discovered that still more papers were missing.

Early the next morning, Selena went back to the Days Inn motel to meet with Saldívar again. Saldívar told Selena that she had been raped in Monterey, Mexico, and needed to go to the hospital; Selena took her. After about an hour, Selena and Saldívar returned to the motel and argued. At 11:48 A.M., Saldívar took out a gun and fired at Selena. The bullet struck her in her right shoulder, severing a major artery. Selena ran toward the lobby to get help. According to the motel's front desk clerk, Shawna Vela, Selena screamed that she needed help because she had been shot. Vela said she and other employees asked Selena who had shot her, and Selena answered, "Saldívar—158." She collapsed on the floor as Vela called 911.

Selena died a short time later at a hospital. After a nine-and-a-half-hour standoff with police, Saldívar was taken into custody for the murder of Selena.

LEGAL ACTION AND OUTCOME

Salivdar's defense in the death of Selena was that it was an accident. Saldívar claimed that she had been threatened and assaulted by Abraham Quintanilla, Jr., Selena's father, which drove her to the final confrontation with Selena. On October 23, 1995, following nine days of testimony and only two hours and twenty minutes of deliberation, Saldívar was found guilty of murder. On October 26, 1995, she was sentenced to life in prison. Saldívar began serving her sentence in Gatesville Prison in Texas; she would be eligible for parole in 2036.

IMPACT

Selena's death was not a leading story in the U.S. mainstream media until Yolanda Saldívar's standoff with police was broadcast live on national television. Although a very well known singer in Mexico, Selena was new to the American market, as she had not made an English-language album yet (she was working on one at the time of her death). Selena's death and the subsequent conviction of Saldívar was followed closely by the Latino community in the United States. After her album was released posthumously, it went double platinum by the end of 1995, making her the first Tejano artist to break through to the mainstream pop music market. A film depicting Selena's life, starring Jennifer Lopez and titled *Selena* (1997), memorialized the singer for her adoring fans.

FURTHER READING

Arraras, Maria Celeste. *Selena's Secret: The Revealing Story Behind Her Tragic Death*. New York: Simon &

SELENA FOREVER

Whether she shot Selena Quintanilla-Perez accidentally or in a fit of rage, Yolanda Saldívar languishes in Gatesville Prison, in Austin, Texas. The prospect of an early release was fought fiercely by Selena's fans, who circulated a "Yolanda Saldívar Not out of Jail" petition on the Internet in 2005 for transmittal to the Texas parole board.

In the months and years following her death, Selena and her music rocketed to stardom. A special service was held in the Los Angeles Coliseum, where Selena was to give a concert, and less than one month following her death, Texas governor George W. Bush declared April 16 "Selena Day" in the singer's honor. *Dreaming of You*, her final album, was released posthumously in early summer, 1995. It became the first Tejano album to reach number one in America and was double platinum by the end of the year. A biographical film, *Selena*, featuring Jennifer Lopez as Selena and Lupe Ontiveros as Saldívar, was released in 1997. Books appeared about Selena and about Saldívar's trial. Moreover, the fan club continued, albeit with a new name: Selena Forever. The home page of its Web site proudly declared,

> The tragic shooting death of Tejano singer Selena spawned a reaction within the Latino community that can be compared to the reactions to the deaths of Elvis Presley and John Lennon. An enormously popular singer in Latino communities across North America, her music crossed cultural boundaries to touch the lives of young and old alike. A flamboyant, sexy stage performer, sometimes hailed as the Latina Madonna, Selena was nonetheless considered a role model, for offstage she was family oriented, active in anti-drug campaigns and AIDS awareness programs. . . .

Schuster, 1996. Examines new details about the life and death of the Tejano superstar and includes never-before-released information on convicted murderer Saldívar.

Marvis, Barbara. *Selena*. Hockessin, Del.: Mitchell Lane, 2003. A book for young adults that covers the life and career of Selena.

Richmond, Clint. *Selena: The Phenomenal Life and Tragic Death of a Tejano Music Queen*. New York: Pocket Books, 1996. Examines every aspect of Selena's life and rise to fame. The first half of the book is in English and the rest is in Spanish. It has eight pages of photographs in the center of the book.

—*Tracie L. Keesee*

SEE ALSO: Mark David Chapman; John E. du Pont; Harry Kendall Thaw.

SALOME
Hebrew princess

BORN: c. 15 C.E.; place unknown
DIED: First century C.E.; place unknown
CAUSE OF NOTORIETY: Salome danced before the court of King Herod of Galilee and, at her mother's urging, requested the head of John the Baptist on a charger.
ACTIVE: c. 30 C.E.
LOCALE: Galilee

EARLY LIFE

The life of Salome (SA-loh-may) is briefly recorded in two ancient sources: the New Testament books of Matthew and Mark (c. 75 C.E.) and *Antiquitates Judaicae* (93 C.E.; *The Antiquities of the Jews*, 1773), by Flavius Josephus. Matthew and Mark fail to name Salome but identify her as the daughter of Herodias (wife of Herod

Salome, as painted by Bernardino Luini c. 1510. (Hulton Archive/ Getty Images)

the tetrarch and former wife of Herod's brother Herod Philip).

Flavius Josephus names Salome as the daughter of Herodias and stepdaughter of Herod Antipas (half brother of Herod Philip and tetrarch of Galilee) at the time of John the Baptist's imprisonment but ascribes to her neither a dance nor a request for John the Baptist's head. Salome is merely named and said to marry Philip the tetrarch of Trachonitis and later to marry and have three sons with Aristobulus (grandson of Herod, brother of Agrippa, senior).

CAREER

According to Matthew and Mark, Salome's dance and request for the head of John the Baptist were done strictly at the urging of her mother, Herodias. Both Herod and Herodias wished to silence John the Baptist, as he proclaimed their marriage to be unlawful. Herod imprisoned him yet dared not kill him, fearing his capacity to incite rebellion. At Herod's birthday celebration, Salome danced and pleased Herod and his court so well that Herod vowed to give her anything she wished, up to half his kingdom. Herod finally regretted his promise but kept it. As a result, John the Baptist was beheaded and the head given to the girl on a charger. She then gave it to her mother. (In Josephus's account, Herod, fearing John the Baptist's ability to create a rebellion, simply had him put to death without any involvement of Salome or Herodias.)

As a result of Salome's actions, the life of John the Baptist was ended. According to Josephus, Herod's army was later destroyed in a war with his former father-in-law, Aretas, and the Jews saw the defeat as punishment from God for having destroyed the life of a holy man.

IMPACT

The impact of the biblical story has proven considerable, Salome being the subject of much art and literature in Christianized cultures up through the Renaissance and reemerging during the late nineteenth and early twentieth centuries, as Western cultures became obsessed with all things Eastern and as medical, social, and psychological discourse viewed the sexuality of women as suspect. Salome's dangerous sensuality, as expressed in dance, became a focal point, and her image as femme fatale was fully realized.

Romantic author Gustave Flaubert rendered perhaps the likeliest account of Salome's dance in "Herodias" (1877), based on his observations of *ghawazee* dancer Kutchuk Hanem. Decadent artist Gustave Moreau produced hundreds of Salome paintings, notably *L'Apparition* (1877) and *Tattooed Salome* (1876). Karl Joris Huysmans's 1884 novel *À rebours* (*Against the Grain*, 1922) describes Moreau's paintings, emphasizing the poisonous nature of Salome's beauty, and inspired Oscar Wilde's 1893 drama *Salome*, in which the central motivation is lust, and later, for Salome, maniacal revenge upon John the Baptist, who repels her advances. Wilde required that Salome kiss the severed head of John the Baptist and named the famed dance "dance of the seven veils," which in time led to more provocative dance performances than had been seen before in European and American society. The dance of the seven veils was immortalized in Richard Strauss's opera *Salome* (1905), based on Wilde's text.

In both Europe and America during the period of "Salomania" (1907-1909) and the rise of modern dance, Salome choreography was performed publicly and privately by such popular figures as Sarah Bernhardt, Gertrude Hoffman, Maud Allan, Isadora Duncan, Aida Walker, Ruth St. Denis, Colette, Ida Rubenstein, and Mata Hari.

SALOME'S DANCE

French novelist Gustave Flaubert, in his story "Hérodias" (collected in Trois contes, *1877), imagines Salome mesmerizing Herod Antipas with this dance:*

She danced like the priestesses of India, like the Nubians of the cataracts, or like the Bacchantes of Lydia. She whirled about like a flower blown by the tempest. The jewels in her ears sparkled, her swift movements made the colors of her draperies appear to run into one another. Her arms, her feet, her clothing even, seemed to emit streams of magnetism, that set the spectators' blood on fire.

Suddenly the thrilling chords of a harp rang through the hall, and the throng burst into loud acclamations. All eyes were fixed on Salome, who paused in her rhythmic dance, placed her feet wide apart, and without bending the knees, suddenly swayed her lithe body downward, so that her chin touched the floor; and her whole audience—the nomads, accustomed to a life of privation and abstinence, the Roman soldiers, expert in debaucheries, the avaricious publicans, and even the crabbed, elderly priests—gazed upon her with dilated nostrils.

Next she began to whirl frantically around the table where Antipas the tetrarch was seated. He leaned towards the flying figure, and in a voice half choked with the voluptuous sighs of a mad desire, he sighed: "Come to me! Come!" But she whirled on, while the music of dulcimers swelled louder and the excited spectators roared their applause. . . .

Again the dancer paused; then, like a flash, she threw herself upon the palms of her hands, while her feet rose straight up into the air. In this bizarre pose she moved about upon the floor like a gigantic beetle; then stood motionless.

The nape of her neck formed a right angle with her vertebrae. The full silken skirts of pale hues that enveloped her limbs when she stood erect, now fell to her shoulders and surrounded her face like a rainbow. Her lips were tinted a deep crimson, her arched eyebrows were black as jet, her glowing eyes had an almost terrible radiance; and the tiny drops of perspiration on her forehead looked like dew upon white marble. . . .

The next moment she . . . pronounced these words: "I ask my lord to give me, placed upon a charger, the head of—" She hesitated, as if not certain of the name; then said: "The head of Iaokanann!"

Source: Gustave Flaubert, *Three Tales* (London: Penguin Classics, 1961).

FURTHER READING

Becker-Leckrone, Megan. "Salome: The Fetishization of a Textual Corpus." *New Literary History* 26, no. 2 (1995): 239-260. Explores the intertextuality of the myth of Salome and how it has been elaborated upon since its inception.

Bentley, Toni. *Sisters of Salome.* New Haven, Conn.: Yale University Press, 2002. Studies several well-known women in the early 1900's whose controversial yet popular performances of Salome provided empowerment.

Gilman, Sander L. "Salome, Syphilis, Sarah Bernhart, and the Modern Jewess." In *The Jew in the Text: Modernity and the Construction of Identity*, edited by Linda Nochlin and Tamar Garb. New York: Thames and Hudson, 1995. Analyzes representations of women and Jews at the turn of the twentieth century and explores interrelationships.

—*Jennifer Cripps Vinsky*

SEE ALSO: Herod Antipas; Flavius Josephus; Mata Hari.

SAVITRI DEVI
Greek activist and Holocaust denier

BORN: September 30, 1905; Lyon, France
DIED: October 22, 1982; Sible Hedingham, Essex, England
ALSO KNOWN AS: Maximiani Portas (birth name); Savitri Devi Mukherji (married name)
MAJOR OFFENSE: Promoting National Socialism in Allied-occupied Germany
ACTIVE: June 15, 1948
LOCALE: Germany
SENTENCE: Two years in prison; served eight months, then was expelled from Germany

EARLY LIFE

Savitri Devi (sa-VEE-tree DEH-vee) was born Maximiani Portas in Lyon, France, to a Greek-Lombard Italian father and an English mother. Her political sympathy for Greece showed early: During World War I, she wrote slogans of protest against the Entente's invasion of neutral Greece. In college, she studied logic and philosophy and earned a doctorate in philosophy. Her fascination with Greco-Roman antiquities prompted her to renounce her French citizenship in 1928 to become a Greek national. She first identified herself as a National Socialist (a vague term in those days that now usually refers to German Nazism) after a visit to Palestine the following year. She felt convinced that Judeo-Christianity had been imposing on the West a sterile monotheism and a servile Semitism.

During her search for a living pagan culture, she traveled to India in 1932. She converted to Hinduism and called herself Savitri Devi, after the Indo-Aryan goddess. She supported Hindu nationalist movements and their campaigns against British colonialism and the spread of Islam. She worked as a lecturer for the Hindu Mission, a National Socialist organization. Her political sympathies for Greece and India gradually pulled her toward Germany. In the swastika, the Aryan sun-wheel, she found a link between Orthodox Hinduism and Adolf Hitler, whom she considered an avatar—a human incarnation—of the Hindu god Vishnu, the sustainer of order. This belief was the foundation for what came to be known as Esoteric Hitlerism.

CRIMINAL CAREER

In 1940, to avoid deportation because of her pro-Axis activities, Savitri Devi married Asit Krishna Mukherji, a Bengali Brahman, editor of *The New Mercury*, a pro-German magazine funded by the German consulate in Calcutta. Mukherji had been instrumental in establishing the connections between the Nazi-Hindutva Congress leader Subhas Chandra Bose and the Axis. After the British ended publication of the magazine, Mukherji launched another, funded by the Japanese.

During World War II, the couple gathered information from British and American servicemen and passed it to the Japanese. The leads they provided resulted in the exploding of several Allied airdromes in Burma. During the first three years after the war, Savitri Devi traveled to various countries in Europe, writing and contacting National Socialist groups.

In 1948, while Germany was still undergoing denazification, Savitri Devi was determined to propagandize on behalf of her belief in Germany and Hitler. On June 15, 1948, she rode a train from Denmark to Germany, distributing leaflets and posting handbills encouraging German people to hold fast to their National Socialist beliefs and to resist the Allied occupation. Germany, in her thinking, was forever the holy land for all Aryans, and the destruction of the Third Reich was nothing but a trial by fire in preparation for an emerging new age.

LEGAL ACTION AND OUTCOME

Savitri Devi was arrested by the British Occupation authorities in February, 1949. She was tried in Düsseldorf, Germany, on April 5, 1949, and convicted of promoting National Socialist beliefs on German territory under the Allied Control Council. Sentenced to two years' imprisonment, she served only eight months in Werl prison and was then released and expelled from Germany.

Savitri Devi spent the rest of her life writing on National Socialist ideas and making contacts with National Socialist and Nazi enthusiasts in Europe and the Americas, among them Colin Jordan, John Tyndall, Matt Köhl, Miguel Serrano, and Ernst Zundel. Holding a Greek passport, she also went on a pilgrimage of National Socialist sites in Germany—sites significant to Hitler's life as well as to the German Nazi Party, including heathen monuments. At the international Nazi conference in Gloucestershire, England, she was a founder-signatory of the Cotswold Agreement, under which the World Union of National Socialists was founded. She was the first to claim that the Nazi genocide of the Jews was an invention of Allied propaganda. Savitri Devi died of myocardial infarction and coronary thrombosis in Essex, England, in 1982.

IMPACT

Savitri Devi connected Esoteric Hitlerism to the occult Green movements. Her writings had a decisive influence on the Libertarian National Socialist Green Party and on activist Bill White. The Chilean writer and diplomat Miguel Serrano praised her as the foremother of Esoteric Hitlerism, which he founded. Savitri Devi's writings have been published by Regin-Verlag in Germany, Historical Review Press in England, and Black Sun Publications in the United States. Her book that has exerted the most influence on National Socialists is *The Lightning and the Sun* (1958), a synthesis of Hinduism, Nazi philosophy, and racial ideology.

FURTHER READING

Elst, Koenraad. *The Saffron Swastika: The Notion of "Hindu Fascism."* New Delhi, India: Voice of India, 2001. Discusses the concept of Hindutva and Hindu nationalism, from the author's examination of Nazism, Fascism, and Communism. He concludes that Hindu Fascism is not an observed reality. Chapter 5 deals with Savitri Devi.

Goodrick-Clarke, Nicholas. *Black Sun: Aryan Cults, Esoteric Nazism, and the Politics of Identity.* New York: New York University Press, 2002. Examines historical and modern-day connections between Nazi ideology and certain religious and cultural oddities. A book for those interested in obscure and puzzling regions of the radical racist right. Chapter 5 considers Savitri Devi.

_____. *Hitler's Priestess: Savitri Devi, the Hindu-Aryan Myth, and Neo-Nazism.* New York: New York University Press, 1998. Examines how Savitri Devi has been lionized by the radical right as a foremother of Nazi ideology.

Savitri Devi. *The Lightning and the Sun.* Buffalo, N.Y.: Samisdat, 1958. The author's synthesis of Hinduism and Nazism.

—*Anh Tran*

SEE ALSO: Willis A. Carto; Dietrich Eckart; Julius Evola; Elisabeth Förster-Nietzsche; Adolf Hitler; David Irving; John Tyndall.

ELIZABETH SAWYER
English witch

BORN: Date unknown; place unknown
DIED: April 19, 1621; Tyburn, London, England
ALSO KNOWN AS: Witch of Edmonton; Mother Sawyer
MAJOR OFFENSES: Witchcraft and murder
ACTIVE: 1614-1621
LOCALE: Edmonton, England
SENTENCE: Death by hanging

EARLY LIFE

Very little is known of the early life of Elizabeth Sawyer (SOY-ur). The only extant biographical information is contained in *The Wonderfull Discoverie of Elizabeth Sawyer, a Witch, Late of Edmonton* (1621), written by Henry Goodcole, a London minister. Goodcole indicates that Sawyer, who was married with children at the time of her arrest, had lived in Edmonton for many years. An impoverished woman with little or no education, Sawyer sold brooms to her neighbors. Her physical appearance suggests that her early life was one of hardship. Her countenance is described as ashen, ghostly, and downcast, and her body as bent and misshapen. As a young mother, Sawyer had also lost an eye when it was pierced by a stick held by one of her children.

CRIMINAL CAREER

Sawyer was long suspected of engaging in witchcraft. Arthur Robinson, a local justice of the peace, interrogated her as early as 1615. Robinson was responding to the accusations of Sawyer's neighbors, who suspected that their refusal to purchase brooms from her had caused her to "witch to death" two nursing infants and a number of cattle. To prove Sawyer's guilt, neighbors relied upon the custom of burning a thatch from her house. If she caused their misfortunes, they believed, she would arrive uninvited at the house of the thatch burner. Sawyer's appearance at homes following such burnings confirmed the neighbors' suspicions. However, it was the death of her neighbor Agnes Ratcleife that led to Sawyer's indictment in 1621. Shortly before her death of a severe illness, Ratcleife told her husband that she had struck Sawyer's pig with a wooden bat for lapping up her soap, prompting Sawyer to threaten her with dire consequences.

THE WITCHCRAFT ACT

Elizabeth Sawyer was found guilty of murder under England's Witchcraft Act, which was not repealed until the 1950's. The act reads in part as follows:

It shall be Felony to practise, or cause to be practised Conjuration, Witchcraft, Enchantment or Sorcery, to get Money; or to consume any Person in his Body, Members or Goods; or to provoke any Person to unlawful Love; or for the Despight of Christ, or Lucre of Money, to pull down any Cross; or to declare where Goods stolen be.

LEGAL ACTION AND OUTCOME

Sawyer was indicted on April 14, 1621, at the Old Bailey in London. She was accused of relying on devilish powers to cause the deaths of Ratcleife, the infants, and cattle. During the trial, Robinson informed the court that Sawyer bore the physical marks of a demoniac alliance, and three women who examined Sawyer discovered a teat-like piece of flesh at the base of her spine. Though acquitted of the deaths of the children and cattle, Sawyer was found guilty, under the Witchcraft Act, of causing Ratcleife's death through witchery and was condemned to death by hanging.

Goodcole visited Sawyer in prison after her conviction and extracted her confession on April 17 in the Chapel of Newgate, which he claims to reproduce verbatim in his pamphlet. Goodcole's titillating examination of Sawyer resulted in her admission that she met the devil in about 1614 (to whom she was vulnerable because of her blaspheming and swearing tongue), that he visited her regularly in the shape of a dog named Tom, that he sucked her blood through the teat above her buttocks, and that she told no one of these encounters because he threatened to rip her to pieces. Ironically, Sawyer admitted to the charges of which she was acquitted but denied causing Ratcleife's death. She was hanged at Tyburn on April 19.

IMPACT

Poets William Rowley, Thomas Dekker, and John Ford dramatized Elizabeth Sawyer's interactions with neighbors, diabolical encounters, and arrest and conviction in *The Witch of Edmonton* (1621), staged not long after her death. In this play, Sawyer is portrayed sympathetically as a victim not only of the devil but also of social prejudice because of her poverty, deformity, old age, and lack of education. While Goodcole's account of Sawyer's life and death is illustrative of the witch-trial literature that proliferated during the witch craze, Sawyer's complex portrayal in *The Witch of Edmonton* reflects the vigorous debate over witchcraft in the period, a subject addressed by James Stewart, later King James I, in *Daemonologie* (1597).

FURTHER READING

Gibson, Marion. "Elizabeth Sawyer." *Oxford Dictionary of National Biography*. Oxford, England: Oxford University Press, 2004. Gibson describes Sawyer's arrest, trial, and execution and discusses her treatment in contemporary works.

_____, ed. *Early Modern Witches: Witchcraft Cases in Contemporary Writing*. London: Routledge, 2000. Goodcole's pamphlet is reproduced in this collection, prefaced by an introduction that situates it in its cultural context.

Rowley, William, Thomas Dekker, and John Ford. *The Witch of Edmonton*. Edited by Peter Corbin and Douglas Sedge. Manchester, England: Manchester University Press, 1999. This edition of the play includes a detailed introduction that considers Sawyer as a figure through which early modern notions of witchcraft are explored and interrogated.

—*Holly Faith Nelson*

SEE ALSO: Tamsin Blight; Mary Butters; Margaret Jones; Florence Newton; Dolly Pentreath; Mother Shipton.

BALDUR VON SCHIRACH
Head of the Hitler Youth and military governor of Vienna (1940-1945)

BORN: March 9, 1907; Weimar, Germany
DIED: August 8, 1974; Kröv-an-der-Mosel, Germany
ALSO KNOWN AS: Baldur Benedikt von Schirach (full name)
MAJOR OFFENSE: Crimes against humanity, specifically sending some sixty thousand people to labor camps, death camps, and ghettos
ACTIVE: December, 1940-May 8, 1945
LOCALE: Vienna, Austria
SENTENCE: Twenty years' imprisonment

EARLY LIFE

Baldur von Schirach (BAHL-duhr fahn SHEE-rakh) was born on March 9, 1907, in Weimar, Germany, to the aristocratic Karl von Schirach, director of the Imperial Theater in Weimar, and his American wife, Emma. When he was ten years old, Baldur joined a military cadet group with the intention of joining the army and fighting in World War I. By 1924 he was studying Germanic art and folklore in Munich, and in that year he became an early member of the Nationalsozialistische Deutsche Arbeiterpartei, or Nazi Party. His anti-Semitism had been stoked by reading works defaming Jews by Henry Ford and Houston Stewart Chamberlain.

POLITICAL CAREER

Quickly gaining the confidence of party leader Adolf Hitler, in 1929 Schirach was named leader of the National Socialist Students' Union, headquartered in Munich. His enthusiasm for Hitler was unbounded, and this zeal, wedded to a natural ability to organize young people, resulted in tremendous success. In 1931 Hitler named Schirach youth leader for the Nazi Party, and in 1933 leader of the youth in the German Reich, or head of the Hitler Youth (Hitler Jugend) organization. In these roles Schirach helped eliminate any rival youth groups, consolidating them all under the Nazi banner. By 1936, the Hitler Youth numbered more than six million young men and women who bonded amid a heady mix of militant Nazi racism and anti-Semitism, romanticized German folklore and history, outright paganism, and Hitler worship.

Through Schirach's leadership of the organization and his propagandistic writings, he played a key role in shaping the new Nazi "superman" in the months leading to World War II. After war broke out, many of the Hitler Youth joined the armed forces, and Schirach was no exception. Under some pressure from members of Hitler's inner circle, Schirach surrendered leadership of the Hitler Youth and joined the army in December, 1939. He served in the infantry regiment Grossdeutschland, attaining the rank of lieutenant. He won an Iron Cross for his staff service in the French campaign in the spring of 1940.

In August, 1940, Hitler appointed Schirach Gauleiter (governor) of Vienna and the surrounding Austrian vicinity. In this position Schirach ran the city, encouraging a seamless continuity of musical and theatrical performances while overseeing the deportation of the city's Jews in fetid cattle cars bound for labor camps and the Auschwitz and Buchenwald concentration camps. Though an anti-Semite, Schirach is on record as having sought to mitigate the position of Jews in Vienna and slow down the pace of the deportations. Nevertheless, his claim that he knew nothing of the conditions or activities at the Nazi death camps is only slightly plausible, as he is known to have attended at least one major meeting at which the so-called final solution was discussed openly. Schirach outspokenly and publicly favored a "Jew-free" Western Europe and is said to have offered a Jew-free Vienna to the führer.

As Gauleiter, Schirach was clearly responsible for the rounding up, dispossessing, and deportation of Vienna's remaining Jews, a number estimated at around sixty thousand by the war's end. Though he arranged for the military defense of Vienna as Soviet troops approached in the spring of 1945, he simply walked away from the city with other refugees, hiding out and finally surrendering to American troops. Schirach was taken to Nuremberg for trial.

LEGAL ACTION AND OUTCOME

Schirach was indicted at the Nuremberg Trials on counts of conspiracy to wage aggressive war and crimes against humanity. The first count was based upon his activity in preparing German youth for offensive armed struggle. He was found not guilty because the court could not connect him directly to the military planning of the offensive campaigns. The second count reflected his duties as Gauleiter, specifically his anti-Jewish activities and role in the deportations. The tribunal recognized that Schirach had not initiated the policy—indeed, much of the Viennese Jewish community had been deported before his arrival—but noted that he had done little to oppose or mitigate its application. Though he denied having known about the extermination of those he sent away, external reports chronicling such activities were found in his office. He was found guilty and sentenced to twenty years' imprisonment, which he served in Spandau Prison. He was released in September, 1966. He lived quietly in southern Germany and died in August, 1974.

IMPACT

Through the international Nuremberg Trials, the victorious Allies, and the rest of the world by extension, sought to make the Nazi leaders accountable for their terrible activities and pay for them, usually with their lives. Baldur von Schirach's role in the Nazi Holocaust was by no means minor, but the court decided that a fair reading of the evidence warranted a lesser sentence than execution. Denunciations of Hitler, the man they had once adored, may have paved the way for the leniency shown Schirach and also Reichminister Albert Speer.

FURTHER READING

Gilbert, G. M. *Nuremberg Diary*. New York: Da Capo Press, 1995. Originally written shortly after the war crime trials, these observations and records of conversations with Schirach (and others) provide a powerful insight into Schirach's mind.

Kater, Michael. *Hitler Youth*. Cambridge, Mass.: Harvard University Press, 2004. Detailed study of the organization for indoctrinating German youth with Nazi values that was founded and run by Schirach.

Overy, Richard. *Interrogations: The Nazi Elite in Allied Hands, 1945*. New York: Penguin Books, 2002. Transcripts of formal interrogations with Schirach and others during the course of the Nuremberg Trials.

Schneider, Gertrude. *Exile and Destruction: The Fate of Austrian Jews, 1938-1945*. New York: Praeger, 1995. Both a personal and historical discussion of the Holocaust in Austria and the roles that Schirach played.

—*Joseph P. Byrne*

SEE ALSO: Houston Stewart Chamberlain; Adolf Hitler; Albert Speer; Julius Streicher.

DUTCH SCHULTZ
American gangster

BORN: August 6, 1902; Bronx, New York
DIED: October 24, 1935; Newark, New Jersey
ALSO KNOWN AS: Arthur Simon Flegenheimer (birth name); the Dutchman; Charles Harman
CAUSE OF NOTORIETY: Despite a mobster career filled with murder, bootlegging, extortion, tax evasion, and gambling, Schultz evaded the law or was acquitted of charges; he served only one brief prison sentence—fifteen months for burglary.
ACTIVE: 1919-1935
LOCALE: New York and New Jersey

EARLY LIFE

Dutch Schultz (shuhlts) was born Arthur Flegenheimer and was a young street tough in the Bronx. Flegenheimer's parents were German-Jewish immigrants; his partner in crime, Joey Noe, was Irish American. Noe and Schultz made money and built their reputations by transporting beer from New Jersey into Manhattan during Prohibition. In 1928, Noe and Flegenheimer set up Bronx speakeasies and supplied beer to Manhattan clubs. They kidnapped competitor Joe Rock, hung him by his thumbs, beat him, and allegedly wrapped a bandage infected with gonorrhea around his eyes. Rock went blind, and the young men's reputation as ruthless gangsters was solidified. Flegenheimer soon began calling himself "Dutch Schultz" after a legendary New York street fighter from the nineteenth century.

CRIMINAL CAREER

Schultz became a gang boss as a result of his focused aggression and his ability to organize. However, when he and Noe expanded their bootlegging operations into midtown Manhattan, the move stirred up trouble with their former associate Jack "Legs" Diamond; Diamond subsequently murdered Noe in 1928. Schultz then hired gangsters Bo and George Weinberg and brothers Vincent "Mad Dog" and Peter Coll as protection and started extorting protection money from restaurants and bars.

Schultz earned public attention in 1931 following the shooting of gangster Charles "Chink" Sherman in a brawl in a speakeasy; he was charged and subsequently acquitted for the crime. Also in 1931, Schultz's men killed Diamond in Albany, New York.

At this time, Vincent Coll then turned on Schultz. Coll was a boyhood friend and a hit man for hire who wanted to be Schultz's partner after Noe's death. Coll sprayed bullets into a speakeasy, wounding five children and killing one. He was acquitted of the crime but was soon arrested again for carrying a concealed weapon. Schultz posted Coll's ten-thousand-dollar bond, but Coll skipped bail and left town. Coll began kidnapping underworld figures and demanded ransom payment from their bosses. Peter Coll was soon gunned down, and Vincent Coll blamed Schultz; in 1932, he killed four of Schultz's deliverymen and went in search of Schultz himself. However, Schultz's gangsters caught Vincent Coll in a telephone booth and murdered him with machine gun fire.

Schultz looked like a gangster, with his broken nose, hooded eyelids, and icy stare. However, he read the works of Charles Dickens and William Shakespeare, rode horses, had a wife and two children, and displayed a rough New York sense of humor in interviews. Such contradictions to his violent profession fascinated the reading public, who

Dutch Schultz. (AP/Wide World Photos)

followed the dramatic saga of American gangsters in daily newspapers. However, this kind of media attention worked adversely for Schultz, who by 1933 had become too high-profile to stay safe. He was charged with tax evasion by prosecutor Thomas Dewey and "hid" from prosecution in plain sight in Manhattan.

Schultz also corrupted police and government officials—notably New York assemblyman Jimmy Hines. Schultz lawyer Dixie Davis made a deal with Dewey to testify against Hines, and Hines went to prison for four years. During this period, he murdered gang member Jules Martin for skimming money. He also took over "policy" in Harlem—penny-ante bets made on three numbers printed in newspapers. Policy became Schultz's most lucrative operation.

LEGAL ACTION AND OUTCOME

In 1934, New York mayor Fiorello Henry La Guardia and the federal government finally agreed to pursue Schultz in earnest and arrest him; they succeeded in their task. The Dutchman, as bribery, offered $100,000 if tax charges were dropped, but his trial proceeded as planned in Syracuse, New York. He gave interviews and passed out money during the court proceedings. The first trial resulted in a hung jury; the second, in Malone, New York, resulted in acquittal.

In 1935, the government charged Schultz with restaurant extortion. Schultz moved to New Jersey and asked his crime syndicate to pursue the assassination of Dewey. The syndicate decided to kill Schultz instead, whom they viewed as unstable and as someone with profitable businesses to absorb. Murder, Inc. (so called by the press), a syndicate specializing in contract killing, got the job.

Schultz and three gang members were fatally shot in the Palace Chop House in Newark, New Jersey, at about 10:15 P.M., on October 23, 1935. Charles Workman and Mendy Weiss entered the restaurant and walked to a back table, where Schultz's gangsters hovered over ledger sheets, and opened fire. Workman shot Schultz in the side with a .45 pistol while Schultz was in the bathroom. Schultz died from an infection because the bullet nicked his stomach. He asked for a priest and was baptized a Roman Catholic. His feverish ravings, which later became famous, were jotted down by a police stenographer. He died on October 24, 1935.

IMPACT

The New York mob, organized by Charles "Lucky" Luciano in 1929, was strong enough by 1935 to eliminate independent gangsters such as Schultz. The Dutchman's scams were absorbed by Luciano's syndicate after his death, giving it control of restaurant unions and policy.

Thomas Dewey estimated that the Schultz gang made twenty million dollars a year from various schemes. Dewey subsequently was elected governor of New York for three terms (1943-1955) and was the Republican candidate for president twice. Schultz was immortalized in popular culture through several films—including *The Cotton Club* (1984), which cast James Remar as a homicidal Schultz, and *Billy Bathgate* (1991), based on a 1989 novel by E. L. Doctorow and starring Dustin Hoffman as the Dutchman. Schultz was typically portrayed as the archetypal gangster: brutish, undereducated, and spontaneously violent—characteristics that the real Schultz masked when he wished.

FURTHER READING

Charyn, Jerome. *Gangsters and Gold Diggers: Old New York, the Jazz Age, and the Birth of Broadway.* New York: Four Walls Eight Windows, 2005. Includes material on Schultz and other Roaring Twenties personalities.

Downey, Patrick. *Gangster City: The History of the New York Underworld, 1900-1935.* Fort Lee, N.J.: Barricade Books, 2004. An accurate record of criminal gangs at war during the 1920's and 1930's.

Sann, Paul. *Kill the Dutchman.* New Rochelle, N.Y.: Arlington, 1971. Written by newspaper reporter Sann, who interviewed persons who knew Schultz during his gangster career, the book is excellent for the details it provides on Schultz's life; other biographies of Schultz borrow heavily from it.

—*Jim Pauff*

SEE ALSO: Vincent Coll; Legs Diamond; Lucky Luciano; Arnold Rothstein.

ASSATA OLUGBALA SHAKUR
Convicted murderer and political exile

BORN: July 16, 1947; New York, New York
ALSO KNOWN AS: JoAnne Deborah Byron (birth name); JoAnne Deborah Chesimard; Jo-Ann Chesimard, Joanne Debra Chesimard; Joanne Byron; Barbara Odoms; Joan Davis; Justine Henderson; Mary Davis; Pat Chesimard; Joanne D. Byron; Joanne Davis; Joann Debra Byron Chesimard; Joanne Deborah Byron Chesimard; Joan Chesimard; Ches Chesimard; Sister-Love Chesimard; Josephine Henderson; Carolyn Johnson; Carol Brown; "Ches"
MAJOR OFFENSE: Murder
ACTIVE: May 2, 1973
LOCALE: New Jersey Turnpike
SENTENCE: Life in prison plus twenty-six to thirty-three years; escaped after two years

EARLY LIFE

Assata Olugbala Shakur (ah-SAH-tah o-LUHG-bah-lah shah-KEWR) was born JoAnne Deborah Byron in New York, New York, and lived with her mother, aunt, and grandparents. In 1950, she moved with her grandparents to Wilmington, North Carolina, where she worked at their restaurant, attended a segregated school, and acquired a strong sense of pride from her entrepreneurial elders. Before entering the third grade, Shakur moved back to New York to live with her mother and new step-father. At age seventeen, after her mother's second divorce, Shakur dropped out of high school and left home. In the late 1960's, after attending community college, she became politically active, married, and became involved in Black Panther Party (BPP) and the Black Liberation Army (BLA).

CRIMINAL CAREER

Shakur became one of the many political activists who were watched by the counterintelligence unit of the Federal Bureau of Investigation (FBI). From 1971 to 1973 she was charged with robbery, kidnapping, murder, and attempted murder and became a fugitive. On May 2, 1973, she and two of her close friends, Sundiata Acoli and Zayd Malik Shakur, were stopped on the New Jersey Turnpike. State Trooper James Harper cited a broken taillight as grounds for their detention and called in troopers Robert Palenchar and Werner Foerster for backup. During roadside questioning, a gunfight began. Malik Shakur and Officer Foerster were killed, while Assata Shakur and Harper were wounded. Assata Shakur was shot once in the left shoulder and once in the back, leaving her with a shattered clavicle and a bullet lodged near her heart. Although the events of that evening would remain in dispute, Shakur said that Harper shot her while she held her hands in the air, and that she was thus too incapacitated to return fire.

LEGAL ACTION AND OUTCOME

Before her conviction in 1977, all the earlier charges against Shakur either were dismissed or resulted in acquittals. After giving birth to her daughter, Kakuya, Shakur was convicted as an accomplice in the murder of State Trooper Foerster and was sentenced to life in prison plus twenty-six to thirty-three years.

There was no hard evidence to support her conviction. Her fingers were clean of gun residue, and no prints of hers were found on the murder weapons. Star witness Harper admitted to perjury in his grand jury testimony that had cited Shakur as one of the shooters. Nonetheless, Shakur was convicted of murder by an all-white jury. In 1979, she escaped from Clinton Correctional Facility and remained in hiding until 1984, when she appeared in Cuba, having been granted political asylum by Fidel Castro.

IMPACT

As late as 2006, Assata Olugbala Shakur remained on the FBI and the state of New Jersey's "Most Wanted" lists. In 1998, the U.S. House of Representatives passed Resolution 254, which called for the immediate extradition of Shakur from Cuba in order to "normalize" Cuban-American relations. On May 2, 2005, the state of New Jersey offered a one-million-dollar reward for the capture of Shakur, while the federal government put her on a domestic terror watch list and furthered its pressure on Castro for extradition. Political activist groups orchestrated several campaigns to protect Shakur's right to asylum, and many of her supporters maintain that she was framed for the murder of Harper. Regardless of her guilt, she became a key voice in the global fight to free political prisoners.

FURTHER READING

Shakur, Assata. *Assata: An Autobiography*. 1987. Reprint. Chicago: L. Hill Books, 2001. Shakur's autobiography vividly describes her childhood, activism, imprisonment, and trial. Incorporating her poetry and introduced by her lawyer, Lennox S. Hinds, *Assata* provides a captivating, if not idealistic, look into the makings of a political revolutionary.

_____. "Assata Shakur: Profiled and on the Run." *The New Crisis* 107, no. 6 (2000). Interview by Ida E. Lewis. Shakur attempts to counter attempts by the U.S. government and mass media to criminalize her.

_____. "Prisoner in Paradise." *Essence* 28, no. 2 (1997): 72-76. Interview by Evelyn C. White. Shakur discusses her political exile in Cuba, family matters, continued activism, and future plans.

—*Lindsay M. Christopher*

SEE ALSO: Fidel Castro; Huey Newton.

CLAY SHAW

New Orleans businessman

BORN: March 17, 1913; Kentwood, Louisiana
DIED: August 14, 1974; New Orleans, Louisiana
ALSO KNOWN AS: Clay Bertrand; Clay Laverne Shaw (full name)
CAUSE OF NOTORIETY: Shaw was the only man to be tried for conspiracy in the assassination of President John F. Kennedy. Found innocent, he was acquitted of these charges and was later revealed to be a CIA operative.
ACTIVE: 1963-1967
LOCALE: New Orleans, Louisiana, and Dallas, Texas

EARLY LIFE

Clay Laverne Shaw (shah) was born in Kentwood, Louisiana, on March 17, 1913. When he was five years old, Shaw, an only child, moved with his parents, Glaris and Alice, to New Orleans. Shaw was a student in the New Orleans public school system and graduated from Warren Easton High School in 1928. Shaw's first love was writing, and during or just after high school he wrote or coauthored several plays. However, with the need for an income, Shaw went to work for the Western Union telegraph company after high school. In 1935, he was transferred to the company's New York City offices. While in New York, Shaw took courses at Columbia University and was eventually promoted to district manager, overseeing around forty city branch offices. Soon, however, he returned to his passion, writing. He left Western Union and accepted a position as a public relations and advertising writer for the Lee-Keedick Lecture Bureau.

In 1942, like many of his generation, Shaw enlisted in the U.S. Army to serve in World War II. He was assigned as a private in the Medical Corps and trained in the officers' candidate school in Abilene, Kansas. He received his commission as a second lieutenant and left for England and the war. After his arrival in England, Shaw rose quickly through the ranks and soon became deputy chief to General Charles Thrasher, the commanding officer of U.S. forces in the southern half of England. Shaw continued to serve with General Thrasher in France and then in Belgium. In 1946, the time of Shaw's honorable discharge, he had attained the rank of major and received decorations from three nations: Belgium, France, and the United States.

ROLE IN THE KENNEDY ASSASSINATION

Upon his return from World War II, Shaw was something of a local hero and celebrity in his New Orleans home. This fact, coupled with the organizational and management skills he had learned stockpiling supplies in the Army, led a group of prominent businessmen to tap Shaw to assist in creating a center for international trade in New Orleans. Shaw would become managing director of the International Trade Mart.

By the time of President John F. Kennedy's assassination in November, 1963, Shaw was a wealthy and respected businessman in Louisiana. In fact, he had attained such a level of social status that he was afforded the opportunity to meet President Kennedy: Shaw had been invited by a friend, De Lesseps "Chep" Morrison, to Kennedy's swearing-in ceremony in Washington, D.C.; he later recalled Shaw referring to Kennedy as "a splendid president." Not three years later, on November 22, 1963, on a sunny afternoon in Dallas, Kennedy was assassinated while traveling in his motorcade through Dealey Plaza.

WARREN COMMISSION HEARINGS

In 1967, in a surprise to the New Orleans community, District Attorney Jim Garrison arrested Shaw and charged him with being part of a conspiracy to assassinate Kennedy. Through the Warren Commission hearings, the name Clay Bertrand repeatedly arose. An attorney named Dean Adams Andrews, Jr., testified that Bertrand had asked him to defend Lee Harvey Oswald, who had been arraigned for the assassination before he was shot dead by Jack Ruby on November 24, 1963. Andrews further described Bertrand as a bisexual man who had brought gay clients to him in the past. Garrison believed Shaw and Bertrand to be the same person. It had long been rumored that Shaw was homosexual and that he was an operative for the Central Intelligence Agency (CIA). Shaw's regular international travel with the International Trade Mart did not help to dispel such rumors.

During the trial, a man named Perry Russo testified that he had seen Shaw with both Oswald and David Ferrie, the latter a CIA operative and also a prominent figure in the Warren Commission Report. Russo also testified that he had heard Smith and Ferrie discussing Kennedy's assassination and noting that it would be blamed on Cuban dictator Fidel Castro. Russo's testimony received criticism when it was discovered that he had been given Pentothal (thiopental, a barbiturate used as a truth serum) before he was interviewed by the prosecution. Shaw was found not guilty in the conspiracy to assassinate Kennedy.

Shaw died in 1974 at the age of sixty-one from lung cancer. Five years later, in 1979, Richard Helms, former director of the CIA, testified under oath that Shaw had, in fact, been a contract agent for the CIA.

IMPACT

Perhaps no event has had as much impact on the American public as the assassination of President Kennedy. The question of who killed the president is passed from generation to generation and is one that, it seems, may never be answered with absolute certainty to the public's satisfaction. Garrison's trial of Clay Shaw, along with Helms's later admission that Shaw had worked for the CIA, served to further the belief held by many Americans that President Kennedy was the victim of an assassination conspiracy. The U.S. Congress Select Committee on Assassinations also found that "President John F. Kennedy was probably assassinated as a result of a conspiracy." Several decades later, a 1991 feature film directed by Oliver Stone, *JFK*, and based on Garrison's 1988 book, fanned the flames of conspiracy theorists.

FURTHER READING

Benson, Michael. *Who's Who in the JFK Assassination: An A-to-Z Encyclopedia.* New York: Kensington, 1992. An enclyclopedic account of more than fourteen hundred individuals linked to Kennedy's assassination and the investigation that followed. The book also explores the differing theories on the assassination.

Garrison, Jim. *On the Trail of the Assassins.* New York: Sheridan Square Press, 1988 This is Garrison's account of his investigation into the assassination of Kennedy. His book traces his growing distrust of the Warren Commission's findings, his individual investigation into the possible connections in the New Orleans area, and his eventual conclusion that the assassination was a conspiracy involving, among others, Shaw.

Posner, G. L. *Case Closed: Lee Harvey Oswald and the Assassination of JFK*. New York: Anchor Books, 2003. Posner writes one of the few books that supports the notion that Oswald was the lone assassin of Kennedy and that there was no conspiracy involved in the killing. In doing so, the author discusses and attempts to dismiss most of the predominant conspiracy theories on the subject.

—Ted Shields

SEE ALSO: Carlos Marcello; Lee Harvey Oswald; Jack Ruby.

JACK SHEPPARD
English thief

BORN: 1702; Spitalfields, London, England
DIED: November 16, 1724; Tyburn, London, England
ALSO KNOWN AS: Jack the Lad; Gentleman Jack; John Sheppard (full name)
MAJOR OFFENSES: Theft and jailbreaking
ACTIVE: Early 1720's
LOCALE: London
SENTENCE: Death by hanging

EARLY LIFE
Before turning to a brief life of crime, Jack Sheppard (SHEHP-uhrd), whose father had died when he and his brother Thomas were very young, was apprenticed to a carpenter, acquiring an expertise in the handling of tools that presumably served him well when he turned into a housebreaker. He was allegedly honest until he began associating with Elizabeth Lyon (also known as Edgeworth Bess), a woman who received stolen goods and later professed to be Sheppard's wife. Sheppard started his career modestly, stealing from houses in which his master was commissioned to carry out repairs. However, he soon progressed to bolder adventures in association with his brother and Bess following his dismissal from his apprenticeship. Sheppard apparently had a speech impediment of some sort and was slight of stature; the notice issued after his famous jailbreak described him as being five feet, four inches in height and very slender.

CRIMINAL CAREER
Sheppard appears to have been an exceedingly incompetent criminal. He owed his eventual arrest to his association with the corrupt magistrate and "thief-taker" Jonathan Wild, whose duplicity became legendary and whose own fall from grace was accomplished within three months of Sheppard's execution. When Wild turned him in, Sheppard gave information against two of his accomplices: his brother Thomas, who was transported to jail, and Joseph Blake (also known as Blueskin), who staked his own claim to fame by attempting to murder Wild in the yard of Old Bailey, London's criminal court.

Although his thefts were relatively minor, Sheppard gained fame—largely by virtue of reports in the *Daily Journal* and other newspapers—because of his two escapes from London's Newgate Prison, although he was swiftly recaptured on each occasion. His speech impediment presumably made it difficult for him to remain unrecognized.

Sheppard's first escape was on August 30, 1724, from the hold in Newgate Prison, where prisoners awaiting execution were held. Bess paid him back for securing her release from Saint Giles's by smuggling in some tools, which Sheppard used to demolish the lock on the hatch in the hold's ceiling. Then, Bess and a female accomplice smuggled Sheppard, clad in a nightgown, past the turnkeys. Once Sheppard escaped, however, he did not seem to have exercised any discretion: He immediately committed further burglaries.

Sheppard's second escape, on October 16, 1724, seemed far more remarkable, since he had been shackled to the floor of a room in Newgate Prison. The fetters on his wrists had not been designed to hold such a thin man, and Sheppard slipped his hands free. He climbed up a chimney to the room above and removed an iron bar en route, which served him as a tool thereafter. Having broken the lock of the upper room, Sheppard made his way to the chapel and broke through another series of doors with the aid of his improvised crowbar and a nail that he had picked up along the way. Finally gaining access to a roof, Sheppard allegedly returned to his cell to fetch his blanket to use as a means to lower himself and escape. Although this second escape made him famous, Sheppard remained at liberty only for a fortnight. He was recaptured shortly after robbing a pawnbroker's shop, where he furnished himself with a sword that he was too drunk to use when he was rearrested.

Two earlier jailbreaking escapades were subsequently

added to the list of Sheppard's notorious acts—the first involved breaking Edgeworth Bess out of Saint Giles's Round House; the second, an alleged escape from another prison. No details of Bess's release or Sheppard's escape from the prison are reliably recorded, although subsequent literary accounts filled in the gaps with various confabulations.

LEGAL ACTION AND OUTCOME

The crowds flocked to see Sheppard when he was returned to Newgate Prison for the third time. He was shackled to the floor of the condemned hold, watched night and day. He had to be tried again in order to prove that he was the same man who had previously been condemned, but the legal proceedings were hurried. A large crowd turned out to see him hanged on November 16, 1724; it rioted afterward and carried Sheppard's body away after smashing the cart of the undertaker who had come to bury him. The body was later recovered and interred at St Martin's-in-the-Fields.

IMPACT

Jack Sheppard's legacy as a notorious thief and remarkable jailbreaker began even before his death. A pamphlet containing an account of his career was published before his execution, on November 4, and another—purportedly written by Sheppard himself—immediately afterward. Both were reprinted for more than a century. On December 5, within three weeks of the execution, a one-act farce titled *Harlequin Sheppard* opened at the Drury Lane Theatre; it was soon followed by a three-act version called *The Prison-Breaker*. The fact that Sheppard was a petty thief, of no distinction whatsoever, was quickly forgotten, and he became the most legendary bandit of his era. Although he bore little resemblance to the character of the dashing highwayman Macheath in John Gay's *The Beggar's Opera* (pr., pb. 1728), reports about Sheppard's career undoubtedly encouraged the composition of that work. Sheppard became the hero of several more plays and a notable novel by William Harrison Ainsworth, *Jack Sheppard* (1839), in which the famous escape was lavishly illustrated by a series of engravings by George Cruikshank. Sheppard was also featured in the 1969 comedy film *Where's Jack?*, in which he was played by Tommy Steele.

FURTHER READING

Ainsworth, William Harrison. *Jack Sheppard: A Romance.* London: Richard Bentley, 1839. A novel originally serialized in Bentley's *Miscellany*. The accounts by Ainsworth were very influential in maintaining Sheppard's legend. Includes a highly elaborate (and, in most editions, copiously illustrated) account of the hero's second escape from Newgate, but the account of the Sheppard's early life is entirely imaginary.

Buckstone, John Baldwin. *Jack Sheppard: A Drama in Four Acts.* London: Webster, 1839. One of many theatrical melodramas based on Sheppard's story and more elaborate than most; it is closely related to Ainsworth's novel and might be regarded as a dramatic version of it.

Hibbert, Christopher. *The Road to Tyburn: The Story of Jack Sheppard and the Eighteenth Century Underworld.* New York: Longmans, Green, 1957. A more modern telling of the Sheppard legend, placing it in context with other crimes and criminals of the era.

The History of Jack Sheppard: His Wonderful Exploits and Escapes. London: James Cochrane, 1839. A Victorian update of the story told in two 1724 pamphlets, which further exaggerated the legend and maintained its currency.

The History of the Surprising Life and Adventures of John Sheppard. London: John Thift, 1724. The first of two pamphlets that gave rise to Sheppard's legend. It was issued in advance of Sheppard's execution.

A Narrative of All the Robberies and Escape of John Sheppard. London: John Applebee, 1724. This second pamphlet claimed that its text was handed to the publisher by Sheppard himself as he was being transported to Tyburn—a claim endorsed by the *Daily Record* but likely untrue.

—*Brian Stableford*

SEE ALSO: William Brodie; Moll Cutpurse; Charles Peace; Rob Roy; Dick Turpin; Jonathan Wild.

SAM SHEPPARD
Surgeon and professional wrestler

BORN: December 29, 1923; Cleveland, Ohio
DIED: April 6, 1970; Columbus, Ohio
ALSO KNOWN AS: Samuel Holmes Sheppard (full name)
CAUSE OF NOTORIETY: Sheppard was convicted of the 1954 murder of his pregnant wife, Marilyn Reese. The conviction was later overturned by the U.S. Supreme Court because of the proliferation of media coverage of the case.
ACTIVE: 1954-1966
LOCALE: Cleveland, Ohio

EARLY LIFE
Samuel Holmes Sheppard (SHEHP-puhrd) and Marilyn Reese were high school sweethearts at Cleveland Heights High School in Cleveland, Ohio. They had originally met at Roosevelt Junior High School in Cleveland. Sheppard played high school football and basketball and ran track. After high school, Sheppard moved to Los Angeles and attended the Los Angeles College of Osteopathic Physicians and Surgeons. While in Los Angeles, he asked Marilyn to come and join him; they were married in February, 1945, and had a son, Samuel Reese Sheppard. After Sheppard's graduation from college, the young couple returned to Cleveland.

MARILYN'S MURDER
At the time that his thirty-one-year-old pregnant wife was slain, thirty-year-old Sheppard was a prominent osteopathic surgeon. He socialized with the mayor and members of the Cleveland Browns. He owned a Jaguar automobile and was a pioneer of waterskiing. On July 4, 1954, Marilyn was found brutally murdered, and Sheppard was tried for her murder. Sheppard maintained his innocence, claiming he had wrestled with Marilyn's murderer, a bushy-haired stranger, and was knocked unconscious.

LEGAL ACTION AND OUTCOME
Sheppard was arrested on charges of killing his wife. During the trial, it was revealed that Sheppard had had an extramarital affair with Susan Hayes, a nurse at the hospital where he was employed. The defense called eighteen character witnesses for Sheppard and two witnesses who said that they had seen a bushy-haired man near the Sheppard home the day of the murder. The defense argued that the crime scene was extremely bloody, and ex-

cept for a small spot on his trousers, Sheppard had no blood on him.

The jury convicted Sheppard of second-degree murder, and he was sentenced to life in prison. The case drew public interest, and special seating for reporters and columnists was installed in the courtroom. Each day, the local newspapers published sensational stories regarding the murder. Sheppard's attorney filed several motions to have the trial moved to a different county, but each was denied. Sheppard's second-degree murder conviction was affirmed on appeal. Sheppard sought review, arguing that the trial court had erred in refusing to grant a change of venue because of the widespread publicity and that the fact that jurors communicated by telephone with their families during deliberations required reversal.

After Sheppard had been confined for almost ten years, the U.S. Supreme Court, in *Sheppard v. Maxwell*, granted Sheppard's petition for release. Defense attorney F. Lee Bailey, whose later fame was based partially on the result of this case, argued on Sheppard's behalf before the Court. The Court concluded that Sheppard had not received a fair trial consistent with the due process clause of the Fourteenth Amendment. It also held that the trial court judge had not fulfilled his duty to protect Sheppard from the inherently prejudicial publicity that saturated the community and had failed to control disruptive influences in the courtroom. Sheppard was retried in 1966 and was acquitted.

Only three days after his release, Sheppard married Ariane Tebbenjohanns, a German divorcée who had corresponded with him during his time in prison. They were later divorced. Because he no longer had a license to practice medicine, he became a professional wrestler. He made his wrestling debut at the Akron Armory in Ohio, teaming with wrestler Hoss Strickland; Sheppard then married (and later divorced) Strickland's daughter. Sheppard's nickname as a wrestler was the Killer. At the age of forty-six, Sheppard died of liver disease.

IMPACT
In the years following Sam Sheppard's death, his son, Samuel Reese Sheppard, worked to clear his father's name in the crime. In 1999, he filed a wrongful imprisonment civil suit against the state of Ohio. At the civil trial, the state argued that Sheppard had not welcomed the news that his wife was pregnant and that her murder was a textbook domestic homicide. The state also questioned

SHEPPARD'S POLICE STATEMENT

On July 10, 1954, Sam Sheppard gave a statement to Cuyahoga County Sheriff's Office detectives regarding the events of July 4. After noting that he had had a long day and spent the evening at his home having dinner with his wife and another couple, Sheppard claimed that he had fallen asleep in front of the television:

I recall very hazily, my wife [Marilyn] partially awoke me in some manner and I think she notified me that she was going to bed.

I eventually continued to sleep. The next thing I recall was hearing [Marilyn] cry out or scream. At this time I was on the couch. I think that she cried or screamed my name once or twice, during which time I ran upstairs, thinking that she might be having a reaction similar to convulsions that she had had in the early days of her pregnancy. I charged into our room and saw a form with a light garment, I believe.

At the same time grappling with something or someone. During this short period I could hear loud moans or groaning sounds and noises. I was struck down. It seems like I was hit from behind somehow but had I grappled this individual from in front or generally in front of me. I was apparently knocked out. The next thing I know I was gathering my senses while coming to a sitting position next to the bed, my feet toward the hallway.

In the dim light I began to come to my senses and recognized a slight reflection on a badge that I have on my wallet. I picked up the wallet and while putting it in my pocket, came to the realization that I had been struck and something was wrong. I looked at my wife, I believe I took her pulse and felt that she was gone. . . . I went down stairs as rapidly as I could, coming down the west division of the steps, I rounded the L of the living room and went toward the dining table situated on the East wall of the long front room on the lake side. I then saw a form progressing rapidly somewhere between the front door toward the lake and the screen door, or possibly slightly beyond the screen door. I pursued this form through the front door, over the porch and out the screen door. All of the doors were evidently open, down the steps to the beach house landing and then on down the steps to the beach, where I lunged or jumped and grappled him in sane manner from the back, either body or leg, it was something solid. However, I am not sure. . . . I had the feeling of twisting or choking and this terminated my consciousness.

The next thing I know I came to a very groggy recollection of being at the water's edge on my face, being wallowed back and forth by the waves. My head was toward the bank, my legs and feet were toward the water. I staggered to my feet and came slowly to some sort of sense. I don't know how long it took but I staggered up the stairs toward the house and at some time came to the realization that something was wrong and that my wife had been injured. I went back upstairs and looked at my wife and felt her and checked for a pulse on her neck and determined or thought that she was Gone. I became or thought that I was disoriented and the victim of a bizarre dream and I believe I paced in and out of the room and possibly into one of the other rooms. I may have reexamined her, finally realizing that this was true. I went downstairs; I believe I went through the kitchen into my study, searching for a name, a number or what to do. . . .

---

why Sheppard had not called out for help and why he had neatly folded his jacket on the daybed on which he said he had fallen asleep. Evidence was also presented that indicated that the family dog did bark on the night of the murder, contrary to earlier reports. After ten weeks of trial and seventy-six witnesses, the eight-person civil jury returned a unanimous verdict that Samuel Reese Sheppard had failed to prove that his father had been wrongly imprisoned. However, in 2002, a court of appeals ruled that the younger Sheppard's case should not have gone to jury since a wrongful imprisonment claim could be made only by the person imprisoned—in this case, the elder Sheppard—and not by a family member. Later that year, the Ohio Supreme Court affirmed this decision.

A 1975 made-for-television film titled *Guilty or Innocent: The Sam Sheppard Murder Case* starred George Peppard as Sheppard. His case inspired a successful television series, *The Fugitive*, that ran between 1963 and 1967; in 1993, the series was used as the basis for a feature film of the same name starring Harrison Ford.

FURTHER READING

DeSario, Jack P., and William D. Mason. *Dr. Sam Sheppard on Trial: The Prosecutors and the Marilyn Sheppard Murder.* Kent, Ohio: Kent State University Press, 2003. A discussion of how the prosecutors argued the case and their involvement with the media.

Entin, Jonathan L. "Being the Government Means (Almost) Never Having to Say You're Sorry: The Sam Sheppard Case and the Meaning of Wrongful Imprisonment." *Akron Law Review* 38, no. 139 (2005). The article discusses whether Sam Sheppard was wrongly convicted for killing his wife.

Neff, James. *Wrong Man: The Final Verdict in the Dr. Sheppard Murder Case*. New York: Random House, 2002. Using interviews and case documents, Neff chronicles the criminal investigation of Sheppard and

discusses the historical shifts in the treatment of suspects following the Sheppard murder case.

—*Cliff Roberson*

SEE ALSO: Seventh Earl of Lucan; Jeffrey MacDonald; Scott Peterson; O. J. Simpson.

SHI HUANGDI
First emperor of China (r. 221-210 B.C.E.)

BORN: 259 B.C.E.; Handan, Zhao, China

DIED: 210 B.C.E.; Shaqiu Prefecture, China

ALSO KNOWN AS: Shih Huang-ti (Wade-Giles); Qin Shi Huangdi (Pinyin); Ch'in Shihn Huang-ti (Wade-Giles); Zheng (Pinyin birth name); Cheng (Wade-Giles birth name)

CAUSE OF NOTORIETY: Shi Huangdi unified China by military conquest, set up a harsh, centralized administration, relied on forced labor for massive public works, burned Confucian books, and had 460 Confucian scholars buried alive.

ACTIVE: 221-210 B.C.E.

LOCALE: China

EARLY LIFE

Shi Huangdi (shih hooahng-dih), who would make himself the first emperor of China, was born in late winter, 259 B.C.E., when China was divided into seven warring states. Named Zheng, he was born in Handan (contemporary Hebei Province), capital of the state of Zhao, where his father, Zichu, a prince of the kingdom of Qin, lived under a hostage exchange agreement. A persistent rumor, discounted by most historians, was that his real father was the wine merchant turned crafty politician Lu Buwei, who promoted Prince Zichu's career. Indeed, Zheng's mother was a former concubine of Lu whom Lu gave to Zheng's father as a gift.

In 250 B.C.E., when Zheng was nine, his father became king of Qin, took the reign name of Zhuang Xiang, and moved with his family to the Qin capital of Xianyang, west of the Yellow River (contemporary Shaanxi Province). When his father died in 246 B.C.E., Zheng was proclaimed king of Qin, but Li Buwei ruled as regent for the thirteen-year-old boy.

POLITICAL CAREER

Aged twenty-one in 238 B.C.E., Zheng assumed personal rule. When he discovered that his mother had a lover,

Lao Ai, who conspired to become king, he executed Lao Ai and his followers and in 237 B.C.E. exiled both his mother and Lu Buwei, who had introduced Lao Ai to her. King Zheng appointed Li Su, his new key adviser, as chief of justice.

Beginning in 236 B.C.E., King Zheng launched a series of wars against the other six Chinese states then in existence. Relying on able generals, intrigues, stratagems,

Shi Huangdi.

bribes, and cruel warfare, Zheng gradually vanquished his enemies. Under his leadership, the Qin army quickly became notorious for cruelty, ruthlessness, and military skill. In 234 B.C.E., reportedly 100,000 enemy prisoners of war were slaughtered by decapitation on Zheng's orders. Internally, Zheng enforced his absolute power by relying on the philosophy of the Legalist scholars, represented by Li Su, who proclaimed that humans were evil and could be controlled only by drastic punishments.

As the kingdom of Qin grew, in 227 B.C.E. a prince of the state of Yen sent the assassin Jing Ke to kidnap or kill Zheng. Making his way into the presence of Zheng, Jing nearly accomplished his goal, chasing Zheng around a pillar until Zheng was able to draw his long sword and defeat Jing, who was put to death.

First Emperor of China

In spite of some military setbacks, by 221 B.C.E. Zheng's army had conquered the last holdout, the state of Qi. At age thirty-eight, Zheng ruled over all of China. He decided to call himself Shi Huangdi, meaning "First August Sovereign Emperor."

Immediately, Shi Huangdi unified his realm. He standardized Chinese script, all weights and measures, currency, and laws. He standardized cart axle gauges, so uniform highways could be built. He abolished all kingdoms, setting up thirty-six provinces. He demilitarized non-Qin troops, melting down their weapons to cast gigantic bells and human figures to adorn his palaces, and ordered 120,000 foreign nobles to move to Xianyang. To execute his massive public works program, which included highways leading from Xianyang to the edges of his realm, Shi Huangdi relied on forced labor. Dissent was punished most commonly by death.

In 200-219, Shi Huangdi set out on his first tour of his new realm. He became obsessed with finding the elixir of immortality and sent thousands of scholars on futile, dangerous search missions. While mountains were dotted with steles celebrating his fame, Shi Huangdi escaped two more assassination attempts. Continuing warfare at the frontiers, in 214 Shi Huangdi ordered work to start on a fortification which in later centuries would become the Great Wall of China.

Disappointed with their astrological forecasts and suspicious of their independent intellectual activities, in 212 Shi Huangdi ordered 460 Confucian scholars buried alive and had all but scientific books burned. He exiled his son Fu-Su, who opposed these measures.

While on an inspection tour, Shi Huangdi fell ill in late summer or early fall of 210 and died in the Shaqiu

palace. Li Su and the eunuch Zhao Gao kept his death a secret until his corpse arrived in Xianyang. They forged his order for Fu-Su to commit suicide and a testament appointing his younger son Hu Hai as second emperor, Er Shi.

Impact

For almost two thousand years, Chinese historians painted an unflattering portrait of the notorious first emperor. They faulted his inability to rule humanely the country he had conquered. Indeed, revolt wiped out Shi Huangdi's family in 206 B.C.E., ushering in the Han Dynasty.

In the twentieth century, under the influence of Mao Zedong, who admired Shi Huangdi for his ruthless unification of China and the persecution of the Confucians, Chinese historiography painted a more favorable picture of the first emperor. His unification of the country and his abolition of all feudal power but his own won praise.

Apart from unifying Chinese culture and society, a feat that survived his dynasty, Shi Huangdi became famous internationally once the huge terra-cotta army of his tomb was discovered in 1974. Thousands of clay soldiers, built to serve him in the afterlife, are considered a cultural treasure of China.

Further Reading

Kern, Martin. *The Stele Inscriptions of Ch'in Shih-huang.* New Haven, Conn.: American Oriental Society, 2000. Presentation and academic analysis of the stone tablets erected to celebrate Shi Huangdi's rule.

Li, Yu-ning, ed. *The First Emperor of China.* White Plains, N.Y.: International Arts and Sciences Press, 1975. Introduction prepares readers for a series of essays by Chinese scholars who evaluate the notorious, disputed legacy of Shi Huangdi. Contains a basic version of Sima Qian's record of the emperor's reign; reprints a Han Dynasty essay condemning him.

Paludan, Ann. *Chronicle of the Chinese Emperors.* London: Thames & Hudson, 1998. Richly illustrated, this work offers a substantial discussion of Shi Huangdi's career and life.

Sima, Qian. *Records of the Grand Historian.* Translated by Burton Watson. Rev. ed. 2 vols. New York: Columbia University Press, 1993. The volume *Qin Dynasty* contains the earliest, detailed record of Shi Huangdi's reign, originally written in China in the first century B.C.E.

—*R. C. Lutz*

See also: Jing Ke.

FUSAKO SHIGENOBU
Leader of the Japanese Red Army

BORN: September 3, 1945; Tokyo, Japan
MAJOR OFFENSES: Kidnapping and attempted murder
ACTIVE: 1971-2005
LOCALE: Japan, the Middle East, South Asia,
   Southeast Asia, and Western Europe
SENTENCE: Twenty years in prison

EARLY LIFE
The father of Fusako Shigenobu (foo-sah-koh shee-geh-noh-boo) was a pharmacist and an ultra-rightist populist activist. Fusako studied in Tokyo public schools. After graduating from high school, she attended Meiji University, working to support herself, and participated in the militant leftist student movement. The early Japanese Red Army (JRA), a paramilitary underground student group that Shigenobu joined, carried out a spectacular plane hijacking in 1970. Internal dissension within the JRA grew thereafter, and Shigenobu left for Beirut in February, 1971, to participate as a JRA member in paramilitary actions led by the Popular Front for the Liberation of Palestine (PFLP).

CRIMINAL CAREER
The JRA group of radical Japanese living overseas, of which Shigenobu was a part, participated in a PFLP armed terrorist attack on the Tel Aviv Lod Airport (now Ben Gurion Airport) on May 30, 1972, resulting in more than twenty dead and eighty wounded. Around this time, Shigenobu married a Palestinian militant and subsequently gave birth to a daughter, Shigenobu Mei. On September 13, 1974, in an action allegedly planned by Shigenobu, the JRA occupied the French embassy in The Hague for two days and took the people there hostage. As a result of these actions, the group obtained the release of a JLA member jailed by the French, Furuya Yutaka, along with $300,000 and a jetliner to take them all back to Beirut.

Other actions involving Shigenobu included a simultaneous takeover of four embassies in Kuala Lumpur, Malaysia, on August 4, 1975; the hijacking of a JAL plane over India on September 28, 1977; a car bomb attack on a U.S. facility in Naples, Italy, on April 14, 1988; and an abortive attempt to blow up a military facility in New Jersey, also on April 14, 1988.

During the 1990's, Shigenobu led a relatively quiet life in the Middle East. She returned to Japan secretly in July, 2000, but was arrested that November. In April, 2001, she disbanded the JRA, calling for continued nonviolent action. Her prison activities included writing and organizing women's prisoners' rights groups.

LEGAL ACTION AND OUTCOME
Shigenobu's trial finally began on September 2, 2005, and concluded on October 31. The prosecution focused on her involvement in the Hague embassy takeover but had difficulty establishing that she was physically present at the various incidents that she was accused of planning. Prosecutors called for life imprisonment, but at sentencing proceedings on February 23, 2006, the presiding judge of the Tokyo District Court, Murakami Hironobu, issued a sentence of twenty years' imprisonment.

IMPACT
Fusako Shigenobu created and led the first, and perhaps the only, Japanese terrorist organization to operate on a worldwide scale; she successfully maintained her position for nearly thirty years. She also began a writing career as early as 1974, publishing both political books and personal accounts of her life as a revolutionary. In April, 2001, at the same time that she publicly renounced violence, she published her autobiography, written in prison and dedicated to her daughter, Mei, who had become a teacher in Japan. Fusako also published a book of poetry in 2005. Mei wrote her own memoirs of her life with her mother in two volumes, published in 2002 and 2003.

At the time of her sentencing, it was thought that Fusako would spend the rest of her life in prison, but through her writings she had succeeded in creating a new image of herself and gaining a certain amount of public acceptance in Japan. Her positive turnabout provided a constructive contrast to the other leading Japanese terrorist, Shoko Asahara, a nihilist, religious fanatic who had not shown any sign of such positive transformation in prison.

FURTHER READING
Farrell, William Regis. *Blood and Rage: The Story of the Japanese Red Army*. Lexington, Mass.: Lexington Books, 1990. A popular account for general readers.
Gallagher, Aileen. *The Japanese Red Army*. New York: Rosen, 2003. A concise study of the Japanese Red Army, including bibliographical references.

Katzenstein, Peter J. *Defending the Japanese State: Structures, Norms, and the Political Responses to Terrorism and Violent Social Protest in the 1970's and 1980's*. Ithaca, N.Y.: Cornell University Press, 1991. Covers the development of terrorism in Japan from the perspective of police responses to internal security threats.

Outman, James L. *Terrorism: Biographies*. Detroit: UXL, 2003. Studies of terrorists who are prominent nationally and internationally, including Fusako Shigenobu.

—Michael McCaskey

SEE ALSO: Shoko Asahara.

HAROLD SHIPMAN
British physician and serial killer

BORN: June 14, 1946; Nottingham, Nottinghamshire, England

DIED: January 13, 2004; Wakefield Prison, Wakefield, West Yorkshire, England

ALSO KNOWN AS: Harold Frederick Shipman (full name); Fred; Freddy; Dr. Death

MAJOR OFFENSE: Murder of fifteen patients

ACTIVE: Early 1970's-1998

LOCALE: Greater Manchester, England

SENTENCE: Life imprisonment; committed suicide while in prison

EARLY LIFE

Harold Frederick Shipman (SHIHP-muhn) was born into a working-class family. He had a very close relationship with his mother, Vera. When he was seventeen, his mother died of lung cancer. In her last days, she suffered a great deal of pain, and her only solace came from the painkillers administered by her family physician. His mother's experience lingered in Shipman's memory for a long time and gave him a strong desire to become a physician. He joined the medical school at University of Leeds. While in medical school, he met a young woman, Primrose. A year later, when Primrose was seventeen and five months pregnant, they married. In 1966, they had a daughter, whom they named Sarah, and later they had three more children.

CRIMINAL CAREER

In 1970, Shipman graduated from medical school and began his practice in Pontefract, a small town southeast of Leeds. Although he was considered a respected physician, he was also seen as rude and wanting a great deal of control. It is believed that it was at Pontefract that he began to kill some of his patients.

After four years, Shipman joined a practice in Todmorden, a town in West Yorkshire. After about a year of work there, he was caught forging prescriptions of pethidine (a morphinelike analgesic) for his own use. He had to undergo drug rehabilitation treatment and was fined, but he was allowed to resume practice in 1977 at Donneybrook Medical Centre in Hyde. He later started his own practice in 1993.

Once Shipman's criminal acts began in the early 1970's, he continued to kill patients with pethidine and morphine. It has been estimated that he was responsible for close to 250 deaths of his patients. Physicians in Shipman's area began to suspect something was wrong at his practice; one doctor, Linda Reynolds, approached the local coroner in early 1998 with concern about the high number of cremation forms for elderly women for which Shipman sought countersigning. Police were contacted and an investigation ensued, but not enough evidence of criminal acts could be found.

Shipman's last murder was of eighty-two-year-old Kathleen Grundy, which occurred on June 24, 1998. A forged will that left Shipman £386,000 led to suspicion about his role in her death. Upon exhumation of Grundy's body and postmortem tests, it was found that Grundy's death was a case of overdose of diamorphine, a legal grade of medical heroin.

LEGAL ACTION AND OUTCOME

Shipman's trial began on October 5, 1999, and was presided over by Justice Thayne John Forbes. Shipman was prosecuted and was found guilty after a six-day deliberation by a jury for murdering fifteen women during the period between 1995 and 1998. On January 31, 2000, he was sentenced to life imprisonment with a recommendation that he never be released. He maintained his innocence in all the crimes. On January 13, 2004, Shipman committed suicide in prison by hanging himself in the cell with bedsheets.

IMPACT

Dame Janet Smith, a judge, was appointed to prepare a dossier of Shipman's activities and develop recommendations. She prepared a six-volume document called *The Shipman Inquiry*, which made recommendations to the General Medical Council, the regulator of the medical profession in the United Kingdom. As a result of the crimes of Harold Shipman and the findings of the inquiry, debates ensued in Britain over several issues: trust between doctors, since several of Shipman's colleagues trusted him; loopholes within medical procedures that physicians can exploit, including the process of cremation certification; and patients' confidence and trust in their doctors. The Shipman case led to the creation of several preventive measures within the United Kingdom so that such criminal activities would be less likely to recur.

FURTHER READING

Baker, Richard. "Implications of Harold Shipman for General Practice." *Postgraduate Medical Journal* 80 (June, 2004): 303-306. This article discusses the implications of the case of Shipman for the medical profession. Issues of accountability, prevention measures, and doctor-patient relationships are discussed.

Pounder, Derrick. "The Case of Dr. Shipman." *American Journal of Forensic Medicine and Pathology* 24 (September, 2003): 219-226. The article discusses the case of Shipman and also presents forensic issues of detection and quantification of morphine in exhumed bodies.

Smith, Dame Janet. *The Shipman Inquiry*. 6 vols. London: The Stationery Office, 2002-2005. A complete account of the inquiry into the case of Harold Shipman in six volumes.

—*Manoj Sharma*

SEE ALSO: Linda Burfield Hazzard; Jack Kevorkian; Michael Swango.

THE WHY OF DR. DEATH

How many people Harold Shipman killed (or "helped die") is uncertain. He was convicted of 15 murders. The Shipman Inquiry tied him to 218 deaths, although its director admitted that the total is probably at least 250. During his medical career, 459 people died under his care. He reportedly told a fellow prison inmate that he was responsible for 508 deaths.

As uncertain is why he killed. The prosecutor at his trial proposed that Shipman "was exercising the ultimate power of controlling life and death, and repeated the act so often he must have found the drama of taking life to his taste." In a similar vein, psychologists identified him as a "health care serial killer" (HCSK), a phenomenon occurring with increasing frequency. Shipman showed several characteristics common to those suffering from HCSK: predicting deaths they later report, preying on those whose health is so poor that their deaths will seem inevitable, and ingratiating themselves with authority figures in order to deflect suspicion. Dr. Richard Badcock, a forensic psychiatrist who interviewed Shipman in prison, concluded that Shipman's murderous medical career may have been inspired by his mother's death. Badcock further described him as a "classic necrophiliac" even though there is no evidence that Shipman found corpses erotic.

Whatever the influence of deviant impulses, Shipman also had more mundane motivations: fraud and theft. He forged a will for his last victim and stole jewelry over an extended period. In 1998, one hundred rings, necklaces, bracelets, brooches, and earrings were found in Shipman's home, worth an estimated ten thousand pounds. Shipman's wife admitted that thirty-four of the pieces did not belong to her. Only one ring was identified by a victim's family; the others were auctioned off to benefit a victims' charity. Such thievery, however, may reflect a desire to dominate and humiliate more than greed. According to police and other sources, Shipman displayed arrogance and often mocked those who had recently died, even laughing at them. He reportedly called one victim a "WOW" (whining old woman), for example.

Shipman himself gave no hints of motivation, although rare flashes of haughty anger during his trial contradicted the image of the kindly old general practitioner that he cultivated. Up to his own death by suicide, he insisted that he was innocent, and his family continued to insist on that fact.

MOTHER SHIPTON
British soothsayer

BORN: 1488; Knaresborough, Yorkshire, England
DIED: 1561; Clifton, Yorkshire, England
ALSO KNOWN AS: Ursula Southeil or Sontheil (birth name)
CAUSE OF NOTORIETY: Mother Shipton is believed to have predicted the Great London Fire of 1666 and the death of Cardinal Thomas Wolsey.
ACTIVE: 1510's-1561
LOCALE: England

EARLY LIFE

Ursula Southeil, later known as Mother Shipton (SHIHP-tuhn), was allegedly born to a single mother in a cave in England. Her mother, Agatha, faced prostitution charges when she was pregnant with Ursula and escaped conviction by reminding the judge in open court that he had mpregnated two of his female servants. Agatha gave Ursula to the care of a foster mother when Ursula was two years old and then spent the remainder of her life in a convent.

Ursula was an intelligent child with a mischievous nature, according to biographers. She suffered some deformity, perhaps a humped back or hooked nose. Such physical attributes have long been associated with the stereotypical image of a witch. Townspeople referred to her as "a devil's child." Ursula married a carpenter named Toby Shipton when she was twenty-four and soon thereafter adopted the name Mother Shipton. After she became famous as a seer, stories developed about her supposed supernatural abilities that she used as a child to get revenge upon anyone who harmed or teased her.

WITCHCRAFT CAREER

Shortly after Mother Shipton's marriage, people from her town started coming to her for help, advice, and knowledge about the future. One such early tale has a neighbor seeking Mother Shipton's counsel after someone stole the neighbor's clothing. Mother Shipton is said to have gotten the thief to confess and return the property. Soon, her prophecies and utterances reached beyond petty thefts in her community. Cardinal Thomas Wolsey, who persuaded King Henry VIII to attack France and harbored papal aspirations, became a primary nemesis for Mother Shipton. After hearing that she had predicted his death, Wolsey threatened that if he came to York, he would burn her at the stake for witchcraft. However, he died before he could carry out the threat; Shipton had

also prophesied that Wolsey would not reach his destination. Other predictions, often in veiled and symbolic language, foretold events in the lives of Henry VIII, as well as his family and advisers. Shipton also is said to have predicted the Great London Fire in 1666. She was believed to have forecast her own death, at the beginning of Queen Elizabeth I's long reign.

Lore about her was spread by word of mouth for at least a century before anything was written down, so it is difficult to know which stories about her were fabricated entirely or exaggerated for dramatic effect over the years. Some prophecies attributed to her were later found to be fictions.

IMPACT

Mother Shipton serves as an example of the folklore and legend that developed around medieval women who spoke the truth to powerful figures and used their intellect to help others and to admonish those in power. The cave where Mother Shipton was born in Knaresborough became a tourist attraction, along with the Petrifying

Mother Shipton. (Courtesy, National Portrait Gallery)

Well near it, which is supposed to turn items thrown into it into stone. The area was said to possess supernatural qualities even before Shipton was born.

FURTHER READING

Briggs, Robin. *Witches and Neighbors: The Social and Cultural Context of European Witchcraft.* New York: Penguin, 1998. Examines court records during Mother Shipton's era and explores regional differences in attitudes toward and beliefs about witchcraft.

Kellet, Arnold. *Mother Shipton, Witch and Prophetess.* Maidstone, Kent, England: George Mann Books, 2002. Written by a Knaresborough-based historian, the book examines the history of Shipton's colorful legend and separates fact from folklore.

Kieckhefer, Richard. *Magic in the Middle Ages.* 2d ed. New York: Cambridge University Press, 2000. Examines magic in the Middle Ages, including a discussion of who practiced it and a survey of magic's development and growth.

—*Elizabeth Jarnagin*

SEE ALSO: Tamsin Blight; Mary Butters; Margaret Jones; Lady Alice Kyteler; Florence Newton; Dolly Pentreath; Elizabeth Sawyer; Joan Wytte.

MUHAMMAD SIAD BARRE
Ruler of Somalia (1969-1991)

BORN: c. 1910; Shiilabbo, Ogaden, Abyssinian Somaliland (now in Ethiopia)

DIED: January 2, 1995; Lagos, Nigeria

ALSO KNOWN AS: Maxamed Siyaad Barre

CAUSE OF NOTORIETY: Siad Barre initiated a war with Ethiopia and a engaged in a consistent pattern of political imprisonment, torture, political killings, and ethnic and tribal discrimination.

ACTIVE: 1969-1991

LOCALE: Somalia

EARLY LIFE

Muhammad Siad Barre (moh-HAHM-ehd SI-ad BEHR-ee) was an orphaned shepherd. He was educated in private schools in Mogadishu and attended the Military Academy in Italy and School of Administration and Politics in Somalia before joining the Italian colonial police force. When the Somali Republic was created in 1960, he was appointed colonel and deputy commandant in the Somali National Army. Siad Barre later rose to brigadier general in 1962 and major general in 1966. On October 21, 1969, General Siad Barre led a successful and bloodless coup and assumed power.

POLITICAL CAREER

As dictator of Somalia, Siad Barre instituted a political system that he called "scientific socialism," which reflected both ideological and economic dependence on the Soviet Union. In reality, Siad Barre ruled as an iron-fisted dictator whose support was heavily based on ethnic and tribal affiliations. The Soviets dropped Siad Barre when, in 1977, he invaded the Ogaden area of southeastern Ethiopia, another Soviet client state. With the help of Cuban troops and Soviet weapons, the Ethiopians successfully defended themselves from an invasion by Somali forces in 1978. Siad Barre then sought and received support from the United States. Despite his well-documented human rights abuses, the United States became a strong supporter of Siad Barre because of Somalia's strategic location in the Indian Ocean near the oil-rich Persian Gulf.

Following the Ogaden war, the Siad Barre regime violently suppressed opposition movements and ethnic groups. For example, various human rights organizations issued reports citing a pattern of political imprisonment, torture, killings, and discrimination against the Isaaks clan. In the late 1980's, an all-out civil war developed in Somalia when rival factional groups—some of which consisted of dissatisfied army officers known as the Somali Salvation Democratic Front (SSDF)—began making substantial territorial gains, especially in the northern Somaliland region. Siad Barre launched an intense counterinsurgency campaign. The war killed thousands, destroyed much of the country, and sent hundreds of thousands of refugees over neighboring borders. The rebellion spread, and Siad Barre was forced to flee the capital on January 26, 1991. He was succeeded by Ali Mahdi Muhammad, who ruled until November, 1991; his government never managed to govern Somalia effectively.

After several attempts to retake Mogadishu failed, Siad Barre went into exile. He initially went to Kenya and then settled in Lagos, Nigeria, where he died in 1995 of a heart attack. He was buried in his hometown in Somalia.

IMPACT

With no effective central authority after Siad Barre's departure, the tribal tensions and conflicts Siad Barre had manipulated resulted in a civil war among feuding clans, and Somalia disintegrated into chaos. Somalia was left with little more than a huge arsenal of weapons, and thus mass starvation was killing more people than the civil war. More than a decade later, Somalia continued to have no real national leader or effective central government and remained a poor Muslim country mired in civil war. Western governments and international organizations feared that it might prove to be a fertile breeding ground or haven for terrorists.

FURTHER READING

Bowden, Mark. *Black Hawk Down: A Story of a Modern War*. East Rutherford, N.J.: Penguin, 2000. A detailed account of the 1993 American mission in Somalia that left eighteen American soldiers dead. The book became the basis for a feature film of the same name.

Fitzgerald, N. J. *Somalia: Issues, History, and Bibliography*. New York: Nova Science, 2002. In addition to providing rich information about the national origin, history, and culture of Somalia, this book extensively covers the human rights abuses and ethnic conflicts during and following the Siad Barre dictatorship.

Little, Peter. *Somalia: Economy Without State*. Bloomington: Indiana University Press, 2003. A readable and informative account of the problems and successes of Somalia since the Siad Barre dictatorship.

Peterson, Scott. *Me Against My Brother: At War in Somalia, Sudan, and Rwanda*. London: Taylor and Francis, 2000. Includes an excellent account of the collapse of Somalia into chaos and civil war beginning with the last days of the Siad Barre dictatorship.

—*Jerome L. Neapolitan*

SEE ALSO: Samuel K. Doe; Mobutu Sese Seko

BUGSY SIEGEL
American gangster and casino owner

BORN: February 28, 1906; Brooklyn, New York
DIED: June 20, 1947; Beverly Hills, California
ALSO KNOWN AS: Benjamin Hymen Siegelbaum (birth name)
CAUSE OF NOTORIETY: A flashy and volatile gangster, Siegel helped bring organized crime to Las Vegas. His taste for celebrity and the spotlight were in large part responsible for his undoing.
ACTIVE: 1920-1947
LOCALE: New York, Hollywood, and Las Vegas

EARLY LIFE

Born in Brooklyn, Benjamin "Bugsy" Siegel (BUHG-zee SEE-guhl) was one of millions of Jewish children born into immigrant poverty during the early years of the twentieth century. Raised on the lower East Side of New York, he became involved in street gangs and fights at an early age. He quickly made friends with a small, older boy named Meyer Lansky, and the two became lifelong partners in crime. Even in his youth, Siegel was known for his white-hot temper and willingness to take violent action. The nickname "Bugsy" was slang for someone who was mentally unstable and was never used to Siegel's face.

CRIMINAL CAREER

During the 1920's, Lansky and Siegel worked with members of the Italian Mafia gangs and for New York gambler Arnold Rothstein. They became part of Rothstein's bootlegging operations that supplied New Yorkers with illegal alcohol during Prohibition, the brief period when the Eighteenth Amendment to the U.S. Constitution was in effect. Lansky and Siegel teamed with young Italians such as Lucky Luciano and Frank Costello to transport and sell bootleg alcohol. After Rothstein's death in 1928 and the organization of the five "crime families" of the New York Mafia, Siegel and Lansky continued to partner with Luciano. Siegel was rumored to be a part of a collection of Jewish and Italian hit men known as Murder, Inc. In later life, Siegel claimed to have killed twelve men, but rumors and myth have conflicted over who the victims were and how they died.

During the mid-1930's, a reform movement swept New York in order to dissolve the older tribes and busi-

SIEGEL AND RAYMOND CHANDLER

Philip Marlowe, the tough-talking detective in Raymond Chandler's novel *The Little Sister* (1949), discusses a photograph that provides the key to a murder mystery:

> Now what did I find? A photo of a movie queen and an ex-Cleveland gangster, maybe, on a particular day. Day when the ex-Cleveland gangster was supposed to be in hock at the Country Jail, also day when ex-Cleveland gangster's onetime sidekick was shot dead on Franklin Avenue in Los Angeles. Why was he in hock? Tip-off that he was who he was, and say what you like against the L.A. cops they do try to run back-East hot shots out of town. Who gave them the tip? The guy they pinched gave it to them himself, because his ex-partner was being troublesome and had to be rubbed out, and being in jail was a first-class alibi when it happened.

The gangster, Steelgrave, bribes a prison doctor to give him a pass to visit his dentist, unbeknownst to the police. The photo pins Steelgrave to a murder, and the plot thickens.

It may sound like a too-convenient plot device, but Chandler was simply refashioning a real incident involving Bugsy Siegel. Like Steelgrave, Siegel was supposed to be in jail when a Los Angeles *Examiner* photographer snapped a picture of him and the deputy escorting him leaving Lindy's, a popular restaurant on Wilshire Boulevard. The newspaper ran the picture the next day, to Siegel's great displeasure and to the embarrassment of city authorities. Dr. Benjamin Blank, the county jail doctor who had written a pass for Siegel to visit the dentist, was discovered to have thirty thousand dollars in checks from the gangster. Siegel had apparently spread his money around freely; he was allowed to roam the jail at will, use the phone whenever he liked, and have restaurant meals delivered.

Doctor Blank was later fired, and the prison guards and escorting deputy got into serious trouble; however, Siegel soon was set free, like the novel's Steelgrave, who is later murdered by a jilted lover.

Chandler recognized the photograph as perfect realism, Los Angeles style. He knew Los Angelinos loved a scandalous murder, that they expected the justice system to be venal, and that they were especially fascinated when a flashy gangster like Siegel was manipulating events. "Sometimes it's a little hard to find out who's making the rules of the ball game," Marlowe says, as understatement.

---

ness partnerships. Thomas E. Dewey was named special prosecutor and quickly began a crackdown on organized crime. In 1935, gangster Dutch Schultz was murdered to prevent him from unleashing an all-out war against the police. In 1936, Luciano was sent to prison; he remained there for nearly forty years. Following the Prohibition era, Siegel and Lansky went their separate ways: Lansky to Florida and then Cuba and Siegel to Los Angeles.

Siegel became part of the Los Angeles scene in the late 1930's and worked his way into bookmaking and controlling the union for film extras. He was handsome and debonair and was seen at many top nightclubs. Contrary to mob protocol, Siegel enjoyed the attention from newspapers and from gossip columnists. He was friends with film actor George Raft and quickly met a young woman named Virginia Hill, who became his permanent girlfriend despite the fact that he was married. Siegel and Hill had a volatile relationship punctuated by fights and mutual jealousies. Hill had won small acting roles in films and also had a string of other mob-connected boyfriends.

THE RISE OF LAS VEGAS

Contrary to popular myth, Siegel did not invent Las Vegas nor did he open its first major hotel. In the early 1940's, he went to Las Vegas to supply a race wire (which provided racing information to bookmakers) to downtown bookmaking parlors. He and his partners invested in small downtown casinos during this time. In 1945, Siegel and his partners bought the El Cortez hotel and casino and sold it six months later for a good profit.

In 1946, Los Angeles publisher Billy Wilkerson was trying to open a hotel casino on Highway 91, twelve miles outside Las Vegas. Two other large hotel-casinos, the El Rancho Vegas and the Last Frontier, were already operating successfully nearby. When Wilkerson ran out of money with the project only half done, Siegel bought into the venture and soon removed Wilkerson from the project.

Siegel completed the hotel-casino using enormous amounts of mob money. The casino, named the Flamingo, was a spectacular resort. However, Siegel's inexperience with legitimate business, his temperamental nature, and the suspicions of his investors proved a lethal combination. The Flamingo opened in December of 1946, but after a successful opening night, it quickly sank into financial instability.

Siegel closed the Flamingo in January, 1947, and reopened it two months later with fresh capital from mob associates. By then, the price of the Flamingo totaled six million dollars, and Siegel's Mafia colleagues began to suspect his intentions. Siegel's mental state was highly

Bugsy Siegel.

agitated and paranoid, and rumors swirled among Mafia members that Hill and Siegel had skimmed money off the project and hidden it in Switzerland. Finally, Siegel's mob associates simply ran out of patience with his lavish spending and volatile temper. On June 20, 1947, during a stay at Hill's Beverly Hills home, Siegel was shot several times through a window while he was sitting on a couch. One bullet famously drove clean through his left eye. Rumors about who ordered and who carried out the hit are numerous, but within hours, some of Siegel's associates took total control of the Flamingo.

IMPACT

Perhaps no other gangster in history has been as romanticized as Bugsy Siegel. A feature film titled *Bugsy* was released in 1991 and starred Warren Beatty as Siegel; Siegel has also been portrayed in television programs and other films. Siegel was a complex and contradictory character. His vision of Las Vegas was prophetic, but he was too limited and mentally unstable to realize it. Unfamiliar with the simplest principles of legitimate business, he squandered money. Unpredictably violent, he could not form and maintain normal business relationships even with longtime criminal associates. The Flamingo would last for more than fifty years while numerous other casino-resorts grew up around it. After Siegel's death, Las Vegas became and remained America's leading tourist resort.

FURTHER READING

Cohen, Rich. *Tough Jews: Fathers, Sons, and Gangster Dreams.* New York: Simon & Schuster, 1998. A good book on Jewish gangster culture during the 1920's and 1930's, showing the milieu from which Siegel emerged and how it influenced his life.

Lacey, Robert. *Little Man: Meyer Lansky and the Gangster Life.* Boston: Little, Brown, 1991. An excellent biography of Lansky, illustrating the similarities and differences between Lansky and Siegel. Details the early efforts of Siegel in Las Vegas.

Smith, John L. *Sharks in the Desert.* Fort Lee, N.J.: Barricade, 2005. Includes stories and anecdotes about the founding and early history of Las Vegas. Not scholarly and prone to exaggeration, it nevertheless offers some good reporting.

—*Charles C. Howard*

SEE ALSO: Albert Anastasia; Louis Buchalter; Frank Costello; Meyer Lansky; Lucky Luciano; Arnold Rothstein; Dutch Schultz.

WILLIAM JOSEPH SIMMONS
Imperial Wizard of the Knights of the Ku Klux Klan (1915-1922)

BORN: 1880; Harpersville, Alabama
DIED: May 18, 1945; Atlanta, Georgia
CAUSE OF NOTORIETY: Simmons, initially a promoter for the fraternal organization Woodmen of the World, led the revival of the white supremacist organization the Knights of the Ku Klux Klan (KKK) and declared himself the Grand Wizard of the new Klan.
ACTIVE: 1915-1922
LOCALE: Georgia

EARLY LIFE

William Joseph Simmons (SIHM-menz) was raised on a farm in central Alabama. His father owned a mill and worked as a doctor. When Simmons was eighteen, he enlisted in the Alabama Volunteers to fight in the Spanish-American War. Following his release from the army, he became a circuit Methodist minister serving small congregations in Alabama and Florida. In 1912, the Alabama Conference denied him a pulpit because of his inefficiency and moral impairment. Simmons eventually became a fraternal promoter for Woodmen of the World, where he rose to the rank of colonel. In 1914, he became a district commander of the organization in Atlanta, Georgia.

KLAN CAREER

In 1915, Simmons worked out the details for a new fraternal organization called the Knights of the Ku Klux Klan. Working from a copy of the 1867 Reconstruction Klan Prescript, Simmons expanded the ritual and hierarchy of the group and copyrighted the document. On October 26, 1915, Simmons and thirty-four other men, including two former Reconstruction-era Klansmen, applied for a charter from the state of Georgia. The Knights of the Ku Klux Klan was described as a purely benevolent and eleemosynary fraternal order. Its program emphasized fraternity, secrecy, and white supremacy.

On Thanksgiving Day, 1915, Simmons led fifteen followers up Stone Mountain, Georgia, torched a cross, and revived the Ku Klux Klan. The revival corresponded with the Atlanta opening of *The Birth of a Nation*—a controversial film directed by D. W. Griffith and based on the novels of Thomas Dixon, Jr.—which glorified the original Klan. Within a month, the Klan had approximately ninety members; by 1919, it had grown to several thousand members.

In June, 1920, Simmons entered into an agreement with Edward Young Clarke and Mrs. Elizabeth Tyler of the Southern Publicity Association to market the Klan. Under the arrangement, Clarke was to receive 80 percent of the ten-dollar fee paid by each recruit. Clarke expanded the program of the KKK to include an aggressive defense of "100 percent Americanism"; as a result, the group began to target Jews, Roman Catholics, Asians, and immigrants. In addition, the Klan emphasized morality and attacked scandalous behavior. Clarke's marketing techniques were successful, and by 1921 Klan membership had increased to 100,000. Soon thereafter, the *New York World* published a series of articles exposing the Klan, and Congress held hearings on the organization. Simmons spent three days testifying before the House Rules Committee, during which time he defended the Klan as a Christian organization. The publicity resulted in even more growth of the Klan, and within a year Klan membership stood at more than one million.

William Joseph Simmons. (Library of Congress)

The success of the Klan eventually resulted in Simmons's demise. Some Klansmen, led by Dallas dentist Hiram Wesley Evans, expressed dissatisfaction with the operation of the national headquarters. In particular, he saw Clarke as using the Klan to get rich and Simmons as incompetent. At the 1922 national meeting of the Klan in Atlanta, the insurgents convinced Simmons to accept a new position—emperor of the Klan—while Evans became Imperial Wizard. Simmons agreed but soon discovered that he had lost his authority. A power struggle followed, and eventually Simmons agreed to an out-of-court settlement whereby he left the Klan and transferred his copyrights to the new leaders in return for a cash settlement of approximately $146,000. Eventually Simmons moved to Luverne, Alabama. He died in May, 1945, in Atlanta, Georgia.

IMPACT

William Joseph Simmons was responsible for the revival of the Ku Klux Klan in 1915. This organization became a nationwide movement in the 1920's with a membership reaching one million through its emphasis on total Americanism and its attacks on religious and ethnic minorities. Throughout its history, the Klan has been the most visible and infamous racist movement in America, and its revival by Simmons resulted in the largest Klan movement in the history of the United States.

FURTHER READING

Blee, Kathleen M. *Women and the Klan*. Berkeley: University of California Press, 1991. This work looks at the role that women played in the 1920's Klan.

MacLean, Nancy. *Behind the Mask of Chivalry*. New York: Oxford University Press, 1994. An examination of the 1920's Klan utilizing internal Klan records from Georgia.

Wade, Wyn Craig. *The Fiery Cross*. New York: Simon & Schuster, 1987. An older work on the history of the Ku Klux Klan that has detailed information on Simmons.

—*William V. Moore*

SEE ALSO: Thomas Dixon, Jr.; David Duke; Nathan Bedford Forrest; Gerald L. K. Smith; J. B. Stoner.

O. J. SIMPSON
African American professional football player and film actor

BORN: July 9, 1947; San Francisco, California
ALSO KNOWN AS: Orenthal James Simpson (full name); the Juice
CAUSE OF NOTORIETY: A successful and popular athlete and actor, Simpson gained notoriety after being accused of the murders of his former wife, Nicole Brown Simpson, and one of her acquaintances, Ronald Goldman. Though ruled not guilty of murder in his criminal trial, Simpson was determined to be liable for the wrongful death of Goldman and assessed a $33.5 million judgment.
ACTIVE: June 12, 1994
LOCALE: Los Angeles, California
SENTENCE: $8.5 million in compensatory damages to the Goldman family and $25 million in punitive damages to the Goldman and Brown families

EARLY LIFE

O. J. Simpson (SIHMP-suhn) was born on July 9, 1947, to a family of modest means; his father abandoned them when Simpson was young, and his mother worked as a hospital orderly. As a child, Simpson developed rickets and was forced to wear leg braces; for much of his youth, he lived close to the streets. At age thirteen, he joined a gang, the Persian Warriors, and by age fifteen he had been arrested for fighting. In high school, he found success on a football field, and after graduation he attended San Francisco City College, where he set national junior college records as a running back.

SPORTS AND ACTING CAREER

In 1967, Simpson attended the University of Southern California, where he was twice named to the All-American football team and, in 1968, won the Heisman Trophy, an award given to college football's top player. The following spring, the Buffalo Bills selected Simpson with the number-one pick in the National Football League (NFL) draft. In eleven seasons in the NFL—nine in Buffalo and two in San Francisco—Simpson ran for more than 11,000 yards, scored 76 touchdowns, and amassed 14,368 net yards. In 1973, he became the first player in league history to run for more than 2,000 yards in one season. He was selected Player of the Year in 1972, 1973, and 1975 and named All-Pro for five straight years, from 1972 through 1976.

Following his retirement from football in 1979, Simpson became a successful television and film actor, surprising many with his comic talents in *The Naked Gun: From the Files of Police Squad!* (1988) and its sequels. He is perhaps best remembered onscreen as spokesperson for Hertz, a car rental company in whose commercials he would run through airports and leap over luggage. He also worked several seasons as a television football commentator.

The Brown-Goldman Murders
On June 12, 1994, Simpson's former wife, Nicole Brown, was murdered outside her home, along with an acquaintance, Ronald Goldman, who was returning an item left that evening at the restaurant where he worked and where Brown had eaten dinner with friends. Brown and Simpson had divorced two years earlier after a difficult seven-year marriage, during which complaints of domestic violence had surfaced; however, the two maintained an amicable relationship and shared custody of their two children. Evidence discovered at the scene of the murders and at Simpson's home implicated Simpson, and when a warrant was issued for his arrest five days later, he attempted to flee. Simpson was spotted in his white Bronco, driven by his friend Al Cowlings, who led police on a slow sixty-mile chase through Los Angeles; Simpson threatened suicide before returning home and surrendering to law enforcement officers.

O. J. Simpson and Nicole Brown in 1980. (AP/Wide World Photos)

Legal Action and Outcome
Simpson was charged with two counts of murder. For his defense, he assembled a team of eleven prominent lawyers, including Hollywood attorney Robert Shapiro; Harvard professor Alan Dershowitz; deoxyribonucleic acid (DNA) expert Barry Scheck; F. Lee Bailey, at the time America's most famous attorney; and Johnnie L. Cochran, whose charisma gave the trial some of its most memorable moments.

The trial began on January 23, 1995, and soon became an American obsession. Although the trial lasted more than nine months and included hundreds of hours of often tedious testimony, 91 percent of Americans watched some of the proceedings on television, including an estimated 150 million viewers on the day of the verdict. The prosecution offered an exhaustive body of evidence outlining the murders and Simpson's involvement, but the defense sought to portray Simpson's arrest as a police conspiracy and to impeach the reliability of the trace evidence. After a four-hour deliberation, the jury declared Simpson not guilty on both counts of murder. Less than one year later, Simpson was sued by Goldman's family for Goldman's wrongful death. After a four-month trial, a jury brought back a $33.5 million judgment against Simpson.

Impact
As the trial dissolved into a media frenzy and real-life soap opera, it raised serious questions regarding justice

---

IF IT DOESN'T FIT . . .

In his closing statement at the criminal trial of O. J. Simpson, lead defense attorney Johnnie Cochran appealed to the jury's sense of racial injustice and distrust of the police investigation:

The Defendant, Mr. Orenthal James Simpson, is now afforded an opportunity to argue the case, if you will, but I'm not going to argue with you, ladies and gentlemen. What I'm going to do is to try and discuss the reasonable inferences which I feel can be drawn from this evidence. . . .

From the very first orders issued by the LAPD so-called brass, they were more concerned with their own images, the publicity that might be generated from this case than they were in doing professional police work. . . . Because of their bungling, they ignored the obvious clues. . . . We think if they had done their job as we have done, Mr. Simpson would have been eliminated early on. . . .

And so as we look then at the time line and the importance of this time line, I want you to remember these words. Like the defining moment in this trial, the day Mr. Darden asked Mr. Simpson to try on those gloves and the gloves didn't fit, remember these words; if it doesn't fit, you must acquit. . . .

And when you are back there deliberating on this case, you're never going to be ever able to reconcile this time line and the fact there's no blood back there. . . . They don't have any mountain or ocean of evidence. It's not so because they say so. That's just rhetoric. We this afternoon are talking about the facts. And so it doesn't make any sense. It just doesn't fit. If it doesn't fit, you must acquit. . . .

Then we come, before we end the day, to Detective Mark Fuhrman. This man is an unspeakable disgrace. He's been unmasked for the whole world for what he is. . . . And they put him on the stand and you saw it. You saw it. It was sickening. . . . Then Bailey says: "Have you used that word, referring to the 'n' word, in the past ten years? . . . I want you to assume that perhaps at some time since 1985 or '86, you addressed a member of the African American race as a Nigger. Is it possible that you have forgotten that act on your part?" . . .

Let's remember this man. . . . Why did they then all try to cover for this man Fuhrman? . . . This man could have been off the force long ago if they had done their job, but they didn't do their job. People looked the other way. People didn't have the courage. One of the things that has made this country so great is people's willingness to stand up and say that is wrong. I'm not going to be part of it. I'm not going to be part of the cover-up. That is what I'm asking you to do. Stop this cover-up. Stop this cover-up. If you don't stop it, then who? Do you think the police department is going to stop it? Do you think the D.A.'s office is going to stop it? Do you think we can stop it by ourselves? It has to be stopped by you. . . .

---

in the United States. The gavel-to-gavel television coverage, watched by millions nationwide, often seemed to affect both the proceedings and the participants. The trial made celebrities of many of the participants, including Judge Lance Ito, prosecutors Marcia Clark and Christopher Darden, much of the defense team, detective Mark Fuhrman, and even Brian "Kato" Kaelin, an aspiring actor who had lived in Simpson's guesthouse and testified about the activity at the Simpson house on the night of the murders. Furthermore, Simpson's extraordinary celebrity prompted accusations that he was, on one hand, receiving special treatment or, on the other, being subjected to overly aggressive prosecution.

The DNA evidence collected from blood found outside Simpson's home, leading toward Simpson's estate, in Simpson's white Bronco, and in the front hall of his home pointed to Simpson. The defense, however, relentlessly attacked the police investigation and cast doubt on the evidence. Althought it is now common knowledge that the DNA eliminated the likelihood of the murderer being anyone other than Simpson, in 1995 the strength of this evidence was not understood by most of the public, including the jurors.

Perhaps most important, the dramatic differences of opinion between white Americans and black Americans over the outcome of the trial highlighted the complex relationship between race and justice in America. The fact that Simpson was black and his victims white magnified the racial overtones of the trial, and coming just four years after the beating of Rodney King by Los Angeles police officers and the subsequent riots when a jury declared the officers innocent, the Simpson trial could not escape its racial implications.

FURTHER READING

Dershowitz, Alan M. *Reasonable Doubts: The Criminal Justice System and the O. J. Simpson Case.* New York: Touchstone, 1996. An analysis of the Simpson trial, along with an explanation of the jury's decision in the context of the American legal system, by a member of Simpson's legal defense team.

Fuhrman, Mark. *Murder in Brentwood.* New York: Zebra Books, 1997. A detailed description of the crime scene and critique of the investigation written by the detective whose impeached testimony at the trial proved devastating for the prosecution.

Hunt, Darnell M. *O. J. Simpson, Facts and Fictions: News Rituals in the Construction of Reality.* New York: Cambridge University Press, 1999. A scholarly study of the differences across racial lines in the pub-

lic perception of the Simpson trial, including the way the media used these perceptions to shape its coverage of the trial.

Toobin, Jeffrey. *The Run of His Life: The People Versus O. J. Simpson.* New York: Random House, 1996. An examination of Simpson's defense team's strategy and the social and legal reasons for its success, written a former prosecutor who covered the trial for *The New Yorker* magazine.

—*Devon Boan*

SEE ALSO: Rodney King; Scott Peterson.

MILES SINDERCOMBE
English conspirator

BORN: Date unknown; Kent, England
DIED: February 13, 1657; London, England
MAJOR OFFENSE: Treason for conspiracy to assassinate Lord Protector Oliver Cromwell
ACTIVE: September 17, 1656-January 9, 1657
LOCALE: London, England
SENTENCE: Death by hanging; committed suicide before sentence could be realized

EARLY LIFE
Very little is known of the early life of Miles Sindercombe (milz SIHN-dur-kohm). It appears that he was born in Kent and was a surgeon's apprentice. During the civil wars of the 1640's, Sindercombe supported Parliament, served in the parliamentary army, and eventually joined with the Levellers, a radical political group that agitated for expanding the right to vote. In May, 1649, he participated in a mutiny in his regiment and did so again in 1654-1655, when he served in a cavalry regiment in Scotland. Sindercombe fled to the European continent and there met Edward Sexby, a former parliamentary soldier who had turned against statesman Oliver Cromwell and had begun to plot Cromwell's assassination together with disaffected republicans.

CRIMINAL CAREER
Sindercombe returned to England with five hundred pounds in funds and recruited several others to the conspiracy: a discontented former soldier, John Cecil; a drifter, William Boyes, who had several aliases; and a member of Cromwell's personal Life-Guards, John Toope (or Toop), who could provide information about

Cromwell's itinerary. These conspirators would make several unsuccessful attempts on Cromwell's life before they were arrested.

Their first attempt involved a plan to shoot Cromwell when he was en route to open the session of Parliament on September 17, 1656. The men rented a house on King Street in Westminster, from which they intended to shoot Cromwell as he passed. The would-be assassins were stymied by the large number of people on the street, which they saw would hinder their escape.

Because the attempt from a fixed location on a city street was unsuccessful, the plotters shifted tactics. Cromwell usually traveled by carriage to Hampton Court for weekends away from crowded London. At a house along the route, they laid in wait to fire on his carriage, but Cromwell stayed in London because of government business—the conspirators were foiled again.

The plotters then attempted to assassinate Cromwell in Hyde Park. Sindercombe was to remain outside the park, while Cecil was stationed inside on his horse. Cromwell's actions thwarted the plot as he asked Cecil to ride over to him so he could admire Cecil's horse. Although in close proximity to Cromwell and with the perfect opportunity, Cecil was unable to shoot.

After these failed attempts, Cromwell's secretary of state and chief "spymaster," John Thurloe, uncovered the plot and had the conspirators arrested. Toope revealed the plotters' biggest plan yet: to burn down Cromwell's residence, Whitehall Palace, on January 8, 1657. After Boyes, Cecil, and Sindercombe planted their incendiary device in the chapel, authorities moved against them. Boyes escaped, Cecil was captured, and Sindercombe was subdued after a bloody scuffle during which he lost a part of his nose to a knife. Cecil quickly confessed, but Sindercombe was unrepentant.

LEGAL ACTION AND OUTCOME
On February 9, 1657, Sindercombe was convicted of treason based on the testimony of Cecil and Toope, but he was able to escape the gruesome death of a traitor by poisoning himself, which resulted in his death on February 13, 1657, a day before he was to be hanged and then drawn and quartered.

IMPACT
Although a relatively minor figure, Miles Sindercombe can be regarded as representative of a segment of England that had significant disagreements with Cromwell's regime. What set Sindercombe apart was his willingness to move beyond mere disaffection and become involved in plots to end Cromwell's rule through assassination. Sindercombe came from the radical republican Leveller element that had opposed King Charles I and worked within the parliamentary army and turned against Cromwell. Occasionally this element made common cause with Royalists, whose goal was to remove Cromwell and restore monarchy under the late king's son, the future Charles II. The fragility of Cromwell's government was demonstrated by the confusion and disorganization that followed his death and resulted in the restoration of monarchy in May, 1660.

FURTHER READING
Davis, J. C. *Cromwell*. London: Arnold, 2001. This analytical work focuses on the object of Sindercombe's plots from the standpoint of his own time and his subsequent historical reputation.

Firth, Charles Harding. *The Last Years of the Protectorate, 1656-1658*. 2 vols. 1909. Reprint. New York: Russell & Russell, 1964. Contains detailed descriptions of Sindercombe's attempts to assassinate Cromwell.

Marshall, Alan. "Killing No Murder." *History Today* 53, no. 2 (February, 2003): 20-26. A very readable, accessible summary of Sindercombe's plots, complete with illustrations.

—*Mark C. Herman*

SEE ALSO: Guy Fawkes; Titus Oates.

BEANT SINGH
Sikh assassin

BORN: Date unknown; Maloya, Punjab, India
DIED: October 31, 1984; New Delhi, India
CAUSE OF NOTORIETY: Singh and an accomplice assassinated Indira Gandhi, prime minister of India.
ACTIVE: October 31, 1984
LOCALE: Garden of the prime minister's house, New Delhi, India

EARLY LIFE
Beant Singh (BEE-ahnt sihng) was born and raised in the Sikh village of Maloya and attended the University of Punjab. Little else is known about his early life. He became a police officer in 1972, and after 1980 he served as part of Prime Minister Indira Gandhi's inner security cordon; his loyalty was never questioned. He was not known for ethnic extremism and had married a Hindu woman, Bimla Devi.

MILITANT CAREER
In June, 1984, Operation Blue Star was carried out by the Indian military under the orders of Prime Minister Gandhi. The operation was an attack designed to oust separatist and militant Sikhs from the Golden Temple complex, the most sacred site of the Sikh religion. The complex was left badly damaged, and many people were killed. The event led to estrangement between the Indian government and large portions of the Sikh community; it also radicalized Singh, and he came under the influence of one of the main conspirators, his uncle Kehar Singh. In turn, Beant brought police constable Satwant Singh to his house on October 16, 1984, in order to recruit him into a conspiracy against the government.

On the morning of October 31, 1984, Gandhi, her staff, and her security aides left her house at No. 1 Safdarjung Road to walk along the path of her garden to her office next door at No. 1 Akbar Road; Gandhi was heading for an interview with documentary filmmakers with the British Broadcasting Company (BBC). She stopped at the gate dividing the two properties to greet Beant and Satwant, who were on security duty. Beant pulled out his .38-bore service revolver and fired five bullets into Gandhi. Like the other security officers who became paralyzed into inaction, Satwant was initially stunned, but Beant ordered him to shoot; he too opened fire, emptying twenty-five bullets into Gandhi. The two men then dropped their weapons as other security men ran to the scene. Beant told them, "I have done what I had to do. Now you do what you have to do." Both men were taken to the guardhouse, where they were shot ten minutes later as they tried to wrest weapons from the guards. At 2:23 P.M., Gandhi was pronounced dead at a nearby hospital.

LEGAL ACTION AND OUTCOME

Justice M. P. Thakkar was appointed to hold an inquiry into the assassination in order to examine whether there was a security lapse and if foreign powers were involved. He submitted his report on February 27, 1986, but it did not become public until March 27, 1989. The report found that the conspiracy involved several people, but the only foreign involvement was training and shelter given by Pakistan to Sikh terrorists.

IMPACT

News that Sikhs had killed Indira Gandhi reached the streets almost immediately following her death. Hindus went on a rampage against Sikhs wherever they could find them, in homes and shops, on buses and trains, and in Sikh-owned buildings and businesses. The carnage lasted three days before the rioting spent itself and police and the army could restore order. More than twenty-five

hundred Sikhs died in Delhi, and thousands more were killed in other cities. The total death toll is unknown. Within hours of her death, Gandhi's son, Rajiv Gandhi, was sworn in as prime minister of India.

FURTHER READING

Anandaram, S. *Assassination of a Prime Minister: As It Happened.* New Delhi: Vision Books, 1994. Offers good details of the assassination by the person who was in charge of the investigation.

Frank, Kathleen. *Indira: The Life of Indira Gandhi.* Boston: Houghton Mifflin, 2002. In this easy-to-read biography, Frank offers a summary of Operation Blue Star and the assassination in chapter 20, "Another Amritsar," and chapter 21, "31 October 1984."

Singh, Anurag, ed. *Giani Kirpal Singh's Eye-Witness Account of Operation Blue Star: Mighty Murderous Army Attack on the Golden Temple Complex.* Amritsar, India: B. Chattar Singh Jiwan Singh, 1999. Useful for an understanding of the outrage felt by many Sikhs at Operation Blue Star and the damage caused to the Golden Temple. The attack was interpreted as an assault on Sikhism itself in a holy war waged by Hindus.

—Roger D. Long

SEE ALSO: Reginald Dyer; Nathuram Vinayak Godse; Thenmuli Rajaratnam; Satwant Singh.

SATWANT SINGH
Sikh assassin

BORN: 1962; Agwaan Kurd village, Gurdaspur, Punjab, India
DIED: January 6, 1989; New Delhi, India
MAJOR OFFENSE: Assassination of Indian prime minister Indira Gandhi
ACTIVE: October 31, 1984
LOCALE: The prime minister's house, New Delhi
SENTENCE: Death by hanging

EARLY LIFE

Satwant Singh (SAT-wahnt sihng) was raised in the Sikh village of Agwaan Kurd and educated to the high school level at Dera Baba Nanak School.

LAW ENFORCEMENT CAREER

On December 5, 1981, Singh became a policeman. After completing his training on December 31, 1983, he was stationed in Uttar Pradesh, north India. In July, 1983, he was transferred to New Delhi, where he served as one of the uniformed members of the personal bodyguard of the prime minister with the rank of police constable. He was engaged to be married to Surinder Kaur, but their marriage was postponed in 1984 because Singh could not get leave from his duties.

In June, 1984, Prime Minister Indira Gandhi ordered Operation Blue Star, an army action designed to oust separatist Sikhs from the Golden Temple Complex, the most sacred site of the Sikh religion. The attack left the complex badly damaged. This act radicalized Singh, as it did many Sikhs, and Singh came under the influence of the conspirators Beant Singh and his uncle Kehar Singh. The three men visited the complex to see for themselves the damage caused by troops. On October 24, Satwant Singh and Beant Singh took part in a Sikh religious service, *Amrit*, at a temple in Delhi.

On October 31, 1984, Gandhi, with staff members, left her house to walk along the path of her garden to her office next door to be interviewed for a British Broadcasting Company documentary. She stopped at the gate dividing the two properties to greet Beant Singh and Satwant Singh, who were on security duty. It was 9:12 A.M. Beant Singh pulled out his .38-bore service revolver and fired five bullets into Gandhi. Satwant Singh was stunned into inaction at first, but Beant Singh told him to shoot. Satwant Singh then opened fire, emptying twenty-five bullets into Gandhi from his Sten gun. The assassins then dropped their weapons as other security personnel ran to the scene. Beant Singh told them, "I have done what I had to do. Now you do what you have to do." Beant Singh and Satwant Singh were taken to the guardhouse, where they were shot ten minutes later as they attempted to escape. Beant Singh was killed, but Satwant Singh survived. At 2:23 P.M. Indira Gandhi was pronounced dead at a nearby hospital.

LEGAL ACTION AND OUTCOME

Justice M. P. Thakkar was appointed to hold an enquiry into the assassination to examine whether there was a security lapse and if foreign powers were involved. He submitted his report on February 27, 1986. The conspiracy involved several people, the report said, but there was no foreign involvement. Satwant Singh was tried for his crime, found guilty, and, along with fellow conspirator Kehar Singh, hanged on January 6, 1989.

IMPACT

Immediately after news reached the streets that Sikhs had killed Gandhi, Hindus went on a campaign of revenge, hunting down Sikhs in an orgy of bloodshed. The carnage lasted three days before law and order was restored. More than twenty-five hundred Sikhs died in Delhi, and thousands more were killed in other cities. The total death toll is unknown. Within hours of Indira Gandhi's death, her son Rajiv Gandhi (1944-1991) was sworn in as prime minister of India.

FURTHER READING

Anandaram, S. *Assassination of a Prime Minister: As It Happened.* New Delhi: Vision Books, 1994. This study offers good details of the assassination by the person in charge of the investigation.

Frank, Kathleen. *Indira: The Life of Indira Gandhi.* Boston: Houghton Mifflin, 2002. In this easy-to-read biography of Gandhi by the biographer who has written books on such renowned women as Mary Kingsley, Emily Brontë, and Lucie Duff Gordon, Frank offers a summary of Operation Blue Star and the assassination in chapter 20, "Another Amritsar," and chapter 21, "31 October 1984."

Singh, Anurag, ed. *Giani Kirpal Singh's Eye-Witness Account of Operation Blue-Star: Mighty Murderous Army Attack on the Golden Temple Complex.* Amritsar: B. Chattar Singh Jiwan Singh, 1999. Useful for an understanding of the outrage felt by many Sikhs at Operation Blue Star and the damage caused to the Golden Temple complex. The attack was interpreted as an assault on Sikhism itself in a holy war waged by Hindus.

—*Roger D. Long*

SEE ALSO: Said Akbar; Thenmuli Rajaratnam; Beant Singh; Sirhan Sirhan; Ramzi Yousef.

Sirhan Sirhan
American assassin

Born: March 19, 1944; Jerusalem, Palestine

Also known as: Sirhan Bisbara Sirhan (full name)

Major offenses: Assassination of Senator Robert F. Kennedy; first-degree murder and five counts of assault with a deadly weapon

Active: June 5, 1968

Locale: Los Angeles, California

Sentence: Death in the gas chamber; reduced to life in prison when the U.S. Supreme Court ruled in *Furman v. Georgia* (1972) that the death penalty was being unconstitutionally applied by the states in violation of the Eighth Amendment's cruel and unusual punishment clause

Early Life

Sirhan Sirhan (SEHR-han SEHR-han) was born into a Jordanian family in Jerusalem. In 1948, Sirhan's family became displaced refugees because of the Arab-Israeli War, and he grew up witnessing horrific violence between Arabs and Jews, including the death of his older brother. From 1948 to 1957, the family lived in a poverty-stricken environment. As Israeli forces quickly began to dominate areas in the Middle East, Sirhan began to doubt whether he would be able to realize his dream of returning to his homeland in Jordan. In 1957, Sirhan and his family emigrated to the United States, settling in Pasadena, California. Sirhan's father abandoned the family and eventually moved back to Palestine.

In high school, Sirhan was viewed as a quiet person with a good sense of humor. He was well liked and fairly popular with young women. He became intrigued by assassinations and once underlined sentences in a high school textbook regarding political assassination, writing in the margin that "many more will come." As a young man, he viewed the assassination of President John F. Kennedy in 1963 as the beginning of the end for the United States.

Political Convictions

Sirhan hated Israel with a passion. When Israel invaded the Sinai Peninsula on June 5, 1967, the Six-Day War began, in which Israeli forces handily defeated the United Arab Republic, Syria, and Jordan. Sirhan was devastated emotionally because he then knew that he could never return to Jordan. He began to hate U.S. politicians and the American media, which he saw as being controlled by wealthy Jews. In particular, Senator Robert F. Kennedy was a focal point for Sirhan's hatred and frustration. As a journalist in 1948, Kennedy had covered the establishment of the new state of Israel for the *Boston Globe*, and a film documentary about Kennedy's trip to Israel happened to air in Los Angeles prior to the 1968 California primary election.

As he campaigned for the presidency in 1968, Robert Kennedy sought to appease Jewish voters for at least two reasons. First, he had formerly worked for Joseph McCarthy, the senator who had vigorously investigated communist sympathizers in the 1950's. The lives and careers of many Jewish people were destroyed by McCarthy's activities. Second, Joseph Kennedy, Robert Kennedy's father and U.S. ambassador to Great Britain in the 1930's, had supported the appeasement of Adolf Hitler. As a U.S. senator, Kennedy began to establish a strong voting record in favor of Israel; for example, he supported the sale of fifty jet fighters to that nation, which greatly angered Sirhan.

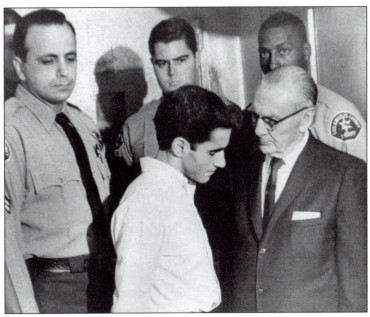

Sirhan Sirhan, in white shirt, talks with his attorney Russel L. Parsons. (AP/Wide World Photos)

CRIMINAL CAREER

In preparation for the assassination of Robert Kennedy, Sirhan began to practice mind control and self-hypnosis in order to make himself an instrument of assassination. He was known to have studied the occult sciences. Over a period of weeks leading up to the California presidential primary, Sirhan stalked Kennedy as he campaigned throughout the state. Sirhan became obsessed with killing Kennedy prior to June 5, 1968, the first anniversary of the Six-Day War. After Kennedy gave a victory speech at the Ambassador Hotel in Los Angeles, Sirhan fatally shot the senator with a .22 caliber handgun as Kennedy was leaving the hotel through a kitchen pantry area.

LEGAL ACTION AND OUTCOME

Sirhan's statements to police after the assassination indicated that his motive for the murder was political. Although a number of psychiatrists evaluating Sirhan questioned his sanity, he was convicted of premeditated first-degree murder on April 17, 1969, and sentenced to death by the gas chamber. Sirhan's sentence was reduced to life in prison after the U.S. Supreme Court ruled in 1972 that the death penalty was unconstitutional. Serving a life sentence in the California state prison at Corcoran, Sirhan was denied parole numerous times.

THE COVER-UP CONSPIRACY THEORY

A confession, abundant witnesses, and evidence notwithstanding, during the 1990's Sirhan Sirhan began denying that he was responsible for killing Senator Robert F. Kennedy. He insisted that he had been brainwashed. In 1998, Sirhan's attorney, Lawrence Teeter, declared that there had been a massive cover-up:

As a result of both (1) the blackmailing of defense attorney [Grant] Cooper and his resultant collaboration with the prosecution and (2) the systematic withholding and falsification of evidence by the prosecution, the jury which convicted Sirhan never knew the following:

1. Senator Kennedy was shot in the back and from behind. Yet all witnesses placed Sirhan as standing face-to-face in front of RFK.
2. Sirhan's gun was placed by all witnesses at between 2 and 5 feet from the victim, but the autopsy report states that the distance between the assailant's gun and the victim was between 1 and 2 inches.
3. The shots entering the victim's body were fired at a sharp upward angle, but the defendant was seen by all witnesses to hold his gun horizontally.
4. The autopsy report which exonerates the defendant was withheld from the court and the defense by prosecutors for at least four months, until after defense counsel had conceded to the jury that their client was the killer—something which the autopsy report demonstrates to be impossible. . . .
8. The police inventory accounted for eight .22 cal. bullets discharged at the crime scene. Seven were removed from victims, and the eighth was described as having been lost in the ceiling. A police officer observed police criminalists dig two bullets out of a door frame in the pantry area within which the victim was killed, bringing to 10 the total number of shots that were fired during the attack.
9. These extra bullets were never disclosed to the defense or the court and were never mentioned in the police property report. The police and prosecution have continued to deny their existence. . . .
17. Although security guards left the scene without their guns being checked, a 15 year old who photographed the attack was thrown to the ground and arrested at gun point. His camera and film were seized. No photographs of the attack were ever made available to the defense or the court.

Source: "The Massive Official Cover-Up," available on the Web site of Lawrence Teeter, www.reopenrfkassassinationcase.com.

IMPACT

The assassination of Robert Kennedy cleared the path to the presidency for other candidates in 1968; the winner in that year's election was Richard Nixon. On September 6, 1970, the hijacking of four commercial airplanes in Europe by Arab terrorists brought international attention to Sirhan Sirhan when the terrorists attempted to offer their captives in exchange for Sirhan's release from prison. In the Arab world, Sirhan remains a symbol of the Arab-Israeli conflict.

Like the assassination of John Kennedy, the murder of Robert Kennedy has spawned a belief in conspiracies. For instance, some have linked Sirhan to organized crime because he worked as a horse trainer at a racetrack in Santa Ana, California. Other conspiracy theorists have focused upon the mind control and self-hypnosis exercises practiced by Sirhan as circumstantial evidence that he may have been used by the intelligence community. No credible evidence has been introduced to prove any of the conspiracy theories.

The House Select Committee on Assassinations in the

late 1970's debated whether to investigate the murder of Robert Kennedy but decided instead to focus upon the murders of John Kennedy and civil rights activist Martin Luther King, Jr. The federal government had not conducted an official investigation into the assassination of Robert Kennedy as of 2006. Attorney Lawrence Teeter gained recognition because he tried to have Sirhan's conviction overturned on appeal based upon faulty evidence introduced at the original trial. After the September 11, 2001, terrorist attacks in the United States, California state prison officials isolated Sirhan from other inmates for his own protection.

FURTHER READING

Clarke, James W. "Sirhan Sirhan." In *American Assassins: The Darker Side of Politics*. Rev. ed. Princeton,

N.J.: Princeton University Press, 1990. Clarke develops a typology for analyzing political assassins throughout American history.

Jansen, Godfrey. *Why Robert Kennedy Was Killed*. New York: Third Press, 1970. Argues that Sirhan's motive for assassinating Robert Kennedy was political.

Kaiser, Robert Blair. *"RFK Must Die": A History of the Robert Kennedy Assassination and Its Aftermath*. New York: Dutton, 1970. A comprehensive analysis of the criminal case from an assistant to the defense attorneys in charge of Sirhan's defense.

—*Scott P. Johnson*

SEE ALSO: Adolf Hitler; Joseph McCarthy; Richard Nixon; Lee Harvey Oswald; James Earl Ray.

JEFFREY SKILLING
American business executive of Enron Corporation

BORN: November 25, 1953; Pittsburgh, Pennsylvania
ALSO KNOWN AS: Jeffrey Keith Skilling (full name)
MAJOR OFFENSES: Fraud, conspiracy, making false statements, and insider trading
ACTIVE: 1990's-early 2000's
LOCALE: Houston, Texas
SENTENCE: Twenty-four years and four months in prison

EARLY LIFE

Jeffrey Skilling (SKIH-ling) was born into a comfortable middle-class family in Pittsburgh, Pennsylvania. His father, Tom Skilling, Jr., was a mechanical engineer who sold valves to power plants. Jeffrey had one older brother, Tom, who later became a well-known meteorologist in Chicago, and two younger siblings. His family moved first to New Jersey and then to the Chicago suburb of Aurora, Illinois, where Skilling was an excellent student. He was admitted to the National Honor Society and served as an alternate on his school's academic quiz team. He graduated near the top of his class from Aurora High School in 1971.

The fall following his graduation, Skilling received an engineering scholarship to study at Southern Methodist University (SMU) in Dallas, Texas. He joined Beta Theta Pi fraternity and graduated in 1975. Even within the generally conservative atmosphere of SMU, Skilling had a reputation for being politically and socially conser-

vative, as well as ambitious. At SMU, he met Susan Long, and the two were married a few days after graduation. They had a daughter and two sons but divorced in 1997. Skilling took a job doing asset and liability management with First National Bank right after his undergraduate years. In 1977, he was admitted to Harvard University's business school and earned an M.B.A. in 1979.

ENRON CAREER

After Harvard, Skilling went to work with McKinsey and Company as a consultant on energy and chemical businesses. During his years at McKinsey, Skilling met Enron chief executive officer (CEO) Kenneth Lay. In 1990, Lay hired Skilling to serve as chairman and chief executive officer of Enron Finance Corporation. A year later, Enron Finance Corporation merged with Enron Gas Marketing to form Enron Gas Services; Skilling served as chairman. Skilling was then named chairman of Enron Capital and Trade Resources. By 1997, Skilling was second in power only to Lay at Enron and in February, 2001, Skilling became CEO of Enron.

Enron had begun as a company focused on energy, mostly through distributing gas and electricity and through forms of construction such as building pipelines and power plants. Under Lay and Skilling, though, Enron used its assets to move into other fields, eventually trading in more than eight hundred products, including communications and financial instruments.

Jeffrey Skilling. (AP/Wide World Photos)

Many analysts now argue that Enron's apparent success was largely a deception. There were rumors throughout the business world that many of Enron's contracts were results of bribery and political pressure. Following the late 1980's, executives with the company had also been accused of engaging in insider trading, or buying and selling stock by individuals engaged in activities that would influence the price of the stock. Under chief financial officer (CFO) Andrew Fastow, hired by Skilling, Enron created companies that were off shore and off the books. This enabled the company to move currency that could not easily be tracked and to hide losses. Moving currency and assets around gave executives the power to make their company appear more profitable than it actually was and thereby drive up its stock price, bringing more money into the company and enriching Enron executives.

By 2000, Enron stock had reached its highest price. Company executives, who knew about their corporation's hidden losses, sold their own stock. Skilling is

reported to have sold millions of dollars in Enron stock at this time. In August, 2001, Skilling resigned, saying that he wanted to devote more time to his family and to charity work. He married former Enron vice president for board communications Rebecca Carter in March, 2002.

LEGAL ACTION AND OUTCOME

Skilling was indicted on thirty-five counts of fraud, conspiracy, insider trading, and lying to auditors by a grand jury in Houston on July 7, 2004. He went on trial, with Lay, in Houston on January 30, 2006. Led by renowned attorney Daniel Petrocelli, Skilling's legal defense team maintained that the executive had not known of fraudulent activities within the company, and he pleaded not guilty on all counts. The attorneys also attempted to delay the legal proceedings and have them moved out of Houston, claiming that the negative publicity and notoriety that their client had received would make it impossible for him to receive a fair trial. Jurors reported that they had difficulty reaching a decision, but on May 25, 2006, Skilling was found guilty of nineteen counts of fraud, conspiracy, making false statements, and insider trading. His sentencing, and that of Lay, was set for October, 2006. The death of Ken Lay on July 5, 2006, from a heart attack suffered during a family vacation automatically led a federal judge to vacate Lay's sentence. Skilling, however, was sentenced to more than twenty-four years in prison; his assets were liquidated, with $45 million earmarked for restitution and most of the balance for legal fees. Skilling expressed remorse but did not admit to guilt, as he and his attorneys prepared an appeal.

IMPACT

The downfall of a highly regarded businessman such as Jeffrey Skilling contributed to a negative popular view of the world of American finance. The Enron scandal was one of several widely publicized corporate scandals in the United States at the beginning of the twenty-first century. As a result, the word "Enron" became virtually synonymous with corporate corruption.

Lawmakers responded to public concern over apparently corrupt practices at Enron and several other companies by passing the Sarbanes-Oxley Act, named after Maryland Democratic senator Paul Sarbanes and Ohio Republican representative Michael Oxley, in July, 2002. The Sarbanes-Oxley Act is generally considered the greatest change to American securities law since the 1930's. It was intended to prevent crimes such as securities fraud by raising accounting requirements, increasing penalties for corporate criminals, and mandating changes in the Securities and Exchange Commission (SEC).

At the time of its collapse, Enron's bankruptcy was the largest bankruptcy in American history. The affair also produced waves throughout American financial circles. The investigation of Enron led to the trial of the Arthur Anderson accounting firm, which in turn incriminated other companies. The widening investigation helped to uncover fraud at Worldcom, and Worldcom's own resulting bankruptcy was even bigger than that of Enron.

FURTHER READING

Eichenwald, Kurt. *Conspiracy of Fools: A True Story.* New York: Random House, 2005. A popular but detailed account of the Enron scandal.

McLean, Bethany, and Peter Elkind. *The Smartest Guys in the Room: The Amazing Rise and Scandalous Fall of Enron.* New York: Portfolio, 2003. The story of the Enron company, written by a *Fortune* reporter who was one of the first to question whether Enron was overvalued.

Skeel, David. *Icarus in the Boardroom: The Fundamental Flaws in Corporate America and Where They Came From.* New York: Oxford University Press, 2005. Inspired by the actions of Skilling, Lay, and other high-profile executives in the early twenty-first century, this book takes a general look at the risk-taking behavior of corporate leaders in American society.

—*Carl L. Bankston III*

SEE ALSO: Bernard Ebbers; Martin Frankel; Kenneth Lay; Michael Milken.

OTTO SKORZENY
Officer in the Nazi Waffen-Schutzstaffel

BORN: June 12, 1908; Vienna, Austria
DIED: July 5, 1975; Madrid, Spain
ALSO KNOWN AS: Most Dangerous Man in Europe
CAUSE OF NOTORIETY: Skorzeny, as the commando leader of the combat arm of the German Waffen-Schutzstaffel (Waffen-SS), engaged in daring exploits, including the rescue of Italian leader Benito Mussolini.
ACTIVE: 1939-1945
LOCALE: Europe

EARLY LIFE

Otto Skorzeny (AH-toh skor-ZEE-nee) was born into a middle-class Austrian family with a long history of military service. He was a gifted student and was an exceptionally skilled fencer, engaging in fifteen duels. During his tenth contest, his opponent smote his cheek, leaving a scar that was quite dramatic. In 1931, he joined the Austrian Nazi Party and quickly joined the Sturm Abteilung (SA, also known as "storm troopers"). He exhibited superior leadership skills and was involved with the Anschluss: He prevented the Austrian president, Wilhelm Miklas, from being shot.

NAZI CAREER

Because of Skorzeny's size (he was six feet, four inches in height), he was appointed as one of Hitler's personal bodyguards. After the war commenced, Skorzeny, then working as a civil engineer, volunteered for service in the Luftwaffe (German air force) but was turned down because he was over the age of thirty. Failing that, he turned to the Waffen-SS, or the combat arm of the Schutzstaffel (SS). On February 21, 1940, Skorzeny went off to war with one of its most famous units, the Leibstandarte-SS Adolf Hitler (loosely translated as Adolf Hitler's SS bodyguard regiment), and fought with distinction in the campaigns against the Soviet Union in 1941 and 1942. He was wounded and returned to Germany in December of 1942, a winner of the Iron Cross for bravery under fire.

As he recuperated, Skorzeny was told about a commando group being formed by Hitler. It was in this capacity that Skorzeny achieved fame by leading the operation to rescue Benito Mussolini, the dictator of Italy and a friend of Hitler, who had been removed from power and imprisoned by the Italian government. The Italians moved Mussolini from place to place in order to frustrate any would-be rescuers. Once he had information regarding Mussolini's location, Skorzeny led a glider-based assault, which rescued Mussolini without a single shot being fired. The exploit earned Skorzeny worldwide fame, promotion to major, and the achievement of the Knight's Cross, a higher order of the Iron Cross.

Skorzeny engaged in numerous daring operations, including Operation Rösselsprung, a paratroop commando operation aimed at capturing Yugoslavia's communist leader, Josip Broz, known as Tito. During the assassination attempt against Hitler in July, 1944, Skorzeny was in Berlin, where he helped put down a rebellion in the capital. During Operation Panzerfaust, Skorzeny kidnapped Romania's regent, Admiral Miklós Horthy de Nagybána's son Nicolas; this move forced Horthy to abdicate.

During the Battle of the Bulge, Skorzeny and his soldiers pretended to be Americans, causing immense problems for the Allies. He spent the first two months of 1945 commanding regular troops in the defense of the German provinces of Prussia and Pomerania as an acting major general. His bravery earned him the Oak Leaves to the Knight's Cross, a high honor.

Skorzeny surrendered to the United States in May, 1945. He was held for more than two years before being tried as a war criminal at the Dachau Military Tribunal, primarily because of his actions in the Battle of the Bulge. He remained a prisoner until July 27, 1948, at which point he escaped. After the war, Skorzeny served as consultant to several countries, including Egypt and Argentina. Moreover, it was rumored that Skorzeny helped many of his SS friends to escape Germany through Odessa.

IMPACT

Otto Skorzeny is notorious for his role in Hitler's Nazi Germany and for his status as a war criminal. Nevertheless, he led a truly fascinating life; likewise, he was incredibly lucky. He never received a prison sentence and was not considered a Nazi by the Allied Powers. At the end of his life, he was a multimillionaire. Furthermore, Skorzeny influenced the way people viewed special forces. Before him, war was won by throwing a massive army against another massive army, resulting in many deaths on both sides. Skorzeny showed that with the right training and skill, a few men could impact a war as greatly as any army.

FURTHER READING

Annussek, G. *Hitler's Raid to Save Mussolini.* New York: Da Capo Press, 2005. Recounts Germany's secret six-week operation to find and rescue the prisoner Mussolini and restore him to power.

Foley, Charles. *Commando Extraordinary.* Rev. ed. New York: Ballantine, 1957. Discusses guerrilla and underground movements during World War II, detailing Skorzeny's exploits in the process.

Skorzeny, Otto. *My Commando Operations: The Memoirs of Hitler's Most Daring Commando.* Translated by David Johnson. Reprint. Atglen, Pa.: Schiffer, 1995. Skorzeny provides behind-the-scenes details of important World War II battles and German and Russian secret military intelligence, among other information.

_____. *Skorzeny's Special Missions.* New York: Greenhill Books, 1997. Skorzeny naturally attempts make himself look benevolent, so he fails to mention anything that could hurt his image. A good read whose source must be taken into account.

Whiting, Charles. *Skorzeny: "The Most Dangerous Man in Europe."* New York: Da Capo Press, 1998. Whiting, an expert on Skorzeny's life and career, brings forth an updated biography on Skorzeny which answers questions that have long been asked about secret details of Skorzeny's missions.

—*Cary Stacy Smith*

SEE ALSO: Heinrich Himmler; Adolf Hitler; Benito Mussolini.

PAMELA ANN SMART
American murderer

BORN: August 16, 1967; Coral Gables, Florida
ALSO KNOWN AS: Pamela Ann Wojas (maiden name);
Pame
MAJOR OFFENSES: Conspiracy to commit murder,
accomplice to first-degree murder, and witness
tampering
ACTIVE: May 1, 1990
LOCALE: Derry, New Hampshire
SENTENCE: Life in prison without parole

EARLY LIFE

Pamela Ann Wojas, later known by her married name, Pamela Ann Smart (PAM-ah-lah an smahrt), was the second of three children for her mother, a stenographer, and her father, an airline pilot. During Wojas's high school years, her family moved from Florida to Windham, New Hampshire, where the petite beauty was described as a charismatic, organized, and popular high school student who participated in varsity cheerleading.

An outstanding college student, she aspired to a career in broadcasting and hosted a popular heavy metal radio show at Florida State University (FSU) that earned her the title "Maiden of Metal." While home in New Hampshire on Christmas break in 1986, Pamela met Gregory William Smart. An immediate attraction ensued between the couple, and they soon became inseparable. Gregg was handsome and athletic, had long brown locks, played the guitar, and shared Pamela's love of heavy metal music. He followed her to FSU, from which she graduated with honors in 1988.

The two were married on May 7, 1989, and appeared to have a perfect life, with Pamela decorating their home with the newest fashions and doting on their dog Halen, named after the rock group Van Halen. Pamela was hired as a media coordinator at Winnacunnet High School in Hampton, New Hampshire. She also participated as a local volunteer for Project Self-Esteem, a group discouraging illicit drug use in high school students. Gregg found early success as an insurance salesman at his father's company. He also adopted a more professional look, cutting his hair and dressing conservatively. The couple began to have serious problems after six months of marriage after Gregg confessed that he had had an affair. Despite Gregg's resolve to celebrate their first anniversary with a party and trip to Florida, a wounded Pamela had not forgiven Gregg's infidelity.

CRIMINAL CAREER

Pamela became romantically involved with William "Bill" Flynn, a fifteen-year-old student. Flynn became enthralled with his older lover, who reportedly told him that the only way they could continue their affair would be for him to kill her husband. Flynn would later testify that he made two botched attempts to kill Gregg at Pamela's urging. He finally succeeded in the murder of Gregg with the assistance of several friends on May 1, 1990, while Pamela attended a school meeting.

Pamela Smart with her husband Gregory Smart on their wedding day. (AP/
Wide World Photos)

Inside the Smart home, Flynn and Patrick "Pete" Randall waited for Gregg. Earlier, the boys had ransacked the house to suggest a burglary. At Pamela's insistence, they had put her cherished dog Halen in the basement to save him from being traumatized by the murder. When Gregg entered his dark home, the two boys overpowered him. After a brief struggle, Flynn killed Gregg execution-style with a single gunshot to the head. The boys ran to a getaway car driven by friend Vance "J. R." Lattime; Raymond Fowler was a passenger in the car.

Upon finding her husband's body later that evening, Pamela immediately ran to a neighbor's home. Suspicion quickly fell upon the young woman, who police later reported seemed to be more concerned with her dog's welfare than with Gregg's homicide. She was further criticized for calling a reporter the day of her husband's wake to give a television interview. Her cool demeanor in interviews and at the crime scene led to the nickname Ice Princess in the media.

LEGAL ACTION AND OUTCOME

On August 1, 1990, Pamela was arrested for first-degree murder. Her trial began on March 5, 1991. Although Pamela acknowledged having an affair with Flynn, she adamantly denied hatching the murder. Perhaps the most damning evidence at trial came from Cecilia Pierce, who was wired by the police. Pierce's recorded conversations with Pamela caught Pamela implying that she was involved in her husband's death. With the testimony of both Flynn and Pete Randall, Pamela was convicted as an accomplice to first-degree murder, conspiracy, and witness tampering and sentenced to life without the possibility of parole. Flynn and Randall were sentenced to forty years and Lattime to thirty years. While serving time at Bedford Hills Correctional Facility for Women in New York, Pamela earned master's degrees in law and English literature. She continued to claim her innocence and asked New Hampshire governor John Lynch to commute her sentence. Lattime was paroled on August 12, 2005.

IMPACT

The Pamela Ann Smart trial was the first fully televised trial in New Hampshire history. The unprecedented media frenzy surrounding the case inspired numerous books and two feature films. The Smart case is viewed by many scholars to mark the advent of live continuous courtroom coverage of sensational criminal trials. The scandalous sexual relationship between Smart and Flynn captivated the public imagination. While some people made light of the affair, others argued Smart was a sexual predator who used her seductive prowess to manipulate her young lover into murder.

The fact that Smart was not an abused woman fighting back at her tormentor also brought public attention to those rare women who kill their spouses for convenience or greed. These "black widows" are notorious for their cold demeanors and matter-of-fact attitude regarding murder. Perhaps because women are a small proportion of all killers, the senseless murder of Gregg Smart garnered a disproportionate amount of media coverage.

FURTHER READING

Fox, James A., Jack Levin, and Kenna Quinet. *The Will to Kill: Making Sense of Senseless Murder.* Boston: Pearson, 2005. The authors are experts in homicide and violence and explore the issues of power and control in various types of senseless murders.

Linedecker, Clifford L. *Babyface Killers.* New York: St. Martin's Press, 1999. Discusses the disturbing cases of juveniles across the country who have killed and explores some of the social reasons for these tragedies.

Maynard, Joyce. *To Die For.* New York: Signet Books, 1995. This novel is loosely based on the Smart case and was made into a major motion picture starring Nicole Kidman in 1996.

—*Denise Paquette Boots*

SEE ALSO: Bambi Bembenek; Marie Hilley; Mary Kay Letourneau; Madeleine Smith; Ruth Snyder.

GERALD L. K. SMITH
American politician and founder of the America First Party

BORN: February 27, 1898; Pardeeville, Wisconsin
DIED: April 15, 1976; Eureka Springs, Arkansas
ALSO KNOWN AS: Gerald Lyman Kenneth Smith (full name)
CAUSE OF NOTORIETY: Smith promoted bigotry and hate with his virulent radio programs and writings aimed at Jews, African Americans, and politicians.
ACTIVE: 1932-1976
LOCALE: United States

EARLY LIFE
Gerald L. K. Smith was born in Pardeeville, in the Kickapoo Valley of rural southwestern Wisconsin. He grew up in a strict Disciples of Christ family in which his mother was the disciplinarian. Smith's father was a farmer and traveling salesman. Smith's education took place in a one-room schoolhouse until his family moved to a larger town, Viroqua, where Smith attended high school and excelled in debate and oratory. He was ordained a minister in 1916 and graduated the following year with a bachelor of oratory degree from Valparaiso University in Indiana. In 1922, Smith married an attractive church singer, Elna Sorenson, who would be his wife for fifty-two years.

After Elna contracted tuberculosis, Smith moved from Indiana to Louisiana in 1928 to become the pastor of a larger church in Shreveport, a city reputed to be a good place for people to recover from tuberculosis. As a minister, Smith effectively used the pulpit to save souls and raise money. He also used a newly developing medium, radio, to attack corruption and local utility companies, as well as to support trade unions.

POLITICAL CAREER
In 1932, Smith met Louisiana governor Huey Long and left the ministry to enter politics. The two noted orators launched the Share Our Wealth movement, which proposed a cap on personal income. After Long was assassinated in 1935, Smith delivered the funeral oration before an audience of 150,000 in the state capitol. For a short time, Smith led the Share Our Wealth society on his own. However, he soon entered into an alliance with two nationally known figures—Francis Townsend, famous for his old-age pension movement, and Father Charles Coughlin, a Roman Catholic priest with the largest radio audience in the nation—to form a new political party, the Union Party. The party nominated Senator William Lemke, a Republican from North Dakota, as its presidential candidate in the 1936 election, but Lemke failed to win a single electoral college vote. Smith's audiences peaked during the campaign, and despite his party's failure, his followers remained loyal. In an era of noteworthy demagogic orators, Smith was acknowledged by many observers to be by far the best.

After the election, Smith moved to Detroit and transformed the Share Our Wealth movement into a racist, white supremacist group. Prior to the United States' entry into World War II, Smith had been active in the most powerful isolationist group in the country, the America First Committee. After the attack on Pearl Harbor in late 1941, Smith formed the America First Party. He ran for the U.S. Senate as a Republican in Michigan but lost in the primary election. In 1942, Smith organized the Christian Nationalist Crusade and began publishing a newspaper, *The Cross and the Flag*, which was to continue for thirty-four years. Smith entered politics again as the America First Party candidate in the 1944 presidential election, in which he received a minuscule number of votes. In 1948, he again sought the presidency in a pathetic campaign based on a platform that included a focus on white supremacy, deporting blacks and Zionist Jews, and constructing ghettos for the Jews who remained. He obviously was more successful as a propagandist, agitator, and fund-raiser than as a candidate. Moreover, Smith, in response to his radio appeals, also received enough money through the mail to become a millionaire.

Too extreme in his views for most rightists, Smith was an equal-opportunity rabble-rouser: Conservatives, liberals, and socialists were all enemies of the Republic in his eyes. He joined with the anti-Semitic automobile tycoon Henry Ford in asserting that "communism is Jewish" and became a Holocaust denier. During the 1940's, Smith barnstormed the nation, crusading against communism, the "Jew-infested" United Nations, the Truman Doctrine, the Marshall Plan, and the North Atlantic Treaty Organization (NATO). Smith moved his crusade headquarters to St. Louis in 1947, Tulsa in 1949, and Los Angeles in 1953.

By the 1960's, Smith had moved to Eureka Springs, Arkansas, where his series of "sacred projects" helped revive the local economy. Smith became a local hero, and in 1964 he began construction of "Holy Land," a planned religious theme park slated to cost $100 million. The park was never completed, but in 1966 its main mon-

---

THE HOLLYWOOD HIGH SCHOOL SPEECH

Gerald L. K. Smith conducted a virulent crusade against Communism throughout the nation, indicting Jews, Hollywood celebrities, and others as "Reds":

On May 25, 1951, a committee, working in cooperation with me and functioning in behalf of the California Anti-Communist League and the American Anti-Communist League, presented the following statement to the Congress of the United States. The statement was formally filed during a hearing of the Un-American Activities Committee. I was present in the hearing room when the statement was presented. It read as follows:

ATTENTION: UN-AMERICAN ACTIVITIES COMMITTEE
The American Anti-Communist League with headquarters at 1533 South Grand Avenue, St. Louis, Missouri, respectfully invited your attention to the following:

1. We are of the opinion that John Garfield has perjured himself and that Senator Jack B. Tenney of Los Angeles should be subpoenaed as an expert witness on this matter.
2. We believe that José Ferrer has perjured himself in pleading a false innocence concerning his association with Communist-front organizations.
3. We believe that Edward G. Robinson is either being neglected in this investigation or has been whitewashed, unless the Committee has plans to reopen the investigation and question Robinson concerning his propaganda activities.
4. We believe that one of the most enigmatic and guilty figures in the film colony is Charles Chaplin. He should be summoned before your Committee and made to give an account of his activities, which go back as far as the historic Bridgman raid in 1922. We have in our possession a book which reveals that Charles Chaplin donated to the Communist Party and that a record of his donations was found in barrels dug up out of the sand dunes following the Bridgman raid.
5. We believe your Committee should investigate the Warner Brothers and they should be called on to explain their use of *Mission to Moscow*, which perhaps made more propaganda for Russia than all the Communist organizations in Hollywood combined.
6. We believe that you should investigate the chief director of MGM, Mr. Dore Schary, who was dismissed from RKO by Howard Hughes because of his pro-Red attitude and hired by MGM to supersede the late Jim McGuinness, a great patriot who dared expose Communism in Hollywood. It is believed by important and intelligent observers in California and elsewhere that McGuinness was put on the shelf and Schary was promoted because of McGuinness' activity in cooperation with your Committee.

Every claim made in this memo can be substantiated by Senator Jack B. Tenney and professional investigators that have worked with him. . . . This statement is endorsed by the California Anti-Communist League. . . .

Source: Gerald L. K. Smith, *Hollywood High School Speech: Exposing Reds and Their Dupes in the Film Colony* (St. Louis, Mo.: Christian Nationalist Crusade, [1951?]).

---

ument, the Christ of the Ozarks—a seven-story, cross-shaped rendition of Jesus overlooking the town—was dedicated. Smith also staged an annual outdoor Passion play, inspired by the Oberammergau productions in Germany; it became the largest outdoor pageant in the United States.

Smith died of pneumonia in 1976 at the age of seventy-eight. He and his wife were buried adjacent to the Christ of the Ozarks statue. Ever the firebrand, Smith went to the grave unrepentant and wrote inflammatory tracts until his death. He had the power to touch people's minds with his splendid gift of oratory. The tragedy of his life is that he chose to use that gift for the cause of bigotry.

IMPACT
It is edifying that many of the reprehensible ideas that were widely held and emphasized by Gerald L. K. Smith and other demagogues became increasingly marginalized in American public life, although it should be remembered how recently such hate speech was condoned. Smith's success at raising considerable money through radio talks, direct mail campaigns, book distribution, and personal appearances may well have inspired later media-savvy televangelists such as Oral Roberts and Pat Robertson. Furthermore, his proposed religious theme park might have provided inspiration for other religious entrepreneurs, such as Jim Bakker with his Heritage USA park.

FURTHER READING

Jeansonne, Glen. *Gerald L. K. Smith: Minister of Hate.* New Haven, Conn.: Yale University Press, 1988. A historian's thoroughly researched biography with an accumulation of details that provides a portrait of both the public and the private man.

Smith, Gerald L. K. *Besieged Patriot: Autobiographical Episodes Exposing Communism, Traitorism, and Zionism from the Life of Gerald L. K. Smith.* Eureka Springs, Ark.: Elna M. Smith Foundation, 1978. Writings from the pen of the demagogue.

_____. *The Story of the Statue the Christ of the Ozarks.* Eureka Springs, Ark.: Elna M. Smith Foundation, 1967. An explanation of the sacred projects in Eureka Springs, Smith's monument to himself, that culminated in a seventy-foot-high sculpture that can be seen from three states.

—*Theodore M. Vestal*

SEE ALSO: Charles E. Coughlin; David Duke; Huey Long; William Joseph Simmons.

MADELEINE SMITH
Accused Scottish murderer

BORN: March 29, 1835; Glasgow, Scotland
DIED: April 12, 1928; New York, New York
ALSO KNOWN AS: Lena Wardle; Lena Wardle Sheehy; Magdalene Hamilton Smith (birth name)
CAUSE OF NOTORIETY: Smith allegedly murdered her lover Pierre L'Angelier, who had refused to return the letters she wrote him.
ACTIVE: March 23, 1857
LOCALE: West End, Glasgow, Scotland
SENTENCE: Found "not proven" (Scotland's so-called third verdict)

EARLY LIFE

Madeleine Smith was the eldest daughter and granddaughter of well-respected and admired architects in Glasgow. After returning from finishing school in London, she was given responsibility for the management of her family's household at the age of eighteen. She was described by contemporaries as being very attractive and confident, with dark hair and gray eyes.

As was customary among upper-class Glaswegians, Smith was expected to make a good marriage. The period between school and marriage could, on occasion, be a time for daring acts that one would never think of doing later. For Smith, such an act was her dalliance with a gardener's son who was working as a warehouse clerk, Émile L'Angelier. Even if L'Angelier's death had not occurred, the revelation of such a relationship between a well-brought-up young woman and a foreign working-class man would have created a scandal throughout Scotland.

The date of Smith and L'Angelier's first meeting and who introduced them is unknown. From the beginning, however, notes passed between them. He ordered her to destroy his letters, he said, so they would not be found by a member of her family. Her letters to him are a major part of the murder case.

The Smiths had searched for and found a suitable husband for Madeleine, one William Minnoch. Madeleine accepted Minnoch's marriage proposal in January of 1857. Knowing that her letters to L'Angelier would not find favor with her fiancé if found, she asked L'Angelier for their return. He refused.

As someone familiar with the gardening business, L'Angelier was well accustomed to the use of arsenic in killing pests. He was known also to use it as a drug. A not-uncommon substance at the time, arsenic was used by women as a form of face powder. To buy it, one had only to sign the "Poison Book" in the apothecary shop.

CRIMINAL CAREER

After the death of L'Angelier, it was assumed by many that Smith poisoned him with arsenic in cocoa. The quantity of arsenic found in the dead man's body, however, was much greater than that which could have been hidden in a simple cup of cocoa. At least one-half ounce of arsenic remained in the deceased after an entire night of stomach upset and diarrhea. Such an amount had never been used to cause the death of a human, except in suicide.

In the weeks preceding his death, L'Angelier stated to his friends and employers that he had been sick very often and that Smith was trying to poison him. He mentioned this to friends so often that after a while they paid no attention to such statements. During this period, L'Angelier continued to see Smith and to take cocoa from her on a regular basis.

L'Angelier had also stated to a friend that he would not allow Smith to marry another man as long as he himself lived. He threatened Smith that he would show all her letters to her father. Smith begged him not to do so, as she could be disowned. She took a great chance and wrote to L'Angelier on Tuesday, February 10, 1857, in an attempt to end their relationship once and for all. L'Angelier's diary, the first entry of which is dated Wednesday, February 11, 1857, is very casual in its recording of his seeing Smith as well as other friends. His regular mentions of illness are virtually afterthoughts in the notations made almost every day.

Smith stated in two of her letters to L'Angelier that she was taking arsenic for her complexion; however she did not make a purchase of arsenic until two days after his first reported illness. Whether Smith committed murder or whether L'Angelier, intentionally or accidentally, committed suicide in such a way as could send his lover to the gallows remains unknown.

LEGAL ACTION AND OUTCOME

Before Smith's trial, at the request of her lead attorney, John Inglis, L'Angelier's diary was not admitted into evidence; however Smith's letters to L'Angelier were. Her fiancé had quickly withdrawn his marriage proposal after she was arrested. During the nine-day trial, many witnesses recalled that L'Angelier had mentioned previous suicide attempts after being jilted by at least one other wealthy woman.

If the jury had found Smith guilty of his death, the sentence would have been death by hanging. Scotland has a distinctive verdict aside from the well-known ones of guilty or innocent: the verdict of "not proven." This is not a statement of innocence, but it is not a statement of guilt, either. The third verdict states that the prosecution has not proven its case, and the individual on trial may go free. In Smith's case, the jury only deliberated thirty minutes before reaching the "not proven" verdict.

Smith went to London and, in 1861, married George Wardle, a draftsman. She and Wardle remained married for many years and had two children. Their marriage ultimately ended in divorce. Smith emigrated to the United States at the age of seventy-one and married again. She died in New York City on April 12, 1928.

IMPACT

Madeleine Smith's audience—the public—applauded her "not proven" verdict, although Inglis, her attorney, considered her to be guilty. So, too, did such observers as Henry James, Jane Carlyle, and George Eliot. Another writer, Belfort Bax, believed that Smith had not received a conviction because of the fact that she was a woman.

FURTHER READING

MacGowan, Douglas. *Murder in Victorian Scotland: The Trial of Madeleine Smith*. Westport, Conn.: Greenwood Press, 1999. A history of young women's waiting years before marriage and the resulting boredom dispelled by affairs with those not of their class.

Morehead, Nigel. *That Nice Miss Smith*. London: F. Muellar, 1957. Smith is given as an example of a woman from a respectable background who became involved with a man far below her social station.

Roughead, William. *Classic Crimes: A Selection from the Works of William Roughead*. New York: Vintage Books, 1976. A humorous account of the Glasgow, Scotland, that produced Madeleine Smith and Émile L'Angelier; an abridgment of the account written by Roughead in 1922.

Trestrail, John H. *Criminal Poisoning*. Grand Rapids, Mich.: Spectrum Health, 2000. A survey of poison as a weapon in cases of murder.

—*Ellen B. Lindsay*

SEE ALSO: Bambi Bembenek; Marie Hilley; Pamela Ann Smart; Ruth Snyder.

SUSAN SMITH
American murderer

BORN: September 26, 1971; Union, South Carolina
ALSO KNOWN AS: Susan Leigh Vaughn (birth name)
MAJOR OFFENSE: Murder of her two children
ACTIVE: October 25, 1994
LOCALE: Union, South Carolina
SENTENCE: Thirty years to life in prison

EARLY LIFE
Susan Smith was born into a dysfunctional family. Her father was a violent alcoholic, and her parents divorced when Susan was six. After the divorce, Susan's mother married Beverly Russell, a local appliance store owner. Five weeks later, Susan's father committed suicide. When Susan was fifteen, Russell began sexually molesting her. Despite these early dysfunctional years, Susan did well in school. She volunteered at the hospital and was named "friendliest female" by peers at her high school. Friends remembered her as cheerful. Despite this seemingly normal existence, her life was in turmoil as she entered into a series of promiscuous love affairs and unsuccessful relationships. In the summer of 1988, Susan began working at a Winn-Dixie market, had an affair with an older married man, became pregnant, and had an abortion. In November, Susan attempted suicide and was hospitalized.

During the summer of 1990, Susan began dating David Smith, who also worked at Winn-Dixie. She became pregnant again, and in January David and Susan got married. In November, 1992, Susan became pregnant again. However, David was distraught about Susan's extramarital affairs, and a few weeks later, the couple agreed to end the marriage.

In 1994, Susan secured a job at Conso Products. There, she met Tom Findlay, the son of the company owner, and they began dating. However, on October 17, Tom wrote a letter explaining that he could no longer see Susan because he did not want a ready-made family.

SLEEPING CHILDREN
Susan was angry and hurt by Tom's letter, and on October 25, 1994, she drove to John D. Long Lake and parked on a boat ramp. Her children, Michael (age three) and Alex (fourteen months), were sleeping in their car seats. Susan stepped from the car, released the hand brake, and watched the car with the children inside disappear into the lake. She then turned and ran to a nearby house and told the occupant that a black man had pointed a gun at her and had driven off with her children.

The story made national headlines. Susan and David appeared on the national television news program *Good Morning America*, and Susan pleaded for help in finding her sons. Initially, people believed her story, and an intense search for the kidnapper followed. Susan described the kidnapper to a sketch artist, and the picture was widely distributed. Meanwhile, the search for Susan's children continued, as did the investigation of her story by law enforcement. After she tested poorly on polygraph exams, police began to dissect Susan's story and confronted her with inconsistencies in her statements. Nine days after her children had disappeared, Susan confessed to murdering her two boys.

LEGAL ACTION AND OUTCOME
Susan's mother and her husband mortgaged their home to pay for attorneys' fees. Beverly hired David Bruck, a

Susan and David Smith. (AP/Wide World Photos)

Harvard-trained attorney, and Bruck hired Judith Clarke to assist. Clarke had worked on the case involving Theodore "the Unabomber" Kaczynski and was considered an expert on death penalty cases. The case was tried by Thomas Pope, who, at age thirty-two, was the youngest prosecutor in the state of South Carolina. Susan underwent a series of psychiatric evaluations and was diagnosed as suffering from dependent personality disorder and depression. However, on July 11, 1995, Susan was ruled mentally competent to stand trial, and the trial commenced on July 18.

The trial was held at Union County Courthouse in Judge William Howard's courtroom. Bruck decided to use hometown sympathy in Susan's trial, hoping it would make it difficult for a jury to implement the death penalty. After two days of testimony, the state rested its case, and the defense began. The defense attorneys argued that Susan suffered from severe mental depression and that the murders were a failed suicide in which Susan planned to drown herself as well as her two sons.

Dr. Seymore Halleck, the psychiatrist who had evaluated Susan, testified that she had suicidal thoughts and depression during the time leading up to murder of her two sons. He also testified that Susan had maintained a series of destructive relationships with at least four different men during the four months preceding the murder and that she had used sex to cure the loneliness in her life. Others testified that Susan had been suicidal most of her life. Afterward, in a move that left the courtroom stunned, Judge Howard allowed the jury to consider a lesser charge of involuntary manslaughter, which carried a lighter penalty. On the last day of the penalty phase of the trial, Russell testified that he had molested Susan when she was a teenager and had consensual sex with her as an adult. After a short deliberation, the jury rejected the death penalty, and Susan was sentenced to thirty years to life in a penitentiary; she would be eligible for parole in 2025.

IMPACT

Susan Smith invented a story about a black man who had kidnapped her two sons at gunpoint. The case had the potential to be racially divisive. The fact that her story was widely accepted indicated a level of latent racism held by many Americans. However, after her confession, the media condemned those who jumped to conclusions about a black kidnapper, and in Union, a series of meetings were held during which black and white residents came together in unity. Black ministers preached messages of love, and racial undertones were quickly dashed.

FURTHER READING

Meyer, C., M. Oberman, with Kelly White et al. *Mothers Who Kill Their Children: Understanding the Acts of Moms from Susan Smith to the "Prom Mom."* New York: New York University Press, 2001. An examination of the motives of several women in killing their children.

Russell, Linda, and Shirley Stephens. *My Daughter Susan Smith.* Brentwood, Tenn.: Authors Book Nook, 2000. Susan Smith's mother explores the facts behind her daughter's crime and elements in her life that led up to it.

Smith, David, with Carol Calef. *Beyond All Reason: My Life with Susan Smith.* New York: Kensington Books, 1995. David Smith takes his turn in examining how the tragedy of his children's deaths occurred and could have been prevented.

—*Jerry W. Hollingsworth*

See also: Darlie Routier; Andrea Yates.

RUTH SNYDER
American murderer

BORN: March 27, 1895; Manhattan, New York
DIED: January 12, 1928; Sing Sing Prison, Ossining, New York
ALSO KNOWN AS: Ruth Brown (birth name); Ruth Brown Snyder (full name); Tommy; Tommie; Momie; Momsie; Tiger Woman; Bloody Blonde; Granite Woman
MAJOR OFFENSE: Murder
ACTIVE: March 20, 1927
LOCALE: Queens Village, Long Island, New York
SENTENCE: Death by electrocution

EARLY LIFE
The only child of a working-class Norwegian father and a Swedish mother, Ruth Snyder (SNI-duhr) was a sickly youngster. She trained at business school instead of finishing high school and held various jobs, including switchboard operator, salesgirl, and stenographer. In 1915, she married Albert Snyder, an art editor for *Motor Boating* magazine. Three years later, their daughter, Lorraine, was born. Shortly after, they moved to suburban Queens Village.

Ruth resisted settling down to the wife-and-mother role expected by her husband and neighbors. Always vivacious and engaging, she resented her older dull and glum husband. Before Albert had met Ruth, his fiancé, Jessie Guishard, had died, and Albert continued to mourn her; he often compared Ruth unfavorably with his first love. Other factors strained the marriage, and the two frequently fought.

In 1925, Ruth met corset salesman Henry Judd Gray, who was also married and had a daughter Lorraine's age. Meeting at hotels (they kept a suitcase at the Waldorf-Astoria) and occasionally at Ruth's home, the couple proceeded with their love affair until the murder of Albert.

CRIMINAL CAREER
Ruth secretly arranged for an insurance policy on her husband that carried a double indemnity clause. Combined with two other policies, Albert's insurance would have amounted to $96,000 in the event of his death. Ruth soon began her attempts to kill him, using gas, sleeping pills, and poisons, but Albert always survived. In the end, she persuaded Gray to help her. Following a late-night party, she and Gray murdered Albert in his bed, battering his head with a sash-weight, strangling him with picture wire, and poisoning him with chloroform. They then ransacked the house, emptying drawers and throwing around household items. After the couple burned their bloody clothing and changed (Gray into one of Albert's new shirts), Gray tied Ruth up, putting a loose gag in her mouth, and left for Syracuse. At dawn and still bound, Ruth woke Lorraine, telling her daughter that she had been attacked by robbers and to get the neighbors to telephone the police.

LEGAL ACTION AND OUTCOME
Police investigators at the crime scene almost immediately suspected Ruth's involvement in the murder. The cover-up was simply unbelievable: Jewels that Ruth claimed had been stolen were found under her mattress, as was the sash-weight in the basement. Although Ruth insisted she had been knocked unconscious, a doctor could find no evidence of a blow. She soon confessed and named Gray. His carefully executed alibi disintegrated under police scrutiny, and he too confessed.

The two were tried jointly in what came to be called the Sash-Weight Murder, although they had separate advocates and blamed each other throughout the proceedings. The appeals process pushed the June 20, 1927, date of execution to January 12, 1928. Ruth's execution occurred shortly after 11:00 P.M., followed by Gray's.

IMPACT
Although legally tried in Queen's County Court, Ruth Snyder was popularly tried by the press as a heartless Nordic murderer and condemned by a bloodthirsty public. Gray fared better: His stoicism, praying, and Bible study were much celebrated. The case made headlines from start to finish, inspiring plays, books, and films, notably *Double Indemnity* (1944) and *The Postman Always Rings Twice* (1946). Photographer Thomas Howard secretly took the shocking photograph of Snyder as she was electrocuted, which was published the next day in the *New York Daily News*, the only such image of a woman.

FURTHER READING
Jones, Ann. *Women Who Kill*. New York: Holt, Rinehart, and Winston, 1980. Contends the fascinating element of the Snyder-Gray crime was the ordinariness of those involved and the vicarious experience of the public as the press painted Snyder a monster and Gray a hero.

Pelizzon, V. Penelope, and Nancy M. West. "Multiple Indemnity: Film Noir, James M. Cain, and Adaptations of a Tabloid Case." *Narrative* 13, no. 3 (2005): 211-237. Explores the relationship between tabloid, pulp fiction crime novel, and film noir generated by the Snyder-Gray case. Includes a strong bibliography.

Ramey, Jessie. "The Bloody Blonde and the Marble Woman: Gender and Power in the Case of Ruth Snyder." *Journal of Social History* 37, no. 3 (2004):

625-650. Argues that the Snyder-Gray case reveals a process-driven gendered discourse reflected in the press coverage during the trial and popular culture responses to it.

—Jennie MacDonald

SEE ALSO: Bambi Bembenek; Marie Hilley; Pamela Ann Smart; Madeleine Smith.

CHARLES SOBRAJ
Vietnamese serial killer

BORN: April 6, 1944; Saigon (now Ho Chi Minh City), Vietnam

ALSO KNOWN AS: Gurhmuk Sobraj (full name); Charles Sobhraj; Bikini Killer; the Serpent

MAJOR OFFENSES: Burglary and murder

ACTIVE: 1975-2004

LOCALE: France, Eastern Europe, Thailand, and India

SENTENCE: Twelve years' imprisonment for one murder; life imprisonment for two other murders

EARLY LIFE

Charles Sobraj (SOH-brahj) was born out of wedlock to a Vietnamese mother and an Indian father, who abandoned the family. Sobraj's mother blamed Charles for his father's abandonment. Eventually, Sobraj was adopted by his mother's French boyfriend; however, he was not given the same treatment as the children whom the couple had together. Because Sobraj's adopted father was in the military, the family moved back and forth between France and Indochina, which created discipline and personality problems for Sobraj. As a teenager, he began committing petty crimes.

CRIMINAL CAREER

Sobraj served his first jail sentence for burglary in 1963 near Paris. While in jail, he became friends with Félix d'Escogne and moved in with him after he was paroled. D'Escogne led a split life between Paris high society and the criminal underworld. Sobraj met and became engaged to Chantal, a Parisian woman who waited for him while he served a sentence for stealing a car. After he was released, Sobraj and Chantal got married. The couple fled France to escape impending arrest on other charges

and moved to Bombay in 1970, where they had a baby girl.

In 1973, Sobraj was arrested for robbing a jewelry store and was imprisoned. He escaped with his wife's help, but the couple were caught and arrested. Sobraj's parents sent money from Saigon for the couple's bail, and Sobraj and Chantal moved to Afghanistan. After Sobraj had twice escaped from prison, the couple parted ways, and Chantal returned to France. Sobraj went to Iran. Sobraj remained on the run for two years, using stolen passports, and traveled throughout Eastern Europe and the Middle East. Sobraj and his brother committed several crimes together; Sobraj was imprisoned in Turkey but again escaped.

Now in Thailand, Sobraj accrued numerous followers—typically foreign tourists following the "hippie trail"—by aiding them in various difficult situations, which, unknown to the travelers, were often created by Sobraj. He met an Indian man named Ajay Chowdhury in this manner, and Chowdhury became his partner in robbery and fraud. Sobraj had illusions of creating a crime family like that of Charles Manson in the United States.

In 1975, Sobraj and Chowdhury drowned their first known murder victim, an American named Jennie Bollivar. Vitali Hakim was the next victim; he was burned at the hands of Sobraj and his followers. Henk Bintanja and Cornelia Hemker, a Dutch engaged couple, were then strangled and burned in December, 1975. Sobraj and Chowdhury drowned another woman, Charmayne Carrou from France. Sobraj would earn the nickname Bikini Killer as a result of his two drowning murders. On December 21-22, 1975, Sobraj and Marie-Andrée Leclerc—one of Sobraj's most devoted followers—murdered Laurent Ormond Carrière, a Canadian national, and Connie Bronzich from California. Afterward, Sobraj went to Calcutta and murdered Israeli scholar Avoni Jacob in order to obtain his passport. Meanwhile, Leclerc and Chowdhury were questioned by the Thai police about the murders but were subsequently released.

Chowdhury, Leclerc, and Sobraj regrouped and stole some gems. However, Chowdhury disappeared after giving the jewels to Sobraj; he was believed to have been murdered by Sobraj, who then went with Leclerc to Geneva, Switzerland. Sobraj gained more followers there and then killed Frenchman Jean-Luc Solomon by poisoning him. In 1976, two American women followers of Sobraj were captured following the drugging of several French tourists. Upon interrogation, the two women told the police everything they knew about Sobraj, and Sobraj was charged with Solomon's murder.

LEGAL ACTION AND OUTCOME

Sobraj was sentenced to twelve years' imprisonment for Solomon's murder. He led a privileged life while in prison as a result of his bribing the guards. He talked about the murders to journalists but never admitted guilt. To avoid his twenty-year-old Thai arrest warrant, Sobraj purposely extended his sentence. In March, 1986, he escaped after drugging prison guards, was recaptured, and his original term was extended by ten years.

Sobraj was released on February 17, 1997. Because most of the warrants and evidence against him were lost by then, and because prosecution witnesses were difficult to locate, Sobraj was allowed to return to France. Numerous people were still seeking justice for other murders he allegedly committed, however; Sobraj was sentenced to life imprisonment on August 20, 2004, for the murders of Bronzich and Carrière.

IMPACT

Charles Sobraj is a testament to the far-reaching hold that the crimes of Charles Manson had on other like-minded, megalomaniacal criminals. He terrorized an entire region of the world, choosing his victims with apparent randomness, just as Manson briefly did in Los Angeles in 1969. In twenty-first century interviews, Sobraj displayed no remorse for his crimes. The brazenness of his murders caught the interest of journalists, who wrote widely of his rituals and escapes, and is reflected in popular culture. The American television program *Law & Order: Criminal Intent* based one of its shows on his life and titled it "Slither." Furthermore, after his return to Paris in the late 1990's, Sobraj hired an agent and allegedly was paid fifteen million dollars for a film deal about his life.

FURTHER READING

Egger, Steven A. *The Killers Among Us*. 2d ed. Upper Saddle River, N.J.: Pearson Education, 2002. Provides a brief description about Sobraj's criminal life and notes that Sobraj did not consider his killings "murder"; rather, he called them "cleaning."

Neville, Richard, and Julie Clarke. *The Life and Crimes of Charles Sobhraj*. Sydney: Jonathan Cape, 1997. Neville and Clarke cover Sobraj's murderous travels across Asia, showing how a charismatic person can enlist followers even in criminal activity.

Newton, Michael. *The Encyclopedia of Serial Killers*. New York: Checkmark Books, 2000. Provides information on Sobraj in a manner that is easily understood by various audiences. Newton describes Sobraj as a nomadic killer.

—*Cassandra L. Reyes*

SEE ALSO: Charles Manson.

VALERIE SOLANAS
American radical feminist author

BORN: April 9, 1936; Ventnor City, New Jersey
DIED: c. April 25, 1988; San Francisco, California
ALSO KNOWN AS: Valerie Jean Solanas (full name)
MAJOR OFFENSE: Assault with a deadly weapon
ACTIVE: June 3, 1968
LOCALE: New York, New York
SENTENCE: Three years' imprisonment

EARLY LIFE

Valerie Solanas (soh-LAH-nuhs) was the first child of Atlantic City bartender Lou Solanas and his wife Dorothy Biondi. Hers was an unhappy childhood, marred by sexual molestation by her father. She also spent much of her youth moving from the home of one family member to another. Valerie's parents divorced in the 1940's, and her mother remarried in 1949 to a piano tuner named Red Moran.

Solanas grew up to be a troubled teenager who shoplifted and was expelled from Holy Cross Academy for striking a nun. In 1953, Solanas became pregnant by a man in the military who refused to marry her. Her son, named David, was adopted by another family.

Solanas graduated from the Oxon Hill School in Maryland in 1954 and enrolled at the University of Maryland that fall. While there, she wrote for the school newspaper, broadcast a radio advice program, and was a member of the Psi Chi honor society. Despite her academic success, Solanas was forced to leave her dormitory after throwing bottles down a flight of stairs. To pay for her education and her apartment, Solanas turned to prostitution, although by this time she was an open lesbian.

During her college years, Solanas, who majored in psychology, began to develop her signature radical feminist theory that women are biologically superior to men. She would later express these ideas in her notorious *SCUM Manifesto*.

After graduating from college in 1958, Solanas began a master's degree program in psychology at the University of Minnesota. By the spring of 1959, however, she had dropped out. She lived briefly in Berkeley, California, where her younger sister recalled Solanas began writing the *SCUM Manifesto*. By the middle of the 1960's, Solanas was living in New York City and hoping for a career as a writer. She supported herself with a combination of panhandling and prostitution, scraping together enough money to rent a room for a few days at a time to write.

MALE-FREE SOCIETY: THE *SCUM Manifesto*

The opening and conclusion of Valerie Jean Solanas's SCUM Manifesto *reads as follows:*

Life in this society being, at best, an utter bore and no aspect of society being at all relevant to women, there remains to civic-minded, responsible, thrill-seeking females only to overthrow the government, eliminate the money system, institute complete automation and destroy the male sex. It is now technically feasible to reproduce without the aid of males (or, for that matter, females) and to produce only females. We must begin immediately to do so. Retaining the male has not even the dubious purpose of reproduction. The male is a biological accident: the Y (male) gene is an incomplete X (female) gene, that is, it has an incomplete set of chromosomes. In other words, the male is an incomplete female, a walking abortion, aborted at the gene stage. To be male is to be deficient, emotionally limited; maleness is a deficiency disease and males are emotional cripples. . . . The few remaining men can exist out their puny days dropped out on drugs or strutting around in drag or passively watching the high-powered female in action, fulfilling themselves as spectators, vicarious livers*[FOOTNOTE: It will be electronically possible for him to tune into any specific female he wants to and follow in detail her every movement. The females will kindly, obligingly consent to this, as it won't hurt them in the slightest and it is a marvelously kind and humane way to treat their unfortunate, handicapped fellow beings.] or breeding in the cow pasture with the toadies, or they can go off to the nearest friendly suicide center where they will be quietly, quickly, and painlessly gassed to death. . . .

The sick, irrational men, those who attempt to defend themselves against their disgustingness, when they see SCUM barreling down on them, will cling in terror to Big Mama with her Big Bouncy Boobies, but Boobies won't protect them against SCUM; Big Mama will be clinging to Big Daddy, who will be in the corner shitting in his forceful, dynamic pants. Men who are rational, however, won't kick or struggle or raise a distressing fuss, but will just sit back, relax, enjoy the show and ride the waves to their demise.

Source: Valerie Jean Solanas, *SCUM Manifesto* (London: Verso, 1970).

CAREER

In New York, Solanas sold self-published copies of the *SCUM Manifesto* on the street. The manifesto blamed men for all of the world's problems and advocated their extermination. A later publisher of the work claimed that "scum" stood for Society for Cutting Up Men, although Solanas herself admitted that no such society existed and that she never devised the acronym. Solanas published an essay, "A Young Girl's Primer," in the men's magazine *Cavalier* in 1966. She also contracted with Maurice Girodias of Olympia Press to publish her first novel. Around this time, she became associated with the circle of artists and performers around the pop artist celebrity Andy Warhol and the studio he called the Factory. Solanas hoped that Warhol would use his fame to promote her writing. In 1967, she appeared in two of Warhol's films, *I, a Man* (1967) and *Bike Boy* (1967). She also gave Warhol a copy of a play she had written, *Up Your Ass*, hoping he would produce it.

ASSAULT ON WARHOL

Solanas gained her greatest notoriety on June 3, 1968. Incensed because she believed that Girodias had tricked her into signing away her rights to all future written work, and armed with two guns, Solanas went looking for Girodias at the Chelsea Hotel. Finding that he was out of town, she went to the Factory and waited for Warhol. She was angry also with Warhol for refusing to produce her play and for misplacing the script she had given him. Convinced that he intended to pass the play off as his own, she shot Warhol and art curator Mario Amaya, then turned herself in to police that evening. Warhol eventually recovered from his wounds, and Girodias capitalized on Solanas's notoriety by publishing the *SCUM Manifesto* later that year.

LEGAL ACTION AND OUTCOME

Defended by the feminist attorney Florynce Kennedy, Solanas was determined incompetent to stand trial and spent a year undergoing psychiatric evaluation, which found that she was a paranoid schizophrenic. In June, 1969, Solanas pleaded guilty to first-degree assault and received a sentence of three years' imprisonment, which included the year she had already spent in psychiatric confinement.

Upon her release, Solanas spent most of the 1970's in New York, likely homeless. Sometime in the 1980's, she relocated to San Francisco, where she worked on a new manuscript. She died of bronchopneumonia; police discovered her body on April 25, 1988, but its condition suggested that she had died several days earlier. Her new manuscript was never published.

IMPACT

Valerie Solanas is remembered as a voice from the most radical edge of American feminism as well as a reflection of the competitive, sometimes cruel, dynamics of Warhol's Factory. Though a handful of women came to her defense after the Warhol shooting, most mainstream feminists have since disavowed her message. British researcher Mary Harron rediscovered the *SCUM Manifesto* in 1987 and rescued Solanas from obscurity, cowriting the script for the 1996 film dramatization of Solanas's life, *I Shot Andy Warhol*. The George Coates Performance Works in San Francisco staged *Up Your Ass* in its 1999-2000 season.

FURTHER READING

Bockris, Victor. *Warhol: The Biography*. New York: Da Capo Press, 2003. This biography places Solanas within the context of Warhol's life and artistic world, describing the effect the shooting had on the artist and his circle.

Heller, Dana. "Shooting Solanas: Radical Feminist History and the Technology of Failure." *Feminist Studies* 27, no. 1 (spring, 2001): 167-189. Heller compares Solanas's life and writings to their depiction in the film *I Shot Andy Warhol* and argues the importance of the *SCUM Manifesto* to the history of feminism.

Jobey, Liz. "Solanas and Son." *The Guardian* 24 (August, 1996), p. T10. This newspaper article offers one of the most thorough accounts of Solanas's early life and teenage pregnancy.

—*Francesca Gamber*

SEE ALSO: Mark David Chapman; John E. du Pont; Theodore Kaczynski; Yolanda Saldívar.

ANASTASIO SOMOZA GARCÍA
Nicaraguan dictator (1937-1956)

BORN: February 1, 1896; San Marcos, Nicaragua

DIED: September 29, 1956; Ancón, Panama Canal Zone (now Panama)

ALSO KNOWN AS: Tacho I; El Yanqui (the Yankee)

CAUSE OF NOTORIETY: Emerging as the most powerful individual in Nicaragua after the period of that country's occupation by U.S. Marines, and enjoying American support during his two decades in power, Somoza was notable for the corruption and repression of civil liberties that characterized his regime.

ACTIVE: 1937-1956

LOCALE: Nicaragua

EARLY LIFE

The son of Anastasio Somoza Reyes and Julia García, Anastasio Somoza García (ah-nahs-TAH-see-oh soh-MOH-sah gahr-THEE-ah) came from a family who was solidly middle-class but not prosperous. His father, a coffee grower, was a member of the Conservative Party and held a seat in the Nicaraguan senate. In 1916, the senator sent his son, who had by then acquired the nickname of Tacho (which he would prefer for the rest of his life), to the Philadelphia home of his cousin, Dr. Desiderio Roman y Reyes, to study at the Pierce School of Business Administration. There Somoza acquired his excellent idiomatic command of the English language, which would later serve him well. He also met Salvadora Debayle Sacasa, whom he married in 1919.

In order to bond with his wife's influential family, Somoza announced that he would transfer his political allegiance to the Liberal Party, which they supported. During the following seven years he and his wife had three children—daughter Lilian and sons Luis and Anastasio—and Somoza attempted several entrepreneurial ventures, all unsuccessful. He masterminded a counterfeiting ring and barely avoided a term of imprisonment. In 1926 Somoza joined a Liberal uprising led by General José Maria Moncada against the

Conservative government of Emiliano Chamorro. Defeated, he fled for a short time to Costa Rica, whence he returned in time to witness his country's occupation by United States Marines.

MILITARY AND POLITICAL CAREER

Somoza's command of American English and his easygoing affability enabled him to ingratiate himself with U.S. authorities, who had their hands full battling a guerrilla insurrection led by the Liberal general Augusto César Sandino. By 1933, Somoza had been placed in a

---

NICARAGUA, PRIVATE PROPERTY

President Franklin D. Roosevelt once said of Anastasio Somoza García, "Somoza may be a son of a bitch, but he's our son of a bitch." The United States' blind-eye policy allowed Somoza to make a fiefdom out of Nicaragua. He once bragged, "It will cost 40,000 lives to drive us from power." In addition to military force, he accumulated the following property and businesses:

- Private sale of cattle to Panama
- Clandestine sale of cattle to Costa Rica
- Monopoly on the distribution of tallow
- Ownership of the San Albino gold mine
- A $175,000 annual income from an "additional contribution" of 2.25 percent of the production of North American mining companies
- Ownership of fifty-one cattle ranches
- Ownership of forty-six coffee plantations
- Ownership of the Montelimar ranch
- Ownership of 50 percent of the shares of the Nicaraguan cement factory
- Ownership of 41 percent of the shares of the cotton mill of the Salvadoran magnate, Gadala María
- Ownership of 50 percent of the shares of the Momotombo National Match Company
- Ownership of the newspaper *Novedades*
- Ownership of most of the nation's sawmills
- Ownership of the buildings that housed the Nicaraguan legations in Mexico and Costa Rica
- Ownership of various apartment houses in Miami
- Ownership of the electrical plants in Chinandega, Tipitapa, Jinotega, Estelí, and La Libertad
- Ownership of the Las Mercedes property adjoining the Managua airport

Source: Data from Claribel Alegría and Darwin Flakoll, *Death of Somoza* (Willimatic, Conn.: Curbstone, 1996).

---

commanding position: Juan Batista Sacasa, his wife's uncle, had been installed as president of Nicaragua. More important, Somoza himself had been appointed commander of the U.S. Marine-trained Guardia Nacional de Nicaragua, which had become the only official military power after the Marines finally left on January 2 of that year. On February 21, 1934, Sandino agreed to meet with Somoza and President Sacasa to sign a peace settlement. Later that same day, Somoza had Sandino treacherously murdered, crushed the Sandinista movement, and became, in effect, the most powerful individual in Nicaragua. Breaking with Sacasa in 1936, Somoza used the Guardia to force his uncle's resignation and was elected president in a rigged election, assuming office on January 1, 1937.

A visit to the United States as the guest of President Franklin D. Roosevelt in 1939 enhanced Somoza's prestige. His staunch support for the American war effort during World War II, and for the Truman and Eisenhower administrations during the Cold War as an avowed enemy of Communism, guaranteed Somoza financial support. He often boasted of having considerably advanced his nation's economic interests and living standards. Often, however, it was his family's enrichment that was most apparent. Under Somoza, Nicaragua was rapidly reduced to a family fiefdom where Somoza's holdings—cattle ranches, coffee and sugar plantations, and factories—dotted the countryside. Financing for education languished, and by the end of 1956, Nicaragua maintained one of the region's highest rates of illiteracy. Officially, Somoza served as president for two terms: 1937-1947 and 1950-1956, though he was always, for all practical purposes, in control of the apparatus of government.

On September 21, 1956, at an election reception in the city of Leon, Somoza was shot four times at close range by the poet Rigoberto López Pérez, who was himself immediately gunned down by members of the Guardia. Transported first to Managua, then to the Panama Canal Zone, the dictator died there a little over a week after being shot.

IMPACT

A consummate manipulator, Anastasio Somoza García was able to play upon international rivalries and fears of possible Communist incursions into Latin America. So firmly entrenched was his regime that it survived his assassination for more than two decades and made possible the perpetuation of a family "dynasty" under his sons Luis Somoza Debayle and Anastasio Somoza Debayle ("Tacho II"), which was finally overthrown by a renewed Sandinista uprising in 1979.

FURTHER READING

Clark, Paul Coe, Jr. *The United States and Somoza, 1933-1956: A Revisionist Look.* Westport, Conn.: Praeger, 1992. The author believes that the notion of massive American support for Somoza has been overplayed and that often Somoza and the U.S. government were at odds.

Diederich, Bernard. *Somoza and the Legacy of U.S. Involvement in Central America.* New York: E. P. Dutton, 1981. Sees the elder Somoza's easygoing affability and command of Americanized English as the key to his lengthy tenure in power.

Gambone, Michael D. *Eisenhower, Somoza, and the Cold War in Nicaragua, 1953-1961.* Westport, Conn.: Praeger, 1997. Somoza is depicted as the arch-manipulator who capitalized on U.S. fears to enable the foundation of his family "dynasty."

Herring, Hubert. *A History of Latin America: From the Beginnings to the Present.* New York: Alfred A. Knopf, 1967. In contrast to other works, Somoza is here presented in a comparatively favorable light as a constructive ruler and an architect of economic resurgence.

Walter, Knut. *The Regime of Anastasio Somoza, 1936-1956.* Chapel Hill: University of North Carolina Press, 1993. Focuses on the political side to Somocismo, and the strongman is pictured as an alliance builder who shifted his emphasis and base of support as changing circumstances dictated.

—*Raymond Pierre Hylton*

SEE ALSO: Fidel Castro; François Duvalier; Jean-Claude Duvalier; Leopoldo Galtieri; Juan Perón; Augusto Pinochet Ugarte; Efraín Ríos Montt; Alfredo Stroessner; Rafael Trujillo; Getúlio Vargas.

RICHARD SPECK
American mass murderer

BORN: December 6, 1941; Kirkwood, Illinois
DIED: December 5, 1991; Stateville Penitentiary, Illinois
ALSO KNOWN AS: Richard Benjamin Speck (full name)
MAJOR OFFENSE: Murder
ACTIVE: July 13, 1966
LOCALE: Chicago, Illinois
SENTENCE: Death penalty, commuted to eight counts of life in prison

EARLY LIFE

Richard Benjamin Speck (spehk) was born on December 6, 1941, into humble beginnings to Margaret and Benjamin Speck. He was the seventh of eight children in his large Baptist family. The family reportedly was raised in a strict environment, with alcohol staunchly forbidden. Speck was close to his father and was devastated by his untimely death when Speck was only six years old. After his father's death, Margaret married Carl Lindberg, a Texan with abusive and alcoholic tendencies. The family relocated to Dallas, Texas, where Richard had severe academic difficulties and gradually adopted a delinquent life filled with crime, alcohol, drugs, and sexual promiscuity.

CRIMINAL CAREER

By his early twenties, Speck had married fifteen-year-old Shirley Malone and had a young son. He often raped and beat his wife at knifepoint and was abusive to his mother-in-law. In 1965, he robbed a woman and served a fifteen-month sentence. His marriage soured and he was being sought for various crimes by Texas police. He moved to Chicago, Illinois, in 1966 to live with his sister, Carolyn. He spent most of his time there working as a merchant seaman, drinking, using drugs, and committing more serious crimes. On April 13, 1966, Chicago police questioned Speck regarding the murder of Mary Kay Pierce, a barmaid at his favorite bar. When Speck did not return for a scheduled interview on April 19, police searched his apartment and found items taken during the rape, robbery, and kidnapping of sixty-five-year-old Mrs. Virgil Harris in Chicago. Before he could be questioned again, Speck would become one of the most notorious murderers in United States history.

On the evening of July 13, 1966, Speck went to a local bar and began drinking heavily. He left the bar sometime later and began the twenty-minute walk toward a townhouse where a group of student nurses lived. At approximately 10:30 P.M., armed with a gun, he entered an open door to the residence. Once inside, he told the young women that he wanted only money. Speck's mood soon changed, however, and he began to bind his hostages with bedsheets. As more of the nurses returned home, he also bound them. Over the course of the next several hours, he began taking the women upstairs one at a time, where he savagely raped, stabbed, suffocated, and bludgeoned them to death. Two nurses were also ambushed and stabbed to death as they returned home in the middle of the killing spree.

Thinking he had killed all the eyewitnesses, Speck fled the crime scene. Unbeknownst to him, a witness named Corazon Amurao was alive and hiding under her bed, paralyzed by fear. Hours later, she crawled outside and saw the carnage in the townhouse. Hysterical, she fled to an outside window ledge and screamed for help until neighbors heard her pleas. Amurao was able to give

Richard Speck. (AP/Wide World Photos)

police a detailed description of her attacker, leading to an extensive search by law enforcement. Speck's six-foot-tall frame, acne-scarred face, southern accent, and Born to Raise Hell tattoo made Speck easily identifiable. He was captured in a seedy hotel after he had attempted suicide by cutting his wrists.

LEGAL ACTION AND OUTCOME

After a massive national manhunt, Speck was captured and then convicted of the heinous murders of the eight student nurses in Chicago. In 1967, in less than one hour, the jury sentenced him to the death penalty. In a subsequent Supreme Court ruling that invalidated death sentences nationally in 1972, Speck's sentence was commuted to eight counts of life in prison. Speck was never charged with any of the other crimes or the murder of the barmaid in Chicago of which he was suspected. Those crimes and other murders Speck was suspected of in Indiana and Michigan remained unsolved.

IMPACT

Richard Speck's crime shocked the national conscience and was one of the worst mass killings in Chicago history. At the time, the murder of these student nurses was called the "crime of the century." On December 5, 1991, Speck died of a massive heart attack after serving nineteen years. Even postmortem, however, Speck continued to cause controversy; a disturbing prison video from within Statesville Correctional Institute in Illinois was uncovered. This video depicted Speck with unusually large breasts, snorting cocaine, bragging about his murders, and having sex with another male inmate. As a result of this exposé and the subsequent public outrage, an intense investigation into the Illinois Department of Corrections was ordered.

FURTHER READING

Altman, Jack, and Marvin Ziporyn. *Born to Raise Hell: The Untold Story of Richard Speck*. New York: Grove Press, 1967. Ziporyn was a medical doctor who served as a defense witness and who interviewed Speck numerous times. This book provides insight into the mind of the notorious killer.

Breo, Dennis L. *The Crime of the Century*. New York: Bantam Books, 1993. Journalist Dennis Breo and prosecutor Bill Martin reconstruct the case against Speck. Includes intimate details of the murders and behind-the-scenes information on the trial and strategies to convict Speck.

Lane, Brian, and Wilfred Gregg. *Encyclopedia of Mass Murder: A Chilling Record of the World's Worst Cases*. New York: Caroll & Graf, 2004. This encyclopedia offers a brief case study of the murders of Speck.

—Denise Paquette Boots

SEE ALSO: Paul Bernardo; Kenneth Bianchi; Ted Bundy; Angelo Buono, Jr.; George Hennard; Karla Homolka; Reginald Kray; Ronald Kray; Marcel Petiot; Charles Starkweather.

ALBERT SPEER

Chief architect and minister of armaments in Nazi Germany

BORN: March 19, 1905; Mannheim, Germany
DIED: September 1, 1981; London, England
ALSO KNOWN AS: Berthold Konrad Hermann Albert Speer (full name); First Architect of the Third Reich
MAJOR OFFENSES: War crimes, specifically employing forced laborers
ACTIVE: 1939-1945
LOCALE: Germany and lands occupied by the Nazis
SENTENCE: Twenty years in prison

EARLY LIFE

Albert Speer (shpeehr) grew up in a middle-class family in Mannheim and Heidelberg. Both his father and his grandfather were architects, and he pursued that same ca-

reer by studying at technical schools in Karlsruhe and Munich and in 1927 completed his architectural studies in Berlin. In 1930 Speer attended a rally of the Nazi Party in a Berlin beer hall (later known as the Beer Hall Putsch) where he heard party leader Adolf Hitler speak. A month later Speer joined the Nazi Party and was given a series of commissions for the party. His talent, efficiency, and enthusiasm so impressed the führer that shortly after Hitler became chancellor of Germany in 1933, Speer was named his personal architect.

POLITICAL CAREER

Hitler was especially interested in art and architecture, and Speer became a personal friend and a prominent

Albert Speer.

member of Hitler's inner circle. One of his first commissions was the design of a Nuremberg stadium as the site for Nazi Party congresses. Speer stage-managed the 1934 party rally on the Nuremberg parade grounds, complete with martial music, swastika flags and banners, and the surrounding of the site with 130 searchlights, creating a "cathedral of light." As documented in Leni Riefenstahl's motion picure *Triumph of the Will* (1935), the Nuremberg rally was one of the Nazis' most successful propaganda feats. Nazi leaders were so pleased with Speer's work that he was given more important commissions.

Together, Hitler and Speer made plans for remodeling Berlin into a new capital of "Greater Germany," *Germania*, a testament to the greatness of the Third Reich. Their audacious construction plans featured enormous boulevards, reflecting ponds, huge public buildings, and a gigantic triumphal arch. Speer's theory of "ruin value" was to govern the construction of new buildings that would leave aesthetically pleasing ruins centuries into the future—symbols of the greatness of German civilization analogous to the ruins of ancient Greece and Rome.

Speer was appointed inspector general of construction for the Reich capital, empowering him to destroy buildings, evict people, and demand materials and labor for the project. To make room for his grand plans and for re-housing Germans affected by this work, Speer allegedly was responsible for the forced eviction and deportation of Jews from the capital. The planned construction of *Germania* came to an abrupt halt, however, during World War II.

Hitler also asked Speer to build the new Reich's chancellery, the official seat of government for Germany. Speer demonstrated his remarkable organizational skills by planning and supervising the project, mobilizing labor to work in shifts, and finishing within a year. The führer admired the chancellery, which included an underground bunker (where Hitler later committed suicide). The building was demolished during the Soviet occupation after World War II.

In 1942, Hitler chose Speer to be minister of armaments and munitions. Speer had never served in the military and knew nothing about armaments, but he had demonstrated that he could create and run highly efficient organizations. Speer attempted to put the German economy on a war footing comparable to that of the Allies, but he was hindered by party politics and the Nazi bureaucracy. Another obstacle was a shortage of workers in German factories, complicated by the Nazis' exclusion of women from factory work. To fill this gap, Speer relied on forced foreign labor and slave labor from concentration camps. Under the threat of severe punishment, such workers were productive. Slowly Speer centralized control of almost all industry and succeeded in dramatically increasing war production, which reached its peak in 1944, matching the armament production of Britain—and this during the height of the Allied strategic bombing campaign. Speer was so successful in mobilizing and streamlining German industry that at one time in late 1943, he was reputed to be Hitler's heir apparent.

After the Battle of the Bulge in late 1944, Hitler issued "scorched earth" orders to destroy Germany's infrastructure to prevent its use by the invading Allies. Speer opposed the führer's policy, and by arguing and pleading with Hitler helped prevent the orders from being carried out until the last days of the war. After Hitler committed suicide in April, 1945, Germany was governed briefly by the so-called Flensburg government headed by Admiral Karl Dönitz. Speer joined Dönitz in northern Germany and remained a part of the government after Germany's unconditional surrender. After the war, U.S. intelligence officers interrogated the cooperative Speer about how

Germany kept increasing its armaments output in the face of accelerated Allied bombings—information that could be useful in the continuing fighting against Japan.

LEGAL ACTION AND OUTCOME

On May 23, 1945, Speer was arrested by British troops, and along with twenty-three other Nazi leaders, was tried for war crimes by the International Military Tribunal. Speer was charged with employing forced laborers and concentration camp prisoners. Although he contended that he was unaware of the killing of millions of Jews and that he was an apolitical, unwitting collaborator in the horror, the prosecution claimed that Speer was well aware of the Holocaust. Of the Nazis convicted at Nuremberg, Speer was one of the few who admitted responsibility for his crimes and expressed repentance. Rather than receiving the death penalty, as did most of the defendants, Speer was sentenced to twenty years' imprisonment in Spandau Prison, West Berlin. While imprisoned, he kept in contact with his family and secretly started writing his memoirs on toilet paper, tobacco wrappings, and any other material he could smuggle out. In 1966 he was released from Spandau.

IMPACT

In 1970, Albert Speer published his memoirs, the first of several semiautobiographical works he wrote. In his books, he claimed that he had no direct involvement in or knowledge of the Holocaust, although he presented himself as someone who should have known what was occurring. In postwar Germany, Speer grew wealthy and became a symbol for people who were involved with the Nazi regime yet claimed not to have had any part in Nazi

atrocities. Speer died of a cerebral hemorrhage in London in 1981. After his death, archival evidence was released indicating that Speer probably knew much more about the atrocities than he admitted.

FURTHER READING

Ramen, Fred. *Albert Speer: Hitler's Architect*. New York: Rosen, 2001. A succinct study of Speer's life in a series of "Holocaust biographies" for a young adult audience.

Schmidt, Matthias. *Albert Speer: The End of a Myth*. New York: St. Martin's Press, 1984. An exposé of Speer's denial of knowledge of the Holocaust, with proof that he was keen to profit from the forcible evacuation of Jewish-owned apartments in Berlin and afterward tried to falsify the records.

Sereny, Gitta. *Albert Speer: His Battle with the Truth*. New York: Knopf, 1995. Based on interviews with Speer, this thorough study humanizes Speer while charging him with indifference to Nazi atrocities.

Speer, Albert. *Inside the Third Reich*. New York: Macmillan, 1970. Memoirs that focus on 1933-1945, when Speer figured prominently in Hitler's government and the German war effort.

Van Der Vat, Dan. *The Good Nazi: The Life and Lies of Albert Speer*. Boston: Houghton Mifflin, 1997. An incriminating portrait of Speer as an opportunist, a "good" dedicated party servant who was the principal exploiter of forced labor.

—*Theodore M. Vestal*

SEE ALSO: Karl Dönitz; Adolf Hitler; Baldur von Schirach.

JOSEPH STALIN
Soviet dictator (1922-1953)

BORN: December 18, 1878; Gori, Georgia, Russian Empire

DIED: March 5, 1953; Kuntsevo, Soviet Union

ALSO KNOWN AS: Joseph Vissarionovich Dzhugashvili (birth name); Koba; Uncle Joe; Man of Steel

CAUSE OF NOTORIETY: As the communist dictator of the Soviet Union, General Secretary Stalin was responsible for creating a totalitarian political system and repressing or liquidating millions of people.

ACTIVE: 1922-1953

LOCALE: Soviet Union

EARLY LIFE

Joseph Stalin (STAH-lihn) was born Joseph Vissarionovich Dzhugashvili. Most Soviet sources on Stalin list his birth date as December 21, 1879; however, Stalin lied about his age. He was actually born on December 18, 1878. He was the only son of a poor cobbler, Vissarion Dzhugashvili. Joseph's mother, Yekaterina, worked as a

Joseph Stalin.

domestic servant in order to enable young Joseph to attend the Tiflis Orthodox Theological Seminary. Though receiving high marks, he had by 1898 entered the growing revolutionary movement in the Russian Empire and was expelled from the seminary forthwith.

As a vocal supporter of Vladimir Lenin's Bolsheviks, the young Dzhugashvili organized strikes and engaged in a train robbery in the Caucasus region of the Russian Empire. Caught on numerous occasions for taking part in such acts, he was exiled or imprisoned by czarist authorities on an intermittent basis between 1902 and 1917. During one of these exiles, Dzhugashvili adopted the name Stalin (in Russian, "man of steel") as his nom de guerre, rejecting a previous pseudonym, Koba.

It was also during this period that Stalin's first wife, Ketevan Svanidze, died from tuberculosis. They had married in 1905; Stalin was extremely distressed by his wife's untimely death in 1907. At her funeral, he reportedly confided to a friend that with her death his "last warm feelings for all human beings" died as well. Later events would certainly prove this correct.

POLITICAL CAREER

In 1917, Stalin returned to Petrograd (now St. Petersburg) from exile and played a significant role in the planning of the coming communist revolution. From 1917 to 1922, he directed the nationalities policy for the newly installed Bolshevik government led by Lenin. In 1922 Stalin was elected general secretary of the Communist Party, at Lenin's behest. Though it was initially thought to be an unimportant post, Stalin deftly used his new powers to appoint loyal subordinates to positions of power and to undermine his rivals. Before his death in 1924, Lenin wrote in his political testament that Stalin (whom Lenin thought to be crude and capricious) had amassed great powers as general secretary, and the ailing Soviet leader pushed for Stalin's removal. After Lenin's death, Stalin's rivals failed to act on Lenin's advice; instead, Stalin remained in his position and strengthened his hold on power.

To gain an unassailable position, Stalin undermined his leading rivals in the Politburo, the principal policy-making body of the Communist Party. Beginning with a theoretical attack against the extremist policies of Leon Trotsky, Grigory Zinovyev, and Lev Kamenev in the mid-1920's, by 1928 Stalin had these "left deviationists" ejected from their positions and had appropriated their ideological plan for heavy industrialization and the collectivization of agriculture.

In the months thereafter, Stalin implemented a policy of full-scale industrialization at breakneck speed. The same year saw the brutal introduction of agricultural collectivization, a policy that pushed millions of peasants onto enormous state or collective farms. Stalin responded to peasant resistance with extraordinary savagery. His security organs, led by the infamous People's Comissariat for Internal Affairs (NKVD), imprisoned or executed those who were branded enemies of the people, removed entire villages to Siberia or Central Asia, and forced an artificial famine upon the agricultural heartland of the Soviet Union. In the end, at least ten million peasants perished.

In 1929, Stalin turned against the remaining members of the Politburo who were opponents of his extremist policies. By 1932, he had totally discredited this "right deviationist" faction led by Nikolay Bukharin, Aleksey Ivanovich Rykov, and Mikhail Tomsky. Shortly thereafter, each was expelled from his position and later shot. The rank and file in party and government apparatuses did not escape similar treatment by Stalin's henchmen. One further victim of Stalin's savagery in the early 1930's was his second wife, Nadezhda Alliuyeva. Having gained knowledge of the many barbaric acts committed by her husband against former friends and innocent Soviet citizens alike, she took her own life under suspicious circumstances in late 1932.

Thus, by the early 1930's, Stalin had vanquished his leading opponents and obtained almost untrammeled powers. Nevertheless, the suspicious and ruthless leader still believed his position to be vulnerable to opposition. Therefore, after ordering the liquidation of Sergei Kirov, a popular leader of the Leningrad party organization, Stalin used Kirov's murder as an excuse to annihilate certain unnamed "enemies of the people" who were re-

---

SEEDS OF THE COLD WAR

On February 9, 1946, Joseph Stalin delivered a speech in Moscow arguing that the world wars were the result of capitalism and that communism was a superior system and would eventually prevail. The speech alarmed Western leaders:

Marxists have more than once stated that the capitalist system of world economy contains the elements of a general crisis and military conflicts, that, in view of that, the development of world capitalism in our times does not proceed smoothly and evenly, but through crises and catastrophic wars. The point is that the uneven development of capitalist countries usually leads, in the course of time, to a sharp disturbance of the equilibrium within the world system of capitalism, and that group of capitalist countries which regards itself as being less securely provided with raw materials and markets usually attempts to change the situation and to redistribute "spheres of influence" in its own favor—by employing armed force. As a result of this, the capitalist world is split into two hostile camps, and war breaks out between them. . . .

The issue now is not whether the Soviet social system is viable or not, because after the object lessons of the war, no skeptic now dares to express doubt concerning the viability of the Soviet social system. Now the issue is that the Soviet social system has proved to be more viable and stable than the non-Soviet social system, that the Soviet social system is a better form of organization of society than any non-Soviet social system.

One of the leaders alarmed by Stalin's speech was British prime minister Winston Churchill, who warned in a speech of his own that Stalin's plan was expansion for Russia. Angered, Stalin struck back, and the Cold War was under way:

In substance, Mr. Churchill now stands in the position of a firebrand of war. And Mr. Churchill is not alone here. He has friends not only in England but also in the United States of America.

In this respect, one is reminded remarkably of Hitler and his friends. . . . Mr. Churchill begins to set war loose, also by a racial theory, maintaining that only nations speaking the English language are fully valuable nations, called upon to decide the destinies of the entire world.

Sources: Joseph Stalin, *Speeches Delivered at Meetings of Voters of the Stalin Electoral District* (Moscow: Foreign Language Publishing, 1950). "Stalin's Reply to Churchill," *The New York Times*, March 14, 1946, p. 4.

---

sponsible for the dastardly deed. An enormous purge of the party, state, and military bureaucracies was unleashed. By the time the "Great Purges" had ended in 1939, Stalin's NKVD had liquidated more than one million party members, as well as thirty-five thousand high-ranking military officers. While these actions certainly cemented Stalin's control of the state, they also negatively affected the functioning of the government and military in the early months of World War II.

After recovering from the trauma caused by Adolf

Hitler's invasion in June, 1941, General Secretary Stalin added three more titles to his name: supreme commander in chief of Soviet armed forces, state defense committee chairman, and generalissimo. As such, Stalin led the Soviet people through the following four years of war, misery, and want. By war's end, the Soviet people had suffered more than twenty-seven million casualties. In the aftermath of such hardship and deprivation, many Soviet citizens believed the excesses of the Stalinist regime would subside.

Instead, their hopes were dashed as the cruel tyrant demanded both further sacrifices and greater devotion from his people. Real or imagined opposition continued to be extinguished with brutal savagery. Moreover, Stalin's cult of personality grew ever grander, as sycophantic lackeys praised the increasingly senile tyrant, granting him numerous honorific titles, even renaming entire cities after him. However, such conduct did not diminish the paranoid suspicions of the autocrat; to be sure, by late 1952 Stalin was laying the foundation for yet another purge of leading party and government officials. Only his death from a cerebral hemorrhage on March 5, 1953, spared the country from further bloodshed.

IMPACT

Joseph Stalin's long reign as the unassailable leader of the Soviet Union witnessed many significant transformations. While Stalin's regime had by 1953 created an industrialized country and military superpower from a largely agrarian and vulnerable state, the economic, developmental, and physical costs of these revolutionary changes were enormous. Stalin's perfection of the totalitarian political regime produced the world's largest system of concentration camps, whose victims numbered in the millions. Millions more perished as a result of Stalin's ruinous, tumultuous drive toward heavy industrialization and collectivization of agriculture. In many ways, the legacies of Stalin's reign continue to constrain political and economic transformation in the postcommunist world even today, more than fifty years after the tyrant's demise.

FURTHER READING

Knight, Amy. *Who Killed Kirov? The Kremlin's Greatest Mystery*. New York: Hill and Wang, 1999. In-depth review of the assassination that plunged the Soviet Union into the "Great Purges."

Service, Robert. *Stalin: A Biography*. Cambridge, Mass.: Harvard University Press, 2004. A comprehensive and exhaustive examination of Stalin, his background, his rise to prominence and power, and his eventual decline.

Viola, Lynne. *Peasant Rebels Under Stalin: Collectivization and the Culture of Peasant Resistance*. New York: Oxford University Press, 1996. Discusses the regime's principal motivations for collectivizing agriculture; also provides an excellent examination of the chief consequences of that policy.

—*Thomas E. Rotnem*

SEE ALSO: Lavrenty Beria; Felix Dzerzhinsky; Francisco Franco; Adolf Hitler; Lazar Kaganovich; Nikita S. Khrushchev; Vladimir Ilich Lenin; Mao Zedong; Vyacheslav Mikhailovich Molotov; Symon Petlyura; Vasili Vasilievich Ulrikh; Andrey Vyshinsky; Genrikh Yagoda; Nikolay Ivanovich Yezhov; Andrey Aleksandrovich Zhdanov.

CHARLES STARKWEATHER
American spree murderer

BORN: November 24, 1938; Lincoln, Nebraska
DIED: June 25, 1959; Lincoln, Nebraska
ALSO KNOWN AS: Charlie Starkweather; Charles Raymond Starkweather (full name)
MAJOR OFFENSES: Multiple murders
ACTIVE: December 1, 1957-January 27, 1958
LOCALE: Lincoln, Nebraska
SENTENCE: Death by electrocution

EARLY LIFE

Charles Starkweather (STARK-weh-ther) was born into a working-class family in Lincoln, Nebraska in 1938. His father, a carpenter, suffered a series of physical ailments that kept him from working consistently, so the family remained relatively poor. Charles resented the teasing he received from his schoolmates about his modest economic condition. He was also teased about his slight speech impediment and bowed legs. At age seventeen, Charles reached a crossroads in his life. He was dating a fourteen-year-old girl, Caril Ann Fugate, whom he wished to marry, but he feared that his life would be similar to that of his father: working as a manual laborer, never having enough money, and then simply dying without anyone caring. Determined to break the cycle, Starkweather turned to crime.

CRIMINAL CAREER

On December 1, 1957, Starkweather committed the first of eleven murders when he robbed a Lincoln gas station and killed the attendant, Robert Colvert. With cash in hand, Starkweather went to the Fugate residence in north Lincoln on January 21, 1958, where he argued with Caril's parents, Velda and Marion Bartlett, who opposed their young daughter's dating the older and ill-bred Starkweather. With Fugate present, Starkweather shot both of her parents to death and strangled to death Fugate's two-year-old sister. Starkweather stuffed the corpses in the outhouse, and he and Fugate remained in the home for two days, pondering their next move. To forestall visits from any curious neighbors, Fugate posted a note on the door warning that the family suffered from influenza and that potential callers should stay away. Three days after the murders, family members became worried and called the police, who found Starkweather and Fugate gone and the corpses concealed in the outhouse.

Fleeing Lincoln, Starkweather and Fugate headed for the rural farm of August Meyer, a Starkweather family friend. Needing a place to hide, Starkweather killed Meyer before he could hear the news of the Fugate murders and alert the police. After hiding at the Meyer residence, on January 27, Starkweather and Fugate set out hitchhiking. They got a ride from a young Lincoln couple, seventeen-year-old Robert Jensen and sixteen-year-old Carol King. Forcing the couple at gunpoint to return to the Meyer farm, Starkweather murdered both Jensen and King in the storm cellar behind the house. Starkweather and Fugate took Jensen's car. With nowhere else to go, they returned to Lincoln. While police combed north Lincoln for Starkweather, the fugitive couple sought refuge in one of the town's affluent neighborhoods. Starkweather selected the home of C. Lauer Ward, one of Lincoln's wealthiest men, in which to hide. Why Starkweather chose that particular home is unknown, and he never provided a reason.

Starkweather knocked on the door, and the maid, Lillian Fencl, answered. Starkweather ordered Fencl at gunpoint back into the house and threatened Ward's wife, Clara. Later that afternoon, Starkweather, convinced that Clara Ward was trying to escape, stabbed her to death in an upstairs bedroom. Shortly afterward, C. Lauer Ward returned home from work and was killed by a shotgun blast. Starkweather then killed Fencl to eliminate her as an eyewitness.

Starkweather and Fugate commandeered Ward's car and fled Lincoln, heading west toward Wyoming. The following day, January 28, authorities discovered the bodies at the Ward residence. Panic arose in the community of Lincoln. Nebraska governor Victor Anderson called out twelve hundred National Guardsmen. Armed parents escorted their children to school. By then, Starkweather and Fugate were in Wyoming. Starkweather murdered Merle Collison, a shoe salesman who was asleep in his car, and tried to drive off in Collison's automobile but was unable to release the parking brake. Starkweather flagged down another car, but the driver struggled with him as a deputy sheriff drove by. Starkweather tried to flee but after a short pursuit surrendered.

LEGAL ACTION AND OUTCOME

After her arrest, Fugate claimed she was Starkweather's hostage, not an active participant in the murders. Angered by Fugate's betrayal, Starkweather insisted that Fugate had committed some of the murders and that she could have escaped any number of times while he was asleep. Starkweather, who refused the advice of his defense attorneys to plead insanity, did little to aid in his own defense at his trial. The jury, after less than twenty-four hours of deliberation, found both Starkweather and Fugate guilty of the first-degree murder of Robert Jensen. On November 28, 1958, Starkweather received the death sentence, while Fugate, a minor at the time of the crimes, was sentenced to life in prison. Again refusing to participate in his own appeals, Starkweather died in the electric chair at the Nebraska State Penitentiary on June 25, 1959. Fugate remained in prison until paroled in June, 1976, all the while claiming her innocence.

IMPACT

Charles Starkweather's murderous spree seemed to foretell of similar murder sprees, like those of Manson Family and David Berkowitz, the Son of Sam, in the 1960's and 1970's. Starkweather, who tried to emulate actor James Dean's image (for which the Lincoln newspapers labeled him a "rebel without a clue"), became a romanticized figure for some disaffected youth. Starkweather's lashing out at society influenced many later artists, from Bruce Springsteen to Quentin Tarantino. His murders have spawned numerous books and television movies, including *Badlands* (1973), directed by Terrence Malik and starring Martin Sheen and Sissy Spacek.

FURTHER READING

Beaver, Ninette, B. K. Ripley, and Patrick Trese. *Caril.* Philadelphia: Lippincott, 1974. Ninette Beaver was a Lincoln newspaper reporter at the time of the Starkweather/Fugate murders; her book concentrates on Caril Fugate's side of the story.

O'Donnell, Jeffrey. *Starkweather: A Story of Mass Murder on the Great Plains.* Lincoln, Neb.: J & L Lee, 1993. A general volume on Starkweather's crimes containing extensive information provided by those involved in the case.

Sargeant, Jack. *Born Bad.* London: Creation Books, 1996. The first half of the book is a summary of the Starkweather/Fugate murders, while the second half concentrates on the cultural influence of the murders since the 1950's.

—Steven J. Ramold

SEE ALSO: David Berkowitz; Charles Manson.

BELLE STARR
American Old West outlaw

BORN: February 5, 1848; near Carthage, Missouri
DIED: February 3, 1889; near Younger's Bend, Indian Territory (now Oklahoma)
ALSO KNOWN AS: Myra Belle Shirley; Myra Maybelle Shirley (birth name); Belle Reed; Bandit Queen; Queen of the Desperadoes; Petticoat Terror of the Plains
MAJOR OFFENSES: Horse stealing and robbery
ACTIVE: July 31, 1882; February, 1886
LOCALE: Indian Territory (now Oklahoma)
SENTENCE: Two consecutive terms of six months each at the House of Corrections in Detroit, Michigan; released after nine months of incarceration

EARLY LIFE

The second of six children in an upper-middle-class family of Southern sympathizers, Myra Maybelle (Belle) Shirley, later known as Belle Starr (stahr), attended the Carthage Female Academy and was educated as a lady. She enjoyed the time spent riding and hunting in the great outdoors with her beloved older brother, Bud, who was eight years her senior. During the Civil War, Bud was killed while serving with Quantrill's Raiders—a pro-Confederate gang led by William Clarke Quantrill. The Shirley family then relocated near Dallas, Texas, after Union forces burned Carthage in 1864 and devastated their holdings. In Texas, the Shirley home became a haven for Missouri outlaws who had ridden with Quantrill, among them Cole Younger, Jim Younger, and Jesse James.

OUTLAW CAREER

On November 1, 1866, Belle married Missouri outlaw Jim Reed; their daughter Rosie was born in September, 1868. They lived in Indian Territory with Cherokee outlaw Tom Starr and also spent time in California, where Belle's son Ed was born in February, 1871. Reed soon relocated to Texas and then headed back to Indian Territory, as he was wanted for passing counterfeit money and for murder. His wife soon joined him, after leaving the children with relatives. Reed was actively involved in several illegal money-procuring ventures with the Younger, James, and Starr gangs and was killed by a deputy sheriff in Paris, Texas, in August, 1874.

Although many legends emerged about Belle, evidence suggests that although often a wife, lover, or companion to nefarious desperadoes and outlaws, Belle herself was tried and found guilty only once, on two counts of stealing horses and robbery with her husband Sam Starr, a Cherokee outlaw she married on June 5, 1880. Her cabin at Younger's Bend in Indian Territory came to be known as a refuge for criminals on the run, and Belle was clearly a woman of shrewd intelligence, gritty determination, and strong will. Following Starr's death in a December, 1886, shoot-out with an Indian police officer, Belle invited a Native American named Bill (Jim) July to share her cabin so that she could maintain the legal right to her homestead.

Shortly before her forty-first birthday in 1889, she was shot and killed in an ambush not far from her home. Her murderer was never found, and different theories arose to suggest that her husband, her neighbor, or her son was the culprit. This unsolved mystery helped accelerate the growth of her legend following her death.

LEGAL ACTION AND OUTCOME
Belle and Sam Starr went to district court at Fort Smith, Arkansas, on November 7, 1882, to confront the horse stealing and robbery charges that two of their neighbors had filed the previous July. The grand jury found cause to suspect larceny, and the pair appeared in March, 1883, before well-known judge Isaac C. Parker, also known as the Hanging Judge for his preferred method of punishment. Belle was found guilty on both counts; Sam was convicted on only one, as the U.S. court lacked jurisdiction in a case when one Native American committed a crime against another. Sam was sentenced to twelve months in prison and Belle to two consecutive six-month terms in prison at the House of Corrections in Detroit. Nine months later, they were both released.

A WOMAN OF SOME NOTORIETY

In an interview that appeared in the June 7, 1886, edition of the Dallas Morning Starr—*datelined from Fort Smith, Arkansas, May 30, 1886—Belle Starr spoke of her life on the frontier:*

After a more adventurous life than generally falls to the lot of woman, I settled permanently in the Indian Territory, selecting a place of picturesque beauty on the Canadian River. There, far from society, I hoped to pass the remainder of my life in peace and quietude. So long had I been estranged from the society of women, whom I thoroughly detest, that I thought I would find it irksome to live in their midst. So, I selected a place that but few have ever had the gratification of gossiping around.

For a time, I lived very happily in the society of my little girl and husband, a Cherokee Indian, son of the noted Tom Starr. But, it soon became noised around that I was a woman of some notoriety from Texas, and from that time on, my home and actions have been severely criticized.

My home became famous as an outlaws' ranch long before it was visited by any of the boys who were friends of mine in times past. Indeed, I never correspond with any of my old associates, and was desirous my whereabouts should be unknown to them. Through rumor, they learned of it. Jesse James first came in and remained several weeks. He was unknown to my husband, who never knew until long afterward, that our home had been honored by Jesse's presence. I introduced Jesse as one Mr. Williams from Texas. But, few outlaws have visited my home, notwithstanding so much has been said. The best people in the country are my friends. I have considerable ignorance to cope with, consequently, my troubles originate mostly in that quarter. Surrounded by a low down class of shoddy whites, who have made the Indian country their home to evade paying tax on their dogs, and, who I will not permit to hunt on my premises, I am the constant theme of their slanderous tongues. In all the world, there is no woman more peaceably inclined than I. . . .

You can just say I am a friend to any brave and gallant outlaw, but have no use for that sneaking, coward class of thieves who can be found in every locality, and who would betray a friend or comrade for the sake of their own gain. There are three or four jolly, good fellows on the dodge now in my section, and when they come to my home, they are welcome, for they are my friends, and would lay down their lives in my defense at any time the occasion demanded it, and go their full length to serve me in any way.

In 1886, Belle Starr was arrested as a suspect in an armed robbery carried out by three individuals but was released when no reliable evidence could be found that a woman was involved.

IMPACT
The mystique of the Wild West took hold on American culture following the Civil War, and the lurid adventures of colorful outlaws became the subject of great attention, both in the popular press and in a highly successful emergent form of literary entertainment, the dime novel. Richard K. Fox was a New York City editor of dime nov-

els who noticed an obituary for Belle Starr in the February 6, 1889, *New York Times* that claimed she had been arrested for murder or robbery twenty times during her life but had always eluded the authorities. Although this was not true, it gave Fox the genesis of a new woman outlaw character for his dime novel empire, and that summer he published *Bella Starr, the Bandit Queen: Or, The Female Jesse James*, a twenty-five-cent paperback written for him by freelancer Alton B. Meyers. The book sold very well, and the following year a fictitious female outlaw character named Belle Starr began to appear in other dime novels.

Italian physician Cesare Lombroso drew upon these imaginary depictions and descriptions of Belle and analyzed her behavior in a book titled *The Female Offender* (1895), which gave a touch of academic validity to her growing legend. Belle became the subject of many poems, plays, novels, and films, and storytellers and writers regularly took great liberty with the facts to adjust Starr's experience or appearance to fit their needs. The ongoing, international appeal of a gun-slinging, stagecoach-

robbing Belle Starr was demonstrated by Akihiro Itou's 1993 Japanese *manga* (comic book) *Belle Starr Bandits*.

FURTHER READING

Shirley, Glenn. *Belle Starr and Her Times*. Norman: University of Oklahoma Press, 1982. The first chapter of this book summarizes the growth of the Belle Starr legend, while the subsequent eighteen chapters carefully try to distinguish fact from fabrication.

Smith, Robert B. *Last Hurrah of the James-Younger Gang*. Norman: University of Oklahoma Press, 2001. A historian carefully tries to work through the many versions of what occurred in some of the James-Younger robberies to discern what the probable truth is. Includes references to Belle Starr and her interactions with gang members.

—*Scot M. Guenter*

SEE ALSO: Jesse James; William Clarke Quantrill; Henry Starr; Cole Younger.

HENRY STARR
American Indian bank robber and bandit

BORN: December 2, 1873; near Fort Gibson, Indian Territory (now in Oklahoma)
DIED: February 22, 1921; Harrison, Arkansas
ALSO KNOWN AS: Cherokee Badman
MAJOR OFFENSES: Bank robbery, train robbery, and murder (later reduced to manslaughter)
ACTIVE: 1892-1921
LOCALE: Indian Territory (later Oklahoma) and Colorado
SENTENCE: More than sixty years in prison for highway robbery; three years for manslaughter

EARLY LIFE

Henry Starr (star) was born near Fort Gibson, in the rugged and dangerous Indian Territory, to George and Mary Scott Starr. His father was half Cherokee, and his mother was Irish and one-quarter Cherokee. Having grown up on Cherokee reservations, Starr was very proud of his heritage.

Henry also came from a long line of criminals and outlaws. His grandfather Tom Starr was a fighter and an outlaw known as the Devil's Own. His uncle Sam Starr was married to Belle Starr, known as the Bandit Queen, who

associated with the Younger Gang. Henry Starr found Belle crude and made it a point when the matter arose to explain that they were related by marriage.

In 1886, when Starr was sixteen, his father died. His mother, who was faced with raising her three children and running the family farm, quickly married C. J. Walker. Starr and Walker fought constantly, and Starr felt Walker was inferior to his family because he had no Cherokee blood. Shortly after his mother's marriage, Starr left home. Relative to other outlaws and bandits of his day, Starr was well educated. He also avoided alcohol, claiming that he needed to be clear-headed and alert at all times.

CRIMINAL CAREER

Starr's criminal career began at age sixteen, when he was arrested for driving a wagon full of whiskey into a dry territory. Starr insisted he had borrowed the wagon and did not know about the whiskey, but he was sent to prison regardless. During this first stint in jail, he became resentful toward the criminal justice system. Upon his release he began committing small robberies and petty thefts.

In 1892, Starr, Ed Newcome, and Jesse Jackson targeted and robbed a train depot in Nowata, Indian Territory, the biggest crime with which Starr had thus far been involved. A warrant was issued for Starr's arrest, and U.S. Marshall Floyd Wilson pursued him. Starr and Wilson exchanged gunfire during the attempted capture. Wilson was fatally injured.

After serving time for bank robberies and murder, Starr was released in January, 1903. Between September, 1914, and January, 1915, Starr and various partners held up at least fourteen banks in Oklahoma. Starr's biggest criminal feat occurred on March 27, 1915, when he and his gang succeeded in robbing two banks simultaneously during broad daylight, something no other criminal gang had managed to do. During the Stroud National Bank and First National Bank heists, Starr was shot and left for dead in the street. He recovered and was sent to McAlester Prison, where he pleaded with outlaws to turn their lives around; these pleas won him favor with authorities and resulted in his parole.

On February 18, 1921, Starr, the first bank robber to use automobiles in committing robberies, attempted to rob the People's National Bank in Harrison, Arkansas. Upon entering the vault, an employee recognized Starr and shot him point-blank with a Winchester rifle kept on hand for such emergencies. Starr died four days later, on February 22, 1921.

Legal Action and Outcome

Starr was constantly in and out of courtrooms and jail cells beginning July 3, 1893, when he was arrested in Colorado Springs, Colorado, on thirteen counts of highway robbery and one count of murder for the death of Floyd Wilson, for which Starr was found guilty and sentenced to death by hanging. He appealed the verdict and received a second trial. Starr was found guilty a second time and again appealed. Upon his third trial, Starr pleaded guilty to manslaughter and received a three-year sentence for Wilson's murder, seven years and seven days for seven counts of robbery, and five years for one count of train robbery.

When Starr applied for a pardon, an incident from his prison days, while he had been awaiting his second trial, reflected favorably upon him. Starr had aided guards in preventing Crawford Goldsby, also known as Cherokee Bill, from breaking out of jail after he had killed a warden. President Roosevelt was so impressed by Starr's assistance in thwarting Cherokee Bill's escape that he pardoned Starr, who was then released on January 16, 1903, after he had served five years.

Starr was again arrested in New Mexico on May 11, 1908, for robbing a bank in Amity, Colorado. He was found guilty and paroled after five years for exemplary behavior. During the Stroud bank robbery, Starr was shot and sent to McAlester Prison, only to be paroled once more in March, 1919.

Impact

After more than fourteen bank robberies were committed by Henry Starr within a four-month period, the Oklahoma state legislature passed the Bank Robber Bill, which set aside fifteen thousand dollars for the capture of bank robbers and enacted a one-thousand-dollar bounty for known outlaws.

Although a true criminal, Starr upheld the outlaw code by never revealing a partner's name and never shooting anyone during the commission of a crime. Following his 1919 parole, Starr encouraged others to abide by the law by starring in the film *A Debtor to the Law* (1919), which illustrated the senseless violence of the Stroud bank robbery.

Further Reading

Drago, Harry S. *Outlaws on Horseback*. Lincoln: University of Nebraska Press, 1998. Focuses on train and bank robbers and offers a well-written account of Henry Starr's role as an outlaw and bank robber in the Wild West.

O'Neal, Bill. *Encyclopedia of Western Gunfighters*. Norman: University of Oklahoma Press, 1991. A factual look at the outlaws who roamed the Old West.

Reasoner, James. *Draw: The Greatest Gunfights of the American West*. New York: Berkley, 2003. Paints a historically accurate picture of the bandits and gunfighters, rather than romanticizing Starr and other Wild West outlaws.

Starr, Henry. *Thrilling Events: Life of Henry Starr*. College Station, Tex.: Creative, 1982. Starr's autobiography gives a personal point of view of the events that shaped his life.

Wellman, Paul I. *A Dynasty of Western Outlaws*. Norman: University of Oklahoma Press, 1998. Focusing on the late 1800's and early 1900's, Wellman's book provides a thorough examination of life in the Wild West. Includes maps and family trees.

—*Sara Vidar*

See also: Apache Kid; Tom Bell; William H. Bonney; Curly Bill Brocius; Butch Cassidy; Bob Dalton; Emmett Dalton; Bill Doolin; John Wesley Hardin; Doc Holliday; Jesse James; Tom Ketchum; Harry Longabaugh; Bill Longley; Joaquín Murieta; Johnny Ringo; Belle Starr; Hank Vaughan; Cole Younger.

ALEXANDRE STAVISKY
French con man

BORN: November 20, 1886; Slobodka, Ukraine,
 Russian Empire (now in Russia)
DIED: January 8, 1934; Chamonix, France
ALSO KNOWN AS: Sacha Stavisky; Serge Alexandre
 Stavisky (full name)
MAJOR OFFENSE: Financial fraud
ACTIVE: Primarily 1928-1932
LOCALE: Orléans and Bayonne, France

EARLY LIFE

Alexandre Stavisky (sta-VIHS-kee), born Sacha Stavisky, was the son of Emmanuel and Dunia Stavisky, Jews from the Ukraine. In 1899 his dentist father moved the family to Paris, where Stavisky attended the prestigious Lycée Condorcet. When he was in his teens, he printed fake business cards in order to get free theater tickets. In 1909, he and his grandfather ran a theater scam in which they sold entrepreneurs bogus concessions in a theater development that was never built.

CRIMINAL CAREER

In 1915 Stavisky served three months in prison for bilking an elderly woman out of twenty-five thousand francs. He also was charged with forgery in 1924 but escaped a jail sentence. In 1925 he met Arlette Simon (a model for fashion designer Coco Chanel), whom he married. As a result of dealing in fraudulent stock transactions and counterfeit treasury bonds, he was arrested in July, 1927, and spent months in La Santé prison awaiting his trial, which was postponed nineteen times. When he was released from prison in late 1927 on medical grounds, he had changed his name to Serge Alexandre.

Stavisky's most significant scam began in 1928 in Orléans, where he pawned jewels at a cooperating crédit municipal, which overvalued the items in exchange for money. By June, 1928, he had taken more than twenty-five million francs for the overvalued and fake goods he had pawned. To cover the funds they extended to Stavisky, the crédit municipal issued bonds to investors who believed that the pawned goods were, in fact, worth what the pawn brokers had listed.

When suspicions were aroused, and before auditors and police were ready to act, Stavisky redeemed the jewels with cash raised from a similar but larger scam in Bayonne. The Bayonne scheme brought him hundreds of millions of francs. Stavisky then placed the relatively worthless bonds with insurance companies and banks in which thousands of unsuspecting people had their money. When in 1933 the Bayonne bonds were due for redemption, there were insufficient funds to pay the investors. To raise funds, Stavisky proposed a new scheme, one that would require the backing of the ministers of foreign affairs and finance and that called for issuing bonds to finance European construction projects.

His failure to gain the necessary political support led to an investigation of the Bayonne crédit municipal and the arrest of its treasurer. With the police at his heels, Stavisky sought to avoid capture by fleeing to Chamonix, where the police caught up with him. Although it was rumored that the police killed him, it is more likely that he took his own life.

LEGAL ACTION AND OUTCOME

Aside from his 1927 arrest, few legal actions were taken against this high-profile con man until 1933, when the police followed him to Chamonix. By currying favor with politicians, some of whom were implicated in his schemes, and by buying favorable newspaper coverage, he was able to evade prosecution most of his life. After his death, he was buried in Père Lachaise cemetery in Paris.

IMPACT

The Stavisky affair was the major political affair of the French interwar period. Not only did many people lose their savings, but the politicians who had abetted Alexandre Stavisky were called to account. Conservative governmental critics accused Prime Minister Camille Chautemps's radical Socialist government of complicity in Alexandre Stavisky's deals and forced his resignation. Although the new premier, Édouard Daladier, succeeded in suppressing the riots (February 6-7, 1934) that ensued after the French people learned the details of the scheme, he, too, had to resign and was replaced by Gaston Doumergue. Jean Chiappe, prefect of police in Bayonne, lost his job, but few influential politicians were charged with crimes. In 1935-1936 twenty defendants, none of whom were important politicians, were tried, and eleven of them, including Stavisky's widow, were acquitted.

The long-term results were some anti-Jewish propaganda and the rise of the Popular Front to oppose the rising tide of fascism in France. Alain Resnais directed the film *Stavisky*, based on the life of the con man, in 1974.

FURTHER READING

Hyman, Paula. *The Jews of Modern France*. Berkeley: University of California Press, 1998. Examines France's evolving attitude toward its Jewish citizens.

Jankowski, Paul. *Stavisky: A Confidence Man in the Republic of Virtue*. Ithaca, N.Y.: Cornell University Press, 2002. Thorough discussion of the web of circumstances that allowed Stavisky's fraud to occur.

Semprun, Jorge. *Stavisky*. New York: Penguin, 1975. Succinct review of the affair followed by a film script of the Alain Resnais film.

—*Thomas L. Erskine*

SEE ALSO: Frank W. Abagnale, Jr.; Bobby Baker; Jim Bakker; Roberto Calvi; Martin Frankel; Victor Lustig; Mou Qizhong; Joseph Weil.

J. B. STONER
American bigot

BORN: April 13, 1924; Walker County, Georgia
DIED: April 23, 2005; Atlanta, Georgia
ALSO KNOWN AS: Jesse Benjamin Stoner, Jr. (full name)
MAJOR OFFENSE: Bombing a church
ACTIVE: 1942-1990
LOCALE: United States
SENTENCE: Imprisoned but paroled after three and one-half years

EARLY LIFE

Jesse Benjamin Stoner (STOH-nuhr), Jr., was born near Lookout Mountain in northern Georgia, the son of Jesse Benjamin Stoner, Sr., and Minerva Pogue Stoner. His father was associated with a sightseeing company and worked as a conductor on the incline railroad train on Lookout Mountain. J. B. Stoner's early years were characterized by tragedy. When he was two years old he was stricken with polio, which crippled him for life. When he was five, his father died in an accident. His mother died when he was seventeen. Although he attended both private and public schools in Chattanooga, he never graduated. As a teenager he admired the segregationist U.S. senator from Mississippi, Theodore Bilbo.

Stoner first garnered attention during World War II when, at the age of sixteen, he wrote to William Joyce, the British propagandist for Radio Berlin called Lord Haw Haw. Stoner was hoping to find a doctor in Germany who could cure his affliction caused by polio. Joyce responded on the air that he would help Stoner secure the services of a German doctor after the war was over. At the time, Stoner denied having Nazi sympathies.

POLITICAL CAREER

Stoner's association with hate groups began when he was a teenager. When he was eighteen he was a kleagle (organizer) for the Ku Klux Klan in Tennessee. In 1944, he petitioned the United States Congress to pass a resolution

J. B. Stoner. (Hulton Archive/Getty Images)

recognizing the "fact" that Jews were the children of the devil, and he urged Congress to take immediate action against what he called "the Jew-devils." In a 1946 interview he stated to a reporter, "I'll never be satisfied as long as there are any Jews here or anywhere. I think we ought to kill all Jews just to save their unborn generations from having to go to hell." Shortly thereafter, Stoner founded the Stoner Anti-Jewish Party. He said he started the party to ouster Adolf Hitler, whom he called a moderate. The stated purpose of the party was to make being a Jew punishable by death.

In the early 1950's, Stoner moved to Atlanta, where he attended Atlanta Law School. There he met Edward R. Fields, who later became one of Stoner's political allies. In 1958, Fields formed the National States Rights Party, of which Stoner became chairman and the most visible member. National States Rights Party members wore white shirts, black ties, and black armbands with the Nazi thunderbolt symbol. The organization also published a newspaper called *The Thunderbolt*.

During the 1950's and 1960's, Stoner and members of the National States Rights Party actively opposed the Civil Rights movement. Stoner frequently made inflammatory speeches in cities such as Birmingham, Alabama, St. Augustine, Florida, and Bogalusa, Louisiana, where opposition to integration was greatest. The Federal Bureau of Investigation and other law enforcement officials suspected Stoner of being involved in church and synagogue bombings. In 1977, Stoner was indicted for the 1958 bombing of the Bethel Baptist Church, an African American church in Birmingham. He was convicted in 1980. After exhausting his appeals, he disappeared. In June, 1983, he surrendered to authorities in Montgomery, Alabama. In 1986, after serving three and one-half years in prison, Stoner was paroled. A year later he was involved in a counterdemonstration over civil rights in Forsyth County, Georgia. Then, in 1998, he attended a Ku Klux Klan leadership meeting with Edward Fields in Zinc, Arkansas.

In addition to illegal means, Stoner used the political process to further his cause. Before he was disbarred, he defended Klansmen and other segregationists charged with racial crimes. For a short time he represented James Earl Ray, the convicted assassin of civil rights leader Martin Luther King, Jr. Ray's brother, Jerry Ray, worked for Stoner as a bodyguard.

Stoner frequently used the electoral process to spread his message of hate. From 1970 through 1990, he ran for various political offices in Georgia on an openly racist platform. In 1970, he ran for governor against Jimmy Carter and fellow segregationist Lester Maddox. Two years later, in 1972, Stoner was an unsuccessful candidate for the United States Senate. In that race, Stoner won a Federal Communications Commission ruling that allowed him to say the word "nigger" in television ads. In 1974, he was a candidate for lieutenant governor of Georgia. In that campaign he received approximately seventy-three thousand votes, nearly 10 percent of the total. Stoner ran for lieutenant governor again in 1990. In the election he received almost thirty-one thousand votes, about 3 percent of the votes cast.

By the late 1990's, Stoner had faded from public view. In 2001, he suffered a stroke that left him partially paralyzed and confined to a nursing home in Walker County in northwest Georgia. A lifelong bachelor, he remained an unapologetic racist and anti-Semite until his death in April, 2005, at the age of eighty-one.

IMPACT

From the early 1940's to the end of the twentieth century, J. B. Stoner used his positions in the Ku Klux Klan, the Stoner Anti-Jewish Party, and the National States Rights Party to spread his message of hate throughout the American South. His rhetoric was so extreme that prosegregation politicians distanced themselves from him. Although some dismissed his ramblings as demented, Stoner may have actually contributed to the success of the Civil Rights movement with his extremism, as his rhetoric made some people reflect on the legitimacy of segregationist policies and those who defended them.

FURTHER READING

Bushart, Howard L., John R. Craig, and Myra Barnes. *Soldiers of God.* New York: Kensington Books, 1998. Analyzes the white supremacist movement in the United States. It includes quotations of Stoner's anti-Semitic statements.

George, John, and Laird Wilcox. *American Extremists: Militias, Supremacists, Klansmen, Communists, and Others.* Amherst, N.Y.: Prometheus Books, 1996. Examines numerous extremist groups, left and right, including a chapter on the National States Rights Party.

—*William V. Moore*

SEE ALSO: Theodore G. Bilbo; Matthew F. Hale; Adolf Hitler; William Joyce; Tom Metzger; James Earl Ray.

JULIUS STREICHER
Nazi newspaper publisher and anti-Semitic propagandist

BORN: February 12, 1885; Fleinhausen, Germany
DIED: October 16, 1946; Nuremberg, Germany
ALSO KNOWN AS: Bloody Czar of Franconia; Chief Jew Baiter
MAJOR OFFENSES: Crimes against humanity, namely his incitement and development of German anti-Jewish sentiment and policies
ACTIVE: May, 1923-April, 1945
LOCALE: Germany
SENTENCE: Death by hanging

EARLY LIFE

Julius Streicher (YEW-lee-uhs SHTRI-kuhr) was born to a schoolmaster in a rural town near Augsburg in southern Germany. Julius followed in his father's footsteps and became a substitute teacher in January, 1904. In 1907 he entered military service for a year, but his rowdiness convinced his superiors he was unfit to become an officer. He returned to teaching and secured a position in Nuremberg. He became active in the local Democratic Party and married in 1913. When World War I broke out a year later, he reentered service and distinguished himself on battlefields in France, Romania, and Italy.

After the war he returned to Nuremberg to resume teaching and was profoundly affected by the problems the postwar German people faced. Unemployment, inflation, occupation, war guilt, and the myth of "Jewish back-stabbing" of the military effort were blended together and in his radicalized mind became the responsibility of Jews not only in Germany but also throughout the world. Raised on traditional German anti-Semitism, he now embraced a rhetorically violent anti-Jewish stance. He joined the Protective and Defensive Society and in 1920 the German Socialist Party, both right-wing political groups, but neither proved anti-Semitic enough for him.

On June 4, 1920, he nonetheless started the *German Socialist*, a party paper in which he ran terse, easily understood articles for the masses of malcontents. Despite internal opposition he carried on, because technically it was *his* paper. The National Socialist (Nazi) Party approached him in May, 1921, but at the time he preferred to create his own racialist coalition, changing the name of the paper to the *Deutscher Volkswille* (German people's will). He also addressed his first mass meeting on April 14, 1922.

CRIMINAL CAREER

In October, 1923, Streicher's small group merged with Adolf Hitler's Nazis, giving the future führer a solid Nuremberg connection. Streicher became blindly loyal to Hitler but never lost his streak of rowdy independence. He renamed his paper *Der Stürmer* (the stormer), and its first edition appeared in May, 1923. Streicher was jailed for complicity in Hitler's Beer Hall Putsch in November, 1923, and joined the German Workers' Party after the Nazis were outlawed. Elected to the Bavarian legislature, he proved a disruptive presence and left to form his own Greater German People's Community. He was equally rowdy as a Nuremberg city councilman (fall, 1924). Upon his release from jail, Hitler appointed Streicher party *Gauleiter* (province leader) of the state of Franconia, a title he would hold for two decades. Known as the Bloody Czar of Franconia for his vocal advocacy in print and at mass rallies of violent anti-Semitic policies and actions, he never took part in anti-Jewish violence.

Julius Streicher.

TEACHING HATE TO CHILDREN

Julius Streicher's publishing house issued Der Giftpilz *(the toadstool), a collection of stories designed to indoctrinate German children into anti-Semitic Nazi thinking. The story below was translated into English by Ernst Hiemer and published in 1938 in London by the Friends of Europe organization.*

"WITHOUT SOLVING THE JEWISH QUESTION, NO SALVATION FOR MANKIND"

Pimpfs of the Hitler Boys' Organization (Jungvolk) are proud of their black uniform. "We are the real Hitler-men" say the Pimpfs. Although "men" is a bit overdone, they are right in one thing: the Pimpfs are loyal to the Führer [Adolf Hitler] in life and death.

The Pimpfs are talking—in this concluding story—among themselves. One of them describes a National-Socialist Party march in Munich on the previous November 9th.

"Next to the Führer was General Göring, who was formerly severely wounded at the Felderrnhalle. I saw, too, Reichministers Dr. Goebbels, Frick, Rust and the Reichsleiter Rosenberg, Amann, Schwarz, our Reich Youth Leader Schirach and many other old campaigners. Before the Führer was carried the Blood-Flag, which received its consecration on November 9th, 1923. And in front of the Blood-Flag marched a man who, in 1923, too, was in the front and the thick of it: Julius Streicher."

Another Pimpf says:

"We know him all right. He is the enemy of the Jews. That is why all the Jews hate him."

"You are right," says another. "The Jews hate and insult only those whom they most fear. And they are afraid of Streicher."

Another Pimpf, hitherto silent, draws attention to a placard, which reads: "Julius Streicher is speaking in the Volk's Hall about 'The Jews are our Undoing!'"

"Let us go" says Konrad. "I've so long wanted to hear him."

Erich says: "I heard him once in a meeting two years ago."

"Tell us about him!" cry the other two Pimpfs.

Erich relates: "The meeting was packed. Thousands of people were there. At first, Streicher spoke about the years of struggle and the great achievements of the Hitler-Reich. Then he came to the Jewish question. What he said was so clear and simple that even we youngsters could understand. He took his examples always from life itself. Once he was very funny and made jokes, so we all had to laugh. Then he became deeply earnest and it was so still in the room, you could have heard a pin drop. He spoke of the Jews and their revolting crimes. He spoke of the great danger the Jews were to the whole world.

'Without a solution of the Jewish question, No salvation for Mankind!'

"That is what he said to us. We all understood. And when at the end he had called Sieg-Heil for the Führer, we had a storm of enthusiasm for him. Streicher had spoken for two hours. It only seemed like a few minutes to us.

"Yes, my dear friends! I shall always think of that meeting. And I shall never forget the speaking-choir which we heard at the end of the gathering:

> From the Germany Hitler created
> Resounds a cry to the whole world:
> Free yourselves from the Jewish hand
> And save both Volk and Fatherland!
> The world awakes in Juda's chains
> Germany alone it knows can save!
> Through German idea and German Being
> Will one day the whole world be restored."

After Nazi Party victories in 1933, *Der Stürmer* grew in circulation, vituperation, and influence. Between 1927 and 1934 circulation doubled to twenty-eight thousand, and from 1934 to 1935 it grew twentyfold to more than half a million copies. Readership was several times that. Streicher retained his control of the publication, making it a semi-official party organ. Its anti-Jewish focus grew increasingly lurid, reviving the ancient "blood libel" of Jews murdering innocent Christians and feeding racist attitudes with pornographic depictions of Jewish sexual brutality. Though appreciated and rewarded by Hitler, Streicher was kept at arm's length and had no role in the infamous major anti-Jewish governmental actions such as the Nuremberg Laws of 1935, Kristallnacht (crystal night) of November, 1938, or the structuring and implementation of the Holocaust itself.

In 1939 a government commission secretly compiled a two-volume record of Streicher's corruption, abuse of power, and sexual misdeeds, and in 1940 a tribunal declared him "unfit for human leadership." Hitler had Streicher placed under house arrest in the *Gauleiter*'s villa outside Nuremberg, allowing him to retain his title and continue publication of *Der Stürmer*. At war's end Streicher fled Franconia for Berchtesgaden, where he was captured by a Jewish officer of the U.S. Army.

LEGAL ACTION AND OUTCOME

Along with leading Nazis, Streicher was tried for war crimes in Nuremberg. The International Military Tribunal accused him of two counts. He was found not guilty of the first, conspiracy to wage aggressive war, because there was no evidence to support it. On the second, crimes against humanity, he was found guilty. Unlike other defendants, however, he was not charged with specific acts of criminal behavior. The charges against him stemmed, rather, from his sustained and hate-filled anti-Semitic rhetoric, both spoken and published. Prosecutors charged—and the court found—that his career as "Chief Jew Baiter" had made the Holocaust and other atrocities possible, even if he had not participated in them. He had poisoned the minds of a generation, and the effects of his propaganda would continue to poison minds "for generations to come."

In his defense, Streicher claimed that before 1933 he had only been a local figure with limited influence, and after the Nazi victory he was merely one of many Nazi proponents of racist ideas and policies. He further claimed that he personally rejected anti-Semitic violence and what little he knew of the Holocaust. Sentenced to death, he was hanged on October 16, 1946, but only after declaring his continuing allegiance to Hitler, the only convict to do so.

IMPACT

Julius Streicher's vile campaign was a watershed of intolerance and hate that mixed interwar German resentment with ancient antipathies that were rooted in Christian mythology. Though many Germans and German leaders shared his anti-Semitism, Streicher's strident popularization of filthy caricatures and racist lies fed the fires of intolerance and no doubt led many more to accept and even condone the policies and atrocities that characterized the Nazi pogrom. His crime was not merely hatred but also the instigation of hatred and ultimately the manifestation of that hatred in the Holocaust.

FURTHER READING

Bytwerk, Randall L. *Julius Streicher: Nazi Editor of the Notorious Anti-Semitic Newspaper Der Stürmer.* New York: Cooper Square Press, 2001. Scholarly biography and study of his propaganda.

Davidowicz, Lucy. *The War Against the Jews, 1933-1945.* New York: Holt, Rinehart and Winston, 1976. Classic account of the Holocaust that sets Streicher's crimes in the context of Nazi atrocities.

Varga, William P. *The Number One Nazi Jew-Baiter: A Political Biography of Julius Streicher, Hitler's Chief Anti-Semitic Propagandist.* New York: Carlton Press, 1981. Biographical study with an emphasis on Streicher's reception by the Nazi hierarchy.

—*Joseph P. Byrne*

SEE ALSO: Klaus Barbie; Martin Bormann; Léon Degrelle; Karl Dönitz; Adolf Eichmann; Hans Michael Frank; Joseph Goebbels; Magda Goebbels; Hermann Göring; Rudolf Hess; Reinhard Heydrich; Heinrich Himmler; Adolf Hitler; Alfred Jodl; Josef Mengele; Joachim von Ribbentrop; Baldur von Schirach; Otto Skorzeny; Albert Speer; Emma Zimmer.

ALFREDO STROESSNER
President of Paraguay (1954-1989)

BORN: November 3, 1912; Encarnación, Paraguay
DIED: August 16, 2006; Brasília, Brazil
ALSO KNOWN AS: Alfredo Stroessner Matiauda (full name)
CAUSE OF NOTORIETY: Stroessner, Paraguay's entrenched dictator for thirty-five years, ruled with an iron hand and ruthlessly suppressed dissent.
ACTIVE: 1954-1989
LOCALE: Paraguay

EARLY LIFE

Alfredo Stroessner (ahl-FRAY-thoh STREHS-nuhr) was born into a middle-class family in Encarnación, across the River Paraná from Argentina; his father, of German origin, was an accountant.

Stroessner joined the Paraguayan Army in 1929 and, by the time he was twenty, was an active infantry combatant in the Chaco War with Bolivia (1932-1935). The Chaco War was the crucial formative experience for Stroessner's generation of Paraguayans. Paraguay had long been demoralized by its catastrophic loss in the War of the Triple Alliance (1865-1870). In Stroessner's generation, however, the military had gained prestige through its role in the Chaco War, in which Paraguay had, to a certain degree, prevailed. The Paraguayan military capitalized on its Chaco prestige even long after its one war hero, General Marshal José Félix Estigarribia, had died.

Estigarribia's premature death in an airplane crash after he had been elected president created opportunities for paid ascension in the Paraguayan political order. Stroessner rapidly rose in army ranks and also associated himself with the conservative Colorado Party. He played an active role in suppressing a coalition of leftist groups in the Paraguayan Civil War of 1947. By 1954, Stroessner was the commanding general of the army. In this role, he led a military coup against President Federico Chávez and became the president of Paraguay in 1954.

POLITICAL CAREER

Stroessner was a modernizer, building roads and encouraging the cultivation of land by retired soldiers. Even his detractors conceded that the dictator had a strong work ethic. Stroessner was well known for sleeping very little and managing the affairs of the country around the clock. This kind of vigilance was necessary for Stroessner to keep control over the military, which, in turn, controlled Paraguay.

Stroessner was intolerant of any opposition and jailed, killed, or exiled anyone who remotely questioned his regime's authority. He seized upon the rise of leftist insurgencies in South America during the late 1960's in order to mount savage "counterterrorism" programs. During this period, similar "bureaucratic-authoritarian" regimes were in place in Argentina, Chile, and Uruguay. Stroessner collaborated with these regimes to form Operation Condor, a campaign of assassination, kidnappings, torture, and secret intelligence against any political dissenters. Paraguay's civil society came under the control of Stroessner's trademark *stronismo*, an umbrella term used by Paraguyans to refer both to the administration's use of torture of opponents and to the opportunistic self-enrichment of Stroessner and his military and political associates. Stroessner especially feared the indigenous Guaraní people (Guaraní speakers make up the majority of Paraguay's population), and his regime sought to withhold all resources from them.

Stroessner's opposition to Cuban leader Fidel Castro and his own anticommunist stance earned him general support from the United States and its allies during most of his presidency. However, in the late 1970's, domestic dissent became more visible and bolder; protesters were perhaps energized by U.S. president Jimmy Carter's call for pro-human rights practices among American allies. Stroessner arrested and exiled opposition leader Domingo Laíno of the Authentic Liberal Radical Party.

In this period, many Western leaders and citizens considered Stroessner a quasi-fascist, as much for his German name and right-wing policies as for the persistent rumors that surviving Nazi war criminals, such as Josef Mengele, had been given asylum in Paraguay. Stroessner therefore attained disrepute among Western leaders greater than that of his neighboring authoritarian rulers, who ran countries that seemed better suited to U.S. strategic needs and were thus treated more gingerly. Stroessner became an international pariah before he was overthrown at the age of seventy-six in a 1989 coup led by General Andrés Rodríguez Pedotti. He fled to Brazil and was granted asylum there. He lived in isolation until his death from a stroke in 2006. Paraguay's current president, Nicanor Duarte, told reporters there were no plans to honor Stroessner publicly.

IMPACT

Alfredo Stroessner will be remembered for bringing Paraguay into modern times; he will continue to be reviled for the oppressive and fraudulent means by which he effected that goal. The legacy of his brutal regime—the longest in Latin American history—is still felt. Though Stroessner's dictatorial regime was overthrown and democratic elections have been held in Paraguay since 1989, Stroessner's right-wing Colorado Party nonetheless continued in power into the twenty-first century. To Latin American scholars, Paraguay's scenario is atypical when considering the region's later-twentieth century democratic transitions: Authoritarian regimes characteristically are succeeded by a set of new parties contending for power. However, Paraguay found it hard to start with a clean slate, and many of its old political patterns seemed to be too entrenched to change very dramatically. The fundamental injustices and inequities in Paraguay have been left unremedied.

FURTHER READING

Bouvier, Virginia. *Decline of the Dictator*. Washington, D.C.: Office on Latin America, 1988. A researcher for a leading Washington organization monitoring Latin American affairs discusses the condition of Paraguay as the end of the Stroessner regime approaches.

Gimlette, John. *At The Tomb of the Inflatable Pig*. New York: Random House, 2004. An irreverent travelogue that contains some anecdotes about the gruesome Stroessner era.

Miranda, Carlos R. *The Stroessner Era: Authoritarian Rule in Paraguay*. Boulder, Colo.: Westview Press, 1990. A comprehensive academic treatment of the Stroessner period.

Roa Bastos, Augusto. "The Exiles of the Paraguayan Writer." *Review: Latin American Literature and Arts*, (September-December, 1981): 24-30. Paraguay's most famous novelist discusses "the two Paraguays": the nation of exiles from the Stroessner regime and those who stayed in the country.

Roett, Riordan. "Paraguay After Stroessner." *Foreign Affairs* 68, no. 2 (Spring, 1989): 124-142. In an article published just after Stroessner's overthrow, a leading international affairs expert assesses the dictator's legacy and the prospects for Paraguayan political renewal.

—*Nicholas Birns*

SEE ALSO: Fidel Castro; François Duvalier; Jean-Claude Duvalier; Leopoldo Galtieri; Augusto Pinochet Ugarte; Miguel Primo de Rivera; Efraín Ríos Montt; Anastasio Somoza García; Rafael Trujillo; Getúlio Vargas; Jorge Rafael Videla.

ROBERT FRANKLIN STROUD
American murderer and ornithologist

BORN: January 28, 1890; Seattle, Washington
DIED: November 21, 1963; Springfield, Missouri
ALSO KNOWN AS: Birdman of Alcatraz
MAJOR OFFENSES: Murders of a bartender and a prison guard
ACTIVE: January 18, 1909, and March 26, 1916.
LOCALE: Juneau, Alaska, and Leavenworth, Kansas
SENTENCE: Twelve years' imprisonment for the first murder; death by hanging for the second, commuted to life imprisonment without parole

EARLY LIFE

Robert Franklin Stroud (strowd) was born into a dysfunctional family. His father had a weakness for alcohol and women, and his mother, who had been badly abused in her first marriage, became distraught when her second husband, during bouts of drunkenness, beat the young boy and threatened to kill the entire family. As a child,

Stroud was often ill, and his mother's oversolicitousness hampered his social development and contributed to his misery in school, which he attended only through the third grade. Stroud often found himself in the role of protector of his two half sisters and younger brother against his father and local bullies. When Stroud was thirteen, the family broke apart over his father's affair with a neighbor woman, and Stroud left home to pursue, as he said, the life of "a great American bum." He returned to Seattle periodically only to discover that his father, who had rejoined the family, continued to drink heavily and mistreat his wife and children. After a particularly violent quarrel with his father in 1908, Robert left for Alaska, where he hoped to get a job in railroad construction.

CRIMINAL CAREER

In Cordova, Alaska, a boom town with twenty-six saloons, Stroud met Kitty O'Brien, a thirty-six-year-old dance-hall entertainer and, according to some accounts, a prostitute. Their relationship continued in Juneau, where Kitty found work in a cabaret, but it ended tragically when Stroud killed their mutual acquaintance, F. K. "Charlie" Von Dahmer, who had viciously beaten and robbed Kitty in Stroud's absence. After turning himself in to the city marshal, Stroud, together with Kitty (whose revolver had been the murder weapon) found himself indicted for first-degree murder. Eventually Stroud's plea of manslaughter was accepted, and the case against Kitty was dropped for lack of evidence. On August 23, 1909, a judge sentenced Stroud to twelve years in the penitentiary on MacNeil Island in Puget Sound.

Frustrated by the harsh sentence for what he considered justifiable homicide, Stroud hurt his chances for parole by such violent acts as stabbing an inmate who had accused him of stealing food and assaulting an orderly who had reported him for trying to obtain drugs. Stroud's hurtful behavior resulted in his transfer to Leavenworth Federal Penitentiary in Kansas on September 5, 1912. There, a prison doctor diagnosed his kidney disease, which was treated through medicines and diet. Stroud also began studying foreign languages, physics, mathematics, and music; he also looked forward to a visit from his younger brother, whom he had not seen in eight years.

Because of a minor infraction, Andrew F. Turner, a new guard, placed Stroud on report, thus vitiating his visiting privileges. On March 26, 1916, in the dining hall filled with more than one thousand inmates, Stroud stabbed and killed Turner.

LEGAL ACTION AND OUTCOME

Stroud was quickly tried and convicted of murder, and on May 27, 1916, he was sentenced to death by hanging. However, because the jury had been improperly charged, the trial and sentence were nullified, precipitating a series of legal battles involving a new trial and various appeals. Finally, in 1920, Stroud was again sentenced to be hanged, but his mother appealed to President Woodrow Wilson and especially to Wilson's wife, Edith Wilson; Edith's influence helped commute Stroud's death sentence to life imprisonment without any possibility of parole.

BIRDMAN OF LEAVENWORTH

Disappointed by the president's action, Leavenworth's warden placed Stroud in isolation. However, it was not long before Stroud had companionship when, in the exercise yard, he found a broken branch that contained a nest of fledgling sparrows. He brought them back to his cell and nursed them to health. He began reading about birds, their food, habits, and diseases, and he soon got permission to raise canaries. A new warden encouraged Stroud's interests by allowing him to obtain cages, chemicals, and other scientific equipment through which he conducted increasingly sophisticated investigations. He was even able to go into business by selling some of the canaries he bred and the remedies he developed for various avian diseases.

Based on his research, Stroud wrote articles for such publications as *Roller Canary Journal*. It was through his piece on "Hemorrhagic Septicemia in Canaries" that he eventually met Della Mae Jones, who later moved from Indiana to Kansas, where she helped manage Stroud's business ventures. In 1933, Jones disclosed that she had secretly married Stroud, but this "contract marriage" alienated both prison officials and Stroud's mother. These officials were also annoyed when the manuscripts of two of Stroud's books were smuggled out of Leavenworth and published: *Diseases of Canaries* (1933), which had been introduced through a bird magazine in 1933, and *Stroud's Digest of the Diseases of Birds*, which was published in 1943, after Stroud had been transferred to Alcatraz in the San Francisco Bay. Stroud's prison transfer may have been caused by these publications, his lack of appreciation for all his privileges, and his continued criminal behavior, including his use of chemicals and apparatus to make alcohol, as well as his physical attacks against guards.

Stroud was not allowed to bring his birds and scientific equipment to Alcatraz. Since he could no longer experiment with birds in his new D Block home, he studied law books with the goal of trying to get his convictions overturned. He also wrote two books—an autobiography and a history of the American penal system, but the warden forbade their publication. Though he did not participate in the prison riot of 1946, which was quelled by eighty Marines, Stroud accused the prison bureau of trying to murder him through its purposeless bombing of D Block.

As he aged, Stroud's health problems multiplied, and in 1959 he was transferred to the Medical Center for Federal Prisoners in Springfield, Missouri, where he died of natural causes in 1963. Morton Sobell, a fellow inmate and a convicted spy, discovered the body.

IMPACT

Although most of his fifty-four years of incarceration were spent in isolation, Robert Franklin Stroud managed, through his ornithological publications, to have a positive influence on bird lovers and avian veterinarians.

However, a year before his death, in 1962, his life and work achieved worldwide fame with the release of a successful film titled *Birdman of Alcatraz,* directed by John Frankenheimer and starring Burt Lancaster as Stroud. Stroud was not allowed to see the film, which was nominated for several Academy Awards and which led to renewed petitions for his release. When an Alcatraz inmate heard of this campaign to free Stroud, he opined: "They don't want to pardon Robert Stroud; they want to pardon Burt Lancaster." Lancaster portrayed Stroud as a gentle and humane amateur scientist and writer, which ran counter to the views of many prison officials that he was an unrepentant killer with a propensity for violence, child pornography, and other unsavory behavior.

In the years following the film and Stroud's death, journalists and biographers have wrestled with the contradictions in the amateur birdman's character. Some have emphasized his intelligence (he did have an IQ of 134), his courage in overcoming obstacles imposed by prison regulations, and his insights on bird diseases. Some of his most important supporters, such as his mother, abandoned him, but others remained loyal to the story of a very bad man who discovered redemption through the pursuit of scientific knowledge.

FURTHER READING

Babyak, Jolene. *Birdman: The Many Faces of Robert Stroud.* Berkeley, Calif.: Ariel Books, 1994. Using Stroud's prison records and interviews with guards and inmates who knew him, Babyak, a warden's daughter, presents a balanced view of his life and scientific contributions.

Esslinger, Michael. *Alcatraz: A Definitive History of the Penitentiary Years.* Ipswich, Mass.: Ocean View, 2003. Praised for its meticulous scholarship, this book contains several pages on the real and fictionalized Stroud. Illustrated with photographs. Index.

Gaddis, Thomas E. *The Birdman of Alcatraz: The Story of Robert Stroud.* Mattituck, N.Y.: Aeonian Press, 1976. This reprint, which contains the author's update covering Stroud's life from 1954 to 1962, also has the original text published by Random House in 1955. This book was the source of the film, but it has to be used cautiously since it depends heavily on Gaddis's conversations with Stroud. No index.

Presnall, Judith Janda. *Life on Alcatraz.* San Diego: Lucent Books, 2001. This book, part of "The Way People Live" series, aims to understand prison culture through an analysis of the daily routine and personal struggles of inmates. Stroud's criminal career, his bird studies at Leavenworth, and his isolation in D Block of Alcatraz are analyzed. Sections on further reading and works consulted. Index.

—*Robert J. Paradowski*

SEE ALSO: Tom Keating.

SUHARTO
Indonesian dictator (1968-1998)

BORN: June 8, 1921; Kemusu, Argamulja, Java, Dutch East Indies (now Indonesia)

ALSO KNOWN AS: Haji Mohammad Soeharto (full name)

CAUSE OF NOTORIETY: Suharto's extensive corruption, brutal killing of dissidents, and other human rights abuses during his presidency ultimately drew scrutiny from international organizations and led to domestic rioting and political upheaval.

ACTIVE: 1968-1998

LOCALE: Indonesia and East Timor

EARLY LIFE

Haji Mohammad Soeharto, known as Suharto (SUH-whahr-toh), was born into a poor farming family in Kemusu village in central Java on June 8, 1921. After graduating from local schools, Suharto worked for a short time as a bank clerk and as a common laborer. At the age of nineteen, he joined the Dutch colonial army. By December, 1941, he had been accepted into a Dutch-run military academy. Within a week, the Japanese entered World War II, and the Dutch rapidly surrendered all of Indonesia to Imperial Japanese forces. With this change in power, Suharto opportunistically joined the occupation police force. By 1943, he had risen to the rank of battalion commander in the Japanese-trained militia.

Following Japan's defeat in World War II and the return of Indonesia to Dutch control, Suharto joined Indonesian forces fighting for independence. By the time of the country's independence in 1949, Suharto had risen to the rank of commander. In his rise through the ranks over

Suharto. (AP/Wide World Photos)

the following fifteen years and under the Guided Democracy rule of President Sukarno (Indonesia's former resistance leader and first president), Suharto earned a reputation for his iron-handed suppression of dissidents. He was chosen to command the army's strategic forces, a sizable elite force stationed in Jakarta, which was maintained to handle national emergencies.

POLITICAL CAREER

Suharto's moment of opportunity came on September 30, 1965, when an alleged communist military coup was derailed. Six generals who shared Suharto's right-wing sentiments were killed in the coup, conveniently leaving few rivals to challenge his control of the military. Suharto's position as supreme military commander was formalized on October 16, 1965. What followed was a series of violent reprisals aimed at communist sympathizers, ethnic Chinese, and those viewed by Suharto as troublesome. At least 500,000 Indonesians were killed, and the army was purged of all potential dissidents.

In poor health, President Sukarno transferred power to General Suharto on March 11, 1966. Exactly one year later, Suharto was appointed by the House of Assembly as acting president; he formally became president in March, 1968. Once he had been given the title of acting president, Suharto announced his New Order program to replace Sukarno's Guided Democracy. Not only was the communist party (Partai Komunis Indonesia, or PKI) banned in this New Order but so too were labor unions, and strict censorship was imposed on the press. Within a short time, 200,000 dissidents were arrested. In 1968, and every five years thereafter, Suharto stood unopposed for election to the presidency by the House of Assembly.

The new anticommunist Suharto regime was a welcome development for the United States, which was reaching its peak of involvement in the Vietnam War. Large development loans were secured for Indonesia from the World Bank (an international lending organization largely controlled by the United States), an estimated 70 percent of which were actually used for development. The remainder fed an extensive network of corruption under Suharto. For instance, as hundreds of companies were formed to handle new business, Suharto, his six children, and a small number of entrepreneurs tied to his family established controlling interests in the companies. This group also acted as intermediaries for purchasing most government imports and for arranging export sales of such major commodities as oil, petrochemicals, and lumber.

Internally, Suharto controlled monopolies of such major commodities as flour, cement, tobacco, and timber. The best real estate for building and industrial development remained in family control. For both foreigners and Indonesians, doing business in Indonesia involved making large contributions to the hundreds of "charities" that Suharto endorsed; these foundations provided slush funds for Suharto and his cronies. Moreover, Suharto's business ventures paid little or no taxes to the government. By the time of his fall from power in 1998, the leader of the fifth most populous nation in the world had become the world's sixth richest individual, and each of his six children controlled a financial empire of their own.

By a strange turn of events, Suharto's interests obtained more than 40 percent of prime land in East Timor. In 1975, after Portugal withdrew from East Timor as a colonial power, an indigenous nationalist movement

(Fretilin) took control. In response, the Indonesian army invaded East Timor, establishing a puppet government that requested immediate absorption into Indonesia. The ensuing conflict, which continued into the twenty-first century, left approximately one-third of the population (200,000 people) dead.

END OF REGIME

In the summer of 1997, the once-soaring economies of the Association of Southeast Nations (ASEAN) plummeted. Economic panic caused bank and corporate failures, the stoppage of construction projects, inflation, and massive unemployment in Indonesia. Riots led to more than one thousand deaths and one billion dollars in property damage. Likewise, Suharto's suspicious wealth and his protectionist policies came under the scrutiny of the World Bank, the International Monetary Fund (IMF), and the United States. In response, Suharto pledged his country to strict austerity measures. However, the resulting economic hardships led to an erosion of domestic confidence in Suharto. By mid-May, 1998, widespread protests over Suharto's corruption became too large to contemplate the use of force. On May 21, Suharto resigned, along with eleven of his ministers.

LEGAL ACTION AND OUTCOME

In late May, 2000, Suharto was placed under house arrest while financial corruption charges were investigated. By July, he was charged with embezzling $571 million from American donations to his charitable foundations. However, Suharto suffered a stroke, along with heart problems and intestinal bleeding, and court-appointed doctors declared him medically unfit to stand trial. If ever declared fit to stand trial by Indonesia's attorney general, Suharto would be subject to charges of human rights violations and corruption. One large portion of Suharto's assets, about nine billion dollars, is said to be in an Austrian bank.

Suharto's son Hutomo Mandala Putra (commonly known as Tommy Suharto) was sentenced to eighteen months for real estate fraud and an additional fifteen years for planning the murder of his judge. Suharto's half brother Probosutedjo was convicted of corrupt practices and received a jail sentence of four years.

IMPACT

Suharto ranks among the most corrupt political leaders of modern history. Dismantling the vast corporate empire controlled by his family members and associates proved to be a complicated process. The killing of hundreds of thousands of Indonesians and East Timorese, as well as the general use of mass torture and arrests, qualifies Suharto as one of the more repressive dictators of the second half of the twentieth century.

FURTHER READING

Elson, R. E. *Suharto: A Political Biography*. New York: Cambridge University Press, 2001. A detailed and scholarly study of Suharto's life, including archival sources and interviews of key individuals. Maps, footnotes, glossary, and select bibliography are included.

"Suharto, Inc." *Time*, May 24, 1999. An extensive exposé of Suharto and his family published on the first anniversary of the Indonesian dictator's resignation.

Vatikiotis, Michael R. *Indonesian Politics Under Suharto: The Rise and Fall of the New Order*. New York: Routledge, 1999. A survey and analysis of Indonesian politics during Suharto's regime. Notes and index are included.

—Irwin Halfond

SEE ALSO: Ferdinand Marcos; Anastasio Somoza García; Than Shwe; Getúlio Vargas.

LUCIUS CORNELIUS SULLA
Roman dictator (82-79 B.C.E.)

BORN: 138 B.C.E.; Rome (now in Italy)
DIED: 78 B.C.E.; Puteoli (now Pozzuoli, Italy)
ALSO KNOWN AS: Lucius Cornelius Sulla Felix (full name)
CAUSE OF NOTORIETY: After Sulla seized power, his Proscriptions brought about the murders of his opponents as well as innocent citizens.
ACTIVE: 88-79 B.C.E.
LOCALE: Rome

EARLY LIFE
The career of Lucius Cornelius Sulla (LOO-shyuhs kohr-NEE-lyuhs SUHL-lah) has to be set in the broader context of the turbulent conditions of Roman politics in the last century of the Roman Republic: the struggle for power between the Senatorial noble families, the Opti-

Lucius Cornelius Sulla. (Library of Congress)

mates, and the Populares, talented individuals who challenged the Senate, supported by the masses. Sulla was born in 138 B.C.E. into an old but not recently distinguished noble family and began his military career under the rising star of the Populairs party. Sulla and the Roman general Marius fought together against Numidia during the Jugurthine War (111-106). Sources indicate some tension between Sulla and Marius as their careers advanced. Sulla had notable success in the Social War and was given the command against Parthia (ruled by Mithridates II) in 88. That same year, he was elected consul, with the support of the powerful Metellus family, to which he joined himself by marriage. This set the stage for a showdown between Senatorial and Populares interest groups, which coalesced around Sulla and Marius, respectively.

POLITICAL CAREER
When the tribune Publius Sulpicius Rufus managed to pass legislation, in the teeth of Optimate opposition, reassigning the command against Mithridates to Marius, Sulla was caught up in the street violence that ensued. He had to seek refuge in, of all unlikely places, Marius's house, and seems to have decided that his situation, and the threat to the state as he saw it, required extreme measures. The action he took had far-reaching consequences: He marched on Rome at the head of his army and essentially seized control of the government. He annulled the actions of Sulpicius and had the Senate declare Sulpicius, Marius, and ten others "enemies of the state." Leaving a largely hostile city behind him, Sulla returned to his campaign against Mithridates.

In the year 87, the pendulum of power swung in favor of Marius and the Roman consul Lucius Cornelius Cinna, who themselves marched on Rome and, after a siege, embarked on a purge of their opponents and declared Sulla an enemy of the state. Marius's death in 86 left Cinna in sole charge and set the stage for a second march on Rome by Sulla, who had repulsed all offers of conciliation.

DICTATORSHIP
In 83-82, Sulla made his way through Italy to Rome, facing surprisingly stiff resistance all the way. Realizing that sterner measures were needed if he were to maintain control this time around, Sulla instituted the "Proscriptions" for which he became notorious: Anyone on the

List of the Proscribed could be killed (rewards were even offered) and his property confiscated. At least five hundred Roman citizens were victims, possibly more, many for no good reason. The Senate appointed Sulla dictator, charged him with restoring law and order, and gave him the name Felix, meaning "fortunate": Sulla always claimed to be favored by Fortune. A series of reactionary measures followed, aimed primarily at strengthening the Senate. After enacting his program of "reform," Sulla retired in 79 to a country villa, where he occupied himself writing his memoirs, hunting, and drinking. He died in 78 of liver failure.

IMPACT

By all accounts a man of violent temper and frightening aspect, Lucius Cornelius Sulla went down in Roman memory as a negative figure, more so than his rival Marius. Sulla's legislation was repealed almost immediately after his death. His choice of violence and military force over constitutional methods, and his success, albeit a short-lived one, set an example that would be imitated by others and ultimately led to the end of the Republican system of government he was trying to "restore."

FURTHER READING

Keaveney, Arthur. *Sulla: The Last Republican.* 2d ed. New York: Routledge, 2005. Survey of Sulla's attempts to shore up the Republican system of government.

Plutarch. *Fall of the Roman Republic: Marius, Sulla, Crassus, Pompey, Caesar, Cicero—Six Lives by Plutarch.* Translated by Rex Warner. Harmondsworth, Middlesex, England: Penguin, 1972. A detailed ancient account of Sulla's life and deeds.

Syme, Ronald. *The Roman Revolution.* New York: Oxford University Press, 2002. Classic analysis of the forces that ended the Roman Republic.

—*David H. J. Larmour*

SEE ALSO: Caligula; Commodus; Cypselus of Corinth; Domitian; Elagabalus; Fulvia; Galerius; Justin II; Nero; Phalaris; Polycrates of Samos; Theodora.

SULLA'S PROSCRIPTIONS

Plutarch's "Life of Sulla," from Parallel Lives, *describes the tyrant's "proscriptions": Those on the list of the proscribed could be killed and their property confiscated. Altogether, at least five hundred (possibly more) Roman citizens were on the list, many innocent:*

Sulla . . . busied himself with slaughter, and murders without number or limit filled [Rome]. Many, too, were killed to gratify private hatreds, although they had no relations with Sulla, but he gave his consent in order to gratify his adherents. At last one of the younger men, Caius Metellus, made bold to ask Sulla in the senate what end there was to be of these evils, and how far he would proceed before they might expect such doings to cease. "We do not ask thee," he said, "to free from punishment those whom thou hast determined to slay, but to free from suspense those whom thou hast determined to save." And when Sulla answered that he did not yet know whom he would spare, "Well, then," said Metellus in reply, "let us know whom thou intendest to punish." This Sulla said he would do. . . .

Sulla at once proscribed eighty persons, without communicating with any magistrate; and in spite of the general indignation, after a single day's interval, he proscribed two hundred and twenty others, and then on the third day, as many more. Referring to these measures in a public harangue, he said that he was proscribing as many as he could remember, and those who now escaped his memory, he would proscribe at a future time. He also proscribed any one who harboured and saved a proscribed person, making death the punishment for such humanity, without exception of brother, son, or parents, but offering any one who slew a proscribed person two talents as a reward for this murderous deed, even though a slave should slay his master, or a son his father. And what seemed the greatest injustice of all, he took away the civil rights from the sons and grandsons of those who had been proscribed, and confiscated the property of all.

Moreover, proscriptions were made not only in Rome, but also in every city of Italy, and neither temple of God, nor hearth of hospitality, nor paternal home was free from the stain of bloodshed, but husbands were butchered in the embraces of their wedded wives, and sons in the arms of their mothers.

Plutarch, "The Life of Sulla," in *The Parallel Lives*, translated by Bernadotte Perrin (New York: Harvard University Press, 1916).

MARY SURRATT
American boardinghouse operator

BORN: May or June, 1823; near Waterloo, Maryland
DIED: July 7, 1865; Washington, D.C.
ALSO KNOWN AS: Mary Elizabeth Jenkins (birth name); Mary Elizabeth Surratt (full name)
MAJOR OFFENSE: Conspiracy and aiding and assisting with the escape of the assassins of President Abraham Lincoln
ACTIVE: October, 1864-April, 1865
LOCALE: Washington, D.C.
SENTENCE: Death by hanging

EARLY LIFE

Born in May or June of 1823 near Waterloo, Maryland, Mary Elizabeth Jenkins, known to history as Mary Surratt (suh-RAT), received a better education than was typical for girls during this era. Her mother enrolled her in a Roman Catholic school when she was twelve, and she became Catholic. In 1840, at age seventeen, Mary married John Harrison Surratt, a man eleven years her senior. Their first home was on land that John's father had inherited from his foster parents, located in Oxon Hill (later the Congress Heights section of Washington, D.C.). Three children were born to the couple: Isaac Douglas, Elizabeth Susanna (Anna), and John Harrison, Jr. After Mary and John's house burned in 1851, John built a home/tavern and post office on 287 acres of land in Prince George's County in a community later called Surrattsville. In August, 1862, when Mary was thirty-nine, she found her husband dead.

CRIMINAL CAREER

About two years after Surratt was widowed, she rented out the tavern site to John Lloyd and moved to a house at 541 High Street in Washington, D.C. There, she began taking in boarders to supplement her income. Among the boarders or frequent visitors was an actor, John Wilkes Booth, as well as Louis Weichmann and others who later would be named as conspirators in the death of President Abraham Lincoln. Between October, 1864, and April 14, 1865, the day of Lincoln's assassination, several suspect actions occurred: private conversations between Surratt, Booth, Weichmann, and Lewis Powell (also known as Lewis Payne); Surratt questioning her son John about the men who had been coming to the house, in turn expressing her uneasiness that something was going on; Surratt hiring a buggy on April 14 to deliver a small package (later said to be Booth's field glasses) to Lloyd and alleg-

edly telling him that "the shooting irons" that had been delivered there some weeks before would soon be needed; and the discovery of a picture of Booth behind another picture that Weichmann had given to Surratt's daughter Anna.

Following the assassination of Lincoln on April 14, 1865, Booth and David E. Herold made a stop at the tavern owned by Surratt. Lloyd is reported to have given the men whiskey, firearms, and the field glasses that Booth had stored at the location. On Monday, April 17, 1865, two Army officers and two detectives came to the Surratt house to question Surratt. While Major H. W. Smith was there, a stranger appeared who told Major Smith that he had come to dig a gutter for Surratt, as requested. The man was Powell, who had attempted to assassinate Secretary of State William Seward on the same night as Lincoln's assassination and whom witnesses placed in the company of Surratt in the past. When Major Smith asked her if she had seen the man before, Surratt swore that she

Mary Surratt.

had not. Defenders of Surratt insisted that she was not lying; rather, because of her poor eyesight, she did not recognize him. Major Smith did not believe the explanations.

LEGAL ACTION AND OUTCOME

Not satisfied with Surratt's answers to his questioning and noting that other suspect persons appeared to be frequenting the boardinghouse, authorities took Surratt to police headquarters for further questioning and then to the Old Capitol Prison. Her defense attorney, Reverdy Johnson, appeared only twice during the trial. Two junior attorneys, Frederick A. Aiken and John Wesley Clampitt, were both in their mid-twenties and were inexperienced; it was the first major case for both men. Among several witnesses brought in to give testimony was Lloyd, who did not say anything against Surratt until he was suspended by his thumbs and the pain was unbearable; thereafter, he provided some of the most damaging evidence against her.

On April 30, Surratt was transferred to the Old Arsenal Penitentiary, where she stood trial along with seven others accused of conspiracy. In spite of some impassioned arguments in her defense, Surratt and three others—George A. Atzerodt, Herold, and Powell—were sentenced to death by hanging; the other prisoners, Samuel Arnold, Samuel A. Mudd, Edward Spangler, and Michael O'Laughlin, received sentences of hard labor at the Penitentiary of Albany, New York. Of the nine members of the Military Commission, five entered a plea for mercy to President Andrew Johnson. After he ordered Surratt's execution, he denied having seen the request. Surratt was hanged on July 7, 1865.

IMPACT

Mary Jenkins Surratt made history as the first woman in American history to be given a death sentence. Throughout the years following the trial, questions have been raised both about Surratt's innocence or guilt and about the issue of the appropriateness of a military trial for a civilian. Historians have also examined the extent to which her inexperienced defense lawyers contributed to her conviction, as well as the reliability of the testimony of Lloyd: He was a known alcoholic and his testimony against Surratt may well have been brought forth by the torture to which he was subjected.

FURTHER READING

Chamlee, Roy Z., Jr. *Lincoln's Assassins: A Complete Account of Their Capture, Trial, and Punishment.* Jefferson, N.C.: McFarland, 1990. Comprehensive treatment of the alleged conspirators and others less directly involved in the assassination plot.

Leonard, Elizabeth D. *Lincoln's Avengers: Justice, Revenge, and Reunion After the Civil War.* New York: Norton, 2004. Focuses largely on Advocate General Joseph Holt, the man who led the investigation and the prosecution of Surratt and other alleged conspirators. The author concludes that Surratt's guilt was questionable and that Holt was unduly eager to have her hanged.

Steers, Edward, Jr., ed. *The Trial: The Assassination of President Lincoln and the Trial of the Conspirators.* Lexington: University Press of Kentucky, 2003. Twelve essays discuss various aspects of the conspiracy cases, such as the legality of a military trial, the development of the cases prior to trial, and the trials of each of the accused. Contains a reprint of the complete record of the military tribunal that convicted Surratt and the seven other alleged conspirators.

Trindal, Elizabeth Steger. *Mary Surratt: An American Tragedy.* Gretna, La.: Pelican, 1996. The author, who researched Surratt for fifteen years, is convinced that Surratt was innocent of conspiracy. Includes copious facts and interjects probable actions or thoughts when facts about personal details in Surratt's life are not known.

—*Victoria Price*

SEE ALSO: John Wilkes Booth; Lewis Powell.

WILLIE SUTTON
American bank robber

BORN: June 30, 1901; Brooklyn, New York
DIED: November 2, 1980; Spring Hill, Florida
ALSO KNOWN AS: Willie "the Actor" Sutton; Slick Willie Sutton; William Sutton (full name)
MAJOR OFFENSE: Bank robbery
ACTIVE: 1920's-1952
LOCALE: East Coast of the United States
SENTENCE: Many, culminating in one for 105 years, another for life

EARLY LIFE

Born in Brooklyn in 1901, Willie Sutton (SUH-tuhn) was the fourth of five children in an Irish American family. He began his schooling at Public School 1 in Brooklyn but left the school the same day he entered it. He transferred to St. James's Parochial School; when he was ten years old, he was again transferred, this time to St. Anne's Parochial School. He was frequently in trouble as a child, robbing grocery stores, and left St. Anne's after getting into a fight and refusing to name his opponent. He then attended Public School 5, where he was caught stealing money from teachers' purses.

After the Sutton family moved, he was enrolled in Public School 10 and graduated in 1916 after completing the eighth grade. He got a job at the Title Guaranty and Trust Company, then worked for Metropolitan Life Insurance Company, and then went to Providence, Rhode Island, to work in a war plant. After World War I, jobs were scarce, and he was employed for a short time by a gardening company. He then stole sixteen thousand dollars from the firm owned by Tom Hurley, his girlfriend's father.

CRIMINAL CAREER

After a week, Sutton and his girlfriend were arrested in Poughkeepsie, New York, but because Hurley did not want his daughter to go to jail, he got Sutton a suspended sentence. Sutton then served as an apprentice to Eddie "Doc" Tate, an accomplished safecracker. Although Sutton was charged with the first-degree murder of "Happy" Gleason, the jury acquitted him. When he was accused of the attempted robbery of the South Ozone National Bank, however, he was convicted and sentenced to five to ten years in Sing Sing Prison but was transferred to Dannemorra Prison after an altercation with a prison guard.

After his release in September, 1929, he married Lou-

ise Leudeman (she later divorced him) and returned to crime. In his robbery of a Western Union office, he used the first of many disguises he would employ throughout his career. His daughter, Jeanne, was born in September of 1930, and he continued to rob. After his arrest for the robbery of Rosenthal's Jewelry Store, he was sentenced to thirty years in Sing Sing. He escaped on December 11, 1932, by scaling the prison walls with a makeshift ladder and then began his career in earnest.

In 1933, Sutton, disguised as a mailman, entered the Corn Exchange Bank and Trust in Philadelphia, but he and his accomplice had to abort their planned bank robbery when a passerby became suspicious. Undaunted, on January 15, 1934, Sutton and two accomplices entered the same bank, this time through a skylight, rounded up the employees, handcuffed them, and put them in a small room. The robbers then gathered up the money. Two weeks later, Sutton was apprehended and sentenced to twenty-five to thirty years in the Eastern State Penitentiary in Philadelphia. On April 3, 1945, after he had made four previous attempts to break out of prison, he and eleven other prisoners escaped, but Sutton was caught the same day. As a fourth-time offender, he was sentenced to life imprisonment and transferred to the maximum-security Holmesburg Prison in Philadelphia.

On February 10, 1947, disguised as a prison guard, Sutton carried a ladder to a prison wall and again escaped. Before he was captured in February of 1952 by police acting on a tip by Arnold Schuster, who was murdered for informing, Sutton had a career total of more than one hundred bank robberies, most of them involving his disguises as a messenger, policeman, or maintenance man, had stolen more than two million dollars, and had been placed on the Federal Bureau of Investigation's "Ten Most Wanted List" on March 20, 1950.

LEGAL ACTION AND OUTCOME

When he was arrested in 1952 and tried for the robbery of the Manufacturers Trust Company in Sunnyside, Long Island, Sutton already owed the legal system one life term and a 105-year sentence. At his trial in the Queens County Court, the jury tacked on an additional thirty years, which he was to serve at Attica Prison in New York State. While incarcerated, Sutton read law books and became a "jailhouse lawyer." When a liberal Supreme Court's decisions in the 1960's granted some concessions to convicts and instituted some curbs on police procedures, Sutton and his determined lawyer succeeded in getting the New York penal system officials to free "Slick Willie" on Christmas Eve, 1969. At the time Sutton was ill, suffering from emphysema and facing an impending operation on the arteries in his legs. After his release he moved to Spring Hill, Florida, where he lived with his sister. Ironically, before his death the Manhattan Bank and Trust Company of New Britain, Connecticut, hired him as their spokesman to promote the company's credit card. Sutton died on November 2, 1980, in Spring Hill. His family later moved his body to Brooklyn, where he was buried in the family plot.

IMPACT

Willie Sutton was a nonviolent criminal who appealed to the masses despite his crimes. He was even seen as a kind of Robin Hood figure. Sutton's notion of "where the money was" later became the "Willie Sutton Rule" of accounting, which states that, in business management, activity-based costing should be applied where the great-

est costs are incurred (where the money is) in order to lower costs. His indirect impact involved a gangland decision not to murder a "citizen," a non-Mob member who is an informer, again.

FURTHER READING

Reynolds, Quentin. *I, Willie Sutton*. 1953. Reprint. New York: Da Capo Press, 1993. Sutton's life story, complete with "lessons" and justifications for his criminal behavior.

Sutton, Willie, with Edward Linn. *Where the Money Was*. New York: Broadway Books, 2004. Update of Reynolds's book to Sutton's release in 1969. Also provides some new material.

Swierczynski, Duane. *This Here's a Stick-Up: The Big Bad Book of American Bank Robbers*. New York: Alpha, 2002. Contains a short discussion of Sutton.
—*Thomas L. Erskine*

SEE ALSO: Henri Charrière.

MICHAEL SWANGO
American serial killer

BORN: October 21, 1954; Tacoma, Washington
ALSO KNOWN AS: Mike Swango; Jackson Michael Kirk; David Jackson Adams; Joseph Michael Swango (full name)
MAJOR OFFENSES: Murder, fraud, and aggravated battery
ACTIVE: January 31, 1984-July 7, 1995
LOCALE: United States, including Illinois, Ohio, and New York, and Zimbabwe, Africa
SENTENCE: Life imprisonment without the possibility of parole

EARLY LIFE

Michael Swango (SWANG-oh) was a well-behaved youngster who excelled at school and graduated as valedictorian of his high school class in 1972. After two years at Millikin University, Swango dropped out and joined the Marine Corps for two years. Afterward he attended Quincy College and majored in biology and chemistry and was then admitted to Southern Illinois University (SIU) medical school in 1979.

As a medical student, Swango was aloof, careless, and morbidly interested in death. Even though he re-

ceived his medical diploma in 1983, he was evaluated by the dean of SIU as mildly incompetent and brimming with attitudinal and professional problems. Swango was granted a yearlong internship in general surgery at the Ohio State University Medical Center but was quickly recognized as inept and brusque with patients.

CRIMINAL CAREER

In early 1984, some patients under Swango's care died inexplicably. Others suffered enigmatic cardiac or respiratory crises but survived and identified Swango as the doctor who had injected them with something just before the onset of their life-threatening episodes. Several nurses also witnessed Swango inject patients who soon thereafter mysteriously died. These observations were reported to Ohio State's head of neurosurgery, but no action was taken against Swango. When Swango was dismissed from Ohio State, the reason given was poor performance.

Swango then worked as a paramedic in Quincy, Illinois. After feeding his coworkers arsenic-laced doughnuts, he was convicted of aggravated battery and sentenced to five years in prison, of which he served only two. Later, Swango used a falsified resume to secure a job as a medical resident at the Veterans Affairs Medical Center in Sioux Falls, South Dakota, but was dismissed in December, 1992, when hospital administrators discovered his felony conviction.

By the end of June, 1993, Swango had moved to New York to work in a psychiatry program at the State University of New York, Stony Brook—a job he secured, once again, through prevarication. On his first day at work, patients under his care began to die of heart failure that followed paralysis. After the dean of Stony Brook discovered Swango's previous felony conviction, Swango was terminated, but he eluded the Federal Bureau of Investigation by leaving the United States for Africa.

In Zimbabwe, Swango worked at Mnene Hospital but was relieved of duty on July 21, 1995, after conclusive evidence emerged that he had poisoned several patients. Swango successfully applied for a position at the Royal Hospital in Dhahran, Saudi Arabia, with another fraudulent application.

LEGAL ACTION AND OUTCOME

While en route to his new job, Swango was arrested in Chicago on June 27, 1997, for fraud. He was escorted to New York for trial. He pleaded guilty to fraud and was sentenced to forty-two months in prison at Florence, Colorado. On September 6, 2000, Swango pleaded guilty to three murder charges as part of a plea bargain and was sentenced to life imprisonment without the possibility of parole.

IMPACT

The Michael Swango incident highlighted the failure of several medical facilities to recognize the danger signs of a killer working within the system. His repeated murders and final capture forced hospitals to play closer attention to suspicious deaths and make better use of practitioner databases such as those of the National Practitioner Data Bank and the Federation of State Medical Boards.

FURTHER READING

Ameringer, Carl F. *State Medical Boards and the Politics of Public Protection.* Baltimore: Johns Hopkins University Press, 1999. An indictment of the ineffectiveness of the National Practitioner Data Bank because participation in it is voluntary.

Lang, Joan. "Swango: The View from the Couch." *The Park Ridge Center Bulletin* 3 (1998): 10. Psychiatrist tells how easily even the best-trained mental health professionals can be fooled by a sociopath.

Robertson, William O. "National Practitioner Data Bank—Still Not Effective After All These Years?" *Western Journal of Medicine* 174 (2001): 148-149. Documents failures of the National Practitioner Data Bank, which it says come largely from underreporting.

Stewart, James B. *Blind Eye: The Terrifying Story of a Doctor Who Got Away with Murder.* New York: Touchstone Books/Simon & Schuster, 1999. Exacting and rigorous reportorial account of Swango's murderous rampage.

—*Michael A. Buratovich*

SEE ALSO: Linda Burfield Hazzard; Harold Shipman.

TA MOK
Commander in chief of the Khmer Rouge army

BORN: 1926; Brakeab, Cambodia
DIED: July 21, 2006; Phnom Penh, Cambodia
ALSO KNOWN AS: Chhit Choeun (probable birth
    name); Ek Choeun; Achar Choeun; Ung choeun;
    Oeung Choeun; Nhuon Kang; Uncle Mok;
    Grandfather Mok; Ta 15; the Butcher
MAJOR OFFENSES: Crimes against humanity
ACTIVE: 1975-1979
LOCALE: Cambodia

EARLY LIFE
Ta Mok (da mohk), born Chhit Choeun, the oldest of seven children, was raised primarily by his grandmother. He attended Pali High School in Phnom Penh. During World War II, with Indochina under Japanese control, Chhit Choeun joined the anticolonial resistance movement. After the war, he served as a Theravada Buddhist monk at Wat Mohamuntri, joining the Khmer Issarak shortly thereafter. The Khmer Issarak was a guerrilla movement of several leftist groups with origins in the anticolonial struggle. Chhit Choeun left the monkhood in his early thirties to marry his cousin, with whom he had two children.

POLITICAL CAREER
By the early 1960's, Chhit Choeun was a member of the Cambodian Communist Party, serving mainly in the southwest. He took the nom de guerre of Ta Mok. By the end of the decade, he was a general in the Khmer Rouge, as the Cambodian Communists styled themselves. In 1968, he rose to the position of secretary of the Southwest Zone. He later joined the Standing and Military Committee of the party, giving him unchallenged power in the Southwest Zone. Around 1970, he lost part of a leg in combat against government troops, but the wound did little to slow him.

THE KILLING FIELDS
In 1975, concurrent with the conquest of South Vietnam by communist North Vietnam, Communists seized power in Laos and Cambodia. Cambodia was renamed "Democratic Kampuchea." Ta Mok was instrumental in the implementation of Cambodian leader Pol Pot's vision of ethnic homogeneity and the elimination of urban areas. With economic collapse, starvation, and rising tensions with the Vietnamese, paranoia grew within the ranks of the Khmer Rouge. Massive purges of cadre and army of-ficers, as well as large-scale murders of ordinary peasants from areas near Vietnam, soon followed. As the party secretary of the Southwest Zone, Ta Mok is believed to have directed the execution of large numbers of people, including some thirty thousand in the Angkor Chey district alone, earning him his nickname, "the Butcher."

Increasingly, the Khmer Rouge drew its senior leadership from Ta Mok's Southwest Zone, as his appointees increasingly replaced the leaders in the Eastern Zone, who were thought to be tainted by association with the Vietnamese and less ruthless in their extermination of suspect populations. In 1977, Ta Mok became commander in chief of the army; his personal power was unchecked in Cambodia.

Fiercely xenophobic, the Khmer Rouge executed an estimated ten thousand Vietnamese who lived in Cambodia as well as others influenced by Vietnamese culture. All Cambodians were placed on starvation rations in order to export a maximal amount of rice to pay for military hardware to deal with the increasingly hostile relations with Vietnam. The repression of Viets brought invasion by Vietnam in December, 1978, which toppled the Khmer Rouge in 1979. Ta Mok continued to be supreme military commander of what remained of the Khmer Rouge and fought an increasingly marginalized guerrilla war against the Vietnamese and, later, Cambodian government forces.

YEARS OUT OF POWER
The Khmer Rouge maintained control over a diminishing area of Cambodia, predominantly along the Thai border. Ta Mok established his headquarters in Anlong Veng and administered the northern section of Khmer Rouge-controlled Cambodia. By 1996, defections had weakened the Khmer Rouge to ineffectiveness. In 1997, Ta Mok named himself commander of one faction. That summer, he arrested Pol Pot for executing a longtime Khmer Rouge loyalist and his family for expressing a desire to seek amnesty. In April, 1998, sweeps by the Cambodian military forced Ta Mok into the jungles along the Thai border. On April 15, 1998, Pol Pot died while under the control of Ta Mok.

LEGAL ACTION AND OUTCOME
On March 6, 1999, the Cambodian army captured Ta Mok just inside the Thai border and transported him to Phnom Penh. Initially, he was charged with tax evasion and membership in the Khmer Rouge. While many other

former Khmer Rouge leaders accepted government amnesty, Prime Minister Hun Sen announced even before Ta Mok's capture that he would not be offered amnesty. In February, 2002, the government of Cambodia charged him with crimes against humanity. Under Cambodian law, the government had six months to try him. As of 2006, Ta Mok was still awaiting trial, although arrangements for a trial involving both Cambodia's judicial system and the international community had been adopted by the United Nations in 2003 and by the Cambodian National Assembly in 2004. On July 21, 2006, Ta Mok died, still awaiting trial.

IMPACT

The Khmer Rouge sought to create a new state based on ethnic "purity" and agriculture. During the four years of its rule over Cambodia, the Khmer Rouge executed its suspected enemies, which included intellectuals, ethnic minorities, and anyone who had traveled abroad, spoke another language, or even wore glasses. Estimates of the number of people who died as a result of the Khmer Rouge vary from 1.5 million to well over 2 million people. The Khmer Rouge executed up to 100,000 people directly, with the remainder dying as a result of starvation, overwork, lack of medical care, and other causes attributable to the Khmer Rouge. Several hundred thousand left the country as refugees. Ta Mok's death under-

scored the urgency of prosecuting those responsible for the "killing fields."

FURTHER READING

Becker, Elizabeth. *When the War Was Over: Cambodia's Revolution and the Voices of Its People.* New York: Public Affairs, 1986. Standard account of the Khmer Rouge from taking power in Cambodia until after its expulsion by the Vietnamese army. Becker traces the implementation of Khmer Rouge's economic and ethnic ideology in Cambodia and the effect of that policy on the people of Cambodia.

Kiernan, Ben. *The Pol Pot Regime: Race, Power, and Genocide in Cambodia Under the Khmer Rouge, 1975-1979.* New Haven, Conn.: Yale University Press, 2002. Scholarly account of the origins, internal workings, and fall from power of the Khmer Rouge.

Morris, Stephen J. *Why Vietnam Invaded Cambodia: Political Culture and the Causes of War.* Stanford, Calif.: Stanford University Press, 1999. Political study of the rise in tensions between the two revolutionary communist regimes and the ensuing invasion of Cambodia and removal of the Khmer Rouge by the Vietnamese.

—*Barry M. Stentiford*

SEE ALSO: Mao Zedong; Ne Win; Pol Pot; Suharto.

ROGER BROOKE TANEY
Chief justice of the United States (1836-1864)

BORN: March 17, 1777; Calvert County, Maryland
DIED: October 12, 1864; Washington, D.C.
CAUSE OF NOTORIETY: Taney's extreme racism was reflected in his legal opinions, most notably in *Dred Scott v. Sandford*, which ignited a firestorm of controversy and contributed to the outbreak of the Civil War.
ACTIVE: c. 1836-1860
LOCALE: Washington, D.C.

EARLY LIFE

Born into a privileged Maryland family, Roger Brooke Taney (TAW-nee) reaped the proceeds of slavery his entire life. The Taneys' wealth, derived from the slave labor of the family plantation, provided for Roger's private education at Dickinson College, training as a lawyer, and

marriage into the prominent Key family of Maryland when he married Anne Key, sister to lawyer Francis Scott Key (who became famous as the author of "The Star Spangled Banner"), in 1806. Taney's social standing led him into state politics, originally as a Federalist. To make himself more politically palatable, Taney freed his slaves, but he retained his convictions that slavery itself was legal and that slaves themselves were less than human. He disagreed with the Federalists over the War of 1812, however, and shifted his allegiance to the Democratic Party. By the 1820's, Taney was a fixture in Maryland politics, becoming the state's attorney general in 1827. Taney campaigned in support of Andrew Jackson for president in 1824 and 1828, and when Jackson won the latter election, he rewarded Taney for his political support by bringing him into his administration.

POLITICAL CAREER

In 1831, Jackson reorganized his cabinet and asked Taney to assume the job of attorney general. Taney's first legal opinions incorporated his views on slavery and the rights of slaves. Most southern states required the captains of ships entering their ports to turn over any free blacks onboard for imprisonment for the duration of the ship's stay. This policy was intended to prevent free blacks from inciting slaves into possible revolt. Great Britain and other European nations protested this violation of their citizens' rights, and the secretary of state asked Taney for a constitutional clarification on the situation. Taney upheld the law, declaring that blacks were a "separate and degraded people" to whom neither the Declaration of Independence nor the Constitution granted any rights, an opinion Taney would reiterate later in his career.

His loyalty to Jackson earned Taney a promotion in 1833, when he became the secretary of treasury. Jackson had determined to dissolve the Bank of the United States, but his secretary of the treasury, William John Duane, refused to transfer federal funds out of the bank. Jackson fired him and put the loyal Taney in his place. Taney dutifully removed the funds to state banks, but an angry Congress refused to approve his nomination as treasury secretary, and Taney returned home to Maryland. In 1836, Jackson nominated Taney to replace recently deceased John Marshall as chief justice of the United States. Congress, now dominated by the Democrats, confirmed the appointment on March 28, 1836.

Taney's long tenure as chief justice was marked by decisions that consistently favored the power of the federal government over that of the states, decisions in marked contrast to his most famous case. He also continued his legal opinions on the status of slavery, such as in *Groves v. Slaughter* (1841) and *Prigg v. Pennsylvania* (1842), even if he was often in the Court minority. In the case of *Dred Scott v. Sandford* (1857), Dred Scott, a Missouri slave, had sued for his freedom in a Missouri court because his owner had lived in Illinois (where slavery was banned by state law) and in Minnesota (then part of the Wisconsin Territory, where slavery was banned by the 1785 Northwest Ordinance). Scott won in local court, lost in the Missouri Supreme Court, and appealed to the U.S. Supreme Court.

Taney used the case to determine Scott's status as a slave and also to decide finally the slavery issue. As

Roger Brooke Taney. (Library of Congress)

Taney opined in the Court's majority decision, Scott did not have jurisdiction to bring suit in the first place, because, as a person of African descent, he was not and could not be a citizen of the United States. As a black person, Taney ruled, Scott had no "rights that a white man was bound to respect." Second, Scott's residence in Illinois did not make him free because Illinois's antislavery law violated the property rights of slave owners to take their property (slaves) into Illinois. Last, Scott's residence in Minnesota did not make him free because the Congress could not limit the property rights of slave owners, and thus the Northwest Ordinance was unconstitutional.

IMPACT

The *Dred Scott* ruling caused a firestorm of protest in the North, which ridiculed Taney's belief that people of African descent could not possibly be citizens of the United States. The overturning of Illinois state law and the Northwest Ordinance also seemed to indicate that local political opinion did not matter, and slave owners could take their property anywhere in America, including the northern states. Taney's extreme viewpoints in favor of slavery and the South damaged his credibility, which made it easier for President Abraham Lincoln to ignore Taney and the other pro-Southern Supreme Court justices during the Civil War.

The best example of Taney's lost influence was the 1861 case of *Ex parte Merryman*, in which Lincoln suspended habeas corpus in Maryland and refused Taney's demands to explain his actions. Rendered powerless by the outbreak of the war he helped to cause, Taney remained an ineffective figure on the Supreme Court until his death on October 12, 1864. His opinions, clearly out of political favor in the North, also greatly diminished the influence of the Supreme Court in the years during and after the Civil War.

FURTHER READING

Fehrenbacher, Don Edward. *Slavery, Law, and Politics: The Dred Scott Case in Historical Perspective.* New York: Oxford University Press, 1981. A wide-ranging examination of the controversial *Dred Scott* case and how different eras view the issues and decisions of the case.

Huebner, Timothy S. *The Taney Court: Justices, Rulings, and Legacy.* Santa Barbara, Calif.: ABC-CLIO, 2003. A full examination of the Taney court, including studies of all of the major cases and information on Taney's fellow justices.

Lewis, Walker. *Without Fear or Favor: A Biography of Chief Justice Roger Brooke Taney.* Boston: Houghton Mifflin, 1965. The standard biography of Taney, this book tries to present a balanced view of the controversial chief justice.

—*Steven J. Ramold*

SEE ALSO: Orval E. Faubus; Arthur de Gobineau; Benjamin Tillman; George C. Wallace.

REACTIONS TO THE DRED SCOTT DECISION

The following are some of the responses by prominent citizens and contemporary newspaper accounts to Chief Justice Taney's decision in the Dred Scott case, in which he famously ruled that Scott, as an African American, had no "rights that a white man was bound to respect":

- *Republican senator Charles Sumner of Massachusetts:* I speak what cannot be denied when I declare that the opinion of the Chief Justice in the case of Dred Scott was more thoroughly abominable than anything of the kind in the history of courts.
- *The Chicago Tribune:* We scarcely know how to express our detestation of [the Supreme Court's] inhuman dicta or fathom the wicked consequences which may flow from it.... To say or suppose, that a Free People can respect or will obey a decision so fraught with disastrous consequences to the People and their Liberties, is to dream of impossibilities.
- *New York Tribune:* It is assumed that Judges, because they are Judges, must always be in the right; that they are so far elevated above the level of ordinary mortality that we not only must not question—nay more, that it is absolutely treason to question the correctness of their decisions; that all we have now to do is to fold our hands and submit without a murmur. Our readers have ere this discovered that we are under the control of no such abject idolatry; that we regard even that awful creature, a Chief-Justice, as a human being, and that we do not mean to submit slavishly to fraud and usurpation because the ermine is interposed to cloak their character.
- *Illinois Democrat Stephen A. Douglas (during a debate with Abraham Lincoln):* Mr. Lincoln goes for a warfare upon the Supreme Court of the United States, because of their judicial decision in the Dred Scott case. I yield obedience to the decisions in that court—to the final determination of the highest judicial tribunal known to our constitution.
- *Cincinnati (Ohio) Daily Enquirer:* The Court of last resort, which has jurisdiction over questions appertaining to the powers of the Federal Government, decided that Congress has no power under the Constitution to legislate upon slavery in the Territories, and that all such legislation as the so-called Missouri Compromise, which undertook to do so, is null and void.
- *Abolitionist Frederick Douglass:* The voice of the Supreme Court has gone out over the troubled waves of the National Conscience. But my hopes were never brighter than now. I have no fear that the National Conscience will be put to sleep by such an open, glaring, and scandalous issue of lies.

CHARLES TAYLOR
Liberian dictator (1997-2003)

BORN: January 28, 1948; Arthington, near Monrovia, Liberia

ALSO KNOWN AS: Charles Ghankay Macarthur Dapkpana Taylor (full name)

CAUSE OF NOTORIETY: Taylor's soldiers perpetrated grave atrocities, and the Revolutionary United Front (RUF) rebel movement that Taylor fostered in neighboring Sierra Leone surpassed his own record of crimes against humanity.

ACTIVE: December, 1989-August 11, 2003

LOCALE: Liberia and Sierra Leone, West Africa

EARLY LIFE

Born of a mother of Gola ancestry and an Americo-Liberian father, Charles Taylor (TAY-luhr) studied in Liberia before proceeding to the United States, where he obtained a B.A. in economics from Bentley College in Waltham, Massachusetts, in 1977.

MILITARY AND POLITICAL CAREER

Taylor returned to Liberia shortly before noncommissioned officers of indigenous Liberian origins overthrew the Americo-Liberian government of William R. Tolbert, Jr., in a bloody coup d'état in April, 1980. Taylor was appointed head of the Government Services Agency, which handled state procurements. However, he soon fell out with Samuel Doe, head of the military junta, who accused Taylor of embezzling $900,000. Taylor fled to the United States, where he was held in the Plymouth County House of Corrections in Massachusetts. He escaped under mysterious circumstances on September 15, 1985. It is strongly suspected that Taylor's escape was part of a plot to bolster opposition to Doe, whose excesses had alienated his friends in Washington.

Taylor subsequently underwent military training in Libya and reemerged in December, 1989, at the head of insurgents from Ivory Coast. The ensuing protracted war engulfed Liberia and its neighbors, especially Guinea and Sierra Leone. Taylor drew support from Libya, Ivory Coast, and Burkina Faso and from the Gio and Mano, who had borne the brunt of Doe's persecution and misrule. Taylor founded a group known as the National Patriotic Liberation Front (NPFL), aimed at toppling Doe. His army, which included boy and girl soldiers whose parents had been murdered by Taylor's marauding soldiers, as well as mercenaries mainly from Burkina Faso,

swept through large swathes of the Liberian hinterland, confining President Doe to Monrovia, the capital city, by 1990.

Meanwhile, several important events took place in 1990 and 1991. First, the escalation of the Liberian conflict prompted other countries in West Africa to organize an interventionist force, the Economic Community of West African States Monitoring Group, better known by its acronym of ECOMOG. It was to be a key, but controversial, actor in the unfolding tragedy in Liberia. Second, one of Taylor's lieutenants, Prince Yormie Johnson, had broken away to form the Independent National Patriotic Liberation Front (INPLF), which established itself in Monrovia. A third major development was the abduction of President Doe by Johnson and his men at the ECOMOG headquarters in Monrovia. Doe was tortured to death on September 9, 1990.

Taylor escalated the Liberian conflict into a regional conflagration by instigating the Revolutionary United

Charles Taylor. (AP/Wide World Photos)

Front of Sierra Leone (RUF) to launch an insurgency against the Sierra Leonean government in 1991. The RUF, under Foday Sankoh and Samuel Bockarie, gained global infamy for cutting off the limbs of their defenseless victims, especially women and children. Taylor and the RUF plundered the mineral resources of Sierra Leone, especially diamonds. Taylor became a major conduit for the "blood diamonds" exported by the RUF to pay for armaments and other supplies.

Meanwhile, the Liberian conflict persisted, with Taylor becoming the most successful Liberian warlord. With Doe out of the way and all but Monrovia in his grip, he was thwarted from seizing power only by the ECOMOG forces stationed in the capital. The impasse was broken by a peace deal in 1995 that installed an interim government. The stage was set for the election of July, 1997, which Taylor won—essentially because the war-weary Liberians feared that he could renew hostilities if he lost the election. He secured 75 percent of the votes cast and assumed office on August 2, 1997.

Like Doe before him, Taylor was a ruthless and corrupt dictator who soon alienated important segments of the society. In 1999, elements opposed to Taylor under the banner of Liberians United for Reconciliation and Democracy (LURD) invaded northern Liberia from the neighboring country of Guinea. While LURD was entrenching itself in the north, the Movement for Democracy in Liberia (MODEL) invaded the country from Ivory Coast to the southeast.

LEGAL ACTION AND OUTCOME

In 2001, the United Nations placed an arms and travel ban on the Taylor government. By June, 2003, the insurgents had seized two-thirds of the country, giving Taylor a taste of his own medicine. In that month, a U.N. tribunal ordered Taylor's arrest in connection with the use of child soldiers and large-scale atrocities in Sierra Leone. Intense pressure from the international community ensured Taylor's resignation and exile on August 11, 2003. As late as 2006 he remained in exile in Calabar, an eastern Nigerian city, at the insistence of the Nigerian president, Olusegun Obasanjo.

IMPACT

Charles Taylor employed child soldiers and terror, caused proliferation of small arms in the West African subregion, escalated regional conflict through the RUF in Sierra Leone, and plundered Liberian and Sierra Leonean diamonds. He caused the deaths of more than 200,000 persons, the displacement and exile of a million others, and the destabilization of neighboring states and governments. Reputed as the most criminal West African ruler of all time, Taylor has been indicted for war crimes, crimes against humanity (including cannibalism), embezzlement of state funds, and human rights violations.

FURTHER READING

Ellis, Stephen. *The Mask of Anarchy: The Destruction of Liberia and the Religious Dimension of an African Civil War.* New York: New York University Press, 1999. An authoritative analysis of the religious and wider undercurrents of the Liberian civil war in which Taylor was a principal actor.

Sawyer, Amos. *Beyond Plunder: Toward Democratic Governance in Liberia.* Boulder, Colo.: Lynne Rienner, 2005. An analysis of the past and future of Liberia by one of its greatest scholars.

Yoder, John C. *Popular Political Culture, Civil Society, and State Failure in Liberia.* Lewiston, N.Y.: Edwin Mellen Press, 2003. An in-depth study of the political context in which Taylor and other Liberian actors operated.

—*Ayodeji Olukoju*

SEE ALSO: Sani Abacha; Idi Amin; Omar al-Bashir; Jean-Bédel Bokassa; Samuel K. Doe; Mengistu Haile Mariam; Mobutu Sese Seko; Robert Mugabe; Muammar al-Qaddafi; Muhammad Siad Barre.

EDWARD TEACH
English pirate

BORN: c. 1680; Bristol, England

DIED: November 22, 1718; Ocracoke Inlet, North Carolina

ALSO KNOWN AS: Blackbeard; Edward Thatch; Edward Thatche; Edward Drummond; Edward Tash; Edward Tatch; Edward Tach

CAUSE OF NOTORIETY: Piracy

ACTIVE: 1717-1718

LOCALE: Caribbean Sea, Atlantic coast of North America

EARLY LIFE

Edward Teach (teech) was born in Bristol, England, c. 1680. Little is known about his early life, but documents show his family was affluent. He was well educated and interacted comfortably with governors, merchants, and members of the upper class.

During his career as a pirate, Teach used many aliases to protect his family. He was best known as Blackbeard. He apparently served as a privateer apprentice in Jamaica during the War of Spanish Succession, although no "letter of marque" was recorded for him. Records of Teach as a pirate date to summer, 1717.

CRIMINAL CAREER

Initially, Teach and pirate Ben Hornigold sailed together and spread great fear throughout the Caribbean. In November, 1717, they captured the French ship *La Concorde* off Martinique. About this time, Britain revoked all privateering licenses and offered amnesty to pirates. Hornigold retired, and Teach began piracy on his own. Teach claimed *La Concorde* for his flagship, renaming it *Queen Anne's Revenge.*

In winter months, Teach sailed off the Atlantic coast and in the summer returned to the Caribbean. His first solo conquest involved the large ship *Great Allen* near St. Vincent. Legend reports that several days later Teach encountered the British man-of-war HMS *Scarborough.* While Teach could have outrun the *Scarborough,* he allegedly engaged in a running duel instead. The British were losing, and Teach allowed retreat because the ship held no valuables. The tale of this skirmish earned Teach much respect for defeating a heavily armed warship and contributed to his image as a fierce pirate. The log of the *Scarborough,* however, shows no encounter. During 1717-1718, Teach terrorized the Caribbean, capturing at least twelve ships and pillaging as many as twenty-five.

In 1718, Royal Governor Woodes Rogers killed or drove away all pirates on Nassau. Consequently, Teach sailed for the Atlantic coast of North America, commanding four vessels and three hundred pirates.

A charismatic leader with a dramatic personality, Teach cultivated an image to intimidate merchants and his crew. Wearing black clothing and carrying multiple swords, knives, and pistols, he appeared ferocious, braiding his long hair and growing a full black beard. For battle, he placed slow-burning fuses in his beard or under his hat, allowing smoke to encircle him. Some say this created the appearance of the devil. Merchants often surrendered at the sight of Blackbeard.

Teach mastered psychological warfare, but Blackbeard was not as cruel as most pirates. His common tactic

Edward Teach.

BLACKBEARD BY FRANKLIN

"The Downfall of Piracy" (1719) was probably written by Benjamin Franklin at age twelve or thirteen, about a year after Blackbeard's death. Although not quite accurate in detail, this bit of youthful doggerel conveys the tone of the times:

Will you hear of a bloody Battle
Lately fought upon the Seas?
It will make your Ears to rattle
And your Admiration cease:

Have you heard of Teach the Rover,
And his Knavery on the Main;
How of Gold he was a Lover,
How he lov'd all ill-got Gain?

When the Act of Grace apeared
Captain Teach, with all his Men,
Unto Carolina steered,
Where they kindly us'd him then;

There he marry'd to a lady,
And gave her five hundred Pound,
But to her he prov'd unsteady,
For he soon march'd off the Ground.

And returned, as I tell you,
To his Robbery as before,
Burning, sinking Ships of value,
Filling them with Purple Gore. . . .

Valliant Maynard as he sailed,
Soon the Pirate did espy,
With his Trumpet he then hailed,
And to him they did reply:

Captain Teach is our Commander,
Maynard said, he is the Man
Whom I am resolv'd to hang, Sir,
Let him do the best he can.

Teach replyed unto Maynard,
You no Quarter here shall see,

But be hang'd on the Mainyard,
You and all your Company;

Maynard said, I none desire
Of such Knaves as thee and thine,
None I'll give, Teach then replyed,
My Boys, give me a Glass of Wine.

He took the Glass, and drank Damnation,
Unto Maynard and his Crew:
To himself and Generation,
Then the Glass away he threw:

Brave Maynard was resolv'd to have him,
Tho' he'd Cannons nine or ten;
Teach a broadside quickly gave him,
Killing sixteen valliant Men.

Maynard boarded him, and to it
They fell with Sword and pistol too;
They had Courage, and did show it,
Killing of the Pirate's Crew.

Teach and Maynard on the Quarter,
Fought it out most manfully,
Maynard's Sword did cut him shorter,
Losing his head, he there did die. . . .

When the bloody fight was over,
We're informed by a Letter writ,
Teach's Head was made a Cover,
To the Jack Staff of the Ship:

Thus they sailed to Virginia,
And when they the Story told,
How they kill'd the Pirates many,
They'd Applause from young and old.

---

was to run ships aground, fire warning shots, take valuables, and let the ship's crew flee. In fact, no record exists of Teach murdering anyone until the battle resulting in his death.

In May, 1718, Teach blockaded Charles Towne, South Carolina. He and his men pillaged every ship in the harbor and took wealthy passengers from *The Crowley* as hostages. Ten ships were destroyed before offi-

cials gave Teach the medical supplies he demanded. Despite numerous threats, all hostages were released unharmed.

In June, 1718, Teach again sailed to North Carolina, planning to surrender to Governor Charles Eden, who represented the British throne. At Topsail Inlet near Beaufort, North Carolina, the *Queen Anne's Revenge* ran aground. The grounding was likely intentional as Teach sought to downsize his fleet. Reports show that while efforts were made to rescue the *Queen Anne's Revenge*, Teach loaded his valuables onto another ship and escaped with riches and select members of his crew.

With his smaller ship, he continued to Bath, North Carolina, and acquired a home. He was pardoned, married Mary of Ormand, and appeared to settle into a planter's life.

When the gold ran out, however, Blackbeard resumed pirating. He joined other pirates on Ocracoke Island for revelry and plundered ships off the Atlantic Coast. Local residents dreaded Blackbeard, distrusted Governor Eden, and feared the offshore islands and surrounding seas were becoming a pirate base. Indeed, Teach likely bribed Eden to overlook his piracy.

LEGAL ACTION AND OUTCOME

North Carolina residents asked the governor of Virginia, Alexander Spotswood, for protection from the general pirate menace and specifically from Blackbeard. Spotswood placed a bounty on Teach's head and sent Lieutenant Robert Maynard to search for him.

Maynard, aboard a small, unarmed sloop, surprised Blackbeard and his crew of twenty-five at Ocracoke Inlet on November 22, 1718. Teach fired on Maynard's ship, and Maynard bluffed by sending his crew below deck. Believing that only a few crew had survived the initial hit, Blackbeard boarded Maynard's sloop. Teach, outnumbered by Maynard's men, was drawn into hand-to-hand combat. He received at least five gunshot wounds and twenty stab injuries before he was decapitated. His head was displayed on the bowsprit of Maynard's ship as a warning to other pirates. Thirteen of Blackbeard' screw were captured and hanged in Williamsburg, Virginia.

IMPACT

Edward Teach's career was glorious but short. The death of Blackbeard was the end of the Golden Age of Piracy.

Separating the man from his legend is difficult. As the most feared pirate in the Western Hemisphere, Blackbeard created an enduring image of piracy. He has been the subject of books, movies, documentaries, and treasure hunts. Benjamin Franklin wrote a poem called "A Sailor's Song on the Taking of Teach," and Robert Louis Stevenson used Blackbeard's crew member Israel Hands as inspiration for his book *Treasure Island* (1883). A tourist industry surrounding Blackbeard developed in Ocracoke, where the remains of the *Queen Anne's Revenge* are believed to have been discovered off the coast.

FURTHER READING

Bond, Constance. "A Fury from Hell or Was He?" *Smithsonium* 30, no. 11 (2000): 62-95. Compares Blackbeard's image with his behavior. Includes information on the discovery of the wreck thought to be the *Queen Anne's Revenge*. Discusses social issues such as race and class in the piracy era.

Butler, Lindley S. *Pirates, Privateers, and Rebel Raiders of the Carolina Coast*. Chapel Hill: University of North Carolina Press, 2000. Examines the lives of eight pirates from the early eighteenth century to Reconstruction, including Blackbeard. Provides useful photos and maps.

Lee, Robert E. *Blackbeard the Pirate: A Reappraisal of His Life and Times*. Winston-Salem, N.C.: Blair, 1974. A well-researched, authoritative study of the life of Teach. Extensive bibliography.

Yetter, George Humphrey. "When Blackbeard Scourged the Seas." *Colonial Williamsburg Journal* 15, no. 1 (1992): 22-28. Provides a good overview of pirate life and specific details of Blackbeard's career and last battle.

—*Barbara E. Johnson*

SEE ALSO: Samuel Bellamy; Stede Bonnet; Anne Bonny; Sir Henry Morgan; John Rackham; Mary Read; Bartholomew Roberts.

THAN SHWE
Burmese junta leader (1992-   )

BORN: February 2, 1933; Kyaukse district, Burma
ALSO KNOWN AS: Senior General
CAUSE OF NOTORIETY: Than led one of the world's most repressive military juntas.
ACTIVE: Beginning 1992
LOCALE: Myanmar (Burma)

EARLY LIFE
Details of the life of Than Shwe (TAH-n sh-WEE) before his rise through the ranks of the Burmese military are largely unknown. He was born in 1933 in the rural district of Kyaukse, which is nestled in a low range of hills thirty kilometers south of Mandalay. He graduated from high school in Kyaukse and remained there, working as a mail clerk, until he joined the military at the age of twenty.

MILITARY AND POLITICAL CAREER
Than rose through the ranks of the military quickly: He attained the rank of captain in 1960 and colonel in 1978. By 1983, he was one of Burma's youngest regional army commanders. He was in Rangoon (now Yangon) as vice chief of staff of the army, brigadier general and vice minister of defense in 1985, and major general in 1986. The Burmese army brutally crushed nonviolent protests against the government in Rangoon on August 8, 1988. Immediately after the bloodshed, Than became deputy commander in chief of the army, deputy defense minister, and the right-hand man of junta ruler General Saw Maung. On April 23, 1992, Than replaced Saw as chairman of the junta and commander in chief of the armed forces.

The new leader took a harder line in Burma's protracted war against ethnic rebels by stepping up the use of the army to destroy ethnic villages. The obliteration of villages was part of a strategy to force civilians in rebel areas to relocate to "new towns." Than's troops forced 800,000 people in southeastern and eastern Burma to abandon their villages. Instead of moving to the new towns, the majority of these refugees went into hiding or sought refuge in Thailand. Muslims from northern Burma numbering about 250,000 fled to Bangladesh.

Eyewitness accounts during 1995-2005 documented routine human rights violations by Than's army against members of minority ethnic groups. Soldiers forced men, women, and children to work as porters or laborers for little or no pay. They used rape as a weapon, and they kidnapped adolescents, selling them in the sex trade or forcing them to serve as "child soldiers" in the Burmese army. Than also did nothing to stop the Burmese military's historic involvement in the Southeast Asia drug trade. The drug trade spurred the spread of illness, such as acquired immunodeficiency syndrome (AIDS), in Burma as well as in neighboring countries.

Than also stifled the democratization of Burma by arresting and holding without trial dozens of prominent politicians and journalists who opposed his regime, including Aung San Suu Kyi, the intensely popular leader of the country's democracy movement.

For many years, Burma watchers thought that Than was a figurehead and that other junta members held most of the power. In October, 2004, Than ousted and arrested Prime Minister Khin Nyunt, the only moderate member of the junta. After this ouster, there was little doubt that Than was in charge. In November, 2005, he announced the transfer of the capital from Yangon to Pyinmana, a sleepy town in the hills of central Burma, presumably feeling that an inland location would make the capital less vulnerable to an attack from the sea. Burmese officials expected the move to take about twelve months' time.

IMPACT
The Burmese people were known to live in fear and heartbreaking poverty under Than Shwe. Not only did his rule oppress his own people, but also the steady flow of refugees, drugs, and disease affected the peace and security of the entire region. Several countries, including the United States, banned trade with Burma to protest the country's human rights violations. In 1997, the United States Congress stopped U.S. businesses from investing in the country.

FURTHER READING
Havel, Václav, and Desmond Tutu. *Threat to the Peace: A Call for the UN Security Council to Act in Burma.* Washington, D.C.: DLA Piper Rudnick Gray Caryl, 2005. A well-documented report on alleged crimes perpetrated by Than Shwe and his fellow junta generals.

Lintner, Bertil. *Outrage: Burma's Struggle for Democracy.* Bangkok, Thailand: White Lotus Books, 1990.

A thorough analysis of circumstances behind the rise of the military junta and its suppression of the democracy movement.

Smith, Martin. *Burma: Insurgency and the Politics of Ethnicity*. New York: Zed Books, 1999. Focuses on the origin and evolution of rebellious groups in Burma's borderlands.

—*Richard A. Crooker*

SEE ALSO: Ne Win; Pol Pot; Ta Mok.

HARRY KENDALL THAW
American murderer

BORN: February 12, 1871; Pittsburgh, Pennsylvania
DIED: February 22, 1947; Miami, Florida
MAJOR OFFENSE: First-degree murder
ACTIVE: June 25, 1906
LOCALE: Madison Square Garden, New York, New York
SENTENCE: Incarceration at an asylum

EARLY LIFE

Harry Kendall Thaw (thaw) spent his childhood being expelled from private schools. While at the University of Pittsburgh and, later, at Harvard, he went on drinking binges and spent most of his time with young showgirls. Thaw's troubles began when Thaw noticed a copper-haired, sixteen-year-old chorus girl on Broadway. Evelyn Nesbit had already been noticed by prominent architect Stanford White. Nesbit's bout of appendicitis (which was initially thought to be a pregnancy) put her in the hospital for a while, and Thaw used this episode to further his attentions toward the young woman. Nesbit admitted to Thaw that White had "deflowered" her, which made Thaw angry; however, he still wished to marry Nesbit. The marriage took place on April 4, 1905.

CRIMINAL CAREER

On June 25, 1906, Mr. and Mrs. Thaw were at Madison Square Garden for the premiere of a new musical revue, *Mamzelle Champagne*. Thaw was wearing a heavy coat that he had refused to check even though the night was warm. At the rooftop theater, Thaw approached White's table and, drawing a gun from his coat, shot White three times in the face. Thaw walked away and met his wife at the elevator, telling her that he had probably saved her life.

LEGAL ACTION AND OUTCOME

After Thaw was arrested, the first trial ended in a hung jury, with seven believing that Thaw was guilty of first-degree murder and the other five ruling that he was not guilty by reason of insanity. Less than a year later, Thaw was found not guilty by reason of insanity by a second jury. He was incarcerated at an asylum at Matteawan, New York, from which he escaped to Canada in 1913. He was later extradited back to the United States, where, in 1915, a jury found him to be sane. Thaw later spent seven more years in an asylum for another offense. Thaw continued his life of chasing showgirls until his death in 1947 at the age of seventy-six.

IMPACT

Because the murder happened during the Gilded Age in the most fashionable city in the United States, several books were written about it specifically, and others mentioned it in detail. While there are any number of murders throughout history that involve the "eternal triangle," this one had three individuals of particular note: Harry Thaw, who was accustomed to getting everything he wanted; Stanford White, the most well-known architect of New York in that era; and Evelyn Nesbit, a young showgirl who was an accomplished actor while still in her teens. Another interesting person is Thaw's mother, who thought that marriage would tame her son's wild impulses. Evelyn Nesbit was promised one million dollars and a divorce if she stood up for Thaw at the trial; she got the divorce but not the money.

FURTHER READING

Lessard, Suzannah. *The Architect of Desire: Beauty and Danger in the Stanford White Family*. New York: Dial Press, 1996. A memoir written by White's great-granddaughter concerning the sexual problems prevalent in generations of the family. The murder itself was a forbidden subject, which made it all the more interesting to the generations that followed.

Lowe, David Garrard. *Stanford White's New York*. New York: Watson-Guptill, 1999. Details the work of the talented architect White and his contribution to the city of New York and gives a description of his murder by Thaw.

Mooney, Michael MacDonald. *Evelyn Nesbit and Stanford White: Love and Death in the Gilded Age.* New York: William Morrow, 1976. Details the pageantry of New York City during the Gilded Age with an emphasis on the murder of Stanford White.

Thaw, Harry K. *The Traitor: Being the Untampered with,*

Unrevised Account of the Trial and All That Led to It. Philadelphia: Dorrance, 1926. Thaw's own account of his life and the social scene of New York before and after his trials.

—*Ellen B. Lindsay*

SEE ALSO: Antoinette Frank; Jean Harris; Sante Kimes; Sam Sheppard; Pamela Ann Smart; Madeleine Smith; Ruth Snyder; Carolyn Warmus.

THEODORA
Empress of Byzantium (r. 527-548)

BORN: c. 497; Constantinople, Byzantine Empire (now Istanbul, Turkey)

DIED: June 28, 548; Constantinople, Byzantine Empire (now Istanbul, Turkey)

CAUSE OF NOTORIETY: Theodora—who could be cruel, was often deceitful, and loved power—used her privileged position as consort to Justinian I to help administer the political machinery of the Byzantine Empire.

ACTIVE: Early 500's

LOCALE: Constantinople, Byzantine Empire (now Istanbul, Turkey)

EARLY LIFE

Theodora (thee-oh-DOHR-ah) experienced a tumultuous life from a young age. In the early sixth century, Constantinople's Hippodrome (racetrack) and arena (circus) had two performing companies, the Blues and the Greens. The Greek Byzantines and Latin Romans shared a love for the circus, and the Hippodrome was frequented by every social class. According to the contemporary historian Procopius of Caesarea's *Anecdota* (c. 550; *The Secret History of the Court of the Emperor Justinian,* 1674; commonly known as *The Secret History*), Theodora's father, Acacius, was the Greens' bearkeeper; he died while Theodora and her sisters were young children. The Greens were about to expel the family, but the girls' mother brought her three daughters out into the arena as suppliants. The Blues took on the family, and from an early age Theodora and her sisters appeared in the circus as performers.

Procopius alleges that Theodora was essentially a prostitute, providing sexual services even before puberty and appearing in bawdy, farcical shows. He claims that she was highly promiscuous and that her sexual desires

were insatiable. She became the mistress of Hecebolus, a governor of the Pentapolis district of Africa, who abandoned her; she made her way back to Constantinople by "practicing her profession in each city."

POLITICAL CAREER

Theodora became the mistress of Justinian I, then nephew of the elderly emperor Justin I (450-527). As she was an

Theodora.

actress, it was illegal for Justinian to marry her; however, he forced Justin to change the law. Justinian and Theodora married around 523, before Justinian's accession in 527.

As empress, Theodora left her circus past behind and was devoted to Justinian (*The Secret History* alleges one infidelity). She was extremely haughty and overbearing, according to Procopius, while Justinian was more affable and approachable. A famous anecdote shows her imperious spirit. In January, 532, as a result of the unjust deaths of Blue and Green faction leaders, the people of Constantinople revolted in the so-called Nika (meaning "conquer") riots. They set afire palace buildings and part of the city and even acclaimed a pretender to the throne. Justinian vacillated, tempted to abandon his empire, but Theodora rebuked his timidity, saying, according to Procopius, "The purple is a glorious shroud." Justinian acted and suppressed the riots, killing more than thirty thousand protesters.

It is uncertain how much Theodora influenced Justinian's policies. Justinian is best known for the reconquest of much of the old Roman Empire, Italy, and Africa, and for the codification of Roman law (the *Corpus Iuris Civilis*). He also reformed much of the imperial government and increased the efficiency of taxation, so that Procopius in *The Secret History* accuses him of "ruining everything" and of unlimited avarice.

Theodora may have influenced Justinian's legislation on women's issues. Justinian mentions that he consulted his "most pious consort" in a law repressing corruption in provincial administration. Theodora attempted to suppress prostitution in Constantinople, providing welfare for former prostitutes and building a convent called Metanoia ("repentance") for these women.

The imperial couple's main difference of policy was theological. Justinian was Orthodox, while Theodora supported the Monophysites, a heretical Christian sect that asserted that Jesus' nature was solely divine. She

---

THE EMPEROR'S CONSCIENCE

Although the Byzantine historian Procopius passed on much scandalous gossip about Theodora, he also shows her bravery and intelligence in a speech before the senate during the Nika riots. (Procopius was her contemporary and may have witnessed the events.)

The Emperor's companions were debating whether it would be better for them to stay or to flee by ship. Many arguments were put forward on both sides. The Empress Theodora said: "As to whether it is unseemly for a woman to be bold among men, or to be daring when others are full o fear, I do not think that the present crisis allows us to consider the matter. For in extreme danger the only vital thing is to deal with the situation in the best way. For my part, I consider that now of all times flight would be bad, even if it brings safety. Once a man is born he cannot escape dying, but for one who has held the imperial power it would be unbearable to become a fugitive. May I never be parted from this purple, and may I never live to see the day when men who meet me will not address me as their sovereign. If you wish to be saved, Emperor, that is not difficult. We have great resources of wealth; there is the sea, here are the boats. But take care lest when you have saved yourself you wish that you could have death instead of your safety. I agree with the old saying, 'Royalty is a good winding sheet.'" At these words from the Empress they were all inspired with courage and began to debate how they could defend themselves if anyone attacked them.

In a later work, Buildings, *Procopius writes of Theodora's role in helping the homeless:*

They all come [to the imperial city] for some task, or some kind of hope, or by chance, and many of them come to supplicate the Emperor, being in some domestic trouble. . . . In addition to their existing distress, they are without a place to live, not being able to pay the price of their stay there. This plight the Emperor Justinian and the Empress Theodora relieved. Near the sea . . . they built large guest houses to provide lodgings for men who came in future in these difficulties.

Source: Procopius, *"History of the Wars," "Secret History," and "Buildings"* (New York: Washington Square Press, 1967).

---

may have been converted to Monophysitism during her travels in the Eastern Empire before her marriage.

Theodora died on June 28, 548, apparently of cancer. Justinian outlived her by many years, but he did not remarry. They had no children, and Procopius alleges that Theodora's jealousies complicated the imperial succession because she persecuted Justinian's blood relatives. Justinian was succeeded by his nephew Justin II (r. 565-578).

IMPACT

Theodora was undoubtedly a strong personality as the Byzantine empress. However, her notoriety depends chiefly upon Procopius's *Secret History*, which vituperates prominent women and emphasizes lurid stories about their sexual behavior. The stories about Theodora resemble those about Valeria Messallina, the wife of the emperor Claudius (r. 41-54 C.E.). However, Messalina practiced her adultery and prostitution while also serving as the empress; Theodora practiced prostitution only in her youth, before her marriage to Justinian. Undoubtedly Theodora was an actor and performer, but Byzantine society assumed such performers were prostitutes.

FURTHER READING

Caretti, Paolo. *Theodora: Empress of Byzantium*. New York: Vendome Books, 2004. A popular biography of Theodora, which is speculative at times.

Evans, James Allan. *The Age of Justinian: Circumstances of Imperial Power*. New York: Routledge, 1996. A general survey of Justinian's reign; discusses Theodora.

_____. *Empress Theodora: Partner of Justinian*. Austin: University of Texas Press, 2002. A good, scholarly biography of Theodora.

Procopius. *The Anecdota*. Translated by H. B. Dewing. Cambridge, Mass.: Loeb Classical Library, 1935. A contemporary of Justinian, Procopius wrote the *Anecdota* soon after Theodora's death. It could not be made public until after Justinian's death.

_____. *The Secret History*. Translated and introduced by G. A. Williamson. New York: Penguin Books, 1966. Translation of the *Anecdota* in which Williamson discusses the problems of this work.

—*Sara Elise Phang*

SEE ALSO: Justin II.

BENJAMIN TILLMAN
South Carolina governor (1890-1894) and U.S. senator (1895-1918)

BORN: August 11, 1847; near Trenton, Edgefield County, South Carolina

DIED: July 3, 1918; Washington, D.C.

ALSO KNOWN AS: Pitchfork Ben; Benjamin Ryan Tillman (full name)

CAUSE OF NOTORIETY: Tillman was instrumental in the implementation and defense of racial segregation in the American South during the late nineteenth and early twentieth centuries

LOCALE: Columbia, South Carolina; Washington, D.C.

EARLY LIFE

The son of wealthy slave owners, Benjamin Ryan Tillman (TIHL-muhn) was born after his father died. He was raised by his mother, who instilled in him the conservative, race-conscious values of the Old South. In 1864 he dropped out of school to join the Confederate army but lost an eye to illness and was unable to serve. He subsequently returned to Edgefield County and the family tradition of farming, becoming a large landowner in his own right.

During the Reconstruction period following the Civil War, Tillman became involved with the Red Shirts, a paramilitary organization formed to resist the rule of northern Republicans and restore the dominance of white southern Democrats in South Carolina government. In 1876 Tillman participated in an event known as the Hamburg Massacre, in which a group of Red Shirts murdered several members of a black militia.

POLITICAL CAREER

Despite his relatively affluent background, Tillman successfully launched a political career by promoting himself as a champion of the common people and an alternative to the "low country" aristocrats, who had traditionally dominated the political culture in South Carolina. During his campaign for governor, he criticized the conservative policies of the "Redemption," or "Bourbon" Democrats, many of which were out of favor with the small-scale, upcountry farmers whose political support Tillman coveted. Tillman's "farmers' movement" coincided with the Agrarian and Populist movements taking place throughout the South in the late nineteenth century in revolt against the aristocracy. Tillman, however, refused to break ranks with Democrats to join the Populist Party, which welcomed African Americans into its ranks. Instead, he sought to combine the economic reforms of Populism with the sectionalist, white supremacist platform of southern Democrats. His pro-Agrarian movement within the South Carolina Democratic Party nearly succeeded in capturing control of

Benjamin Tillman.

state government in 1886. Tillman was elected governor in 1890.

As governor, Tillman was an advocate of economic reform and an opponent of social progress, particularly with regard to the treatment of African Americans. Having already successfully lobbied the state to establish an agricultural college, Tillman increased state funding for public education, a concern of the Agrarian Populists, but did little else of substance to advance a Populist agenda. An adherent of the paternalistic conventions of the Old South, Tillman used governmental power to control a variety of social and economic institutions, creating a state monopoly for the distribution of liquor, increasing the regulation of railroads, and stripping African Americans of their voting rights.

"Pitchfork Ben"

Elected to the United States Senate in 1894, Tillman arrived in Washington with a new nickname, having promised to admonish President Grover Cleveland, a pro-industry northern Democrat, by sticking a pitchfork into his ribs. Tillman continued to declare his support for small farm holders but largely ignored the populist causes that they favored, focusing instead upon advancing a white supremacist agenda designed to limit further the rights of blacks to vote, receive equal protection of

the law, and access public accommodations. Tillman was instrumental in organizing a state constitutional convention in South Carolina in 1895, which instituted poll taxes and literacy tests designed to prevent blacks from voting as well as laws mandating separate schools for white and black students, forbidding interracial marriage, and tightening the hold of plantation owners over their sharecroppers by creating a form of virtual-debt slavery.

Tillman openly and unapologetically expressed contempt for African Americans and advocated violence and intimidation as means of ensuring their inequality with whites, declaring on the Senate floor in 1900 that black men suspected of sexual relations with white women should be lynched. Occasionally, the propensity toward physical violence that Tillman exhibited early in life would resurface; the Senate censured him in 1902 after he assaulted fellow senator John L. McLaurin on the Senate floor.

Despite his self-professed radicalism and obsession with racial politics, Tillman managed to reach across lines of party and ideology to contribute to the passage of progressive legislation, cooperating with his nemesis Theodore Roosevelt in 1906 by leading Senate debate over a bill regulating railroad rates. Racial politics, however, continued to dominate Tillman's agenda. Tillman served in the Senate until his death in 1918, but his influence was greatly diminished after strokes in 1908 and 1910 impaired his ability to speak.

Impact

By combining a Populist economic agenda with the white supremacist social agenda of southern Democrats, Benjamin Tillman derailed the emerging Populist movement, resulting in a restoration of white Democratic dominance that would endure for generations in the southern United States. As a state governor and later as a U.S. Senator, Tillman played a prominent role in establishing the system of Jim Crow laws that segregated the races in the American South, preserving a racial caste system that ensured the secondary status of southern blacks well into the twentieth century. Often regarded as one of the most outspoken racists ever to serve in the U.S. Congress, his vehement defense of segregation on the national stage reinforced the institution and emboldened its adherents, contributing to the further subjugation of southern blacks. His encouragement of the use of violence to enforce the South's racial order resulted in the continued practice of lynching, leading to the murder of numerous African Americans during the segregation era.

FURTHER READING
Kantrowitz, Stephen. "Ben Tillman and Hendrix Mc-
Lane: Agrarian Rebels, White Manhood, 'The Farmers,' and the Limits of Southern Populism." *Journal
of Southern History* 66, no. 3 (August, 2000): 497-
524. Placing Tillman's pseudopopulist Democratic
agenda in the broader context of southern Agrarian
Populism, this article discusses how race politics
disrupted the Populist movement and ensured the
continuation of white Democratic dominance.
_____. *Ben Tillman and the Reconstruction of White
Supremacy.* Chapel Hill: University of North Carolina Press, 2000. Examines Tillman's rise to power as

a case study of the resurgence of white supremacist
politics in the post-Reconstruction South.
Simkins, Francis Butler. *Pitchfork Ben Tillman: South
Carolinian.* 1944. Reprint. Columbia: University of
South Carolina Press, 2002. The classic biography of
Tillman, one of the few comprehensive accounts of
his life and career.

—*Michael H. Burchett*

SEE ALSO: Theodore G. Bilbo; Orval E. Faubus; William Joseph Simmons; Roger Brooke Taney: George
C. Wallace.

TITO
Dictator of post-World War II Yugoslavia (1945-1980)

BORN: May 7, 1892; Kumrovec, Croatia (then part of
the Austro-Hungarian Empire)
DIED: May 4, 1980; Ljubljana, Yugoslavia (now in
Slovenia)
ALSO KNOWN AS: Josip Broz (birth name)
CAUSE OF NOTORIETY: Although sometimes praised
for his leadership of Yugoslavia's resistance to the
Nazi occupation and success in keeping the Soviet
Union out of postwar Yugoslavia, Tito was also
noted for his brutality, dictatorial rule of
Yugoslavia, and steadfast commitment to
communism.
ACTIVE: 1945-1980
LOCALE: Yugoslavia, principally Belgrade

EARLY LIFE
Even by the standards of the last, tumultuous days of the
Austro-Hungarian Empire and the subsequent, often violent interwar years in the Balkans, Tito (TEE-toh) led the
strong-willed, adventurous, and eventually successful
life of a self-made man.

Tito, born Josip Broz in the northeastern corner of
what later became Croatia, left school at age twelve. After learning a locksmith's trade, the young Broz embarked on an odyssey through Central Europe. He was
inducted into the empire's army in 1913 and eventually
sent to the Russian front in World War I. He then resided
briefly in Slovenia, Bohemia, and Germany; in one job
he worked as a test driver for Daimler motor works in
Vienna.

In April of 1915, his battalion captured and imprisoned by the Russians, Broz organized protests by his
fellow prisoners of war and twice escaped captivity.
He also became a member of the Russian Communist
Party.

POLITICAL CAREER
By the 1930's, Broz had become a leading member of
Yugoslavia's outlawed Communist Party (CPY), then
headquartered in Vienna. It was there, while directing the
Yugoslav underground against the Yugoslav state created after World War I at Versailles, that he adopted his
code name, Tito.

By the time Germany bombed Yugoslav's capital of
Belgrade in June of 1941, and shortly thereafter overran
and dissolved the country, the Soviet Union had named
Tito as the secretary general of the still-banned CPY
and military commander of Yugoslavia's resistance to
German occupation. By 1944, the brutal underground
campaign waged by Tito's partisans had taken the lives
of approximately 800,000 Germans and 350,000 (dis-
proportionately Croatian) Yugoslav collaborators and
liberated all of Yugoslavia. Tito was beginning to fashion a government for postwar Yugoslavia.

Four years later, following a split with the Soviet
Union, which had wanted Yugoslavia to function as another of its post-World War II satellite states in Central
Europe, Tito's new, independent Communist state was
under his dictatorial rule. Indeed, the break with the Soviet Union forced Tito to conduct a postwar purge of not

only former Nazi collaborators and opponents to Communism but also many of his former associates. To do this, Tito created his own loyal but brutal army and secret police. His opponents quickly came under his control or were ruthlessly dispatched from the political scene.

IMPACT

Tito's iron-fisted regime made the Yugoslavian state possible. In many ways he was synonymous with the nation, knit together from traditionally disparate nationalities. Despite Tito's concerted efforts during the last fifteen years of his life to enable his country to hold together indefinitely, with Tito's death in 1980 Yugoslavia began to unravel. The fear of Soviet intervention held its diverse Croat, Serbian, and other nationalities together for a decade. When this fear disintegrated with the Soviet Union's fall in 1991-1992, so did the Yugoslav state.

FURTHER READING

Djilas, Milovan. *Tito: The Story from Inside*. New York: Harcourt Brace Jovanovich, 1980. Very interesting work by a former Tito aide who later became a jailed critic of his regime.

Ramet, Sabrina P. *Balkan Babel: The Disintegration of Yugoslavia from the Death of Tito to Ethnic War*. Boulder, Colo.: Westview Press, 2002. Excellent treatment of the impact of Tito's death on the state he fashioned.

West, Richard. *Tito and the Rise and Fall of Yugoslavia*. New York: Carroll and Graf, 1996. Excellent follow-up reading on Tito's life and legacy.

—*Joseph R. Rudolph, Jr.*

SEE ALSO: Francisco Franco; Adolf Hitler; Radovan Karadžić; Slobodan Milošević; Benito Mussolini; Joseph Stalin.

SWEENEY TODD
English serial killer

BORN: October 16, 1756; London, England
DIED: January 25, 1802; Newgate Prison, London, England
ALSO KNOWN AS: Demon Barber of Fleet Street
MAJOR OFFENSE: Murder
ACTIVE: c. 1801
LOCALE: London, England
SENTENCE: Death by hanging

EARLY LIFE

Not much is known for certain about the life of Sweeney Todd (SWEE-nee tawd). It is suggested that he was born into poverty on October 16, 1756, in London. He was born to alcoholic parents who abandoned him when he was young. They left, it is speculated, to find liquor and never returned. Young Todd was turned over to the local parish, which was responsible for finding apprenticeships for orphans. He was assigned as an apprentice to a cutler, the trade responsible for making, repairing, or selling knives or other cutting instruments. Not long afterward, Todd was arrested for petty larceny.

While in prison, Todd managed to earn an apprenticeship with the prison barber. After his release, Todd set up trade as a "flying barber," a tradesman with no permanent address who participates in his craft wherever and whenever he can. After several years, Todd purchased a shop at 186 Fleet Street.

CRIMINAL CAREER

Todd employed the use of his barbershop both to lure and to dispatch his victims. He fashioned a barber chair that, when reclined, would rotate into the basement. Once it rotated, the client was dropped though a trapdoor into the basement, and the empty barber chair was restored to the shop.

The motive behind his crimes was monetary. He murdered numerous men for profit, for the items in their possession. One man was killed for his gold pocket watch and one for a pearl necklace that he was in charge of delivering. It was the necklace that later sealed Todd's conviction.

Todd was engaged in his macabre activities before he met his accomplice, Margery or Sarah Lovett (her first name is uncertain). Lovett owned a pie shop in Bell Yard. Before the two of them conspired, Todd had been disposing of the bodies of his victims within the catacombs and family crypts of St. Dunstan's Church, which was located next door to his barbershop. When the corpses became too numerous to hide, Lovett used their remains in her meat pies.

A repugnant odor eventually emanated from the catacombs of St. Dunstan's Church, and authorities launched an investigation. They discovered the fresh remains of numerous men and the tunnel that led from Fleet Street to Bell Yard. This investigation resulted in the arrest of both Todd and Lovett.

LEGAL ACTION AND OUTCOME

Todd and Lovett were arrested in 1801 and held at Newgate Prison. Lovett poisoned herself before she went to trial. Todd, however, was tried for only one murder: that of Francis Thornhill, who was killed for the pearl necklace in his possession. Although Todd probably killed numerous men, a conviction in one of those murders was sufficient to sentence him to hanging. During the trial it was suggested that he killed nearly 160 men. The jury took no time in convicting him and on January 25, 1802, Todd was hanged in the prison yard at Newgate.

IMPACT

Sweeney Todd's trial and conviction drew wide public attention and became the basis for a plethora of books, movies, and even a Broadway musical. The gruesome nature of the case and involvement of so many innocent people fueled its sensationalism. Todd's victims were the men who entered his barbershop and the countless individuals who consumed Lovett's meat pies. Some suggest that the story of Sweeney Todd is purely fictitious and exists only in legend and lore.

FURTHER READING

Haining, Peter. *Sweeney Todd: The Real Story of the Demon Barber of Fleet Street*. London: Robson Books, 2003. Haining separates fact from fiction and reveals a ghastly story about this unique criminal.

Hazel, Harry. *Sweeney Todd: Or, The Ruffian Barber*. New York: H. Long, 1865. A romanticized work of fiction that embellishes the lives of Todd and various other characters.

—*Alison S. Burke*

SEE ALSO: H. H. Holmes; Jack the Ripper; Henri Désiré Landru.

HIDEKI TOJO
Japanese prime minister (1941-1944)

BORN: Officially registered as December 30, 1884; Tokyo, Japan

DIED: December 23, 1948; Tokyo, Japan

ALSO KNOWN AS: Kamisori; the Razor; Tōjō Hideki

CAUSE OF NOTORIETY: Prime minister of Japan at the time of its attack on Pearl Harbor and for the majority of the Pacific War, Tojo was later executed as a war criminal.

ACTIVE: 1941-1944

LOCALE: Japan and Asia

SENTENCE: Death by hanging

EARLY LIFE

Hideki Tojo (hee-deh-kee toh-joh) was born in Tokyo. His father, Hidenori Tojo, was a lieutenant general in the imperial Japanese army. Tojo's family had roots in the Morioka feudal domain. After the Meiji Restoration and the transformation of Japan from a collection of fiefdoms to a centralized, modern nation-state, former residents of the Satsuma and Choshu domains gained ascendancy over the new military. As a result, Tojo's father, despite his ability, was unable to advance to the highest levels of the military command. This sparked the young Tojo's ambition, and he decided to pursue a military career in his father's footsteps. He attended the Military Youth School from the age of fifteen and went on to attend the Military Academy. Tojo graduated in 1905, earning the rank of second lieutenant at the age of twenty-one. In 1909, at the age of twenty-five, he married Ito Katsuko. As his career progressed, Tojo advanced steadily in rank and became a member of the inner circle of the Kodo (control) faction of the army elite.

POLITICAL CAREER

Before gaining political power, Tojo enjoyed a long and distinguished military career, which included periods abroad in Germany and Switzerland. In the mid-1930's, he held a number of important military posts in Manchuria, an area of northern China controlled by the Japanese army. These included the posts of commander of the military police and, eventually, chief of staff of the Kantogun—a force that was seen as Japan's elite army on the continent. Japan's imperial constitution contained no prohibition on active military officers taking up important political posts. As the nation began all-out war with China in 1937 and moved further toward militarism in the late 1930's, more and more army and navy personnel began to occupy key political positions.

In the first stages of the Japan-China War, Tojo acted as a field commander on the continent. Subsequently, however, he moved into the political sphere, holding several important posts, including the position of army minister in 1940 as a part of the second Konoe Fumimaro cabinet. Tojo became prime minister in October 18, 1941, less than two months before Japan's attack on Pearl Harbor, Hawaii, and supported the final decision to begin hostilities against the United States. Tojo remained as prime minister and filled several other important positions, such as foreign minister and minister of education, during the Pacific War until a series of military defeats led him to accept responsibility and resign his political posts on July 22, 1944.

LEGAL ACTION AND OUTCOME

Following Japan's defeat and unconditional surrender on August 15, 1945, the occupation authorities began to arrest Japanese soldiers and statesmen for crimes committed in wartime. Tojo, facing arrest because of his role in beginning the war with the United States, attempted suicide but survived and was tried for "crimes against peace" as a Class-A war criminal in the International Military Tribunal for the Far East. Tojo was found guilty of waging aggressive war against China, the United States, and other nations. He was sentenced to death by hanging on November 12, 1948. The sentence was carried out on December 23 of that year.

IMPACT

Hideki Tojo presided over the beginning of a war that ended with the atomic bombings of Hiroshima and Nagasaki and Japan's unconditional surrender as well as the deaths of millions in Asia and in the Pacific region. He also supported Japan's disastrous war in China both as a politician and as a direct participant. His personal impact, however, has been downplayed by some historians, who stress the group character of Japanese military decision making in the 1930's and 1940's.

Tojo remains an extremely controversial figure. Revisionist historians in Japan have painted him as a martyr and claim that he acted to defend Japan. While these

Hideki Tojo.

views are not mainstream, they have gained considerable attention, both inside and outside Japan. In addition, in 1978, Tojo and the other Japanese statesmen executed as Class-A war criminals were enshrined at Yasukuni Shrine—a shrine of Japan's native Shinto religion devoted to the spirits of those killed in Japan's modern wars—as "The Martyrs of the Showa Period." While this action was taken by the shrine and not officially endorsed by the Japanese government, China, Korea, and other countries have interpreted visits to Yasukuni by Japanese prime ministers as the worship of Tojo and other executed war criminals and as the justification or even glorification of past war crimes and aggression. Japanese leaders insist that the visits are simply to offer prayers for world peace. However, Tojo's place in Japanese history remains a contentious issue.

FURTHER READING

Butow, Robert. *Tojo and the Coming of the War*. Princeton, N.J.: Princeton University Press, 1961. An authoritative English-language biography of Tojo. The work pays special attention to the buildup to the war with the United States and Tojo's role in World War II.

Dower, John. *Embracing Defeat: Japan in the Wake of World War II*. London: Penguin Books, 2000. The leading English-language work on the American occupation of Japan and the aftermath of World War II in Asia. Contains detailed coverage of the Tokyo Trial and the last days of Tojo Hideki's life.

Wilmott, H. P. *The Second World War in the Far East*. New York: Smithsonian Books, 2004. A detailed yet accessible survey history of World War II in Asia and the Pacific region. Provides strong coverage of Tojo's role.

—*Matthew Penney*

SEE ALSO: Hirohito; Kuniaki Koiso.

TOKYO ROSE
Japanese American traitor

BORN: July 4, 1916; Los Angeles, California
DIED: September 26, 2006; Chicago, Illinois
ALSO KNOWN AS: Ikuko Toguri (birth name); Iva Toguri (school name); Ikuko Toguri d'Aquino (married name)
MAJOR OFFENSE: Transmission of wartime propaganda
ACTIVE: Late 1943-August, 1945
LOCALE: Japan
SENTENCE: Ten years' imprisonment plus a fine of $100,000; paroled after six years, two months

EARLY LIFE
The name "Tokyo Rose" (toh-kee-oh rohz) has been associated with a Japanese American named Ikuko Toguri. Her parents, who came to the United States from Japan, raised her to become an American. As a result, Toguri was ignorant of the Japanese culture and language. She attended the University of California and graduated with a degree in zoology in 1940.

Toguri left for Japan on July 5, 1941, with only a certificate of identity from San Pedro, California, reportedly to visit a seriously sick aunt, whom she had never before met. Three months later, she applied for an American passport in order to return to the United States. The U.S. Consulate forwarded her application to the U.S. Department of State for consideration. On December 7, 1941, Japan attacked Pearl Harbor, and the United States declared war on Japan.

Lacking a U.S. passport, Toguri applied for repatriation to the United States through the Swiss Legation in Japan. Meanwhile, to support herself, she started working as a typist for the Domei News Agency in June, 1942. Radio Tokyo hired her as a part-time English-language typist in August, 1943.

CRIMINAL CAREER
In late 1943, Toguri was reportedly coerced into working as an announcer for a radio program called *Zero Hour*. Among the prisoners of war who produced the program was Charles Hugh Cousens, who had been a radio personality in Sydney before the war. *Zero Hour* was broadcast from 6:00 P.M. to 7:15 P.M., Tokyo time, six

Tokyo Rose. (NARA/Harry S. Truman Library and Museum)

days a week. The purpose of the program was to demoralize American soldiers in the South Pacific region. It was the soldiers listening to the propaganda transmissions who gave Toguri the name Tokyo Rose. She usually addressed the soldiers as "orphans of the Pacific" and identified herself as "orphan Ann (or Annie)," "your favorite enemy Ann" or "your favorite playmate and enemy Ann."

In one of her propaganda broadcasts in October, 1944, she told the soldiers that their wives and sweethearts were having romances back in the States, while they were marooned in the South Pacific, all their ships having been sunk by the Japanese Navy. Her voice was heard in a total of 340 programs during her twenty-one months with *Zero Hour*. After the war and Japan's surrender in August, 1945, Toguri was arrested by U.S. authorities. She was kept in various prisons before being returned to the United States in September, 1948.

LEGAL ACTION AND OUTCOME

Toguri's trial began in July, 1949, and lasted three months. The jury at the Federal District Court in San Francisco found her guilty of only one out of eight overt acts. The overt act VI was concerned with her propaganda transmission in October, 1944, when she talked about the loss of American ships. On October 6, 1949, U.S. District Judge Michael Roche sentenced Toguri to ten years in prison and fined her $100,000. She was sent to the Federal Reformatory for Women in Alderson, West Virginia.

Because of her good behavior in prison, Toguri served only six years and two months. She was released on January 28, 1956, and her parole ended in April, 1959. She succeeded in fighting the U.S. government's efforts to deport her and also in filing for presidential pardon. President Gerald Ford gave her a pardon on January 19, 1977. The seventh person convicted of treason in U.S. history, she is to date the only one to be pardoned. Her last recorded residence was in Chicago.

VETERANS HONOR TOKYO ROSE

The injustice of Iva Toguri's conviction for treason as "Tokyo Rose" is widely accepted, and efforts persist to clear her name. One of the most remarkable came from the World War II Veterans Committee. In the winter 2004/2005 issue of its magazine *World War II Chronicles*, the committee published "Convicting a Myth: Debunking the Legend of Tokyo Rose," by Tim Holbert. The response from its readership of veterans was large and favorable—so much so that the Federal Bureau of Investigation removed its damning version of Toguri's trial from its Web site. On January 15, 2006, the committee went further, presenting its Edward J. Herlihy Citizenship Award to Toguri in a Los Angeles ceremony. The annual award goes to members of the World War II generation who exemplify the ideals of American citizenship, especially paying tribute to those whose patriotism has been unjustly questioned.

Even before the war, Toguri did not find Japan congenial. Homesick, she wrote to her family on October 13, 1941,

> I have gotten used to many of the things over here and I think that in a few more months that I will be able to say that I don't mind living in Japan. It has been very hard and discouraging at times but from now on it will be all right I'm sure . . . but for the rest of you, no matter how bad things get and how much you have to take in the form of racial criticisms and no matter how hard you have to work, by all means remain in the country you learn to appreciate more after you leave it.

During the war, Japanese authorities put great pressure on her to give up her American citizenship and even threatened her to do so. Moreover, her pro-American views made her unpopular among Japanese coworkers and neighbors, yet she steadfastly refused to renounce her native land. When Emperor Hirohito announced Japan's surrender in 1945, Toguri cheered, not suspecting the trouble in store for her.

Toguri was visibly moved during the awards ceremony. She responded, "This is a great honor. . . . I am embarrassed to be able to receive this award, but at the same time I thank you very much. . . . I thank all of the World War II veterans."

Source: Quotations from "Iva Toguri (Tokyo Rose) Receives Citizenship Award," *Nikkei*, February 15, 2006. Available at http:/www.discovernikkei.org.

IMPACT

At its time, the Tokyo Rose trial, which cost $750,000, was the most expensive one in U.S. history. To build the case against Toguri, the Federal Bureau of Investigation had interviewed hundreds of U.S. Army personnel serving in the South Pacific and searched for Japanese documents and recordings of propaganda broadcasts. Witnesses from Japan were identified and brought to the United States. Toguri maintained that she had not betrayed the United States because she was forced to work for Japan. In 1976 she appeared on television's *60 Minutes* and told the Tokyo Rose story from her point of view. She has been the subject of several documentary films.

The Tokyo Rose case revealed the problem of interpreting the meaning of "treason." Toguri's lack of choice, her circumstances, and the questionable success of her propaganda broadcasts have convinced many people that she should have been given a lighter sentence. Cousens was also arrested after the war; he was tried and acquitted.

FURTHER READING

Ben-Yehuda, Nachman. *Betrayals and Treason*. Boulder, Colo.: Westview Press, 2001. Part of the book examines the radio traitor cases of Tokyo Rose and William Joyce (Lord Haw Haw) and claims that though the cases were different, both persons violated trust and loyalty.

Pfau, Ann Elizabeth. *Miss Yourlovin: Women in the Culture of American World War II Soldiers*. Rutgers, N.J.: Rutgers University Press, 2001. Tokyo Rose is here portrayed as one of the women of an ambivalent cult

of womanhood found among World War II soldiers.

Simpson, Caroline Chung. *An Absent Presence: Japanese Americans in Postwar American Culture, 1945-1960*. Durham, N.C.: Duke University Press, 2001. Connects the internment of Japanese Americans during World War II to broader themes of the culture and argues that the Tokyo Rose trial revealed a residual fear of the Japanese fifth column and fears about women's proper role and sexuality.

Yoo, David K. *Growing up Nisei: Race, Generation, and Culture Among Japanese Americans of California, 1924-49*. Chicago: University of Illinois Press, 2001. Examines the emergence of the Japanese American second-generation subculture, from the Immigration Act to the Tokyo Rose trial.

—*Anh Tran*

SEE ALSO: Charles E. Coughlin; Mildred Gillars; William Joyce.

TOMÁS DE TORQUEMADA
First grand inquisitor of the Spanish Inquisition (1484-1498)

BORN: 1420; Valladolid, Torquemada, near Castile (now in Spain)

DIED: September 16, 1498; Ávila, Spain

ALSO KNOWN AS: Hammer of Heretics

CAUSE OF NOTORIETY: Torquemada is remembered for his suppression of religious dissent in Spain and the judicial torture and execution of thousands of Jews and others whom he deemed heretical.

ACTIVE: 1482-1496

LOCALE: Spain

EARLY LIFE

The son of Pedro Fernandez de Torquemada and nephew of Juan de Torquemada, a prominent theologian and Dominican cardinal, Tomás de Torquemada (toh-MAWS day tohr-kay-MAW-dah) was born in 1420. Tomás took vows to become a Dominican himself and also earned a doctorate to teach canon law and theology. His asceticism and piety impressed his contemporaries, and eventually Torquemada was elected prior of the Santa Cruz monastery in Segovia, probably where he made the acquaintance of the future Queen Isabella and became her confessor.

A perhaps apocryphal story claims that he obtained a vow from Isabella that if she became queen, she would

stamp out heresy in Castile. Whether true or not, the account reflects the religious intolerance and social turmoil that beset Spain in the late 1400's and Torquemada's fanatical orthodoxy. Christians, Jews, and Muslims inhabited the Iberian Peninsula in disharmony. The success of Christian armies was bringing the Reconquest of the peninsula from the Muslims to a close. Thousands of Jews and Muslims had converted to Christianity, often because of coercion. Many of these converts (*conversos*) continued to practice their ancestral religions in secret, to the outrage of Old Christians, who resented the wealth and prominence of the *marranos* (a term of opprobrium used by the Christians to denote crypto-Jews). To the Roman Catholic clergy, anyone who accepted Christian baptism and then hypocritically continued to practice Judaism was a heretic. Pressure mounted for the establishment of the Inquisition to eliminate the judaizers and other heretics.

INQUISITOR CAREER

In 1478, the pope authorized Isabella to create the Holy Office of the Inquisition in Castile (it already existed in her husband Ferdinand's realms). After some delay, the monarch established the tribunal and on February 11, 1482, named Torquemada one of the inquisitors. The following year, she and Ferdinand named him grand inquisitor to direct the Inquisition in both Castile and Aragon. Torquemada quickly set up offices of the Inquisition in Sevilla, Jaen, Ávila, Valladolid, Córdoba, and Ciudad Real and later extended it to other cities. In 1484, he sent out twenty-eight articles outlining investigative and judicial procedures of the tribunal. These authorized the use of torture to extract confessions, although those confessions obtained during torture were not acceptable: The accused had to confess when not under such duress. In 1488, he established a five-member council, known as the Suprema (Consejo de la Suprema y General Inquisición), to oversee the provincial tribunals and hear appeals from them. Devout, intolerant, and legalistic by temperament, Torquemada was determined to crush the heretics yet prevent the Holy Office from lapsing into unregulated violence and mayhem.

Under Torquemada, the Inquisition concentrated on ferreting out and punishing judaizers. Ironically descended himself from a *converso* ancestor, Torquemada labored with energy and diligence. He saw all *conversos* as potential heretics. While the grand inquisitor allowed a grace period upon establishing tribunal in the city for heretics to confess and be reconciled, he demanded that the repentant reveal the names of all other judaizers of whom they were aware. Heretics forfeited their properties to the Inquisition and the crown, an economic temptation that led to widespread abuse. Torquemada financed the St. Thomas monastery in Ávila from such seizures, and Ferdinand and Isabella used confiscated properties to help wage war against the Muslim kingdom of Granada.

Torquemada also influenced the monarchs' decision to expel all the Jews from Spain. Following the 1350's, anti-Semitism had intensified in Spain, which had the largest Jewish population in Europe and where many noble families profited from rich dowries obtained through marriages to Jews. The uproar grew in 1490, when Jews were accused of kidnapping and crucifying a Christian child in the town of La Guardia and then cutting out his heart for a magical spell to destroy the Christians. The whole story was a fraud, but the Inquisition tortured confessions out of several Jews and burned them at the stake. In such hysteria, the monarchs responded to the prodding of Torquemada and others that as long as Jews lived in Spain, they were a threat, especially to the Christian orthodoxy of the *conversos*. The monarchs consequently decided to expel the Jews, whereupon several leading Jews offered Ferdinand thirty thousand ducats if he changed his mind. Learning of the meeting, Torquemada allegedly burst into the room, crucifix in hand. Re-

minding Ferdinand that Judas Iscariot had sold Jesus for thirty pieces of silver, he asked if the king was also going to sell Christ. Ferdinand and Isabella expelled the Jews on March 31, 1492.

IMPACT

The name Tomás de Torquemada became synonymous with the Inquisition's fanaticism, religious bigotry, and cruelty. However, although Torquemada did not create the intolerance and frenzy that led to establishment of the Inquisition and the expulsion of Spain's 160,000 Jews, nevertheless, he did preside over the Inquisition's period of most savage repression. During his fourteen years as grand inquisitor, up to two thousand Jews and Muslims were killed, and many others were burned in effigy because they had already died or fled Spain. Many thousands more suffered inhumane punishment or had their valuable property seized.

By the time he died in semiretirement in 1498, Torquemada had established the institutions that perpetuated religious orthodoxy at the cost of intolerance, brutality, and fanaticism. To his contemporaries, he was the Hammer of the Heretics. His tomb in the St. Thomas monastery of Ávila bore the epitaph: "He put heretics to flight" (*pestem fugat haereticam*). Some modern historians have compared him with Adolf Hitler.

FURTHER READING

Kamen, Henry. *The Spanish Inquisition: A Historical Revision*. New Haven, Conn.: Yale University Press, 1997. While not pardoning Torquemada or the Inquisition's anti-Semitism, Kamen argues that the tribunal's torture was less brutal than that of contemporary civil courts and that it executed far fewer than died in the witch crazes in England and Germany.

Lea, Henry Charles. *A History of the Inquisition of Spain*. 4 vols. New York: Macmillan, 1922. A classic study based on broad reading of documents generated by the Inquisition, it describes Torquemada's role in the early years of the tribunal and provides important detail on how it functioned.

Pérez, Joseph. *The Spanish Inquisition: A History*. New Haven, Conn.: Yale University Press, 2005. A short, balanced overview of the tribunal, from the surge in late medieval Spanish anti-Semitism to the Inquisition's abolition in the nineteenth century.

—*Kendall W. Brown*

SEE ALSO: Charles II; Clement VII; Joan the Mad; Pedro the Cruel.

LEON TROTSKY
Social theorist, revolutionary, and Soviet commissar (1917-1924)

BORN: November 7, 1879; Yanovka, Kherson Province, district of Yelizavetgrada, Ukraine, Russian Empire

DIED: August 21, 1940; Coyoacán, near Mexico City, Mexico

ALSO KNOWN AS: Lev Davidovich Bronstein (birth name)

CAUSE OF NOTORIETY: Trotsky was a leader in the first (1905) and second (1917) Russian Revolutions; his rival for power, Joseph Stalin, sought to eliminate him on grounds of treason and conspiracy.

ACTIVE: 1905-1940

LOCALE: Russia, later the Soviet Union

SENTENCE: Banished from Russia, 1929; later tried and sentenced to death in absentia

EARLY LIFE

Lev Davidovich Bronstein, later known as Leon Trotsky (TROTS-kee), was born at Yanovka, a small town in southern Ukraine, to David and Anna Bronstein, who were of Jewish origin. Lev was one of eight children, four of whom died in infancy. The Bronsteins sent Lev to the port city of Odessa for schooling, where he stayed with a relative of his mother. At Odessa, with its rich German culture, he was influenced by liberal ideas. A bright student, Lev excelled in academics while also demonstrating a propensity to question authority, with the result that he was once expelled from school.

After six years of schooling at Odessa, he moved to Nikolayev to continue his education and joined a clandestine socialist organization there that introduced him to Marxist ideas. Upon completion of his secondary schooling, he attended the University of Odessa and then returned to Nikolayev in 1897 to help organize the South Russian Workers Union and, later, the Russian Democratic Labor Party. These revolutionary activities led to his arrest and imprisonment in Odessa in 1898, and he was exiled to Siberia in 1900. During his captivity in Siberia, he married Aleksandra Sokolovskaya, a corevolutionary, and fathered two girls. In 1902, Bronstein, with the help of a forged passport with an assumed name, Trotsky, which was the name of the head jailer in the Odessa prison in which he was imprisoned, escaped from Siberia and traveled to London to meet Vladimir Ilich Lenin, leaving his family behind. From that point Lev Bronstein was known as Leon Trotsky.

POLITICAL CAREER

Although Trotsky's political career began to take shape in Nikolayev, he rose to prominence after he met Lenin in London. Trotsky's membership in the London Social Democrats helped position him to become a leader in the first Russian Revolution, which broke out in 1905.

Although the collaboration between Trotsky and Lenin continued until Lenin's death in 1924, there were sharp differences in their thinking and approach to the course of the Russian Revolution. These differences became pronounced when Lenin supported the Bolsheviks (members of the majority), while Trotsky supported the Menshevik (minority) faction of the Russian Democratic Workers Party. The Mensheviks argued for a more democratic and broad-based approach for implementing socialism, while the Bolsheviks advocated a revolution led by a relatively small but well-disciplined, action-oriented group of the proletariat and peasantry, supported by sympathizers.

In 1905, Trotsky traveled to Russia to help organize the workers against Czar Nicholas II, demanding political and economic reforms. Trotsky was arrested and incarcerated and, in 1907, once again deported to Siberia. After escaping from Siberia a second time, he made his way through several European countries and eventually settled in Vienna, where he worked as a correspondent until the beginning of World War II. When the war broke out, he was expelled from one European country after another because of his antiwar stance. Eventually he arrived in New York in 1917, the year the second Russian Revolution began. Welcoming the revolution as an opportunity, Trotsky reached Petrograd and assisted Lenin, despite his theoretical differences with him. Trotsky soon assumed the military leadership for the revolution.

Following the revolution, Trotsky was appointed commissar of foreign affairs in the Bolshevik government and was regarded as the most powerful official, second only to Lenin. He also joined the five-member Politburo, the powerful policy-making body of the Communist Party. Eventually, Trotsky resigned from the position of foreign commissar to assume the position of commissar of war and built the Red Army from the remnants of the old Russian army.

Lenin's declining health and death in 1924 precipitated a power struggle between Joseph Stalin and Trotsky for the leadership of the Communist Party, a struggle that Stalin won. Trotsky was soon removed from his position as commissar of war. Eventually, Stalin succeeded in expelling him not only from the Politburo and the Central Committee but also from the Communist Party itself. To remove any possible threat from Trotsky, Stalin banished him from the country in 1929. After having failed to secure permanent domicile in any European country, Trotsky found asylum in Mexico in 1936 and lived at Coyoacán, outside Mexico City. His troubles did not end there.

LEGAL ACTION AND OUTCOME

Trotsky was at the center of the political opposition, called the Trotskyite-Zinovyevite Terrorist Center, that Stalin sought to suppress. In the notorious Moscow Trials (1936-1938), which Stalin used to eliminate his opponents, forced confessions aided in obtaining convictions. Trotsky was tried in absentia and sentenced to death for treason. Historians have found no evidence to support the charge.

There were two attempts against Trotsky's life during his stay in Mexico. The second one succeeded when Ramón Mercader, believed to be an agent of Stalin, struck and killed Trotsky with an ice ax in 1940.

PERMANENT REVOLUTION

In a 1932 speech delivered in Copenhagen, "In Defense of October," Trotsky reached a visionary conclusion:

Only a powerful increase in productive force and a sound, planned, that is, socialist organisation of production and distribution can assure humanity—all humanity—of a decent standard of life and at the same time give it the precious feeling of freedom with respect to its own economy.

Freedom in two senses—first of all man will no longer be compelled to devote the greater part of his life to physical toil. Second, he will no longer be dependent on the laws of the market, that is, on the blind and obscure forces which work behind his back. . . .

Man calls himself the crown of creation. He has a certain right to that aim. But who has asserted that present day man is the last and highest representative of the species Homo Sapiens? No, physically as well as spiritually he is very far from perfection, prematurely born biologically, with feeble thought, and has not produced any new organic equilibrium.

It is true that humanity has more than once brought forth giants of thought and action, who tower over their contemporaries like summits in a chain of mountains. The human race has a right to be proud of its Aristotle, Shakespeare, Darwin, Beethoven, Goethe, Marx, Edison and Lenin. But why are they so rare?

Above all, because almost without exception they came out of the middle and upper classes. Apart from rare exceptions, the sparks of genius in the suppressed depths of the people are choked before they can burst into flame.

But also because the processes of creating, developing and educating a human being have been and remain essentially a matter of chance, not illuminated by theory and practice, not subjected to consciousness and will. . . .

Once he has done with the anarchic forces of his own society man will set to work on himself, in the pestle and retort of the chemist. For the first time mankind will regard itself as raw material, or at best as a physical and psychic semi-finished product. Socialism will mean a leap from the realm of necessity into the realm of freedom in this sense also, that the man of today, with all his contradictions and lack of harmony, will open the road for a new and happier race.

IMPACT

Leon Trotsky was one of the most prolific and powerful Russian writers; his contribution to literature and culture is enormous, as acknowledged even by those who oppose his theoretical perspective. Trotskyism represents the more idealistic and democratic version of communism. Trotsky vigorously argued for a broad-based, worldwide revolutionary process that, he believed, would become permanent. The concept of permanent revolution, one that eventually encompasses all nations and achieves the final victory of the working class everywhere, sharply contrasts with Stalin's view of socialism in one country. Despite the dissolution of the Soviet Union in 1991 and the demise of Russian communism, some still believe in Trotsky's theory of a permanent revolution.

FURTHER READING

Deutscher, Isaac. *The Prophet Unarmmed*. New York: Verso, 2003. Deutscher provides a well-documented account of the struggle between Stalin and Trotsky that led to Trotsky's defeat and expulsion from Russia in 1929.

Gilbert, Helen. *Leon Trotsky: His Life and Ideas*. Seattle, Wash.: Red Letter Press, 2003. This short primer on Trotsky serves as an accessible introduction to his life and thinking.

Trotsky, Leon. *My Life: An Attempt at an Autobiogra-*

phy. New York: Charles Scribner and Sons, 1930. Trotsky recalls and interprets the events that transformed his life and, in the process, contributes to the understanding of twentieth century world history.

—*Mathew J. Kanjirathinkal*

SEE ALSO: Nikita S. Khrushchev; Vladimir Ilich Lenin; Ramón Mercader; Joseph Stalin; Vasili Vasilievich Ulrikh; Andrey Vyshinsky; Yakov Mikhailovich Yurovsky; Andrey Aleksandrovich Zhdanov; Grigory Yevseyevich Zinovyev.

RAFAEL TRUJILLO
Dictatorial head of the Dominican Republic (1930-1961)

BORN: October 24, 1891; San Cristóbal, Dominican Republic

DIED: May 30, 1961; Ciudad Trujillo (now Santo Domingo), Dominican Republic

ALSO KNOWN AS: Rafael Leónidas Trujillo Molina (full name); El Benefactor

CAUSE OF NOTORIETY: By developing a cult of personality and using brutality against his opponents, Trujillo ruled the Dominican Republic with absolute political control for more than thirty years.

ACTIVE: 1930-1961

LOCALE: Dominican Republic

EARLY LIFE

Rafael Leónidas Trujillo Molina (rah-fah-ehl lay-aw-NEE-dahs troo-HEE-yoh moh-LEE-nah) was born to José Trujillo Valdez and Altagracia Julia Molina. When he was five years old, he contracted diphtheria and came close to dying. His teachers considered him a normal student who was attentive and whose main concern was to appear clean and sharp. At age sixteen, Trujillo worked at the Santo Domingo telegraph office, where he was employed for three years. After this period, Trujillo became involved with a gang, La 44, and was arrested for forging checks.

POLITICAL CAREER

Trujillo was trained by U.S. Marines during the United States' occupation of the Dominican Republic (1916-1924) at the Escuela Militar de Haina. The U.S. military trained the Policía Nacional (National Police) to maintain order after its departure. In 1919, Trujillo was promoted to lieutenant. When the U.S. troops left the Dominican Republic in 1924, they left Horacio Vásquez as president and Trujillo as lieutenant colonel. In 1927, Trujillo became brigadier general and commander in chief of the Dominican Republic army. Vásquez was overthrown in a coup in 1930, and on May 16, 1930,

Trujillo was elected president of the Dominican Republic. He had persecuted, blackmailed, or murdered any opposition to gain his position.

His terror continued directly after he took office. On June 1, 1930, Trujillo ordered the murder of Virgilio Martínez Reyna and his wife. Martínez had suggested to Vásquez's vice president, José Dolores Alfonseca, that he do away with Trujillo. In vengeance, Martínez was shot, stabbed, and mutilated with machetes. His pregnant wife received two gunshots to her stomach. Trujillo also established a secret police force, the Military Intelligence Service (SIM). This force was in charge of gathering information, torturing enemies, and carrying out murders as Trujillo saw fit.

Trujillo quickly created a personality cult and insisted that people support and praise him. He believed himself to be a messiah to his people and called himself "El Benefactor" (The Benefactor). He changed the name of the capital from Santo Domingo to Ciudad Trujillo. He controlled the radio, newspapers, and television; in schools, he made children pray for "God, country, and Trujillo." He made his rule legitimate by altering the constitution so that he would win all elections (his party was the only participant). Through these various acts, he succeeded in being the president from 1930 to 1938 and 1942 to 1952; he was then foreign minister—a position that still afforded him rule of the country—from 1953 to 1961.

Trujillo brought a level of stability and prosperity to the Dominican Republic. In 1930, after a devastating hurricane, Trujillo promised to rebuild the country. To this end, he appropriated and monopolized all industries and commerce, strengthening the economy and encouraging foreign investment in the Dominican sugar, cocoa, and banana industries. Because of Trujillo's absolute political control, the United States felt secure in investing in the island nation. During a period of war and strife in Europe, Trujillo also allowed Jewish refugees and Spanish Republican exiles to immigrate to the Dominican Republic. Trujillo established a federal school and health system and also built roads. By expanding government services, he created a middle class of professional workers. The Dominican economy prospered, the quality of life improved, and mortality rates lowered during his dictatorship.

However, the president also pursued a policy of *blanquismo*, or the whitening of the race. In October, 1937, he ordered the massacre of fifteen to twenty thousand dark-skinned Haitians who lived and worked in the not-yet-defined border between Haiti and the Dominican Republic. Haitian farmers were killed for, among other reasons, not being able to pronounce the "r" in *perejil*, the Spanish word for parsley. According to Trujillo, this massacre was his response to Haiti for supporting exiled Dominicans who were presumably planning to overthrow him. The massacre established the Haitian-Dominican border at Rio Masacre. However, the United States forced Trujillo to pay $750,000 in reparations to Haiti.

During World War II, Trujillo sided with the Allied Forces and gained American support for being anticommunist. Trujillo leveraged his anticommunist position to persecute any political opposition. His regime subsequently became known for its brutality against anyone who opposed it, whether a suspected communist or not. In one of Trujillo's more notorious acts, Jesús de Galíndez—a Columbia University instructor and exiled Basque who also worked as an informer for the Federal Bureau of Investigation (FBI) and the Central Intelligence Agency (CIA)—was tortured and killed in 1956. Galíndez was kidnapped from New York City on March 12, one day before his doctoral dissertation defense. His dissertation, titled "The Age of Trujillo," disclosed the criminal acts of Trujillo's dictatorship. In 1960, Trujillo allegedly attempted the murder of Venezuelan president Rómulo Betancourt. On November 25 of the same year, Trujillo ordered the murder of the Mirabal sisters (Patria, Minerva, and María Teresa), who were political activists. They were driving home from seeing their imprisoned husbands (the men had been arrested for opposing Trujillo's regime) when they were kidnapped, taken to a field, beaten, and strangled. Trujillo established torture chambers throughout the Dominican Republic during the last years of his regime.

After the failed attempt on the life of President Be-tancourt, the United States, along with the Organization of American States (OAS), established harsh economic sanctions and ended diplomatic ties in an effort to destabilize Trujillo's power. The United States provided arms and support to Trujillo's opposition. Trujillo was assassinated May 30, 1961, while driving his car. He was succeeded by his son Rafael Leónidas Trujillo, Jr. (Ramfis), who rounded up his father's assassins, tortured and shot them, and cut up their bodies and fed them to sharks. Five months after taking power, he died from injuries in a car accident.

IMPACT

During his reign, Rafael Trujillo established a healthy economy, paid off external debt, and built a national bank. He also supported urban development and in 1940 opened the Universidad de Santo Domingo. However beneficial these public works were, they were made possible only by complete tyrannical oppression.

FURTHER READING

Roorda, Eric Paul. *The Dictator Next Door: The Good Neighbor Policy and the Trujillo Regime in the Dominican Republic, 1930-1945*. Durham, N.C.: Duke University Press, 1998. This book examines the American Good Neighbor Policy and questions whether the United States should have intervened during Trujillo's dictatorship.

Scheina, Robert L. *Latin America's Wars: Age of the Professional Soldier, 1900-2001*. Washington, D.C.: Brassey's, 2003. A very comprehensive and thorough historical account of Latin America's wars and military governments.

Wiarda, Howard J. *Dictatorship and Development: The Methods of Control in Trujillo's Dominican Republic*. Gainesville: University of Florida Press, 1968. Wiarda analyzes the Trujillo dictatorship through political science theories and thus provides the theoretical background to understand Trujillo's system of control.

—*Kim Díaz*

SEE ALSO: Fidel Castro; François Duvalier; Jean-Claude Duvalier; Leopoldo Galtieri; Manuel Noriega; Augusto Pinochet Ugarte; Efraín Ríos Montt; Anastasio Somoza García; Alfredo Stroessner; Getúlio Vargas.

KARLA FAYE TUCKER
American murderer

BORN: November 18, 1959; Houston, Texas
DIED: February 3, 1998; Huntsville State Prison, Huntsville, Texas
ALSO KNOWN AS: Karla Faye Tucker Brown
MAJOR OFFENSE: Murder
ACTIVE: June 13, 1983
LOCALE: Houston, Texas
SENTENCE: Death by lethal injection

EARLY LIFE

Karla Faye Tucker (KAHR-lah fay TUHK-uhr) was the illegitimate daughter of a Houston firefighter of Greek ethnicity from whom Karla presumably inherited her dark complexion and black hair. Her mother, Carolyn Moore Tucker, was married to Larry Tucker, a Houston longshoreman turned small-time businessman. Karla lived in the Tucker household with two older sisters, Kathi Lynne and Kari Ann. Tucker was precocious. Not only did she learn to drive a car and a motor boat at an early age, but that was also the time she started smoking marijuana, which later became an addiction. Moreover, by early puberty, she had become sexually active.

Eventually, the Tuckers divorced, and the girls were placed in the custody of their father. Larry Tucker catered to their every wish, and he could not control the boisterous girls. They eventually drifted back to their mother, whose libertarian lifestyle was more to their liking. Soon, Tucker paid for her drugs by touring with bands and engaging in prostitution. Among the many men she met at parties was Jerry Lynn Dean (who married her best friend, Shawn Jackson) and Danny Garrett, several years older, who became Tucker's boyfriend. For Dean, she developed an early dislike which turned into intense hatred when she discovered that he had abused Jackson.

CRIMINAL CAREER

On June 13, 1983, under the influence of drugs after a dope party, Tucker and Garrett decided to steal Dean's motorcycle, or at least some spare parts. They entered Dean's bed-room using Jackson's key, which Tucker had found in her friend's clothing. Tucker jumped on Dean, and they struggled. Garrett started bludgeoning him with a hammer. Tucker grabbed one of Dean's work tools, a pickax, and hit Dean first; Garrett completed the killing. Tucker then noticed a woman, Deborah Ruth Thornton, cowering nearby. Tucker came at Thornton with the pickax, and Garrett again finished the murder.

LEGAL ACTION AND OUTCOME

To help convict the twosome, Detective J. C. Mosier convinced Garrett's brother, Doug, who had heard the pair talk about their crimes and tipped off the Houston police, to wear a hidden tape-recorder to get Tucker's testimony of the events. The subsequent tape-recording was used as evidence at their trial in April, 1984. Tucker and Garrett were convicted of the murders by a jury.

The sentencing phase of the trial took place immediately thereafter. The jury found that Tucker's crimes were deliberate and that she continued to pose a threat to society. On that basis, she was sentenced to death by lethal injection. Garrett died in prison from a liver ailment in 1993 before he could be executed.

Eventually, after numerous appeals, the United States

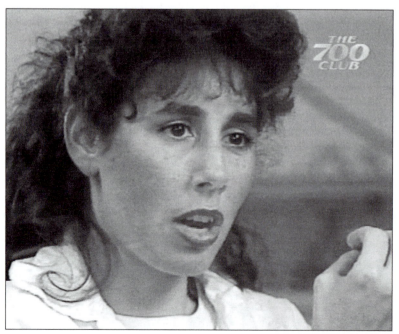

Karla Faye Tucker. (AP/Wide World Photos)

Supreme Court refused to overturn earlier rulings. Tucker's own impassioned petitions to the Texas Board of Paroles and Pardon and to then-governor George W. Bush for a thirty-day reprieve of the death sentence and its commutation to life imprisonment were turned down. Despite many other pleas for mercy by people such as Sister Helen Prejean, a leading advocate for the abolition of the death penalty, and Pope John Paul II, Tucker became the first woman to be executed in Texas since the Civil War.

IMPACT

Karla Faye Tucker's execution not only reignited the controversy about capital punishment but also raised a moral question that the prisoner had voiced in her petitions to the Board of Paroles and Governor Bush: If a bad person ultimately turns genuinely good and acquires a new, remorseful, God-fearing identity, should that fact not be taken into account in reconsidering her punishment? By 1998, when Tucker was executed, society had still not made up its mind.

FURTHER READING

Butts, J. Lee. "A Bad Girl Gone Good: Karla Faye Tucker." In *Texas Bad Girls: Hussies, Harlots, and Horse Thieves*. Plano, Tex.: Wordware, 2001. A discussion that clearly sides with Tucker and her appeals to avoid the death penalty. Includes illustrations, bibliography, and index.

Hornberger, Francine. *Mistresses of Mayhem: A Book of Women Criminals*. Indianapolis: Alpha-Pearson, 2002. A short, objective biographical profile of women deviants, such as Tucker. Includes bibliography and index.

Lowry, Beverly. *Crossed Over: A Murder, a Memoir*. New York: Knopf, 1992. A sympathetic profile based on several personal contacts between the author and Tucker.

—Peter B. Heller

SEE ALSO: Velma Margie Barfield; Jean Harris; Bonnie Parker; Pamela Ann Smart; Ruth Snyder; Andrea Yates.

DICK TURPIN
English highwayman and cattle thief

BORN: Probably September, 1705; Hempstead, Essex, England
DIED: April 7, 1739; York, North Yorkshire, England
ALSO KNOWN AS: John Palmer; Richard Turpin (full name)
MAJOR OFFENSES: Horse stealing, housebreaking, highway robbery, and murder
ACTIVE: 1730-1738
LOCALE: Mostly Essex and Lincolnshire, England
SENTENCE: Death by hanging

EARLY LIFE

Dick Turpin (TUR-pihn) was the son of John Turpin, a farmer and keeper of The Bell Inn (now the Bluebell Inn) in Hempstead, Essex. Dick received a basic education and was apprenticed to a butcher, but throughout his youth he was known to be disorderly and violent. At some uncertain date he married Elizabeth ("Bess") Millington and opened a butcher's shop near Thaxted, in Epping Forest, Essex. He soon found it easier to steal cattle than acquire them legitimately and so entered a life of crime.

CRIMINAL CAREER

Turpin's early cattle thieving was apparently cut short when he was identified by a local man, and Turpin fled into the Essex countryside. He is alleged to have spent time as a smuggler along the Essex coast until caught by revenue men, but he escaped and returned to Epping. He fell in with a band of deer thieves who turned their attention to housebreaking. They were known as the Gregory Gang, after the group's leader. The *Newgate Calendar* catalogs a long sequence of their crimes, which became steadily more vicious. Their method was to barge into the house, bind and gag the occupants, and ransack the place. They expected the occupants to reveal the locations of items of special value; if they did not, the gang would inflict harm. Turpin once threatened to lay an old woman across the fire.

LEGAL ACTION AND OUTCOME

After one violent robbery in February 1735, where a maidservant was raped and the owner had near-boiling water thrown on him, a warrant was issued for the gang's arrest, with a reward of fifty pounds, later increased to

Dick Turpin.

one hundred pounds. This was sufficient for most of the gang to be captured over the following few months. Only Turpin and Thomas Rowden remained at large.

During the rest of 1735, Turpin and Rowden turned to highway robbery, with known offenses in Barnes and Southwark and on roads north and south of London. During the winter of 1735 Rowden left for Gloucester, where he was eventually caught and later hanged. Turpin went into hiding, possibly in Holland, but was back operating as a highwayman in February, 1737, now in conjunction with Matthew King. The two had a hideaway in a cave in Epping Forest, near Loughton.

In April, 1737, Turpin stole a horse at gunpoint, but Richard Bayes, a local landlord who was helping the victim, learned of the horse's whereabouts and sought to recover it. A struggle ensued in which Turpin, trying to shoot Bayes, shot his partner King instead. King died a week later, after he had revealed Turpin's whereabouts. During that week Turpin was recognized by Thomas Morris, who sought to apprehend him, but Turpin shot and killed Morris. A reward of two hundred pounds was now placed on Turpin's head, the warrant stating that he was "about five feet nine inches high, very much marked with the small-pox . . . and broad about the shoulders."

Turpin fled north to Brough in Yorkshire, adopted the name John Palmer, and operated as a horse trader. Turpin crossed into Lincolnshire, where he would steal cattle and horses and then sell them. However, on October 2, 1738, Turpin made the mistake of shooting a domestic

chicken, and when a witness threatened to inform, Turpin threatened to shoot him. The informant sought a warrant for John Palmer's arrest. Taken before the justice of the peace, Turpin was unable to provide surety for good behavior and was committed to the house of corrections in Beverley.

Investigations into Palmer's background were undertaken, and it was learned that Palmer was wanted in Lincolnshire for stealing sheep. He was moved to the prison at York Castle. From there, in February, 1739, Turpin wrote to his brother-in-law in Essex beseeching him to provide evidence of good character. His brother-in-law refused to accept the letter, and it remained at the local post office, where, remarkably, it was seen by Turpin's old schoolmaster, who had taught him to write. He recognized the handwriting and, consulting a local magistrate, read the letter and made the connection between Palmer and Turpin.

This sealed Turpin's fate. He was tried at York Assizes on March 22, 1739, convicted on two indictments of horse stealing, and condemned to hang.

It was only now that Turpin became the flamboyant character of legend. He acquired a new frock coat and shoes to wear for his execution and hired five men to act as mourners. He gave away his personal belongings to local people. On the day of his execution he chatted with the executioner before throwing himself off the ladder to his death by hanging.

IMPACT

An account of Dick Turpin's life was recorded in the *Newgate Calendar* from which Turpin's notoriety grew. However, he might have been forgotten had it not been for the writer William Harrison Ainsworth, who used Dick Turpin as a character in his novel *Rookwood* (1834). It was Ainsworth who made Turpin a gallant, almost heroic villain and who created the legend of Turpin's overnight ride from London to York on his horse Black Bess. This account captured the public imagination and turned Turpin's image into that of a romantic daredevil. The success of *Rookwood* gave impetus to the genre of the Newgate novel, which drew upon and often glorified villains recorded in the *Newgate Calendar*. These included such "penny dreadfuls" of Victorian

Britain as *Dick Turpin* by Henry Downes Miles (1840) and *Black Bess: Or, The Knight of the Road* by J. F. Smith (1868), which created the romantic image that endures to this day.

FURTHER READING

Barlow, Derek. *Dick Turpin and the Gregory Gang*. London: Phillimore, 1973. A basic starting place for a detailed study of Turpin's crimes.

Day, Julius E., and Arty Ash. *Immortal Turpin*. London: Staples Press, 1948. The first thorough biography with detailed sources and dispassionate analysis.

Sharpe, James. *Dick Turpin*. London: Profile Books, 2004. As well as examining the historical Turpin, Sharpe seeks to explore why the highwayman has been so romanticized.

Spraggs, Gillian. *Outlaws and Highwaymen: The Cult of the Robber in England*. London: Pimlico, 2001. This shows how Turpin was absorbed into an existing English tradition of creating robber heroes.

—*Mike Ashley*

SEE ALSO: Claude Duval; Robin Hood; Jack Sheppard.

WILLIAM MARCY TWEED
American politician

BORN: April 3, 1823; New York, New York
DIED: April 12, 1878; New York, New York
ALSO KNOWN AS: Boss Tweed
MAJOR OFFENSES: Embezzlement and forgery
ACTIVE: 1852-1878
LOCALE: New York, New York
SENTENCE: Twelve years' imprisonment, serving one year; served two more years in prison before his death

EARLY LIFE

William Marcy Tweed (tweed) received some elementary schooling before becoming an apprentice in the chair-making business. He also held small jobs in his father's brush factory and served as a bookkeeper and volunteer firefighter. Tweed was one of the original members of a fire engine company known as Big Six. There, he gained experience and popularity and soon became an influential foreman of this company. This early success catapulted him into the world of politics.

POLITICAL CAREER

From 1852 to 1853, Tweed was a member of the New York board of aldermen and then served for two years in the U.S. House of Representatives. In 1856, he was elected to a new, bipartisan city board of supervisors. He held other important positions in city government, such as school commissioner and deputy street commissioner. In 1862, he became president of the board of supervisors. Two years later, when the city's department of public works was first established, Tweed became its head. Shortly after the American Civil War concluded, he be-

came a member of the New York State Senate, serving until 1871. He was an aspiring member of the Tammany Hall organization, and from 1869 to 1871 he held the position of "grant sachem," which was the principal leader of the Democratic Party of New York City's executive committee. Tweed's numerous appointed and elected

William Marcy Tweed. (Library of Congress)

TWEED IN WORD AND DEED

Remarks attributed to Boss Tweed appear to reflect an arrogant disregard for public opinion and intelligence. Consider these often repeated quotations:

- I don't care a straw for your newspaper articles, my constituents don't know how to read.
- I don't care who does the electing, so long as I get to do the nominating.
- As long as I count the votes, what are YOU going to do about it? (This is eerily similar to something Joseph Stalin is supposed to have said: "It's not the people who vote that count. It's the people who count the votes.")
- The fact is New York politics were always dishonest—long before my time. There never was a time you couldn't buy the Board of Aldermen. . . . A politician coming forward takes things as they are.
- Government: Buy the people, gull the people, fool the people.

Reportedly, when Tweed was processed into the prison on Blackwell Island in 1875, the clerk asked him to state his religion. "None," Tweed replied. Asked to name his occupation, he said, "Statesman."

However, his biographers portray a Tweed who was intimately concerned with New Yorkers' opinions, needs, and moods. He won the hearts of the city's large, impoverished Irish community by distributing government funds; whether he did it legally or illegally hardly mattered. His patronage created jobs. The money also went to schools (including the growing Roman Catholic parochial school system) and hospitals, and in the form of direct aid to needy families, such as gifts of coal. "Because of Tweed," concludes Kenneth D. Ackerman in *Boss Tweed: The Rise and Fall of the Corrupt Pol Who Conceived the Soul of Modern New York* (2005), "New York got better, even for the poor."

Moreover, Tweed was not simply a manipulator. He risked his life on at least two occasions. Just after he became the Tammany Hall leader, riots broke out in New York over the recently enacted draft law conscripting troops during the Civil War. Although he sympathized with the antidraft sentiment, he went through the strife-torn streets trying to calm the situation. During the street battles between Irish Catholics and Irish Protestants in 1870 and 1871, Tweed was seriously injured trying to quell the violence.

When he took to wearing a 10.5-carat diamond stickpin, as if to call attention to his power, the poor whom he helped did not appear to mind.

of patronage and controlling and manipulating the voting process in order to ensure compliance with the wishes of the boss. A hierarchy was established and maintained (which included precinct captains, ward heelers, and the board chair). Bossism became a major target of upper-class municipal reform groups, which also sought to separate politics from administration and instill more professionalism in local government.

The oldest and most famous combination of ethnic and machine politics occurred in the Tammany Hall machine of Manhattan. The Tammany Society had existed since 1789 and originally was mainly a social fraternal organization. However, it gradually evolved and became more politicized, especially under the dominant Irish leadership, and eventually served as a central control for activities conducted by neighborhood district clubs. While these clubs were the core of the organization, citywide control was needed for settling disputes among these clubs, determining citywide nominations, and distributing patronage. Tammany Hall filled that gap effectively from 1860 to 1900.

The group of cronies whom Tweed selected as political allies became known as the Tweed Ring, and it siphoned millions of dollars from the public's funds in city government. For example, in 1870, Tweed's amendment to the city charter facilitated a new board of audit, allowing the Tweed Ring to gain control of the city treasury. Thereafter, vastly overpaid contracts for public works and services, amounting to millions of dollars, were skimmed off by the group.

In 1869, *The New York Times* began to editorialize constantly against the Tammany Hall machine, which in turn sparked interest in coalitions of reformers. However, since many people could not read, Boss Tweed's base remained intact. Nonetheless, *New York Times* political cartoonist Thomas Nast was very effective with his popular caricatures of Tweed in exposing Tweed's excesses and his organization to New York and national audiences.

public service positions and networking capacity made him especially knowledgeable about the use of power and influence.

"Bossism" flourished as a dominant system of U.S. city government after the Civil War. It was an informal system of local government in which public power was concentrated in the hands of a few strong and influential persons. The leader was referred to as a political boss, who may or may not have had a formal governmental position. Power was thereby concentrated through the use

LEGAL ACTION AND OUTCOME

Railroad tycoon and advocate of reform Samuel J. Tilden proved to be an effective contributor to the downfall of the "ring of thieves." Tilden pushed for control of the party leadership at Tammany while successfully guiding the prosecution of Tweed in a civil case.

In November of 1873, Tweed was convicted of embezzlement, sentenced to twelve years' imprisonment, and ordered to pay a heavy fine. He was confined to Blackwell's Island until June, 1875, when he was released on a technicality. He was again arrested on a civil charge and immediately committed to the Ludlow Street Jail because he was unable to pay the substantial three-million-dollar bail.

On December 4, 1875, Tweed escaped and somehow made his way, after months of being "underground," to Cuba and eventually Spain. Subsequently, he was arrested by the Spanish authorities, brought back to New York, and imprisoned again. He died in jail on April 12, 1878. Between $20 and $200 million were estimated to have been stolen by the infamous ring; less than $1 million was ever recovered. Only Tweed and one other ring member went to jail for their sustainable graft schemes and blatant corruption activities.

IMPACT

William Marcy Tweed was one of the most colorful figures of the boss era and set the standard for dishonesty and corruption. He was followed by bosses Charles Murphy and Richard Croker.

Reformers had clearly routed the Tweed Ring. However, the model of the machine was replicated in future New York City regimes, as well as many other cities, especially in the Northeast. Revisionist historians and some political scientists have argued that one legacy of the bossism and machine era was that it held the nation's cities together in periods of rapid immigration and urbanization, while social unrest and revolution mounted in Europe under similar conditions in the late nineteenth and early twentieth centuries.

FURTHER READING

Burrows, Edwin G., and Mike Wallace. *Gotham: A History of New York City to 1898*. New York: Oxford University Press, 1999. A massive historical treatise that devotes much coverage to Tammany Hall and the life and times of Boss Tweed.

Callow, Alexander B., Jr. *The Tweed Ring*. New York: Oxford University Press, 1966. An exhaustive study of Tweed by a professor of history at the University of California, Santa Barbara.

_____, ed. *The City Boss in America: An Interpretive Reader*. New York: Oxford University Press, 1976. Twenty-seven authors discuss the rise of bossism, the challenge from reformers, and modern political machines. Tweed is featured in several sections.

Solomon, Noal. *When Leaders Were Bosses: An Inside Look at Political Machines and Politics*. Hicksville, N.Y.: Exposition Press, 1975. Brings together thirteen chapters on different bosses and their machines. Chapter 2, "Tammany Hall," features discussions of Tweed and his cronies.

—*G. Thomas Taylor*

SEE ALSO: Thomas Joseph Pendergast; James J. Walker.

JOHN TYNDALL
British neo-Nazi politician and founder of the British National Union

BORN: July 14, 1934; London, England
DIED: July 19, 2005; Hove, Sussex, England
ALSO KNOWN AS: John Hutchyns Tyndall (full name)
MAJOR OFFENSES: Organizing a paramilitary force and inciting racial hatred
ACTIVE: 1957-2005
LOCALE: Burnley, Lancashire, England
SENTENCE: Several months' imprisonment for organizing a paramilitary force; one year in prison for inciting racial hatred

EARLY LIFE

John Hutchyns Tyndall (TIHN-duhl) was born the son of a Young Men's Christian Association (YMCA) warden in south London. His father's side of the family had come from Ireland, where his grandfather had been an inspector in the Royal Irish Constabulary and was active in fighting the Catholic rebels in Northern Ireland and the Republic of Ireland. Before him, an ancestor had been a well-known Victorian scientist, and another, the famous William Tyndale, in the sixteenth century was the first translator of the English Bible.

After an undistinguished school career at Penge and Beckenham Grammar School, Tyndall served two years with the Royal Horse Artillery. He then spent a little time as a salesman. His first interest in politics was shown when he attended a Communist youth rally in Moscow in the mid-1950's, but he quickly swung to the other extreme and spent the rest of his life involved in far-right activist politics.

POLITICAL CAREER

Tyndall first joined the League of Empire Loyalists (LEL), led by the far-right Arthur Kenneth Chesterton. Through the league, Tyndall met John Bean, one of Chesterton's disciples, while campaigning in a London by-election in 1957. The two men developed an interest in direct action and were once arrested outside the house of a Conservative member of Parliament with a paint can and brushes. Tyndall did not think the LEL was active enough, so he formed his own party, the National Labour Party. However, the official Labour Party banned the use of its name. Tyndall then merged his party with the White Defence League in 1960 to form the British National Party (BNP), a party that was to have several different manifestations. Tyndall became its deputy national organizer.

Tyndall's violent, neo-Nazi oratory frequently resulted in direct clashes with left-wing groups. When, in 1962, British socialist Colin Jordan set up a private army called Spearhead—based on Adolf Hitler's Brownshirts (Hitler's storm troopers, who wore brown uniforms)—Tyndall became its deputy commander. He was jailed for several months for organizing a paramilitary force, along with Jordan. Tyndall split with Jordan when Jordan suddenly married Tyndall's fiancé, Françoise Dior.

It was in prison that Tyndall formulated his own political theories, which he published as *The Authoritarian State*. In this twenty-three-page pamphlet, he states his contempt for all democratic procedures, even within his own party. His views had a platform in the magazine he edited for many years, also called *Spearhead*. In the 1970's, he married a co-activist and had one daughter with her.

After severing his ties with the old BNP, Tyndall set up his own National Socialist movement and then founded the Greater Britain movement in 1964. In 1966, he was again arrested, this time for carrying a gun and bullets. In 1967, the disparate group of far-right organizations were brought together as the National Front (NF) under Chesterton's leadership. When Chesterton resigned, Tyndall assumed leadership. Tyndall came to power during a period when many working-class and lower-middle-class British citizens felt alienated by the Conservative Party's acceptance of large-scale immigration. However, they were also alienated by Tyndall's preferred method of violent street fighting and general thuggishness, as well as his obvious adherence to Nazi ideology, and therefore, the NF failed to make inroads into this collective dissatisfaction. In 1979, the year prime minister Margaret Thatcher came to power, NF candidates lost their deposits in every one of the 303 constituencies in which they contested.

Internal dissent again fractured the NF, and Tyndall left to form a new NF party, again named the British National Party, in 1982. In 1986, he was jailed for a year for inciting racial hatred. He stood as a BNP candidate in the 1994, 1997, and 2001 elections but never received many votes. In 1996, he met a young Cambridge graduate, Nick Griffin, and offered him the editorship of *Spearhead*. In the 1999 leadership election, he lost to Griffin—whom he criticized for his more democratic leanings—and was expelled. Reinstated, he was expelled a second time and forbidden to participate in local elections.

LEGAL ACTION AND OUTCOME

By the turn of the twenty-first century, Tyndall had been arrested and charged three times. The laws against racial incitement in Britain had been strengthened, but Tyndall continued to disregard them in the name of freedom of speech. In 2003, a British Broadcasting Corporation (BBC) undercover investigative reporter infiltrated the BNP in Lancashire, where the party had a strong following. He taped a number of party members, including Griffin and Tyndall, making very explicit racist remarks and boasting of racist attacks. When the show, titled *The Secret Agent*, was shown on BBC-TV in 2004, the police decided to act against the men. Tyndall was arrested on suspicion of inciting racial hatred and formally charged on April 6, 2005. The trial was due to have its first hearing at Leeds Crown Court on July 21, 2005. Two days before that date, however, Tyndall died of a heart attack at his house in Sussex.

IMPACT

John Tyndall's main impact was not in his offenses but in his oratory, which could be mesmerizing, and in his organizational energy, which perpetuated the momentum of the far-right movement even in its periods of greatest dis-illusion and fracture. He was personally very courageous, but his adherence to Nazi ideology, his penchant for uniforms and jackboots, and his arrogance caused him to lose friends and, in the end, to become a hindrance to the BNP.

FURTHER READING

Copsey, Nigel. *Contemporary British Fascism: The British National Party and the Search for Legitimacy*. London: Palgrave Macmillan, 2004. This discussion sets Tyndall in the wider context of the growth of far-right parties.

Sykes, Alan. *The Radical Right in Britain*. London: Palgrave Macmillan, 2004. A volume in the British History in Perspective series, this title covers the rise of extreme conservatism in twentieth century Britain.

Tyndall, John. *Eleventh Hour: A Call for British Rebirth*. London: Albion Press, 1988. A long, rambling work, part autobiography, part political philosophy. A classic National Front text.

—*David Barratt*

SEE ALSO: Françoise Dior.

VASILI VASILIEVICH ULRIKH
Soviet military judge

BORN: July 13, 1889; Riga, Latvia, Russian Empire (now in Latvia)

DIED: May 7, 1951; Moscow, Soviet Union (now in Russia)

CAUSE OF NOTORIETY: As chairman of the Military Collegium of the Supreme Court of the Soviet Union, Ulrikh served as presiding judge over all the major show trials of the Great Terror.

ACTIVE: 1926-1948

LOCALE: Former Soviet Union, mostly Russia and Ukraine

EARLY LIFE

Vasili Vasilievich Ulrikh (va-SEE-lee va-SEE-lyeh-vihch EWL-rihk) was the son of a Baltic German father and a Russian mother from the service nobility. Both his parents were involved in socialist organizations, and as a result the family was sentenced to a five-year term of exile to the region of Irkutsk in 1905. In 1910, Ulrikh returned to Riga to take a technical degree at the Riga Polytechnical Institute.

No sooner had Ulrikh received his degree than Russia entered World War I. Because he possessed a college education, Ulrikh was selected as an officer by the czarist army and was sent to the front. He appears to have served honorably but without distinction. He was married and divorced twice, although his second marriage appears to have been a common-law liaison of the sort often practiced by the early Bolsheviks, who rejected all forms of sacramental marriage. He had a son with one of his wives but paid little attention to him.

POLITICAL CAREER

After the Bolshevik Revolution, Ulrikh used his father's record as a Socialist sympathizer to gain the trust of Leon Trotsky, at the time the war commissar, and become not only a member of the Communist Party but also a military judge. Almost at once he began his long career of issuing death sentences followed by immediate executions. Although he had no legal training whatsoever, it did not matter, for what passed as legality during the Russian civil war was identifying individuals and groups as "class enemies," according to the Bolshevik understanding of Marxist theory, to condemn them to death. Joseph Stalin, general secretary of the Communist Party, soon saw the possibilities in such a judge.

In 1926 Ulrikh became chairman of the Military Collegium of the Supreme Court of the Soviet Union. This judicial body was, in theory, the highest court of appeals for military cases, but in practice it quickly became a special court for political cases. Ulrikh was the presiding judge at all the major show trials of the Great Terror, but he can in no way be considered to have run the trials. His authority was limited to opening and closing the trials and calling recesses as needed. The real authority belonged to the prosecutor, Andrey Vyshinsky, a handsome and charismatic man with a subtle legal mind and phenomenal oratorical ability who could be trusted to match wits with the brilliant minds of the Old Bolshevik leaders.

In addition to his role in the Moscow Trials, Ulrikh presided over enormous numbers of secret trials. The best-known trial was that of Marshal Mikhail Tukhachevsky and other leaders of the Red Army, but in most Ulrikh did not make even a pretense of any real judicial procedure. The accused would enter; be told the charges, the verdict, and the sentence in rapid-fire succession; and be marched out to be shot, in a horrifying clockwork. When allowed a little more time, Ulrikh often enjoyed tormenting his victims, joking cruelly with them or leaving them sitting all night while he and his fellow judges left to "confer." Furthermore, he appears to have had an unusual fascination with executions, to the point of carrying them out himself.

Throughout World War II Ulrikh tried and executed numerous defeated military officers as well as leaders of conquered areas such as the Baltic states and Poland. He even participated in some of the early trials of the Zhdanovshchina, the postwar repressions led by Andrey Zhdanov.

In 1948 Ulrikh suddenly fell from Stalin's favor as the result of having exiled to Siberia a number of Ukrainian peasants whom Stalin wanted shot. Forced to tender his resignation as chairman of the Military Collegium of the Supreme Court of the Soviet Union, Ulrikh was made course director at the Military Law Academy. His tenure there coincided with his descent into alcoholism, and he would regale his listeners (often prostitutes whom he had summoned) with tales of the executions he had witnessed in his heyday.

It is possible that Stalin intended to follow his old pattern of purging the purgers and make Ulrikh one of the prime defendants in a future round of show trials (particularly if the Doctors' Plot, which was halted by Stalin's

1953 death, was intended to be the beginning of a new terror). However, Ulrikh died suddenly of a heart attack in 1951 while still at his new post. He was subsequently buried without honors at the Novodevichy Cemetery.

IMPACT

Although Vasili Vasilievich Ulrikh was a figurehead under the real control of Vyshinsky and Stalin, his role as the hanging judge who could always be relied upon to return guilty verdicts made him an active participant in Stalin's murderous system. Many of Ulrikh's trials were mere parodies of justice, minutes-long shams in which one accused after another was condemned, often on absurd charges.

FURTHER READING

Conquest, Robert. *The Great Terror: A Reassessment.* New York: Oxford University Press, 1990. A postglasnost reissuing of the most authoritative volume on the era.

Montefiore, Simon Sebag. *Stalin: The Court of the Red Tsar.* New York: Alfred A. Knopf, 2003. Includes information on Stalin's use of Ulrikh and other henchmen to run the Terror while deflecting attention from himself.

Rayfield, Donald. *Stalin and His Hangmen: The Tyrant and Those Who Killed for Him.* New York: Random House, 2004. A study of the relationship of Stalin and his chief henchmen.

Vaksberg, Arkady. *Stalin's Prosecutor: The Life of Andrei Vyshinsky.* New York: Grove Weidenfeld, 1991. Includes information on Ulrikh's role in the Moscow Trials as related to Vyshinsky's.

—*Leigh Husband Kimmel*

SEE ALSO: Lavrenty Beria; Felix Dzerzhinsky; Francisco Franco; Adolf Hitler; Lazar Kaganovich; Nikita S. Khrushchev; Vladimir Ilich Lenin; Mao Zedong; Vyacheslav Mikhailovich Molotov; Symon Petlyura; Joseph Stalin; Leon Trotsky; Andrey Vyshinsky; Genrikh Yagoda; Nikolay Ivanovich Yezhov; Andrey Aleksandrovich Zhdanov.

URBAN VI
Italian pope (1378-1389)

BORN: c. 1318; Naples (now in Italy)
DIED: October 15, 1389; Rome (now in Italy)
ALSO KNOWN AS: Bartolomeo Prignano (birth name)
CAUSE OF NOTORIETY: Protagonist of the so-called Great Schism (1378-1417), during which the papacy was divided into two, Urban VI was known for his authoritarian attitude and raging temper toward church dignitaries. He had his cardinal opponents tortured and executed for allegedly plotting against him in 1385.
ACTIVE: 1378-1389
LOCALE: Rome and Nocera

EARLY LIFE

Bartolomeo Prignano (bahr-to-lo-MAY-o prih-NYAH-noh), who would become Urban (UR-bahn) VI, began his ecclesiastic career as a brilliant jurist and was part of the circle around the French cardinal Guy de Boulogne, himself a prominent jurist and diplomat.

Prignano was first elevated to the rank of bishop of Acerenza, then of Bari. In 1377, Pope Gregory XI (1371-1378), a Frenchman elected in Avignon, was induced to bring the papacy back to Rome by the prayers of Saint Catherine of Siena. Gregory entered the Eternal City on January 17 of that year. Prignano followed and became responsible for the apostolic chancellery. After Gregory died on March 27, 1378, the conclave gathered on April 7 while the crowd noisily manifested its determination to have a Roman pope elected, threatening to kill the sixteen cardinals of the conclave if they did not elect an Italian pope. The following day, Prignano was elected, and he was crowned on April 18.

POLITICAL AND PASTORAL CAREER

Urban VI immediately began to act with extreme brutality, accusing the cardinals of corruption, simony, and absenteeism. He alienated them, causing the majority to flee to the nearby city of Agnani. Later the cardinals moved to Fondi under the jurisdiction of the Neapolitan kingdom, where they declared the April election invalid. Therefore, they elected the former condottiere Robert of Geneva as new pope under the name of Clement VII. In this troubled situation, Urban intervened in the affairs of the kingdom of Naples, taking the side of Charles of Durazzo against Queen Jane I.

In the frenzy of the struggle against his rival Clement

VII, he committed all the offenses that he had so bitterly attributed to the cardinals. He, too, practiced nepotism, giving the principality of Capua to his nephew Butillo Prignano and covering all his misdemeanors. He then obtained for his "protégé" the town of Nocera, where he fixed his residence. He later broke his alliance with Durazzo, who declared that the pope was mad and determined to place him under the custody of his cardinals.

Fearing betrayal, Urban had six of the cardinals imprisoned and tortured until the bishop of L'Aquila confessed he had been part of a plot to capture the pope. Urban decided to punish the cardinals heavily with the help of his nephew Butillo. One of them was attached to a tree trunk and flayed. The cardinal of Venice was crucified, and salt and vinegar were poured on his wounds. While these horrors were perpetrated, the pope is said to have walked in a nearby alley, reciting his rosary and only interrupting his reading from time to time to encourage the torturers to get on with their task.

Besieged in Nocera by the Neapolitan troops, he succeeded in escaping to Genoa, where he gave orders to his nephew to put to death the prisoners he had brought with him. More and more isolated, while his rival Clement VII was strengthened by the conquest of Naples by French troops, Urban eventually returned to Rome. He died a few days after his return to the Vatican and was buried in the Saint Andrew chapel in Saint Peter's Church.

IMPACT

Urban VI is considered responsible for the Great Schism, and many modern Church historians have adopted the harsh judgment of some of his contemporaries who called him *homo furiosus* (madman).

FURTHER READING

Kelly, J. N. D., ed. *The Oxford Dictionary of Popes*. New York: Oxford University Press, 1986. An essential, synthetic sequence of biographies of the popes.

Maillard-Luypaert, Monique. "Urbain VI." In *Dictionnaire historique de la papauté*, edited by Philippe Levillain. Paris: Fayard, 2003. An accurate and well-

Urban VI.

balanced compendium of the life and career of Urban VI, by a modern specialist. Bibliography.

Ullmann, Walter. *The History of the Great Schism: A Study in XIVth Ecclesiastical History*. 1948. Reprint. Hamden, Conn.: Archon Books, 1972. Study of the intricate implications of this fundamental episode in the history of occidental Christianity, in which Urban played an important part.

—*Frank La Brasca*

SEE ALSO: Alexander VI; Cesare Borgia; Clement VII; Leo X.

VOLKERT VAN DER GRAAF
Dutch animal rights activist

BORN: July 9, 1969; Middelburg, Netherlands
MAJOR OFFENSES: Premeditated murder in the assassination of right-wing politician Pim Fortuyn, illegal weapons possession, and threatening a man's life
ACTIVE: May 6, 2002
LOCALE: Hilversum, Netherlands
SENTENCE: Eighteen years in prison

EARLY LIFE

Volkert van der Graaf (FOLK-urt fahn duhr KRAF) was the second child of a Dutch father and a British mother. In a 2000 interview with nonprofit organization Animal Freedom, he discussed being committed to animal rights from an early age. For example, participating at age fifteen in the rescue of seabirds following a major oil spill in Zeeland made an enormous impression on him. He was upset by the "slow and horrible way" that the birds died. While a student in environmental studies at the University of Wageningen, he was active in the Inter-University Coalition on Animal Use and a member of an activist animal rights group, but no evidence ties him to illegal activities.

In 1992, van der Graaf cofounded the Vereniging Milieu-Offensief (VMO, translated as environmental offensive), dedicated to fighting bioindustry using the law. With VMO, he challenged land developers before planning boards and brought charges against farmers who were violating environmental regulations. VMO's Web site claimed winning about two-thirds of more than two thousand legal cases.

CRIMINAL CAREER

The year before his murder of politician Pim Fortuyn, van der Graaf, his girlfriend, and their baby moved to Harderwijk, in the Dutch "Bible belt." No evidence suggests that he was particularly religious, although court-appointed psychiatrists characterized him as rigidly moralistic. After the murder, colleagues at the VMO described him as "overstressed" following his baby's birth but were otherwise unable to explain his act.

Speculation in the press suggested that van der Graaf was upset by Fortuyn's claim that he would lift bans on breeding animals for fur and by his contempt for environmental movements. Fortuyn had also recently added the head of the national pig farmers' association to his party's candidates. At VMO, van der Graaf had filed many complaints against this particular man.

On May 6, 2002, nine days before the national elections, van der Graaf shot Fortuyn to death as the politician left a radio interview. Polls suggested that Fortuyn was on track to become prime minister. Van der Graaf was arrested within minutes of the shooting, thanks to bystanders who alerted police by cell phone. He had the gun in his pocket at the time of the arrest. Evidence gathered by the police included a printout of Fortuyn's schedule from his party's Web site, maps of the media complex, and addresses of other ranking officials in the party. Although conspiracy theories abounded, including one tying van der Graaf to the terrorist group al-Qaeda, the police found no evidence to support such claims.

LEGAL ACTION AND OUTCOME

Van der Graaf initially refused to make any statement, but in November the public ministry announced that van der Graaf had confessed to the murder. Following a court-ordered, seven-week period of psychiatric observation, he was tried for premeditated murder, illegal weapons possession, and threatening a man's life. The trial took place in Amsterdam-Osdorp's high-security court known as the Bunker in early spring, 2003.

Psychiatric evaluation found van der Graaf fully competent to stand trial despite having obsessive-compulsive personality disorder. Van der Graaf confessed in court, saying he shot Fortuyn to defend Dutch Muslims from persecution. He equated Fortuyn's rise with that of Adolf Hitler in the 1930's but expressed remorse for taking a life.

He was convicted on all counts and sentenced to eighteen years in prison. Under Dutch law, he had to serve a minimum of twelve years. The prosecution appealed the sentence, requesting a life term, but on July 18, 2003, the court resentenced him to eighteen years, stating that the threat to democracy was not serious enough to justify lifelong imprisonment.

IMPACT

The Dutch have a long tradition of tolerance, consensus politics, coalition governments, and political stability. Pim Fortuyn was an outspoken, confrontational, anti-immigration, and conservative populist. The rapid rise of his political party and his subsequent assassination, the first in modern Dutch history, disrupted this political and social consensus. Fortuyn's influence brought concerns about immigration into public discussion. As a result, most Dutch political parties have taken a much tougher stance against immigration than before Fortuyn's murder at the hands of Volkert van der Graaf.

FURTHER READING
Amir, Abedi. *Political Establishment Parties: A Comparative Analysis*. London: Taylor & Francis, 2003. An examination of how extremist political parties, such as Fortuyn's Lijst, can rise in popularity and power in traditionally tolerant countries.

Andeweg, Rudy B., and Galen A. Irwin. *Governance and Politics of the Netherlands*. New York: Palgrave-Macmillan, 2005. An analysis of how the assassination of Fortuyn could happen in a country dedicated to political consensus and stability.

—*Rebecca Lovell Scott*

SEE ALSO: Roy Cohn; Byron Looper; Dan White.

BARTOLOMEO VANZETTI
Italian anarchist

BORN: June 11, 1888; Villafaletto, Italy
DIED: August 23, 1927; Boston, Massachusetts
MAJOR OFFENSES: Robbery and murder
ACTIVE: April 15, 1920
LOCALE: South Braintree, Massachusetts
SENTENCE: Death

EARLY LIFE
Bartolomeo Vanzetti (bahr-toh-loh-MAY-oh vahn-ZEHT-tee) was born in Villafaletto, Italy, in 1888. His father was a farmer and café owner. Vanzetti ended his primary school education at thirteen when he was apprenticed at a local pastry shop. Though skilled at this trade, Vanzetti was taken ill with pleurisy. During his convalescence, he read spiritual and philosophical works. After the death of his beloved mother, Vanzetti emigrated to the United States in 1908.

POLITICAL SYMPATHIES
In New York City, Vanzetti worked in restaurants. Moving to Massachusetts, he worked at a brick mill but soon left and took various other jobs. He went back to New York in 1909 and was employed as a pastry chef. He became disillusioned, as employers would summarily dismiss workers and then agencies would charge unreasonable fees for finding new work. At one point, unemployed for months, Vanzetti was forced to sleep outside. Eventually, he took a job as a laborer in Massachusetts. Vanzetti found this job attractive because it involved working outdoors, although he preferred to spend his time indoors reading political and philosophical works.

Vanzetti read many works on politics and especially on anarchism, a political philosophy popular during his generation. Immersing himself in local anarchist circles, Vanzetti made new friends. From 1913 to 1917, he lived and worked in Massachusetts among com-

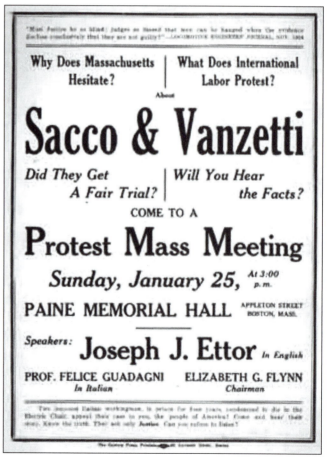

Protests were held in support of Sacco and Vanzetti. (Courtesy, Massachusetts Historical Society)

FROM THE DEATH HOUSE

On August 22, 1927, Bartolomeo Vanzetti wrote the following letter from Massachusetts State Prison on the day before he and Nicola Sacco were executed. The letter is addressed to lecturer and former Harvard professor H. W. L. Dana.

DEAR FRIEND DANA:

Rosa [Sacco's second wife] and my sister Liugi paid us a visit just now and told us of your letter to us, which they had forgotten home. They will bring it to us this afternoon, if they will come back. But they told us the contents of your letter, and I am writing now because it seems that nothing and no one is going to stop our execution after this midnight; so we may have no chance to see your letter.

Judge [Oliver Wendell] Holmes repelled our appeal on the ground that the State Supreme Court had passed on the case and he does not want to invade the State Court ground.

Yesterday, Judge [Louis D.] Brandeis repelled our appeal on the ground of personal reasons; to wit, because he or members of his family are favorably interested in our case, as demonstrated by the facts that after our arrest Rosa and her children went to live for a month in an empty house of Justice Brandeis in Dedham, Mass.

These two justices are the symbols of liberalism in the Federal Supreme Court and they turned us their shoulders.

Now our lawyers are presenting the appeal to justice [Harlan Fiske] Stone. Since the other Federal Supreme justices are reactionary, well, that will be a good ground on which to repel our appeal. So that it is coming to pass that some justices repel our appeal because they are friendly with us and the other justices repel our appeal because they are hostile to us, and through this elegant Forche Caudine, we are led straight to the electric chair. . . .

The Defense Committee, the Defense, our friends here . . . are working frantically day and night in a desperate effort to avoid our execution, and they fail second by

second and our execution appears always nearer and unavoidable. There are barely 12 hours to its moment, and we are lost—if we refuse to hope against reason.

And in our coffin will lay our friends' optimism and our pessimism. What I wish more than all in this last hour of agony is that our case and our fate may be understood in their real being and serve as a tremendous lesson to the forces of freedom—so that our suffering and death will not have been in vain.

I do not enter into particulars because I know you will learn of them before receiving this letter. But the situation appears to be in this moment as follows: All the Federal justices will repel our appeal and from hence the other few hours our fate will be completely in the hands of Governor [of Massachusetts Alvan T.] Fuller. To me this means—death. So much the better if I will be wrong.

So, dear friend and comrade Dana, I wish to thank you for all that you have done for Nicola, I, and for our families. My sister brought me your regards and informs me of your going to Italy and to our families. Please salute for us all the friends and comrades you will meet in Europe, and express to them what you know that we have in our hearts. And to you we send our extreme good-bye and brotherly embrace. Be brave and of good cheer, brother Dana.

Also for Nicola, we are yours,
NICOLA AND BARTOLOMEO

P.S. . . . I wish and hope you will lend your faculties in inserting our tragedy in the history under its real aspect and being.

Source: The Letters of Sacco and Vanzetti, edited by Marion D. Frankfurter and Gardner Jackson (New York: Viking Press, 1928).

rades who were convinced of the need to radically alter society. Although the United States and Italy were allied during World War I, Vanzetti and his friends believed that the war only promoted the interests of ruling elites. Faced with being drafted into the American military, Vanzetti, his friend Nicola Sacco, and a handful of others went to Mexico. Vanzetti eventually returned to Massachusetts, where he sold fish to the public until his arrest in 1920.

Vanzetti soon became entangled in one of the most infamous political trials in American history. Vanzetti and

Sacco were alleged to have murdered two shoe factory employees, paymaster F. A. Parmenter and company guard Alessandro Berardelli, in South Braintree, Massachusetts, on April 15, 1920. In addition, Vanzetti was also believed to have committed a separate attempted robbery on December 24, 1919.

LEGAL ACTION AND OUTCOME
Vanzetti and Sacco were arrested on May 5, 1920. Vanzetti was tried first for the attempted robbery and, despite many witnesses who testified to his innocence, was

found guilty and sentenced to prison. Shortly thereafter, Vanzetti and Sacco were brought before Judge Webster Thayer for the South Braintree offense. Both defendants were found guilty and sentenced to death.

However, because of Judge Thayer's obvious prejudice against the defendants and his known hostility toward immigrants, as well as the political radicalism of the defendants and contradicted prosecution testimony, the trial of Vanzetti and Sacco was met with national and international criticism. Writers and political leaders on virtually every continent criticized the defendants' conviction as a mockery of justice. Federal and state authorities received countless letters and telegrams in protest.

In 1925, a gang member admitted to the crime and declared Sacco and Vanzetti innocent. The Massachusetts judiciary ignored this admission. In response to heated criticism and protestations, Governor Alvan T. Fuller created an investigatory committee. Chaired by the president of Harvard University, A. Lawrence Lowell, the committee came to defend the governor's refusal to grant clemency. As a result, many American and international cities experienced protest demonstrations. Although the trial had been manifestly unfair and mounting evidence pointed to the guilt of others, the authorities disregarded all criticisms and the defendants' assertions of innocence and finally executed Sacco and Vanzetti on August 23, 1927.

IMPACT

The Vanzetti and Sacco criminal conviction was a significant event in United States and working-class history. The successful prosecution of Vanzetti and Sacco marks the final days of a once-formidable American anarchist movement. This trial also had other significant political and social dimensions, because prejudice against immigrants and political radicals permeated American society; many people understood that the moral quality of society and the American judicial system was also on trial. The larger issue was whether the search for justice would overcome the palpable antiradicalism and xenophobia of the age. The execution of the two Italian immigrants seemed to confirm it could not.

To many working-class persons, the case was simply a political execution that was to be expected from the forces of order. Many intellectuals, on the other hand, saw the trial as an attack on fundamental rights. Leading legal scholars, such as Harvard law professor and future Supreme Court justice Felix Frankfurter, criticized the conduct of police, the prejudice of the judge, the jury membership, the prosecution's evidence, and the impeached witness testimony.

The Vanzetti and Sacco trial remained controversial decades later. Many modern-day legal analysts conclude that though the men were innocent, they were victims of a judicial process corrupted by a xenophobia and exacerbated by antianarchist and anti-Italian bias. Some, however, contend that one or both of the defendants may indeed have been guilty. No studies to date have firmly established the guilt of either Vanzetti or his comrade Sacco. What is clear is that the conviction of Vanzetti and Sacco more likely resulted from their ethnicity and political radicalism than from the weight of evidence. Their execution came at a time when, paradoxically, the anarchism about which both men were so passionate no longer posed a threat to the forces that sought to extinguish its ideals by prosecuting its adherents.

FURTHER READING

Avrich, Paul. *Sacco and Vanzetti: The Anarchist Background.* Princeton, N.J.: Princeton University Press, 1991. This preeminent scholar gives a definitive assessment of the case and of the anarchist movement.

Binelli, Mark. *Sacco and Vanzetti Must Die!* Normal, Ill.: Dalkey Archive Press, 2006. The work presents an intriguing review of the controversy surrounding the case.

Feuerlicht, Roberta Strauss. *Justice Crucified: The Story of Sacco and Vanzetti.* New York: McGraw-Hill, 1977. The author presents a very readable assessment of the characters involved in the trial.

Frankfurter, Felix. *The Case of Sacco and Vanzetti: A Critical Analysis for Lawyers and Laymen.* Boston: Little, Brown, 1927. This indispensable work did much to reveal the trial's unfairness.

Topp, Michael, ed. *The Sacco and Vanzetti Case: A Brief History with Documents.* New York: Macmillan, 2005. This work offers varied views and essential documents concerning the case.

—*Pietro Lorenzini*

SEE ALSO: Emma Goldman; Nicola Sacco.

GETÚLIO VARGAS
Brazilian dictator (1930-1945, 1951-1954)

BORN: April 19, 1883; São Borja, Rio Grande do Sul, Brazil

DIED: August 24, 1954; Rio de Janeiro, Brazil

ALSO KNOWN AS: Father of the Poor; Father Getúlio Dornelles Vargas (full name)

CAUSE OF NOTORIETY: While Vargas's quasifascist dictatorship created some reforms that benefited Brazil, it also supported a brutal secret police force and repressed free speech and other civil liberties.

ACTIVE: 1930-1945

LOCALE: Brazil

EARLY LIFE

Born in the southernmost state of Brazil, Getúlio Vargas (zhay-TOO-lee-oh VAR-gahs) was from a prosperous gaucho (cowboy) ranching family. He abandoned his early military career, finished law school in 1909, and became state attorney general in 1910. He rose through the Brazilian political ranks, always supporting the boss in power.

POLITICAL CAREER

In 1928 Vargas became governor of the state. In 1930 he ran for president as the Liberal Alliance candidate. When the other candidate won, Vargas led an army to Rio de Janeiro to depose the ruling president, Washington Pereira, to prevent him from inaugurating the president-elect, Julio Prestes. Vargas assumed the presidency of a provisional government.

In 1933 Vargas was elected to a four-year term as president of Brazil, and in 1934 he initiated a new constitution. An attempt by the Communist Party to take control of the country led Vargas to declare a state of emergency and assume autocratic powers. Vargas's term of office was due to end in 1937; Brazilian law prohibited him from succeeding himself. Loath to surrender power, he used the fear of communism to carry out a coup d'état and create a new government called the Estado Novo (new state), modeled after the similarly named government of António de Oliveira Salazar, dictator of Portugal, and borrowing elements of European fascism.

The Estado Novo favored the ruling oligarchies but drew support from urban workers by enacting a minimum wage law and codifying all labor reforms into a single labor act. Vargas also enacted reforms in social security and granted women the right to vote. He initiated economic reforms that benefited Brazil. He also abolished all political parties, developed a centralized police force, jailed political dissidents, and encouraged a sense of nationalism that included anti-Semitism. The press was censured, and the secret police repressed dissidents through torture and assassination.

During World War II, despite his fascist tendencies and his early notion of sending troops to support Adolf Hitler, Vargas supported the Allies. His term of power was to end in 1943, but he used the war as a rationale for continuing in office, stating that elections would be held when possible. He made the same claim in 1944. When he showed no intention of stepping down from the presidency, he was overthrown in a coup d'état in October, 1945.

Vargas, who had maintained widespread popular support, was freely elected president in 1950. However, he no longer had the autocratic power of his Estado Novo days. He again created some economic reforms, focusing on energy resources, creating the Brazilian Petroleum Corporation in 1953 and beginning the Brazilian Electric Power Company. Inflation, however, was rampant, and Vargas no longer had the support of the military, which demanded that he resign. On August 24, 1954, Vargas wrote a lengthy suicide note to the people of Brazil, suggesting that his was a sacrifice for the nation. He then shot himself through the heart.

IMPACT

Getúlio Vargas strengthened the military, stimulated the economy, and promoted international trade and international relations. He accomplished some labor reforms, gave women suffrage, and encouraged a sense of Brazilian nationalism. However, he also repressed free speech and supported a brutal secret police. Every August Brazil sees memorial celebrations in honor of "Father Getúlio," friend of the poor.

FURTHER READING

Levine, Robert. *Father of the Poor? Vargas and His Era.* New York: Cambridge University Press, 1998. A narrative portrait of Vargas; includes translations of Vargas's diary and suicide note, a chronology, and a bibliographic essay.

Rose, R. S. *One of the Forgotten Things: Getúlio Vargas and Brazilian Social Control, 1930-1954.* Westport, Conn.: Greenwood Press, 2000. An effort to correct the "restricted memory" of Brazilians who honor Vargas each August 24 by reminding readers of the brutality and repressiveness of the Vargas regime.

Williams, Daryle. *Culture Wars in Brazil: The First*

Vargas Regime, 1930-1945. Durham, N.C.: Duke University Press, 2001. An investigation into the politics of culture and the state in the construction of a Brazilian identity.

—*Linda Ledford-Miller*

SEE ALSO: Francisco Franco; Adolf Hitler; Benito Mussolini; Augusto Pinochet Ugarte; Eva Perón; Juan Perón; António de Oliveira Salazar; Alfredo Stroessner; Jorge Rafael Videla.

HANK VAUGHAN
American outlaw and gunslinger

BORN: April 27, 1849; near Coburg, Oregon
DIED: June 15, 1893; Pendleton, Oregon
ALSO KNOWN AS: Henry Clay Vaughan (full name)
MAJOR OFFENSES: Cattle rustling, robbery, murder, and bigamy
ACTIVE: 1864-1893
LOCALE: Oregon, Idaho, Nevada, Arizona, and Washington

EARLY LIFE

Henry "Hank" Vaughan (vawn) was born April 27, 1849, in the southern Willamette Valley, Oregon. Both his parents were settlers who traveled the Oregon Trail. Hank was one of seven children and spent most of his time helping on the family farm. In 1861, the Vaughan family left the Willamette Valley, moving to The Dalles in eastern Oregon along the Columbia River. Several years later, the family moved to Canyon City, Oregon, in the hope of profiting by starting a ranch that sold horses and beef to gold miners moving into the region. Vaughan shed the innocence of youth early: By age fifteen, he was facing his first criminal charge of murder.

CRIMINAL CAREER

In 1864, Vaughan had a drunken argument with a man who refused to pay fees to Vaughan for tending his horse. Vaughan pulled a revolver and shot the man through the head, killing him. Vaughan was arrested, and while out on bail he tracked down and shot the man who had filed murder charges against him. Vaughan was rearrested, but his family convinced a judge to allow him to enlist in the army rather than face trial and punishment. Vaughan was a problem recruit and dishonorably discharged after six weeks.

In early 1865, Vaughan teamed with Dick Burton and headed to the Idaho goldfields. While traveling through Umatilla County, Oregon, the two men rustled horses and were pursued by a sheriff's posse. The posse caught the rustlers camping and a shoot-out ensued. Burton was killed, and Vaughan killed a deputy and wounded the sheriff. The sheriff was able to wound Vaughan in the arm, slowing Vaughan's escape; he was quickly captured.

LEGAL ACTION AND OUTCOME

Vaughan was tried in Baker County, Oregon, on charges of murder and horse theft, found guilty, and sentenced to life in prison at hard labor. A lynch mob marched on the jail, thinking Vaughan got off easy. Vaughan was immediately transported to the penitentiary in Portland and six months later moved to the penitentiary in Salem.

The Salem prison was under construction, and inmates were made to build their own facility. During his incarceration, Vaughan learned blacksmithing, carpentry, and bricklaying, as well as how to read and write. In 1870, Vaughan was pardoned for good behavior.

CATTLE RUSTLING

Within months of his release, Vaughan established an operation near Toano, Nevada, where he made enough money, between rustling and blacksmithing, to buy land near Elko, Nevada. In 1875, he married Lois McCarty, sister of the outlaw McCarty brothers. The Vaughans had two sons, but Lois soon left Hank, taking the boys with her. Shortly after Lois left, Hank was shot in the head during a gunfight in Arizona. After this injury, Vaughan moved to Pendleton, Oregon, and married Louisa Ditty, despite not being divorced from his first wife.

Vaughan set up rustling operations on the Umatilla Indian Reservation and at nearby Spokane Falls; both locations were along cattle-drive routes. Because Vaughan was never home and was a philanderer, Louisa soon left him. In 1881, Vaughan arrived in Prineville, Oregon, a town whose history of frontier violence and lawlessness was worse than that of Dodge City, Kansas, or Tombstone, Arizona. The local Prineville cattlemen's association established a vigilante posse to hunt down rustlers, and Vaughan wanted to see how this might affect his operations. He approached a veteran gunslinger from New Mexico, Charlie Long, who had been hired as a ranch boss and "troubleshooter" by the vigilante posse. The two men played cards until Long refused a drink bought by Vaughan. Insulting words escalated into one of the most famous gunfights in American history. Long shot Vaughan in the head and twice in the chest; Vaughan hit Long four times in the chest. Unbelievably, both men survived.

After recovering from his wounds, Vaughan met the widow Martha Robie. Robie was relatively wealthy and owned a large tract of land on the Umatilla Reservation. Vaughan married her, though at the time he was not divorced from either of his previous wives. The couple established a successful farming operation, but Vaughan continued to rustle livestock using reservation natives and his former brothers-in-law as confederates.

In 1886, Vaughan humiliated a man by shooting at his feet to make him "dance." The man ambushed Vaughan the next day and seriously wounded him in the right arm. During his recovery, Vaughan learned to draw and shoot left-handed and spent much of his time gambling. In Centerville, Washington, Vaughan severely beat a man he accused of cheating and was arrested. Before his trial, Vaughan bribed the principal witness into not testifying. Later that year, he and Martha sold their farm for a profit and spent time traveling the country, seeking out spas and hot springs to help speed Vaughan's recovery.

On June 2, 1893—while Vaughan was drunk and galloping his horse up and down Main Street in Pendleton, Oregon, and shooting out streetlights—his horse stumbled on a concrete sidewalk. Vaughan was thrown headfirst onto the road, fracturing his skull. He survived two weeks in a coma before dying.

LEGAL ACTION AND OUTCOME

Although Vaughan engaged in cattle rustling, robbery, and murder, as well as bigamy, during his storied career, he managed to avoid legal punishment with the exception of the five years he served on his life sentence for murder.

IMPACT

Hank Vaughan was a man whose quick temper and antisocial attitudes typify legendary desperadoes of the Old West. Vaughan seemed to take everything in life as a personal challenge: He had a disregard for any law he found

---

THE WORSE FOR LIQUOR

Contemporary descriptions of Hank Vaughan, such as this newspaper account from the December 18, 1922, issue of the Wenatchee, Washington, Daily World, *suggest he was personable enough until he got riled or drunk:*

He weighed about 165 pounds, erect and straight as an Indian and had peculiar blue gray eyes that held you in a grip as it were, when thinking seriously in contemplation or after imbibing a few drinks. He wore his hair and whiskers well groomed. They were of a brown, red cast. A broad rim hat, fashioned after the cowboy's style, high heeled boots, a well fitting suit of clothes of the Prince Albert style and invariably of a snuff colored cloth composed his makeup. When Vaughan was not under the influence of liquor he was possessed of not an ungentlemanly or uncourteous manner. He was quite charitable, and usually pleasant. He was an interesting talker, and an entertainer, as a witty story teller, a quick thinker and judge of human nature. He did not seem to know the word fear and when in a state of intoxication or in a bad mood nothing daunted him.

---

personally troublesome—whether it involved marriage, rustling, or murder—and seemed to see no difference between his legitimate and illegal operations. Vaughan took pride in aggressively taking advantage of the lawless period of the early Pacific Northwest. However, stories abound that, when not drunk, Vaughan was a friendly, outgoing man who willingly helped neighbors and local law enforcement. Tales of Vaughan riding horses into saloons and shooting up towns, his unmatched quick-draw speed, his rustling activities, and his survival of thirteen bullet wounds made him a mythic figure in the Pacific Northwest.

FURTHER READING

Ontko, Gale. *Thunder over the Ochoco: And, The Juniper Trees Bore Fruit*. Bend, Oreg.: Maverick, 1999. The fifth volume in a series documenting the history and settlement of Oregon, with one of the best accounts of the criminal activities of Vaughan.

Skovlin, Jon M. *Hank Vaughan, 1849-1893: A Hell-Raising Horse Trader of Bunchgrass Territory*. Cove, Oreg.: Reflections, 1996. Well-documented and illustrated biography of Vaughan, albeit slightly romanticized.

_____. *In Pursuit of the McCartys*. Cove, Oreg.: Reflections, 2001. A historical biography of the McCartys, a family that produced three outlaw sons and were allies and in-laws of Hank Vaughan during the period of his criminal activities.

—*Randall L. Milstein*

SEE ALSO: Apache Kid; Tom Bell; William H. Bonney; Curly Bill Brocius; Butch Cassidy; Bob Dalton; Emmett Dalton; Bill Doolin; John Wesley Hardin; Doc Holliday; Jesse James; Tom Ketchum; Harry Longabaugh; Bill Longley; Joaquín Murieta; Johnny Ringo; Belle Starr; Henry Starr; Cole Younger.

VEERAPPAN
Indian poacher and gangster

BORN: January 18, 1952; Gopinatham Village, Karnataka, India
DIED: October 18, 2004; Dharmapuri, India
ALSO KNOWN AS: Tamil Bandit; Koose Muniswamy Veerappa Gounder (birth name); Vīrappan; Molakai
MAJOR OFFENSES: Elephant poaching, illegal trading in ivory and sandalwood, kidnapping, and murder
ACTIVE: Late 1960's-2004
LOCALE: Southern India

EARLY LIFE

Veerappan (VUR-ah-pan), which translates as "brave," was born Koose Muniswamy Veerappa Gounder in the village of Gopinatham in Karnataka, India. He came from a family of modest cattle grazers and was nicknamed Molakai for much of his youth and adolescence. By age eighteen, Veerappan had joined a gang of elephant poachers, and he was reported to have killed his first elephant at fourteen. He quickly became a strong force in the ivory- and sandalwood-smuggling trades by killing off rival gang members and smugglers. In 1991, Veerappan married Muthulaakshmi, a shepherdess, and the couple had three daughters: Yuvarania, Prabha, and a third who died in infancy in 1993.

CRIMINAL CAREER

Veerappan lived, and plotted his activities, in undisclosed locations within the Biligirirangan and Malai Mahadeswara Hills, and the forests of Sathyamangalam and Gundiyal, which border the southern state regions of Karnataka, Tamil Nadu, and Kerala. By the late 1960's, he had amassed a gang of forty men who either killed or incorporated other elephant poachers. Veerappan and his gang developed an international ivory and sandalwood ring that has been accused of smuggling some $2.6 million in ivory and $22 million in sandalwood.

Veerappan's activities escalated from poaching and smuggling to kidnapping and murder. He was accused of committing more than 124 murders throughout his career. For the most part, his victims were police officers, forest service officials, informants, or people thought to be informants. Veerappan was arrested in 1986 but escaped before he was formally charged and brought to trial. It is alleged that he bribed a police officer with two thousand dollars. During his escape, he killed four policemen and a forest official while they were sleeping.

In addition, Veerappan kidnapped government officials. He beheaded Karnataka deputy conservator of forests Srinivas in revenge for his sister Mari's suicide in 1990. In 1993 he blew up a bus, killing twenty-two passengers, including police and civilians. This was followed by the murder of a police officer in 1996 as revenge for his brother Arjunan, who committed suicide while being held in police custody. Veerappan kidnapped the former Karnataka state minister H. Nagappa, who was later found dead in the forest in 2002. Veerappan also kidnapped people of celebrity, including one of India's most famous actors, Rajkumar, whom he held for ransom for 109 days in 2000. From the 1980's until his death in 2004, Veerappan kidnapped more than fourteen forest officials, killing at least two of them, and killed at least twenty-seven policemen, along with countless rival gang members and informants.

LEGAL ACTION AND OUTCOME

By 2000 police were creating a special task force to apprehend Veerappan and put an end to his reign of terror. The task force cultivated informants by posing as prisoners and talking to Veerappan's former associates in prisons, as well as placing Veerappan's family members under surveillance. Members of the force were planted as operatives within Veerappan's gang and, over time, learned to think like their target. By 2004, the task force was able to influence Veerappan through the use of such moles.

Upon learning of severe cataracts in his left eye,

Veerappan was convinced by moles to leave the forest and seek treatment. The task force, monitoring his movements, prevented his vehicle from continuing its course. When asked to surrender, Veerappan started a gun battle in which he and three of his associates were killed.

IMPACT

Some reports state that Veerappan killed up to two thousand elephants throughout his criminal career; his biographer Sunaad Raghuram maintains the number is closer to two hundred.

Veerappan had been one of India's most wanted bandits. There were estimates of bounties on Veerappan's head that topped $1.1 million. It is also unofficially estimated that during the decade of hunting Veerappan, the government spent the equivalent of millions of dollars in the attempt to capture him.

After Veerappan's death, commissions were developed to investigate not only the police's involvement in the gang leader's death but also human rights violation charges that were levied against the police force concerning the way in which police questioned and allegedly tortured witnesses.

Veerappan played the role of a modern-day Robin Hood to the villagers of Gopinatham. He had an arrangement with the villagers in which he would pay them well for services and necessities, such as food and clothing for his gang, and they would keep him apprised of all police activity. The villagers agreed to this arrangement, many speculate, out of fear. Veerappan would brutally harm anyone he considered an informer or those who did not abide by his wishes.

Veerappan's criminal career, spanning decades, was so extraordinary that it held India's imagination during his life and has continued to intrigue the country after his death. Although he kept communities in fear, thousands turned out for his funeral, and more were turned away. Questions surrounding his death—including the rumor that he was actually killed not by police but by one of his own men (at his request) and that he was not killed at all but committed suicide—continue to fascinate India. A film directed by Ram Gopal Varma, *Let's Kill Veerappan* (previously titled *Let's Catch Veerappan*), was in production as of 2006.

Veerappan. (AP/Wide World Photos)

FURTHER READING

Raghuram, Sunaad. *Veerappan: India's Most Wanted Man.* St. Paul, Minn.: Ecco, 2002. An unbiased account of Veerappan's criminal career and his battles with the law. Raghuram presents a factual biography without romanticizing the life of his subject. Examines Veerappan's forest living conditions and theorizes about why the bandit was so difficult to catch.

_____. *Veerappan: The Untold Story.* New York: Viking, 2001. Offers well-researched information on Veerappan's activities in the wild and helps explain why he remained at large for decades.

Sharma, Ravi. "The End of Veerappan." *Frontline* 21, no. 23 (November 6, 2004). A detailed account of the special task force and Veerappan's last days.

—*Sara Vidar*

SEE ALSO: Phoolan Devi.

HENDRIK FRENSCH VERWOERD
Prime minister of South Africa (1958-1966)

BORN: September 8, 1901; Weesp, near Amsterdam, the Netherlands

DIED: September 6, 1966; Cape Town, South Africa

CAUSE OF NOTORIETY: Verwoerd, as editor of the Afrikaner newspaper *Die Transvaler*, took a pro-Nazi position during World War II. Later, as prime minister of the National Party government, he energetically implemented apartheid and Bantustan policies, pulling South Africa out of the British Commonwealth in the face of mounting international criticism.

ACTIVE: 1958-1966

LOCALE: Union of South Africa (now Republic of South Africa)

EARLY LIFE

The son of Dutch Reformed Church evangelist and businessman Wilhelmus Johannes Verwoerd and his wife, Anje Strik, Hendrik Frensch Verwoerd (HEHN-drihk frehnsh fehr-VEWRT) was taken from the Netherlands to join the Afrikaner community in South Africa at the age of two. He proved to be exceptionally gifted academically, rising rapidly through the University of Stellenbosch, which he entered in 1919. He eventually earned a B.A. degree in 1921, a master's degree in 1922, and a doctorate in psychology and philosophy in 1924. The following year, he took post-doctoral courses in Germany following an offer to study at Oxford—he had an aversion to British education and institutions. While in Germany, Verwoerd attended universities at Hamburg, Leipzig, and Berlin and likely made contact with supporters of Adolf Hitler's Nazi movement during this period. Nazi ideology may have influenced Verwoerd's later thinking on racial policy in South Africa. At Hamburg, he married Betsie Shoeman, an Afrikaner student whom he had met years earlier at Stellenbosch.

POLITICAL CAREER

Returning to South Africa in 1927, Verwoerd joined the faculty at the University of Stellenbosch, where his rise again proved meteoric. He was appointed to the chair of applied psychology and eventually assumed a professorship in sociology and social work. When Jewish refugees from Nazi Germany began to apply for asylum in South Africa, Verwoerd conspicuously spearheaded a protest among certain university faculty members to oppose their admittance into the country.

Verwoerd left academia in 1937 to become founder and chief editor of the Afrikaner newspaper *Die Transvaler*. Verwoerd's publication became noteworthy for its extreme views on race, and it also became an organ for white supremacy, consistently espousing anti-Semitic, anti-British, and pro-Nazi ideas. Verwoerd came afoul of the authorities for his opposition to South Africa's entry into World War II on the Allied side. Politically, he became increasingly identified with the more fanatically racist elements within Daniel François Malan's mainly Afrikaner National Party.

Though he lost the race for a seat in the South African legislative assembly during the 1948 elections, Malan's party swept into power, and Verwoerd was appointed to the Senate. He received the cabinet post of minister for native affairs and began planning and pressing for a

Hendrik Verwoerd. (AP/Wide World Photos)

"Bantustan" policy through the Native Laws Amendment Act of 1952. Under this arrangement, Black Africans were to be moved out of urban areas and into specially assigned tribal "homelands," or "Bantustans," where they would develop independently of the white population in South Africa and eventually be granted separate statehood. Verwoerd became even more influential under the ministry of Johannes Gerhardus Strijdom, who succeeded Malan, serving from 1954 to 1958.

Upon Strijdom's death in 1958, Verwoerd became prime minister and zealously promoted his ideas on apartheid and Bantustan creation. On January 20, 1960, annoyed by British criticism of apartheid, Verwoerd announced a referendum on the question of the Union of South Africa becoming a republic and severing its ties with the British Commonwealth. On March 21, 1960, at Sharpeville, a crowd protesting apartheid was fired on by police; sixty-nine people were killed. The Sharpeville Massacre, while triggering a wave of international condemnation, only served to make Verwoerd adhere to his course all the more rigidly. On April 16, 1960, in Johannesburg, a farmer named David Pratt fired two shots in Verwoerd's face. The prime minister recovered and survived this assassination attempt.

On October 5, 1960, a well-managed referendum made South Africa a republic. This was officially proclaimed on May 31, 1961, and Verwoerd announced the expected break with the Commonwealth. Increasing internal protests were met with more vigorous countermeasures; among those arrested and eventually sentenced to life imprisonment during the crackdown was African National Congress leader Nelson Mandela, who would not be released until 1990.

Long before that, however, Verwoerd fell victim to a second assassination attempt. On September 6, 1966, at the legislative assembly room in Cape Town, a demented parliamentary messenger named Dimitri Tsafendas, claiming to be acting on the commands of a large tapeworm in his stomach, stabbed the prime minister to death while he sat waiting to make a speech.

IMPACT

If Hendrik Frensch Verwoerd did not originate apartheid in South Africa, he nonetheless wholeheartedly endorsed it and gave it an edge and an inflexibility that would spawn international isolation for his nation. He also helped usher in a long and vicious spiral of protest and repression that would not subside until the release of Nelson Mandela and his subsequent election to the South African presidency in 1994.

FURTHER READING

Clark, Nancy L., and William H. Worger. *South Africa: The Rise and Fall of Apartheid*. New York: Pearson Longman, 2004. Attributes to Verwoerd the sharpest definition and the most rigorous legal application of the apartheid doctine.

Denoon, Donald, with Balam Nyeko and J. B. Webster. *Southern Africa Since 1800*. New York: Praeger, 1973. This study takes in a broad perspective and somewhat downplays the significance of apartheid, and thus the importance of Verwoerd's ministry, in the larger context.

Lacour-Gayet, Robert. *A History of South Africa*. Translated by Stephen Hardman. London: Cassell, 1977. An unconventional characterization of Verwoerd, who seems to be depicted more as a misdirected idealist than as a doctrinaire racist.

Sparks, Allister. *The Mind of South Africa*. New York: Ballantine Books, 1990. Details apartheid's historical and intellectual basis and its conflict with the rising movements for decolonialization and racial equality.

Thompson, Leonard. *A History of South Africa*. New Haven, Conn.: Yale University Press, 1995. Contains a very detailed but quite comprehensible description of the Bantustan policy and the rationale put forward by Verwoerd and his party in their support of this particular initiative.

—*Raymond Pierre Hylton*

SEE ALSO: Eugene de Kock; Winnie Mandela.

JORGE RAFAEL VIDELA
President of Argentina (1976-1981)

BORN: August 2, 1925; Mercedes, Buenos Aires
Province, Argentina

MAJOR OFFENSES: Homicide, deprivation of liberty,
torture, and kidnapping

ACTIVE: 1976-1983

LOCALE: Argentina

SENTENCE: Life in prison, then pardoned; held under
house arrest for his role in kidnapping infants of
"subversives" and making them available for
adoption to military families

EARLY LIFE

Jorge Rafael Videla (HOR-hay rah-fah-EHL vee-DEH-
lah) was born into a military family on August 2, 1925, in
the province of Buenos Aires. At the age of sixteen, he
entered the prestigious National Military College, where
he later served as an instructor and was popular with his
students. He served in a variety of posts in his early career, including time in the Fourteenth Infantry Regiment
and the Motorized Army Regiment, as an adviser in the
Argentine embassy in the United States, and as a member
of the Inter-American Defense Board. By the early
1970's, Videla had been promoted to brigadier general
and was made head of the Argentine army.

POLITICAL CAREER

Much of Videla's career corresponded with the political,
economic, and social crises of Cold War-era Argentina.
During his career, the military overthrew elected civilian
presidents in 1955, 1962, and 1966, which provoked
growing opposition from student activists, labor unions,
and armed Marxist rebels. In 1973, the aging Juan Perón
(who was overthrown in 1955) returned to the presidency, only to die the next year. His vice president and
third wife, Isabel Perón, then became president. As the
violence continued to escalate, Isabel secretly ordered
the military to annihilate armed rebels throughout the
country. In August of 1975, she appointed General
Videla as commander in chief of the army, and he declared that much blood would need to be spilled in order
to cleanse the nation.

On March 24, 1976, the armed forces overthrew
Isabel Perón, established a three-man junta with General
Videla as president, and began "the process of national
reorganization." Many Argentines welcomed Videla's
coup, including the famed writer Jorge Luis Borges, who
was grateful that true "gentlemen" were finally govern-

ing the country. The junta suspended all political activity
while pledging to observe ethics and human rights. Subversives, however, were not considered authentic Argentines and did not merit rights, and armed groups were
hunted down. However, people with subversive ideas,
including union leaders, student activists, and many intellectuals, were also considered threats to the nation.
Soldiers and policemen kidnapped people off the street
or in late-night raids, blindfolded them, and took them to
secret detention centers where beatings, torture, rape,
and death awaited. Relatives could find no information
about the whereabouts of their "disappeared" loved ones.
In reality, the military was disposing of thousands of victims in mass graves, while others were drugged, taken up
in airplanes, and hurled into the sea. More than twelve
thousand Argentines were killed, although some analysts put estimates much higher.

Videla presided over the most intense period of repression. However, chronic economic problems during
his regime led to the removal of Videla from the presidency in 1981, and he was not a part of the junta that led
Argentina into its disastrous war with Great Britain over
the Malvinas, or Falkland, Islands in 1982. Disgraced,
the military called for civilian elections. The military declared amnesty for all participants in the war against sub-
version before transferring power to the newly elected civilian president, Raúl Alfonsín, in 1983.

LEGAL ACTION AND OUTCOME

Days after taking office, Alfonsín ordered the trial of
Videla and the other junta members for homicide, deprivation of liberty, and torture. The new congress also
overturned the military's amnesty decree. Alfonsín
formed the National Commission on the Disappeared
(CONADEP) to investigate military crimes and to provide evidence for the trials. The trials began on April 22,
1985, and lasted until December. Using the massive
amounts of evidence gathered by CONADEP, the judges
found that although junta members did not themselves
engage in torture and murder, they were responsible for
the clear pattern of such behavior that occurred under
their supervision. Nevertheless, different levels of guilt
were assigned according to level of involvement. Of the
nine junta leaders tried, General Videla and Admiral
Emilio Eduardo Massera received life sentences. Three
others received lesser sentences, and four were acquitted.

IMPACT

The trial and conviction of Jorge Rafael Videla and other commanders provided a catharsis for many Argentines and demonstrated that no government is above the law. However, the verdicts were less satisfactory for many and showed the difficulty that countries often have in moving forward after violent dictatorships. After convicting the junta leaders, Alfonsín's government walked a very delicate line between demands by human rights groups and much of the populace to prosecute all who had committed atrocities, and the need for the country to bury its past. Even as additional trials proceeded, various military rebellions erupted after 1987 as disgruntled officers tried to stop the trials and restore dignity to the armed forces. Those rebellions led Alfonsín's government to enact a statute of limitations on prosecutions, as well as a "due obedience" decree that absolved lower officers from prosecution.

Tensions still simmered when Carlos Saúl Menem was elected president in 1989. A victim of military repression himself as a Peronist governor in the 1970's, Menem decided that he had the moral authority to heal the country's wounds by pardoning the convicted military commanders, which he did in 1989 and 1990. Videla felt vindicated. However, the pardoning of Videla and the others outraged many in Argentina and around the world; under increasing pressure, Videla was rearrested in 1998 under different charges: kidnapping the infants of disappeared individuals, children who were then given through adoption to military families or friends. An ailing Videla remained under house arrest in Argentina into the twenty-first century.

FURTHER READING

Argentine National Commission on the Disappeared. *Nunca Más*. New York: Farrar, Straus, Giroux, 1986. Selections from the CONADEP report, including a useful introduction and graphic testimony from witnesses regarding their treatment by the military. In Spanish.

Feitlowitz, Marguerite. *A Lexicon of Terror: Argentina and the Legacies of Torture*. New York: Oxford University Press, 1998. A gripping account of the attitudes of the military and the horrors it committed.

Seoane, Maria. *El Dictador: La historia secreta y pública de Jorge Rafael Videla*. Buenos Aires: Editorial Sudamericana, 2001. A comprehensive history of Videla's career, with documents. In Spanish.

—*Jeffrey M. Shumway*

SEE ALSO: Juan Perón.

EUGÈNE FRANÇOIS VIDOCQ
French bandit

BORN: July 23 or 24, 1775; Arras, France
DIED: May 11, 1857; Paris, France
ALSO KNOWN AS: Captain Rousseau
MAJOR OFFENSES: Theft, assault, forgery, fraud, and smuggling
ACTIVE: 1795-1843
LOCALE: France, Belgium, England, and the Netherlands
SENTENCE: Three months in jail for assault; eight years in the galleys for forgery; sixteen years in the galleys for failure to produce identification; five years in prison and a fine of three thousand francs for fraud

EARLY LIFE

Eugène François Vidocq (yew-zhehn frahn-swah vee-dok) was born to a respected baker who supplied bread to the town inns at Arras, France. As a youth, Vidocq excelled in the Franciscan school, and by befriending soldiers he learned to fence—and to steal. After having tricked his mother so he could steal the week's earnings, he knew he could not return home. His goal was to see the New World, but a pretty actress used her wiles to rob him. Penniless, he joined the royalist regiment, where he was constantly beaten. He managed to achieve the rank of corporal, but after hitting a sergeant major Vidocq deserted the army to avoid death.

In Arras, Vidocq saved two noblewomen from the guillotine and was nearly guillotined himself. A family friend arranged for Vidocq to wed his daughter, but when Vidocq caught her being unfaithful he left for Belgium under the assumed name of Captain Rousseau. Once recognized, he escaped to Paris, where he enjoyed the company of beautiful women, supporting them through his thievery.

CRIMINAL AND POLITICAL CAREER

A master of disguise, Vidocq on several occasions was arrested, sentenced, and imprisoned, but he always escaped. One unforgettable incident involved his forging a pardon for a father who had stolen food for his family. Vidocq was caught but escaped. Smuggling was his next adventure, but he was arrested for not having proper identification papers. Sentenced to eight years in the galleys, he escaped by filing through his chains and donning a sailor's uniform. Captured again and sent to Toulon to the galleys, he paid a guard to allow him to escape. Betrayed by robbers, Vidocq was sentenced to the galleys for life.

Luck appeared in the person of the Lyon police chief, who, recognizing Vidocq's great intelligence, offered him clemency in exchange for becoming a police informant. When Vidocq left Lyon, he had legitimate papers; he then worked in a dry-goods shop in Arras. His past caught up with him, however: He was recognized, and he fled to Rouen. The pattern of capture and escape continued.

Vidocq offered to become an informant for the Paris police, in which capacity he invented the technique of fingerprinting criminals. In 1815, King Louis XVIII appointed him to a high post in the Sûreté (the security police), where according to biographer John Philip Stead, he oversaw a staff of twelve former convicts and in 1817 made 811 arrests of assassins, thieves, fences, forgers, and swindlers.

Resigning his Sûreté post in the late 1820's or early 1830's, Vidocq went on to establish the world's first detective agency, the Bureau des Renseignements (Bureau of Information), to help poor people who had been swindled. His success created envy and a desire for revenge, leading to a police campaign against Vidocq's agency. While Vidocq was serving a sentence, his agency was ransacked. Upon his release, Vidocq slowly revived his business while enjoying elegant dinners and parties at private homes.

He prized his acquaintances with literary giants Victor Hugo, Théophile Gautier, and especially Honoré de Balzac. Vidocq also enjoyed the company of pretty girls but occasionally visited his wife at their country house. He closed the bureau he had founded and turned to writing novels. At seventy, Vidocq set out for England, where he arrived on March 24, 1845, after some near captures by police. In London he hoped to sell his inventions, write new memoirs, promote his ideas about manufacturing paper, and perhaps start a new information office. He never could set himself down to write more memoirs, but the sale of his inventions allowed him to return to France, where he spent Christmas with his wife in Saint Mandé. Upon his return to London, he was able to make a lucrative sale of some of his paintings but was surprised to read twice his own obituary, the first in a Paris journal and the second in London. His wife managed to correct the Paris paper.

In May, 1846, Vidocq went to the Brunswick Hotel to meet Prince Louis Napoleon Bonaparte, who was registered as the Count Arenenberg. Louis Napoleon had escaped from prison disguised as a laborer. King Louis-Philippe had incarcerated him for six years, and it was Vidocq who had given some escape plans to Louis Napoleon's brother's best friend. Shortly after that visit, Vidocq returned to France because of financial difficulties with his two properties, his wife's illness, and a lack of clients. When his wife died in 1847, Vidocq, though a constant adulterer, was truly saddened by the death of his loyal and faithful friend. He sold his properties and moved to an old house in the Marais district of Paris. At eighty years of age, Vidocq would move again in the Marais to number 2 rue Saint-Pierre-Popincourt, where he still courted the generous and willing ladies of the theater by promising to make each of them his heiress. He continued to serve as an agent for the police until an attack paralyzed him two weeks before he died.

LEGAL ACTION AND OUTCOME

Vidocq served or partially served a variety of sentences throughout his life: He was sentenced to the galleys multiple times. Charged on December 29, 1839, of swindling clients, corrupting government employees, and usurping governmental prerogatives, he was acquitted and released after spending two months in prison. In 1842, convicted of stealing and fraud, he was sentenced to five years in the Conciergerie. The court of appeals exonerated him in 1843.

IMPACT

Despite his notoriety as a criminal, Eugène François Vidocq became more famous for establishing the science of criminology and is now considered at least its nominal founder: He supposedly introduced not only fingerprinting but also advanced record-keeping, footprinting (through the use of plaster casts), and the use of indelible ink. He became the world's first modern detective and founder of its first detective agency, the Bureau des Renseignements.

Vidocq also inspired many great writers, including Victor Hugo, who based two of his fictional protagonists

(Jean Valjean and Inspector Javert) on him, and Honoré de Balzac, whose character Vautran in *Père Goriot* (1834-1835) was also modeled after Vidocq. He is considered to be the prototype for Edgar Allan Poe's Auguste Dupin and Sir Arthur Conan Doyle's Sherlock Holmes as well. The 1946 feature film *A Scandal in Paris*, directed by Douglas Sirk, purports to tell Vidocq's story.

FURTHER READING

Edwards, Samuel. *The Vidocq Dossier: The Story of the World's First Detective*. Boston: Houghton Mifflin, 1977. A factual and entertaining account of Vidocq's life as a criminal, a police informer, and inventor of the first dectective agency.

Morton, James. *The First Detective: The Life and Revolutionary Times of Eugène Vidocq, Criminal, Spy, and Private Eye*. London: Ebury Press, 2005. Entertainingly relates the story of Vidocq by reference to his memoirs as well as the authors and stories he inspired.

Vidocq, Eugène François. *Memoirs of Vidocq: Master of Crime*. 1935. Reprint. Oakland, Calif.: AK Press, 2003. Vidocq's autobiography, in which it is difficult to distinguish fact from fiction; anecdotes reveal the ingenuity of a master criminal.

—*Patricia J. Siegel*

SEE ALSO: Cartouche; Henri Charrière; Jacques Mesrine; Alexandre Stavisky.

PANCHO VILLA
Mexican bandit and revolutionary

BORN: June 5, 1878; Hacienda de Río Grande, San Juan del Río, Durango, Mexico
DIED: July 20, 1923; near Parral, Chihuahua, Mexico
ALSO KNOWN AS: Francisco Villa; Doroteo Arango (birth name)
CAUSE OF NOTORIETY: Although a hero to some for his role in the Mexican Revolution, Villa became notorious for his indiscriminate killings and for his invasion of the United States.
ACTIVE: 1910-1923
LOCALE: Northern Mexico and New Mexico

EARLY LIFE

The early life of Pancho Villa (PON-choh VEE-yah) is shrouded in mystery. Legends abound, some spread by Villa himself, but few details are known for certain. He was born Doroteo Arango to poor sharecroppers on a large estate in the Mexican state of Durango. In his teens, he ran off and joined a band of outlaws and became involved in robberies and assaults. He was arrested in 1901 and sentenced to serve in the army, which he deserted a year later.

After his desertion, he moved to the neighboring state of Chihuahua. To avoid the authorities, he changed his name to Francisco Villa but was usually referred to as Pancho (a common nickname for Francisco). He held some legitimate jobs over the next few years but did not give up crime entirely, and in 1910 he was being sought

Pancho Villa. (Library of Congress)

THE PUNITIVE EXPEDITION

On March 9, 1916, Pancho Villa led five hundred men in an attack on Columbus, New Mexico. The raid did not go well for him. Colonel Frank Tompkins of the U.S. Thirteenth Cavalry, initially surprised, managed to gather thirty-two men and fight back. He lost fourteen of his soldiers but killed an estimated seventy-five to one hundred of Villa's troops after pursuing them for eight hours. For his trouble, Villa's band made their getaway with only a few dollars and goods for all their looting.

However, Villa's men killed ten civilians and set Columbus on fire, leaving part of the town in smoking ruins. The raid caused panic along the American side of the border. To prevent further raids, President Woodrow Wilson sent Brigadier General John J. Pershing and a 4,800-man brigade, much of it cavalry, and began mobilization of 15,000 National Guardsmen. This military venture became known as the Punitive Expedition.

What ensued, however, would sound more like comic opera were lives not lost and much property destroyed. His forces assembled, Pershing went on the offensive. Within a month, however, his reconnaissance aircraft, Curtiss JN-2 "Jennies," had all crashed. His scouts misled him, while Villa's men kept the Mexican leader well informed of Pershing's movements. When Pershing headed into the desert, Villa circled behind and followed, obscured from the American column by the dust that their heavy armored vehicles raised. Once Pershing's forces were tricked into attacking Mexico's federal troops, while, according to legend, Villa watched in glee.

There were some modest successes. The most celebrated was a daring raid led by Lieutenant George S. Patton that killed three of Villa's men, including a top deputy. For the most part, however, those who saw the most success were the people on both sides of the border who supplied the U.S. Army: merchants, barkeepers, and brothel owners.

By the end of 1916, the pursuit had run out of momentum, and Pershing was having trouble with troop morale. The battle with the Mexican federal troops—known as the Carrizal Affair after the village nearby—briefly moved the countries closer to a border war, but in January, 1917, Pershing's forces were recalled. A much larger war for the United States loomed on the horizon in Europe.

Huerta staged a coup against Madero, leading to a new round of the revolution.

This time the revolutionary movement was led by Venustiano Carranza, the governor of the state of Coahuila. Returning from Texas, Villa took up arms on the side of Carranza and created a legendary military unit known as the División del Norte (the Division of the North).

Villa's forces won several notable victories and eventually took over the whole state of Chihuahua. Villa became governor of the state in December, 1913, but stepped down after a month to concentrate on the fight against Huerta, who was finally defeated in July, 1914.

After Huerta's defeat, a civil war broke out among the revolutionaries which lasted for more than five years and which was noted for its atrocities. During this period, Villa was involved in several unsavory incidents. Even before the civil war, Villa had committed some questionable acts. For instance, he expelled all Spaniards from Chihuahua on pain of death. He issued discriminatory orders against the Chinese. He invaded the British consulate in Chihuahua City and kidnapped a member of the wealthy Terrazas family in order to extort money. He or his henchman, Rodolfo Fierro, killed a British landowner in an argument. During the civil war, especially when things were going badly for his side, Villa would become enraged and order arbitrary executions. One time he had ninety women villagers shot after one of them protested the death of her husband.

THE RAID ON COLUMBUS

Villa had originally been pro-American and had enjoyed American support. However, the U.S. government eventually decided to support the other side in the Mexican Civil War. In response, Villa became almost blindly anti-American. He swore to kill as many Americans as he could, and in January, 1916, some of his men massacred a group of American mining engineers on a train at Santa Isabel.

---

by the authorities, first for cattle rustling and then for the murder of a police informant.

REVOLUTIONARY CAREER

In 1910, Villa entered politics for the first time, joining the movement led by the political reformer Francisco Madero against the dictatorship of Porfirio Díaz. Villa took part in several battles against government forces in Chihuahua and was instrumental in Madero's victory in 1911.

In 1912, Villa was imprisoned for desertion after clashing with Madero's army commander, General Victoriano Huerta. He escaped from prison in December, 1912, and fled to Texas, where he remained until General

In March, 1916, Villa led an attack on the New Mexico town of Columbus. Seventeen Americans died, and the American government sent an expeditionary force into Mexico under General John J. Pershing to hunt for Villa. The American force destroyed some of Villa's bands but could not find Villa himself. He eventually emerged from hiding and had some successes but committed further atrocities, which cost him popular support. Eventually he agreed to cease hostilities and went into retirement on an estate in Durango in 1920. He was assassinated in 1923 after threatening to raise men to fight again.

IMPACT

Pancho Villa inspired both adulation and hatred. Among radicals such as the left-wing journalist John Reed, he became a symbol of the romance of revolution. Others, however, saw him as a bandit who simply got caught up in the revolution or used the revolution for his own ends. He inspired numerous folk songs and many Hollywood movies, the earliest of which was *The Life of General Villa* (1914). Villa himself took part in it.

With his big, bristling moustache and his acts of daring, he seemed a romantic figure, and his supporters saw in him a true reformer interested in improving the lot of the poor. In some ways he was a forerunner of the widely celebrated Cuban revolutionary Che Guevara. He might also be seen as a forerunner of the anti-American terrorist Osama Bin Laden.

Several observers have commented on Villa's dualities. He could be generous and compassionate but also brutal and cruel. He seemed at times to be genuinely committed to opposing oppression but at other times simply to be interested in violence for its own sake. The dualities themselves may account for some of the fascination he still inspires.

FURTHER READING

Katz, Friedrich. *The Life and Times of Pancho Villa*. Stanford, Calif.: Stanford University Press, 1998. A massively detailed account of Villa's life and of the Mexican Revolution. Sympathetic to Villa, this work sees him as a genuine reformer.

Machado, Manuel A., Jr. *Centaur of the North: Francisco Villa, the Mexican Revolution, and Northern Mexico*. Austin, Tex.: Eakin Press, 1988. Short biography emphasizing Villa's atrocities. Provides details on Villa's anti-Spanish and anti-Chinese acts.

McLynn, Frank. *Villa and Zapata: A History of the Mexican Revolution*. New York: Carroll & Graf, 2001. Attempts to analyze Villa's complicated personality and also analyzes the socioeconomic forces in the revolution. Does not see him as a true reformer, but says he and Zapata were the heart and soul of the revolution.

Tuck, Jim. *Pancho Villa and John Reed: Two Faces of Romantic Revolution*. Tucson: University of Arizona Press, 1984. Sees both Villa and Reed as bringing dash and excitement to revolution.

—*Sheldon Goldfarb*

SEE ALSO: Osama Bin Laden; Porfirio Díaz; Che Guevara; Emiliano Zapata.

VLAD III THE IMPALER
Walachian prince (r. 1448, 1456-1462, 1476)

BORN: Late 1431; Sighisoara, Transylvania (now in
Romania)

DIED: December, 1476; near Bucharest, Walachia
(now in Romania)

ALSO KNOWN AS: Vlad Tepes; Vlad the Impaler; Vlad
Dracula; Vlad Tepesch; Vlad Tzepes

CAUSE OF NOTORIETY: Vlad the Impaler was known
for his sadistic cruelty, especially the mass
impalement of his enemies.

ACTIVE: 1456-1476

LOCALE: Walachia (now Romania)

EARLY LIFE

The father of Vlad (vlahd) III, Vlad II (r. 1436-1447), secured the throne of Walachia as a protégé of the Holy Roman Emperor Sigismund of Hungary. However, after the
emperor's death in 1437, Vlad II submitted to Ottoman
sultan Murad II (r. 1421-1444 and 1446-1451) and thereafter oscillated in his allegiance between Hungary and
the Ottomans. Hungary's emerging strongman, János
Hunyadi (1407-1456), profoundly mistrusted Vlad II
and replaced him with a rival in 1442. Vlad fled to Murad
for protection, and Murad restored him to power in 1443
but insisted that Vlad's two younger sons, Vlad III and
Radu II, remain Ottoman hostages. The younger Vlad inherited his nickname Dracul from his father, who was
also called Vlad II Dracul; "drac" in Romanian means
both dragon and devil.

Hunyadi, enraged by what he regarded as Vlad's
treachery, caused his death in 1447. Murad then placed
Prince Vlad (now Vlad III) on the Walachian throne in
October, 1448, as vaivode (military governor), but Vlad
III was expelled a month later and fled back to the sultan.
After further upheavals in Walachia, Vlad returned in
1456, swearing allegiance both to the Hungarian king
and to the sultan. By this time, Murad was dead and the
new sultan was Mehmed II (r. 1444-1446 and 1451-
1481), an energetic leader who had conquered Constantinople in 1453.

CAREER AS VAIVODE

In his midtwenties, Vlad III embarked upon his second
period of rule, which lasted for the next six years (1456-
1462), the period during which he acquired his reputation for monstrous cruelty. From one point of view,
Vlad's conduct during these years differed little from
that of other fifteenth century European rulers who

sought to consolidate their power over states torn by aristocratic factions. He sought to enhance the authority of
the ruler, to rein in the pretension of the boyars (nobles),
to elevate new men from the ranks of the nonnoble, to
strengthen the throne as the source of justice, and to
spend generously on military and ecclesiastical patronage. All this would have been praiseworthy had it not
been accompanied by manifestations of sadism on an un-
paralleled scale, with mass impalements as the preferred
form of retribution against his enemies, reflecting a personal delight in human suffering. His victims numbered
in the thousands.

Like his father, Vlad III oscillated between loyalty to
his Ottoman overlord and allegiance to Hungary. Eventually, Mehmed II resolved to punish him for his devastating raid into Ottoman Bulgaria. Mehmed crossed the
Danube in early June, 1462, with an enormous army
and accompanied by Vlad's younger brother, Radu the

Vlad III the Impaler.

Handsome, Vlad's designated replacement. The sultan marched on Tîrgovişte, which Vlad abandoned, and although Vlad subsequently launched a daring (if ineffectual) night attack upon the sultan's encampment, Mehmed continued into the foothills of the Transylvanian Alps before turning east toward the Danube delta. He invested Radu as the new vaivode and recrossed the Danube.

By mid-July, Mehmed was back in Edirne, this remarkable campaign to dethrone Vlad having taken little more than a month to complete. Overwhelmed by Ottoman might and abandoned by the boyars whom he had so savagely persecuted, Vlad fled westward to his aerie on the Argeş River, hotly pursued by Radu with a mixed force of Turks and Walachians, and crossed into southeastern Transylvania, where he submitted to the new Hungarian king Matthias I Corvinus (r. 1458-1490).

Matthias mistrusted Vlad and imprisoned him in Visegrád, although it may not have been an onerous captivity. Matthias himself was more focused on Vienna and Prague than the Ottoman borderlands, but the death of Radu in January, 1475, left a vacuum in Walachia. Matthias saw Vlad as the only possible candidate for the throne. Vlad was released from captivity, married into the powerful Hungarian Szilágyi family, and was required to abandon Orthodoxy for Roman Catholicism. Meanwhile, the Ottomans had appointed Besarab the Old to succeed the dead Radu.

Vlad had been a prisoner in Hungary since 1462, but now Matthias provided the troops with which Vlad could regain his throne. They crossed the frontier in summer, 1476, and on August 8, Vlad entered Tîrvogişte. On November 16 he entered Bucharest, and on November 26 he was invested for a third time as vaivode. Retribution soon followed. Vlad's supporters were attacked near Bucharest by a superior force of Turks, Walachians loyal to Besarab, and Vlad's boyar enemies. He was slaughtered during or after the battle, and his headless body was taken to the island-monastery of Snagov, where it was secretly buried.

IMPACT

Vlad III the Impaler's career would not have been different from that of other medieval Balkan tyrants and would soon have been forgotten but for a curious coincidence. His atrocities had been directed at, among others, the Saxon communities of Sibiu and Brasov, the two southernmost German settlements in Transylvania. From these, tales of Vlad's cruelty spread to Germany at the very time of the invention of the printing press. A pamphlet printed in Nuremberg in 1499 and another in Strasbourg in 1500 showed "Dracole" seated at a table eating his dinner as an executioner dismembers heads and limbs in front of him; in the background can be seen a forest of stakes with writhing bodies. Much later, the legend of the Walachian monster became conflated with the villain of Bram Stoker's *Dracula*, published in 1897, although Stoker's fictitious vampire was located not in Walachia but in northern Moldavia. Still later, Romanian nationalists in the twentieth century turned Vlad into a symbolic "freedom fighter" against the Turks, and in the twenty-first century, the state tourist agency exploited Vlad's residences as tourist sites.

FURTHER READING

Babinger, Franz. *Mehmed the Conqueror and His Times*. Princeton, N.J.: Princeton University Press, 1978. A definitive study, describing Vlad's campaigns from the Ottoman viewpoint.

Boia, Lucian. *Romania, Borderland of Europe*. London: Reaktion Books, 2001. Discusses the modern cult of Vlad the Impaler.

Heid, Joseph. *Hunyadi: Legend and Reality*. New York: Columbia University Press, 1985. Useful for information about Vlad's father and the general historical background.

McNally, Raymond T., and Radu Florescu. *In Search of Dracula*. Greenwich, Conn.: New York Graphic Society, 1972. A wide-ranging account that addresses the many bases for the Dracula legend.

Treplow, Kurt W. *Vlad III Dracula*. Oxford, England: Center for Romanian Studies, 2000. A newer study on both the history and the legend.

—*Gavin R. G. Hambly*

SEE ALSO: Elizabeth Báthory.

ANDREY ANDREYEVICH VLASOV
Soviet army general and Nazi collaborator

BORN: September 14, 1900; Lomakino, near Nizhny Novgorod, Russia

DIED: August 1, 1946; Moscow, Soviet Union (now in Russia)

ALSO KNOWN AS: Andrei Andreyevich Vlasov (full name); Andrey Volkhov

MAJOR OFFENSE: Treason

ACTIVE: July, 1942-May, 1945

LOCALE: Russian front during World War II

SENTENCE: Death by hanging

EARLY LIFE

Little is known about the early years of Andrey Andreyevich Vlasov (AN-dray an-DRAY-yuh-vich VLAS-ahv). He was the youngest son of a Byelorussian farmer who earned money on the side as a tailor. As such, Vlasov's father was the kind of prosperous middle-class farmer that Soviet leader Joseph Stalin identified as a kulak, a repressed group. Vlasov sought betterment through education, first as a student in a seminary and then in an agricultural college. Events of the Russian Civil War (1918-1922) forced the seminary to close and interrupted his agricultural studies. In 1919, Vlasov was drafted into the Red Army.

MILITARY CAREER

Throughout his Red Army career, Vlasov avoided politics and was a military technician; his career advanced in a steady, unspectacular manner. Between 1938 and 1939, he served as military adviser to Chiang Kai-shek's Chinese government and thus avoided Stalin's purges (the systematic political repression and persecution of Soviet citizens). Subsequent postings earned Vlasov the Order of Lenin for his ability to rebuild and renovate substandard units.

When Germany invaded Russia in 1941, Vlasov held corps and then army commands. His desperate defense near Kiev and last-minute breakout resulted in his promotion to command of the Twentieth Army near Moscow. Under Vlasov, this army played a significant role in the Russian counterattack and eventual German defeat.

Awarded the Order of the Red Banner for his actions, Vlasov was transferred to the Second Shock Army outside Leningrad, where he was ordered to break the siege. With too few troops and limited artillery, failure was inevitable. Stalin forbade retreat and doomed Vlasov's forces to encirclement and annihilation. Disillusioned, Vlasov was ready to surrender and denounce the Soviet purges and incompetence, as well as Stalin's criminal negligence.

Vlasov's fame in the Moscow battles made him an attractive catch for German propagandists. The most persuasive was Captain Wilfried Strik-Strikfeldt, Vlasov's German interpreter and confidant. German authorities sought to convince Vlasov to lead the anti-Stalinist Russians and dismantle the Soviet state.

From the beginning of World War II, thousands of angry and vengeful Russians saw the war as an opportunity to destroy the Stalinist system. After bloody fighting depleted many German units, German officers willingly incorporated Russian volunteers as auxiliaries in both combatant and noncombatant roles. Strik-Strikfeldt and others wanted to use Vlasov's name and reputation to spur Russian desertions and raise a vast "anti-Bolshevik army." Such a dream was antithetical to the racial ideology of Adolf Hitler, which denigrated Slavs and realized that any Russian state, communist or not, would naturally oppose German efforts at colonization in Russia.

Although opposed to the actual formation of a Russian anti-Bolshevik army, Hitler allowed Vlasov to write propaganda leaflets. Germany's dwindling troop strength in the fall of 1944 convinced Nazi official Heinrich Himmler to utilize the military power of a Russian anti-Bolshevik army. Himmler thus engineered the creation of the Committee for the Liberation of the Peoples of Russia (the Komitet Osvobozhdyeniya Narodov Rossi, known as the KONR), with Vlasov as its commander. Although more than one million Russians changed sides during the war, Himmler allowed the KONR to form only two divisions. Created too late to have an impact on the fighting, the KONR forces had little effect on the war's outcome. Vlasov and other defectors were either captured by the Russians or, after surrendering to the Western allies, transferred to Russia for trial.

LEGAL ACTION AND OUTCOME

Vlasov and high-ranking KONR officers were interrogated, tried, and sentenced to death for treason by Russian authorities and then hanged. The trials were typical Stalinist show trials, held to demonstrate the fate of collaborators. Such trials were essential if the Soviet state were to prevent further disloyalty nurtured by Soviet mismanagement during the war. Most of the lower ranks of the KONR and other collaborationist groups were either executed or condemned to penal servitude in Russian labor camps.

IMPACT

Andrey Andreyevich Vlasov was the best known and highest ranking of the more than one million Soviets who fought as German auxiliaries in the anti-Stalin resistance during World War II. While certain German officers convinced Vlasov that Germany would support the KONR movement, the nature of Nazi Germany's structure and leadership ensured that this was a fantasy and doomed Vlasov.

Nevertheless, Vlasov represented the most significant and dangerous threat to Stalin's control of Russia. Because he was an accomplished, famous, and decorated general, Vlasov's repudiation of Stalin's leadership and communist ineptitude resonated with thousands of Russians. Even in the war's last days, propaganda appeals issued in Vlasov's name enticed many Russian soldiers to desert and join the KONR. Because German propagandists used Vlasov's name so widely in their efforts to destabilize Soviet Russia, Vlasov became, for Stalin, the face of treason. During the Cold War, many in the West portrayed Vlasov as Russia's lost hope for a leader who might have overthrown Stalin and eliminated communism, which made Vlasov famous. However, Hitler's policies ensured that Vlasov could never be anything but a propaganda contrivance.

FURTHER READING

Anders, Wladyslaw. *Russian Volunteers in Hitler's Army*. Bayside, N.Y.: Axis Europa, 1998. A good overview of the organization and history of German units built upon Russian defectors, including the KONR.

Andreyev, Catherine. *Vlasov and the Russian Liberation Movement*. Cambridge, England: Cambridge University Press, 1987. One of the most insightful studies of Vlasov's ideology and the objectives of the anti-Stalinist Russians.

Munoz, Antonio J. *The Osttruppen*. Vol. 2 in *Hitler's Eastern Legions*. Bayside, N.Y.: Axis Europa, 1997. A good treatment of the organization, equipment, and history of the Russian volunteer forces.

Strik-Strikfeldt, Wilfried. *Against Stalin and Hitler: A Memoir of the Russian Liberation Movement, 1941-1945*. New York: Macmillan, 1970. As Vlasov's confidant, Strik-Strikfeldt provides contemporary insight into Vlasov's personality and ideology.

—*Kevin B. Reid*

SEE ALSO: Heinrich Himmler; Adolf Hitler; Joseph Stalin; Vasili Vasilievich Ulrikh.

CLAUS VON BÜLOW
Accused murderer

BORN: August 11, 1926; Copenhagen, Denmark
ALSO KNOWN AS: Claus Cecil Borberg (birth name); Klaus von Bülow
CAUSE OF NOTORIETY: Von Bülow was accused of attempting to murder his wife by giving her an overdose of insulin. In his first trial, he was found guilty and sentenced to thirty years in prison. At the second trial in 1985, he was found not guilty on all charges.
ACTIVE: 1982-1985
LOCALE: Newport, Rhode Island

EARLY LIFE

Claus von Bülow (klows vawn BYEW-loh) was born to playwright Svend Borberg and Ionna von Bülow Borberg. He was educated at Swiss schools and was known for using his charm and intelligence to make contacts among his extremely rich young schoolmates and others. Claus had the look and personal style of someone with enormous amounts of money, but his family's fortunes had been lost after World War I. After the Nazis invaded Denmark in 1940, he escaped to England by hiding inside a British airplane. He graduated from Cambridge University and went to work as an assistant to oil magnate J. Paul Getty.

BUSINESS CAREER

After marrying Martha (Sunny) Crawford von Auersperg on June 6, 1966, he continued working for Getty. The marriage had considerable problems because Claus worked as an art adviser when Sunny wanted him to stay with her. Sunny had continuous drug and alcohol problems, which exacerbated her hypoglycemia. Claus and Sunny talked of separating; their plans were known only

Claus von Bülow, left, with his attorney Alan Dershowitz. (AP/Wide World Photos)

to them, not to their daughter or to Sunny's two adult children from her first marriage. The family celebrated Christmas together in Rhode Island in 1979, and Sunny became inebriated, her movements becoming uncoordinated. She fell down, was taken to the hospital, and returned home after being stabilized.

On the morning of December 22, 1980, Sunny was discovered on her bathroom floor, unconscious. She was rushed to a hospital, where her body temperature was found to be 81 degrees. An insulin-encrusted needle was found near her body; Sunny took insulin by injection to keep her weight down.

LEGAL ACTION AND OUTCOME

Thanks to insistent petitioning by his stepchildren, Claus was put on trial for attempted murder. He was found guilty and sentenced to thirty years in prison. He then hired famed attorney Alan M. Dershowitz to file his ap-

peal. Dershowitz cast doubt on the most important evidence, including the needle. Dershowitz also stated that his client's stepchildren, aided by their lawyer, could have framed von Bülow. In equally interesting accounts, he speculated on Sunny's drug habits.

IMPACT

In 1985, Claus von Bülow was found not guilty. The von Bülows' daughter, Cosima von Bülow, was disowned by her maternal grandmother for maintaining her father's innocence. Claus's two stepchildren sued him for fifty-six million dollars. As a result of this, he renounced all claims to Sunny's personal fortune. As of 2006, Sunny von Bülow remained in a coma at Columbia-Presbyterian Hospital in New York.

In 1990, the film *Reversal of Fortune* (starring Jeremy Irons as Claus and Glenn Close as Sunny von Bülow), based on Dershowitz's book of the same title, depicted the case, posing many questions and then leaving viewers to make their own decisions. Irons portrays the fear of a man facing thirty years in prison. The film also brings forth a woman who takes various drugs to control her weight.

FURTHER READING

Dershowitz, Alan M. *America on Trial: Inside the Legal Battles That Transformed Our Nation*. New York: Warner Books, 2004. A comprehensive history of trials, beginning with America's Salem witch trials, through the scandal-ridden cases of Jean Harris, O. J. Simpson, and Dershowitz's most famous case, that of von Bülow.

_____. *Reversal of Fortune: Inside the Von Bülow Case*. New York: Random House, 1986. After being convicted of attempting to kill his wife, von Bülow

hired Dershowitz to begin his appeal process. In the best tradition of great lawyers, Dershowitz asked the important question: "Who benefits [if Claus goes to prison]?" The answer was Sunny's two adult children by her previous marriage.

Weed, Frank J. *Certainty of Justice: Reform in the Crime Victim Movement*. New York: Aldine de Gruyter, 1995. Details changes in state and federal laws designed to benefit each individual crime victim, even those, as in the case of Sunny von Bülow, in an irreversible coma.

—*Ellen B. Lindsay*

SEE ALSO: Bambi Bembenek; Ira Einhorn; Jean Harris; Seventh Earl of Lucan; Scott Peterson; Sam Sheppard; Pamela Ann Smart; Madeleine Smith; Ruth Snyder; Carolyn Warmus.

ANASTASE VONSIATSKY
American fascist leader and spy

BORN: June 12, 1898; Warsaw, Poland, Russian Empire
DIED: 1965; Florida
ALSO KNOWN AS: Anastase Andreievitch Vonsiatsky (full name); Count Anastase Andreievitch Vonsiatsky; Prince Anastase Andreievitch Vonsiatsky; V-V; Count Annie; the Czar
MAJOR OFFENSE: Espionage
ACTIVE: 1930's-1942
LOCALE: Thompson, Connecticut
SENTENCE: Five years in prison

EARLY LIFE

Anastase Vonsiatsky (ah-nah-STAH-zee vahn-ZYAHT-skee) was born in Warsaw (then a part of the Russian Empire) in 1898. His family consisted of minor nobility and zealous supporters of the czar. His father was assassinated by Polish terrorists when Vonsiatsky was twelve years old. Vonsiatsky was studying in the prestigious Emperor Nicholas Military Academy when the Russian Revolution broke out in 1917. He became a lieutenant in the "White Russians" counterrevolutionary forces (who were opposed to the Bolsheviks). Wounded in 1920, he was taken to Constantinople for treatment. In June, 1921, he emigrated to the United States, becoming a naturalized citizen in 1927.

CRIMINAL CAREER

Supported in the United States by his wealthy heiress wife, Vonsiatsky was able to devote his time to building a network of fascist sympathizers. In 1927, he became the American leader of the Brotherhood of Russian Truth, dedicated to the overthrow of Soviet communism. In 1932, Vonsiatsky founded the Russian National Revolutionary and Labor and Workers Peasant Party of Fascists (known as the Russian Revolutionary Party) with the purpose of instituting a fascist regime in Russia. At its height in the 1930's, this party consisted of fourteen members, with Vonsiatsky as its *vozhd* (leader). Chief among party activities were paramilitary training on Vonsiatsky's extensive estate in Thompson, Connecticut, and publishing a periodical titled *The Fascist*.

Vonsiatsky traveled throughout the world, organizing a network of party sympathizers, cultivating contacts in the fascist governments of Germany and Japan, and meeting with Adolf Hitler and Hermann Göring. With the outbreak of World War II, Vonsiatsky became associated with a ring of pro-Nazi sympathizers and spies headed by Gerhard Wilhelm Kunze, a leader of the German American Bund. Vonsiatsky supplied money to the ring and made contact with Nazi and Japanese agents.

LEGAL ACTION AND OUTCOME

With American entry into World War II, Vonsiatsky's activities came under increased scrutiny. In May, 1942, the Federal Bureau of Investigation (FBI) searched his Connecticut estate and found rooms full of incriminating evidence, including correspondence with fascists throughout the world, swastika emblems and apparel, and ample ammunition usable for street violence. On June 6, 1942, Vonsiatsky was indicted for conspiracy to violate the Espionage Act for his involvement with the Kunze espionage ring. On June 22, 1942, Vonsiatsky pleaded guilty and was sentenced to a term of five years in a federal penitentiary and fined five thousand dollars.

IMPACT

As the leader of the faction of White Russian émigrés who proposed violent means to institute a fascist regime in Russia, Anastase Vonsiatsky was attracted to the Nazi war effort and was eventually convicted of espionage in assistance of the Axis Powers. History seems to indicate that Vonsiatsky was a minor figure in the actual world of World War II espionage, but his flamboyant persona and imposing stature, as well as his tales of counterrevolutionary terrorism and practice of having paramilitary groups marching across his palatial Connecticut estate, were a sensation in his day. Some have speculated, improbably, that he was the prototype for "Big Daddy" Warbucks of the "Little Orphan Annie" cartoon strip and that he was later involved in the conspiracy to assassinate John F. Kennedy. In any case, his conviction in 1942 was seen as a successful coup for the FBI in breaking a major pro-German espionage ring.

FURTHER READING

Higham, Charles. *American Swastika*. Garden City, N.Y.: Doubleday, 1985. Outlines ties to Nazi groups among native-born Americans and White Russians such as Vonsiatsky.

Jenkins, Philip. *Hoods and Shirts: The Extreme Right in Pennsylvania, 1925-1950*. Chapel Hill: University of North Carolina Press, 1997. Chapter 8, on the World War II years, details Vonsiatsky's role as an intermediary between Ukrainian anticommunists in the United States and native American fascist leaders.

Sayers, Michael, and Albert Kahn. *Sabotage! The Secret War Against America*. New York: Harper and Brothers, 1942. A sensationalized account of Nazi and Jap-

anese spies, saboteurs, and sabotage in the United States, which details Vonsiatsky's extensive contacts with Nazi officials in the years leading up to his arrest.

—*Howard Bromberg*

SEE ALSO: Jacques Doriot; William Joyce; Sir Oswald Mosley.

VONSIATSKY ON THE RUSSIAN REVOLUTIONARY PARTY

In June-July, 1940, the periodical The Fascist *ran this statement by Vonsiatsky concerning his Russian Revolutionary Party:*

The Russian National Revolutionary Party, of which I am the leader, does not support either Germany's or Japan's ambition for hegemony in Europe or the Far East.

The Germans and the Japanese have never made clear their attitude toward a replacement of the present Stalinist rule by a Russian National Government.

The sole aim of our organization is to return Russia to a free people with a government elected by the people, of the people and for the people.

Our intention is to form in Russia a truly DEMOCRATIC government.

Our Party is not anti-Semitic.

Our Party has no membership dues; it is financed solely by voluntary contributions from its members and sympathizers. It is not subsidized by any FOREIGN POWER or foreign individuals.

Our organization is BANNED in Germany and Japan.

Only in the United States can we enjoy freedom of action and thought within the laws of the country.

I HEREWITH STATE EMPHATICALLY THAT THE ACTIVITIES OF OUR ORGANIZATION ARE AGAINST THE PRESENT SOVIET GOVERNMENT ALONE AND THAT IN NO WAY WHATSOEVER DOES IT ACT AGAINST THE CONSTITUTION OF THE UNITED STATES OR VIOLATE ITS LAWS WHICH WE LOYALLY SUPPORT.

ANASTASE A. VONSIATSKY
Thompson, Conn.
July 4, 1940

Source: Federal Bureau of Investigation, U.S. Department of Justice.

ANDREY VYSHINSKY
Soviet jurist and foreign minister

BORN: December 10, 1883; Odessa, Russia
DIED: November 22, 1954; New York, New York
ALSO KNOWN AS: Andrey Yanuarievich Vyshinsky (full name)
CAUSE OF NOTORIETY: As procurator of Joseph Stalin's infamous show trials, Vyshinsky presided over the death sentences of dozens of innocent defendants.
ACTIVE: 1933-1939
LOCALE: Moscow

EARLY LIFE

Three years after the birth of Andrey Vyshinsky (AHN-dray vih-SHIHN-skee) in Odessa, his family moved to Baku, where Andrey earned excellent grades at the gymnasium (secondary school) and enjoyed the cultural activities hosted by his parents. It was in Baku that Vyshinsky met Kapitolina Isidorovna Mikhailova, with whom he enjoyed a happy marriage until his death. Vyshinsky left Baku to study law at Kiev University, from which he was soon dismissed because of his illegal Marxist activities. Returning to Baku, he joined the Social Democratic Party and in 1905 played a major role in a railway workers' strike. During this period Vyshinsky was organizing his party's armed forces and directing the assassinations of police collaborators.

Vyshinsky's part in the railway strike led to his arrest in January, 1906, but he remained free until February, 1908, when the Tiflis court sentenced him to a year in Baku's Bailovka Prison. It was there that he first met and debated politics with Koba, or Joseph Vissarionovich Dzhugashvili, who would later be known as Joseph Stalin. Vyshinsky was released in October, 1908, and Stalin a few days later; it would be ten years before the two met again.

Vyshinsky reenrolled at Kiev University. Despite his brilliant performance in law studies, he became a tutor in a private gymnasium. He then went to Moscow and became an assistant to a prominent attorney and labored in the service of the February, 1917, revolution as a member of the moderate minority wing of the Russian Social Democratics, the Mensheviks, who called for gradual social reform. Attaining the rank of militia commissar in Moscow, he then became chairman of the Yakimanka district's first division. Stalin by now was an influential Bolshevik and people's commissar on nationality affairs, and after the October Revolution Vyshinsky became a deputy special commissar of food and transport. With a nod from the powerful Stalin, Vyshinsky abandoned the Mensheviks and in February, 1920, joined the Russian Communist Party of the more radical Bolsheviks. With this change in ideologies, Vyshinsky was poised to become the enforcer of Stalin's purges.

POLITICAL CAREER

Vyshinsky's first nefarious chore came in 1928 when, as chairman of an ad hoc "Special Judicial Presence," he presided over the trial of fifty-three engineers accused of being a "wrecking organization" in the town of Shakhty in the Rostov region. Eleven of the defendants were sentenced to death. Thus having demonstrated his abilities in his new career, Vyshinsky assumed in 1930 the same role in the trial of eight prominent scientists. His biographer Arkady Vaksberg sees this trial as Stalin's "important rehearsal for what was to go down in history as 'The Great Terror'" and as a precedent to "pave the way for a psychological attack on the population." For his superb

Andrey Vyshinsky. (Hulton Archive/Getty Images)

orchestration of these two trials, in May, 1931, Vyshinsky was appointed procurator of the Supreme Court of the Russian Federation (RSFSR) and deputy people's commissar of justice of the RSFSR.

The murder of Sergei Kirov—probably at Stalin's order—in December, 1934, led to the important trial of Grigory Yevseyevich Zinovyev and Lev Kamenev in August, 1936, the first of those show trials in which the defendants would be coerced into pleading guilty and Vyshinsky would be responsible for masterminding the bogus testimony. According to witnesses, Vyshinsky took a personal role in threatening the two victims, both of whom were subsequently executed.

The most infamous show trial was that of Nikolay Bukharin and Aleksey Ivanovich Rykov in 1938. Bukharin had been close to Vladimir Ilich Lenin and enjoyed a high position in the Bolshevik hierarchy, and it was certainly his status and prestige that condemned him. Vaksberg quotes Vyshinsky's telling remark in 1937 that "One has to remember Comrade Stalin's instruction that there are sometimes periods . . . when the laws prove obsolete and have to be set aside." Bukharin was courageous in remarks to Vyshinsky but succeeded only in eliciting Vyshinsky's crudest insults.

With these public trials for world consumption completed, Vyshinsky continued as procurator general until June, 1939, when Stalin appointed him deputy chairman of the Soviet People's Commissariat. In March, 1949, Stalin replaced Vyacheslav Molotov as foreign minister with Vyshinsky, who gave scurrilous speeches at the United Nations and, shortly after Stalin's death in March of 1953, became the Soviet Union's permanent delegate to that body.

On Saturday, November 20, 1954, the Soviet diplomatic delegation left for Glen Cove, New York, where Vyshinsky had planned to prepare a speech arguing that the International Atomic Energy Agency should be accountable to the United Nations and the Security Council. Vyshinsky remained in his Park Avenue apartment, fell ill the next day, and died on the morning of November 22 of a heart attack.

IMPACT

Of all the baleful figures in Stalin's entourage, none was more destructive of civic freedom than Andrey Vyshinsky. It was in his role as the mastermind behind the show trials that Vyshinsky had the strongest effect on Soviet history. Vyshinsky also used his post as deputy chairman of the Soviet People's Commissariat to demoralize Soviet artists and publicize Socialist Realism in such films as *Lenin* (1918) and *Traktoristy* (1939; *Tractor-Drivers*). His influence in this appointment cast a dark shadow over Soviet art of the decade.

FURTHER READING

Bukharin, Nikolay. *How It All Began: The Prison Novel.* Translated by George Shriver. New York: Columbia University Press, 1998. The distinguished Bolshevik Bukharin was probably Vyshinsky's most important victim, and Stephen F. Cohen's introduction to this novel is informative.

Koestler, Arthur. *Darkness at Noon.* Translated by Daphne Hardy. London: Jonathan Cape, 1940. This famous novel, reprinted many times, focuses on the plight of the old Bolsheviks.

Sebag Montefiore, Simon. *Stalin: The Court of the Red Tsar.* New York: Alfred A. Knopf, 2004. Outstanding biography of the Russian dictator, with many appearances by Vyshinsky.

Vaksberg, Arkady. *Stalin's Prosecutor: The Life of Andrei Vishinsky.* Translated by Jan Butler. New York: Grove Weidenfeld, 1990. An excellent biography by a lawyer who knew Vyshinsky personally.

—*Frank Day*

SEE ALSO: Lavrenty Beria; Felix Dzerzhinsky; Lazar Kaganovich; Nikita S. Khrushchev; Vladimir Ilich Lenin; Vyacheslav Mikhailovich Molotov; Symon Petlyura; Joseph Stalin; Vasili Vasilievich Ulrikh; Genrikh Yagoda; Nikolay Ivanovich Yezhov; Andrey Aleksandrovich Zhdanov; Grigory Yevseyevich Zinovyev.

WINIFRED WAGNER
British Nazi supporter

BORN: June 23, 1897; Hastings, England
DIED: March 5, 1980; Überlingen, Germany
ALSO KNOWN AS: Winifred Williams (birth name)
CAUSE OF NOTORIETY: Through her close association with Adolf Hitler's Nazi regime, Wagner debased the esteemed Wagner Festival at Bayreuth by making it a Nazi Party nationalist propaganda tool.
ACTIVE: 1923-1950
LOCALE: Germany

EARLY LIFE

Born in Britain and orphaned before the age of two, Winifred Wagner (VAHG-nuhr) was adopted at age ten by Karl and Henriette Klindworth, who gave her some musical training and a thoroughly German education. Through long association with German composer Richard Wagner and his family, Klindworth was a familiar figure at Bayreuth, where annual presentations of Wagner's operas and others' composed works drew crowds. The Klindworths visited the Wagners in 1914 and brought seventeen-year-old Winifred, who was introduced to Siegfried Wagner, the composer's only son. Siegfriend and Winifred were immediately drawn to each other and married the following year.

In 1906, Siegfried's formidable but enfeebled mother yielded the direction of the festival to him. However, his potentially scandalous homosexual tendency prompted the family's concern over maintaining its traditions and controlling it. With heirs required to run the festival, Winifred was accepted, despite hostility from her sisters-in-law. Though Siegfried preserved a quasi-bachelor existence through the marriage, he and Winifred did have four children: sons Wieland and Wolfgang and daughters Friedelind and Verena.

NAZI CAREER

In 1924, Siegfried revived the annual festivals, which had been suspended during and after World War I. The poisons of reactionary nationalism and anti-Semitism were already at work. Both had been elements of Wagner's thinking and more virulently of the thinking of his widow, Cosima. In 1908, their daughter Eva (Siegfried's sister) married Houston Stewart Chamberlain (1855-1927), who was an ardent Wagnerite and passionate anti-Semite and turned Bayreuth into a beacon of anti-Jewish nationalism. Although personally conservative and anti-Semitic, Siegfried was also politically naïve and sensi-

tive to Jewish sources of financial backing. Winifred, on the other hand, was nurtured in anti-Semitism by Klindworth. However, the couple mutually detested the liberal Weimar Republic and its disorders.

In September, 1923, Winifred first met the still-obscure Adolf Hitler. She was immediately captivated by him and welcomed him to Bayreuth and its inner circle. When Hitler's Beer Hall Putsch failed in Munich two months later, Winifred ostentatiously aided the jailed conspirators. The 1924 festival reopening was rife with Nazi associations. Siegfried, less captivated personally by Hitler, formally distanced the festival from Hitler, but Winifred, who became a party member in 1926, deepened her cordial relationship with the Nazi leader.

Siegfried died suddenly in August, 1930, four months after his mother's death at age ninety-two. Winifred, despite being only thirty-three, became his legal heir and assumed control of the festival. Her leadership began tumultuously but was transformed when Hitler came to power in 1933. Identifying himself with Wagner and his music, the dictator turned Bayreuth into a focus of Nazi cultural ideology, a grand propaganda machine, while Winifred's close friendship made him a virtual member of the Wagner family. Hitler meddled constantly, attending each festival and conceiving a vast architectural program for Bayreuth. Artistic standards slipped and then collapsed in the war years amid factional struggles and Wagner family infighting.

In 1945, with the war's end and the subsequent American occupation of Germany, all the Wagners' property in Bayreuth was confiscated. Eventually, plans emerged to revive the festival. Badly tarred during denazification, Winifred in 1950 finally renounced her legal rights in favor of her two sons. She remained, however, an unrepentant Nazi, outspoken in her devotion to Hitler, his memory, and his lingering partisans. In 1975, she spoke out in a belligerent documentary film titled *Winifred Wagner und die Geschichte des Hauses Wahnfried von 1914-1975*. Allowed to resume residence in Bayreuth, she was a recurrent embarrassment to her son's regime until her death in 1980.

IMPACT

The festivals resumed in 1951. Wolfgang was soon pushed aside by Wieland, a formerly fervent Nazi and theatrical reactionary who became politically respectable and notoriously progressive in his productions. Upon

Wieland's death in 1966, amid recurrent family squabbles, Wolfgang resumed control, fending off challenges to his leadership. Despite full artistic revival, Bayreuth remained shadowed by memories of the Nazi associations that Winifred Wagner had fostered so disastrously.

FURTHER READING

Hamann, Brigitte. *Winifred Wagner: A Life at the Heart of Hitler's Bayreuth.* Translated by Alan Bance. London: Granta Books, 2005. A fully documented account of Winifred's career.

Köhler, Joachim. *Wagner's Hitler: The Prophet and His Disciple.* Translated by Ronald Taylor. Malden, Mass.: Blackwell, 2000. A controversial argument for Hitler's profoundly Wagnerian background.

Spotts, Frederic. *Bayreuth: A History of the Wagner Festival.* New Haven, Conn.: Yale University Press, 1994. A commanding study, with full exposition of Winifred's career.

Wagner, Friedelind, with Page Cooper. *Heritage of Fire: The Story of Richard Wagner's Granddaughter.* New York: Harper, 1945. Winifred's staunchly anti-Nazi daughter describes her Bayreuth youth and her escape from it and her mother in 1938.

Wagner, Nike. *The Wagners: The Dramas of a Musical Dynasty.* London: Weidenfeld & Nicolson, 1998. Winifred's granddaughter considers family history and interprets her great-grandfather's works.

—*John W. Barker*

SEE ALSO: Houston Stewart Chamberlain; Elisabeth Förster-Nietzsche; Adolf Hitler; Ludwig II.

JAMES J. WALKER
Mayor of New York City (1926-1932)

BORN: June 19, 1881; New York, New York
DIED: November 18, 1946; New York, New York
ALSO KNOWN AS: James John Joseph Walker (full name); Jimmy Walker; Beau James; Night Mayor
CAUSE OF NOTORIETY: As mayor of New York City, Walker faithfully served the interests of Tammany Hall—the corrupt Democratic Party machine of the time—through cronyism in political appointments and favoritism in the awarding of contracts.
ACTIVE: 1926-1932
LOCALE: New York, New York

EARLY LIFE

James J. (Jimmy) Walker (WAH-kuhr) was born June 19, 1881, to William Walker, a Democratic assemblyman and alderman from Greenwich Village. Before entering politics, Jimmy Walker was an aspiring actor and fairly successful songwriter; his most popular composition was "Will You Love Me in December (As You Do in May)?" He studied law, and his first successful foray into politics was his election to the New York State Assembly in 1909. He married chorus girl Janet Allen in 1912, but they were divorced in 1933. He then married actress Betty Compton, whom he divorced in 1942.

POLITICAL CAREER

In 1914, Walker won election to the New York State Senate. While still a state senator, he had helped pass legislation that legalized after-church entertainment on Sundays, including baseball, boxing, and filmgoing. This move won him the approval of many working-class people and helped his election to mayor in 1926.

Walker was a flamboyant and charismatic mayor, more interested in nightclubbing, showgirls, and gambling than in governing. Despite frequent vacations, a showgirl mistress (Compton), and rumors of corruption, the people loved "Beau James," as Walker was often called. Walker represented the city's rebellious "anything goes" attitude toward the social repression of the times. Although Walker operated within the context of the Volstead Act, which had enacted Prohibition, the youth of the Roaring Twenties found a way around Prohibition in speakeasies and black-market liquor.

Despite the lack of attention to his job, Walker was a surprisingly shrewd and effective politician. He was part of Tammany Hall, the name given to the corrupt Democratic Party machine of the time. He was an effective machine boss and knew how to find votes for himself and his cronies. For example, some tax revenues from questionable and private real estate deals, which brought in a half-billion dollars annually to the city, were used for better wages for city employees. Actions like this greatly endeared him to New Yorkers. In 1929, he won reelection by an overwhelming margin.

However, the Great Depression that began in 1929 exposed Walker's neglect of essential city services and made his flamboyant lifestyle less palatable to the masses. Furthermore, the gangland murder of organized crime kingpin Arnold Rothstein exposed the weakness and corruption of the district attorney and the police department. Resultant social unrest led to investigations in 1931 into Walker's administration. They revealed an enormous amount of corruption at all levels of the Walker administration, particularly in the city's court system and the police vice squad.

In 1932, Walker was charged with accepting hundreds of thousands of dollars in payoffs and bribes from people who had business ties to the city. He was called before Governor Franklin D. Roosevelt to answer the charges. On September 1, 1932, Walker resigned from office and fled the country to live in Europe.

There were some notable accomplishments of the Walker administration, including the creation of the Department of Sanitation and the beginnings of construction on the Triborough Bridge, the West Side Highway, and the Queens Midtown Tunnel. Walker returned to New York City in 1935 and eventually became head of Majestic Records, where he remained until his death in New York on November 18, 1946.

IMPACT

In the mid-1990's, political historian Melvin G. Holli polled 160 journalists, historians, and social scientists about the ten best and ten worst mayors in the history of the United States between 1820 and 1993. Because of the massive corruption of the Walker administration and Walker's contributions to the greatest economic collapse in the city's history, he was ranked as the third worst. However, in his time, Walker was loved by many New Yorkers. As the mayoral election approached in 1945, *Daily News* straw pollsters showed the voters in New York City favored him as Mayor Fiorello La Guardia's

successor. A romanticized version of Walker's life appeared in the 1957 film *Beau James*, starring Bob Hope.

The investigation and eventual downfall of Walker played a crucial role in Franklin Delano Roosevelt's ascendance to the presidency. Governor Roosevelt, who was in the midst of his first presidential campaign in 1932, became personally involved in the investigations of Walker. A former Tammany Hall man himself, Roosevelt recast himself as a "goo-goo" (advocate of good government), which greatly contributed to his successful run for the presidency that year.

FURTHER READING

Fowler, Gene. *Beau James: The Life and Times of Jimmy Walker*. New York: Viking, 1949. This book is considered by many to be the best biography of Walker.

Holli, Melvin G. *The American Mayor: The Best and the Worst Big-City Leaders*. University Park: Pennsylvania State University Press, 1999. Includes the results of Holli's poll and gives biographies for each mayor who ranked in the poll. Also discusses what qualities distinguish good from bad city leaders.

Leinwand, Gerald. *Mackerels in the Moonlight: Four Corrupt American Mayors*. Jefferson, N.C.: McFarland, 2004. Four of America's most corrupt mayors, including Walker, are profiled and analyzed.

Mitang, Herbert. *Once upon a Time in New York: Jimmy Walker, Franklin Roosevelt, and the Last Great Battle of the Jazz Age*. New York: Free Press, 2000. This book traces the political downfall of Mayor Walker and rise of Governor Roosevelt to the presidency.

—Jerome L. Neapolitan

SEE ALSO: Thomas Joseph Pendergast; Arnold Rothstein; William Marcy Tweed.

WILLIAM WALKER
American filibuster

BORN: May 8, 1824; Nashville, Tennessee
DIED: September 12, 1860; Trujillo, Honduras
ALSO KNOWN AS: General Walker
MAJOR OFFENSE: Aggressive invasion
ACTIVE: 1853-1860
LOCALE: Baja California and Sonora, Mexico; Costa
    Rica; El Salvador; Guatemala; Honduras; Nicaragua
SENTENCE: Death by firing squad

EARLY LIFE
Born in 1824 in Tennessee, William Walker (WAH-
kuhr) graduated from the University of Nashville at the
age of fourteen. After studying medicine in Europe,
Walker later received his medical degree from the University of Pennsylvania at age nineteen. In the following
years, Walker lived in New Orleans, were he studied law
and worked as journalist. Then, in 1849, he moved to
Northern California and settled in Marysville, where he
established a law practice. While living there, he became
fascinated by the idea of taking over a weak Latin American nation. At the time such campaigns, as well as their
perpetrators, were called filibusters.

William Walker. (Library of Congress)

FILIBUSTER CAREER
In 1853, at the age of twenty-nine, Walker and an army of
forty-five men sailed to Baja California in northern Mexico and captured the town of La Paz. Soon thereafter,
Walker declared himself president of Lower California
and then established the Republic of Sonora by laying
claim to the Mexican territory of Sonora. His conquest
was short-lived as his followers deserted, causing
Walker to surrender to authorities following charges of
violating U.S. neutrality laws. He was tried but quickly
acquitted thanks to popular support for the ideals of
manifest destiny, the notion that the United States was
destined to dominate the North American continent. As a
result of Walker's incursion into Mexico, the United
States later purchased a portion of Sonora from Mexico
in the Gadsden Purchase.

Walker next turned his attention to Nicaragua after he
was hired as a mercenary by a rebel Nicaraguan faction.
In May, 1855, Walker sailed to Nicaragua with an army
of fifty-eight men. In a few months, Walker and his army
defeated the Nicaraguan army, captured the capital city
of Granada, and took control of the nation. Patricio Rivas
was appointed president of Nicaragua, but it was Walker,
as commander of the army, who held authority. In 1856,
U.S. president Franklin Pierce recognized Walker's legitimacy. Seeking additional conquests, Walker sent one
thousand mercenaries to Guatemala, El Salvador, Costa
Rica, and Honduras. In response, the Costa Rican government sent a force to invade Nicaragua. Walker's army
fended off the invasion, but a poorly executed counterattack on Costa Rica failed, and Walker suffered major
losses.

LEGAL ACTION AND OUTCOME
Shipping magnate Cornelius Vanderbilt had previously
supported Walker's tactics in the interest of controlling
the San Juan River-Lake Nicaragua route from the Caribbean to the Pacific. Vanderbilt retaliated against Walker,
however, after Walker revoked his charter to conduct
business in Nicaragua. Vanderbilt successfully pressured
the U.S. government to withdraw recognition of Walker's
political legitimacy. Meanwhile, the British navy regularly intercepted shipments of supplies to Walker.

In July, 1856, Walker became president of Nicaragua
in an uncontested election. His attempts to reinforce his
popularity in the United States by legalizing slavery were
moderately successful. However, Vanderbilt's public

opposition, harassment by the British navy, a weakened army facing serious attrition, and the strengthening alliance of countries opposed to him caused Walker to surrender. He returned to the United States in mid-1857, where he was greeted as a hero.

Walker visited President James Buchanan as well as financiers in New York, seeking support for a return trip to Nicaragua. In late November, he initiated a second expedition, and upon his arrival he declared himself commander of the Nicaraguan army. The invasion was short-lived, however, as Walker was rearrested by Commodore Hiram Paulding of the U.S. Navy and returned to the United States.

In 1860, Walker published a book, *The War in Nicaragua*, to strengthen his base of Southern support by assuming a pro-slavery position. This device proved successful, and that same year Walker returned to Nicaragua. The British at this time controlled the Mosquito Coast (now in Nicaragua), and the British navy thwarted Walker's plan to land there. He instead went ashore at Trujillo, Honduras, also controlled by the British, who considered Walker an impediment to their enterprises in the region. A British navy captain captured Walker and handed him over to the Hondurans. Six days later, at the age of thirty-six, Walker was executed by firing squad.

THE GRAY-EYED MAN OF DESTINY

William Walker was the most flagrant of a type of mid-nineteenth century adventurer known as a "filibuster." Although now associated primarily with an oratorical maneuver in the U.S. Senate, the word derives from Spanish *filibustero*. Its variant, *freebooter*, retains the original meaning—buccaneer or pirate. In particular, it was applied to pirates in the Caribbean during the seventeenth and eighteenth centuries. When piracy died out there, the word fell from usage, but it was revived in the next century to describe private adventurers who attacked foreign nations for money or power and without their own nations' authorization.

Walker started filibustering (the verb form also existed) in Baja California in 1853, but he was far from the only one. At almost exactly the same time and place, France's Count Gaston Raousset-Boulbon tried to set up the Independent State of Sonora. Henry Crabb likewise tried to carve out a Republic of Sonora three years later. A decade earlier, Colonel Samuel W. Jordon of Texas participated in attempts to create the Republic of the Rio Grande. The successful Texas Revolution of 1836 was itself a product of filibustering. The brief Bear Flag revolt in California following the Mexican-American war is yet another example.

In the United States, considerable support for filibusters existed. They were seen as people who put in practical application the government's doctrine of manifest destiny, a noble-sounding term for an assumption held by many Americans: The United States had the right to expand its borders if it so desired. Political turmoil and lawlessness in other countries provided the pretext for interference, on the further assumption that superior American culture and democratic values would be a blessing for the locals. Indeed, among fellow Southerners, Walker was known as the "gray-eyed man of destiny," a hero and inspiration, especially because he sought to extend slavery to Central America.

On the other hand, among Central Americans—Nicaraguans in particular—Walker still symbolizes all that is to be feared from the United States. Some historians date the deep Latin American suspicion of gringos from Walker's shenanigans in Nicaragua.

IMPACT

Walker remains America's most notorious filibuster. Remembered far more in Latin America than in the United States, William Walker and his grandiose schemes might have led several Central American countries into the United States as pro-slavery states, which could have postponed the Civil War.

FURTHER READING

Carr, Albert Z. *The World and William Walker*. 1963. Reprint. Westport, Conn.: Greenwood Press, 1975. Provides a comprehensive and engaging biography of Walker. The author does a good job of detailing the man and the history of Nicaragua in the 1850's.

May, Robert E. *Manifest Destiny's Underworld*. Chapel Hill: University of North Carolina Press, 2004. Provides a well-researched and thoughtful analysis of an underemphasized portion of American history, during which filibusters invaded parts of Latin America using terrorist tactics.

Scroggs, William O. *Filibusters and Financiers*. 1916. Reprint. New York: Macmillan, 1969. This classic work provides an authoritative narrative on American filibustering activities before 1860.

—*Wayne J. Pitts*

SEE ALSO: Aaron Burr; Porfirio Díaz; James Wilkinson.

RACHEL WALL
American pirate

BORN: 1760; near Carlisle, Pennsylvania
DIED: October 8, 1789; Boston, Massachusetts
ALSO KNOWN AS: Rachel Schmidt (birth name)
MAJOR OFFENSES: Highway robbery and accessory to murder
ACTIVE: 1781, 1782, 1787-1789
LOCALE: Atlantic Ocean near the Isles of Shoals; Boston, Massachusetts
SENTENCE: Death by hanging

EARLY LIFE
Rachel Wall (RAY-chehl wahl) grew up in rural Pennsylvania on her family's farm. Few biographical facts other than those in her 1789 confession were recorded. Her pious Presbyterian parents expected their children to conform to their religious expectations for moral behavior. Wall disliked the rigidity of their lifestyle. She met fisherman George Wall, a veteran of the American Revolution, who convinced her to elope.

After the couple wed, they resided in Philadelphia, then New York City, before settling in Boston. During her husband's periodic absences on a fishing vessel, Wall worked as a maid on Beacon Hill. She overheard gossip that her husband was robbing commercial vessels, not fishing. He boasted about riches he had obtained from plundering when he returned to Boston.

CRIMINAL CAREER
Wall's involvement in piracy began in 1781 when George Wall schemed how he and five friends, all veteran revolutionary privateers, could use their wartime experiences seizing vessels to obtain cargoes to sell for profit. He selected the Isles of Shoals as a base. The pirates' tactic was to steal a sloop and pretend to be a fishing family. During stormy weather, they would anchor their craft in an inlet. After the storm dissipated, the group knocked their masts askew, displayed a distress flag, and drifted into open water near New England trade routes. Rachel's role was to stand on the deck of the sloop and plead for assistance.

George and his crew raided the ship that attempted to rescue them, murdering the captain and crew, stealing money and cargo, and sinking the vessel. Rachel and her fellow pirates then sold the stolen goods in New England towns. She accompanied her husband and his raiders on pirating sprees during which twelve ships were seized, twenty-four people murdered, and six thousand dollars in cash plus cargo looted. According to several sources, a September, 1782, hurricane swept George to sea and ended the Walls' piracy. However, in her confession, Rachel commented that she had aided her husband's escape from Boston's jail in 1785 before he abandoned her.

After that time, Rachel resumed honest employment as a maid. Although she vowed to behave morally, she found thievery difficult to resist. Starting in the spring of 1787, she robbed vessels anchored at Boston's harbor. She stole gold, money, and jewelry from ships while captains and crews slept.

LEGAL ACTION AND OUTCOME
The precise crime resulting in Wall's execution was unclear. Her confession referred to robbing travelers. Some sources indicated that a witness identified Wall as the culprit who had mugged a woman in the summer of 1789. Wall proclaimed her innocence. A judge ruled Wall guilty at an August 25, 1789, trial.

On October 7, with her execution scheduled for the next day, Wall signed a confession and apologized for various sins but asserted she had not committed the robbery for which she had been convicted. In her cautionary statement, Wall hoped her execution might prevent vulnerable women from associating with immoral people encouraging them to become corrupt. On October 8, 1789, authorities hanged Wall during a public execution on Boston Common's gallows.

IMPACT
According to the New England Pirate Museum, Rachel Wall is the only woman pirate on record who plundered solely in the New England region. Other women pirates preyed mostly on vessels in the Caribbean Sea or in English waters, occasionally traveling to New England for choice captures.

Wall was not as well known as other women pirates, especially Anne Bonny and Mary Read. Some historians suggest that perhaps this is because Wall apologized for her actions and was less bloodthirsty than her contemporaries. Writers have romanticized Wall's exploits and have incorporated them into pirating lore.

FURTHER READING
Druett, Joan. *She Captains: Heroines and Hellions of the Sea.* New York: Simon & Schuster, 2000. Discusses

the credibility of accounts portraying Wall and suggests why her crimes remain less known than those of more famous women pirates.

Lorimer, Sara. *Booty: Girl Pirates on the High Seas.* San Francisco: Chronicle Books, 2002. Biographical chapter featuring Wall is based on an interpretation of her confession. Map and art elaborate Wall's pirating experiences.

Williams, Daniel E. *Pillars of Salt: An Anthology of* *Early American Criminal Narratives.* Madison, Wis.: Madison House, 1993. Scholarly study includes text of *Life, Last Words, and Dying Confession of Rachel Wall* and an illustration of that broadside preserved by the American Antiquarian Society.

—*Elizabeth D. Schafer*

SEE ALSO: Charlotte de Berry; Anne Bonny; Grace O'Malley; Mary Read.

GEORGE C. WALLACE
Governor of Alabama (1963-1967, 1971-1979, 1983-1987)

BORN: August 25, 1919; Clio, Alabama
DIED: September 13, 1998; Montgomery, Alabama
ALSO KNOWN AS: George Corley Wallace (full name)
CAUSE OF NOTORIETY: Wallace was known for his advocacy of racial segregation and white supremacy. He became an icon of southern cultural heritage and, following an assassination attempt on his life, a more sympathetic figure.
ACTIVE: 1960's-1980's
LOCALE: Alabama

EARLY LIFE
Born into modest means in Clio, Alabama, George Wallace (WAH-lihs) demonstrated a fighting spirit as a successful high school boxer. He received his law degree in 1942 before enlisting in the U.S. Army Air Force during World War II. He flew combat missions over Japan, serving under General Curtis LeMay, who later was Wallace's presidential running mate in 1968.

POLITICAL CAREER
Wallace began his political career in 1946 in the Alabama state legislature. While he is largely remembered as a staunch conservative and for his inflammatory segregationist advocacy, his first election was as a progressive liberal, particularly on racial issues. He was a delegate to the 1948 Democratic National Convention, refusing to join the vast majority of old-style southern Democrats who staged a walkout in protest of desegregation initiatives. However, his liberalism and racial tolerance proved major factors in his failed 1958 gubernatorial bid, and he quickly executed an ideological reversal that would define him politically from that point forward. John Patterson, Wallace's opponent in the Democratic primary, received strong support from the Ku Klux Klan, leading Wallace to state, "I'll never be out-niggered again." His adoption of a hard-line segregationist style proved successful, and he won the 1962 gubernatorial race.

Wallace was propelled into the national spotlight in 1963 for blocking the doors to prevent racial integration at the University of Alabama. On June 11, 1963, federal marshals and the National Guard were called to assist in

George C. Wallace. (Library of Congress)

WALLACE AT THE SCHOOLHOUSE DOOR

Standing before the University of Alabama to prevent two African American students, Vivian Malone and James Hood, from registering, Governor George Wallace protested the actions of the federal government, which had nationalized Alabama's National Guard in order to ensure that the students would be able to register:

The unwelcomed, unwanted, unwarranted and force-induced intrusion upon the campus of the University of Alabama today of the might of the Central Government offers a frightful example of the oppression of the rights, privileges and sovereignty of this State by officers of the Federal Government. . . . This nation was never meant to be a unit of one . . . but a united [*sic*] of the many . . . [T]his is the exact reason our freedom loving forefathers established the states, so as to divide the rights and powers among the states, insuring that no central power could gain master government control. . . .

I stand here today, as Governor of this sovereign State, and refuse to willingly submit to illegal usurpation of power by the Central Government. I claim today for all the people of the State of Alabama those rights reserved to them under the Constitution of the United States. Among those powers so reserved and claimed is the right of state authority in the operation of the public schools, colleges and Universities. My action does not constitute disobedience to legislative and constitutional provisions. It is not defiance—for defiance sake, but for the purpose of raising basic and fundamental constitutional questions. My action is raising a call for strict adherence to the Constitution of the United States as it was written—for a cessation of usurpation and abuses. My action seeks to avoid having state sovereignty sacrificed on the altar of political expediency. . . .

Now, therefore, in consideration of the premises, and in my official capacity as Governor of the State of Alabama, I do hereby make the following solemn proclamation:

WHEREAS, the Constitution of Alabama vests the supreme executive powers of the State in the Governor as the Chief Magistrate, and said Constitution requires of the Governor that he take care that the laws be faithfully executed; and,

WHEREAS, the Constitution of the United States, Amendment 10, reserves to the States respectively or to the people, those powers not delegated to the United States; and,

WHEREAS, the operation of the public school system is a power reserved to the State of Alabama under the Constitution of the United States and Amendment 10 thereof; and,

WHEREAS, it is the duty of the Governor of the State of Alabama to preserve the peace under the circumstances now existing, which power is one reserved to the State of Alabama and the people thereof under the Constitution of the United States and Amendment10 thereof.

NOW, THEREFORE, I, George C. Wallace, as Governor of the State of Alabama . . . do hereby denounce and forbid this illegal and unwarranted action by the Central Government.

Source: Statement and Proclamation of Governor George C. Wallace, issued at the University of Alabama, June 11, 1963. Alabama Department of Archives & History.

---

the desegregation of the university after Wallace was steadfast in his refusal to allow two black students to enroll. He remained well remembered for his infamous slogan Segregation Today, Segregation Tomorrow, Segregation Forever.

Wallace eventually served four terms as governor of Alabama, both before and after his presidential bid in 1968 as a candidate of the American Independent Party. As an Independent, Wallace was a serious threat to split the conservative vote with Nixon in 1968. Wallace hoped to carry enough electoral votes to force the U.S. House of Representatives to determine the election and, although ultimately he fell short, he almost succeeded, winning five southern states and finishing strong in Maryland and Michigan.

On May 15, 1972, Wallace had again undertaken the presidential race and was on the campaign trail in Maryland when his bid was halted by the attempt of Arthur Bremer on his life. The bullet wounds led to Wallace's paralysis, and he remained bound to a wheelchair for the rest of his life, continuing to serve as governor of Alabama to 1979 and again from 1983 to 1987.

IMPACT

The legacy of George Wallace is, somewhat ironically, as split as his life. As noted in a Public Broadcasting Service (PBS) documentary *George Wallace: Settin' the Woods on Fire* (2000), he advocated unequivocal segregation but later asked to be forgiven. Always one to speak his mind and a constant lightning rod for controversy, Wallace had a major influence on the political and social landscape both of the South and of the United States as a whole. He is most notorious for attempting to prevent enrollment of African Americans at the University of Alabama and, as a result, for solidifying and extending the pro-segregation movement. Consequently, Wallace is largely remembered in the context of race relations and bigotry. He was indeed racist in his political ideology during the formative and most notable years as Alabama's governor and during his presidential campaign.

However, Wallace came to be viewed in a mixed light. His conversion to born-again Christianity and direct apologies to the black community may have softened his lingering notoriety. Late in life, he was apologetic with regard to his hard-line racial views and displayed an attitude more similar to his early, relatively liberal days.

Regardless of Wallace's repentance, however, his legacy is more commonly associated in the popular culture with defining southern values. A line from the well-known southern song "Sweet Home Alabama," by America's Confederate rock band Lynyrd Skynyrd and which includes the words "where the Governor is true," memorializes Wallace's segregationist stance during the Civil Rights movement. To many, Wallace remains associated with contemporary states' rights champions, such as the late senators Strom Thurmond and Howell Heflin. While he remains revered by southern heritage groups and is widely seen as a regional champion of the people, he is nonetheless viewed as a controversial figure.

FURTHER READING

Carter, Dan T. *The Politics of Rage: George Wallace, the Origins of the New Conservatism, and the Transfor-mation of American Politics*. Baton Rouge: Louisiana State University Press, 2000. This interpretive biography of the Alabama governor argues that he was an evil and politically incorrect figure and is at odds with most biographies that contend Wallace embraced a reversal of ideology concerning race relations during his later years.

Healey, Thomas S. *The Two Deaths of George Wallace: The Question of Forgiveness*. Montgomery, Ala.: Black Belt Press, 1996. A detailed account of the events leading up to would-be assassin Arthur Bremer's shooting of the presidential candidate in 1972, concentrating on the psychological makeup of Bremer, who is portrayed as obsessed and deranged, not necessarily anti-Southern or even personally opposed to Wallace.

Lesher, Stephan. *George Wallace: American Populist*. Reading, Mass.: Addison-Wesley, 1994. Compared with most Wallace biographies, this one is pointedly positive in portraying Wallace. The governor is presented as the inspiration for a cult of personality whose racist political posturing overshadowed his career. The author provides an objective account of how Wallace used racist politics to benefit his campaigns and tap into a once-viable strain of populism. Despite the ugliness of his once-racist views, Wallace is shown as an influential politician whose experience helped shape numerous American political figures, from Strom Thurmond to Ronald Reagan and Bill Clinton.

—*J. Mitchell Miller*

SEE ALSO: Theodore G. Bilbo; Arthur Bremer; Willis A. Carto; Orval E. Faubus.

CAROLYN WARMUS
American murderer

BORN: January 8, 1964; Detroit, Michigan
ALSO KNOWN AS: Carolyn Marie Warmus (full name)
MAJOR OFFENSES: Murder in the second degree; criminal possession of a weapon
ACTIVE: January 15, 1989
LOCALE: Greenburgh, Westchester County, New York
SENTENCE: Twenty-five years to life for second-degree murder; concurrent five to fifteen years for criminal possession of a weapon; concurrent one to three years for criminal possession of a forged instrument

EARLY LIFE

The eldest daughter of a wealthy, self-made insurance executive, Carolyn Warmus (WAHR-muhs) was the eldest of three children. Her parents, Thomas and Elizabeth Warmus, divorced in 1972, when Carolyn was eight. Because of Elizabeth's drinking problem, Thomas Warmus was granted custody of the children. Both parents remarried subsequently.

Carolyn was raised as a spoiled socialite in her father's luxurious, six-bedroom home in the exclusive Detroit suburb of Franklin Hills. She attended elite private schools and eventually Teachers College, Columbia University in New York City, where she earned a master's degree in elementary school education.

She was hired by Scarsdale's elite Greenville Elementary School in 1987 in Westchester County, New York. Paul Solomon, a sixth-grade teacher, also worked there. Solomon, thirty-nine, was married to Betty Jeanne Solomon, a credit card account executive. The couple had a fifteen-year-old daughter, Kristan. Warmus soon developed a seeming "fatal attraction" for Paul Solomon. Blond and attractive, sassy and affluent, Warmus had earlier tried to latch onto other men, developing obsessions but rarely relationships with them.

CRIMINAL CAREER

By early 1989, Paul Solomon was trying, halfheartedly, to disencumber himself of what had become an uncomfortable association, as his wife was becoming suspicious of Warmus's frequent calls and egregious solicitude for the Solomons' daughter, Kristan. Warmus persisted in pursuing the relationship. On Sunday, January 15, 1989, she called Paul at home, asking him to meet her that evening. Telling his wife that he was going out bowling, Paul made his way to the Treetops Restaurant in Yonkers, New York. Warmus arrived there around 7:45 P.M., late but characteristically so. When Paul got home after 11:30 P.M., he found his wife slumped on the living-room floor, dead. She had been hit on the head with a blunt instrument and shot nine times with a .25-millimeter handgun, four times in the back as she lay on the floor.

At first, because of a possible motive, Paul Solomon was the prime suspect. Eventually it was discovered that Carolyn Warmus had hired a New York City private detective, Vincent Parco, among others, to provide her with a handgun equipped with a silencer for her "personal security." Police traced the .25-millimeter ammunition to a New Jersey outlet. Warmus had used the misappropriated driver's license of a former coworker for identification when purchasing the gun.

LEGAL ACTION AND OUTCOME

Warmus's first trial, beginning in January, 1991, ended with a hung jury and a mistrial. At her second trial, a year later, a bloody cashmere left-hand woman's glove, noted under Betty Jeanne Solomon's body at the crime scene but subsequently mislaid, could now be produced as evidence. It was positively identified as having belonged to Warmus by Kristan Solomon. This, together with the handgun and silencer and Warmus's probable motivation, was sufficient for the jury to convict Warmus of second-degree murder in June, 1992. Under her twenty-five-years-to-life sentence, Warmus would be eligible for parole in 2017.

IMPACT

The story of a poor little rich girl having an obsessive affair with a philandering husband—a deadly love triangle, a tale of "fatal attraction"—galvanized public attention. So had the fact that it involved a femme fatale who had never been denied anything she had ever wanted—except for the husband of another woman. The voyeuristic public and media, especially within the entertainment industry, found the case irresistible. The story's rendering as a television movie in 1992 was no surprise. More thoughtful observers, however, may have reflected on such issues as parental responsibility (or lack of it) or family or psychological dysfunction to explain Carolyn Warmus's deviance.

FURTHER READING

Gallagher, Mike. *Lovers of Deceit: Carolyn Warmus and the "Fatal Attraction" Murder*. New York: Doubleday, 1993. A detailed account of Betty Jeanne Solomon's murder, its complicated twists and turns, and the roles of numerous individuals involved in the case. Illustrations.

Knappmann, Edward W. *Sex, Sin, and Mayhem: Notorious Trials of the '90's*. Detroit, Mich.: Visible Ink Press, 1995. Includes a factual summary of Warmus's two trials in 1991 and 1992. Illustrations, index.

Time-Life Books. *Crimes of Passion*. Alexandria, Va.: Author, 1994. The Warmus case is narrated in easy-flowing, language, though less colorful than Gallagher's. Illustrations, bibliography, index.

—*Peter B. Heller*

SEE ALSO: Bambi Bembenek; Joey Buttafuoco; Jean Harris.

RANDY WEAVER

American white separatist

BORN: January 3, 1948; Villisca, Iowa
ALSO KNOWN AS: Randall Claude Weaver (full name)
CAUSE OF NOTORIETY: Weaver, charged with possession and sale of two sawed-off shotguns to undercover government agents, failed to appear in court, which led to an incident on Weaver's property in which a U.S. deputy marshal was murdered and a lengthy standoff with federal agents ensued.
ACTIVE: 1989-1992
LOCALE: Sandpoint, Boise, and Ruby Ridge, Idaho

EARLY LIFE

Randall Claude Weaver (WEE-vuhr) was one of four children born to Clarence and Wilma Weaver. The Weavers were farmers in Villisca, Iowa. After graduating from high school in 1966, Randy enrolled in Iowa Central Community College. In the fall of 1968, Weaver quit college and enlisted in the Army. There he did well and was selected for the Green Berets. His true desire was to go to Vietnam. When his assignments kept him in the United States, he became disillusioned and decided to get out of the military and return to Iowa.

Upon returning to Iowa, he married Vicki Jordison in November, 1971. Randy enrolled in the University of Northern Iowa. The couple made a living selling Amway products. Weaver decided that school was too expensive, so he quit school and got a job at a John Deere tractor plant. Vicki got a job as a secretary. The two seemed to be doing well and purchased a small home and settled down.

In August, 1983, the couple sold their home in Iowa and moved west. They bought twenty acres of land at Ruby Ridge, Idaho, for five thousand dollars. Randy built a cabin there, in which the family—now including three children, Sara, Samuel, and Rachel—settled. It was after their move to northern Idaho that the Weavers developed their white separatist and antigovernment philosophies. Both Randy and Vicki came to believe that the government was watching them. Weaver allegedly began to participate in Aryan Nations activities and to display "white power" signs.

CRIMINAL CAREER

Weaver's first brush with the law was his January 17, 1991, arrest on a 1990 indictment for selling altered shotguns. Weaver was released on ten-thousand-dollar bail. He was to appear in court again on February 20, 1991. However, he was mistakenly sent a notice that his appearance date was March 20, 1991. Weaver did not appear in court on either of those dates.

In August, 1991, deputy U.S. marshals were sent out to arrest Weaver and bring him to court. Deputies from the U.S. Marshals Service Special Operations Group (SOG) were assigned to conduct surveillance of Weaver's house and to try to arrest him without anyone being injured. The deputies assessed the situation and determined that any action by the government would result in the serious injury or death of Weaver, law enforcement officers, or both. They recommended to the United States attorney that no action be taken.

However, at the insistence of the United States attorney, SOG deputies again began surveillance of the Weaver house on August 21, 1992. It was a chance encounter between deputies and Randy's son Samuel and friend Kevin Harris that led to the shoot-out that left both Samuel and Deputy William Degan mortally wounded. As a result of the death of Degan, numerous law enforcement agencies descended on Ruby Ridge.

Weaver believed that the law enforcement officers wanted him and his family dead. He declared that he would fight the officers. The result was a standoff between the Weaver family and Federal Bureau of Investigation (FBI) Hostage Rescue Team agents. On August 22, 1992, an FBI sniper shot and killed Vicki while she was holding the family's baby, Elisheba Anne, and wounded both Weaver and Harris. As the standoff continued, the FBI used retired Green Beret colonel Bo Gritz as a negotiator. The FBI believed that Gritz, who had ties to right-wing groups, might be trusted by Weaver. The standoff ended with the surrender of Weaver and Harris on August 30, 1992.

LEGAL ACTION AND OUTCOME

In March, 1993, Weaver was tried on several counts: his indictment for selling illegally altered shotguns to an Alcohol, Tobacco, and Firearms (ATF) informant on December 13, 1990; failure to appear in court in February, 1991; and assault, conspiracy, and murder in August, 1992. Weaver was represented by the well-known attorney Gerry Spence, who reportedly had not lost a case

since the 1960's. Weaver was convicted only of failure to appear in court, and the jury found him not guilty on all other charges. He was sentenced to eighteen months in custody and a ten-thousand-dollar fine. He was given credit for the fourteen months' time that he had served prior to sentencing.

IMPACT

If not for the relatively minor offenses that Randy Weaver committed between 1989 and 1991, the well-publicized incident at Ruby Ridge might not have occurred. For some Americans, Weaver became a symbol of the right to individual freedoms, including the right to own firearms. For others, his ties to the white separatist movement earned him contempt. Moreover, the shoot-out at Ruby Ridge became a rallying point for some right-wing extremists—including Timothy McVeigh, who was convicted of and executed for the 1996 Oklahoma City bombing that left 168 people dead—who considered the Weaver family victims of government oppression. Weaver sued the federal government for the wrongful death of his wife and son. In an out-of-court

Randy Weaver, displaying evidence before a Senate judiciary subcommittee. (AP/Wide World Photos)

STATE OF IDAHO V. HORIUCHI

Lon Horiuchi, the FBI sniper whose bullet felled Randy Weaver's wife, Vicki, was indicted for involuntary manslaughter. In the case State of Idaho v. Horiuchi, *the federal district court dismissed the indictment, holding that Horiuchi was protected by the Supremacy Clause of the U.S. Constitution, which grants immunity from criminal prosecution to federal law enforcement agents who, acting in the scope of official duty, reasonably and honestly believe their actions were necessary under the circumstances. That decision was affirmed by the Ninth Circuit Court of Appeals, whose ruling, written by District Judge William B. Shubb, reads in part:*

[T]here is nothing in the record to dispute the district court's finding that Horiuchi's subjective belief that his actions were necessary and proper was honestly held. The State has presented no evidence of evil or malicious intent, nor has the State shown any facts to dispute Horiuchi's state of mind. In fact, the state only charged Horiuchi with manslaughter, a crime that is specifically charged as being "without malice." . . .

Horiuchi knew it would be difficult, if not impossible, to apprehend the man once he re-entered the cabin, due to the presence of the Weaver children. Had he hesitated for even a few seconds or called out a warning (even assuming that Harris could have heard him from 200-300 yards away), Harris could have fled into the cabin, taking up a defensive, armed position.

Courts must avoid the temptation to dissect the events which flashed before a police officer in a matter of seconds and to over scrutinize the officer's response to those events. It is all too easy for judges pondering a cold record in the sanctity of their chambers to second guess the split-second decisions of the officer on the scene. . . . Faced with a dangerous armed man who was running to an area where he would present a greater danger, Horiuchi had less than a few seconds to make a decision. . . . Harris was a suspect in the shooting of a federal marshal; he was threatening a helicopter; he was running to a place where he could rearm, regroup, and take up a defensive position. Horiuchi did not see Vicki Weaver standing behind the open door with the curtains closed. He had no reason to believe that a woman holding a baby would be standing outside the threshold of the cabin, but hidden by the open door, after her husband had been shot at by an unknown agent. Horiuchi saw no danger to others, and he shot. He only intended to hit Harris.

The district court's finding that Horiuchi reasonably believed that shooting Harris was necessary and proper under the circumstances is supported by the evidence. Today, all must regret the tragic result. However, given the circumstances at the time, Horiuchi made an objectively reasonable decision.

Source: Office of the Circuit Executive U.S. Court of Appeals for the Ninth Circuit. Ruling. *State of Idaho v. Horiuchi.* Case no. 98-30149, filed June 14, 2000.

settlement, Weaver was awarded $100,000 for his losses. His three daughters were awarded $1 million each. In 1998, Weaver published a book titled *The Federal Siege at Ruby Ridge: In Our Own Words* with his daughter Sara and later made appearances on the gun-show circuit to promote the book.

FURTHER READING

Bock, Alan. *Ambush at Ruby Ridge*. New York: Berkley Books, 1996. Approaches the Ruby Ridge incident as a highly critical episode of overzealous government.

Klaidman, Daniel. "The Standoff Never Ends." *Newsweek*, September 1, 1997. Report of continued litigation against the FBI sniper who shot and killed Vicki Weaver.

Stern, Kenneth. *A Force upon the Plain: The American Militia Movement and the Politics of Hate*. New York: Simon & Schuster. 1996. Critical of right-wing groups, this book proposes federal legislation banning private militias.

Walter, Jess. *Every Knee Shall Bow*. New York: HarperCollins. 1996. Critical of actions taken on both sides of the Ruby Ridge incident.

Weaver, Randy, and Sara Weaver. *The Federal Siege at Ruby Ridge: In Our Own Words*. Marion, Mont.: Ruby Ridge, 1998. An account of the events of Ruby Ridge in the words of Randy and Sara Weaver.

Wells, Robert. "ATF Criticized for Actions in Ruby Ridge Shootout." *Congressional Quarterly Weekly Report*, September 9, 1995. Report on congressional hearings that criticized the actions of the ATF and FBI at Ruby Ridge.

—*Gerald P. Fisher*

SEE ALSO: David Koresh; Timothy McVeigh; Terry Nichols.

JOSEPH WEIL
American swindler and con artist

BORN: 1875 or 1877; Chicago, Illinois
DIED: February 26, 1976; Chicago, Illinois
ALSO KNOWN AS: Joseph R. Weil; Yellow Kid
MAJOR OFFENSE: Mail fraud
ACTIVE: c. 1900-1941
LOCALE: Chicago, Illinois
SENTENCE: Three years in prison

EARLY LIFE
Joseph Weil (weel or wil) was the son of honest, hard-working German American grocers in Chicago, born either in 1875 (according to Weil) or in 1877 (as indicated in official records). Weil watched his parents struggle for a meager living and was determined to have a much better life. Despite being a gifted student, he dropped out of high school at age seventeen. His first job was as a collector for a firm at which the bookkeepers and cashiers robbed their employer. Being observant and clever, Weil noticed their embezzlement and confronted them. To protect themselves, they paid him to keep quiet. Later, Weil acknowledged that his first job taught him that cunning and blackmail paid much better than his parents' ethical lifestyle.

Weil was offered a job by con man Doc Meriwether that entailed helping Doc sell phony elixirs composed of rainwater and alcohol that were touted as a cure for tapeworm.

CRIMINAL CAREER
From his first two jobs, Weil learned how to prey on people's greed and fears. He became a high-earning confidence man who swindled both urban and rural people out of eight million dollars over his forty-year career. He earned the nickname the Yellow Kid because he frequently read the comic strip "Hogan's Alley" featuring a country bumpkin character of the same name.

Most of Weil's victims were leading bankers, businessmen, doctors, and lawyers with the common desire to make money quickly. Many of his frauds involved horse races. Weil would convince others that the races were fixed. Wanting to get in on a sure thing, people would give him money to bet. Weil would collect the bets but leave with the money.

Weil's scams were staged in such a way that his victims would not report him to the police. For example, he persuaded victims that he had a duplicating machine that created legitimate-looking copies of their money. During the duplicating process, his accomplices would arrive in the guise of police raiding the premises. His victims would depart the premises to avoid jail but without their money.

In 1907, Weil staged an illegal boxing match during which a boxer, who was guaranteed to win, was pronounced "dead" by an accomplice posing as a doctor. Frightened bettors left without their money. Weil also set up buildings to look like legitimate banks or brokerage houses and hired accomplices to pose as employees. After conning people into making investments, he would take off with the money, leaving only empty offices.

LEGAL ACTION AND OUTCOME
In 1926, when members of Weil's gang believed that he had swindled them out of their share of income from selling stolen bonds, they reported him to police. Weil was jailed for three years. He was again jailed briefly in 1941 before ending his criminal career and going straight.

IMPACT
After giving up his life of crime, Joseph Weil lectured on swindlers and their methods. He wrote a book on "practical successful salesmanship." In 1956, he testified in the U.S. Senate as an expert witness before the Kefauver Committee, which was investigating American crime. The 1973 film *The Sting*, which received the Academy Award for Best Picture, is widely considered to have been inspired by Weil's life.

FURTHER READING
Algren, Nelson. *Chicago: City on the Make*. Fiftieth anniversary ed. Chicago: University of Chicago Press, 2001. An account of the history of Chicago. Annotated, with explanations of the people, events, and scandals that shaped Chicago's history.
Haller, Mark H. "Urban Crime and Criminal Justice: The Chicago Case." *Journal of American History* 57, no. 3 (December, 1970): 619-635. A historical review of the relationships between urban crimes, the social lives of ethnic groups in urban slums, and attempts to reform the criminal justice system.
Klapp, Orrin E. "The Clever Hero." *Journal of American Folklore* 67, no. 263 (January-March, 1954): 21-34. An account of criminals who were admired by the public for their ability to use power over others and who became social forces in their communities.

Weil, Joseph R., and W. T. Brannon. *Con Man: A Master Swindler's Own Story*. 1948. Reprint. New York: Broadway Books, 2004. Weil's account of how he swindled the public.

—Linda Volonino

SEE ALSO: Frank W. Abagnale, Jr.; Billy Cannon; Janet Cooke; Tino De Angelis; Billie Sol Estes; Susanna Mildred Hill; Megan Louise Ireland; Clifford Irving; Victor Lustig; Arthur Orton; Alexandre Stavisky.

CARL WEISS
Assassin of U.S. senator Huey Long

BORN: December 6, 1906; Baton Rouge, Louisiana
DIED: September 8, 1935; Baton Rouge, Louisiana
ALSO KNOWN AS: Carl Austin Weiss (full name)
CAUSE OF NOTORIETY: Weiss, a physician and family man, shot Senator Huey Long and was himself immediately shot dead by Long's bodyguards.
ACTIVE: September 8, 1935
LOCALE: Baton Rouge, Louisiana

EARLY LIFE
Carl Weiss (kahrl wis) was the eldest of three children born to prominent Baton Rouge physician Carl Adam and Viola (née Maine) Weiss. Weiss rapidly began a distinguished medical career after graduating from Tulane University Medical School, interning at Touro Hospital in New Orleans, American Hospital in Paris, and Bellevue Hospital in New York and doing postgraduate work in Vienna.

Most reports state that he was a scholarly gentleman and regular church attendee at St. Joseph's Catholic Church. In 1933, Weiss married Louise Yvonne Pavy, the daughter of Benjamin Pavy, a longtime Opelousas judge and a political opponent of Huey Long. Weiss developed a successful medical practice in Baton Rouge, and in 1935 Yvonne gave birth to their son, Carl Austin Weiss, Jr.

CRIMINAL CAREER
On the evening of September 8, 1935, Weiss told his family that he was going to check on patients at the local hospital. Instead, he went to the state capitol and quickly approached U.S. senator Huey Long. While there is no universally accepted eyewitness account of the shooting, the most commonly accepted version is that of state police officer Murphy Roden. Roden's account was that Weiss approached Long rapidly and shot him once. Roden wrestled the gun from Weiss as state police officers shot Weiss between thirty and seventy times. At the time, Weiss was not known by any of those around the

scene of the shooting and was referred to as "the man in the white linen suit."

Observers recounted that Long voiced his wonder at having been shot. Some accounts have Long stating that he did not know Weiss at all. Weiss did not fit the profile of many other political assassins. There was no record of his being a political zealot, nor was there any recorded evidence that would suggest that he was psychotic. By most accounts, Weiss was a dedicated husband and father with a successful medical practice. Others have hypothesized that Weiss never actually shot Long and that Long was killed in the barrage of gunfire from Long's bodyguards. Several reports cite poor medical attention as a contributing factor in the senator's death. Regardless of these theories, Long died two days later, on September 10, after emergency surgery to save him proved unsuccessful.

IMPACT
The death of Huey Long remains questionable to this day. Much of the confusion and controversy regarding this case comes from the facts that there was no autopsy performed on Long's body and there was significant delay in the investigation of the incident. Carl Weiss was buried the day after he died.

Part of the confusion of the stories may have been perpetuated by the significant popularity of Robert Penn Warren's book *All the King's Men* (1946). The book was a thinly veiled biography of Huey Long (referred to as Willie Stark), including his assassination by Dr. Adam Stanton. Although Long's political machine was powerful, there was no clear line of succession after his death. Part of the way to solidify the political machine was to make Long a martyr. In order to keep the legend alive, his supporters may have spread several conspiracy stories that President Franklin D. Roosevelt and other anti-Long parties set Long up to die.

Some claim that Carl Weiss killed Long as an act of patriotism out of fear that Long was leading the United

States to a fascist governmental system similar to those in Europe at the time. Others claim that Weiss was motivated by other factors. Long was known aggressively to slander political opponents and their families, and Pavy family members were targeted by Long.

FURTHER READING

Clarke, James W. *American Assassins: The Darker Side of Politics*. Princeton, N.J.: Princeton University Press, 1982. One chapter on Weiss explains that his lack of pathology or political zealotry makes him an "atypical" assassin.

Deutsch, Hermann B. *The Huey Long Murder Case*. Garden City, N.Y.: Doubleday, 1963. Describes details in the lives of Weiss and Long to explain how this unforeseen act most likely occurred.

Zinman, David H. *The Day Huey Long Was Shot: September 8, 1935*. Jackson: University Press of Mississippi, 1993. Zinman questions that Weiss actually fired the bullet that killed Long.

—*John C. Kilburn, Jr.*

SEE ALSO: Huey Long.

HYMIE WEISS
American gangster

BORN: 1898; Chicago, Illinois
DIED: October 11, 1926; Chicago, Illinois
ALSO KNOWN AS: Earl Wojciechowski (birth name)
CAUSE OF NOTORIETY: As one of the leaders of Chicago's infamous Northside Gang, Weiss engaged in bootlegging and murder and tangled several times with rival gangsters Johnny Torrio and Al Capone.
ACTIVE: 1913-1926
LOCALE: Chicago, Illinois

EARLY LIFE

Hymie Weiss (HI-mee wis) was born Earl Wojciechowski in Chicago in 1898 to William and Mary Wojciechowski. His parents' devout Catholic families originally came to Buffalo, New York, by way of Poland before the nineteenth century. After they married, his parents moved to Chicago sometime before Earl was born. During this period and for reasons that are unclear, Earl's father changed the family surname to a more Jewish-sounding name, Weiss. During his early teens, Earl became known as Hymie to his friends, a name that stuck with him throughout his criminal career.

Early on, Hymie became friends with Dean (Dion) O'Banion, a tough Irish boy six years his senior with a penchant for crime. Throughout their teens, the boys engaged in various forms of crime, including burglary, car theft, muggings, bootlegging, armed robberies, and even murder. Together, Weiss and O'Banion, along with other infamous mobsters such as Bugs Moran, built one of the most nefarious criminal gangs of Prohibition-era Chicago—the Northside Gang. The gang's criminal headquarters was a flower shop on North State Street on Chicago's north side, across from the Holy Name Cathedral. However, the gang's arch rivals, Italian mobsters Johnny Torrio and Al Capone, who ran the rackets in Chicago during this time, would ultimately bring about the untimely demise of O'Banion and Weiss.

CRIMINAL CAREER

Weiss has been credited with being responsible for the creation and success of his gang's bootlegging enterprise. His business acumen, coupled with his loyalty to both O'Banion and their crew, helped spearhead the Northsiders as one of the front-runners in the bootlegging industry during Prohibition. Weiss was also an established hit man; his murder of fellow mobster Stephen Wisniewski propelled him into organized crime fame. Reportedly, Wisniewski had hijacked beer trucks belonging to the Northsiders, and to teach him a lesson, O'Banion ordered Weiss to kill him. Weiss decided to take Wisniewski on a drive along Lake Michigan; Wisniewski never returned. After returning from the murder, Weiss openly joked to other members of the gang that he took "Stevie" for a "one-way ride," a phrase that gained notoriety in and of itself.

From 1920 to 1926, Weiss and O'Banion attempted to absorb small-time rival gangs, gain their rightful stake in the illegal booze business, and start an all-out gang war with rivals Capone and Torrio. As tensions grew between the Northsiders and the Capone and Torrio gang, violence erupted on the streets of Chicago. In fact, this particular six-year period has been labeled as one of the bloodiest times in Chicago history. During this tumultuous period, dozens of men from both gangs were brutally murdered, including O'Banion in November, 1924.

Following O'Banion's death, Weiss took the helm of the Northsiders and slowly plotted his revenge against Capone and Torrio. After waiting nearly two months to avenge his friend's death, Weiss and his crew attempted numerous times to assassinate Capone and Torrio; these attempts only wounded Torrio and forced him into retirement, which in turn enraged the unscathed Capone and prompted him to seek his own revenge. After his failed assassination attempts, Weiss himself became a victim of the Prohibition gang war. On October 11, 1926, Capone's henchmen gunned down Weiss as he was entering the gang headquarters on North State Street. It was later discovered that the assailants had shot Weiss from a second-story window across the street from the Northsider headquarters.

At age twenty-eight, Weiss became a victim of a bootlegging war that he had helped create. After his death, the Northsiders continued to operate under the leadership of Moran and other members; however, Capone proved to be too powerful and the Northsiders disbanded. At the time of his death, Weiss had mounted an estate worth an estimated $1.3 million, all of which he willed to his wife.

IMPACT

Hymie Weiss, Polish American mobster and bootlegger, is remembered as one of the most notorious gangsters of the Prohibition era. With his street smarts and his business knowledge, Weiss helped create one of the most successful illegal operations in Chicago history. He will be remembered as one of the cofounders of the Northside Gang, which attempted but failed to topple the mighty Al Capone.

FURTHER READING

Abadinsky, Howard. *Organized Crime*. 7th ed. Belmont, Calif.: Wadsworth/Thomson Learning, 2003. A textbook that offers a unique account of the history of organized crime in America and how criminals such as Weiss and O'Banion operated during the Prohibition era.

Keefe, Rose. *Guns and Roses: The Untold Story of Dean O'Banion, Chicago's Big Shot Before Al Capone*. Nashville, Tenn.: Cumberland House, 2003. Provides detailed information about the criminal life of O'Banion and offers insight into the friendship between O'Banion and Weiss.

Reppetto, Thomas. *American Mafia: A History of Its Rise to Power*. New York: Henry Holt, 2004. A detailed look at the history of the Mafia in the United States. Sheds light on the gangs of the Prohibition era, including Chicago's infamous Northside Gang.

—*Paul M. Klenowski*

SEE ALSO: Al Capone; Sam Giancana; Bugs Moran; Dion O'Banion.

HORST WESSEL
German Nazi and lyricist

BORN: September 9, 1907; Bielefeld, Westphalia, Germany
DIED: February 23, 1930; Berlin, Germany
CAUSE OF NOTORIETY: Wessel, a member of the Nazi Sturmabteilung (SA, or assault section of the Nazi storm troopers), rallied morale by writing patriotic song lyrics and was glorified as a Nazi martyr in the early years of the movement.
ACTIVE: 1926-1930
LOCALE: Berlin, Germany

EARLY LIFE

Horst Wessel (hohrst VEHS-sehl) came from a respectable bourgeois family. His father, Dr. Ludwig Wessel, was a Lutheran minister who later served in the pastorate at St. Nikolai, Berlin's oldest church. During World War I, he became chaplain at the headquarters of Field Marshal Paul von Hindenburg and died while on duty. Young Wessel was raised with the ideal of sacrificing for "the Fatherland."

Wessel became an ardent nationalist and was active in the Bismarck Bund, the German youth section of the German Nationalist People's Party, as well as in the Free Corps Viking youth organization. After taking a degree at a humanistic gymnasium (a school preparatory to the university), he started to study law in 1926 at the University of Berlin. He joined a fraternity that was a training ground for the professional elite but found its aristocratic aspirations and political passivity irrelevant to Germany's troubled political scene. He also came in contact

THE HORST WESSEL SONG

"Die Fahne hoch" ("The Flag on High") was the signature anthem of the Nazi Party, a paean to bravery and self-sacrifice for the Fatherland. It was banned in Germany at the end of World War II.

Flag high, ranks closed,
The S.A. marches with silent solid steps.
Comrades shot by the red front and reaction
march in spirit with us in our ranks.

The street free for the brown battalions,
The street free for the Storm Troopers.
Millions, full of hope, look up at the swastika;
The day breaks for freedom and for bread.

For the last time the call will now be blown;
For the struggle now we all stand ready.
Soon will fly Hitler-flags over every street;
Slavery will last only a short time longer.

Flag high, ranks closed,
The S.A. marches with silent solid steps.
Comrades shot by the red front and reaction
march in spirit with us in our ranks.

with Marxism at the university, and he found it as reprehensible as bourgeois hypocrisy. He found his political awakening when he joined the Nazi Party in 1926.

NAZI CAREER

While smart and politically astute, Wessel was also restless and violent. After Nazi propaganda minister Joseph Goebbels sent him to Vienna in 1928 to organize the Nazi youth movement there, Wessel returned to Berlin, where he transformed a small pack of intimidated, riffraff Brownshirts (members of the SA, so called because of their brown uniforms) into a reckless fighting force called Storm Section 5. This group worked mostly in the East Berlin section of Friedrichshain, a largely communist area of dangerous streets, newly arrived immigrants, and thugs. Under Wessel's command, the Nazis successfully challenged the communists on their home ground by using terrorism and counterterrorism. The communist leadership of the district was angry that the Berlin Nazis were campaigning in a once solidly communist district and had even managed to convert many former communists and supporters to the Nazi cause. The Red Front Fighters League counterattacked by launching brutal assaults on Nazis in the streets and in the pubs they frequented.

Wessel understood the power of music to rally people in political battle. It was customary for the Brownshirts to sing as they marched through the streets of Berlin, both to raise their own morale and to spread propaganda. Wessel's creation of a wind instrument band won considerable renown as a propaganda ploy in the neighborhoods. In 1929, he wrote his own lyrics titled "Die Fahne hoch" ("The Flag on High") to the tune of an old German patriotic song called "Wacht am Rhein" ("The Watch on the Rhine").

MARTYRDOM

Wessel died the way he had lived, violently. In mid-1929, after falling in love with a prostitute named Erna Jaenicke, he moved out of his mother's house and into a sublet room in Friedrichshain, not far from the streets that he roamed with his thugs. This move caused his work for the Nazi Party to deteriorate. Although Goebbels sent someone to talk to him, Wessel considered it a show of disdain for his beloved Erna, his future bride. He continued to exist on the fringes of poverty, supporting Erna and himself on his wages as a construction worker. Also in 1929, his brother, Werner, was killed in a skiing accident with several of his friends. Wessel's physical and psychological health began to decline, while the communists circulated flyers in the neighborhood calling for his murder.

The facts of Wessel's death were never clear because they were quickly distorted by both the Nazis and the communists. What is clear is that on January 14, 1930, he had an argument with his landlady, Frau Salm. They argued over the rent and the presence of Erna, as well as the frequent disturbances from the gatherings of Wessel's Brownshirts in his apartment. Unable to handle the situation alone, Frau Salm went to a local tavern and asked for help from the Red Front Fighters League, whose members were eager to avenge themselves on Wessel. Two men, Ali Hohler, who had underworld contacts, and Erwin Ruckert, an active party member, went to Wessel's apartment, where Hohler shot him several times in front of Erna. Wessel died a few weeks later from his injuries.

IMPACT

Horst Wessel's death fit perfectly into Goebbels's propaganda machine, and he turned it into a unifying symbol of the Nazi Party. Wessel was glorified as a martyr to the Nazi cause. He was celebrated in myth and song, biography and film. Units in the German and Italian armed forces were named after him, as were public streets and squares. "The Flag on High" became known as the "Horst Wessel Lied" (Horst Wessel song) and was an anthem of the Nazi Party. It was considered a paean to bravery and to self-sacrifice for the führer and the Fatherland. Wessel's grave was a Nazi shrine until 1945, the year the song was banned in Germany.

FURTHER READING
Baird, Jay W. "Goebbels, Horst Wessel, and the Myth of Resurrection and Return." In *To Die for Germany: Heroes in the Nazi Pantheon*. Bloomington: Indiana University Press, 1992. Details the way in which Goebbels elevated Wessel as a Nazi martyr.

Bytwerk, Randall L. *Bending Spines: The Propaganda of Nazi Germany and the German Democratic Republic*. East Lansing: Michigan State University Press, 2004. This book provides an analysis of the material of the German Propaganda Archive.

Delarue, Jacques. *The Gestapo: A History of Horror*. Translated by Mervyn Savill. New York: William Morrow, 1964. An overview of the German secret police during the Nazi regime.

—*Sheila Golburgh Johnson*

SEE ALSO: Joseph Goebbels; Adolf Hitler.

DAN WHITE
American killer

BORN: September 2, 1946; San Francisco, California
DIED: October 21, 1985; San Francisco, California
ALSO KNOWN AS: Daniel James White (full name)
MAJOR OFFENSE: Voluntary manslaughter
ACTIVE: November 27, 1978
LOCALE: San Francisco, California
SENTENCE: Seven years and eight months in prison; served less than five years

EARLY LIFE
San Franciscan Dan White (wit) came from a blue-collar, working-class family. Good-looking, religious, and self-righteous, White served San Francisco as both a police officer and a firefighter. His future seemed assured by his election to the post of San Francisco city supervisor, representing District 8, the city's most conservative district and home to many working-class Roman Catholics. White vowed to wage war against political and social radicals, sexual deviates, and incorrigibles. He promised to fight to restore traditional values to city government.

CRIMINAL CAREER
Despite his promises to reform San Francisco's government, White had difficulty supporting his wife and newborn child on a supervisor's $9,600 yearly salary. On November 10, 1978, he submitted his resignation from the Board of Supervisors to San Francisco mayor George Moscone. Shortly thereafter, with urging from various conservative groups, White reconsidered and asked Moscone to reappoint him.

An underlying cause of White's resignation was his opposition to the gay rights bill introduced by supervisor Harvey Milk and passed by a ten-to-one vote by the Board of Supervisors. The dissenting vote was White's. Mayor Moscone, who was dedicated to equal rights for all citizens, signed the bill into law immediately.

Moscone, about to announce the appointment of one of his political supporters, Don Horanzy, to fill White's seat, turned a deaf ear to White's request for reappointment. White falsely assumed that Milk was responsible for Moscone's failure to reappoint him. (He did not realize that there was some friction between Moscone and Milk.) White brooded about Moscone's silence over the weekend. Unable to sleep, White gorged himself on so-called junk food.

On the morning of Monday, November 27, an enraged White entered City Hall through a basement window, to avoid passing through metal detectors at the main entrance. He burst into Moscone's office and, after confronting him, drew a .38-caliber handgun from his pocket and pumped four bullets into the mayor's body at close range, two into his head.

White then reloaded his weapon, using devastating dumdum bullets, and proceeded to Milk's office. Milk maneuvered White into White's former office. White, standing between Milk and the door, drew the revolver from his tan jacket and pumped five bullets into the supervisor, killing him instantly. He fled and was soon found with his wife in Saint Mary's Church, praying.

LEGAL ACTION AND OUTCOME

White was arrested and brought to trial charged with the premeditated first-degree murders of Moscone and Milk. Although it was obvious that White had killed the two, many San Franciscans felt great sympathy for the accused. Police officers and firefighters raised a defense fund of more than $100,000 on White's behalf.

When the White jury was impaneled, it excluded gays, blacks, and members of other minority groups. However, the jury selected was largely white and blue-collar, was politically and socially conservative, and clearly was homophobic. The capital charges against White were reduced to voluntary manslaughter, of which he was eventually found guilty.

White's defense was the so-called Twinkie defense. It asserted that White was overstimulated by the high-carbohydrate foods he consumed the night before the killings. This defense, designed to reduce his culpability, succeeded: He was sentenced to seven years and eight months in prison, which, with reductions for good behavior, resulted in his serving slightly less than five years.

Released from Soledad Prison on January 6, 1984, White, plagued by financial problems, went to Los Angeles but found the atmosphere there inhospitable. He returned to San Francisco, where, on October 21, 1985, he ended his life by attaching a garden hose to the exhaust pipe of his wife's Buick Le Sabre and inhaling the carbon monoxide fumes.

IMPACT

The immediate impact of Dan White's killing of Moscone and Milk was to divide the city of San Francisco. Thousands of protesters marched to City Hall to honor the two dead politicians. The day of their deaths is commemorated annually by a march in the Castro district, which Milk represented.

The verdict in the White trial was announced on May 21, 1979. That evening, thousands of protesters marched on City Hall and, in what is termed the "White Night" ri-ots, fought with police and burned a number of police cars. The protesters broke into City Hall and created more than a million dollars in damage.

Police officers, covering their shields, dealt brutally with the protesters and invaded several gay bars, whose patrons they beat. In the long term, however, this violence focused attention on the inhumanity of mistreating gays in the name of justice.

FURTHER READING

Krakow, Kari. *The Harvey Milk Story*. Ridley Park, Pa.: Two Lives Publishing, 2001. A valuable account of White's killing spree in San Francisco. Comments on the aftermath of the murders.

Marcus, Eric. *Making History: The Struggle for Gay and Lesbian Equal Rights*. New York: HarperCollins, 1992. Focuses on how the killings in San Francisco's City Hall helped gays achieve civil rights gains both in San Francisco and throughout the United States.

Ridinger, Robert B. Marks. *The Gay and Lesbian Movement: References and Resources*. New York: G. K. Hall, 1996. Ridinger cites accounts of Dan White's killing of Moscone and Milk from the standpoint of White's conflicted views of homosexuality.

Shilts, Randy. *The Mayor of Castro Street: The Life and Times of Harvey Milk*. New York: St. Martin's Press, 1982. Assesses Harvey Milk's contributions to the lesbian/gay movement, emphasizing how his death galvanized segments of mainstream society to support equal rights.

Weiss, Mike. *Double Play: The San Francisco City Hall Killings*. Reading, Mass.: Addison-Wesley, 1984. The most comprehensive account in print of the city hall killings. At 422 pages, the book contains very useful documentation and information.

—*R. Baird Shuman*

SEE ALSO: Byron Looper; Volkert van der Graaf.

CHARLES WHITMAN
American mass murderer

BORN: June 24, 1941; Lake Worth, Florida
DIED: August 1, 1966; Austin, Texas
ALSO KNOWN AS: Charles Joseph Whitman (birth name); Texas Sniper
CAUSE OF NOTORIETY: Whitman, who murdered seventeen people in a one-day killing spree, was killed by authorities before he could be brought to trial.
ACTIVE: August 1, 1966
LOCALE: Austin, Texas

EARLY LIFE
Charles Joseph Whitman (WHIHT-muhn) was born to Charles A. and Margaret E. Whitman in Lake Worth, Florida, and was raised Roman Catholic. In grade school, Whitman demonstrated superior intelligence, and at the early age of twelve he became an Eagle Scout. Despite their affluence and social prominence, the Whitman family suffered internal discord. Whitman's father was physically and verbally abusive toward Charles and his mother. Whitman graduated from high school in June, 1959, and, after a serious confrontation with his father in July, enlisted in the U.S. Marine Corps, where he became a sharpshooter. In 1961, Whitman applied for and received a scholarship from the Naval Enlisted Science Education Program and began study at the University of Texas, Austin. The following summer he married.

Haunted by his father's berating, Whitman's academic performance as an engineering student began to suffer despite his best efforts. His scholarship was revoked in February, 1963, and he was forced to return to Camp Lejeune, South Carolina. While stationed there, he was court-martialed for unlawful possession of a firearm and usury. Notwithstanding these infractions, Whitman was honorably discharged from the Marines in December, 1964, and he returned to the University of Texas engineering program.

In early 1966, Whitman's mother and youngest brother, John, left his abusive father and other brother, Patrick, and moved to Austin. Whitman began to receive harassing phone calls from his father.

CRIMINAL CAREER
In March, 1966, Whitman met with a doctor at the university health center to discuss recurring feelings of rage and hostility. He failed to return as directed for subsequent visits but was prescribed Dexedrine by his psychiatrist. Later it was discovered that he had a cancerous brain tumor.

On July 31, 1966, Whitman stabbed and killed his mother, leaving a note describing his actions. In the predawn hours of August 1, Whitman stabbed his wife in her sleep, leaving another note expressing his reasons and his final wishes. Dressed as a maintenance worker, Whitman entered the Clock Tower of the University of Texas at about 11:30 A.M. and ascended to the observation deck, carrying a footlocker containing several high-powered semiautomatic rifles, handguns, and ammunition. In the process, Whitman killed a tower employee and two visitors. At 11:48 A.M., Whitman began firing a rifle from the 307-foot tower, killing the first random victim on the main mall of the campus. During the following ninety-six minutes, Whitman killed eleven (including an unborn child) and wounded thirty-one people from his barricaded position; three decades later, the day's seventeenth victim would die from wounds sustained during the spree.

LEGAL ACTION AND OUTCOME
The massacre ended when two Austin police officers, Houston McCoy and Ramiro Martinez, and one deputized citizen, Allan Crum, crept out onto the observation deck to confront Whitman. As Martinez emptied his .38-caliber revolver in the direction of Whitman, McCoy fired on Whitman twice with a 12-gauge shotgun, killing him. Martinez waved a white towel when the murderous rampage finally ended at 1:24 P.M. Whitman's body was returned to Florida, where he was buried.

IMPACT
Charles Whitman's mass murders significantly affected Austin's first responders. The Austin Police Department and Brackenridge Hospital's emergency room were quickly overwhelmed during the murder spree. In the following months and years, police administrators established special weapons and tactics (SWAT) units, and hospitals developed protocols for mass casualty incidents.

The University of Texas Clock Tower was closed for two years after the shootings. It reopened to the public in 1968, but after a series of suicides, it again closed in 1975. After twenty-four years, the tower's observation deck, replete with guided tours and physical security features, reopened on September 15, 1999.

The shock of Austin's darkest ninety-six minutes had local and national media implications. Word of the massacre spread quickly via television, newspapers, and word of mouth. Nationally, the story was featured on the August, 1966, covers of *Time* and *Life* magazines. Surviving victims, suffering short- and long-term disabilities, were interviewed for years after the incident. David Gunby, one of the first gunshot victims of Whitman on August 1, 1966, died from kidney complications on November 12, 2001, the result of wounds he had sustained during the shooting spree.

FURTHER READING

Helmer, William J. "The Madman in the Tower." In *Crime Chronicles*. New York: Warner Books, 2000. Part of a larger collection of true crime events that occurred in Texas, this concise analysis of Whitman shows the historical context and magnitude of the murder spree.

Lavergne, Gary M. *A Sniper in the Tower: The Charles Whitman Murders*. Denton: University of North Texas Press, 1997. Using primary sources and photographs, this is an in-depth factual account of Charles Whitman's father's "tough love," Whitman's hate for his father, and how it shaped his life leading up to the mass murders.

Nevin, David. "Texas Sniper's Murder Rampage." *Life* 61, no. 7 (August 12, 1966): 24-31. Published eleven days after the incident, the cover story traces Whitman's early life through his murderous rampage as depicted in photographs.

—Anthony J. Luongo III

SEE ALSO: Baruch Goldstein; John Allen Muhammad and Lee Boyd Malvo.

JONATHAN WILD
British gang leader

BORN: c. 1682; Wolverhampton, Staffordshire, England
DIED: May 24, 1725; Tyburn, London, England
ALSO KNOWN AS: Thief-Taker General of Great Britain and Ireland
MAJOR OFFENSE: Returning stolen goods under false pretenses
ACTIVE: January, 1725
LOCALE: London, England
SENTENCE: Death by hanging

EARLY LIFE

Born in Wolverhampton, Jonathan Wild served a brief apprenticeship as a buckle maker before venturing to London in 1704. After losing his money at the gaming tables, he was imprisoned for debt. During four years of confinement, he gained extensive knowledge of London's criminal underworld under the tutelage of prostitute Mary Milliner, his future wife.

CRIMINAL CAREER

Wild developed a sophisticated criminal network in London in which he directed thefts of goods, then extorted "rewards" for their return from their original owners. As self-styled "thief taker," he effectively controlled London's criminal underclass by arresting and providing evidence against those operating outside his network.

Wild began his criminal career at a time of rapid population expansion in London, where the antiquated criminal justice system was inadequate to deal with the rise in urban crime. Ironically, measures intended to curb crime led to Wild's rise. In the 1710's authorities passed ordinances making it illegal to harbor or sell stolen goods (formerly not a crime). Wild turned the situation to his advantage by offering to serve as middleman between thieves and their victims. For thieves, he offered a better return for their stolen goods and protection from prosecution. To victims, he offered restoration of goods for less than the cost of their replacement, with no questions asked. Wild's organizational genius soon had him planning and directing thefts, maintaining warehouses of stolen goods, and managing agents involved in the return of the goods or their sale on the black market.

By 1715 Wild had abandoned his humble residence with Milliner in Cock Alley for an office in the Old Bailey, London's famed criminal court. By 1718 he had taken control of the criminal network of corrupt City Marshal Charles Hitchens, whose fall from grace Wild orchestrated. Having reached the height of his power and public approbation, Wild styled himself "Thief-Taker General of Great Britain and Ireland." Wild maintained his facade as a crime fighter by arresting well-known criminals such as members of the Carrick gang and Jack Sheppard (a former compatriot).

LEGAL ACTION AND OUTCOME

In 1725 Wild suffered a reversal of fortune: His participation in the jailbreak of one of his own confederates landed him in Newgate Prison. Though he attempted to carry on his business from behind bars, his reputation as thief taker was destroyed, and the full extent of his criminal operations soon came to light. Tried on almost a dozen counts, including broad crimes such as extortion and racketeering, Wild was convicted on a single charge of fraudulently returning some expensive lace whose theft he had planned. His death sentence was carried out at London's Tyburn gallows to the evident pleasure of the large crowd.

IMPACT

While Jonathan Wild was not the first to create an organized crime network in eighteenth century London, he established the most all-encompassing criminal enterprise of his time. His use of the public persona of crime fighter to cover his increasingly brazen crimes led to his lasting infamy. His approach to crime as a lucrative business also heralded the rise of the organized crime syndicates of the twentieth century.

In death, Wild the criminal became Wild the fictional villain. While Daniel Defoe wrote a relatively straightforward account of Wild's life in 1725, John Gay transposed Jack Sheppard and Wild into Mack the Knife and Peachem in *The Beggar's Opera* (1729). Henry Fielding used Wild's Machiavellian genius to satirize the corrupt ministry of Robert Walpole in his novel *Jonathan Wild* (1743).

FURTHER READING

Beattie, J. M. *Policing and Punishment in London, 1660-1750: Urban Crime and the Limits of Terror*. New York: Oxford University Press, 2001. Provides an overview of the development of a criminal justice system and the role of "thief taker."

Fielding, Henry. *Jonathan Wild the Great*. Edited by Peter Ackroyd. London: Hesperus Press, 2004. This edition of Fielding's classic uses Wild's life to satirize Robert Walpole. Ackroyd provides a valuable introduction, which separates the historical Wild from the fictional.

Linebaugh, Peter. *The London Hanged: Crime and Civil Society in the Eighteenth Century*. 2d ed. London: Verso, 2003. A broad discussion of the evolution of the criminal underworld as an aspect of the development of modern capitalistic society. The work discusses a number of famous criminals including Wild.

—*Luke Powers*

SEE ALSO: Eugene Aram; William Brodie; William Dodd; Jack Sheppard; Dick Turpin.

JAMES WILKINSON
American traitor

BORN: 1757; Calvert County, Maryland
DIED: December 28, 1825; Mexico City, Mexico
CAUSE OF NOTORIETY: Wilkinson was involved in an attempt to overthrow George Washington as commander of the Continental army during the American Revolution, in spying for the Spanish government, and in the treasonous activities of Aaron Burr.
ACTIVE: 1787-1811
LOCALE: Kentucky and Louisiana

EARLY LIFE

James Wilkinson (WIHL-kihn-suhn) was the son of Joseph Wilkinson, a merchant-planter in Calvert County, Maryland. After studying medicine at the University of Pennsylvania, Wilkinson joined the Continental army at the outbreak of the American Revolution in 1775. He was a captain in 1776 under Benedict Arnold and a brigadier general in 1777, at age twenty, serving as an aid to Horatio Gates. His involvement in several controversies, including a plot to replace George Washington with Gates, led to Wilkinson's resignation from the army in 1781.

ESPIONAGE CAREER

Wilkinson moved to Kentucky in 1783, and by 1784 he was a paid agent of Spanish authorities in New Orleans, advising Spain about American plans in the West. Although his actual benefit to Spain was minimal, he allegedly took an oath of loyalty to the Spanish crown in 1787 and had a role in the so-called Spanish Conspiracy of 1787-1790. His secret contacts with Spain continued through the War of 1812.

Wilkinson rejoined the army in 1791, serving under

General Anthony Wayne in the Ohio River Indian campaigns. In 1796, upon the death of Wayne, Wilkinson became the ranking officer of the U.S. Army. In 1803 he was military governor in the Southwest and participated in the transfer of the Louisiana Territory from France to the United States. He was governor of Louisiana in 1805-1806. In this capacity he began his involvement with Aaron Burr.

In the winter of 1804, Burr was serving his last months as vice president of the United States. He met often in Washington with Wilkinson, whom he had known since 1776, when both served under Benedict Arnold. The meetings included close study of maps of the Louisiana Territory and Mexico. On June 8, 1805, three months after Burr left office, the two met again at Fort Massac on the Ohio River. Wilkinson's position as Louisiana governor, as well as his similarity to Burr in character, made him an ideal accomplice for Burr's scheme to separate Louisiana and form his own nation.

When Burr's plans became known, Wilkinson denounced him as a traitor and testified against him before a grand jury in 1807. Burr was indicted but later acquitted; Wilkinson escaped indictment by one vote and again testified at Burr's trial for treason.

Wilkinson's military career resumed during the War of 1812, in which he led the disastrous Canadian invasion in 1813. Reportedly still on the payroll of Spain, he retired from the U.S. Army in disgrace in 1815. In Mexico City, seeking a land grant in Texas, Wilkinson died on December 28, 1825.

LEGAL ACTION AND OUTCOME

Wilkinson was twice court-martialed, in 1811 and in 1815, but never convicted. Proof of his involvement with Spain was not collected until after his death.

IMPACT

James Wilkinson's military career was less successful than his legal battles. Critics at the time said that he never won a battle or lost a court-martial. John Randolph, a contemporary of Wilkinson and a congressman from Virginia, called Wilkinson a "finished scoundrel." Royal Shreve's 1933 book states as part of its title that Wilkinson "made intrigue a trade and treason a profession."

FURTHER READING

Green, Thomas Marshall. *The Spanish Conspiracy.* 1891. Reprint. Gloucester, Mass.: P. Smith, 1967.

James Wilkinson.

Puts Wilkinson in the center of Spanish intrigue in America from 1763 to 1812. Also includes the involvement of Kentucky senator John Brown. Gives a good picture of Wilkinson's character.

Melton, Buckner F. *Aaron Burr: Conspiracy to Treason.* New York: John Wiley and Sons, 2002. Evaluates Burr's involvement with, and betrayal by, Wilkinson. Includes testimony by Wilkinson at Burr's treason trial.

Montgomery, M. R. *Jefferson and the Gun-Men: How the West Was Almost Lost.* New York: Crown, 2000. Covers the interaction of all the men involved in the affairs regarding land west of the Mississippi River in the first decade of the nineteenth century: Thomas Jefferson, Meriwether Lewis, William Clark, Burr, and Wilkinson. Artist sketches of each.

Shreve, Royal Ornan. *The Finished Scoundrel: General James Wilkinson, Sometime Commander-in-Chief of the Army of the United States, Who Made Intrigue a Trade and Treason a Profession.* Indianapolis: Bobbs-Merrill, 1933. Very critical of Wilkinson; details the route of his deception.

—*Glenn L. Swygart*

SEE ALSO: Benedict Arnold; Aaron Burr; William Walker.

HENRY WIRZ
Swiss American commandant of Andersonville prison during the Civil War

BORN: November 25, 1823; Zurich, Switzerland
DIED: November 10, 1865; Washington, D.C.
ALSO KNOWN AS: Hartmann Heinrich Wirz (full name)
MAJOR OFFENSES: Murder and violation of the laws and customs of war
ACTIVE: March 27, 1863-April 17, 1865
LOCALE: Andersonville, Sumter County, Georgia
SENTENCE: Death by hanging

EARLY LIFE

Hartmann Heinrich Wirz (vuhrts) was born in Switzerland in 1823; his father, Hans, was a tailor by trade. As a young man, Wirz dreamed of becoming a physician, but Hans objected, insisting that his son enter the growing mercantile trade. Wirz married in 1845, but the marriage ended in divorce after he ran into trouble with the law a few years later. After the Swiss government banished him, Wirz emigrated to the United States in 1849. In the United States, Wirz first worked as a weaver in Lawrence, Massachusetts, but eventually relocated to Kentucky, where he sought employment as a doctor's assistant. Wirz settled in the small town of Cadiz to practice medicine and met a widow named Elizabeth Wolfe. They were married on May 28, 1854. By the late 1850's, the couple had moved to Milliken's Bend, Louisiana, where Wirz was hired as a doctor for the slaves on the Marshall Plantation.

When the Civil War broke out, Wirz enlisted as a private in the Fourth Louisiana Regiment, and he moved in the summer of 1861 to guard prisoners around the Confederate capital of Richmond, Virginia. Wirz received a severe wound just above his right wrist during the Battle of Seven Pines. This debilitating injury changed the course of Wirz's military career, and with the help of Brigadier General John H. Winder, the commander in charge of overseeing Richmond's prison population, Wirz received a promotion to sergeant and was placed in charge of the Tuscaloosa, Alabama, prison. The position lasted less than a year. Wirz underwent another change in duty by December, 1862, when Southern officials sent him overseas to carry dispatches to Confederate commissioners in Europe. After spending two years abroad, Wirz returned in February, 1864, and received a promotion to captain. Winder then ordered him to assume command of the interior stockade at Andersonville near Macon, Georgia.

CRIMINAL CAREER

Wirz inherited a chaotic situation after taking command. The guard force at Andersonville was a group consisting of Georgia Reserves and teenagers. Prison officials depended on a crude wooden fence 15 feet within the stockade, known as the "deadline," to stop prisoners. If prisoners approached the deadline, guards warned them to leave the area; if the men refused the order, the sentries would shoot them.

Overcrowding caused mortality rates to skyrocket within the stockade as the prison population grew dramatically over a six-month period. When the camp began operations in March, 1864, the prison camp contained seventy-five hundred men; by August, Andersonville confined approximately thirty-two thousand men on twenty-six acres of land. Congestion also affected sanitation within the stockade. A small creek five feet in width bisected the prison, and it eventually became a breeding ground for infectious diseases. The poor quality of rations contributed to sickness within the compound as well. Of the forty-five thousand men confined at Andersonville during its fourteen months of operation, it is estimated that thirteen thousand died from disease, malnutrition, and exposure.

By mid-April, 1865, a Union column captured Columbus, and three weeks later, the liberation of Andersonville took place. Wirz was placed under arrest for conspiring to deliberately impair the lives of Union prisoners of war.

LEGAL ACTION AND OUTCOME

Wirz awaited trial by military commission in Old Capitol Prison. A military commission derived its authority from the international laws of war and special executive or congressional legislation that tried nonmilitary offenses. By the conclusion of the war, Union forces occupied most of the South, and officials viewed the section as a de facto belligerent nation. Wirz was a member of the Confederate Army, so military rules that governed Union soldiers could not be applied to him.

The Wirz commission consisted of nine men: Major General Lewis "Lew" Wallace, best remembered for his 1880 novel, *Ben-Hur*, became the president of the commission. The prosecuting attorney depicted Wirz as a brutal fiend who maliciously intended to destroy the prisoners by subjecting them to inhumane conditions. The defense counsel, to the contrary, claimed that Wirz was a victim of circumstance because the camp's situation worsened beyond his control, experiencing costly delays and shortages in supplies.

The trial riveted Americans and made newspaper headlines for its two-month duration. In a unanimous decision, commission members found Wirz guilty of deliberately impairing the lives of prisoners and of eleven of thirteen counts of individual acts of murder. He was sentenced to death by hanging. Wirz went to the gallows on November 10, 1865, at 10:30 A.M.

IMPACT

As commandant of Andersonville, Henry Wirz was connected to the horrendous conditions of the prison and thus charged with war crimes committed during the Civil War. Wirz constituted a convenient scapegoat because he was the victim of a hostile Northern press that reported conditions at Andersonville months before Wirz was charged and brought to trial. Wirz was also a victim of circumstance. Winder, his superior, had died a few months before the end of the war and could not testify to Wirz's actions as commandant. Lastly, he was the victim of a system that relied on contemporary military law. Moreover, the Wirz trial served as a showcase for Judge Advocate General Joseph Holt to get former high-ranking members of the Confederacy before military commissions. Holt felt that Jefferson Davis, the declared president of the Confederacy during the war, in particular, should answer for his war crimes, and he believed the Wirz trial would implicate the former Confederate president.

FURTHER READING

Futch, Ovid. *History of Andersonville Prison*. Gainesville: University of Florida Press, 1968. Scholarly treatment of conditions at Andersonville; argues that mismanagement by Southern officials caused supply shortages that devastated the efficient administration of the prison.

Hesseltine, William Best. *Civil War Prisons: A Study in War Psychology*. Columbus: University of Ohio Press, 1930. Classic work by a historian regarding military prisons located in the North and South.

Laska, Lewis L., and James M. Smith. "Hell and the Devil: Andersonville and the Military Trial of Henry Wirz, C.S.A, 1865." *Military Law Review* 68 (Spring, 1975): 77-132. The authors explain the difference between courts-martial and military commissions. They contend that Wirz was a scapegoat because of a variety of legal, political, and social factors.

Marvel, William. *Andersonville: The Last Depot*. Chapel Hill: University of North Carolina Press, 1994. Marvel asserts that Wirz confronted bias and a prejudicial court from the onset of his trial. The author contends that Norton Parker Chipman, judge advocate, manipulated Wirz and impeded the defense at every opportunity.

—*Gayla Koerting*

SEE ALSO: Belle Boyd; Simon Cameron; Pauline Cushman; William Clarke Quantrill.

ADAM WORTH

German American thief and swindler

BORN: 1844; eastern Germany
DIED: January 8, 1902; London, England
ALSO KNOWN AS: Napoleon of Crime; Henry James Raymond, Esq.; Adam Wirth; Little Adam; Prince of the Safecrackers; Napoleon of the Criminal World
MAJOR OFFENSE: Robbery
ACTIVE: c. 1869-1892
LOCALE: Liege, Belgium
SENTENCE: Seven years of solitary confinement and hard labor; served five years

EARLY LIFE

Adam Worth (wurth) was born in Germany to Jewish parents in 1844. When Worth was five, his family, including a brother, John, and a sister, Harriet, emigrated to the United States, settling in Cambridge, Massachusetts, where Worth's father set up shop as a tailor. Meanwhile, "Little Adam" developed a reputation as a con artist in the Boston area. When the American Civil War (1861-1865) broke out, Worth enlisted numerous times, receiving a Union enlistment bonus or payment each time.

CRIMINAL CAREER

After the war, Worth settled in New York City and began his criminal career in earnest. He started as a pickpocket and soon found himself robbing banks in league with the infamous "Queen of Fences," Frederika "Marm" Mandelbaum. In 1869, he moved to Liverpool, then London, adopting the name and persona of Henry James Raymond, Esq., a wealthy English gentleman. Worth organized and contracted out assignments for robbery, burglary, swindling, mail theft, and forgery throughout England and the Continent, from which he would collect a sizable commission. Worth's lust for affluent respectability led him to purchase a 110-foot yacht, which he also used for criminal operations in South America.

Worth's most famous exploit was his 1876 theft of the painting *Duchess of Devonshire* (painted in 1783 by the famous artist Thomas Gainsborough), which Worth would hide for twenty-five years before returning it in 1901 for twenty-five thousand dollars in cash.

LEGAL ACTION AND OUTCOME

Worth's mystique as a criminal mastermind was enhanced by his ability to escape prosecution for two decades, while directing a web of criminal activities. However, on October 5, 1892, while supervising a robbery in Liège, Belgium, he was arrested. On March 20, 1893, he was convicted of robbery and sentenced to seven years of solitary confinement and hard labor in the infamous Prison de Louvain. He served five years before his release and then died two years later, a broken man.

IMPACT

An organizer and mastermind of crime spanning several continents and the ocean seas, Adam Worth has acquired a certain literary notoriety. Robert Anderson, a Scotland Yard detective, described the diminutive Worth as the "Napoleon of the Criminal World." Worth's greatest impact was to serve as a model of evil genius. Arthur Conan Doyle revealed that he modeled in part the criminal genius and foe of Sherlock Holmes, Professor James Moriarty, after Worth. In the Sherlock Holmes 1893 story "The Final Problem," Doyle describes Moriarty as the "Napoleon of Crime," at the center of evil in London, like a spider in the middle of its web. It has been speculated that T. S. Eliot's *Old Possum's Book of Practical Cats* (1939) drew inspiration from the same source in describing the "mystery cat" Macavity, who organizes the criminal cats and "who all the time/ Just controls their operations: the Napoleon of Crime!"

FURTHER READING

Doyle, Arthur Conan. *The New Annotated Sherlock Holmes*. Edited by Leslie S. Klinger. New York: W. W. Norton, 2004-2005. A three-volume, 2,900-page collection of the Sherlock Holmes novels and short stories, including the stories featuring Professor James Moriarty, with extensive notes explaining the source and background of characters and incidents.

Horan, James D. *The Pinkertons: The Detective Dynasty That Made History*. New York: Crown, 1967. Devotes a chapter to Worth based on the Pinkerton archives. For three days in 1899, Worth gave a complete account of his life to his former nemesis, Detective William Pinkerton, in the course of negotiations for return of the *Duchess of Devonshire*.

Macintyre, Ben. *The Napoleon of Crime: The Life and Times of Adam Worth, Master Thief*. New York: Farrar, Straus and Giroux, 1997. An engrossing, comprehensive modern biography, sympathetic to Worth and emphasizing the strict code of nonviolence he adopted for himself and enforced on his gang members.

—*Howard Bromberg*

SEE ALSO: Jules Bonnot; Cartouche; Frederika Mandelbaum; Jack Sheppard; Dick Turpin; Jonathan Wild.

AILEEN CAROL WUORNOS
American serial killer

BORN: February 29, 1956; Rochester, Michigan
DIED: October 9, 2002; Florida State Prison, Starke, Florida
ALSO KNOWN AS: Aileen Carol Pittman (birth name); Lee
MAJOR OFFENSES: Prostitution, robbery, and murder
ACTIVE: December 1, 1989-November 19, 1990
LOCALE: Northern and central Florida
SENTENCE: Death by lethal injection in six separate sentences

EARLY LIFE
Aileen Carol Wuornos (WUHR-nohs) was born into a troubled family. Her parents were teenagers and separated not long after her birth. Her father, Leo Pittman, was a child molester who was committed to mental hospitals in Kansas and Michigan before committing suicide. Her mother, Diane, abandoned Aileen and her brother Keith in 1960. Diane's parents, Lauri and Britta Wuornos, legally adopted the children later that year. Wuornos later claimed that Lauri, her grandfather, had sexually molested her and that Britta, her grandmother, was an alcoholic.

Wuornos was sexually active from an early age and later reported that one of her partners was her brother. In 1971, she gave birth to a son at a Detroit maternity home; her brother may have been the father. During the summer of that year, Britta died, officially of liver failure. Aileen's mother then accused Lauri of killing Britta, claiming that he had also threatened to kill his grandchildren. The two Wuornos children became wards of the court, but Aileen dropped out of school and became a wanderer, supporting herself by prostitution. During the 1970's and 1980's, she was arrested for numerous petty crimes, including disorderly conduct, drunk driving, assault, and shoplifting, as well as prostitution.

CRIMINAL CAREER
On her brother's death in 1976, Wuornos received an insurance payment of ten thousand dollars, but she spent the money on her legal fines and on a car that she wrecked. Later that year, she hitchhiked to Florida,

Aileen Carol Wuornos. (AP/Wide World Photos)

where she lengthened her record with arrests for armed robbery of a convenience store, passing forged checks, auto theft, and other charges. From May, 1982, to June, 1983, she was imprisoned on an armed robbery charge. While in Florida, Wuornos formed one of the few close relationships in her life. She met Tyria Moore, a woman originally from Ohio, in a gay bar in Daytona, Florida. The two women became lovers and friends, traveling together and sharing difficult lives.

Police officers who arrested Wuornos, under various aliases, frequently noted her hostile attitude. She seemed to seek out confrontation and traveled with a loaded pistol when she picked up customers in bars and truck stops or hitchhiked to sell sex to truck drivers. On November 30, 1989, she took a ride with Richard Mallory, a fifty-one-year-old electrician. Two weeks later, Mallory was found dead in the woods outside Daytona, shot three times in the chest with a .22-caliber pistol. Over the course of the next year, a number of additional dead men, some nude and some clothed, were discovered in similar circumstances.

LEGAL ACTION AND OUTCOME

Wuornos became a suspect in the crimes when she tried to pawn items belonging to Mallory and another victim, Walter Gino Antonio. Although she used an alias, police identified her by the fingerprints on pawn shop cards. Wuornos confessed almost immediately to six killings, but she claimed that the men had attempted to assault her sexually and that she had shot them in self-defense. Wuornos was sentenced to death by legal injection in 1992.

The appeal of the death sentence lasted more than a decade. In November, 1992, *Dateline NBC* reporter Michele Gillens discovered that Mallory had served ten years in prison for violent rape, giving some credibility to Wuornos's claim that she had been assaulted. During her trial, Wuornos also obtained an advocate in the person of Arlene Pralle. Reporting that she had received instructions in a dream to help Wuornos, Pralle and her

---

> ## FEMALE SERIAL KILLERS
>
> *Reporters claimed for Aileen Wuornos the distinction of being America's first female serial killer. That claim is not correct, nor was she the most prolific. While Caucasian males vastly outnumber all other types of serial killers, women have been represented since late in the nineteenth century. Some of them were partners with men—typically their husbands or lovers—in the killings, but several acted entirely on their own. Here are examples:*
>
> - **Jane Toppan**, who worked as a private nurse, confessed in 1901 to having murdered thirty-one people with morphine injections. She may actually have killed as many as one hundred. She said, "That is my ambition, to have killed more people—more helpless people—than any man or woman who has ever lived."
> - **Belle Gunness**, after killing two husbands and two of her children for insurance money, lured wealthy men to her Chicago home, murdered them, and fed their bodies to her pigs. From bones found after a fire there in 1908, investigators estimated that she killed at least fourteen and as many as one hundred with the help of her farmhand, Ray Lamphere. She is thought to have faked her own death in the fire and escaped with money stolen from her victims.
> - **Martha Beck** and Raymond Fernandez were known as the "lonely-hearts killers." During the 1940's, they targeted elderly single women, bilking them of their savings before killing them. They confessed to twelve murders but may have killed as many as twenty. They were executed together in 1951.
> - **Caril Ann Fugate**, fourteen years old, helped or approved of eleven murders by her boyfriend, Charles Starkweather, in Nebraska during 1958 and 1959; she perhaps killed some on her own. Her father, mother, and baby sister were among the victims.
> - **Dorothea Puente** poisoned at least eight elderly people in her Sacramento, California, boardinghouse and then cashed their social security checks as if they were still living. She was arrested in 1988 after police dug up corpses in her garden.
> - **Lyda Catherine Ambrose** murdered five husbands and lovers for insurance money before she went to jail in Idaho in 1931. She escaped in 1932 but was recaptured in Kansas and spent the rest of her life imprisoned.

---

husband legally adopted the troubled woman. Nevertheless, the United States Supreme Court denied the appeal in 1996, and the State of Florida executed Wuornos on October 9, 2002.

IMPACT

The trial and conviction of Aileen Wuornos drew wide public attention and became the basis of numerous books, plays, an award-winning film, and even an opera. Part of the impact of the Wuornos case was due simply to the fact that the offender was a woman who killed men. Serial killers are generally identified as men, often killing for sexual motivations, with women or younger men as the victims. Thus, Wuornos was frequently billed as the first female serial killer, although there have been many women who have killed multiple victims.

Part of the impact of the Wuornos case was also a result of her defense. Wuornos maintained that she had been sexually abused throughout her life and that the men she had killed were attempting to sexually assault her. The troubled childhood raised questions about the degree of responsibility held by someone who has been repeatedly attacked. Moreover, the revelation that her first victim had been a rapist suggested that there may have been some element of truth to her claims.

Some feminist social critics took the Wuornos case as an illustration of the condition known as battered women's syndrome, a psychological reaction to repeated brutality. The moral complexity of the Wuornos case appeared in the acclaimed 2003 film *Monster*, which told the killer's story from the time she met her female lover until she was convicted of murder. The film portrayed Wuornos as an individual who had been abused by everyone in her life except the lover and as someone who deserved a certain amount of sympathy.

FURTHER READING

Reynolds, Martin. *Dead Ends: The Pursuit, Conviction, and Execution of Female Serial Killer Aileen Wuornos, the Damsel of Death*. New York: St. Martin's Press, 2004. An account of Wuornos's killing spree by the reporter who broke the story. The book follows the story from Wuornos's accounts through the trial and conviction.

Russell, Sue. *Lethal Intent*. New York: Kensington, 2002. An internationally syndicated journalist examines Wuornos's early life and background to determine why this woman, who wanted to do something "no woman has ever done before," turned to homicide.

Shipley, Stacey L., and Bruce A. Arrigo. *The Female Homicide Offender: Serial Murder and the Case of Aileen Wuornos*. Upper Saddle River, N.J.: Prentice Hall, 2003. A psychological and criminological investigation of what leads to female homicidal behavior that goes well beyond the Wuornos case. Challenges the conventional view of women serial killers as victims of abuse and analyzes the social and cultural context in which violence evolves.

Wuornos, Aileen, and Christopher Berry-Dee. *Monster: My True Story*. London: John Blake, 2004. Wuornos's own story as told to the editor of *The New Criminologist*, who is also the director of the Criminology Research Centre.

—*Carl L. Bankston III*

SEE ALSO: Karla Homolka.

JOAN WYTTE
English witch, seer, and healer

BORN: 1775; Bodmin, Cornwall, England
DIED: 1813; Bodmin, Cornwall, England
ALSO KNOWN AS: Fighting Fairy Woman of Bodmin
CAUSE OF NOTORIETY: Although Wytte never ran afoul of the legal establishment for her practice of witchcraft, her corpse was displayed as a museum piece until 1998.
ACTIVE: 1790's-1813
LOCALE: Cornwall, England

EARLY LIFE

Little is known of Joan Wytte (WI-eht) during her early years, though it is fairly safe to assume that in her youth she learned some of the healing skills common to "cunning women" of her era. Several other Cornish women of about the same time frame are also remembered for skills associated with witchcraft. These include Dolly Pentreath (1692-1777), Tamsin Blight (1798-1856), and Granny Boswell (1813-1906).

HEALING CAREER

Wytte was credited with several skills common to witches or "cunning women" of her day: clairvoyance, divining, and healing. Neighbors would come to her for help and advice. Wytte's particular method of healing, clouties, is still used by pagans in Cornwall today. In clouties, a piece of cloth from the sick person's clothing is made into a charm and hung on a tree branch. As the fabric decays, the person is supposed to become healed.

None of Wytte's practices aroused enough attention for her to receive legal censure. Rather, a toothache led to her demise. After her death, an autopsy revealed a badly abscessed wisdom tooth. Apparently the agony it caused her made her quarrelsome and combative. These characteristics led to her being dubbed "The Fighting Fairy Woman of Bodmin." Shortly before her death, Wytte got into a particularly fierce fight in which she reportedly threw people across the room; these assaults led to her being jailed. She died in 1813 as a result of poor treatment she received in prison.

IMPACT

Joan Wytte is most famous for what happened to her after her death, which augmented and perpetuated her legend. Her corpse was used as a prop for a séance and was then displayed in a Cornwall museum until 1998. Legend has it Wytte's fiery spirit was no calmer in death than it had been in her pain-afflicted life. Witnesses to the séance claimed that the lid of Wytte's coffin flew around the room, hitting people.

Her corpse's next home, the Cornwall Museum of Witchcraft, allegedly experienced disturbances thought to be poltergeist activity. Local legend says that the museum brought in a witch to analyze the cause, which was traced to Wytte's expressing her desire to rest in a peaceful spot. Museum of Witchcraft staff decided in 1998 to give Wytte a long-overdue burial, and her body was interred in a nearby wood. The empty coffin that once held Wytte is still displayed in the museum, along with a memorial stone stating that she is "no longer abused." Local residents often place flowers on this memorial stone.

FURTHER READING

Briggs, Robin. *Witches and Neighbors: The Social and Cultural Context of European Witchcraft*. New York: Penguin, 1998. Examines court records of Wytte's time and explores regional differences in attitudes toward and beliefs about witchcraft.

Davies, Owen. *Cunning-Folk: Popular Magic in English History*. New York: Hambledon, 2003. An examination of the tradition of cunning folk and the key social roles they played in nineteenth century British life. The author estimates that there were thousands of such individuals across the British isles. Illustrated, with a detailed bibliography and index.

Jones, Kelvin I. *The Wise Woman: Her Lives, Charms, Spells, and Cures*. Corpusty, Norwich, England: Oakmagic, 2000. Argues that the wise or cunning woman is not the same as a witch, as is commonly supposed.

Kieckhefer, Richard. *Magic in the Middle Ages*. 2d ed. New York: Cambridge University Press, 2000. Examines how magic was practiced in the Middle Ages, including who practiced it. Surveys magic's development and growth.

—Elizabeth Jarnagin

SEE ALSO: Tamsin Blight; Mary Butters; Margaret Jones; Florence Newton; Dolly Pentreath; Elizabeth Sawyer; Mother Shipton.

GENRIKH YAGODA
Soviet secret police chief

BORN: 1891; Lodz, Poland, Russian Empire (now in Poland)

DIED: March 15, 1938; Moscow, Soviet Union (now in Russia)

ALSO KNOWN AS: Enon Gershonovich Yagoda (full name); Genrikh Gregorievich Yagoda (Russian full name); Enoch Yehuda

CAUSE OF NOTORIETY: During the Soviet Great Terror, Yagoda oversaw the first two Moscow Trials and the subsequent deaths of political figures and other, lesser-known Soviet citizens. Joseph Stalin ultimately charged Yagoda with poisoning Soviet leaders and had him tried in the third Moscow Trial; Yagoda was found guilty.

ACTIVE: 1922-1938

LOCALE: Former Soviet Union, particularly Moscow and Leningrad (now St. Petersburg)

SENTENCE: Death

EARLY LIFE

Genrikh Yagoda (GEHN-rihk yah-GOH-dah) was the son of a Jewish jeweler who moved to Nizhniy Novgorod early in the son's life, and there is evidence that the family's original name was Yehuda (Judah) before it was changed to the more Russian-sounding "Yagoda," which means "berry" in Russian. Yagoda studied to be a pharmacist, and in 1907 he became a member of the Bolsheviks, a socialist political faction.

In personal appearance, Yagoda was short and balding, with devious eyes behind thick glasses. Perhaps because of his small stature and unimpressive appearance, he always insisted on appearing in public in full uniform and designed impressive uniforms for the Soviet secret police. As his career progressed, he became increasingly debauched in his personal life and amassed a substantial collection of women's lingerie and sex toys. He also was fascinated with horticulture and claimed that he had more than one thousand orchids and roses at his dacha, or country house.

During the early years of the Soviet Union, Yagoda was associated with the group that would ultimately be condemned by Soviet dictator Joseph Stalin as the "right deviationist" wing of the Bolshevik Party. In particular, Yagoda was a close friend of Yakov Sverdlov, the first Soviet head of state, with whom Stalin had quarreled.

POLITICAL CAREER

Although Yagoda had held a variety of positions in the Bolshevik Party from the beginning of the Bolshevik regime in 1917, his true rise to power began at the close of the Russian Civil War (1918-1922). By this time, he had risen to the upper echelons of the Cheka, the earliest form of the Soviet secret police. On June 6, 1921, Cheka chief Felix Dzerzhinsky recommended him as a deputy to Vyacheslav Menzhinsky, an important section head. In this position, Yagoda worked consistently to solidify his own position, appointing friends and associates to significant positions. However, he made several serious mistakes, including allowing the head of the old czarist secret police, Alexei Lopukhin, to escape to France. This and other defections annoyed Stalin, who disliked anything that signified a possible loss of control.

When Dzerzhinsky died in 1926, Menzhinsky succeeded to his position, and Yagoda was put in line to take the top position in turn. That opportunity came in 1934 upon Menzhinsky's death. Yagoda was put in charge of the Soviet secret police when Leningrad party secretary Sergei Kirov was shot on December 1, 1934. Historians have long debated the exact extent to which Stalin was involved in the assassination of his friend and rival. It is known that the secret police units guarding Leningrad's party headquarters were aware of Kirov's assassin, Leonid Nikolaev, and even briefly detained him.

MOSCOW TRIALS

Stalin ordered Yagoda to search out and destroy all the people who were responsible for Kirov's death. That Nikolaev had acted alone on an unhealthy obsession was not an acceptable answer, and Stalin soon provided specific names of enemies who were to be linked to the murder as a part of a grand conspiracy, led from abroad by his hated rival Leon Trotsky. Yagoda became one of the principal organizers of the first two of the infamous Moscow Trials—parodies of justice with predetermined verdicts against Soviet officials, which nonetheless thoroughly convinced many Western observers, who praised the trials as exemplary. In addition, Yagoda saw to the arrests and secret trials of thousands of other, lesser figures.

However, Stalin soon grew dissatisfied with Yagoda for developing the purges too slowly and for failing to look within his own organization for possible counterrevolutionaries and foreign agents. In an example of the dictator's twisted sense of humor, he had Yagoda not only dismissed but also arrested and made him one of the defendants at the third and final Moscow Trial. Yagoda was accused of having poisoned various Soviet leaders, a charge that was not entirely false. There is evidence that Stalin used Yagoda's knowledge of chemistry and poisons to eliminate various rivals who could not be discredited and publicly destroyed. On March 13, 1938, Yagoda was condemned to death, and the sentence was duly carried out a mere two days later.

IMPACT

Genrikh Yagoda was instrumental in creating the apparatus of Soviet state terror and setting it into motion at the beginning of the Great Terror. However, he underestimated the sheer extent of Stalin's ambition to destroy all enemies, real and possible. As a result, Yagoda was, in the end, consumed by the monster he had created. Rather than being interred in the Kremlin Wall as had been his two predecessors, his ashes were thrown into an unmarked grave along with uncounted numbers of his own victims.

FURTHER READING

Conquest, Robert. *The Great Terror: A Reassessment*. New York: Oxford University Press, 1990. A post-glasnost reissuing of the most authoritative volume on the era.

Montefiore, Simon Sebag. *Stalin: The Court of the Red Tsar*. New York: Alfred A. Knopf, 2003. Includes information on Stalin's use of Yagoda and other henchmen to run the Terror while deflecting attention from himself.

Rayfield, Donald. *Stalin and His Hangmen: The Tyrant and Those Who Killed for Him*. New York: Random House, 2004. A study of the relationship between Stalin and his chief henchmen.

Rogovin, Vadim Z. *1937: Stalin's Year of Terror*. Translated by by Frederick S. Choate. Oak Park, Mich.: Mehring Books, 1998. A Trotskyist perspective on the Great Terror.

Vaksberg, Arkady: *Stalin's Prosecutor: The Life of Andrei Vyshinsky*. New York: Grove Weidenfeld, 1990. Includes information on Yagoda's role in the Moscow Trials as related to that of Vyshinsky.

—*Leigh Husband Kimmel*

SEE ALSO: Felix Dzerzhinsky; Vladimir Ilich Lenin; Joseph Stalin; Vasili Vasilievich Ulrikh; Nikolay Ivanovich Yezhov.

ANDREA YATES
American murderer

BORN: July 2, 1964; Houston, Texas
ALSO KNOWN AS: Andrea Pia Kennedy (birth name)
MAJOR OFFENSE: Murder of her five children
ACTIVE: June 20, 2001
LOCALE: Houston, Texas
SENTENCE: Life sentence; conviction overturned in 2005

EARLY LIFE

Andrea Pia Kennedy, known by her married name of Andrea Yates (AN-dree-ah yayts), was born on July 2, 1964, in Houston, Texas. Raised in a Roman Catholic family, Andrea had a happy childhood. She was high school class valedictorian, and she jogged and swam regularly. After graduating from Milby High School in 1982, Andrea attended the University of Houston and University of Texas at Houston, where she majored in nursing. She worked as a registered nurse at a Houston cancer center from 1986 until 1994.

Andrea met Russell "Rusty" Edison Yates in Houston in 1990. They were married on April 17, 1993. Rusty was employed as an engineer with the National Aeronautics and Space Administration (NASA), and Andrea continued to work as a nurse until she had her first child, Noah Jack, in 1994.

Andrea and Rusty lived in a house in Houston until 1993; they then lived in a travel trailer and bus. During this time Andrea had four other children and one miscarriage. She reportedly became increasingly reclusive and overtly religious while she homeschooled her children. Her husband subscribed to a fundamentalist philosophy of marriage, insisting that his wife defer to him, give up her job, and not use birth control. The couple believed that a woman's children would go to hell for her sins if she did not repent, and Andrea was consumed with guilt for her inability to deal with her struggles with mental illness. The family did not have babysitters, and Rusty later admitted that he never changed a diaper for any of his children.

Andrea Yates. (AP/Wide World Photos)

CRIMINAL CAREER

During the course of their marriage, Andrea was treated for her deteriorating mental state. After the birth of her first child, she reported seeing Satan and images of death. She became increasingly thin, evasive, detached, isolated, and consumed with religious righteousness; she attempted suicide during depressive episodes. During her first suicide attempt, on June 17, 1999, Andrea was hospitalized for overdosing on pills. After being treated in a psychiatric unit and being diagnosed with major depressive disorder, she was released with a prescription for antidepressants. However, she did not take the medication.

Andrea soon stopped feeding her children and began to report hallucinations to her husband. She later threatened to slit her own throat with a knife and was hospitalized after going into a catatonic state. While there, she was successfully treated with antipsychotic medication and therapy for postpartum depression, and she was released from the hospital after being warned by doctors that having more children could put her health at risk.

She returned to the bus to care for her four children and became increasingly obsessed with fundamentalist Christian teachings.

Rusty purchased a home at Andrea's family's urging later in 1999, and her mental state appeared to improve dramatically. Andrea was healthy until March, 2000, when she stopped taking her medication as a result of another pregnancy. Four months after the birth of her daughter, her father died suddenly, sending Andrea into a deep depression. She mutilated herself, lost her appetite, stopped caring for her children, and refused to speak to her family.

After two more brief hospitalizations and treatment with antipsychotic medications, Andrea was again released. Two days after her meeting with her psychiatrist, Andrea brought her children one by one to her bathroom, where she drowned them; she then laid them out on her bed. When she was done killing her four sons and one daughter, ages six months to seven years, she calmly called police to request an officer and then called her husband and told him to come home.

LEGAL ACTION AND OUTCOME

Yates was charged with five counts of capital murder for the drowning of her children. She gave a detailed confession to police, saying that she killed her children to save them from Hell. During her seventeen-day trial, numerous psychiatrists testified that Yates was not competent, was mentally defective, and was in a psychotic state when she killed her children. California psychiatrist Park Dietz, a prosecution witness, testified that Yates was mimicking an episode of the television series *Law and Order* during which a woman was acquitted of killing her children by drowning them. Yates was convicted of capital murder on March 12, 2002, for the deaths of three of her children but was spared the death penalty. Instead, she was sentenced to life in prison on March 15. Americans were torn over the verdict, with many arguing for treatment for her mental illness instead.

However, in early 2005, the Texas Court of Appeals reversed Yates's sentence after finding that Dietz's testimony about the *Law and Order* episode was factually incorrect; no such episode ever aired, and the court found that Dietz's testimony might have influenced the jury. A new trial was ordered, and on January 9, 2006, Yates pleaded not guilty by reason of insanity to the murder charges. On July 26, 2006, Yates was found not guilty by reason of insanity by a jury of six men and six women. Yates underwent several months of evaluation prior to being assigned to a mental health facility for treatment.

IMPACT

The Yates case was a polarizing one for many Americans and brought discussions of homeschooling, the isolation of the mentally ill woman, and the role of fundamentalist Christianity in the tragic deaths of the children into a public forum. Some, including many feminists, characterized Rusty Yates as an abuser for "forcing" his wife to continue to have children despite warnings from medical professionals. Rusty was also vilified by public opinion, as many considered him an accessory to his children's deaths. Others were shocked that a mother could bring such lethal harm to her own children.

Rusty in turn blamed the deaths of his children on poor medical care of Andrea and on insurance companies; he supported his wife throughout her trials but maintained that her insanity case was "built on lies." Andrea's family blamed Rusty for Andrea's mental deterioration and called him insensitive and apathetic. They supported charges of negligent homicide and child endangerment being brought against Rusty, but prosecutors never pursued these charges. Rusty had divorced Andrea in March, 2005, and remarried in March, 2006.

FURTHER READING

O'Malley, Suzanne. *Are You There Alone? The Unspeakable Crime of Andrea Yates*. New York: Simon & Schuster, 2004. The author offers a detailed account of Yates's crime, psychiatric analyses, and information about the false testimony of the prosecution witness that Andrea was trying to escape punishment.

Spencer, Suzy. *Breaking Point*. New York: St. Martin's Press, 2002. This true-crime novelist presents the story of how Andrea Yates changed from a loving mother to a woman tormented by the darkness of mental illness. Provides inside information from police on the scene and background on the family.

—*Denise Paquette Boots*

SEE ALSO: Diane Downs; Magda Goebbels; Marie Hilley; Darlie Routier; Susan Smith.

NIKOLAY IVANOVICH YEZHOV
Head of Soviet secret police (1936-1938)

BORN: May 1, 1895, or possibly 1892; St. Petersburg, Russia, or possibly Suwałki, Poland

DIED: Probably February 2, 1940; Moscow, Soviet Union (now in Russia)

ALSO KNOWN AS: Nikolai Ivanovich Ezhov; the Dwarf; Karlik; Kol'ka Knizhnik (Nicky the Bookworm); Kolya; Kostya; Kolyushenka

CAUSE OF NOTORIETY: Yezhov carried out the Great Purges of the Communist Party and of Soviet citizens accused of opposing Joseph Stalin's rule until he himself came under suspicion and was killed for treason and espionage following a show trial.

ACTIVE: 1936-1938

LOCALE: Former Soviet Union, particularly Moscow

SENTENCE: Death

EARLY LIFE

According to his official biography, Nikolay Ivanovich Yezhov (NIHK-oh-li ee-VAH-noh-vitch yeh-ZHOFF) was born in St. Petersburg on May 1, 1895. Some believe that he may in fact have been born as early as 1892, likely in the area of Suwałki, a town on the border of Poland and Lithuania. Although his official biography claimed that he was of purely Russian ethnic origin, his mother was apparently Polish or Lithuanian, and Yezhov was able to speak some Polish and Lithuanian. Later, as the xenophobia of Soviet dictator Joseph Stalin began to color Soviet life, Yezhov would disavow knowing any language except Russian.

Yezhov's education was spotty at best, described in his Communist Party documents as elementary and incomplete. However, he was a determined autodidact, and his extensive reading resulted in his being labeled with the nickname Kol'ka Knizhnik, or Nicky the Bookworm. He held various lowly positions in St. Petersburg's industries and began to experiment sexually with both men and women. During World War I, his small stature (five feet, one inch) and fragile health led to his being exempted from service in the czar's army; however, he later obtained the ribbon for a St. George Cross and passed himself off as a war veteran.

POLITICAL CAREER

After service as a radio technician in the Red Army during the Russian Civil War (1918-1922), Yezhov spent several years moving from one position to another, always with good reports about the energy with which he tackled each assignment. People recalled him as a shy but personable young man, fond of singing and hardly the monster he later became.

By the early 1930's, Stalin took a personal interest in Yezhov. In 1936, Yezhov was made assistant to Genrikh Yagoda, head of the Soviet secret police, and placed in charge of the work of arranging the first two show trials, or legal proceedings of political opponents of Stalin during the Great Purge. Yezhov also purged the rank and file of the secret police. Finally, Yagoda was accused of deliberately slowing the progress of the purges and was sentenced to death in the last of the three show trials.

Throughout 1937, Yezhov, serving as chief of the secret police, brought the Great Terror to a frantic peak known as the *Yezhovshchina*, or "Yezhov-thing." Soviet citizens were being arrested and shot for the flimsiest of reasons. Yezhov often prepared lists of people to be executed on random scraps of paper rather than official stationery of the Narodnyi Komissariat Vnutrennikh Del (NKVD; the People's Commissariat of Internal Affairs). He also began to drink so heavily that it affected his ability to work. He was said to spend the entire morning drinking in his Lubyanka office.

By 1938, the purges had reached the point that the Soviet Union was teetering on the brink of disaster. In the fields of science and industry, so many trained specialists had been eliminated that there was literally no one left who understood how to operate the equipment. Officials began to realize that the purges had to be slowed down before the country fell apart. Stalin brought in Lavrenty Pavlovich Beria, a fellow man of the Caucasus, as Yezhov's assistant. Yezhov immediately recognized a scenario eerily similar to that which had taken place between Yagoda and him in 1936: Yezhov had been appointed Yagoda's assistant until Yagoda was killed for impeding with the purges. Yezhov now went to Beria with his fears of impending execution, apparently not realizing that Beria despised him and relished the opportunity to destroy him. In April, 1938, Yezhov was made commisar of water transportation, which he recognized as a demotion and a prelude to destruction. He spent the next year in a diminished position, spending entire meetings silently folding paper airplanes and flying them, then retrieving them from under chairs.

The last publicly acknowledged act of Yezhov occurred on April 19, 1939, a day on which he signed three orders as People's Commissar of Water Transportation. The next day, he vanished from public view. Perhaps Stalin did not want to publicize that a second secret police chief had been found an enemy of the people. As a result, many people suggested that Yezhov had been spared and allowed to live out his natural life under a false name. In fact, he was imprisoned until February 2, 1940, at which time he was given a brief and perfunctory trial as a "spy" by Vasili Vasilievich Ulrikh, Stalin's hanging judge, and shot that evening.

IMPACT

Along with prosecutor Andrey Vyshinsky and military judge Vasili Vasilievich Ulrikh, Nikolay Ivanovich Yezhov was one of the men most responsible for the mass murders of the Great Terror. He purged heedlessly, hoping to impress Stalin with his zeal and thus preserve his own life. However, in the end, he outwitted himself, destroying so many people that the terror had to be brought to a halt before it rendered the Soviet Union unable to function; Yezhov was removed from power and executed. The sheer viciousness of Yezhov's action, however, had allowed Stalin to shift the blame for his crimes onto Yezhov, a deception that proved so successful that Soviets often complained that if Stalin only knew what was going on, he would put a stop to it.

FURTHER READING

Conquest, Robert. *The Great Terror: A Reassessment.* Rev. ed. New York: Oxford University Press, 1990. A post-glasnost reissuing of the most authoritative volume on the era.

Montefiore, Simon Sebag. *Stalin: The Court of the Red Tsar.* New York: Alfred A. Knopf, 2003. Includes information on Stalin's use of Yezhov and other henchmen to run the Great Terror while deflecting attention from himself.

Rayfield, Donald. *Stalin and His Hangmen: The Tyrant and Those Who Killed for Him.* New York: Random House, 2004. A study of the relationship between Stalin and his chief henchmen.

Rogovin, Vadim Z. *1937: Stalin's Year of Terror.* Translated by Frederick S. Choate. Oak Park, Mich.: Mehring Books, 1998. A Trotskyist perspective on the Great Terror.

Vaksberg, Arkady. *Stalin's Prosecutor: The Life of Andrei Vyshinsky.* New York: Grove Weidenfeld, 1990. Provides information on Yezhov's role in the Moscow Trials as related to that of Vyshinsky.

—*Leigh Husband Kimmel*

SEE ALSO: Lavrenty Beria; Felix Dzerzhinsky; Joseph Stalin; Vasili Vasilievich Ulrikh; Andrey Vyshinsky; Genrikh Yagoda.

DOMINIQUE YOU
Caribbean pirate and privateer

BORN: c. 1772; Haiti
DIED: November 15, 1830; New Orleans, Louisiana
ALSO KNOWN AS: Frederick Youx; Captain Dominique; Johnness
CAUSE OF NOTORIETY: A highly successful pirate and privateer operating in the Gulf of Mexico and Caribbean Sea, You worked in close coordination with the pirate community headed by Jean Laffite and, as a result, helped defend the city of New Orleans when the British invaded it in January, 1815.
ACTIVE: 1805-1830
LOCALE: Gulf of Mexico and Caribbean Sea

EARLY LIFE

Little is known about the early life of Dominique You (dahm-ih-NEEK yoo). He may have been the older half brother of the most famous American pirates, Jean and Pierre Laffite. There is evidence that, as a young man, You had experience at sea. By the 1790's, he had made his way to France, where he served as an artilleryman in Napoleon Bonaparte's army. By 1802, he was a member of the expeditionary force led by General Charles Le-Clerc to put down a slave rebellion in San Dominique (now Haiti). When the French force was defeated, You remained in the New World and eventually made his way to New Orleans, which became part of the United States in 1803.

PIRATING CAREER

Shortly after arriving in New Orleans, You joined forces with the Laffite brothers, who had established a stronghold for smugglers south of the city in Barataria Bay. By 1805, he was captain of a ship that preyed on merchant vessels from countries doing business in the region. At times, You operated as a privateer, commissioned by one of the governments with interests in the region to capture vessels of hostile nations. At other times, he sailed as a simple pirate, carrying on his activities purely for personal profit. Like other Gulf pirates and privateers, You and his comrades made little effort to distinguish among the nationalities of ships that they captured, and the Laffites' network in and around New Orleans provided You a ready market for the goods he obtained. Their success eventually provoked an outcry from Spanish, French, British, and American merchants, who were losing fortunes to these audacious nautical bandits.

In the summer of 1814, reacting to the disruption and political scandal caused by the Gulf pirates, the United States government sent a naval force to destroy the Laffites' headquarters. You was captured, and in November, 1814, he was indicted for his crimes. He was never tried, however, as he and the Laffites agreed to assist U.S. forces under the command of General Andrew Jackson in defending New Orleans against an impending British attack. You's actions in January, 1815, as commander of an artillery battery earned him a personal commendation from Jackson and a pardon for past transgressions.

After the Battle of New Orleans, You went back to pirating for a time, but some financial reverses caused him to give up the trade. Although he was engaged briefly in a plot to free Napoleon Bonaparte from exile and bring him to America, You spent most of the last decade of his life working as a local politician in New Orleans, where he had purchased a home. During his final years, he became increasingly destitute, and though he was revered by the local populace, he died penniless. Nevertheless, the city paid for an elaborate funeral, and businesses were closed on the day he was buried.

IMPACT

Along with his fellow pirates and privateers, Dominique You had a major hand in disrupting commerce in the Gulf of Mexico and the Caribbean for more than twenty years. He helped create the legend of the privateer as a heroic daredevil, an image that lived on despite the realities of the profession. His actions at the Battle of New Orleans were certainly instrumental in the Americans' victory, thereby helping to establish Andrew Jackson's reputation as a military hero and launch a political career that eventually led Jackson to the White House.

FURTHER READING

Davis, William C. *The Pirates Laffite: The Treacherous World of the Corsairs of the Gulf.* New York: Harcourt, 2005. Brief discussion of You's dealings with the Laffite brothers during his career as a privateer.
Lagarde, François, ed. *The French in Texas: History, Migration, Culture.* Austin: University of Texas Press, 2003. A chapter on French pirates and privateers sketches You's association with the Laffite brothers and his career after the Battle of New Orleans.
Remini, Robert. *The Battle of New Orleans.* New York:

Viking, 1999. Concentrates on You's role in supporting the Americans at the Battle of New Orleans and on his personal relationship with Andrew Jackson.

—*Laurence W. Mazzeno*

SEE ALSO: Samuel Bellamy; Stede Bonnet; Anne Bonny; Jean Laffite; Sir Henry Morgan; John Rackham; Mary Read; Bartholomew Roberts.

COLE YOUNGER
American outlaw

BORN: January 15, 1844; Lee's Summit, Missouri
DIED: March 21, 1916; Lee's Summit, Missouri
ALSO KNOWN AS: Thomas Coleman Younger (full name)
MAJOR OFFENSES: Accessory to murder, attack with the intent to do bodily harm, and bank robbery
ACTIVE: 1866-1876
LOCALE: Missouri, Kansas, Minnesota, and other states
SENTENCE: Life in prison; paroled after twenty-five years; pardoned two years later

EARLY LIFE
Cole Younger (YUNG-gur) was the seventh of fourteen children born to Henry Washington and Bursheba Younger. Southern sympathizers and slave owners, the affluent Youngers owned several businesses and homes and were prosperous farmers in western Missouri.

The bloody Border Wars, in which Kansas and Missouri fought over Kansas's right to be a slave state, marked Cole Younger's boyhood. In 1862, members of the Missouri Militia killed his father. In 1863, one of his family's homes was burned during the implementation of Union Brigadier General Thomas Ewing, Jr.'s General Order 11, which mandated the destruction of Missouri and Kansas homes in the border areas of the two states. Union officers believed the area's residents were harboring William Clarke Quantrill's guerrillas, who were responsible for killing more than 150 civilians in Lawrence, Kansas.

In 1862, Younger joined Quantrill's Raiders and rode under the Black Flag. He participated at the Centralia Massacre, robbed mail coaches, and helped terrorize areas deemed pro-Union. He left Quantrill in 1864 and became a captain in the Confederate Army. After the war, he returned to his mother's farm.

Younger, who could not forget the danger and excitement of his guerrilla days, agreed to join Jesse and Frank James to form the James-Younger Gang.

CRIMINAL CAREER
Younger earned success and notoriety as an outlaw and member of the James-Younger Gang. During his tenure with the gang from 1866 until 1876, he helped rob nine banks, three trains, two stagecoaches, two omnibuses, and a state fair. The first robbery took place in Liberty,

Clockwise, from top: Henrietta Younger, Cole Younger, James Younger, and Robert Younger. (Library of Congress)

AN INTERVIEW WITH COLE YOUNGER

On November 7, 1880, J. W. Buel conducted a lengthly interview with the Younger brothers—Cole, Jim, and Bob—while they were serving prison sentences in Stillwater, Missouri. During the interview, Buel asked Younger about the Northfield robbery and prison life:

BUEL: Will you explain the causes and circumstances which led you to Northfield; also, explain, please, how you became separated from the two comrades who succeeded in escaping? I have been told that the shooting of Jim Younger, in the mouth, caused such profuse hemorrhage that the pursuers could trail you by the blood; that one of the two who escaped insisted on killing Jim in order to destroy the trail, and that it was this proposition which caused the separation.

YOUNGER: Positively, I will have nothing to do with writing or furnishing any information concerning the Northfield robbery, or any other robbery. I do not say this through any unkindness. . . .

BUEL: How long was each of you in the surgeon's care after your capture ?

YOUNGER: Jim and I are still receiving surgical attention, and will be the remainder of our lives.

BUEL: How often have you and your brothers been wounded?

YOUNGER: I have been wounded altogether twenty times; eleven of these wounds were received at Northfield. Jim was wounded four times at Northfield, and six times in all. Bob was never wounded until the pursuit in Minnesota, where he was struck three times. . . .

BUEL: What are your respective duties in the penitentiary?

YOUNGER: We have no special duties. Jim and I being on the hospital list do very little, while Bob performs various duties. I occupy much of my time in theological studies for which I have a natural inclination. It was the earliest desire of my parents to prepare me for the ministry, but the horrors of war, the murder of my father, and the outrages perpetrated upon my poor old mother, my sisters and brothers, destroyed our hopes so effectually that none of us could be prepared for any duty in life except revenge. . . .

BUEL: How do you regard your treatment in the prison?

YOUNGER: I will say that since our capture we have met with uniform kindness, and while in the penitentiary our relations with the officers have been cordially pleasant. . . . While I think of it, I should like to ask a favor. . . . In the first place, many of my old comrades are married and settled down in Missouri, where they are living peaceful lives. I want it understood that all these men fought for principle, not for plunder, and that they were true-hearted, honorable soldiers, fighting for what they esteemed was a righteous cause. In relation to me giving corn, and also pork and beef, to the poor during that hard winter, when food was so difficult to obtain, I will only say that I was following an example set by my blessed and sainted mother, whose charitable heart never failed to respond to distress. These facts I desire you to make understood in your book. . . .

Source: James William Buel, *The Border Outlaws: An Authentic and Thrilling History of the Most Noted Bandits of Ancient or Modern Times* (St. Louis, Mo.: Historical Publishing Company, 1881).

Missouri, and became known as the first non-wartime bank robbery. After the success of that robbery, Younger followed the gang through eight states and shared in more than $100,000 in stolen assets. He later convinced three of his brothers, James (or Jim), Robert (Bob), and John Younger, to join the gang.

DEFEAT AT NORTHFIELD
On September 7, 1876, Younger, his brothers Bob and Jim, and five other members of the James-Younger Gang rode into Northfield, Minnesota, to rob the First National Bank. During the robbery, assistant bank cashier Joseph Lee Haywood and passerby Nicholas Gustavson were killed. Outraged townsmen wounded Younger and his brothers and killed two of the gang. A posse chased the gang and surrounded the Youngers at Madelia, Minnesota. Jim was shot five times, Cole was shot eleven times, and Bob bore two bullet wounds. Only Frank and Jesse James, who separated from the Youngers, escaped to Missouri.

LEGAL ACTION AND OUTCOME
The captured Younger brothers pleaded guilty to robbery and murder and were sentenced to life at the Minnesota State Penitentiary at Stillwater. Cole Younger served twenty-five years before he was paroled in 1901, but the requirements of his parole prevented him from leaving Minnesota. Fully pardoned in 1903, he returned to Missouri and in that year published his memoirs as *The Story of Cole Younger by Himself.* He also renewed his ac-

quaintance with Frank James, and the two of them started the Cole Younger and Frank James Historical Wild West Show, which closed seven months later. Younger obtained other short-term jobs, including president of the Hydro-Carbon Oil Burner Company, president of an electric railroad construction company, and featured consultant for the Lew Nichols Carnival Company. He finally succeeded as a self-styled lecturer delivering cautionary advice to young people around the United States. He died at home in Lee's Summit in 1916.

IMPACT

Cole Younger will always be known as a member of the James-Younger Gang, never as its leader. In the annals of outlaw history, he did not gain the infamy accorded Jesse James. Although one film bears his name, *Cole Younger, Gunfighter* (1958), his character is featured in many films about James. Younger also is the focus of numerous books, magazine and newspaper articles, ballads, and poems.

During his long incarceration in Minnesota, Younger worked to become a model prisoner. He and Jim Younger initiated a funding drive to start a prison newsletter, *The Prison Mirror*, which continues today as the oldest continuously published prison newsletter in the United States.

His rehabilitation gained the admiration of influential Missourians and Minnesotans who worked to secure his parole. Several bills, including the Bennett Bill and the Deming Bill, were introduced and passed to obtain the release of the Youngers and set aside their life sentences. The passage of the Deming Bill by the Minnesota legislature in 1901, and its acceptance by the Board of Prison and the Board of Pardons, secured the parole of Cole and Jim Younger.

FURTHER READING

Brant, Marley. *The Illustrated History of the James-Younger Gang*. Montgomery, Ala.: Black Belt Press, 1997. More than two hundred photographs of the James-Younger Gang illustrate this historical treatment, which aims to separate fact from the fiction and reveal unexplored reasons for the gang's outlawry.

_____. *The Outlaw Youngers: A Confederate Brotherhood*. Lanham, Md.: Madison Books, 1995. The Civil War is the catalyst for the descent of four young men from an all-American family into a maelstrom of violence and crime; greed and thrill seeking become their reasons for pursuing the lifestyle after the war.

Bronaugh, Warren C. *The Youngers' Fight for Freedom*. Columbia, Mo.: E. W. Stephens, 1906. This is a historical and personal account of how Bronaugh, a Missourian and former Confederate soldier, fought to secure parole, then a full pardon for the Younger brothers.

Younger, Cole. *The Story of Cole Younger by Himself*. 1903. Reprint. St. Paul: Minnesota Historical Society, 2000. Younger attempts to defuse the negative aspects of his life story but manages to include just as many myths and lies as any other written account of his criminal exploits.

—*Cathy M. Jackson*

SEE ALSO: Apache Kid; Tom Bell; William H. Bonney; Curly Bill Brocius; Butch Cassidy; Bob Dalton; Emmett Dalton; Bill Doolin; John Wesley Hardin; Doc Holliday; Jesse James; Tom Ketchum; Harry Longabaugh; Bill Longley; Joaquín Murieta; William Clarke Quantrill; Johnny Ringo; Belle Starr; Hank Vaughan.

RAMZI YOUSEF
Kuwaiti-born terrorist

BORN: May 20, 1968; Fahaeel, Kuwait

ALSO KNOWN AS: Abdul Basit Mahmoud Abdul Karim Fahaheel; Abdul Basit Balochi; Abdul Basit Mahmoud Kareem; Ramzi Ahmed Yousef (full name)

MAJOR OFFENSES: Airline bombings and seditious conspiracy to bomb the World Trade Center

ACTIVE: 1993-1995

LOCALE: World Trade Center, New York City; Pakistan; Thailand; and the Philippines

SENTENCE: 240 years in solitary confinement

EARLY LIFE

Ramzi Yousef (RAM-zee YEW-sehf) was born and raised in Kuwait. His father was reportedly a Pakistani from the Baluchistan province. After he finished his schooling in Kuwait, Yousef's family moved to Turbat, Baluchistan, in 1986, but he went to Oxford, England, where he studied English at the Oxford College of Further Education. After a summer trip to his family's home, he returned to Wales in 1987 to study electrical engineering at the West Glamorgan Institute of Higher Education (later known as the Swansea Institute of Higher Education). After his graduation, he returned to Kuwait, where he was employed by the National Computer Center in Kuwait's Planning Ministry. He apparently escaped from Kuwait when Iraq invaded Kuwait in 1990, but there remain questions about whether the man who studied in England was the Ramzi Yousef who would become the mastermind behind the 1993 bombing of the World Trade Center.

Yousef reportedly was active, at the behest of Osama Bin Laden, in terrorist training and activities as he made his way to the United States on September 1, 1992, using a fake Iraqi passport. When immigration officials discovered bomb materials, suicide-bomb videotapes, and a manual concerning ways to handle immigration authorities in the luggage of his traveling companion, Ahmed Ajaj, the two men were arrested. Yousef, who appealed for political asylum, was freed and given a November 9 hearing date. He then told police that he was Abdul Basit Mahmod Abdul Karim, a Pakistani who had been raised in Kuwait and who had lost his passport. The Pakistani consulate in New York issued him a temporary Pakistani passport on December 31, 1992. In the interim he contacted Sheikh Abdel Rahman, a fundamentalist Muslim cleric, and made several calls to Baluchistan.

TERRORIST CAREER

Although his terrorist activities were conducted internationally, Yousef's most notorious crime was the bombing of the World Trade Center in 1993. After his arrival in the United States, he and Mohammed Salameh moved into an apartment at 251 Virginia Avenue in Jersey City, New Jersey. They were later joined by Nidal Ayyad, who helped Salameh open bank accounts in which funds from Germany and the Middle East were deposited. The funds were then used to acquire chemicals (urea, nitric acid, and sulfuric acid) which were stored in a storage locker Salameh had rented. After Yousef and Salameh moved to 40 Pamrapo Avenue in Jersey City, they used the apartment as a bomb factory. On February 26, 1993, the terrorists rented a Ryder van, which Salameh then reported as stolen. Three days later they drove the van, packed with four boxes of explosives, to the World Trade Center, where it exploded seventeen minutes after noon. Hours later, Yousef flew to Pakistan on a commercial airliner.

In the summer of 1993, Yousef attempted to assassinate Benazir Bhutto, the Pakistani prime minister, but he and his accomplice, Abdul Hakim Murad, were interrupted by police as they planted the bomb. When the bomb accidentally detonated, Yousef was injured, and Murad took him to a hospital. The following year Yousef was involved in another bombing attempt, this time involving the Israeli embassy in Bangkok, Thailand. On the way to the embassy, the car containing the bomb became involved in an accident, and Yousef left the scene, leaving the bomb behind. In 1994 he planted a bomb aboard a Philippine Airlines jet leaving Manila. Although the bomb exploded and killed a passenger, the plane landed at its destination safely. At this time the confident Yousef also was making plans to assassinate Pope John Paul II and U.S. president Bill Clinton.

Yousef was next involved in a plan, known as the Bojinka plot, to plant explosive devices in toy cars in suitcases aboard United and Northwest Airlines flights from Bangkok. He enlisted the assistance of Istaique Parker, a South African Muslim student in Pakistan, but Parker (who called himself "Hamid" when he was interrogated), was frightened by the enormity of the projected crime and contacted the American embassy in Pakistan. Parker was also influenced by the two-million-dollar reward offered for Yousef's capture.

LEGAL ACTION AND OUTCOME

Yousef was taken prisoner by agents from the American Diplomatic Security Service in Pakistan, and Prime Minister Bhutto, whom he had attempted to kill, approved his extradition to the United States. At his trial for the bombing of the Philippine airliner and the Bojinka plot, Yousef acted as his own attorney. He was found guilty in September, 1996, of both charges. He was tried again in 1997 for his involvement in the World Trade Center bombing and was again convicted. On January 8, 1998, Judge Kevin Duffy sentenced him to 240 years in solitary confinement. Yousef began serving his sentence in a high-security prison in Florence, Colorado.

IMPACT

Although Ramzi Yousef was imprisoned for his terrorist activity, the ripple effect of his crimes has been considerable. His bombing of the Philippine aircraft and his plans for hijacking airplanes and destroying Americans and the symbols of their power were instrumental in the events of September 11, 2001, and the aftermath of the destruction of the twin towers at the World Trade Center. He had shown that airplanes could be bombed and had made plans for hijacking planes. His links to Bin Laden and al-Qaeda, as well as tenuous connections to Iraq, also contributed to President George W. Bush's decision not only to bomb Afghanistan but also to invade Iraq. Yousef was a hero to the insurgents battling American forces in Iraq in the early 2000's and those throughout the world.

Thousands of young Muslim radicals have followed his career, which involved training in Afghanistan and Pakistan, experience with explosives, and a determination to battle American hegemony.

FURTHER READING

Katz, Samuel M. *Relentless Pursuit: The DSS and Their Manhunt for the al-Qaeda Terrorists.* New York: Forge, 2002. Chapter 5 deals with Yousef's capture in Pakistan.

Lance, Peter. *One Thousand Years for Revenge.* New York: Regan Books, 2003. Extensive coverage of Yousef's activities and a discussion of the Federal Bureau of Investigation's failures to respond to evidence about terrorist anti-American plans. Also contains an illustrated time line.

Mylroie, Laurie. *Study of Revenge.* Washington, D.C.: AEI Press, 2001. Good coverage of Yousef's life and activities, including a convincing case for Yousef having assumed Karim's identity, plus an attempt to tie Yousef to Saddam Hussein.

Reeve, Simon. *The New Jackals.* Boston: Northeastern University Press, 1999. Places Yousef in the context of Islamic militants and ties him to Iraq, albeit a bit tangentially.

—*Thomas L. Erskine*

SEE ALSO: Mohammed Atta al-Sayed; Osama Bin Laden; Khalid Shaikh Mohammed; Zacarias Moussaoui.

YUAN SHIKAI
President of China (1912-1916)

BORN: September 16, 1859; Zhangying, Henan Province, China

DIED: June 6, 1916; Beijing, China

ALSO KNOWN AS: Yüan Shih-le'ai; Weiting; Rong'an Jung'an; Father of the Warlords

CAUSE OF NOTORIETY: A power-hungry warlord, Yuan built China's first modern army and enacted a series of betrayals in order to pursue his own ambition to create a new Chinese dynasty.

ACTIVE: 1898-1916

LOCALE: China

EARLY LIFE

Yuan Shikai (yew-ahn shih-ki) was born on September 16, 1859, in Zhangying, Henan Province, China, into a

modestly successful family with a fairly high number of civil and military figures in its genealogy. Yuan twice attempted to pass the *juren* (traditional civil service) exam but failed both times. Denied entry into the more prestigious civil officialdom, Yuan joined the military. Through family connections, he was posted to Korea, where he excelled in complicated politics while Korea was slipping under Japanese control. Many traditional Chinese officials above him failed to survive, and he adeptly advanced to become the highest Chinese representative in Korea.

MILITARY CAREER

Yuan left Korea and returned to China after twelve years. He began to restructure the Chinese military forces using the Westernized techniques that he had observed while in the Japanese military. By 1899, Yuan commanded the best armed forces in China. As a military reformer, he was attractive to Guangxu, the young Chinese emperor, who assumed he could trust Yuan, a person theoretically under his control. However, real power remained in the hands of Cixi, the empress dowager of the Qing Dynasty, who had been unofficially running China since the death of Emperor Xianfeng in 1861. Cixi had been Xianfeng's favorite concubine and had the good fortune to bear a son for him when his wife, Empress Cian, was unable to bear children. Officially, Cixi was only a co-regent for her son Tongzhi until he reached adulthood. However, Tongzhi died mysteriously in his teen years in 1874, and Cixi managed to have her nephew, Guangxu, appointed as her son's successor so that she could remain regent.

By 1898, Guangxu, now in his early twenties, sought to take control of China and move the country in a modern direction. From the middle of June to September 21, 1898, during the Hundred Days' Reform, Guangxu issued several dramatic reform edicts. However, Guangxu foolishly trusted Yuan with his plans to eliminate traditional officials who held significant influence over Cixi. Sensing that Cixi was still the real power, Yuan informed her of Guangxu's plans. In turn, Cixi had Guangxu placed under house arrest, rescinded his reform edicts, and executed several of his liberal reform officials.

While Yuan betrayed Emperor Guangxu for Cixi and the traditionalists in 1898, in 1911 he sold out the traditionalists. Although Yuan was briefly out of favor with the traditionalists after Cixi died in 1908, the Nationalist Party of Sun Yat-sen (a political leader) began a revolution in the fall of 1911 which threatened to overthrow the Chinese dynasty. The dynasty's traditionalists turned to Yuan for help. However, because Sun Yat-sen had promised to make Yuan the president of the Republican government, Yuan betrayed the traditionalists: He joined the revolution and forced the abdication of the boy emperor Puyi. Effective January 1, 1912, Yuan became China's new president, presumably of a constitutional, democratic regime complete with its own elected legislature.

Elections were held in 1913 and are probably the most democratic elections ever held in China even though the franchise was limited to property owners who paid a fee or tax to vote. Sung Chiao-jen, a deputy to Yung, challenged him for control and was assassinated in March, 1913. There was widespread speculation that Yuan was behind the murder. Yuan expected the new legislature to be under his control, while the legislature assumed it

Yuan Shikai.

could control Yuan. However, Yuan held power over the troops, and he quickly betrayed the Republican revolution and attempted to make himself the head of a new dynasty. The endless machinations of the 1912-1916 era led Yuan to betray nearly everyone not under his direct control in his ruthless pursuit of power.

The stress and turmoil of the four years in which Yuan ruled proved to be too much for him. Although he officially died of uremia on June 6, 1916, in Beijing, China, many scholars have speculated that the intense pressure of those four years was the real cause of the destruction of Yuan's health and his death.

IMPACT

Yuan Shikai was a Chinese military and political leader who was infamous for his betrayal of every Chinese authority to whom he owed allegiance. He betrayed his responsibility to the Chinese emperor in 1898 and his responsibility to the Chinese officials in 1911. However, his greatest impact came when he betrayed Sun Yat-sen's democratic revolutionary forces in 1912-1916 by accepting the role as democratic president of China, only to attempt to reinstate an imperial dynasty with himself at the head. When he died, he ushered in the infamous warlord period which weakened China for most of the following decade until Chiang Kai-shek seized power in 1927.

Many historians believe that Yuan set an example of duplicity that provided a model for all future warlords during the era that divided China until its reunification under the Communists in 1949.

FURTHER READING

Fairbank, John King. *China: A New History.* Cambridge, Mass.: Harvard University Press, 1992. This was the last book written by the leading historian of China in the twentieth century. Clear and insightful.

Pye, Lucian W. *Warlord Politics.* New York: Praeger, 1976. This outstanding account of the warlord period contains a great deal of information about Yuan Shikai.

Spence, Jonathan. *The Search for Modern China.* New York: Norton, 1990. This insightful account by one of the greatest living China scholars provides a concise history of recent Chinese history, including the activities of Yuan Shikai.

Young, Ernest. *The Presidency of Yuan Shi-k'ai: Liberalism and Dictatorship in Early Republican China.* Ann Arbor: University of Michigan Press, 1977. Remains one of the best and most complete biographies of Yuan Shikai.

—*Richard L. Wilson*

SEE ALSO: Mao Zedong; Puyi.

YAKOV MIKHAILOVICH YUROVSKY
Soviet secret policeman

BORN: June 19, 1878; Tomsk, Siberia, Russian Empire (now in Russia)

DIED: August 2, 1938; Moscow, Soviet Union (now in Russia)

CAUSE OF NOTORIETY: Yurovsky executed Czar Nicholas II and the royal family during the Russian Civil War.

ACTIVE: July 17, 1918

LOCALE: Yekaterinburg, Siberia, Soviet Union (now Russia)

EARLY LIFE

Yakov Mikhailovich Yurovsky (YA-kof mihk-HAY-loh-vihch yer-OF-skee) was born in the Siberian city of Tomsk to a working-class family whose values included a strong loyalty to the Romanov Dynasty. Yurovsky's father was a glazier, and his mother was a seamstress. Yakov was the eighth of ten children; with so many mouths to feed, his hardworking parents never had much to spare. The family, however, was not totally destitute and even had a dacha on the banks of the Ob River out of town. Little more than a wooden hut, it was nonetheless an escape from the summer swelter that would turn their regular abode over a butcher shop into a sweatbox. Even so, what they had seemed only to underline what they lacked and bred in Yurovsky a sense of resentment both of the hardships of his life and of the folk piety that regarded life's travails as sent from heaven.

His father forced him to leave school early and to enter a trade, apprenticing him to the city's best watchmaker. Yurovsky remained in that profession for ten years, until he became swept up in the 1897 strikes and as a result was blacklisted. Unable to find work in Tomsk, he wandered about Siberia, eventually settling in Yekaterinburg, where he found work and a wife. However, in the aftermath of the 1905 Russian Revolution, he decided to take definite action against his frustration and joined the Bolshevik Party. He subsequently had to flee the country and lived in Berlin for a time, developing an interest in photography. When he returned to Russia in 1912 he was quickly arrested, but instead of prison he received exile back to Yekaterinburg. After a brief stint in the army as a medical orderly during World War I, Yurovsky deserted.

POLITICAL CAREER

After the Bolshevik Revolution, Yurovsky quickly established himself as a political leader in Yekaterinburg, helping to found the Ural Regional Soviet. He also joined the regional Cheka, or secret police. By 1918, the situation in Bolshevik Russia was becoming increasingly desperate because of the civil war against the White Russians, or counterrevolutionaries. Thanks to efforts by monarchists to rescue them, the deposed Czar Nicholas II and his family had been moved repeatedly to areas more distant from the capital, ultimately ending up in

Yekaterinburg. However, by July of 1918, much of Siberia was in White hands, and Yekaterinburg was in danger. Rather than let the royal family be recaptured by the Whites, the Bolsheviks decided to execute them all, and that duty fell to Yurovsky.

In the early hours of July 17, 1918, Yurovsky marched the royal family into a basement room of the House of Special Purpose, their prison for the past several months, and lined them up against a wall. There he read them the orders condemning them to death. Nicholas, never overly quick on the uptake, could not understand what was happening until Yurovsky shot him in the chest. At that point, all Yurovsky's men opened fire, but in an undisciplined way that turned the execution into a brutal massacre. Several of the royals were wearing large numbers of jewels sewn into their clothes, which served as bulletproof vests. As a result, they had to be bludgeoned to death. Yurovsky then had the bodies taken to a nearby pit for a crude burial.

Although Yurovsky was richly rewarded and ultimately moved to Moscow, he became a pariah for his role in the deaths of the Romanovs. However proud the Soviets might have been of their revolution, there remained a sense of guilt about that act of regicide, and Yurovsky became its principal scapegoat. Near the end of his life, he came to regret bitterly his actions. He died on August 2, 1938, in the Kremlin hospital and was buried at the Novodevechy Cemetery outside Moscow.

IMPACT

By killing the czar and the rest of the immediate royal family, Yakov Mikhailovich Yurovsky eliminated a possible rallying point for White forces during the Russian Civil War. As a result, the White forces were disunited and frequently worked at cross-purposes, a factor that furthered the Bolshevik victory. The Soviet Union would not face another serious threat to its existence until the Nazi invasion in World War II.

Furthermore, the loss of all Czar Nicholas's children

meant that any possibilities for a royal restoration following the 1991 breakup of the Soviet Union would have to fall back upon the collateral heirs who had escaped to the West and their descendants. Because of questions about the relative strengths of the various claims and arguments that some heirs had become disqualified for the throne, there was no real chance that the various monarchist groups in post-Soviet Russia would agree on any one heir to support. As a result, the Russian Federation remained republican in its form of government by default.

FURTHER READING

Grabbe, Paul, and Beatrice Grabbe. *The Private World of the Last Tsar*. Boston: Little, Brown, 1984. A photographic record of Czar Nicholas II and the royal family, including many personal pictures.

King, Greg, and Penny Wilson. *The Fate of the Romanovs*. New York: John Wiley and Sons, 2003. A reexamination of the last days of the Russian royal family, taken from previously secret Soviet archival documents.

Maylunas, Andrei, and Sergei Mironenko. *A Lifelong Passion: Nicholas and Alexandra, Their Own Story*. New York: Doubleday, 1997. A biography of the last czar and his wife.

Perry, John Curtis, and Constantine Pleshakov. *The Flight of the Romanovs: A Family Saga*. New York: Basic Books, 1999. Describes members of both the immediate and extended royal family of Russia and their fates.

—*Leigh Husband Kimmel*

SEE ALSO: Lavrenty Beria; Felix Dzerzhinsky; Lazar Kaganovich; Nikita S. Khrushchev; Vladimir Ilich Lenin; Vyacheslav Mikhailovich Molotov; Symon Petlyura; Joseph Stalin; Vasili Vasilievich Ulrikh; Andrey Vyshinsky; Genrikh Yagoda; Nikolay Ivanovich Yezhov; Andrey Aleksandrovich Zhdanov.

FELIX YUSUPOV
Russian aristocrat and leader of the plot to assassinate Grigori Rasputin

BORN: March 23, 1886; St. Petersburg, Russia
DIED: September 27, 1967; Paris, France
ALSO KNOWN AS: Feliks Feliksovich Yusupov (full name); Feliks Feliksovich Iusupov; Prince Yusupov
CAUSE OF NOTORIETY: Yusupov was a decadent member of the Russian royal family who confessed to, but remained unconvicted of, the murder of the Russian mystic Grigori Rasputin.
ACTIVE: December 16, 1916
LOCALE: St. Petersburg, Russia

EARLY LIFE
Felix Yusupov (yoo-suh-POV) was born to a life of extreme privilege. A member of the nobility, he married the niece of Czar Nicholas II and amassed a fortune, which arguably was second only to that of the czar. He owned a beautiful estate, Moika Palace, near the bank of the Neva River in St. Petersburg, but traveled extensively and was educated at Oxford College in England. Handsome and articulate, Yusupov was also pompous, patronizing, and openly effeminate, rarely attempting to hide his homosexuality. His beautiful wife, Irina, and he were a favored couple and often visited the czar and czarina at the Winter Palace. However, the Yusupov marriage was troubled by the prince's blatant infidelity.

POLITICAL CAREER
In his political thinking, Yusupov was an abject reactionary, still clinging to concepts long abandoned by Westerners, such as the divine right of kings and absolute monarchy. While at Oxford, Yusupov was befriended by Oswald Raynor and John Scales, two young men who seemed to share his interests and ideas. However, Yusupov was unaware that Raynor and Scales were clandestine members of the British Secret Intelligence Service, an organization that was keenly aware of the prince's close ties to the czar. Russia had recently aligned itself with England and France, and British intelligence wanted reassurance that Russia would maintain the pact in the likely case of war with Germany.

Upon his return to St. Petersburg, Yusupov became aware of what he perceived as the malignant presence of the rogue, self-proclaimed man of God, Grigori Rasputin, who was from Siberia. Rasputin had become an infamous person in St. Petersburg. Despite his filthy clothes and poor hygiene, countless women surrendered to his seductive will. He also developed a reputation for faith healing, and he possessed an inordinate amount of charisma and self-confidence. The prince instinctively felt superior to the poorly educated and coarse peasant. He also felt envious of the clearly growing but apparently incomprehensible influence that Rasputin now enjoyed over the royal Romanov family. Finally, Yusupov was angered by the obvious lust that Rasputin felt toward Irina, a feeling that might well have been reciprocated. For all of his other failings, Yusupov had shown little inclination toward physical violence, but this temperament was about to change.

Yusupov was most bothered by the peasant's close ties to the royal couple, particularly Empress Alexandra. Rasputin's alleged healing of Alexandra's son, Alexei, from the uncontrolled bleeding of hemophilia likely explained the holy man's closeness to and influence over the royal family; however, the young man's hemophilia was a state secret, so Rasputin's influence remained a mystery. In 1914, Rasputin advised the czar to stay out of World War I; once Russia entered the war, Rasputin advised the czar to seek a unilateral peace with Germany. These two views infuriated nationalists such as Yusupov. After listening to several rabidly anti-Rasputin speeches in the Russian Duma, Yusupov took the initiative in organizing a plot to kill the monk. His coconspirators included the grand duke Dmitri Pavlovich (the czar's cousin), Vladimir Purishkevich (an outspoken member of the Duma), Lieutenant Sukhotin (a wounded but recovering army officer), and a Dr. Lazavert (friend of Purishkevich). The timing of the murder was set for late in the evening of December 16, 1916, and the site would be the basement of Moika Palace.

Rasputin was lured to the Yusupov residence by the promise of a tryst with Irina, who in reality was not present that evening. The victim was led to an ornate room, which looked to be prepared for a party. Rasputin was told that Irina would be down shortly, and in the meantime he was offered and unwittingly consumed a substantial quantity of pastries and wines laced with the highly poisonous potassium cyanide. The conspirators felt that the use of guns might alert the St. Petersburg police, whose headquarters were nearby; however, when Rasputin showed few ill effects as a result of the poison, Yusupov shot him twice. Rasputin was also beaten, and his body was then rolled up in an old rug and dropped through a hole chopped in the ice of the frozen Neva River. When Rasputin's body was recovered and autopsied, water was found in his lungs, proving that, remarkably, he was a drowning victim. Speculation also existed that Raynor and Scales, Yusupov's intelligence friends, were also present that evening. Rasputin had suffered a third gunshot wound, delivered to the forehead at point-blank range, a sign of a professional assassin.

IMPACT

The czar and czarina were shocked and saddened by the murder of Rasputin, but Yusupov never faced charges because of his close ties to the Romanovs. Many monarchists supported the act, seeing it as the removal of a malignant influence, but peasants were upset by the loss of their only voice in government. Rasputin had prophesied that if he was assassinated by royalty or the nobility, then the czar and his immediate family would be swept from power and all would be dead within two years. His prediction came true in 1916; the Russian Revolution occurred in 1917, and the czar, the czarina, and their five children were executed in 1918.

FURTHER READING

Cowles, Virginia. *The Last Czar*. New York: G. P. Putnam's Sons, 1977. This work features another recounting of the murder and the preceding speeches in the Duma that aroused Yusupov to action.

Massie, Robert K. *Nicholas and Alexandra*. New York: Atheneum, 1967. An outstanding source, which particularly excels at describing Yusupov's youth and upbringing. It also gives a chilling account of Rasputin's murder.

Taylor, Edmond. *The Fall of the Dynasties*. Garden City, N.Y.: Doubleday, 1963. This is a rather pedestrian retelling of the events, but it does include some interesting theories and analyses.

—*Thomas W. Buchanan*

SEE ALSO: Grigori Yefimovich Rasputin; Yakov Mikhailovich Yurovsky.

GIUSEPPE ZANGARA
Italian American bricklayer and attempted assassin

BORN: September 7, 1900; Ferruzzano, Reggio
  Calabria Province, Italy
DIED: March 20, 1933; Railford, Florida
ALSO KNOWN AS: Joe Zangara
MAJOR OFFENSES: Attempted assassination and first-
  degree murder
ACTIVE: February 15, 1893
LOCALE: Bayfront Park, Miami, Florida
SENTENCE: Death by electrocution

EARLY LIFE

Born in Ferruzzano, Italy, Giuseppe Zangara (zhyew-SEHP-pay zehn-GAR-uh) seemed to have bad luck for most of his short life. He suffered from an ear ailment at birth, which led physicians to operate immediately. His mother died when he was two from complications of another childbirth. At three years old, Zangara fell down two flights of stairs; at four, he burned his leg in a fire; and at five, he broke his wrist in another fall down the stairs. Shortly after he started school at age six, his father insisted that he quit school to work on a farm in order to make money for the family. The combination of hard labor at such a young age and the many beatings administered by his father left Zangara with severe stomach pains—an ailment that he would complain about for the rest of his life—and a deep-seated hatred of capitalists, whom he blamed for his family's economic plight.

At the age of twenty-one, Zangara began compulsory service in the Italian military. He had a series of low-level assignments. During his five-year stint, he contemplated killing King Victor Emmanuel III of Italy but never got the opportunity. After leaving the military, Zangara worked briefly as a brick mason. He decided to go to the United States and arrived in Brooklyn, New York, in September, 1923. Eventually, he found his way to Paterson, New Jersey, where he lived with an uncle who resided there. Zangara found work as a bricklayer. During the next several years, he joined a union and applied for U.S. citizenship, which he achieved in 1929. At just five feet, one inch tall and a little over one hundred pounds, Zangara kept to himself socially. He lived in a series of rooming houses in Paterson, East Paterson, Passaic, and Hackensack while in New Jersey. He spent one year in California before going to Miami in 1931.

CRIMINAL CAREER

By early 1933, Zangara was running out of money and was in constant pain from his stomach ailment. He bought a .32-caliber pistol with the intent of killing President Herbert Hoover but balked at going to Washington, D.C., because of the cold weather there. Then he found out that president-elect Franklin D. Roosevelt would be coming through Miami on his way back from vacation in the Bahamas. On the night of February 15, 1933, he waited for Roosevelt to speak from his car in front of the bandstand at Bayfront Park. However, Zangara's inability to get through the crowd and his diminutive stature led him to stand on an unstable chair in an attempt to kill Roosevelt. Zangara missed Roosevelt, and the five shots he fired hit five bystanders instead, including Chicago mayor Anthony Cermak, who had come down from the stage to talk to the soon-to-be chief executive. Cermak was by far the most seriously injured.

LEGAL ACTION AND OUTCOME

Originally sentenced to four twenty-year terms after pleading guilty to charges of assault with intent to kill, Zangara was indicted for first-degree murder following Mayor Cermak's death from injuries on March 6, 1933. Once again entering a guilty plea and expressing no remorse, Zangara was sentenced to death by electrocution at the Florida State Penitentiary in Railford. As he was strapped into the electric chair on March 20, 1933, he called witnesses "lousy capitalist sons of bitches." He was buried in an unmarked prison grave when no person claimed his remains.

IMPACT

There are several points to consider about the bizarre life and death of Giuseppe Zangara. First, his execution just five weeks after the shooting at Miami's Bayfront Park set a modern-day record for the rapidity of the justice system, even though Zangara pleaded guilty and displayed no regret for his actions other than missing the intended target. Still, some legal experts question the quality of his legal counsel, while others believe Zangara's status as an Italian immigrant resulted in discrimination against him.

The second issue in the case is the determination of Zangara's mental and physical state at the time of the shootings. Various psychiatrists argued over whether Zangara met the definition of insanity. What analysts do know is that he was not an ideological extremist, such as a communist or an anarchist. He was an atheist and anti-capitalist whose target became the political leader of a nation that embraced capitalism. While some accuse Zangara of having a death wish, he never attempted to commit suicide. Perhaps his desperate economic situation, isolated social status, and ever-present stomach pains contributed to his decision to kill. Interestingly, a postexecution autopsy determined that Zangara had a chronically infected gallbladder, though physicians could not agree on what effect that may have had on his stomach or abdomen.

Zangara's failure to hit president-elect Franklin Roosevelt allowed Roosevelt to flourish as a leader who led America through the Great Depression and World War II. Before he did that, however, he had to take the train back to Washington and be inaugurated as the nation's thirty-second president. In a strange twist of history, his train picked up several dignitaries on the way out of Florida, one of whom was Joseph P. Kennedy, whose son would later become President John F. Kennedy, who would be assassinated in 1963.

FURTHER READING

Clarke, James W. *American Assassins: The Darker Side of Politics*. Princeton, N.J.: Princeton University Press, 1982. This book contains a chapter that compares Zangara to Arthur Bremer, who attempted to assassinate Alabama governor George Wallace during his presidential run in 1972.

Picchi, Blaise. *The Five Weeks of Giuseppe Zangara, the Man Who Attempted to Assassinate FDR*. Chicago: Academy Chicago, 1998. This is the definitive account of Zangara's life and death, which includes extensive eyewitness accounts together with Zangara's memoir, written shortly before his execution.

Ray, Jo Anne. *American Assassins*. Minneapolis, Minn.: Lerner, 1974. This text contains a biographical chapter about Zangara.

—*Samuel B. Hoff*

SEE ALSO: John Wilkes Booth; Arthur Bremer; Samuel Joseph Byck; Leon Czolgosz; Lynette Fromme; Charles Julius Guiteau; Lee Harvey Oswald; Gavrilo Princip; Sirhan Sirhan.

EMILIANO ZAPATA
Mexican bandit and revolutionary

BORN: August 8, 1879; Anenecuilco, Morelos, Mexico
DIED: April 10, 1919; Hacienda Chinameca, Morelos, Mexico
ALSO KNOWN AS: Attila of the South
CAUSE OF NOTORIETY: A bandit in the eyes of the Mexican and U.S. governments of his time, Zapata led a revolutionary movement on behalf of peasants to enact fair landownership laws.
ACTIVE: 1910-1919
LOCALE: Morelos, Mexico

EARLY LIFE

Emiliano Zapata (ay-meel-YAH-noh sah-PAH-tah) was the son of a Mexican farmer. Skilled in handling horses, he worked as a trainer for some of the hacienda owners near his home. With government backing, many of these property owners appropriated land from peasants and villages and incorporated it into their own estates. This troubled Zapata, who saw that the rich men's horses he trained ate better and lived better than did his neighbors. Zapata determined to fight the injustice. Now under the scrutiny of governmental officials, he assumed leadership positions in his home village of Anenecuilco.

REVOLUTIONARY CAREER

Zapata first attempted to rectify unjust landownership policies through the Mexican legal system. The government, led by President Porfirio Díaz, backed the hacienda owners; sugarcane grown on the plantations was crucial to Mexico's economy.

In 1910 Francisco Madero initiated a revolution designed to rectify inequities he saw in northern Mexican social systems, and Zapata gathered a group of men from Morelos to lend support from the south to that revolution. Zapata hoped to see the reforms he favored become a part of Madero's program. Madero succeeded in forcing Díaz into exile but then seemed to lose interest in the reforms important to Zapata. Zapata continued his revolution, now against Madero. In November, 1911, Zapata proposed the Plan de Ayala, which laid out the goals of the Morelos revolutionaries. The most fundamental of these were fair landownership laws, liberty, and justice for all Mexicans, including peasants.

General Victoriano Huerta also led opposition against Madero, tricked him, and had him assassinated. Huerta became president but did not address issues of land reform, and Zapata continued to lead a revolutionary movement against the government. Two northern Mexican groups also fought against Huerta. One was led by Pancho Villa, another early supporter of Madero, and the other by Venustiano Carranza, a politician intent on gaining the presidency for himself. The three groups were never well coordinated, but Huerta was defeated, at least in part, because his forces were divided by the three-way conflict.

Carranza, whose forces were supported by the United States government, was the first to reach the capital, Mexico City. He began to set up a new government with no indication that he would incorporate the reforms sought by either Zapata or Villa. Zapata and Villa drove Carranza's forces out of Mexico City. The two men, however, never came to trust each other enough to coordinate their efforts. At one stage, Villa failed to supply

Emiliano Zapata. (Library of Congress)

armaments he had promised Zapata. At another, Zapata failed to open a southern battle front when Villa's forces were crushed by Carranza's army under General Álvaro Obregón. Carranza moved back into Mexico City and set up his government.

After initiating a vicious campaign in southern Mexico, Carranza's forces, under General Pablo González, killed and displaced the peasants and drove Zapata's troops into hiding in the hills. Zapata resorted to guerrilla warfare, which, combined with Carranza's disregard of revolutionary reforms and González's ruthlessness, destroyed any support Carranza had in rural Mexico, weakening his ability to govern. For Carranza, getting rid of Zapata now became a priority.

The opportunity came when Colonel Jesús Guajardo, one of González's officers, was rumored to be unhappy with González. Zapata attempted to contact Guajardo to see if he could be enticed to bring his men and armaments to the revolutionary side. Zapata's contact letter was intercepted and delivered to González, who used it to accuse Guajardo of treason, a crime punishable by death. Guajardo's choices were limited under these conditions, and he followed González's mandate to kill Zapata. Guajardo set up a meeting with Zapata near Chinameca in April of 1919, leading Zapata to believe they would discuss Guajardo's change of allegiance. Instead, Guajardo's men ambushed and killed Zapata.

Zapata's followers, instead of disbanding as expected by Carranza and González, continued the resistance. Meanwhile, seizing what he saw as his opening to the presidency, Obregón initiated his own rebellion against Carranza. Zapata's followers became an important part of Obregón's success, driving Carranza into exile. As Carranza fled, he was assassinated by traitors, perhaps acting on Obregón's behalf. Obregón assumed the presidency of Mexico.

IMPACT

This sequence of events was a part of the Mexican Revolution, a major landmark in Mexican history. The legacy of the revolution is still being debated, but Emiliano Zapata is thought of as the most sincere and idealistic revolutionary, the one least interested in self-aggrandizement. There is no evidence that he desired the presidency or other high office for himself. Instead, he was thrust into a leadership role by the people of Anenecuilco, to whom he became a hero.

THE PLAN OF AYALA

On November 25, 1911, Emiliano Zapata and Pancho Villa, along with several other revolutionary leaders, published their Plan of Ayala. After withdrawing their support for President Francisco I. Madero, they promised to improve life for peasants, a cause dear to Zapata:

As an additional part of the plan, we invoke, we give notice: that [regarding] the fields, timber, and water which the landlords, científicos, or bosses have usurped, the pueblos or citizens who have the titles corresponding to those properties will immediately enter into possession of that real estate of which they have been despoiled by the bad faith of our oppressors, maintain at any cost with arms in hand the mentioned possession; and the usurpers who consider themselves with a right to them [those properties] will deduce it before the special tribunals which will be established on the triumph of the revolution.

In virtue of the fact that the immense majority of Mexican pueblos and citizens are owners of no more than the land they walk on, suffering the horrors of poverty without being able to improve their social condition in any way or to dedicate themselves to Industry or Agriculture, because lands, timber, and water are monopolized in a few hands, for this cause there will be expropriated the third part of those monopolies from the powerful proprietors of them, with prior indemnization, in order that the pueblos and citizens of Mexico may obtain ejidos, colonies, and foundations for pueblos, or fields for sowing or laboring, and the Mexicans' lack of prosperity and well-being may improve in all and for all.

[Regarding] The landlords, científicos, or bosses who oppose the present plan directly or indirectly, their goods will be nationalized and the two-third parts which [otherwise would] belong to them will go for indemnizations of war, pensions for widows and orphans of the victims who succumb in the struggle for the present plan.

In order to execute the procedures regarding the properties aforementioned, the laws of disamortization and nationalization will be applied as they fit, for serving us as norm and example can be those laws put in force by the immortal Juárez on ecclesiastical properties, which punished the despots and conservatives who in every time have tried to impose on us the ignominious yoke of oppression and backwardness.

Source: Quoted in John Womack, *Zapata and the Mexican Revolution* (New York: Knopf, 1969).

How effective was the revolution in achieving Zapata's overarching goal of land reform? Zapata was able to affect landownership policy, but his changes were reversed when Carranza recaptured Mexico City. Obregón's presidency saw some land reform, and in 1935 President Lázaro Cárdenas brought radical land reform to Mexico. Despite this progress, the plight of the Mexican poor was negligibly improved.

In 1994, the Indians of the state of Chiapas in rural Mexico initiated a rebellion based on landownership inequities. They called themselves Zapatistas, the name used by Zapata's followers throughout the Mexican Revolution. While Zapata and the revolution did not correct Mexico's problems of landownership or other social issues, they did bring attention to the abuses and perhaps started Mexico on a tortuous course to more equitable practices.

FURTHER READING

Benjamin, Thomas. *La Revolución: Mexico's Great Revolution as Memory, Myth, and History.* Austin: University of Texas Press, 2000. Analysis of the revolution and its impact, including Zapata's role.

Brunk, Samuel. *Emiliano Zapata: Revolution and Betrayal in Mexico.* Albuquerque: University of New Mexico Press, 1995. Analysis of Zapata's role in the revolution.

McLynn, Frank. *Villa and Zapata: A History of the Mexican Revolution.* New York: Carroll and Graf, 2000. Analysis of the two men and their interactions and impacts on the revolution.

Womack, John, Jr. *Zapata and the Mexican Revolution.* New York: Vintage Books, Random House, 1968. The classic study of Zapata's role in the revolution.

—*Carl W. Hoagstrom*

SEE ALSO: Porfirio Díaz; Pancho Villa.

ABU MUSAB AL-ZARQAWI
Jordanian-born terrorist

BORN: October 20, 1966; Zarqa, Jordan
DIED: June 7, 2006; Hibhib, Iraq
ALSO KNOWN AS: ʾAbū Muṣʿab al-Zarqāwī (full name); Ahmad Fadil al-Khalayleh (birth name); al-Gharib (the Stranger); Abū Musʾab Zarqāwī; Ahmad Fadil al-Khalaylah; Ahmad Fadil al-Khalailah; Abu Ahmad; Sakr Abu Suwayd; Abu Muhammad
CAUSE OF NOTORIETY: Considered a major player in the jihad movement (holy war) and founder of Jama'at al-Tawid w'al-Jihid (Unity and Jihad Group), Zarqawi also arguably led terrorist organization al-Qaeda in Osama Bin Laden's absence.
ACTIVE: Beginning 1984
LOCALE: Middle East
SENTENCE: Sentenced in absentia to death

EARLY LIFE
The son of a native Jordanian family, Abu Musab al-Zarqawi (AH-bew mew-SAHB al zhahr-KAW-wee) grew up in a shabby two-story dwelling in a dusty mining town seventeen miles north of Amman. His depressed neighborhood and town were mostly made up of working-class citizens. He attended the local schools, where his teachers described him as an average but rebellious student. In his free time, he used the neighborhood cemetery as a playground. At the age of seventeen, he dropped out of school and immediately began working.

Zarqawi was looking to fill the void in his life; he searched for purpose and in 1984 joined the military for two years. In 1986, however, he was back in Zarqa leading a dissolute life. Soon thereafter he was arrested on several occasions for petty crimes and at one time was even sentenced to four months in prison.

In 1989, he traveled to Afghanistan to join the insurgency against the Soviet invasion. By the time Zarqawi arrived, however, the Soviets' Red Army had withdrawn. Zarqawi now felt out of place among the Arab warriors who roamed the streets. He began collecting the stories of these fighters and prepared them for publication in

Abu Musab al-Zarqawi. (AP/Wide World Photos)

Al-Bunyan al-Marsus (the solid edifice), a propaganda tool of al-Qaeda. In 1993, Zarqawi returned to Jordan and began preaching a revolutionary creed against the Jordanian regime. He founded a terrorist group, financed in part by al-Qaeda, whose goal was to topple the Jordanian government. Soon Zarqawi was arrested and imprisoned for possession of weapons.

In prison, Zarqawi met the Islamic scholar Mohammed al-Maqdisi, who taught him the principles of the extreme separatist sect known as the Salafi, which advocated total elimination of Western, particularly U.S., influence in the Islamic world.

TERRORIST CAREER

Upon the death of Jordan's King Hussein in 1999, his son, the new king Abdullah, decreed amnesty for Jordanian prisoners. Shortly after his release, Zarqawi proved himself to be an important part of the al-Qaeda apparatus in Afghanistan. In 2001, Osama Bin Laden and Zarqawi became allies. It was at this time that the Kurdish secret service drew American attention to Zarqawi. The long list of crimes of which Zarqawi was accused was revealed, and the list continued to grow in the following years. In 2001, a U.S.-Jordanian investigation accused Zarqawi of being part of the plot to carry out attacks in Jordan during the millennium celebrations in 2000. Zarqawi was also charged with the assassination of Yitzhak Snir, an Israeli citizen, along with the assassination of the U.S. diplomat Laurence Foley, who was gunned down in Amman. In 2003, Zarqawi was also blamed for a truck bomb explosion at the United Nations headquarters in Baghdad and the explosives driven into the Imam Ali Mosque.

Various sources report that U.S. secretary of state Colin Powell's February, 2003, speech before the United Nations Security Council—in which he presented evidence that Iraqi dictator Saddam Hussein was hiding attempts to develop weapons of mass destruction—put Zarqawi's name in the limelight for the first time. Almost

---

THE DEATH OF ZARQAWI

Early during the insurgency that followed the American invasion of Iraq in 2003, Abu Musab al-Zarqawi arose as a viciously efficient terrorist leader. After the capture of Saddam Hussein, Zarqawi became enemy number one for the United States military. A bounty of twenty-five million dollars was put on his head. It was not the money, however, that led to Zarqawi's death. It was a little luck on the part of American special forces and some mistakes by the terrorist himself.

On June 7, 2006, two U.S. Air Force F-16's dropped five-hundred-pound bombs on a small house in a palm grove outside the village of Hibhib, near the town of Baquba and north of Baghdad. When Iraqi police, followed by U.S. special forces, reached the scene, they found six bodies in the destroyed house and a mortally wounded Zarqawi. He died shortly afterward.

Over several weeks U.S. intelligence had traced Zarqawi to the village based upon information from electronic and signal intelligence and possibly from the interrogation of a Zarqawi aide, Kassim al-Ani. Then, a key tip pinpointed him. According to a Bush administration spokesperson, when Zarqawi moved into Baquba, he had angered the villagers by executing nine locals. The tip may have come as revenge. In any case, it put special forces on the trail of Sheikh Abd-al-Rahman, Zarqawi's spiritual adviser. The sheikh's movements led special forces to Zarqawi, and the air strike was called in quickly to prevent him from escaping.

Zarqawi was identified first by scars and tattoos and later by fingerprint and deoxyribonucleic acid (DNA) evidence. There was no possibility of mistake, and his organization did not even try to deny the death. Within weeks, the Iraq branch of al-Qaeda had named a new leader, Abu Hamza al-Muhajir.

By then the organization was in serious trouble. Along with Zarqawi's death, the Hibhib raid also turned up tactical information from papers and computer discs found in the house. Special forces moved rapidly, conducting seventeen simultaneous raids on Zarqawi's network within hours of the air strike. These raids netted yet further intelligence; thirty-nine raids took place the following night.

Over the next week, according to the U.S. military, the captured information led to 450 raids, during which 104 insurgents were killed and 759 people arrested.

---

overnight, Zarqawi rose from his humble beginnings to be seen in the West as the new leader of the jihad movement. However, some believe that Zarqawi's role in the insurgency movement within Iraq was exaggerated by the U.S. government as part of a propaganda campaign designed to promote the image of an enemy figure, which in turn served U.S. government political goals. On the other hand, many feel that regardless of his leadership position, Zarqawi did indeed play an important role in several key events during the ensuing Iraq War, including the 2004 beheadings of Nicholas Berg, an American hostage, and Ken Bigley, a British citizen, and the 2005 bombings in Amman, Jordan, which killed approximately seventy people in three hotels. Moreover, U.S.

officials point to Zarqawi as the mastermind behind more than seven hundred killings in Iraq, mostly from suicide and roadside bombings.

Throughout the war in Iraq, periodic reports surfaced of Zarqawi's death or severe injury from U.S. attacks. Authorities also claimed he had to have a leg amputated—the result of a missile attack in Afghanistan in 2002—and was fitted with a prosthetic leg. In May, 2005, the Iraqi government confirmed that Zarqawi had been wounded by U.S. forces, and debates ensued both about the truth of these claims and about how severely Zarqawi was injured.

On June 7, 2006, reports of Zarqawi's death proved true. After tracking him for several weeks, U.S. troops had identified his exact location and dropped a laser-guided, five-hundred-pound bomb into his hideout in the small village of Hibhib, Iraq. A second bomb followed immediately thereafter. Zarqawi was found alive but badly wounded. Iraqi police were the first to arrive on the scene and quickly placed Zarqawi on a stretcher. He survived fifty-two minutes after the bombing. Before his death, he mumbled a few indistinguishable words and tried to turn himself away from the stretcher; as soon as he was secured back on the stretcher, he died almost immediately from severe injuries to his lungs.

IMPACT

Starting as a small player in a wider jihad movement, Abu Musab al-Zarqawi proved himself to be a leader among leaders. Experts believe that better-educated jihadists became his followers after seeing that the United States christened Zarqawi a powerful player. As Bin Laden remained trapped near the border of Afghani-

stan and Pakistan, Zarqawi became the symbolic leader of the fight against the United States and a magnet for whoever wished to join the jihad movement. Not only did this affect military strategies, but Zarqawi's tactics themselves also changed the way the world engaged in military warfare. Immediately following Zarqawi's death, a new successor was appointed: Abu Hamza al-Muhajir, a man about whom little was known.

FURTHER READING

Brisard, Jean-Charles, and Damien Martinez. *Zarqawi: The New Face of al-Qaeda*. New York: Other Press, 2005. Experts in international terrorism and terrorism financing, the authors chronicle Zarqawi's career from his humble impoverished beginnings to his leadership of the jihad movement.

Clarke, Richard. *Defeating the Jihadists: A Blueprint for Action*. New York: The Foundation Press, 2004. Details the various jihad groups across the globe. Highlights the jihad organization created by Zarqawi and identifies measures for defeating it.

Napoleoni, Loretta. *Insurgent Iraq: Al Zarqawi and the New Generation*. London: Constable and Robinson, 2005. Examines the life of the most notorious insurgent in Iraq, Zarqawi. Zarqawi was able to spread the jihad movement into Iraq with the help of the American war.

—*John Jacob Rodriguez*

SEE ALSO: Mohammed Atta al-Sayed; Osama Bin Laden; Khalid Shaikh Mohammed; Zacarias Moussaoui; Ayman al-Zawahiri.

AYMAN AL-ZAWAHIRI
International terrorist

BORN: June 19, 1951; Maadi, near Cairo, Egypt

ALSO KNOWN AS: Abu Muhammad; Abu Fatima; Muhammad Ibrahim; Abu Abdallah; Mengele of the Islamic Fundamentalist Movement; the Doctor; the Teacher

CAUSE OF NOTORIETY: Although Zawahiri has been linked to the assassination of Egyptian president Anwar el-Sadat, bombings of U.S. embassies, and the 2001 terrorist attacks on the United States, he has had few charges brought against him and has served little jail time.

ACTIVE: October 6, 1981; August 7, 1998; September 11, 2001

LOCALE: Throughout the Middle East, Africa, and the United States

EARLY LIFE

Ayman al-Zawahiri (AY-mahn ahl-zah-wah-HEE-ree) was born in Maadi, Egypt. His parents were from two prominent families in Egypt who had established a dynasty of medical doctors in the country. His father was a professor of pharmacology at Ain Sham University in Cairo, but Zawahiri pursued a more radical direction as a teenager by joining an Islamic militant group called the Muslim Brotherhood. It is believed that Zawahiri and his generation of Muslim young men were radicalized even further by the defeat of Egypt at the hands of Israel in the Six-Day War of 1967.

In 1968, Zawahiri graduated from a secondary school in Maadi and then enrolled in medical school at Cairo University, where he eventually graduated cum laude with a medical degree in 1974. Zawahiri's medical degree listed a specialty in psychology and pharmacology. In 1978, he obtained a master's degree in surgery. As a college student at Cairo University, Zawahiri began following the teachings of a Muslim scholar named Sayyid Qutb, who wrote about the need to rid Islam of secular influences from Western culture. Zawahiri became interested in Qutb because his teachings focused on a creating a worldwide movement of Islamic fundamentalism. At Cairo University, Zawahiri was considered highly intelligent and was well respected by his teachers.

TERRORIST CAREER

In 1979, Zawahiri became the founder of a radical militant group called Islamic Jihad and recruited young Muslim men to join the organization. The goal of Islamic Jihad was to overthrow the Egyptian government and establish a government based on a type of Muslim fundamentalism that might eventually become a global model

---

THE ZAWAHIRI-BIN LADEN FATWA

On February 12, 1998, Ayman al-Zawahiri and Osama Bin Laden issued a religious decree, "World Islamic Front for Jihad Against Jews and Crusaders," declaring war on the United States. Here are extracts:

The Arabian Peninsula has never—since Allah made it flat, created its desert, and encircled it with seas—been stormed by any forces like the crusader armies spreading in it like locusts, eating its riches and wiping out its plantations. All this is happening at a time in which nations are attacking Muslims like people fighting over a plate of food. . . .

All these crimes and sins committed by the Americans are a clear declaration of war on Allah, his messenger, and Muslims. And ulema [Islamic scholars] have throughout Islamic history unanimously agreed that the jihad is an individual duty if the enemy destroys the Muslim countries. . . .

On that basis, and in compliance with Allah's order, we issue the following fatwa [religious decree] to all Muslims:

The ruling to kill the Americans and their allies—civilians and military—is an individual duty for every Muslim who can do it in any country in which it is possible to do it, in order to liberate the al-Aqsa Mosque and the holy mosque [Mecca] from their grip, and in order for their armies to move out of all the lands of Islam, defeated and unable to threaten any Muslim. This is in accordance with the words of Almighty Allah, "and fight the pagans all together as they fight you all together," and "fight them until there is no more tumult or oppression, and there prevail justice and faith in Allah."

We—with Allah's help—call on every Muslim who believes in Allah and wishes to be rewarded to comply with Allah's order to kill the Americans and plunder their money wherever and whenever they find it. We also call on Muslim ulema, leaders, youths, and soldiers to launch the raid on Satan's U.S. troops and the devil's supporters allying with them, and to displace those who are behind them so that they may learn a lesson. . . .

Almighty Allah also says: "So lose no heart, nor fall into despair. For ye must gain mastery if ye are true in faith."

Source: Federation of American Scientists Web site, www.fas.org.

---

for Arab countries everywhere. In the 1980's, Zawahiri participated in the Soviet-Afghanistan War as a physician attending to Afghan refugees and as a mujahideen fighter resisting the Soviets in their attempt to occupy Afghanistan. During this time, Zawahiri met Osama Bin Laden and became an important mentor to him. Together, in 1998, the two men became leaders of the terrorist organization called al-Qaeda; Zawahiri joined the Islamic Jihad with al-Qaeda in a merger that would prove to have serious ramifications for the United States and the rest of the world.

Both Bin Laden and Zawahiri studied religion under Palestinian Shaikh Abdullah Azzam while serving in Afghanistan. In February, 1998, Zawahiri and Bin Laden issued a fatwa, or a religious decree, titled *World Islamic Front for Jihad Against Jews and Crusaders* in an attempt to create a global movement of terrorism. In August, 1998, Zawahiri ordered the truck bombings that killed 224 people at the U.S. embassies in Kenya and Tanzania. It is believed that Zawahiri also played a key role in the September 11, 2001, terrorist attacks on U.S. soil, which killed nearly three thousand Americans.

LEGAL ACTION AND OUTCOME

Zawahiri has been arrested several times in connection with his terrorist activities, but he has rarely served significant jail time. In 1981, he was arrested and served jail time for conspiracy charges in the assassination of Egyptian president Anwar el-Sadat but was later released for a lack of evidence connecting him to the crime. The Russian government detained Zawahiri in 1996 for attempting to recruit jihadists in Chechnya to carry out suicide terrorist attacks. On June 16, 1999, a United States district court charged Zawahiri with murder in the embassy bombings in East Africa that killed more than two hundred people. Also in 1999, Zawahiri was sentenced to death in absentia by an Egyptian court for his part in a terrorist attack by his organization, Islamic Jihad, in which sixty-two tourists were killed in Luxor, Egypt.

Following the September 11, 2001, terrorist attacks on the United States, the International Criminal Police Organization (Interpol) issued an arrest warrant for Zawahiri. After the United States' invasion of Afghanistan in December, 2001, Zawahiri went into hiding with Bin Laden, presumably in a mountainous area in the border region between Pakistan and Afghanistan. In 2004 and 2006, it was believed that U.S. and Pakistani troops had surrounded Zawahiri in a tribal area of Pakistan near the mountains of the Afghanistan border, but he escaped. Zawahiri has appeared on video with Bin Laden mocking President George W. Bush and the U.S. government and promising more terrorist attacks on American soil. U.S. authorities have issued a twenty-five-million-dollar reward for information leading to the capture of Zawahiri.

IMPACT

In the mid-1990's, Ayman al-Zawahiri was identified as the most significant terrorist threat against the United States. He is regarded as a pioneer in the development of the strategy of suicide bombers, which became a trademark of jihad assassinations and terrorist attacks. Zawahiri is considered the number-two person behind Osama Bin Laden within al-Qaeda. He is viewed as Bin Laden's closest adviser and mentor. Zawahiri is often called the Mengele of the Islamic Fundamentalist Movement in reference to the Nazi physician under Adolf Hitler, Josef Mengele, who experimented on Jewish prisoners; Zawahiri has been known to experiment on human prisoners in the past using chemical and biological agents.

FURTHER READING

Aboul-Enein, Youssef. "Ayman al-Zawahiri's 'Knights Under the Prophet's Banner': The al-Qaeda Manifesto." *Military Review* 85, no. 1 (January 1, 2005): 83. Examines the teachings of Zawahiri expressed in his short manuscript *Knights Under the Prophet's Banner* (2001), which discusses the evolution and the accomplishments of the Islamic Jihad and his association with the Islamist movements in Egypt, as well as with Bin Laden.

Dennis, Anthony. *Osama Bin Laden: A Psychological and Political Portrait*. Lima, Ohio: Wyndham Press, 2002. Dennis documents the close relationship between Bin Laden and Zawahiri.

Gerges, Fawaz A. *The Far Enemy: Why Jihad Went Global*. Cambridge, England: Cambridge University Press, 2005. In a well-researched discussion, Gerges explores the history of the jihadist movements within the Middle East, their internal divisions and debates, and their plans for a global shift in power.

Wright, Lawrence. "The Man Behind Bin Laden." *The New Yorker*, September 16, 2002. Wright discusses the evolution of Ayman al-Zawahiri from an Egyptian physician to an international terrorist.

Zayyat, Montasser al-. *The Road to Al-Qaeda: The Story of Bin Laden's Right-Hand Man*. Sterling, Va.: Pluto Press, 2004. Montasser provides a biography of Zawahiri.

—*Scott P. Johnson*

SEE ALSO: Abu Nidal; Osama Bin Laden; Josef Mengele.

ANDREY ALEKSANDROVICH ZHDANOV
Soviet bureaucrat

BORN: February 26, 1896; Mariupol, Ukraine, Russian Empire

DIED: August 31, 1948; Moscow, Soviet Union (now in Russia)

CAUSE OF NOTORIETY: Zhdanov led the intellectual crackdown in the Soviet Union that followed the relaxations during World War II.

ACTIVE: 1934-1947

LOCALE: Former Soviet Union, particularly Moscow and Leningrad (St. Petersburg)

EARLY LIFE

Andrey Aleksandrovich Zhdanov (AN-dray al-ehk-ZAN-dro-vich ZHDAN-of) was born in the Black Sea port city of Mariupol on February 26, 1896, to a family of the hereditary service nobility. His father, like the father of Vladimir Ilich Lenin, was an inspector of schools. His mother, a graduate of the Moscow Musical Conservatory, taught her son to sing and play the piano. Thus he was the only representative of the old intelligentsia among the rude peasants of Joseph Stalin's court. Perhaps because of that awkward class origin, he took pains to be very proper in his personal life and relationship with the dictator Stalin, to the point that other members of the Politburo scorned him as a prig.

POLITICAL CAREER

Although Zhdanov had held various minor positions from the beginning of the Bolshevik regime, his career really took off after the 1934 murder of Leningrad party secretary Sergei Kirov. Appointed by Stalin to take the murdered Kirov's place, Zhdanov participated in the purging of Leningrad's Party apparat with frantic zeal. During World War II, while Leningrad was surrounded and besieged by Nazi forces for nine hundred days, Zhdanov administered the starving city with brutal efficiency.

However, it was after the close of the war that he made his permanent mark on Soviet history. Locked in a political struggle with Georgi Malenkov for control of the overall party apparat, Zhdanov needed to prove his credentials as a doctrinaire hard-liner. As a result, he took the lead in a new wave of repressions that cracked down on the intellectual elite, particularly in Leningrad. He called poet Anna Akhmatova a "nun-harlot" and regarded Mikhail Zoshchenko's satire "Prikliucheniia obeziany" ("The Adventures of a Monkey") as intolera-bly offensive. Zhdanov also sought to portray the world as divided into two irreconcilable camps, communist and capitalist.

Always a heavy drinker, Zhdanov began to display symptoms of alcoholism, to the point that even Stalin ordered him to stop drinking. Nikita S. Khrushchev recalled in his memoirs that Zhdanov regularly drank himself under the table solely because it pleased Stalin to see him drunk. After Zhdanov argued with Stalin and fell out of favor in 1947, he went downhill quickly. Never graced with a strong constitution in spite of his burly build, Zhdanov finally succumbed to a heart attack in 1948.

IMPACT

Andrey Aleksandrovich Zhdanov's attacks on Akhmatova and Zoshchenko were so critical in signaling the end of the wartime relaxation on Soviet control of literature that the subsequent repression was named the *Zhdanovshchina*, literally "the Zhdanov-thing," paralleling the *Yezhovshchina* for the height of the 1930's Great Terror, named for secret police chief Nikolay Ivanovich Yezhov. Even after Zhdanov died, his baleful influence did not end, for accusations that he had been murdered by medical malpractice formed, in part, the foundation for claims of the "Doctor's Plot," which appears to have been intended as the opening round of a new cycle of purges, interrupted only by Stalin's unexpected death on March 5, 1953. Zhdanov's "two-camp" schema of international relations survived him in the person of ideologist Mikhail Suslov.

FURTHER READING

Conquest, Robert. *The Great Terror: A Reassessment.* New York: Oxford University Press, 1990. A postglasnost reissuing of an authoritative volume on the era.

Khrushchev, Nikita S. *Khrushchev Remembers.* Translated by Strobe Talbott. Boston: Little, Brown, 1970. A revealing primary source, although with certain predictable blind spots regarding Khrushchev's own complicity in many of the crimes he describes.

Montefiore, Simon Sebag. *Stalin: The Court of the Red Tsar.* New York: Alfred A. Knopf, 2003. Includes information on Stalin's use of Zhdanov and other henchmen to run the Terror while deflecting attention from himself.

Rayfield, Donald. *Stalin and His Hangmen: The Tyrant and Those Who Killed for Him.* New York: Random House, 2004. A study of the relationship between Stalin and his chief henchmen.

—*Leigh Husband Kimmel*

SEE ALSO: Lavrenty Beria; Felix Dzerzhinsky; Lazar Kaganovich; Nikita S. Khrushchev; Vladimir Ilich Lenin; Vyacheslav Mikhailovich Molotov; Symon Petlyura; Joseph Stalin; Vasili Vasilievich Ulrikh; Andrey Vyshinsky; Genrikh Yagoda; Nikolay Ivanovich Yezhov.

GRIGORY YEVSEYEVICH ZINOVYEV
Bolshevik revolutionary and Soviet Communist politician

BORN: September 23, 1883; Yelizavetgrad, Russian Empire (now Kirovohrad, Ukraine)

DIED: August 25, 1935; Moscow, Soviet Union (now in Russia)

ALSO KNOWN AS: Ovel Gershon Aronov Radomyslsky (birth name); Hirsh Apfelbaum

MAJOR OFFENSE: Conspiracy to overthrow the Soviet state and to assassinate Joseph Stalin

ACTIVE: 1901-1935

LOCALE: Russia

SENTENCE: Death by pistol shot

EARLY LIFE

Grigory Yevseyevich Zinovyev (grih-GAW-ree yehv-SAY-oh-vihch zih-NOHV-yehv) was born Ovel Gershon Aronov Radomyslsky, the son of a Jewish dairy farmer. He had no formal education but was taught at home. In 1901, he joined the infant Russian Social Democratic Party and began labor organizing. He left the Russian Empire because of police harassment and moved successively to Berlin, Paris, and finally Switzerland. There he met Georgy Plekhanov and Vladimir Ilich Lenin, Russian socialists who edited the newspaper *Iskra* (meaning "spark"), the most orthodox Marxist organ of the party at a time when European socialism was rife with revisionism. In the split between the misnamed Bolsheviks (meaning "majority faction") led by Lenin and the Mensheviks ("minority faction"), Zinovyev sided with the former.

POLITICAL CAREER

In 1903, Zinovyev returned briefly to Russia and worked on *Iskra*, but he soon went back to Switzerland. During the revolution of 1905, he served as an agitator for Lenin's faction, trying to convince members of the party to support the Bolshevik program. He also helped organize the General Strike, which closed down the country and forced Czar Nicholas II to promise a parliament (duma) for Russia. Suffering from heart trouble, Zinovyev left to seek medical attention abroad.

In 1907, Zinovyev was elected by Lenin's faction to the Central Committee of the Party. Because Mensheviks (who, in fact, had the majority support of the party) did not recognize this election, Lenin formed a separate party of the Bolsheviks. Zinovyev was his second leader of the party. He became close to Bolshevik revolutionary Lev Borisovich Kamenev, and from this period onward they worked together. After serving a brief jail sentence, Zinovyev went into exile abroad, where he worked closely with Lenin and helped to organize the Bolshevik press.

Zinovyev returned to Petrograd (now St. Petersburg) with Lenin in May, 1917, and was recognized by the party, public, and government as Lenin's closest associate. Thus, in August, 1917, when the provisional government ordered the arrest of the Bolshevik leaders as German spies, Lenin and Zinovyev went into hiding together in the Finnish suburbs of Petrograd. In October, the Bolshevik Central Committee met in secret, and on Lenin's motion it determined to carry out a coup d'état against the government of Aleksandr Fyodorovich Kerensky. Zinovyev and Kamenev objected because they believed the coup would violate democratic principles, and they published their objections in the press, thereby revealing the secret plans. The government unsuccessfully acted against the Bolsheviks, but the party—under the military leadership of Leon Trotsky—overthrew the government and established Bolshevik (now called Communist) rule. Zinovyev and Kamenev briefly fell into disgrace, and Trotsky (who had just joined the Bolsheviks that summer) and a heretofore minor figure on the Central Committee, Joseph Stalin, assumed more leading roles on the committee.

Nevertheless, in the following months, Zinovyev

once again regained his important posts within the party. He was elected to the seven-member Central Committee Political Bureau (Politburo), which became the top leadership of the party. He also became the chief of the party's Petrograd district and the executive secretary of the Communist International (Comintern), which was organized to unite Communist parties around the world. Zinovyev, as leader of the Comintern, was often blamed by opponents of communism, socialism, and labor unions around the world for fomenting labor and political unrest in their countries. The most notorious example was the so-called Zinovyev letter (later found to be forged), which the British Conservative Party said incited British workmen in 1924 to organize a general strike. The Conservatives ousted the British Labour government, using the letter as campaign propaganda.

During the Russian Civil War (1918-1922), Trotsky, who was the leader of the Red Army, and Zinovyev had a falling out because of Trotsky's impatience with the way in which Zinovyev handled the defense of Petrograd. When Lenin fell ill in 1922 and it appeared that Trotsky might succeed him as leader of the party, Zinovyev and Kamenev joined with Stalin in a triumvirate and reduced Trotsky's power considerably. Stalin, linking himself with more conservative leaders of the Politburo, then turned against Zinovyev.

In the period between 1925 and 1927, Zinovyev and Kamenev reversed their stances and joined Trotsky in an alliance called the Left Opposition. The right wing of the Politburo (aligned with Stalin) easily defeated them, however, and had them expelled from the party. Stalin expelled Trotsky from the country but allowed Zinovyev and Kamenev to return to party membership. In the meantime, Stalin turned on the members of the right wing and emerged as the dictator of the Soviet Union.

LEGAL ACTION AND OUTCOME

In 1933, with his popularity falling because of his stringent economic policies and brutal suppression of the peasantry, Stalin turned on the original Bolsheviks as scapegoats. In the first of a bizarre series of public trials in 1935, prosecutors accused Zinovyev and Kamenev of conspiring both with Trotsky and with Adolf Hitler to overthrow the Soviet state and of plotting to assassinate Stalin and other leaders. The court sentenced Zinovyev to ten years' imprisonment.

The next year, in a more sensational case called the Trial of the Fifteen, the court sentenced Zinovyev and Kamenev to death. They were executed by pistol shot almost immediately afterward in the basement of the secret police building.

IMPACT

As a Bolshevik and a leader of the Soviet Communists, Grigory Yevseyevich Zinovyev was instrumental in establishing the worldwide communist movement and the Comintern. As a high-profile victim of Stalin's purge trials, he helped shed light on Stalin as a dictator rather than a leader of a democratic political system.

FURTHER READING

Radzinsky, Edvard. *Stalin*. Translated by H. T. Willetts. London: Sceptre, 1997. An excellent biography of Stalin using Soviet archives opened after the fall of

Grigory Zinovyev.

communism in the early 1990's. Contains details of his relationship to and attitude toward Zinovyev.

Schapiro, Leonard B. *The Communist Party of the Soviet Union*. 2d ed. New York: Vintage, 1971. The standard academic, English-language history of the Soviet Communist Party. Gives details of Zinovyev's career and fate.

Volkogonov, Dmitri. *Trotsky: The Eternal Revolution-ary*. Translated and edited by Harold Shukman. New York: Free Press, 1996. A biography of Leon Trotsky that paints a rather unfavorable portrait of him and also gives details about Zinovyev's career.

—*Frederick B. Chary*

SEE ALSO: Vladimir Ilich Lenin; Joseph Stalin; Leon Trotsky; Yakov Mikhailovich Yurovsky.

Great Lives from History

Appendixes

CHRONOLOGICAL LIST OF ENTRIES

All personages appearing in this list are the subjects of articles in *Great Lives from History: Notorious Lives*. The arrangement of personages in this list is chronological on the basis of birth years. Subjects of multiperson essays are listed separately.

Ancient World to 475 C.E.

Jezebel (c. 800 B.C.E.)
Cypselus of Corinth (early seventh century B.C.E.)
Phalaris (c. 610-600 B.C.E.)
Polycrates of Samos (c. 500 B.C.E.?)
Alcibiades of Athens (c. 450 B.C.E.)
Shi Huangdi (259 B.C.E.)
Jing Ke (mid-third century B.C.E.)
Lucius Cornelius Sulla (138 B.C.E.)
Catiline (c. 108 B.C.E.)
Judas Iscariot (first century B.C.E.)
Marcus Junius Brutus (c. 85 B.C.E.)
Fulvia (c. 85/80 B.C.E.)
Herod the Great (73 B.C.E.)

Herod Antipas (before 20 B.C.E.)
Pontius Pilate (c. 10 B.C.E.)
Barabbas (early first century C.E.)
Cassius Chaerea (c. 1 C.E.?)
Caligula (August 31, 12 C.E.)
Salome (c. 15 C.E.)
Flavius Josephus (c. 37 C.E.)
Nero (December 15, 37 C.E.)
Domitian (October 24, 51 C.E.)
Commodus (August 31, 161 C.E.)
Elagabalus (203/204 C.E.)
Galerius (c. 250 C.E.)
Attila (c. 406 C.E.)

Middle Ages, 476-1400

Theodora (c. 497 C.E.)
Justin II (c. 520 C.E.)
Marozia (c. 890 C.E.)
al-Ḥākim (August 14, 985 C.E.)
Genghis Khan (between 1155 and 1162)
King John (December 24, 1166)
Boniface VIII (c. 1235)

Robin Hood (fl. thirteenth century?)
Lady Alice Kyteler (1280)
John Parricida (1290)
Urban VI (c. 1318)
Peter the Cruel (August, 30, 1334)
Charles VI (December 3, 1368)

1401-1500

Gilles de Rais (September or October, 1404)
Tomás de Torquemada (1420)
Vlad III the Impaler (late 1431)
Alexander VI (January 1, 1431)
Richard III (October 2, 1452)
ʿAruj (c. 1473)
Leo X (December 11, 1475)

Cesare Borgia (1475 or 1476)
Clement VII (May 26, 1478)
Joan the Mad (November 6, 1479)
Lucrezia Borgia (April 18, 1480)
Mother Shipton (1488)
Johnnie Armstrong (c. 1490's)

1501-1600

Nostradamus (December 14, 1503)
Roderigo Lopez (1525)
Grace O'Malley (c. 1530)
Ivan the Terrible (August 25, 1530)
Erik XIV (December 13, 1533)
Francis Drake (c. 1540)
Balthasar Gérard (1557)
Fyodor I (May 31, 1557)
Elizabeth Báthory (August 7, 1560)

Jacques Clément (c. 1567)
Guy Fawkes (April 15, 1570)
Beatrice Cenci (February 6, 1577)
François Ravaillac (1578)
Elizabeth Sawyer (c. 1580?)
Moll Cutpurse (c. 1584)
John Felton (c. 1595)
Margaret Jones (c. 1600)
Florence Newton (c. 1600?)

1601-1700

Jean Martinet (c. 1620?)
Miles Sindercombe (c. 1620?)
Sir Henry Morgan (c.1635)
Charlotte de Berry (1636)
Claude Duval (1643)
William Kidd (c. 1645)
Titus Oates (September 15, 1649)
William Dampier (August, 1651)
Charles II (November 6, 1661)
John Quelch (c. 1665)
Ivan V (September 6, 1666)
Rob Roy (baptized March 7, 1671)

John Law (April 21, 1671)
Dolly Pentreath (c. 1675)
Edward Teach (c. 1680)
Jonathan Wild (c. 1682)
Bartholomew Roberts (May 17, 1682)
Mary Read (c. 1685)
Stede Bonnet (1688)
Nadir Shah (October 22, 1688)
Samuel Bellamy (1689)
Cartouche (1693)
Anne Bonny (c. 1697)
John Rackham (c. 1700)

1701-1800

Jack Sheppard (1702)
Eugene Aram (1704)
Dick Turpin (probably September, 1705)
William Dodd (May 29, 1729)
Charles Lee (February 6, 1732)
Benjamin Church (August 24, 1734)
Marquis de Sade (June 2, 1740)
Ivan VI (August 23, 1740)
Benedict Arnold (January 14, 1741)
William Brodie (September 28, 1741)
Jean-Paul Marat (May 24, 1743)
Maurycy Beniowski (September 20, 1746)
Christian VII (January 29, 1749)
William Bligh (September 9, 1754)
Marie-Antoinette (November 2, 1755)
Aaron Burr (February 6, 1756)
Sweeney Todd (October 16, 1756)
James Wilkinson (1757)

Robespierre (May 6, 1758)
Rachel Wall (1760)
Charlotte Corday (July 27, 1768)
Dominique You (c. 1772)
Mary Butters (late 1700's)
Cheng I Sao (1775)
Joan Wytte (1775)
Eugène François Vidocq (July 23 or 24, 1775)
John Bellingham (1776)
Roger Brooke Taney (March 17, 1777)
Jean Laffite (c. 1780)
Giuseppe Fieschi (December 3, 1790)
William Burke (1792)
Marie Laveau (1794)
Nicholas I (July 6, 1796)
Tamsin Blight (1798)
Simon Cameron (March 8, 1799)

1801-1810

Richard Lawrence (1800 or 1801)

Oakes Ames (January 10, 1804)

1811-1820

Madame Restell (May 6, 1812)
Daniel M'Naghten (1814)

James Donnelly (March 7, 1816)
Arthur de Gobineau (July 14, 1816)

1821-1830

Nathan Bedford Forrest (July 13, 1821)
Schuyler Colfax (March 23, 1823)
William Marcy Tweed (April 3, 1823)
Mary Surratt (May or June, 1823)
Johannah Donnelly (September 22, 1823)
Henry Wirz (November 25, 1823)

James W. McCord, Jr. (January 26, 1824)
William Walker (May 8, 1824)
Tom Bell (1825)
Konstantin Petrovich Pobedonostsev (May 21, 1827)
Frederika Mandelbaum (c. 1830)
Porfirio Díaz (September 15, 1830)

1831-1840

Joaquín Murieta (c. 1832)
Charles Peace (May 14, 1832)
Pauline Cushman (June 10, 1833)
Arthur Orton (March 20, 1834)
Jim Fisk (April 1, 1834)
Madeleine Smith (March 29, 1835)

Leopold II (April 9, 1835)
Jay Gould (May 27, 1836)
William Clarke Quantrill (July 31, 1837)
John Wilkes Booth (May 10, 1838)
George A. Custer (December 5, 1839)
Curly Bill Brocius (c. 1840)

1841-1850

Charles Julius Guiteau (September 8, 1841)
James Donnelly, Jr. (December 8, 1841)
Molly Maguires (formed 1843)
Adam Worth (1844)
Cole Younger (January 15, 1844)
Anthony Comstock (March 7, 1844)
Lewis Powell (April 22, 1844)
Belle Boyd (May 4, 1844)
William Donnelly (1845)
Ludwig II (August 24, 1845)
Elisabeth Förster-Nietzsche (July 10, 1846)

John Donnelly (1847/1848)
Benjamin Tillman (August 11, 1847)
Jesse James (September 5, 1847)
Ferdinand Walsin Esterhazy (December 16, 1847)
Belle Starr (February 5, 1848)
Wyatt Earp (March 19, 1848)
Patrick Donnelly (April 15, 1849)
Hank Vaughan (April 27, 1849)
Lou Blonger (May 13, 1849)
Johnny Ringo (May 3, 1850)
Michael Donnelly (September, 1850)

1851-1860

Sam Bass (July 21, 1851)
Doc Holliday (August 14, 1851)
Bill Longley (October 6, 1851)
John Wesley Hardin (May 26, 1853)
Robert Donnelly (November 9, 1853)
Eusapia Palladino (January 21, 1854)
Thomas Donnelly (August 30, 1854)
Ned Kelly (December, 1854)
Houston Stewart Chamberlain (September 9, 1855)

Philippe Pétain (April 24, 1856)
Jenny Donnelly (October, 1856)
Cassie L. Chadwick (October 10, 1857)
Bill Doolin (1858)
Yuan Shikai (September 16, 1859)
William H. Bonney (November 23, 1859)
Apache Kid (c. 1860)
Lizzie Borden (July 19, 1860)

1861-1870

H. H. Holmes (May 16, 1861)
Albert B. Fall (November 26, 1861)
Jack Ketch (October 31, 1863)
Thomas Dixon, Jr. (January 11, 1864)
Reginald Dyer (October 9, 1864)
Butch Cassidy (April 13, 1866)
Harry Longabaugh (Spring, 1867)
Linda Burfield Hazzard (1868)
Salvatore Maranzano (1868)
Dietrich Eckart (March 23, 1868)

Bill Haywood (February 4, 1869)
Henri Désiré Landru (April 12, 1869)
Bob Dalton (May 13, 1869)
Emma Goldman (June 27, 1869)
Mary Mallon (September 23, 1869)
Eligiusz Niewiadomski (December 1, 1869)
Grigori Yefimovich Rasputin (c. 1870)
Miguel Primo de Rivera (January 8, 1870)
Vladimir Ilich Lenin (April 22, 1870)
Albert Fish (May 19, 1870)

1871-1880

Ma Barker (c. 1871)
Harry Kendall Thaw (February 12, 1871)
Ioannis Metaxas (April 12, 1871)
Emmett Dalton (May 3, 1871)
Thomas Joseph Pendergast (July 22, 1872)
Leon Czolgosz (1873)
Sante Jeronimo Caserio (September 8, 1873)
Henry Starr (December 2, 1873)
Joseph Weil (1875 or 1877)
Aleister Crowley (October 12, 1875)
Ada Everleigh (February 15, 1876)
Mata Hari (August 7, 1876)
Jules Bonnot (October 14, 1876)
Felix Dzerzhinsky (September 11, 1877)

Theodore G. Bilbo (October 18, 1877)
Pancho Villa (June 5, 1878)
Yakov Mikhailovich Yurovsky (June 19, 1878)
Joseph Stalin (December 18, 1878)
Joe Masseria (1879)
Symon Petlyura (May 10, 1879)
Gaston Bullock Means (July 11, 1879)
Emiliano Zapata (August 8, 1879)
Leon Trotsky (November 7, 1879)
William Joseph Simmons (1880)
Susanna Mildred Hill (c. 1880)
Dorothy Clutterbuck (January 19, 1880)
Kuniaki Koiso (March 22, 1880)

1881-1890

James J. Walker (June 19, 1881)
François Darlan (August 7, 1881)
Irish Invincibles (formed late 1881)
Father Divine (c. 1882)
Arnold Rothstein (January 17, 1882)
Charles Ponzi (March 3, 1882)
Ion Antonescu (June 15, 1882)
Getúlio Vargas (April 19, 1883)
Pierre Laval (June 28, 1883)
Benito Mussolini (July 29, 1883)
Grigory Yevseyevich Zinovyev (September 23, 1883)
Andrey Vyshinsky (December 10, 1883)
Hideki Tojo (December 30, 1884)
Julius Streicher (February 12, 1885)
John R. Brinkley (July 8, 1885)
Béla Kun (February 20, 1886)
Felix Yusupov (March 23, 1886)

Alexandre Stavisky (November 20, 1886)
Fanya Kaplan (1887)
Roscoe Arbuckle (March 24, 1887)
Shoeless Joe Jackson (July 16, 1887)
Vidkun Quisling (July 18, 1887)
Jack the Ripper (fl. 1888)
Bartolomeo Vanzetti (June 11, 1888)
Adolf Hitler (April 20, 1889)
António de Oliveira Salazar (April 28, 1889)
Vasili Vasilievich Ulrikh (July 13, 1889)
Ante Pavelić (July 14, 1889)
Tommy Lucchese (December 1, 1889)
Victor Lustig (January 4, 1890)
Robert Franklin Stroud (January 28, 1890)
Vyacheslav Mikhailovich Molotov (March 9, 1890)
Alfred Jodl (May 10, 1890)
Aimee Semple McPherson (October 9, 1890)

1891-1900

Genrikh Yagoda (1891)
Frank Costello (January 26, 1891)
Wallace Dodd Fard (February 25, 1891)
Nicola Sacco (April 22, 1891)
Leander Perez (July 16, 1891)
Bugs Moran (August 21, 1891)
Karl Dönitz (September 16, 1891)
Rafael Trujillo (October 24, 1891)
Charles E. Coughlin (October 25, 1891)
Tito (May 7, 1892)
Dion O'Banion (July 8, 1892)
Francisco Franco (December 4, 1892)
Hermann Göring (January 12, 1893)
Joachim von Ribbentrop (April 30, 1893)
Huey Long (August 30, 1893)
Lazar Kaganovich (November 22, 1893)
Mao Zedong (December 26, 1893)
Nikita S. Khrushchev (April 17, 1894)
Rudolf Hess (April 26, 1894)
Dave Beck (June 16, 1894)
Gavrilo Princip (July 25, 1894)
J. Edgar Hoover (January 1, 1895)
Ruth Snyder (March 27, 1895)
Nikolay Ivanovich Yezhov (May 1, 1895)
Richard Walther Darré (July 14, 1895)

Machine Gun Kelly (July 17, 1895)
Juan Perón (October 8, 1895)
Joe Ball (January 7, 1896)
Anastasio Somoza García (February 1, 1896)
Andrey Aleksandrovich Zhdanov (February 26, 1896)
Sir Oswald Mosley (November 16, 1896)
Legs Diamond (1897)
Marcel Petiot (January 17, 1897)
Louis Buchalter (February 6, 1897)
Joseph Darnand (March 19, 1897)
Winifred Wagner (June 23, 1897)
Joseph Profaci (October 2, 1897)
Elijah Muhammad (October 7, 1897)
Joseph Goebbels (October 29, 1897)
Lucky Luciano (November 24, 1897)
Vito Genovese (November 27 1897)
Hymie Weiss (1898)
Gerald L. K. Smith (February 27, 1898)
Julius Evola (May 19, 1898)
Anastase Vonsiatsky (June 12, 1898)
Jacques Doriot (September 26, 1898)
Trofim Lysenko (September 29, 1898)
Al Capone (January 17, 1899)
Lavrenty Beria (March 29, 1899)
John Reginald Halliday Christie (April 8, 1899)

Puniša Račić (c. 1900?)
Hans Michael Frank (May 23, 1900)
Martin Bormann (June 17, 1900)
Giuseppe Zangara (September 7, 1900)

Andrey Andreyevich Vlasov (September 14, 1900)
Heinrich Himmler (October 7, 1900)
Mildred Gillars (November 29, 1900)

1901-1910

Fulgencio Batista y Zaldívar (January 16, 1901)
Whittaker Chambers (April 1, 1901)
Hirohito (April 29, 1901)
Willie Sutton (June 30, 1901)
Hendrik Frensch Verwoerd (September 8, 1901)
Magda Goebbels (November 11, 1901)
Albert Anastasia (February 26, 1902)
Meyer Lansky (July 4, 1902)
Dutch Schultz (August 6, 1902)
Carlo Gambino (August 24, 1902)
Ayatollah Khomeini (May 17, 1900 or September 24, 1902)
Joe Adonis (November 22, 1902)
John Dillinger (June 22, 1903)
Pretty Boy Floyd (February 3, 1904)
Reinhard Heydrich (March 7, 1904)
Alger Hiss (November 11, 1904)
Nathan F. Leopold, Jr. (November 19, 1904)
Albert Speer (March 19, 1905)
Richard A. Loeb (June 11, 1905)
Savitri Devi (September 30, 1905)
Henri Lemoine (fl. 1905-1908)
Elmyr de Hory (1906)
Puyi (February 7, 1906)
Bugsy Siegel (February 28, 1906)
Adolf Eichmann (March 19, 1906)
William Joyce (April 24, 1906)
Léon Degrelle (June 15, 1906)

Ed Gein (August 27, 1906)
Henri Charrière (November 16, 1906)
Carl Weiss (December 6, 1906)
Virginia McMartin (c. 1907)
Baldur von Schirach (March 9, 1907)
François Duvalier (April 14, 1907)
Yoshiko Kawashima (May 24, 1907)
Horst Wessel (September 9, 1907)
Anthony Blunt (September 26, 1907)
Otto Skorzeny (June 12, 1908)
Sam Giancana (June 15, 1908)
Vincent Coll (July 20, 1908)
Alvin Karpis (August 10, 1908)
Jim Folsom (October 9, 1908)
Enver Hoxha (October 16, 1908)
Joseph McCarthy (November 14, 1908)
Adam Clayton Powell, Jr. (November 29, 1908)
Baby Face Nelson (December 6, 1908)
Clyde Barrow (March 24, 1909)
Wilbur Mills (May 24, 1909)
Muhammad Siad Barre (c. 1910)
Orval E. Faubus (January 7, 1910)
Carlos Marcello (February 6, 1910)
Carmine Galante (February 21, 1910)
Nathuram Vinayak Godse (May 19, 1910)
Abe Fortas (June 19, 1910)
Bonnie Parker (October 1, 1910)

1911-1920

L. Ron Hubbard (March 13, 1911)
Josef Mengele (March 16, 1911)
Jack Ruby (March 25, 1911)
Guy Burgess (April 16, 1911)
Ne Win (May 24, 1911)
Klaus Fuchs (December 29, 1911)
Kim Philby (January 1, 1912)
Eva Braun (February 6, 1912)

Kim Il Sung (April 15, 1912)
Alfredo Stroessner (November 3, 1912)
Richard Nixon (January 9, 1913)
Jimmy Hoffa (February 14, 1913)
Clay Shaw (March 17, 1913)
Donald Duart Maclean (May 25, 1913)
John Cairncross (July 25, 1913)
John Mitchell (September 15, 1913)

Klaus Barbie (October 25, 1913)
Jiang Qing (1914)
Ramón Mercader (February 7, 1914)
Tino De Angelis (1915)
Paul Castellano (June 20, 1915)
Ethel Rosenberg (September 28, 1915)
Augusto Pinochet Ugarte (November 25, 1915)
Tokyo Rose (July 4, 1916)
Tom Keating (March, 1917)
Ferdinand Marcos (September 11, 1917)
Nicolae Ceauşescu (January 26, 1918)
Richard Girnt Butler (February 23, 1918)

George Lincoln Rockwell (March 9, 1918)
Julius Rosenberg (May 12, 1918)
E. Howard Hunt (October 9, 1918)
David Berg (February 18, 1919)
Eva Perón (May 7, 1919)
George C. Wallace (August 25, 1919)
Mohammad Reza Shah Pahlavi (October 26, 1919)
Said Akbar (c. 1920's?)
Sun Myung Moon (January 6, 1920)
Roberto Calvi (April 13, 1920)
Timothy Leary (October 22, 1920)
Byron De La Beckwith (November 9, 1920)

1921-1930

Nexhmije Hoxha (February 7, 1921)
Jean-Bédel Bokassa (February 22, 1921)
Suharto (June 8, 1921)
Lyndon H. LaRouche, Jr. (September 8, 1922)
Salvatore Giuliano (November 16, 1922)
Jean Harris (April 27, 1923)
Joe Colombo (June 16, 1923)
Wojciech Jaruzelski (July 6, 1923)
Elisabeth Becker (July 20, 1923)
Sam Sheppard (December 29, 1923)
Bonnie Nettles (1924)
Madame Nhu (1924)
Robert Mugabe (February 21, 1924)
J. B. Stoner (April 13, 1924)
D. B. Cooper (mid-1920's)
Idi Amin (c. 1925)
John DeLorean (January 6, 1925)
Billie Sol Estes (January 10, 1925)
John D. Ehrlichman (March 20, 1925)
Pol Pot (May 19, 1925)
Jorge Rafael Videla (August 2, 1925)
Ta Mok (1926)
Efraín Ríos Montt (June 16, 1926)

Leopoldo Galtieri (July 15, 1926)
Willis A. Carto (July 17, 1926)
Claus von Bülow (August 11, 1926)
Fidel Castro (August 13, 1926 or 1927)
Ruth Ellis (October 9, 1926)
H. R. Haldeman (October 27, 1926)
Roy Cohn (February 20, 1927)
Jean-Marie Bastien-Thiry (October 19, 1927)
Bobby Baker (1928)
James Earl Ray (March 10, 1928)
Vincent Gigante (March 29, 1928)
Jack Kevorkian (May 26, 1928)
Che Guevara (June 14, 1928)
Jean-Marie Le Pen (June 20, 1928)
Joe Gallo (April 7, 1929)
Imelda Marcos (July 2, 1929)
Ronnie Biggs (August 8, 1929)
Samuel Joseph Byck (January 30, 1930)
Anton Szandor LaVey (April 11, 1930)
Mobutu Sese Seko (October 14, 1930)
Laud Humphreys (October 16, 1930)
Clifford Irving (November 5, 1930)
G. Gordon Liddy (November 30, 1930)

1931-1940

Jim Jones (May 13, 1931)
Marshall Applewhite (May 17, 1931)
Khieu Samphan (July 27, 1931)
Albert DeSalvo (September 3, 1931)
Charles W. Colson (October 16, 1931)
Françoise Dior (April 7, 1932)

Meir Kahane (August 1, 1932)
Velma Margie Barfield (October 29, 1932)
Than Shwe (February 2, 1933)
Marie Hilley (June 4, 1933)
Stanley Milgram (August 15, 1933)
William Luther Pierce III (September 11, 1933)

Reginald Kray (October 24, 1933)
Ronald Kray (October 24, 1933)
Judith Campbell Exner (January 11, 1934)
Bettino Craxi (February 24, 1934)
John Tyndall (July 14, 1934)
Sante Kimes (July 24, 1934)
Angelo Buono, Jr. (October 5, 1934)
Ulrike Meinhof (October 7, 1934)
Charles Manson (November 12, 1934)
Seventh Earl of Lucan (December 18, 1934)
James Porter (January 2, 1935)
Richard Kuklinski (April 11, 1935)
Werner Erhard (September 5, 1935)
Margita Bangová (c. 1936)
Horst Mahler (January 23, 1936)
Valerie Solanas (April 9, 1936)
Winnie Mandela (September 26, 1936)
Andrei Chikatilo (October, 16, 1936)
Abbie Hoffman (November 30, 1936)

Jacques Mesrine (December 28, 1936)
Mengistu Haile Mariam (1937)
Ivan Boesky (March 6, 1937)
Saddam Hussein (April 28, 1937)
Abu Nidal (May, 1937)
Billy Cannon (August 2, 1937)
Manuel Noriega (February 11, 1938)
David Irving (March 24, 1938)
Tom Metzger (April 9, 1938)
Alberto Fujimori (July 28, 1938)
Charles Starkweather (November 24, 1938)
John E. du Pont (c. 1939)
Jim Bakker (January 2, 1939)
Lee Harvey Oswald (October 18, 1939)
Saparmurat Niyazov (February 19, 1940)
Ira Einhorn (March 15, 1940)
John Gotti (October 27, 1940)
Gary Gilmore (December 4, 1940)

1941-1950

Mou Qizhong (1940 or 1941)
Kim Jong-il (February 16, 1941)
Aldrich Ames (June 16, 1941)
Charles Whitman (June 24, 1941)
Slobodan Milošević (August 20, 1941)
Bernard Ebbers (August 27, 1941)
Richard Speck (December 6, 1941)
Muammar al-Qaddafi (1942)
Huey Newton (February 17, 1942)
John Wayne Gacy (March 17, 1942)
Kenneth Lay (April 15, 1942)
Theodore Kaczynski (May 22, 1942)
James Oliver Huberty (October 11, 1942)
Ratko Mladić (March 12, 1943)
Andreas Baader (May 6, 1943)
William Calley (June 8, 1943)
Henry Hill (June 11, 1943)
Sani Abacha (September 20, 1943)
Jeffrey MacDonald (October 12, 1943)
Omar al-Bashir (January 1, 1944)
Sirhan Sirhan (March 19, 1944)
Charles Sobraj (April 6, 1944)
Robert Philip Hanssen (April 18, 1944)
Frank Collin (November 3, 1944)
Gilbert Gauthe (1945)

Dennis Rader (March 9, 1945)
Sammy Gravano (March 12, 1945)
Radovan Karadžić (June 19, 1945)
Fusako Shigenobu (September 3, 1945)
Harold Shipman (June 14, 1946)
Michael Milken (July 4, 1946)
Leonard Lake (July 20, 1946)
Dan White (September 2, 1946)
Ted Bundy (November 24, 1946)
Bernhard Goetz (1947)
O. J. Simpson (July 9, 1947)
Assata Olugbala Shakur (July 16, 1947)
Randy Weaver (January 3, 1948)
Charles Taylor (January 28, 1948)
Eugene de Kock (January 29, 1948)
Frank W. Abagnale, Jr. (April 27, 1948)
Lynette Fromme (October 22, 1948)
Pablo Escobar (January 12, 1949)
Ilich Ramírez Sánchez (October 12, 1949)
Beant Singh (c. 1950?)
Jeffrey Lundgren (May 3, 1950)
Samuel K. Doe (May 6, 1950)
David Duke (July 1, 1950)
Arthur Bremer (August 21, 1950)
Larry C. Ford (September 29, 1950)

1951-1960

Kenneth Bianchi (May 22, 1951)
Ayman al-Zawahiri (June 19, 1951)
Jean-Claude Duvalier (July 3, 1951)
Daulton Lee (1952)
Sydney Barrows (January 14, 1952)
Veerappan (January 18, 1952)
Dennis Levine (1953)
Robert Jay Mathews (January 16, 1953)
Christopher John Boyce (February 16, 1953)
David Berkowitz (June 1, 1953)
Jeffrey Skilling (November 25, 1953)
Patty Hearst (February 20, 1954)
Richard Allen Davis (June 2, 1954)
Janet Cooke (July 23, 1954)
Jonathan Pollard (August 7, 1954)
Michael Swango (October 21, 1954)
Martin Frankel (November 21, 1954)
Terry Nichols (April 1, 1955)

Shoko Asahara (May 2, 1955)
Mark David Chapman (May 10, 1955)
John Hinckley, Jr. (May 29, 1955)
Diane Downs (August 7, 1955)
Aileen Carol Wuornos (February 29, 1956)
Joey Buttafuoco (March 11, 1956)
George Hennard (October 15, 1956)
Baruch Goldstein (December 9 or 12, 1956)
Osama Bin Laden (March 10, 1957)
Leslie Nelson (September 26, 1957)
Mehmet Ali Ağca (January 9, 1958)
Bambi Bembenek (August 15, 1958)
David Koresh (August 17, 1959)
Karla Faye Tucker (November 18, 1959)
Jeffrey Dahmer (May 21, 1960)
Yolanda Saldívar (September 19, 1960)
Charles Ng (December 24, 1960)
John Allen Muhammad (December 31, 1960)

1961-1970

Satwant Singh (1962)
Mary Kay Letourneau (January 30, 1962)
Phoolan Devi (August 10, 1963)
Byron Looper (1964)
Carolyn Warmus (January 8, 1964)
Khalid Shaikh Mohammed (March 1, 1964, or April 14, 1965)
Uday Hussein (June 18, 1964)
Andrea Yates (July 2, 1964)
Paul Bernardo (August 27, 1964)
Marc Lépine (October 26, 1964)
Rodney King (April 2, 1965)
Heidi Fleiss (December 30, 1965)
Qusay Saddam Hussein (May 17, 1966)
Eric Rudolph (September 19, 1966)

Abu Musab al-Zarqawi (October 20, 1966)
Nick Leeson (February 25, 1967)
Pamela Ann Smart (August 16, 1967)
Megan Louise Ireland (August 18, 1967)
Timothy McVeigh (April 28, 1968)
Ramzi Yousef (May 20, 1968)
Zacarias Moussaoui (May 30, 1968)
Mohammed Atta al-Sayed (September 1, 1968)
Volkert van der Graaf (July 9, 1969)
Andrew Cunanan (August 31, 1969)
Antoinette Frank (January 1, 1970)
Darlie Routier (January 4, 1970)
Karla Homolka (May 4, 1970)
George Rivas (May 6, 1970)
Yigal Amir (May 23, 1970)

1971-

Matthew F. Hale (July 27, 1971)
Susan Smith (September 26, 1971)
Scott Peterson (October 24, 1972)
Thenmuli Rajaratnam (1974?)

Mijailo Mijailovic (December 6, 1978)
John Walker Lindh (February 9, 1981)
Lee Boyd Malvo (February 18, 1985)

BIBLIOGRAPHY

CONTENTS

GENERAL STUDIES AND REFERENCE

Alexander, Gemma, ed. *Heroic and Outrageous Women*. Edison, N.J.: Castle Books, 2002.

Ballinger, Anette. *Dead Woman Walking: Executed Women in England and Wales, 1900-1955*. Aldershot, England: Ashgate, 2000.

Barmash, Isadore. *Great Business Disasters: Swindlers, Burglars, and Frauds in American Industry*. Chicago: Playboy, 1972.

Bauman, Richard A. *Women and Politics in Ancient Rome*. New York: Routledge, 1992.

Benoit, Tom. *Where Are They Buried? How Did They Die? Fitting Ends and Final Resting Places of the Famous, Infamous, and Noteworthy*. New York: Black Dog & Leventhal, 2003.

Block, Lawrence, ed. *Gangsters, Swindlers, Killers, and Thieves: The Lives and Crimes of Fifty American Villains*. New York: Oxford University Press, 2004.

Bondeson, Jan. *The Great Pretenders: The True Stories Behind Famous Historical Mysteries*. New York: W. W. Norton, 2004.

Bryant, Mark. *Private Lives: A True Compendium of Curious Facts, Bizarre Habits and Fascinating Anecdotes About the Lives of the Famous and Infamous Throughout History*. New York: Cassell, 2002.

Butts, Ed. *She Dared: True Stories of Heroines, Scoundrels, and Renegades*. Toronto, Ont.: Tundra Books, 2005.

Chessman, Clive. *Rebels, Pretenders, and Imposters*. New York: St. Martin's Press, 2000.

Clarke, James W. *American Assassins: The Darker Side of Politics*. 1982. Rev. ed. Princeton, N.J.: Princeton University Press, 1990.

DeVito, Carto. *The Encyclopedia of International Organized Crime*. New York: Facts On File, 2005.

Drago, Sinclair. *Road Agents and Train Robbers: Half a Century of Western Banditry*. New York: Dodd, 1973.

Farquhar, Michael. *A Treasury of Deception: Liars, Misleaders, Hoodwinkers, and the Extraordinary True Stories of History's Greatest Hoaxes, Fakes, and Frauds*. New York: Penguin Books, 2005.

Flowers, H. Lorraine, and R. Barri Flowers. *Murder in the United States: Crimes, Killers, and Victims of the Twentieth Century*. Jefferson, N.C.: McFarland, 2001.

Foreman, Laura, ed. *Mass Murderers*. Alexandria, Va.: Time-Life Books, 1993.

George, John, and Laird Wilcox. *American Extremists: Militias, Supremacists, Klansmen, Communists, and Others*. Amherst, N.Y.: Prometheus Books, 1996.

Guiley, Rosemary Ellen. *The Encyclopedia of Witches and Witchcraft*. 2d ed. New York: Checkmark Books, 1999.

Gutman, Roy. *Crimes of War*. New York: W. W. Norton, 1999.

Herman, Arthur. *The Idea of Decline in Western History*. New York: Free Press, 1997.

Hickey, Eric, ed. *Encyclopedia of Murder and Violent Crime*. Thousand Oaks, Calif.: Sage, 2003.

Hornberger, Francine. *Mistresses of Mayhem: A Book of Women Criminals.* Indianapolis: Alpha-Pearson, 2002.

Hyde, Stephen, and Geno Zanetti, eds. *Players: Con Men, Hustlers, Gamblers, and Scam Artists.* New York: Thunder's Mouth Press, 2002.

Jackman, Ian, ed. *Con Men: Fascinating Profiles of Swindlers and Rogues from the Files of the Most Successful Broadcast in Television History.* New York: Simon & Schuster, 2003.

Jones, Ann. *Women Who Kill.* New York: Holt, Rinehart, and Winston, 1980.

Kelly, Robert J. *Encyclopedia of Organized Crime in the United States: From Capone's Chicago to the New Urban Underworld.* Westport, Conn.: Greenwood Press, 2000.

Knappmann, Edward W. *Sex, Sin, and Mayhem: Notorious Trials of the '90's.* Detroit, Mich.: Visible Ink Press, 1995.

Kohn, George C. *Dictionary of Culprits and Criminals.* 2d ed. Lanham, Md.: Scarecrow Press, 1995.

Linebaugh, Peter. *The London Hanged: Crime and Civil Society in the Eighteenth Century.* 2d ed. London: Verso, 2003.

Mathew, H. C. G., and Brian Harrison, eds. *Oxford Dictionary of National Biography, from the Earliest Times to the Year 2000.* New York: Oxford University Press, 2004.

Nash, Jay Robert, ed. *Bloodletters and Badmen: A Narrative Encyclopedia of American Criminals, from the Pilgrims to the Present.* New York: J. B. Lippincott, 1973.

_____. *World Encyclopedia of Organized Crime.* New York: Paragon House, 1992.

Newton, Michael. *Bad Girls Do It: An Encyclopedia of Female Murderers.* Port Townsend, Wash.: Loompanics Unlimited, 1993.

_____. *The Encyclopedia of Serial Killers.* New York: Checkmark Books, 2000.

Norris, Joel. *Serial Killers.* New York: Doubleday Anchor, 1989.

O'Neal, Bill. *Encyclopedia of Western Gunfighters.* Reprint. Norman: University of Oklahoma Press, 1991.

Outman, James L. *Terrorism: Biographies.* Detroit: UXL, 2003.

Ray, Jo Anne. *American Assassins.* Minneapolis, Minn.: Lerner, 1974.

Robinson, Daniel. *Wild Beasts and Idle Humors: The Insanity Defense from Antiquity to the Present.* Cambridge, Mass.: Harvard University Press, 1998.

Roughead, William. *Classic Crimes: A Selection from the Works of William Roughead.* New York: Vintage Books, 1976.

Schechter, Harold. *The Serial Killer Files.* New York: Ballantine Books, 2003.

Sifakis, Carl. *The Mafia Encyclopedia.* 2d ed. New York: Facts On File, 1999.

Snow, Robert L. *Deadly Cults: The Crimes of True Believers.* Westport, Conn.: Praeger, 2003.

Spraggs, Gillian. *Outlaws and Highwaymen: The Cult of the Robber in England.* London: Pimlico, 2001.

Swierczynski, Duane. *This Here's a Stick-Up: The Big Bad Book of American Bank Robbers.* New York: Alpha, 2002.

Time-Life Books, ed. *Crimes of Passion.* Alexandria, Va.: Time-Life Books, 1994.

Vronsky, Peter. *Serial Killers: The Method and Madness of Monsters.* Goleta, Calif.: Berkley Trade, 2004.

Williams, Roger M. *The Super Crooks: A Rogue's Gallery of Famous Hustlers, Swindlers, and Thieves.* Chicago: Playboy Paperbacks, 1974.

Wilson, Colin. *The History of Murder.* New York: Carroll & Graf, 2000.

Wilson, Colin, and Donald Seaman. *The Encyclopedia of Modern Murder, 1962-1982.* New York: G. P. Putnam's Sons, 1983.

Wilson, Colin, and Kirk Wilson. *Unsolved Crimes.* London: Carroll & Graf, 2002.

ASSASSINS

Ackerman, Kenneth D. *Dark Horse: The Surprise Election and Political Murder of President James A. Garfield.* New York: Carroll & Graf, 2003.

Anandaram, S. *Assassination of a Prime Minister: As It Happened.* New Delhi: Vision Books, 1994.

Barrett, Anthony A. *Caligula: The Corruption of Power.* New Haven, Conn.: Yale University Press, 1989.

Belli, Melvin M. *Dallas Justice: The Real Story of Jack Ruby and His Trial.* New York: McKay Press, 1964.

Benson, Michael. *Who's Who in the JFK Assassination: An A-to-Z Encyclopedia.* New York: Kensington, 1992.

Biondich, Mark. *Stjepan Radić, the Croat Peasant Party, and the Politics of Mass Mobilization: 1904-1928.* Toronto, Ont.: University of Toronto Press, 2000.

Bonnie, Richard, Joseph Jeffries, and Peter Low. *A Case Study in the Defense of John W. Hinckley, Jr.* New York: Foundation Press, 2000.

Bremer, Arthur H. *An Assassin's Diary.* New York: Harper's Magazine Press, 1973.

Caplan, Lincoln. *The Insanity Defense and the Trial of John W. Hinckley, Jr.* Boston: David R. Godine, 1984.

Cassels, Lavender. *The Archduke and the Assassin: The Road to Sarajevo.* New York: Stein and Day, 1985.

Chamlee, Roy Z., Jr. *Lincoln's Assassins: A Complete Account of Their Capture, Trial, and Punishment.* Jefferson, N.C.: McFarland, 1990.

Cheetham, Anthony. *The Life and Times of Richard III.* London: Weidenfeld and Nicolson, 1992.

Clark, Champ. *The Assassination: Death of the President.* Alexandria, Va.: Time/Life, 1987.

Clark, James C. *The Murder of James A. Garfield: The President's Last Days and the Trial and Execution of His Assassin.* Jefferson, N.C.: McFarland, 1993.

Clark, Martin L. *The Noblest Roman: Marcus Brutus and His Reputation.* London: Thames and Hudson, 1981.

Clarke, Asia Booth. *John Wilkes Booth: A Sister's Memoir.* Edited and with an introduction by Terry Alford. Jackson: University of Mississippi Press, 1996.

Clarke, James W. *American Assassins: The Darker Side of Politics.* 1982. Rev. ed. Princeton, N.J.: Princeton University Press, 1990.

Cooper, H. H. *The Murder of Olaf Palme: A Tale of Assassination, Deception, and Intrigue.* Lewiston, N.Y.: Edwin Mellen Press, 2003.

Deutsch, Hermann B. *The Huey Long Murder Case.* Garden City, N.Y.: Doubleday, 1963.

Dolph Owings, W. A., ed. *The Sarajevo Trial.* Chapel Hill, N.C.: Documentary, 1984.

Frank, Kathleen. *Indira: The Life of Indira Gandhi.* Boston: Houghton Mifflin, 2002.

Garrison, Jim. *On the Trail of the Assassins.* New York: Sheridan Square Press, 1988.

Godse, Nathuram. *Why I Assassinated Mahatma Gandhi.* Delhi, India: Surya Bharti, 2003.

Goodrich, Thomas. *The Darkest Dawn: Lincoln, Booth, and the Great American Tragedy.* Bloomington: Indiana University Press, 2005.

Grabbe, Paul, and Beatrice Grabbe. *The Private World of the Last Tsar.* Boston: Little, Brown, 1984.

Hamilton, Sue. *The Killing of a Rock Star: John Lennon (Days of Tragedy).* Edited by John Hamilton. Minneapolis, Minn.: Abdo & Daughters, 1989.

Higham, Charles. *Murdering Mr. Lincoln: A New Detection of the Nineteenth Century's Most Famous Case.* Beverly Hills, Calif.: New Millennium Press, 2004.

Johns, A. Wesley. *The Man Who Shot McKinley.* South Brunswick, N.J.: A. S. Barnes, 1970.

Jones, Jack. *Let Me Take You Down: Inside the Mind of Mark David Chapman, the Man Who Shot John Lennon.* New York: Villard Books, 1992.

Kaarthikeyan, D. R., and Radhavinod Raju. *Triumph of Truth: The Rajiv Gandhi Assassination—The Investigation.* Chicago: New Dawn Press, 2004.

Kantor, Seth. *The Ruby Cover-Up.* New York: Kensington, 1978.

Karpin, Michael, and Ina Friedman. *Murder in the Name of God: The Plot to Kill Yitzchak Rabin.* New York: Metropolitan Books, 1998.

Kendall, Paul, ed. *Richard III: The Great Debate.* London: Allen and Unwin, 1955.

Khosla, Gopal Das. *Murder of the Mahatma and Other Cases from a Judge's Notebook.* Bombay: Jaico, 1968.

King, Greg, and Penny Wilson. *The Fate of the Romanovs.* New York: John Wiley and Sons, 2003.

Krakow, Kari. *The Harvey Milk Story.* Ridley Park, Pa.: Two Lives Publishing, 2001.

Lawrence, Richard. *Shooting at the President!* New York: W. Mitchell, 1835.

Legge, Alfred O. *The Unpopular King: The Life and Times of Richard III.* 2 vols. London: Ward and Downey, 1885.

Leonard, Elizabeth D. *Lincoln's Avengers: Justice, Revenge, and Reunion After the Civil War.* New York: Norton, 2004.

Levick, Barbara. *Claudius.* New Haven, Conn.: Yale University Press, 1990.

Lockyer, Roger. *Buckingham: The Life and Political Career of George Villiers, First Duke of Buckingham, 1592-1628.* London: Longman, 1981.

Mahoney, Harry Thayer, and Marjorie Locke Mahoney. *The Saga of Leon Trotsky: His Clandestine Operations and His Assassination.* London: Austin & Winfield, 1998.

Mailer, Norman. *Oswald's Tale: An American Mystery.* New York: Random House, 1995.

Maylunas, Andrei, and Sergei Mironenko. *A Lifelong Passion: Nicholas and Alexandra, Their Own Story.* New York: Doubleday, 1997.

Moran, Richard. *Knowing Right from Wrong: The Insanity Defense of Daniel McNaughtan.* New York: Free Press, 1981.

Morstein-Marx, Robert. *Mass Oratory and Political Power in the Late Roman Republic.* Cambridge, England: Cambridge University Press, 2004.

Mousnier, Roland. *The Assassination of Henry IV.* Translated by Joan Spencer. New York: Scribner, 1973.

Munir, M. *Assassination of Mr. Liaquat Ali Khan: Report of the Commission of Enquiry.* Karachi: Government of Pakistan, February 28, 1952.

Ownsbey, Betty. *Alias "Paine": Lewis Thorton Powell, the Mystery Man of the Lincoln Conspiracy.* Jefferson, N.C.: McFarland, 1993.

Perry, John Curtis, and Constantine Pleshakov. *The Flight of the Romanovs: A Family Saga.* New York: Basic Books, 1999.

Picchi, Blaise. *The Five Weeks of Giuseppe Zangara: The Man Who Attempted to Assassinate FDR.* Chicago: Academy Chicago, 1998.

Posner, Gerald L. *Case Closed: Lee Harvey Oswald and the Assassination of JFK.* New York: Random House, 1993.

_____. *Killing the Dream: James Earl Ray and the Assassination of Martin Luther King, Jr.* New York: Random House, 1998.

Ray, James Earl. *Who Killed Martin Luther King, Jr.? The True Story by the Alleged Assassin.* New York: Marlowe, 1992.

Ray, Jo Anne. *American Assassins.* Minneapolis, Minn.: Lerner, 1974.

Rosenberg, Charles E. *The Trial of Assassin Guiteau.* Chicago: University of Chicago Press, 1968.

Ross, Charles. *Richard III.* London: Eyre Methuen, 1981.

Ross, Stewart. *Assassination in Sarajevo: The Trigger for World War I.* Chicago: Heinemann Library, 2001.

Shearing, Joseph. *The Angel of the Assassination: Marie-Charlotte de Corday d'Armont, Jean-Paul Marat, Jean-Adam Lux: A Study of Three Disciples of Jean-Jacques Rousseau.* New York: H. Smith and R. Haas, 1935.

Shelton, Vaughan. *Mask for Treason: The Lincoln Murder Trial.* Harrisburg, Pa.: Stackpole Books, 1965.

Shilts, Randy. *The Mayor of Castro Street: The Life and Times of Harvey Milk.* New York: St. Martin's Press, 1982.

Simon, Rita, and David Aaronso. *The Insanity Defense: A Critical Assessment of Law and Policy in the Post-Hinckley Era.* New York: Praeger, 1988.

Steadman, Henry, et al. *Before and After Hinckley: Evaluating Insanity Defense Reform.* New York: Guilford Press, 1993.

Steers, Edward, Jr. *The Trial: The Assassination of President Lincoln and the Trial of the Conspirators.* Lexington: University Press of Kentucky, 2003.

Swanson, James, and Daniel Weinberg. *Lincoln's Assassins: Their Trial and Execution.* Santa Fe, N.Mex.: Arena, 2001.

Trindal, Elizabeth Steger. *Mary Surratt: An American Tragedy.* Gretna, La.: Pelican, 1996.

U.S. Congress. *Compilation of the Statements of James Earl Ray: Staff Report by House Select Committee on Assassinations.* Washington, D.C.: Government Printing Office, 2001.

Warren Commission. *The Official Warren Commission Report on the Assassination of President John F. Kennedy.* Garden City, N.Y.: Doubleday, 1964.

Weigel, George. *Witness to Hope: The Biography of Pope John Paul II, 1920-2005.* New York: Harper-Perennial, 2005.

Weiss, Mike. *Double Play: The San Francisco City Hall Killings.* Reading, Mass.: Addison-Wesley, 1984.

Williams, Charles. *The Last Great Frenchman: A Life of General de Gaulle.* New York: John Wiley and Sons, 1997.

Wills, Garry, and Ovid Demaris. *Jack Ruby.* New York: New American Library, 1967.

Wolpert, Stanley. *Nine Hours to Rama.* New York: Random House, 1962.

Youssoupoff, Felix. *Lost Splendor: The Amazing Memoirs of the Man Who Killed Rasputin.* Translated by Ann Green and Nicolas Katkoff. 1953. Reprint. Chappaqua, N.Y.: Turtle Point Press, 2003.

Zinman, David H. *The Day Huey Long Was Shot: September 8, 1935.* Jackson: University Press of Mississippi, 1993.

BIBLICAL VILLAINS

Beach, Eleanor Ferris. *Jezebel Letters: Religion and Politics in Ninth Century Israel.* Minneapolis, Minn.: Fortress Press, 2005.

Beasley-Murray, George. *John.* 2d ed. Waco, Tex.: Word Books, 1999.

Bond, Helen K. *Pontius Pilate in History and Interpretation.* Cambridge, England: Cambridge University Press, 1998.

Brown, Raymond E. *The Death of the Messiah.* 2 vols. Garden City, N.Y.: Doubleday, 1999.

Carter, Warren. *Pontius Pilate: Portraits of a Roman Governor.* Collegeville, Minn.: Liturgical Press, 2003.

Crossan, John Dominic. *Who Killed Jesus? Exposing the Roots of Anti-Semitism in the Gospel Story of the Death of Jesus.* San Francisco: Harper, 1996.

Dutcher-Walls, Patricia. *Jezebel: Portraits of a Queen.* Collegeville, Minn.: Liturgical Press, 2004.

Edersheim, Alfred. *The Life and Times of Jesus the Messiah.* Grand Rapids, Mich.: Eerdmans, 1981.

Harlow, Victor E. *The Destroyer of Jesus*. Oklahoma City, Okla.: Modern, 1954.

Hoehner, Harold W. *Herod Antipas*. Cambridge, England: Cambridge University Press, 1972. Reprinted as *Herod Antipas: A Contemporary of Jesus Christ*. Grand Rapids, Mich.: Zondervan, 1983.

Horsley, Richard A., and J. S. Hanson. *Bandits, Prophets, and Messiahs*. Minneapolis, Minn.: Fortress, 1985.

Josephus, Flavius. *Josephus: The Complete Works*. Translated by William Whiston. Nashville, Tenn.: Thomas Nelson, 1998.

Kokkinos, Nikos. *The Herodian Dynasty: Origins, Role in Society, and Eclipse*. Sheffield, England: Sheffield Academic Press, 1998.

Lagerkvist, Pär. *Barabbas*. Reprint. New York: Vintage Books, 1989.

McBirnie, William. *The Search for the Twelve Apostles*. Wheaton, Ill.: Tyndale House, 1982.

Maier, Pail. *Pontius Pilate*. Garden City, N.Y.: Doubleday, 1968.

Morris, Leon. *The Gospel According to John*. Rev. ed. Grand Rapids, Mich.: Eerdmans, 1995.

Myers, Carol L. *Discovering Eve: Ancient Israelite Women in Context*. New York: Oxford University Press, 1988.

Phillepfontallie, Jean, and Sheldon Lee Gosner. *The Coins of Pontius Pilate*. Warren Center, Pa.: Shangri-La, 2001.

Rhoads, David M. *Israel in Revolution, 6-74 C.E.: A Political History Based on the Writings of Josephus*. Philadelphia: Fortress, 1976.

Richardson, Peter. *Herod*. Columbia: University of South Carolina Press, 1996.

Witherington, Ben. *New Testament History*. Grand Rapids, Mich.: Baker Academic, 2001.

Wroe, Anne. *Pontius Pilate: The Biography of an Invented Man*. New York: Modern Library, 2001.

CON ARTISTS, CHEATS, AND FRAUDS

Abagnale, Frank W. *The Art of the Steal: How to Protect Yourself and Your Business from Fraud*. New York: Broadway Books, 2001.

Abagnale, Frank W., and Stan Redding. *Catch Me if You Can*. 1980. Reprint. New York: Broadway Books, 2000.

Algren, Nelson. *Chicago: City on the Make*. Fiftieth anniversary ed. Chicago: University of Chicago Press, 2001.

Ambrose, Stephen E. *Nothing Like It in the World: The Men Who Built the Transcontinental Railroad, 1863-1869*. New York: Simon & Schuster, 2000.

Ames, Charles Edgar. *Pioneering the Union Pacific: A Reappraisal of the Builders of the Railroad*. New York: Appleton-Century-Crofts, 1969.

Bailey, Fenton. *Fall from Grace: The Untold Story of Michael Milken*. Secaucus, N.J.: Carol, 1992.

Bain, David Haward. *Empire Express: Building the First Transcontinental Railroad*. New York: Viking, 1999.

Bakker, Jay. *Son of a Preacher Man: My Search for Grace in the Shadows*. San Francisco: Harper, 2002.

Barmash, Isadore. *Great Business Disasters: Swindlers, Burglars, and Frauds in American Industry*. Chicago: Playboy, 1972.

Belton, Brian A. *Gypsy and Traveller Ethnicity: The Social Generation of an Ethnic Phenomenon*. London: Routledge, 2004.

Boese, Alex. *Museum of Hoaxes*. New York: Penguin Putnam, 2002.

Boesky, Ivan. *Merger Mania: Arbitrage, Wall Street's Best Kept Money-Making Secret*. New York: Holt, Rinehart, and Winston, 1985.

Bondeson, Jan. *The Great Pretenders: The True Stories Behind Famous Historical Mysteries*. New York: W. W. Norton, 2004.

Brody, Keith, and Sancha Dunstan. *The Great Telecoms Swindle: How the Collapse of WorldCom Finally Exposed the Technology Myth*. Oxford, England: Capstone, 2003.

Bruck, Connie. *Predators' Ball: The Inside Story of Drexel Burnham and the Rise of the Junk Bond Raiders*. New York: Simon & Schuster, 1988.

Chessman, Clive. *Rebels, Pretenders, and Imposters*. New York: St. Martin's Press, 2000.

Cornwell, Rupert. *God's Banker: The Life and Death of Roberto Calvi*. London: Unwin, 1984.

Crosbie, John S. *The Incredible Mrs. Chadwick: The Most Notorious Woman of Her Age*. New York: McGraw-Hill Ryerson, 1975.

Davia, Howard R. *Fraud 101: Techniques and Strategies for Detection*. New York: John Wiley, 2000.

Deford, Frank. *Everybody's All-American*. New York: Viking Press, 1981.

De Grave, Kathleen. *Swindler, Spy, Rebel: The Confidence Woman in Nineteenth-Century America*. Columbia: University of Missouri Press, 1995.

De Jonge, Alex. *The Life and Times of Grigorii Rasputin*. New York: Coward, 1982.

Estes, Pam. *Billie Sol: King of Texas Wheeler-Dealers*. Abilene, Tex.: Noble Craft Books, 1983.

Farquhar, Michael. *A Treasury of Deception: Liars, Misleaders, Hoodwinkers, and the Extraordinary True Stories of History's Greatest Hoaxes, Fakes, and Frauds*. New York: Penguin Books, 2005.

Fay, Stephen, Lewis Chester, and Magnus Linklater. *Hoax: The Inside Story of the Howard Hughes-Clifford Irving Affair*. New York: Viking Press, 1972.

Feilding, Everard. *Sittings with Eusapia Palladino, and Other Studies*. New Hyde Park, N.Y.: University Books, 1963.

Fischel, Daniel. *Payback: The Conspiracy to Destroy Michael Milken and His Financial Revolution*. New York: Harper Business, 1995.

Fleitz, David L. *Shoeless: The Life and Times of Joe Jackson*. Jefferson, N.C.: McFarland, 2001.

Fogel, Robert William. *The Union Pacific Railroad: A Case in Premature Enterprise*. Baltimore: The Johns Hopkins University Press, 1960.

Fuhrmann, Joseph T. *Rasputin: A Life*. New York: Praeger, 1990.

Gleeson, Janet. *Millionaire: The Philander, Gambler, and Duelist Who Invented Modern France*. New York: Simon & Schuster, 2000.

Gropman, Donald. *Say It Ain't So, Joe! The True Story of Shoeless Joe Jackson*. New York: Carol, 2001.

Gurwin, Larry. *The Calvi Affair: Death of a Banker*. London: Macmillan, 1983.

Howson, Gerald. *The Macaroni Parson: Life of the Unfortunate Doctor Dodd*. London: Hutchinson, 1973.

Hunt, Luke, and Karen Heinrich. *Barings Lost: Nick Leeson and the Collapse of Barings*. London: Butterworth-Heinemann, 1996.

Hyde, Stephen, and Geno Zanetti, eds. *Players: Con Men, Hustlers, Gamblers, and Scam Artists*. New York: Thunder's Mouth Press, 2002.

Iggers, Jeremy. *Good News, Bad News: Journalism Ethics and the Public Interest*. Boulder, Colo.: Westview Press, 1998.

Irving, Clifford. *Fake: The Story of Elmyr de Hory, the Greatest Art Forger of Our Time*. New York: McGraw Hill, 1969.

_____. *The Hoax*. New York: Permanent Press, 1981.

Jackman, Ian, ed. *Con Men: Fascinating Profiles of Swindlers and Rogues from the Files of the Most Successful Broadcast in Television History*. New York: Simon & Schuster, 2003.

Jankowski, Paul. *Stavisky: A Confidence Man in the Republic of Virtue*. Ithaca, N.Y.: Cornell University Press, 2002.

Jeter, Lynne. *Disconnected: Deceit and Betrayal at WorldCom*. New York: Wiley, 2003.

Johnson, J. A., Jr. *Thief: The Bizarre Story of Fugitive Financier Martin Frankel*. New York: Lebhar-Friedman Books, 2000.

Johnson, James F. *The Man Who Sold the Eiffel Tower*. New York: Doubleday, 1961.

Juhnke, Eric S. *Quacks and Crusaders: The Fabulous Careers of John Brinkley, Norman Baker, and Harry Hoxsey*. Lawrence: University Press of Kansas, 2002.

Keating, Tom, with Geraldine and Frank Norman. *Fake's Progress*. London: Hutchinson, 1977.

Lacková, Ilona. *A False Dawn: My Life as a Gypsy Woman in Slovakia*. Edited and translated by Milena Hübschmannová. Hatfield, England: University of Herfordshire Press, 1999.

Lee, R. Alton. *The Bizarre Careers of John R. Brinkley*. Lexington: University Press of Kentucky, 2002.

Leeson, Nick, with Ivan Tyrell. *Back from the Brink: Coping with Stress*. London: Virgin Books, 2005.

Leeson, Nick, with Edward Whitley. *Rogue Trader*. London: Little, Brown, 1996.

Levine, Dennis B., with William Hoffer. *Inside Out: An Insider's Account of Wall Street*. New York: Putnam, 1991.

Malik, Om. *Broadbandits: Inside the $750 Billion Telecom Heist*. New York: Wiley, 2003.

Maugham, Sir Frederick H. *The Tichborne Case*. Westport, Conn.: Hyperion Press, 1936.

Miller, Norman C. *The Great Salad Oil Swindle*. New York: Coward-McCann, 1965.

Nemeth, Neil. *News Ombudsmen in North America: Assessing an Experiment in Social Responsibility*. Westport, Conn.: Praeger, 2003.

Oudard, Georges. *The Amazing Life of John Law, the Man Behind the Mississippi Bubble*. Translated by G. E. Massé. New York: Payson & Clar, 1928.

Pollock, Ellen Joan. *The Pretender: How Martin Frankel Fooled the Financial World and Led the Feds on One of the Most Publicized Manhunts in History*. New York: Simon and Schuster, 2002.

Ponzi, Charles. *The Rise of Mr. Ponzi*. Reprint. Naples, Fla.: Inkwell, 2001.

Radnstis, Sandor. *The Fake: Forgery and Its Place in Art*. Lanham, Md.: Rowman and Littlefield, 1999.

Radzinsky, Edvard. *The Rasputin File*. New York: Doubleday, 2000.

Randi, James. *The Mask of Nostradamus: The Prophecies of the World's Most Famous Seer*. Buffalo, N.Y.: Prometheus Books, 1993.

Rasputin, Maria. *Rasputin: The Man Behind the Myth.* Englewood Cliffs, N.J.: Prentice Hall, 1977.

Raw, Charles. *The Moneychangers: How the Vatican Bank Enabled Roberto Calvi to Steal $250 Million for the Heads of the P2 Masonic Lodge.* London: Harvill, 1992.

Richardson, Michael. *The Edge of Disaster: The Story of Jim and Tammy Bakker.* New York: St. Martin's Press, 1987.

Sagert, Kelly Boyer. *Joe Jackson: A Biography.* Westport, Conn.: Greenwood Press, 2004.

Semprun, Jorge. *Stavisky.* New York: Penguin, 1975.

Shepard, C. E. *Forgiven: The Rise and Fall of Jim Bakker and the PTL Ministry.* New York: Atlantic Monthly Press, 1989.

Sifakis, Carl. *Hoaxes and Scams: A Compendium of Deceptions, Ruses, and Swindles.* London: Michael O'Mara Books, 1994.

Sobel, Robert. *Dangerous Dreamers: The Financial Innovators from Charles Merrill to Michael Milken.* Rev. ed. New York: John Wiley and Sons, 2000.

Stein, Benjamin J. *License to Steal: The Untold Story of Michael Milken and the Conspiracy to Bilk the Nation.* New York: Simon & Schuster, 1992.

Stewart, James B. *Den of Thieves.* New York: Simon & Schuster, 1991.

Tidwell, Gary. *Anatomy of a Fraud: Inside the Finances of the PTL Ministries.* New York: John Wiley & Sons, 1993.

Van Cise, Philip S. *Fighting the Underworld.* 1936. Reprint. New York: Greenwood Press, 1968.

Walker, Kent, with Mark Schone. *Son of a Grifter: The Twisted Tale of Sante and Kenny Kimes, the Most Notorious Con Artists in America.* New York: William Morrow, 2001.

Watts, Jill. *God, Harlem, USA: The Father Divine Story.* Berkeley: University of California Press, 1992.

Weil, Joseph R., and W. T. Brannon. *Con Man: A Master Swindler's Own Story.* 1948. Reprint. New York: Broadway Books, 2004.

Weisbrot, Robert. *Father Divine and the Struggle for Racial Equality.* Urbana: University of Illinois Press, 1983.

Weisman, Stewart L. *Need and Greed: The True Story of the Largest Ponzi Scheme in American History.* Ithaca, N.Y.: Syracuse University Press, 1999.

Williams, Roger M. *The Super Crooks: A Rogue's Gallery of Famous Hustlers, Swindlers, and Thieves.* Chicago: Playboy Paperbacks, 1974.

Wilson, Ian. *Nostradamus: The Man Behind the Prophecies.* New York: St. Martin's Press, 2003.

Zuckoff, Michael. *Ponzi's Scheme: The True Story of a Financial Legend.* New York: Random House, 2005.

CULT LEADERS

Atack, Jon. *A Piece of Blue Sky.* New York: Lyle Stewart, 1990.

Bahr, Robert. *Least of All Saints: The Story of Aimee Semple McPherson.* Englewood Cliffs, N.J.: Prentice Hall, 1979.

Bartley, W. W., III. *Werner Erhard, the Transformation of a Man: The Founding of Est.* New York: Clarkson N. Potter, 1978.

Bednarowski, Mary Farrell. *New Religions and the Theological Imagination in America.* Bloomington: Indiana University Press, 1989.

Blumhofer, Edith L. *Aimee Semple McPherson: Everybody's Sister.* Grand Rapids, Mich.: William B. Eerdmans, 1993.

Bugliosi, Vincent. *Helter Skelter: The True Story of the Manson Murders.* New York: W. W. Norton, 1974.

Corydon, Bent. *L. Ron Hubbard: Messiah or Madman?* Fort Lee, N.J.: Barricade Books, 1992.

Earley, Pete. *Prophet of Death: The Mormon Blood-Atonement Killings.* New York: William Morrow, 1991.

Epstein, Daniel Mark. *Sister Aimee: The Life of Aimee Semple McPherson.* Florida: Harcourt Brace, 1993.

Evanzz, Karl. *The Messenger: The Rise and Fall of Elijah Muhammad.* New York: Pantheon Books, 1999.

Gregg, Claude A. *An Original Man: The Life and Times of Elijah Muhammad.* New York: St. Martin's Press, 1997.

Hall, John R. *Gone from the Promised Land: Jonestown in American Cultural History.* New Brunswick, N.J.: Transaction, 1987.

Hong, Nansook. *In the Shadow of the Moons.* Boston: Little, Brown, 1998.

House, Wayne H.. *Charts of Cults, Sects, and Religious Movements.* Grand Rapids, Mich.: Zondervan, 2000.

Hubbard, L. Ron, ed. *What Is Scientology?* Los Angeles: Bridge, 1993.

Jenkins, Philip. *Mystics and Messiahs: Cults and New Religions in American History.* New York: Oxford University Press, 2000.

Karpf, Jason, and Elinor Karpf. *Anatomy of a Massacre.* Waco, Tex.: WRS, 1994.

Koopmans, Andy. *Charles Manson.* San Diego, Calif.: Lucent Books, 2005.

Lalich, Janja. *Bounded Choice: True Believers and Charismatic Cults*. Berkeley: University of California Press, 2004.

Lee, Martha F. *Nation of Islam: An American Millenarian Movement*. Syracuse, N.Y.: Syracuse University Press, 1996.

Lewis, James R. *Sex, Slander, and Salvation: Investigating the Family/Children of God*. Goleta, Calif.: Center for Academic Publication, 1994.

Lincoln, C. Eric. *The Black Muslims in America*. Trenton, N.J.: Africa World Press, 1961.

Linedecker, Clifford L. *Massacre at Waco, Texas: The Shocking Story of Cult Leader David Koresh and the Branch Davidians*. New York: St. Martin's Press, 1993.

Maaga, Mary M. *Hearing the Voice of Jonestown: Putting a Human Face on an American Tragedy*. Syracuse, N.Y.: Syracuse University Press, 1998.

Melton, J. Gordon. *The Church of Scientology*. Salt Lake City: Signature Books, 2000.

Monsma, Stephen. *When Sacred and Secular Mix: Religious Nonprofit Organizations and Public Money*. Lanham, Md.: Rowman & Littlefield, 2000.

Moon, Sun Myung. *Divine Principle*. 2d ed. Washington, D.C.: Holy Spirit Association for the Unification of World Christianity, 1984.

Pressman, Steven. *Outrageous Betrayal: The Real Story of Werner Erhard from Est to Exile*. New York: St. Martin's Press, 1993.

Pritchett, W. Douglas. *The Children of God, Family of Love: An Annotated Bibliography*. New York: Garland, 1985.

Reavis, D. J. *The Ashes of Waco: An Investigation*. Syracuse, N.Y.: Syracuse University Press, 1998.

Rhodes, Ron. *The Challenge of the Cults and New Religions*. Grand Rapids, Mich.: Zondervan, 2001.

Sanders, Ed. *The Family*. Rev. ed. New York: Thunder's Mouth Press, 2002.

Shupe, Anson. *In the Name of All That's Holy: A Theory of Clergy Malfeasance*. Westport, Conn.: Praeger, 1995.

Singer, Margaret Thaler. *Cults in Our Midst: The Continuing Fight Against Their Hidden Menace*. San Francisco: Jossey-Bass, 2003.

Snow, Robert L. *Deadly Cults: The Crimes of True Believers*. Westport, Conn: Praeger, 2003.

Sontag, Frederick. *Sun Myung Moon and the Unification Church*. Nashville, Tenn.: Abingdon Press, 1977.

Wessinger, Catherine. *How the Millennium Comes Violently: From Jonestown to Heaven's Gate*. New York: Seven Bridges Press, 2000.

Wright, S. A., ed. *Armageddon in Waco: Critical Perspectives on the Branch Davidian Conflict*. Chicago: University of Chicago Press, 1995.

DICTATORS, TYRANTS, AND BAD RULERS

Abrahamian, Ervand. *Khomeinism: Essays on the Islamic Republic*. Berkeley: University of California Press, 1993.

Aburish, Said. *Saddam Hussein: The Politics of Revenge*. New York: Bloomsbury USA, 2000.

Afshar, Haleh, ed. *Iran: A Revolution in Turmoil*. Albany: State University of New York Press, 1985.

Alexander, Robert. *Juan Domingo Perón: A History*. Boulder, Colo.: Westview Press, 1979.

Allen, John. *Idi Amin*. Farmington Hills, Mich.: Thomson Gale, 2003.

Andrewes, Antony. *The Greek Tyrants*. New York: Harper & Row, 1963.

Aquino, Belinda. *Politics of Plunder: The Philippines Under Marcos*. Manila: University of the Philippines College of Public Administration, 1999.

Aram, Bethany. *Juana the Mad: Sovereignty and Dynasty in Renaissance Europe*. Baltimore: Johns Hopkins University Press, 2005.

Argentine National Commission on the Disappeared. *Nunca Más*. New York: Farrar, Strauss, Giroux, 1986.

Argote-Freyre, Frank. *Fulgencio Batista: From Revolutionary to Strongman*. New Brunswick, N.J.: Rutgers University Press, 2004.

Arnold, Guy. *The Maverick State: Gaddafi and the New World Order*. New York: Cassell, 1996.

Ascherson, Neal. *The King Incorporated: Leopold the Second and the Congo*. 1963. Reprint. London: Granta Books, 1999.

Aung San Suu Kyi. *Letters from Burma*. London: Penguin, 1998.

Axworthy, Michael. *Sword of Persia: Nadir Shah, from Tribal Warrior to Conquering Despot*. London: I. B. Tauris, 2006.

Bakhash, Shaul. *The Reign of the Ayatollahs: Iran and the Islamic Revolution*. New York: Basic Books, 1984.

Ball, Patrick, Paul Kobrak, and Herbert F. Spirer. *State Violence in Guatemala, 1960-1996: A Quantitative Reflection*. Washington, D.C.: American Association for the Advancement of Science, 1999.

Ball, Warwick. *Rome in the East: The Transformation of an Empire*. London: Routledge, 2000.

Batista y Zaldívar, Fulgencio. *Cuba Betrayed*. New York: Vantage Press, 1962.

Becker, Elizabeth. *When the War Was Over: Cambodia's Revolution and the Voices of Its People*. New York: Public Affairs, 1986.

Becker, Jasper. *Rogue Regime: Kim Jong-il and the Looming Threat of North Korea*. New York: Oxford University Press, 2005.

Bellonci, Maria. *Lucrezia Borgia*. London: Phoenix Press, 2003.

Ben-Ami, Shlomo. *Fascism from Above: The Dictatorship of Primo de Rivera in Spain, 1923-1930*. New York: Oxford University Press, 1983.

Blunt, Wilfrid. *The Dream King*. New York: Viking Press, 1970.

Boatwright, Mary T., Daniel J. Gargola, and Richard J. A. Talbert. *The Romans from Village to Empire*. New York: Oxford University Press, 2004.

Bouvier, Virginia. *Decline of the Dictator*. Washington, D.C.: Office on Latin America, 1988.

Bowden, Mark. *Black Hawk Down: A Story of a Modern War*. East Rutherford, N.J.: Penguin, 2000.

Braham, R. L. *The Destruction of the Romanian and Ukrainian Jews During the Antonescu Period*. New York: Columbia University Press, 1997.

Breen, Michael. *Kim Jong-il: North Korea's Dear Leader*. New York: John Wiley & Sons, 2004.

Brown, John. *Memoirs of the Courts of Sweden and Denmark: During the Reign of Christian VII of Denmark and Gustavus III and IV of Sweden*. New York: Grolier Society, 1818.

Brumberg, Daniel. *Reinventing Khomeini: The Struggle for Reform in Iran*. Chicago: University of Chicago Press, 2001.

Burbach, Roger. *The Pinochet Affair: State Terrorism and Global Justice*. New York: Zed Books, 2003.

Burghart, Daniel L., and Teresa Sabonis-Hall, eds. *In the Tracks of Tamerlane: Central Asia's Path to the Twenty-First Century*. Washington, D.C.: Center for Technology and National Security Policy, National Defense University, 2001.

Burzanovich, Tihomir-Tiho. *Two Bullets for Pavelić: The Story of Blagoje Jovovic*. Translated by Sinisa Djuric. Banja Luka, Bosnia: Pavelić Papers, 2003.

Bushkovitch, Paul. *Peter the Great: The Struggle for Power, 1671-1725*. New York: Cambridge University Press, 2001.

Cardoza, Anthony L. *Benito Mussolini: The First Fascist*. New York: Pearson Longman, 2006.

Caretti, Paolo. *Theodora: Empress of Byzantium*. New York: Vendome Books, 2004.

Carr, Albert Z. *The World and William Walker*. 1963. Reprint. Westport, Conn.: Greenwood Press, 1975.

Carr, Raymond. *Spain, 1808-1975*. Oxford, England: Clarendon Press, 1982.

Cerf, Christopher, and Micah Sifry, eds. *The Iraq War Reader: History, Documents, Opinions*. Carmichael, Calif.: Touchstone, 2003.

Chan, Stephen. *Robert Mugabe: A Life of Power and Violence*. London: I. B. Tauris, 2003.

Chartrand, René. *Louis XIV's Army*. 1988. Reprint. Oxford, England: Osprey, 2002.

Church, S. D., ed. *King John: New Interpretations*. Rochester, N.Y.: Boydell Press, 1999.

Clapham, Christopher. *Transformation and Continuity in Revolutionary Ethiopia*. Cambridge, England: Cambridge University Press, 1988.

Clark, Martin. *Mussolini*. New York: Pearson Longman, 2005.

Clark, Paul Coe, Jr. *The United States and Somoza, 1933-1956: A Revisionist Look*. Westport, Conn.: Praeger, 1992.

Condit, Erin. *François and Jean-Claude Duvalier*. New York: Chelsea House, 1989.

Corcoran, Simon. *The Empire of the Tetrarchs: Imperial Pronouncements and Government, A.D. 284-324*. New York: Oxford University Press, 1996.

Coughlin, Con. *Saddam: King of Terror*. New York: HarperCollins, 2002.

Cummings, Sally N., ed. *Power and Change in Central Asia*. New York: Routledge, 2002.

Dale, Peter Scott, and Jonathan Marshall. *Cocaine Politics: Drugs, Armies, and the CIA in Central America*. Berkeley: University of California Press, 1998.

Danziger, Danny, and John Gillingham. *1215: The Year of the Magna Carta*. New York: Simon and Schuster, 2004.

Davidson, Eugene. *The Unmaking of Adolf Hitler*. Columbia: University of Missouri Press, 1996.

Decalo, Samuel. *Psychoses of Power: African Personal Dictatorships*. Gainesville: Florida Academic Press, 1998.

De Kock, Eugene. *A Long Night's Damage: Working for the Apartheid State*. Saxonwold, South Africa: Contra Press, 1998.

Dennis, Amarie. *Seek the Darkness: The Story of Juana la Loca*. 5th ed. Madrid: Impresores Sucesores de Rivadeneyra, 1969.

Diederich, Bernard. *Somoza and the Legacy of U.S. Involvement in Central America*. New York: E. P. Dutton, 1981.

Dinges, John. *The Condor Years: How Pinochet and His Allies Brought Terrorism to Three Continents*. New York: The New Press, 2004.

_____. *Our Man in Panama: The Shrewd Rise and Brutal Fall of Manuel Noriega*. New York: Random House, 1991.

Djilas, Milovan. *Tito: The Story from Inside*. New York: Harcourt Brace Jovanovich, 1980.

Doder, Dusko, and Louise Branson. *Milosević: Portrait of a Tyrant*. New York: Free Press, 1999.

Dormann, Knut. *Elements of War Crimes Under the Rome Statute of the International Criminal Court*. New York: Cambridge University Press, 2003.

Duke, Lynne. *Mandela, Mobutu, and Me*. New York: Doubleday, 2003.

Ellis, Stephen. *The Mask of Anarchy: The Destruction of Liberia and the Religious Dimension of an African Civil War*. New York: New York University Press, 1999.

Elson, R. E. *Suharto: A Political Biography*. New York: Cambridge University Press, 2001.

Emerson, Barbara. *Leopold II of the Belgians: King of Colonialism*. New York: St. Martin's Press, 1979.

Emerson, Caryl. *Boris Godunov*. Bloomington: Indiana University Press, 1986.

Estow, Clara. *Pedro the Cruel of Castile, 1350-1369*. New York: E. J. Brill, 1995.

Evans, James Allan. *The Age of Justinian: Circumstances of Imperial Power*. New York: Routledge, 1996.

_____. *Empress Theodora: Partner of Justinian*. Austin: University of Texas Press, 2002.

Ewans, Martin. *European Atrocity, African Catastrophe: Leopold II, the Congo Free State, and Its Aftermath*. New York: Routledge, 2002.

Fairbank, John King. *China: A New History*. Cambridge, Mass.: Harvard University Press, 1992.

Feitlowitz, Marguerite. *A Lexicon of Terror: Argentina and the Legacies of Torture*. New York: Oxford University Press, 1998.

Ferguson, James. *Papa Doc, Baby Doc: Haiti and the Duvaliers*. New York: Basil Blackwell, 1987.

Ferril, A. *Caligula: Emperor of Rome*. London: Thames & Hudson, 1991.

Fink, Christina. *Living Silence: Burma Under Military Rule*. London: Zed Books, 2001.

Fitzgerald, N. J. *Somalia: Issues, History, and Bibliography*. New York: Nova Science, 2002.

Gambone, Michael D. *Eisenhower, Somoza, and the Cold War in Nicaragua, 1953-1961*. Westport, Conn.: Praeger, 1997.

Garner, Paul. *Porfirio Díaz*. New York: Longman, 2001.

Gerson, Lennard D. *The Secret Police in Lenin's Russia*. Philadelphia: Temple University Press, 1976.

Giblin, James Cross. *The Life and Death of Adolf Hitler*. New York: Clarion, 2002.

Glay, Marcel Le, Jean-Louis Voisin, and Yann Le Bohec. *A History of Rome*. 3d ed. London: Blackwell, 2005.

Glenny, Misha. *The Fall of Yugoslavia: The Balkan War*. New York: Penguin, 1996.

Gobodo-Madikizela, Pumla. *A Human Being Died That Night*. Boston: Houghton Mifflin, 2002.

Grant, Michael. *The Collapse and Recovery of the Roman Empire*. New York: Routledge, 1999.

_____. *The Roman Emperors: A Biographical Guide to the Rulers of Imperial Rome, 31 B.C.-A.D. 476*. New York: Barnes and Noble, 1997.

Grey, Ian. *Catherine the Great: Autocrat and Empress of All Russia*. Philadelphia: Lippincott, 1962.

Gwyn, David. *Idi Amin: Death-Light of Africa*. Boston: Little, Brown, 1977.

Hardman, John. *Robespierre*. New York: Addison Wesley Longman, 1999.

Harris, David. *The Crisis: The President, the Prophet, and the Shah—1979 and the Coming of Militant Islam*. Boston: Little, Brown, 2004.

Harrold, Michael. *Comrades and Strangers: Behind the Closed Doors of North Korea*. New York: John Wiley & Sons, 2004.

Havel, Vacláv, and Desmond Tutu. *Threat to the Peace: A Call for the UN Security Council to Act in Burma*. Washington, D.C.: DLA Piper Rudnick Gray Caryl, 2005.

Haydon, Colin, and William Doyle, eds. *Robespierre*. Cambridge, England: Cambridge University Press, 1999.

Heder, Stephen. *Pol Pot and Khieu Samphan*. Clayton, Australia: Centre of Southeast Asian Studies, 1991.

Heinl, Robert Debs, and Nancy Gordon Heinl. *Written in Blood: The Story of the Haitian People, 1492-1995*. Rev. ed. Lanham, Md.: University Press of America, 1996.

Hekster, Olivier. *Commodus: An Emperor at the Crossroads*. Amsterdam: Gieben, 2002.

Henneman, John Bell. *Olivier de Clesson and Political Society in France Under Charles V and Charles VI*. Philadelphia: University of Pennsylvania Press, 1996.

Henze, Paul B. *Layers of Time: A History of Ethiopia*. New York: Palgrave, 2000.

Hochschild, Adam. *King Leopold's Ghost: A Story of Greed, Terror, and Heroism in Colonial Africa.* New York: Houghton Mifflin, 1998.

Hodges, Gabrielle Ashford. *Franco: A Concise Biography.* New York: Thomas Dunne Books, 2002.

Holland, Richard. *Nero: The Man Behind the Myth.* London: Sutton, 2000.

Ioanid, R. *The Holocaust in Romania: The Destruction of Jews and Gypsies Under the Antonescu Regime, 1940-1944.* New York: Ivan Dee, 2000.

Jackson, Gabriel. *The Spanish Republic and the Civil War, 1931-1939.* Princeton, N.J.: Princeton University Press, 1972.

Janos, Andrew C., and William B. Slottman, eds. *Revolution in Perspective: Essays on the Hungarian Soviet Republic of 1919.* Berkeley: University of California Press, 1971.

Jaroslavsky, Andrés. *The Future of Memory: Children of the Dictatorship in Argentina.* London: Latin America Bureau, 2003.

Joachim, Joachim G. *Ioannis Metaxas: The Formative Years, 1871-1922.* Mannheim, Germany: Bibliopolis, 2000.

Johnson, Douglas. *The Root Causes of Sudan's Civil Wars.* Oxford, England: International African Institute, 2004.

Johnson, James Turner. *The War to Oust Saddam Hussein: The Context, the Debate, the War, and the Future.* Lanham, Md.: Rowman & Littlefield, 2005.

Jones, J. A. P. *King John and the Magna Carta.* London: Longman, 1971.

Jordan, David P. *The Revolutionary Career of Maximilien Robespierre.* New York: Free Press, 1985.

Kamen, Henry. *The Spanish Inquisition: A Historical Revision.* New Haven, Conn.: Yale University Press, 1997.

Kapcia, Antoni. *Fulgencio Batista, 1933-1944: From Revolutionary to Populist.* Westport, Conn.: Greenwood Press, 1996.

Karsh, Efraim, and Inari Rautsi. *Saddam Hussein: A Political Biography.* 1991. Reprint. New York: Grove Press, 2002.

Keaveney, Arthur. *Sulla: The Last Republican.* 2d ed. New York: Routledge, 2005.

Keegan, John. *The Iraq War.* New York: Knopf, 2004.

Kern, Martin. *The Stele Inscriptions of Ch'in Shih-huang.* New Haven, Conn.: American Oriental Society, 2000.

Khomeini, Ruhallah. *Islam and Revolution: Writings and Declarations.* Translated by Hamid Algar. Berkeley: University of California Press, 1981.

Khrushchev, Nikita S. *Memoirs of Nikita Khrushchev: Commissar (1918-1945).* Translated by George Shriver and Stephen Shenfield. University Park: Pennsylvania State University Press, 2005.

Kiernan, Ben. *The Pol Pot Regime: Race, Power, and Genocide in Cambodia Under the Khmer Rouge, 1975-1979.* 1996. Reprint. New Haven, Conn.: Yale University Press, 2002.

King, Greg. *The Mad King: The Life and Time of Ludwig II of Bavaria.* Secaucus, N.J.: Carol, 1996.

Kinzer, Stephen. *All the Shah's Men: An American Coup and the Roots of Middle East Terror.* New York: Wiley, 2003.

Kirkpatrick, Ivone. *Mussolini: A Study in Power.* New York: Hawthorne Books, 1964.

Knight, Amy. *Who Killed Kirov? The Kremlin's Greatest Mystery.* New York: Hill and Wang, 1999.

Lane, George. *Genghis Khan and Mongol Rule.* Westport, Conn.: Greenwood Press, 2004.

Langdon-Davies, John. *Carlos: The King Who Would Not Die.* Englewood Cliffs, N.J.: Prentice-Hall, 1963.

Lankov, Andrei. *From Stalin to Kim Il Sung: The Formation of North Korea, 1945-1960.* Philadelphia: Rutgers University Press, 2003.

Larkin, Emma. *Finding George Orwell in Burma.* New York: Penguin Press, 2005.

Leggett, George. *The Cheka: Lenin's Political Police—The All-Russian Extraordinary Commission for Combating Counter-Revolution and Sabotage.* New York: Oxford University Press, 1981.

Levine, Robert. *Father of the Poor? Vargas and His Era.* New York: Cambridge University Press, 1998.

Levytsky, Boris. *The Uses of Terror: The Soviet Secret Police, 1917-1970.* New York: Coward, McCann and Geoghegan, 1972.

Lewis, W. H. *The Splendid Century: Life in the France of Louis XIV.* Reprint. Long Grove, Ill.: Waveland Press, 1997.

Li, Yu-ning, ed. *The First Emperor of China.* White Plains, N.Y.: International Arts and Sciences Press, 1975.

Li Zhisui. *The Private Life of Chairman Mao.* New York: Random House, 1997.

Lincoln, W. Bruce. *Nicholas I: Emperor and Autocrat of All the Russians.* De Kalb: Northern Illinois University Press, 1989.

Lintner, Bertil. *Outrage: Burma's Struggle for Democracy.* Bangkok, Thailand: White Lotus Books, 1990.

Little, Peter. *Somalia: Economy Without State.* Bloomington: Indiana University Press, 2003.

Lockhart, Laurence. *Nadir Shah*. London: Luzac, 1938.

Lynn, John A. *The Wars of Louis XIV, 1667-1714*. New York: Longman, 1999.

MacFarquhar, Roderick, ed. *The Politics of China: The Eras of Mao and Deng*. 2d ed. New York: Cambridge University Press, 1997.

McIntosh, Christopher. *The Swan King: Ludwig II of Bavaria*. 1982. Reprint. London: Tauris Park, 2003.

Mack Smith, Denis. *Mussolini*. New York: Vintage Books, 1981.

Madariaga, Isabel de. *Ivan the Terrible: First Tsar of Russia*. New Haven, Conn.: Yale University Press, 2005.

Maier, Karl. *This House Has Fallen: Nigeria in Crisis*. London: Penguin, 2000.

Man, John. *Attila: The Barbarian King Who Challenged Rome*. London: Bantam, 2005.

Marcos, Ferdinand. *Notes on the New Society of the Philippines*. Manila, Philippines: Marcos Foundation, 1973.

Marcus, Harold. *A History of Ethiopia*. Berkeley: University of California Press, 1994.

Maxwell, Robert. *Jaruzelski*. New York: Pergamon Press, 1985.

Meredith, Martin. *Our Votes, Our Guns: Robert Mugabe and the Tragedy of Zimbabwe*. Cambridge, Mass.: Public Affairs, 2002.

Michta, Andrew. *The Soldier-Citizen*. New York: St. Martin's Press, 1997.

Mignone, Emilio. *Witness to the Truth: The Complicity of Church and Dictatorship in Argentina, 1976-1983*. Translated by Phillip Berryman. Maryknoll, N.Y.: Orbis Books, 1988.

Miller, John, and Aaron Kenedi, eds. *Inside Iraq: The History, the People, and the Politics of the World's Least Understood Land*. New York: Marlow, 2002.

Miranda, Carlos R. *The Stroessner Era: Authoritarian Rule in Paraguay*. Boulder, Colo.: Westview Press, 1990.

Moin, Baqer. *Khomeini: Life of an Ayatollah*. New York: St. Martin's Press, 2000.

Montejo, Victor. *Voices from Exile: Violence and Survival in Modern Maya History*. Norman: University of Oklahoma Press, 1999.

Morris, Stephen J. *Why Vietnam Invaded Cambodia: Political Culture and the Causes of War*. Stanford, Calif.: Stanford University Press, 1999.

Moseley, Ray. *Mussolini: The Last Six Hundred Days of Il Duce*. Dallas: Taylor, 2004.

_____. *Mussolini's Shadow: The Doubled Life of Count Galeazzo Ciano*. New Haven, Conn.: Yale University Press, 1999.

Murray, O. *Early Greece*. 2d ed. Cambridge, Mass.: Harvard University Press, 1993.

Neville, Peter. *Mussolini*. London: Routledge, 2003.

Nicholls, David. *Haiti from Dessalines to Duvalier: Race, Colour, and National Independence in Haiti*. Rev. ed. New Brunswick, N.J.: Rutgers University Press, 1996.

Norman, Andrew. *Robert Mugabe and the Betrayal of Zimbabwe*. Jefferson, N.C.: McFarland, 2004.

Nors, P. *The Court of Christian VII of Denmark*. London: Hurst & Blackett, 1928.

Nzongola-Ntalaja, Georges. *The Congo: From Leopold to Kabila, a People's History*. London: Zed Books, 2002.

O'Donnell, James S. *A Coming of Age: Albania Under Enver Hoxha*. Boulder, Colo.: East European Monographs, 1999.

Omara-Otunnu, Amii. *Politics and the Military in Uganda, 1890-1985*. New York: St. Martin's Press, 1987.

Orizio, Riccardo. *Talk of the Devil: Encounters with Seven Dictators*. Translated by Avril Bardoni. New York: Walker, 2003.

Osaghae, Eghosa. *Crippled Giant: Nigeria Since Independence*. London: Hurst, 1998.

Pavlov, Andrei, and Maureen Perrie. *Ivan the Terrible*. London: Pearson-Longman, 2003.

Paxton, John. *Leaders of Russia and the Soviet Union: From the Romanov Dynasty to Vladimir Putin*. New York: Fitzroy Dearborn, 2004.

Payne, Stanley. *The Franco Regime, 1936-1975*. London: Phoenix Press, 1987.

Peimani, Hooman. *Failed Transition, Bleak Future? War and Instability in Central Asia and the Caucasus*. Westport, Conn.: Praeger, 2002.

Pérez, Joseph. *The Spanish Inquisition: A History*. New Haven, Conn.: Yale University Press, 2005.

Perrie, Maureen. *The Cult of Ivan the Terrible in Stalin's Russia*. London: Palgrave, 2001.

Perry, Laurens Ballard. *Juárez and Díaz: Machine Politics in Mexico*. De Kalb: Northern Illinois University Press, 1978.

Peterson, Scott. *Me Against My Brother: At War in Somalia, Sudan, and Rwanda*. London: Taylor and Francis, 2000.

Pham, John-Peter. *Liberia: Portrait of a Failed State*. Chicago: Reed Press, 2004.

Pinto, Antonio Costa. *Salazar's Dictatorship and Euro-*

pean Fascism: Problems of Interpretation. New York: Columbia University Press, 1996.

Pipes, Richard, ed. *The Unknown Lenin: From the Secret Archive*. New Haven, Conn.: Yale University Press, 1998.

Platonov, S. F. *Boris Godunov: Tsar of Russia*. Gulf Breeze, Fla.: Academic International Press, 1973.

Plutarch. *Fall of the Roman Republic: Marius, Sulla, Crassus, Pompey, Caesar, Cicero—Six Lives by Plutarch*. Translated by Rex Warner. Harmondsworth, Middlesex, England: Penguin, 1972.

Price, Munro. *The Road from Versailles: Louis XVI, Marie Antoinette, and the Fall of the French Monarchy*. New York: St. Martin's Press, 2003.

Procopius. *The Secret History*. Translated and introduced by G. A. Williamson. New York: Penguin Books, 1966.

Prunier, Gérard. *Darfur: The Ambiguous Genocide*. Ithaca, N.Y.: Cornell University Press, 2005.

Pu Yi, Aisin-Gioro. *From Emperor to Citizen*. Translated by W. J. F. Jenner. 1964-1965. Reprint. Beijing, China: Foreign Languages Press, 2002.

Pye, Lucian W. *Mao Tse-tung: The Man in the Leader*. New York: Basic Books, 1976.

_____. *Warlord Politics*. New York: Praeger, 1976.

Ramet, Sabrina P. *Balkan Babel: The Disintegration of Yugoslavia from the Death of Tito to Ethnic War*. Boulder, Colo.: Westview Press, 2002.

Recovery of Historical Memory Project. *Guatemala: Never Again!* Maryknoll, N.Y.: Orbis Books, 1999.

Reshetar, John S. *Ukrainian Revolution, 1917-1920: A Study in Nationalism*. Manchester, N.H.: Ayer Company, 1972.

Rial, James H. *Revolution from Above: The Primo de Rivera Dictatorship in Spain, 1923-1930*. Fairfax, Va.: George Mason University Press, 1986.

Riccardo, Orizio. *Talk of the Devil: Encounters with Seven Dictators*. London: Secker and Warburg, 2003.

Roberts, Michael. *The Early Vasas: A History of Sweden, 1523-1611*. New York: Cambridge University Press, 1986.

Romero, Luis Alberto. *History of Argentina in the Twentieth Century*. Translated by James P. Brennan. University Park: Pennsylvania State University Press, 2002.

Romula, Beth Day. *Inside the Palace: The Rise and Fall of Ferdinand and Imelda Marcos*. New York: Putnam, 1987.

Roorda, Eric Paul. *The Dictator Next Door: The Good Neighbor Policy and the Trujillo Regime in the Do-minican Republic, 1930-1945*. Durham, N.C.: Duke University Press, 1998.

Rose, R. S. *One of the Forgotten Things: Getúlio Vargas and Brazilian Social Control, 1930-1954*. Westport, Conn.: Greenwood Press, 2000.

Rosenbaum, Ron. *Explaining Hitler: The Search for the Origins of His Evil*. New York: Random House, 1998.

Roux, Jean-Paul. *Genghis Khan and the Mongol Empire*. New York: Harry N. Abrams, 2003.

Rowlands, Guy. *The Dynastic State and the Army Under Louis XIV: Royal Service and Private Interest, 1661-1701*. New York: Cambridge University Press, 2002.

Rutledge, Steven H. *Imperial Inquisitions: Prosecutors and Informants from Tiberius to Domitian*. London: Routledge, 2001.

Scarre, Chris. *Chronicle of the Roman Emperors: The Reign-by-Reign Record of the Rulers of Imperial Rome*. London: Thames and Hudson, 1995.

Scroggs, William O. *Filibusters and Financiers*. 1916. Reprint. New York: Macmillan, 1969.

Seagrave, Sterling. *The Marcos Dynasty*. New York: Harper & Row, 1988.

Sell, Louis. *Slobodan Milosević and the Destruction of Yugoslavia*. Durham, N.C.: Duke University Press, 2003.

Service, Robert. *Lenin: A Biography*. Cambridge, Mass.: Harvard University Press, 2000.

Shorris, Earl. *The Life and Times of Mexico*. New York: W. W. Norton, 2004.

Short, Philip. *Pol Pot: Anatomy of a Nightmare*. New York: Henry Holt, 2005.

Smith, George Ivan. *Ghosts of Kampala: Rise and Fall of Idi Amin*. New York: St. Martin's Press, 1980.

Smith, Martin. *Burma: Insurgency and the Politics of Ethnicity*. New York: Zed Books, 1999.

Sohn, Won Tai. *Kim Il Sung and Korea's Struggle: An Unconventional History*. Jefferson, N.C.: McFarland, 2003.

Southern, Pat. *Domitian: Tragic Tyrant*. New York: Routledge, 1997.

Spence, Jonathan. *Mao Zedong*. New York: Viking Penguin, 1999.

Stanik, Joseph T. *El Dorado Canyon: Reagan's Undeclared War with Qaddafi*. Annapolis, Md.: Naval Institute Press, 2003.

Stojadinović, Ljubodrag. *Ratko Mladić: Tragic Hero*. Translated and edited by Milo Yelesiyevich. New York: Unwritten History, 2006.

Suetonius. *Lives of the Caesars*. Translated by Catherine Edwards. New York: Oxford University Press, 2000.

Suh, Dae-Sook. *Kim Il Sung: The North Korean Leader.* New York: Columbia University Press, 1988.

Tanter, Raymond. *Rogue Regimes: Terrorism and Proliferation.* New York: St. Martin's Press, 1998.

Taubman, William. *Khrushchev: The Man and His Era.* New York: W. W. Norton, 2003.

Terrell, Ross. *Mao: A Biography.* New York: Harper and Row, 1980.

Thompson, J. M. *Robespierre.* 1935. Reprint. New York: Blackwell, 1988.

Titley, Brian. *Dark Age: The Political Odyssey of Emperor Bokassa.* Montreal, Que.: McGill-Queen's University Press, 1997.

Tökés, Rudolf L. *Béla Kun and the Hungarian Soviet Republic.* New York: Frederick A. Praeger, 1967.

Treadgold, Warren. *A History of the Byzantine State and Society.* Stanford, Calif.: Stanford University Press, 1997.

Troubetzkoy, Alexis S. *Imperial Legend: The Mysterious Disappearance of Tsar Alexander I.* New York: Arcade, 2002.

Troyat, Henri. *Catherine the Great.* New York: Meridian, 1994.

Turnbull, Stephen. *Genghis Khan and the Mongol Conquests: 1190-1400.* New York: Routledge, 2004.

Turner, Frederick C. *Juan Perón and the Reshaping of Argentina.* Pittsburgh, Pa.: University of Pittsburgh Press, 1983.

Turyahikayo-Rugyema, Benomi. *Idi Amin Speaks: An Annotated Selection of His Speeches.* Madison: University of Wisconsin Press, 1998.

Udovicki, Jasminka, and James Ridgway, eds. *Yugoslavia's Ethnic Nightmare: The Inside Story of Europe's Unfolding Ordeal.* New York: Lawrence Hill Books, 1995.

Ure, P. N. *The Origin of Tyranny.* New York: Russell and Russell, 1962.

Vandewalle, Dirk, ed. *Qadhafi's Libya, 1969-1994.* New York: St. Martin's Press, 1995.

Vatakiotis, P. J. *Popular Autocracy in Greece, 1936-1941: A Political Biography of General Ioannis Metaxas.* London: Frank Cass, 1998.

Vatikiotis, Michael R. *Indonesian Politics Under Suharto: The Rise and Fall of the New Order.* New York: Routledge, 1999.

Viola, Lynne. *Peasant Rebels Under Stalin: Collectivization and the Culture of Peasant Resistance.* New York: Oxford University Press, 1996.

Walker, Paul E. *Exploring an Islamic Empire, Fatmid History and Its Sources.* London: I. B. Tauris, 2002.

Walter, Knut. *The Regime of Anastasio Somoza, 1936-1956.* Chapel Hill: University of North Carolina Press, 1993.

Warnes, David. *Chronicle of the Russian Tsars: The Reign-by-Reign Record of the Rulers of Imperial Russia.* London: Thames & Hudson, 1999.

Watson, L. *Antonescu, Marshal of Romania: From the Great War to World War II.* London: Center for Romanian Studies, 2003.

Weatherford, Jack. *Genghis Khan and the Making of the Modern World.* New York: Crown, 2004.

Webb, Gary. *Dark Alliance: The CIA, the Contras, and the Crack Cocaine Explosion.* New York: Seven Stories Press, 1999.

West, Richard. *Tito and the Rise and Fall of Yugoslavia.* New York: Carroll and Graf, 1996.

Whitney, Robert. *State and Revolution in Cuba: Mass Mobilization and Political Change, 1920-1940.* Chapel Hill: University of North Carolina Press, 2001.

Wiarda, Howard J. *Dictatorship and Development: The Methods of Control in Trujillo's Dominican Republic.* Gainesville: University of Florida Press, 1968.

Williams, Daryle. *Culture Wars in Brazil: The First Vargas Regime, 1930-1945.* Durham, N.C.: Duke University Press, 2001.

Yahyá, Latif, and Karl Wendl. *I Was Saddam's Son.* New York: Arcade, 1997.

Young, Ernest. *The Presidency of Yuan Shi-k'ai: Liberalism and Dictatorship in Early Republican China.* Ann Arbor: University of Michigan Press, 1977.

GANGSTERS AND ASSOCIATES

Abadinsky, Howard. *Organized Crime.* 7th ed. Belmont, Calif.: Wadsworth/Thomson Learning, 2003.

Asbury, Herbert. *The Gangs of New York: An Informal History of the New York Underworld.* New York: Thunder's Mouth Press, 2004.

Barnes, Bruce. *Machine Gun Kelly: To Right a Wrong.* Perris, Calif.: Tipper, 1991.

Bergreen, Laurence. *Capone: The Man and the Era.* New York: Simon & Schuster, 1994.

Binder, John J. *Images of America: The Chicago Outfit.* Charleston, S.C.: Arcadia, 2003.

Bonanno, Bill. *Bound by Honor: A Mafioso's Story.* New York: St. Martin's Press, 1999.

Bonanno, Rosalie, and Beverly Donofrio. *Mafia Marriage.* New York: St. Martin's Paperbacks, 2003.

Bowden, Mark. *Killing Pablo: The Hunt for the World's Greatest Outlaw.* New York: Atlantic Monthly Press, 2001.

Brashler, William. *The Don: The Life and Death of Sam Giancana*. New York: Harper & Row, 1977.

Bruno, Anthony. *The Iceman: The True Story of a Cold-Blooded Killer*. New York: Dell, 1993.

Burrough, Bryan. *Public Enemies: America's Greatest Crime Wave and the Birth of the FBI, 1933-1934*. New York: Penguin Books, 2004.

Capeci, Jerry. *The Complete Idiot's Guide to the Mafia*. 2d ed. Indianapolis, Ind.: Alpha Books, 2002.

_____. *Jerry Capeci's Gang Land*. New York: Alpha Books, 2003.

Chandler, Billy Jaynes. *King of the Mountains: The Life and Death of Salvatore Giuliano*. De Kalb: Northern Illinois University Press, 1988.

Charyn, Jerome. *Gangsters and Gold Diggers: Old New York, the Jazz Age, and the Birth of Broadway*. New York: Four Walls Eight Windows, 2005.

Clarke, Donald H. *In the Reign of Rothstein*. New York: Grosset and Dunlap, 1929.

Cohen, Rich. *Tough Jews: Fathers, Sons, and Gangster Dreams in Jewish America*. New York: Simon and Schuster, 1998.

Cummings, John, and Ernest Volkman. *Gombata: The Improbable Rise and Fall of John Gotti and His Gang*. New York: Avon Books, 1990.

Davis, John H. *Mafia Dynasty: The Rise and Fall of the Gambino Crime Family*. New York: HarperCollins, 1993.

_____. *Mafia Kingfish*. New York: McGraw-Hill, 1989.

Delap, Breandán. *Mad Dog Coll: An Irish Gangster*. Dublin: Mercier Press, 1999.

DeVito, Carto. *The Encyclopedia of International Organized Crime*. New York: Facts On File, 2005.

Dickie, John. *Cosa Nostra: A History of the Sicilian Mafia*. New York: Palgrave Macmillan, 2004.

Downey, Patrick. *Gangster City: The History of the New York Underworld, 1900-1935*. Fort Lee, N.J.: Barricade Books, 2004.

Exner, Judith Campbell. *My Story*. New York: Grove Press, 1977.

Feder, Sid, and Burton Turkus. *Murder, Inc.: The Story of the Syndicate*. Cambridge, Mass.: Da Capo Press, 2003.

Fido, Martin. *The Krays: Unfinished Business*. London: Carlton Books, 2000.

Fox, Stephen. *Blood and Power: Organized Crime in Twentieth-Century America*. New York: William Morrow, 1993.

Franco, Joseph, with Richard Hammer. *Hoffa's Man: The Rise and Fall of Jimmy Hoffa as Witnessed by His Strongest Arm*. New York: Prentice Hall, 1987.

Gentry, Curt. *J. Edgar Hoover: The Man and the Secrets*. 1991. Reprint. New York: W. W. Norton, 2001.

Giancana, Antoinette, John R. Hughes, and Thomas H. Jobe. *JFK and Sam: The Connection Between the Giancana and Kennedy Assassinations*. Nashville, Tenn.: Cumberland House, 2005.

Giancana, Antoinette, and Thomas C. Renner. *Mafia Princess: Growing Up in Sam Giancana's Family*. New York: Morrow, 1984.

Giancana, Sam, and Chuck Giancana. *Double Cross: The Explosive, Inside Story of the Mobster Who Controlled America*. New York: Warner Books, 1993.

Girardin, G. Russell, with William J. Helmer. *Dillinger: The Untold Story*. Bloomington: University of Indiana Press, 1994.

Gosch, Martin A., with Richard Hammer. *The Last Testament of Lucky Luciano*. New York: Dell, 1978.

Hamilton, Stanley. *Machine Gun Kelly's Last Stand*. Lawrence: University Press of Kansas, 1993.

Hamilton, Sue, and John Hamilton. *Public Enemy Number One: The Barkers*. Bloomington, Minn.: Abdo and Daughters, 1989.

Hanna, David. *Vito Genovese: The Godfather Series*. New York: Belmont Tower Books, 1974.

Helmer, William J., and Art Bilek. *The St. Valentine's Day Massacre: The Untold Story of the Gangland Bloodbath That Brought Down Al Capone*. Nashville, Tenn.: Cumberland House, 2004.

Hersh, Seymour. *The Dark Side of Camelot*. Boston: Little, Brown, 1997.

Hill, Gregg, and Gina Hill. *On the Run: A Mafia Childhood*. New York: Warner, 2004.

Hill, Henry, with Gus Russo. *Gangsters and Goodfellas: Wiseguys, Witness Protection, and Life on the Run*. New York: M. Evans, 2004.

Jacobs, James B. *Mobsters, Unions, and Feds: The Mafia and the American Labor Movement*. New York: New York University Press, 2006.

Jacobs, James J., Coleen Friel, and Robert Radick. *Gotham Unbound: How New York City Was Liberated from the Grip of Organized Crime*. New York: New York University Press, 1999.

Karpis, Alvin, with Bill Trent. *The Alvin Karpis Story*. New York: Berkley, 1971.

Karpis, Alvin, with Robert Livesay. *On the Rock: Twenty-Five Years in Alcatraz*. Toronto, Ont.: Beaufort Books, 1980.

Katcher, Leo. *The Big Bankroll: The Life and Times of*

Arnold Rothstein. Reprint. New York: Da Capo Press, 1994.

Katz, Leonard. *Uncle Frank: The Biography of Frank Costello*. New York: Drake, 1973.

Kavieff, Paul. *The Life and Times of Lepke Buchalter: America's Most Ruthless Labor Racketeer*. Fort Lee, N.J.: Barricade Books, 2006.

Keefe, Rose. *Guns and Roses: The Untold Story of Dean O'Banion, Chicago's Big Shot Before Al Capone*. Nashville, Tenn.: Cumberland House, 2003.

_____. *The Man Who Got Away: The Bugs Moran Story*. Nashville, Tenn.: Cumberland House, 2005.

Kelly, Robert J. *Encyclopedia of Organized Crime in the United States: From Capone's Chicago to the New Urban Underworld*. Westport, Conn.: Greenwood Press, 2000.

Kennedy, Robert. *The Enemy Within: The McClellan Committee's Crusade Against Jimmy Hoffa and Corrupt Labor Unions*. 1960. Reprint. Westport, Conn.: Greenwood Press, 1982.

King, Jeffery S. *The Life and Death of Pretty Boy Floyd*. Kent, Ohio: Kent State University Press, 1998.

Kirk, Robin. *More Terrible than Death: Massacres, Drugs, and America's War in Colombia*. Cambridge, Mass.: Public Affairs, 2002.

Kobler, John. *Capone: The Life and World of Al Capone*. 1971. Reprint. Cambridge, Mass.: Da Capo Press, 2003.

Kray, Charlie, and Colin Fry. *Doing the Business*. London: Blake, 1999.

Kuklinski, Barbara, and John Driver. *Married to the Iceman: A True Account of Life with a Mafia Hitman and the Inside Story of His Crimes*. New York: E. P. Dutton, 1994.

Lacey, Robert. *Little Man: Meyer Lansky and the Gangster Life*. Boston: Little, Brown, 1991.

Lewis, Norman. *The Honoured Society: The Sicilian Mafia Observed*. London: Eland, 2003.

Lyman, Michael D., and Gary W. Potter. *Organized Crime*. Upper Saddle River, N.J.: Pearson/Prentice Hall, 2004.

Maas, Peter. *Underboss: Sammy the Bull Gravano's Story of Life in the Mafia*. New York: HarperCollins, 1997.

_____. *The Valachi Papers*. 1968. Reprint. New York: HarperCollins, 2003.

Maccabee, Paul. *John Dillinger Slept Here: A Crook's Tour of Crime and Corruption in St. Paul, 1920-1936*. St. Paul: Minnesota Historical Society Press, 1995.

Macintyre, Ben. *The Napoleon of Crime: The Life and Times of Adam Worth, Master Thief*. New York: Farrar, Straus and Giroux, 1997.

Matera, Dary. *John Dillinger: The Life and Death of America's First Celebrity Criminal*. New York: Carroll & Graf, 2004.

Morton, James. *Gangland: The Early Years*. London: Time Warner Books, 2003.

Mustain, Gene, and Jerry Capeci. *Mob Star: The Story of Gotti*. Royersford, Pa.: Appha Books, 2002.

Nash, Jay Robert, ed. *Bloodletters and Badmen: A Narrative Encyclopedia of American Criminals, from the Pilgrims to the Present*. New York: J. B. Lippincott, 1973.

_____, ed. *World Encyclopedia of Organized Crime*. New York: Paragon House, 1992.

Nickel, Steven, and William J. Helmer. *Baby Face Nelson: Portrait of a Public Enemy*. Nashville, Tenn.: Cumberland House, 2002.

O'Brien, Joseph, and Andris Kurins. *Boss of Bosses: The FBI and Paul Castellano*. New York: Dell, 1991.

Owen, Richard, and James Owen. *Gangsters and Outlaws of the 1930's: Landmarks of the Public Enemy Era*. Shippensburg, Pa.: White Mane, 2003.

Pearson, John. *The Cult of Violence: The Untold Story of the Krays*. London: Orion, 2001.

Pietrusza, David. *Rothstein: The Life, Times, and Murder of the Criminal Genius Who Fixed the 1919 World Series*. New York: Carroll and Graf, 2003.

Pileggi, Nicholas. *Wiseguy: Life in a Mafia Family*. New York: Simon & Schuster, 1985.

Raab, Selwyn. *Five Families: The Rise, Decline, and Resurgence of America's Most Powerful Mafia Empires*. New York: St. Martin's Press, 2005.

Ragano, Frank, and Selwyn Raab. *Mob Lawyer*. New York: Scribner's, 1994.

Reppetto, Thomas A. *American Mafia: A History of Its Rise to Power*. New York: H. Holt, 2004.

Ruth, David E. *Inventing the Public Enemy: The Gangster in American Culture, 1918-1934*. Chicago: University of Chicago Press, 1996.

Sann, Paul. *Kill the Dutchman*. New Rochelle, N.Y.: Arlington, 1971.

Sifakis, Carl. *The Mafia Encyclopedia*. 2d ed. New York: Facts On File, 1999.

Smith, John L. *Sharks in the Desert*. Fort Lee, N.J.: Barricade, 2005.

Stewart, Tony. *Dillinger: The Hidden Truth*. Philadelphia: Xlibris, 2002.

Stille, Alexander. *Excellent Cadavers*. New York: Random House, 1995.

Talese, Gay. *Honor Thy Father*. New York: World, 1971.

Volkman, Ernest. *Five Families: Gangbusters—The Destruction of America's Last Great Mafia Dynasty*. New York: Avon Books, 1998.

Wallis, Michael. *Pretty Boy: The Life and Times of Charles Arthur Floyd*. New York: St. Martin's Press, 1992.

Wills, Garry. *The Kennedy Imprisonment*. Boston: Little, Brown, 1982.

Winter, Robert. *Mean Men: The Sons of Ma Barker*. Danbury, Conn.: Routledge Books, 2000.

MILITARY FIGURES

Alden, J. R. *General Charles Lee: Traitor or Patriot?* Baton Rouge: Louisiana State University Press, 1951.

Alexander, Caroline. *The Bounty: The True Story of the Mutiny on the Bounty*. New York: Viking, 2003.

Anders, Wladyslaw. *Russian Volunteers in Hitler's Army*. Bayside, N.Y.: Axis Europa, 1998.

Andreyev, Catherine. *Vlasov and the Russian Liberation Movement*. Cambridge, England: Cambridge University Press, 1987.

Argentine National Commission on the Disappeared. *Nunca más = Never Again: A Report*. London: Faber and Faber, 1986.

Axworthy, Michael. *Sword of Persia: Nadir Shah, from Tribal Warrior to Conquering Despot*. London: I. B. Tauris, 2006.

Barnett, Louis. *Touched by Fire: The Life, Death, and Mythic Afterlife of George Armstrong Custer*. New York: Henry Holt, 1996.

Brandt, Clare. *The Man in the Mirror: A Life of Benedict Arnold*. New York: Random House, 1994.

Browning, Robert M. *Forrest: The Confederacy's Relentless Warrior*. Washington, D.C.: Brassey's, 2004.

Carr, Albert Z. *The World and William Walker*. 1963. Reprint. Westport, Conn.: Greenwood Press, 1975.

Chartrand, René. *Louis XIV's Army*. 1988. Reprint. Oxford, England: Osprey, 2002.

Clark, Paul Coe, Jr. *The United States and Somoza, 1933-1956: A Revisionist Look*. Westport, Conn.: Praeger, 1992.

Collett, Nigel. *The Butcher of Amritsar: General Reginald Dyer*. London: Hambledon & London, 2005.

Colvin, Ian Duncan. *The Life of General Dyer*. Edinburgh, Scotland: W. Blackwood & Sons, 1929.

Curtis, Michael. *Verdict on Vichy: Power and Prejudice in the Vichy France Regime*. New York: Arcade, 2002.

Dale, Peter Scott, and Jonathan Marshall. *Cocaine Politics: Drugs, Armies, and the CIA in Central America*. Berkeley: University of California Press, 1998.

Dening, Greg. *Mr. Bligh's Bad Language: Passion, Power, and Theatre in the Bounty*. Cambridge, England: Cambridge University Press, 1992.

Diederich, Bernard. *Somoza and the Legacy of U.S. Involvement in Central America*. New York: E. P. Dutton, 1981.

Dinges, John. *Our Man in Panama: The Shrewd Rise and Brutal Fall of Manuel Noriega*. New York: Random House, 1991.

Ellis, Walter M. *Alcibiades*. London: Routledge, 1989.

Fein, Helen. *Imperial Crime and Punishment: The Massacre at Jallianwala Bagh and British Judgment, 1919-1920*. Honolulu: University Press of Hawaii, 1977.

Feitlowitz, Marguerite. *A Lexicon of Terror: Argentina and the Legacies of Torture*. New York: Oxford University Press, 1998.

Fink, Christina. *Living Silence: Burma Under Military Rule*. London: Zed Books, 2001.

Flexner, James Thomas. *The Traitor and the Spy: Benedict Arnold and John André*. 1975. Reprint. Syracuse, N.Y.: Syracuse University Press, 1991.

Fuchs, Richard L. *An Unerring Fire: The Massacre at Fort Pillow*. Mechanicsburg, Pa.: Stackpole Books, 2002.

Gabriel, Richard. *Subotai the Valiant, Genghis Khan's Greatest General*. Westport, Conn.: Praeger, 2004.

Gambone, Michael D. *Eisenhower, Somoza, and the Cold War in Nicaragua, 1953-1961*. Westport, Conn.: Praeger, 1997.

Glenny, Misha. *The Fall of Yugoslavia: The Balkan War*. New York: Penguin, 1996.

Goodrich, Thomas. *Black Flag: Guerrilla Warfare on the Western Border, 1861-1865*. Bloomington: Indiana University Press, 1995.

Gordon, C. D. *The Age of Attila: Fifth-Century Byzantium and the Barbarians*. Ann Arbor: University of Michigan Press, 1960.

Havel, Vacláv, and Desmond Tutu. *Threat to the Peace: A Call for the UN Security Council to Act in Burma*. Washington, D.C.: DLA Piper Rudnick Gray Caryl, 2005.

Herring, Hubert. *A History of Latin America: From the Beginnings to the Present*. New York: Alfred A. Knopf, 1967.

Hesseltine, William Best. *Civil War Prisons: A Study in War Psychology*. Columbus: University of Ohio Press, 1930.

Hough, Richard. *Captain Bligh and Mr. Christian: The Men and the Mutiny*. London: Hutchinson, 1972.

Hurst, Jack. *Nathan Bedford Forrest: A Biography*. New York: A. A. Knopf, 1993.

Kennedy, Gavin. *Bligh*. London: Duckworth, 1978.

Kukah, Matthew Hassan. *Democracy and Civil Society in Nigeria*. London: Spectrum, 1999.

Larkin, Emma. *Finding George Orwell in Burma*. New York: Penguin Press, 2005.

Leonard, Elizabeth D. *All the Daring of the Soldier: Women of the Civil War Armies*. New York: W. W. Norton, 1999.

Leslie, Edward E. *The Devil Knows How to Ride: The True Story of William Clarke Quantrill and His Confederate Raiders*. New York: Da Capo Press, 1998.

Lewis, W. H. *The Splendid Century: Life in the France of Louis XIV*. Reprint. Long Grove, Ill.: Waveland Press, 1997.

Lintner, Bertil. *Outrage: Burma's Struggle for Democracy*. Bangkok, Thailand: White Lotus Books, 1990.

Lockhart, Laurence. *Nadir Shah*. London: Luzac, 1938.

Lottman, Herbert R. *Pétain: Hero or Traitor? The Untold Story*. New York: Morrow, 1985.

Lynn, John A. *The Wars of Louis XIV, 1667-1714*. New York: Longman, 1999.

Maenchen-Helfen, Otto. *The World of the Huns: Studies in Their History and Culture*. Berkeley: University of California Press, 1973.

Maier, Karl. *This House Has Fallen: Nigeria in Crisis*. London: Penguin, 2000.

Man, John. *Attila: The Barbarian King Who Challenged Rome*. London: Bantam, 2005.

Martin, James Kirby. *Benedict Arnold, Revolutionary Hero: An American Warrior Reconsidered*. New York: New York University Press, 2000.

Martin, Jane A., and Jeremy Ross, eds. *Spies, Scouts, and Raiders: Irregular Operations*. Alexandria, Va.: Time-Life Books, 1985.

Nichols, Bruce. *Guerrilla Warfare in Civil War Missouri, 1862*. Jefferson, N.C.: McFarland, 2004.

Osaghae, Eghosa. *Crippled Giant: Nigeria Since Independence*. London: Hurst, 1998.

Patterson, S. M. *Knight Errant of Liberty: The Triumph and Tragedy of General Charles Lee*. New York: Lantern Press, 1958.

Plutarch. *The Rise and Fall of Athens*. Translated by Ian Scott-Kilvert. London: Penguin Books, 1960.

Pye, Lucian W. *Warlord Politics*. New York: Praeger, 1976.

Rowlands, Guy. *The Dynastic State and the Army Under Louis XIV: Royal Service and Private Interest, 1661-1701*. New York: Cambridge University Press, 2002.

Sale, Richard T. *Traitors: The Worst Acts of Treason in American History, from Benedict Arnold to Robert Hanssen*. New York: Berkley, 2003.

Sawyer, Amos. *Beyond Plunder: Toward Democratic Governance in Liberia*. Boulder, Colo.: Lynne Rienner, 2005.

Schultz, Duane. *Quantrill's War: The Life and Times of William Clarke Quantrill, 1837-1865*. New York: St. Martin's Press, 1996.

Scroggs, William O. *Filibusters and Financiers*. 1916. Reprint. New York: Macmillan, 1969.

Sklenar, Larry. *To Hell with Honor: Custer and the Little Bighorn*. Norman: University of Oklahoma Press, 2000.

Smith, Martin. *Burma: Insurgency and the Politics of Ethnicity*. New York: Zed Books, 1999.

Strik-Strikfeldt, Wilfried. *Against Stalin and Hitler: A Memoir of the Russian Liberation Movement, 1941-1945*. New York: Macmillan, 1970.

Thayer, T. *The Making of a Scapegoat: Washington and Lee at Monmouth*. Port Washington, N.Y.: Kennikat Press, 1976.

Thompson, E. A. *The Huns*. Rev. ed. Oxford: Basil Blackwell, 1999.

Toohey, John. *Captain Bligh's Portable Nightmare*. New York: HarperCollins, 1998.

Utley, Robert M. *Cavalier in Buckskin: George Armstrong Custer and the Western Military Frontier*. Norman: University of Oklahoma Press, 1988.

Walter, Knut. *The Regime of Anastasio Somoza, 1936-1956*. Chapel Hill: University of North Carolina Press, 1993.

Webb, Gary. *Dark Alliance: The CIA, the Contras, and the Crack Cocaine Explosion*. New York: Seven Stories Press, 1999.

Welch, James. *Killing Custer: The Battle of the Little Bighorn and the Fate of the Plains Indians*. New York: W. W. Norton, 1994.

Wyeth, John A. *That Devil Forrest*. 1899. Reprint. Baton Rouge: Louisiana State University Press, 1989.

MURDERERS AND ACCUSED MURDERERS

Alexander, Shana. *Very Much a Lady: The Untold Story of Jean Harris and Dr. Herman Tarnower*. Boston: Little, Brown, 1983.

Altman, Jack, and Marvin Ziporyn. *Born to Raise Hell: The Untold Story of Richard Speck*. New York: Grove Press, 1967.

Arraras, Maria Celeste. *Selena's Secret: The Revealing Story Behind Her Tragic Death*. New York: Simon & Schuster, 1996.

Babyak, Jolene. *Birdman: The Many Faces of Robert Stroud*. Berkeley, Calif.: Ariel Books, 1994.

Bailey, Brian. *Burke and Hare: The Year of the Ghouls*. Edinburgh, Scotland: Mainstream, 2002.

Ballinger, Anette. *Dead Woman Walking: Executed Women in England and Wales 1900-1955*. Aldershot, England: Ashgate, 2000.

Barrow, Blanch Caldwell. *My Life with Bonnie and Clyde*. Norman: University of Oklahoma Press, 2004.

Beaver, Ninette, B. K. Ripley, and Patrick Trese. *Caril*. Philadelphia: J. B. Lippincott, 1974.

Bird, Anne. *Blood Brother: Thirty-Three Reasons My Brother Scott Peterson Is Guilty*. New York: Regan Books, 2005.

Bortnick, Barry. *Polly Klaas: The Murder of America's Child*. New York: Pinnacle Books, 1995.

Breo, Dennis L. *The Crime of the Century*. New York: Bantam Books, 1993.

Brottman, Nikita. *Meat Is Murder! An Illustrated Guide to Cannibal Culture*. New York: Creation, 2001.

Brown, Christopher Wayne. *Media Tried, Justice Denied: Behind the Truth and Lies of the Darlie Lynn Routier Murder Case*. Lewisville, Texas: Ad Vice Marketing, 1999.

Bugliosi, Vincent. *Helter Skelter: The True Story of the Manson Murders*. New York: W. W. Norton, 1974.

Bulwer-Lytton, Edward. *Eugene Aram: A Tale*. 3 vols. London: Henry Colburn and Richard Bentley, 1831-1832.

Crier, Catherine. *A Deadly Game: The Untold Story of Scott Peterson*. New York: Regan Books, 2005.

Davis, Barbara. *Precious Angels: A True Story of Two Slain Children and a Mother Convicted of Murder*. New York: Onyx, 1999.

Davis, Don. *Hush Little Babies: The True Story of a Mother Who Murdered Her Own Children*. New York: St. Martin's Press, 1997.

DeLaughter, Bobby. *Never Too Late: A Prosecutor's Story of Justice in the Medgar Evers Case:* New York: Simon & Schuster, 2001.

Dershowitz, Alan M. *Reasonable Doubts: The Criminal Justice System and the O. J. Simpson Case*. New York: Touchstone, 1996.

————. *Reversal of Fortune: Inside the von Bülow Case*. New York: Random House, 1986.

DeSario, Jack P., and William D. Mason. *Dr. Sam Sheppard on Trial: The Prosecutors and the Marilyn Sheppard Murder*. Kent, Ohio: Kent State University Press, 2003.

Douglas, Hugh. *Burke and Hare: The True Story*. London: Robert Hale, 1973.

Douglas, John, and Mark Olshaker. *The Anatomy of Motive*. New York: Scribner, 1999.

Downs, Elizabeth Diane. *Diane Downs: Best Kept Secrets*. Springfield, Oreg.: Danmark, 1989.

Earley, Pete. *Prophet of Death: The Mormon Blood-Atonement Killings*. New York: William Morrow, 1991.

Edwards, Owen Dudley. *Burke and Hare*. Edinburgh, Scotland: Polygon, 1981.

Eglin, Peter, and Stephen Hester. *The Montreal Massacre: A Story of Membership Categorization Analysis*. Waterloo, Iowa: Wilfrid Laurier University Press, 2003.

Ellis, Georgie. *A Murder of Passion: A Daughter's Memoir of the Last Woman to Be Hanged*. London: Blake, 2003.

Fletcher, G. *A Crime of Self-Defense: Bernhard Goetz and the Law on Trial*. Chicago: University Of Chicago Press, 1990.

Flowers, H. Lorraine, and R. Barri Flowers. *Murder in the United States: Crimes, Killers, and Victims of the Twentieth Century*. Jefferson, N.C.: McFarland, 2001.

Foreman, Laura, ed. *Mass Murderers*. Alexandria, Va.: Time-Life Books, 1993.

Fox, James A., Jack Levin, and Kenna Quinet. *The Will to Kill: Making Sense of Senseless Murder*. Boston: Pearson, 2005.

Frey, Amber. *Witness for the Prosecution of Scott Peterson*. New York: Regan Books, 2005.

Fryer, Michael, of Reeth. *The Trial and Life of Eugene Aram*. Richmond, England: M. Bell, 1832.

Fuhrman, Mark. *Murder in Brentwood*. New York: Zebra Books, 1997.

Gaddis, Thomas E. *The Birdman of Alcatraz: The Story of Robert Stroud*. Mattituck, N.Y.: Aeonian Press, 1976.

Gallas, John, and Clifford Harper. *The Ballad of Santo Caserio*. London: Agraphia Press, 2003.

Gatrell, V. A. C. *The Hanging Tree*. New York: Oxford University Press, 1994.

Gilmore, Mikal. *Shot in the Heart*. New York: Doubleday, 1994.

Ginsburg, Philip E. *Poisoned Blood: A True Story of Murder, Passion, and an Astonishing Hoax*. New York: Charles Scribner's Sons, 1987.

Hanchett, William. *The Lincoln Murder Conspiracies.* Urbana: University of Illinois Press, 1983.

Harris, Jean. *They Always Call Us Ladies.* New York: Macmillan, 1988.

Havill, Adrian. *The Mother, the Son, and the Socialite: The True Story of a Mother-Son Crime Spree.* New York: St. Martin's Paperbacks, 1999.

Hickey, Eric, ed. *Encyclopedia of Murder and Violent Crime.* Thousand Oaks, Calif.: Sage, 2003.

Higdon, Hal. *Leopold and Loeb: The Crime of the Century.* Urbana: University of Illinois Press, 1999.

Hood, Thomas. *The Dream of Eugene Aram: The Murderer.* London: Charles Tilt, 1832.

Hunt, Darnell M. *O. J. Simpson, Facts and Fictions: News Rituals in the Construction of Reality.* New York: Cambridge University Press, 1999.

Hustmyre, Chuck. *Killer with a Badge.* New York: Berkley, 2004.

Jack, Belinda. *Beatrice's Spell: The Enduring Legend of Beatrice Cenci.* New York: Other Press, 2005.

Jansen, Godfrey. *Why Robert Kennedy Was Killed.* New York: Third Press, 1970.

Jenkins, Philip. *Moral Panic: Changing Concepts of the Child Molester in Modern America.* New Haven, Conn.: Yale University Press, 1998.

Jones, Ann. *Women Who Kill.* New York: Holt, Rinehart, and Winston, 1980.

Jones, Ian. *Ned Kelly: A Short Life.* Rev. ed. South Melbourne, Victoria, Australia: Lothian Books, 2003.

King, Gary C. *The Texas 7: A True Story of Murder and a Daring Escape.* New York: St. Martin's Press, 2001.

King, Jeanne. *Dead End: The Crime Story of the Decade: Murder, Incest, and High-Tech Thievery.* New York: M. Evans, 2002.

Lavergne, Gary M. *A Sniper in the Tower: The Charles Whitman Murders.* Denton: University of North Texas Press, 1997.

Leavitt, Judith Walzer. *Typhoid Mary: Captive to the Public's Health.* New York: Beacon Press, 1996.

Leopold, Nathan Freundenthal, Jr. *Life Plus Ninety-Nine Years.* New York: Doubleday, 1958.

Lessard, Suzannah. *The Architect of Desire: Beauty and Danger in the Stanford White Family.* New York: Dial Press, 1996.

Levy, Steven. *The Unicorn's Secret: Murder in the Age of Aquarius—A True Story.* 1988. Reprint. New York: Penguin, 1999.

Linedecker, Clifford L. *Babyface Killers.* New York: St. Martin's Press, 1999.

Lowe, David Garrard. *Stanford White's New York.* New York: Watson-Guptill, 1999.

Lowry, Beverly. *Crossed Over: A Murder, a Memoir.* New York: Knopf, 1992.

McDonald, R. Robin. *Black Widow: The True Story of the Hilley Poisonings.* Far Hills, N.J.: New Horizon Press, 1986.

McGinniss, Joe. *Fatal Vision.* New York: Penguin Putnam, 1984.

MacGowan, Douglas. *Murder in Victorian Scotland: The Trial of Madeleine Smith.* Westport, Conn.: Greenwood Press, 1999.

Mailer, Norman. *The Executioner's Song.* Boston: Little, Brown, 1979.

Malcolm, Janet. *The Journalist and the Murderer.* London: Granta Books, 2004.

Malette, Louise, and Marie Chalouh, eds. *The Montreal Massacre.* Translated by Marlene Wildeman. Charlottetown, P.E.I.: Gynergy, 1991.

Marnham, Patrick. *Trail of Havoc: In the Steps of Lord Lucan.* New York: Viking Penguin, 1988.

Marvis, Barbara. *Selena.* Hockessin, Del.: Mitchell Lane, 2003.

Masterton, Willie L. *Lizzie Didn't Do It!* Boston: Brandon, 2000.

Maynard, Joyce. *To Die For.* New York: Signet Books, 1995.

Meyer, C., M. Oberman, with Kelly White et al. *Mothers Who Kill Their Children: Understanding the Acts of Moms from Susan Smith to the "Prom Mom."* New York: New York University Press, 2001.

Molony, John. *Ned Kelly.* Rev. ed. Melbourne, Australia: Melbourne University Press, 2002.

Mooney, Michael MacDonald. *Evelyn Nesbit and Stanford White: Love and Death in the Gilded Age.* New York: William Morrow, 1976.

Moore, Sally. *Lucan: Not Guilty.* London: Sedgwick and Jackson, 1987.

Morehead, Nigel. *That Nice Miss Smith.* London: F. Muellar, 1957.

Morgan, Wendy. *Ned Kelly Reconstructed.* Cambridge, England: Cambridge University Press, 1994.

Morris, W. *Ghosts of Medgar Evers: A Tale of Race, Murder, Mississippi, and Hollywood.* New York: Random House, 1998.

Neff, James. *Wrong Man: The Final Verdict in the Dr. Sheppard Murder Case.* New York: Random House, 2002.

Newton, Michael. *Bad Girls Do It: An Encyclopedia of*

Female Murderers. Port Townsend, Wash.: Loompanics Unlimited, 1993.

O'Donnell, Jeffrey. *Starkweather: A Story of Mass Murder on the Great Plains.* Lincoln, Neb.: J & L Lee, 1993.

Olsen, Gregg. *Starvation Heights.* New York: Warner Books, 1997.

O'Malley, Suzanne. *Are You There Alone? The Unspeakable Crime of Andrea Yates.* New York: Simon & Schuster, 2004.

Ordine, Bill, and Ralph Vigoda. *Fatal Match.* New York: Avon Books, 1998.

Payment, Simone. *The Trial of Leopold and Loeb: A Primary Source Account.* New York: Rosen, 2004.

Potter, Jerry Allen, and Fred Bost. *Fatal Justice: Reinvestigating the MacDonald Murders.* New York: W. W. Norton, 1995.

Presnall, Judith Janda. *Life on Alcatraz.* San Diego: Lucent Books, 2001.

Radish, Kris. *Run, Bambi, Run: The Beautiful Ex-Cop and Convicted Murderer Who Escaped to Freedom and Won America's Heart.* New York: Carol, 1992.

Ranson, Roy. *Looking for Lucan: The Final Verdict.* London: Smith Gryphon, 1994.

Rathjen, Heidi, and Charles Montpetit. *December 6: From the Montreal Massacre to Gun Control—The Inside Story.* Toronto, Ont.: McClelland & Stewart, 1999.

Ricci, Corrado. *Beatrice Cenci.* 2 vols. Translated by Morris Bishop and Henry Longan Stuart. New York: Boni and Liveright, 1925.

Richmond, Clint. *Selena: The Phenomenal Life and Tragic Death of a Tejano Music Queen.* New York: Pocket Books, 1996.

Rocha, Sharon. *For Laci: A Mother's Story of Love, Loss, and Justice.* Landover, Md.: Crown Books, 2006.

Roddick, Bill. *After the Verdict: A History of the Lawrencia Bembenek Case.* Milwaukee, Wis.: Composition House, 1999.

Rule, Ann. *Small Sacrifices: A True Story of Passion and Murder.* New York: Signet, 2003.

Russell, Linda, and Shirley Stephens. *My Daughter Susan Smith.* Brentwood, Tenn.: Authors Book Nook, 2000.

Sargeant, Jack. *Born Bad.* London: Creation Books, 1996.

Scherr, Marie. *Charlotte Corday and Certain Men of the Revolutionary Torment.* New York: AMS Press, 1970.

Smith, Carleton. *Blood Money: The Du Pont Heir and the Murder of an Olympic Athlete.* New York: St. Martin's Press, 1996.

Smith, David, with Carol Calef. *Beyond All Reason: My Life with Susan Smith.* New York: Kensington Books, 1995.

Smith, Dame Janet. *The Shipman Inquiry.* 6 vols. Manchester, England: Shipman Inquiry, 2002-2005.

Snow, Robert L. *Deadly Cults: The Crimes of True Believers.* Westport, Conn.: Praeger, 2003.

Spencer, Suzy. *Breaking Point.* New York: St. Martin's Press, 2002.

Springer, Patricia. *Flesh and Blood.* New York: Pinnacle, 1997.

Steele, Phillip W., and Marie Barrow Scoma. *The Family Story of Bonnie and Clyde.* Gretna, La.: Pelican, 2000.

Thaw, Harry K. *The Traitor: Being the Untampered with, Unrevised Account of the Trial and All That Led to It.* Philadelphia: Dorrance, 1926.

Time-Life Books, ed. *Crimes of Passion.* Alexandria, Va.: Author, 1994.

Toobin, Jeffrey. *The Run of His Life: The People Versus O. J. Simpson.* New York: Random House, 1996.

Trestrail, John H. *Criminal Poisoning.* Grand Rapids, Mich.: Spectrum Health, 2000.

Ward, David. *King of the Lags: The Story of Charles Peace.* Foreword by Richard Whittington-Egan. 1964. Reprint. London: Souvenir, 1989.

Watson, Eric R. *Eugene Aram: His Life and Trial.* Edinburgh, Scotland: William Hodge, 1913.

Williams, Stephen. *Karla: A Pact with the Devil.* Toronto: Random House of Canada, 2003.

Wilson, Colin, and Donald Seaman. *The Encyclopedia of Modern Murder, 1962-1982.* New York: G. P. Putnam's Sons, 1983.

NAZIS AND FASCISTS

Aharoni, Zvi. *Operation Eichmann: The Truth About the Pursuit, Capture, and Trial.* Translated by Helmut Bögler. New York: John Wiley & Sons, 1997.

Anderson, Ken. *Hitler and the Occult.* Amherst, N.Y.: Prometheus Books, 1995.

Annussek, G. *Hitler's Raid to Save Mussolini.* New York: Da Capo Press, 2005.

Arendt, Hannah. *Eichmann in Jerusalem: A Report on the Banality of Evil.* New York: Viking Press, 1963.

Barnett, Correlli, ed. *Hitler's Generals.* New York: Grove Press, 2003.

Berenbaum, Michael. *The World Must Know: The History of the Holocaust as Told in the United States*

Holocaust Memorial Museum. Boston: Little, Brown, 1993.

Bloch, Michael. *Ribbentrop*. London: Abacus, 2003.

Bormann, Martin. *The Bormann Letters*. New York: AMS Press, 1981.

Botwinick, Rita Steinhardt. *A History of the Holocaust: From Ideology to Annihilation*. Upper Saddle River, N.J.: Pearson Prentice Hall, 2004.

Bower, Tom. *Klaus Barbie: The Butcher of Lyons*. New York: Bookmoat, 1984.

Bramwell, Anna. *Blood and Soil: Richard Walther Darré and Hitler's Green Party*. Abottsbrook, England: Kensal Press, 1985.

Breitman, Richard. *The Architect of Genocide: Himmler and the Final Solution*. New York: Alfred A. Knopf, 1991.

Butler, Rupert. *An Illustrated History of the Gestapo*. Osceola, Wis.: Motorbooks International, 1992.

Bytwerk, Randall L. *Bending Spines: The Propaganda of Nazi Germany and the German Democratic Republic*. East Lansing: Michigan State University Press, 2004.

Cesarani, David. *Eichmann: His Life and Times*. New York: Vintage Books, 2005.

Curtis, Michael. *Verdict on Vichy: Power and Prejudice in the Vichy France Regime*. New York: Arcade, 2002.

Davidowicz, Lucy. *The War Against the Jews, 1933-1945*. New York: Holt, Rinehart and Winston, 1976.

Davidson, Eugene. *The Unmaking of Adolf Hitler*. Columbia: University of Missouri Press, 1996.

Delarue, Jacques. *The Gestapo: A History of Horror*. Translated by Mervyn Savill. New York: William Morrow, 1964.

Dönitz, Karl. *Ten Years and Twenty Days*. Translated by R. H. Stevens. Annapolis, Md.: Naval Institute Press, 1990.

Edwards, Bernard. *Dönitz and the Wolf-Packs: U-Boats at War*. London: Brockhampton Press, 1999.

Evans, Richard J. *The Third Reich in Power*. New York: Penguin, 2005.

Finkielkraut, Alain. *Remembering in Vain the Klaus Barbie Trial and Crimes Against Humanity*. New York: Columbia University Press, 1992.

Foley, Charles. *Commando Extraordinary*. Rev. ed. New York: Ballantine, 1957.

Giblin, James Cross. *The Life and Death of Adolf Hitler*. New York: Clarion, 2002.

Gilbert, G. M. *Nuremberg Diary*. New York: Da Capo Press, 1995.

Gilbert, Martin. *The Holocaust: A History of the Jews of Europe During the Second World War*. New York: Owl Books, 2004.

Gildea, Robert. *Marianne in Chains: In Search of the German Occupation 1940-45*. London: Pan, 2003.

Goldhagen, Daniel Jonah. *Hitler's Willing Executioners: Ordinary Germans and the Holocaust*. New York: Vintage Books, 1997.

Griffin, Robert S. *The Fame of a Dead Man's Deeds: An Up-Close Portrait of White Nationalist William Pierce*. Lavergne, Tenn.: Lightning Source, 2001.

Hamann, Brigitte. *Winifred Wagner: A Life at the Heart of Hitler's Bayreuth*. Translated by Alan Bance. London: Granta Books, 2005.

Harris, Whitney R. *Tyranny on Trial: The Trial of the Major German War Criminals*. Dallas: Southern Methodist University Press, 1999.

Harvey, Elizabeth. *Women and the Nazi East: Agents and Witnesses of Germanization*. New Haven, Conn.: Yale University Press, 2003.

Housden, Martyn. *Hans Frank, Lebensraum, and the Final Solution*. New York: Palgrave Macmillan, 2004.

Kater, Michael. *HitlerYouth*. Cambridge, Mass.: Harvard University Press, 2004.

_____. *The Nazi Party: A Social Profile of Members and Leaders, 1919-1945*. Cambridge, Mass.: Harvard University Press, 1983.

Kershaw, Ian. *Hitler, 1889-1936: Hubris*. New York: Norton, 1999.

Kilzer, Louis. *Hitler's Traitor*. Novato, Calif.: Presidio, 2000.

Klabunde, Anja. *Magda Goebbels*. New York: Time Warner Trade, 2004.

Knopp, Guido. *Hitler's Henchmen*. Translated by Angus McGeoch. Phoenix Mill, England: Sutton, 2000.

_____. *Hitler's Women*. New York: Routledge, 2003.

Köhler, Joachim. *Wagner's Hitler: The Prophet and His Disciple*. Translated by Ronald Taylor. Malden, Mass.: Blackwell, 2000.

Lagnado, Lucette Matalon, and Sheila Cohn Dekel. *Children of the Flames: Dr. Josef Mengele and the Untold Story of the Twins of Auschwitz*. New York: Penguin Books, 1992.

Lavenda, Peter. *Unholy Alliance: A History of Nazi Involvement with the Occult*. New York: Continuum, 2002.

Lee, Asher. *Goering: Air Leader*. New York: Hippocrene, 1972.

Lemmons, Russel. *Goebbels and Der Angriff*. Lexington: University Press of Kentucky, 1994.

Lifton, Robert Jay. *The Nazi Doctors: Medical Killing and the Psychology of Genocide*. New York: Basic Books, 1986.

Manvell, Roger, and Heinrich Fraenkel. *Hess: A Biography*. New York: Drake, 1973.

Meisner, Hans-Otto. *Magda Goebbels: First Lady of the Third Reich*. New York: The Dial Press, 1980.

Munoz, Antonio J. *The Osttruppen*. Vol. 2 in *Hitler's Eastern Legions*. Bayside, N.Y.: Axis Europa, 1997.

Murphy, Brendan. *The Butcher of Lyon: The Story of Infamous Nazi Klaus Barbie*. New York: Empire Books, 1983.

Nicholls, David. *Adolf Hitler: A Biographical Companion*. Santa Barbara, Calif.: ABC-CLIO, 2000.

Ousby, Ian. *Occupation: The Ordeal of France, 1940-1944*. London: Pimlico, 1999.

Overy, Richard. *Interrogations: The Nazi Elite in Allied Hands, 1945*. New York: Penguin Books, 2002.

Padfield, Peter. *Dönitz, the Last Führer: Portrait of a Nazi War Leader*. New York: Harper and Row, 1984.

_____. *Himmler, Reichsführer*. London: Macmillan, 1991.

Paxton, Robert O. *Vichy France*. New York: Columbia University Press, 2001.

Perisco, Joseph E. *Nuremberg: Infamy on Trial*. New York: Penguin, 1995.

Piotrowski, Tadeusz. *Poland's Holocaust: Ethnic Strife, Collaboration with Occupying Forces, and Genocide in the Second Republic, 1918-1947*. Jefferson, N.C.: McFarland, 1998.

Posner, Gerald. *Mengele: The Complete Story*. New York: Cooper Square Press, 2000.

Rabinovici, Schoschana. *Thanks to My Mother*. Translated by James Skofield. New York: Dial Books, 1998.

Ramen, Fred. *Albert Speer: Hitler's Architect*. New York: Rosen, 2001.

Reed, Anthony. *The Devil's Disciples: Hitler's Inner Circle*. New York: W. W. Norton, 2003.

Reuth, Ralf Georg. *Goebbels*. Translated by Krishna Winston. New York: Harcourt Brace, 1993.

Ribbentrop, Joachim von. *Documents on the Events Preceding the Outbreak of the War*. Honolulu: University Press of the Pacific, 2004.

Rockwell, George Lincoln. *This Time the World*. New York: Parliament House, 1963.

Rosenbaum, Ron. *Explaining Hitler: The Search for the Origins of His Evil*. New York: Random House, 1998.

Sayer, Ian, and Douglas Botting. *The Women Who Knew Hitler: The Private Life of Adolf Hitler*. New York: Carroll & Graf, 2004.

Schmaltz, William H. Hate: *George Lincoln Rockwell and the American Nazi Party*. Washington, D.C.: Brossey's, 1999.

Schmidt, Matthias. *Albert Speer: The End of a Myth*. New York: St. Martin's Press, 1984.

Schmittroth, Linda, and Mary Kay Rosteck. *People of the Holocaust*. Detroit: UXL, 1998.

Schneider, Gertrude. *Exile and Destruction: The Fate of Austrian Jews, 1938-1945*. New York: Praeger, 1995.

Sereny, Gitta. *Albert Speer: His Battle with the Truth*. New York: Knopf, 1995.

Sigmund, Anna Maria. *Women of the Third Reich*. Ontario, Canada: NDE, 2000.

Simonelli, Frederick J. *American Fuehrer: George Lincoln Rockwell and the American Nazi Party*. Urbana: University of Illinois Press, 1999.

Skorzeny, Otto. *My Commando Operations: The Memoirs of Hitler's Most Daring Commando*. Translated by David Johnson. Reprint. Atglen, Pa.: Schiffer, 1995.

_____. *Skorzeny's Special Missions*. New York: Greenhill Books, 1997.

Smelser, Ronald, and Rainer Zitelmann. *The Nazi Elite*. Translated by Mary Fischer. New York: New York University Press, 1993.

Smith, Bradley F. *Heinrich Himmler: A Nazi in the Making, 1900-1926*. Palo Alto, Calif.: Hoover Institution Press, 1971.

Snyder, Louis L. *Hitler's Elite: Shocking Profiles of the Reich's Most Notorious Henchmen*. New York: Berkley Books, 1989.

Speer, Albert. *Inside the Third Reich*. New York: Macmillan, 1970.

Spotts, Frederic. *Bayreuth: A History of the Wagner Festival*. New Haven, Conn.: Yale University Press, 1994.

Stegmann-Gall, Richard. *The Holy Reich: Nazi Conceptions of Christianity, 1919-1945*. New York: Cambridge University Press, 2003.

Van Der Vat, Dan. *The Good Nazi: The Life and Lies of Albert Speer*. Boston: Houghton Mifflin, 1997.

Varga, William P. *The Number One Nazi Jew-Baiter: A Political Biography of Julius Streicher, Hitler's Chief Anti-Semitic Propagandist*. New York: Carlton Press, 1981.

Vizulis, Izidors. *The Molotov-Ribbentrop Pact of 1939*. New York: Praeger, 1990.

Wagner, Friedelind, with Page Cooper. *Heritage of Fire: The Story of Richard Wagner's Granddaughter*. New York: Harper, 1945.

Wagner, Nike. *The Wagners: The Dramas of a Musical Dynasty*. London: Weidenfeld & Nicolson, 1998.

Waller, John H. *The Devil's Doctor: Felix Kersten and the Secret Plot to Turn Himmler Against Hitler*. New York: John Wiley and Sons, 2002.

Warlimont, Walter. *Inside Hitler's Headquarters*. New York: Presidio Press, 1991.

Weisberg, Richard H. *Vichy Law and the Holocaust in France*. New York: New York University Press, 1996.

Weitz, John. *Hitler's Diplomat: Joachim von Ribbentrop*. London: Weidenfeld and Nicolson, 1992.

Zimmerman, Joshua. *Poles, Jews, and the Politics of Nationality: The Bund and the Polish Socialist Party in Late Czarist Russia, 1892-1914*. Madison: University of Wisconsin Press, 2003.

OUTLAWS AND GUNSLINGERS

Armstrong, William, A. *The Armstong Borderland: A Reassessment of Certain Aspects of Border History*. Edinburgh: John McQueen, 1960.

Ash, Russell. *Discovering Highwaymen*. Princes Risborough, Buckinghamshire, England: Shire, 1999.

Barlow, Derek. *Dick Turpin and the Gregory Gang*. London: Phillimore, 1973.

Barndollar, Lue Diver. *What Really Happened on October 5, 1892: An Attempt at an Accurate Account of the Dalton Gang and Coffeyville*. Coffeyville, Kans.: Coffeyville Historical Society, 2001.

Barra, Allen. *Inventing Wyatt Earp: His Life and Many Legends*. New York: Carroll & Graf, 1998.

Barrow, Blanche, and John Neal Phillips. *My Life with Bonnie and Clyde*. Norman: University of Oklahoma Press, 2004.

Barton, Barbara. *Den of Outlaws*. San Angelo, Tex.: Rangel Printing, 2000.

Biggs, Michael, and Neil Silver. *The Biggs Time: Ronnie and Michael, Man and Boy*. London: Virgin Books, 2002.

Biggs, Ronald. *Odd Man Out*. London: Bloomsbury, 1994.

Blackwood, Gary L. *Highwaymen (Bad Guys)*. Salt Lake City, Utah: Benchmark Books, 2001.

Block, Lawrence, ed. *Gangsters, Swindlers, Killers, and Thieves: The Lives and Crimes of Fifty American Villians*. New York: Oxford University Press, 2004.

Boessenecker, John. *Badge and Buckshot: Lawlessness in Old California*. Norman: University of Oklahoma Press, 1988.

Brant, Marley. *The Illustrated History of the James-Younger Gang*. Montgomery, Ala.: Black Belt Press, 1997.

_____. *Jesse James: The Man and the Myth*. New York: Berkley Books, 1998.

Breakenridge, William M. *Helldorado: Bringing the Law to the Mesquite*. New York: Houghton Mifflin, 1928.

Bronaugh, Warren C. *The Youngers' Fight for Freedom*. Columbia, Mo.: E. W. Stephens, 1906.

Brooks, L. T. *The Last Gamble of Doc Holliday*. Raleigh, N.C.: Pentland Press, 2004.

Bruns, Roger. *The Bandit Kings from Jesse James to Pretty Boy Floyd*. New York: Crown, 1995.

Burns, Walter Nobel. *The Robin Hood of El Dorado: The Saga of Joaquín Murrieta, Famous Outlaw of California's Age of Gold*. Albuquerque: University of New Mexico Press, 1999.

_____. *The Saga of Billy the Kid*. New York: Grosset and Dunlap, 1926.

Burrows, Jack. *John Ringo: The Gunfighter Who Never Was*. Tucson: University of Arizona Press, 1987.

Dalton, Emmett. *Beyond the Law*. 1918. Reprint. Gretna, La.: Pelican, 2002.

_____. *When the Daltons Rode*. Garden City, N.Y.: Doubleday, Doran, 1931.

Day, Julius E., and Arty Ash. *Immortal Turpin*. London: Staples Press, 1948.

Dobson, R. B., and J. Taylor. *Rymes of Robyn Hood: An Introduction to the English Outlaw*. Pittsburgh: University of Pittsburgh Press, 1976.

Drago, Harry S. *Outlaws on Horseback*. Lincoln: University of Nebraska Press, 1998.

Drago, Sinclair. *Road Agents and Train Robbers: Half a Century of Western Banditry*. New York: Dodd, 1973.

Drewe, Robert. *Kelly Gang*. New York: Penguin Books, 2003.

Durham, Keith. *The Border Reivers*. Toronto, Ont.: Osprey, 1995.

Dyer, Robert L. *Jesse James and the Civil War in Missouri*. Columbia: University of Missouri Press, 1994.

Edwards, Peter. *Night Justice: The True Story of the Black Donnellys*. Toronto, Ont.: Key Porter Books, 2004.

Feltes, Norman N. *This Side of Heaven: Determining the Donnelly Murders, 1880*. Toronto, Ont.: University of Toronto Press, 1999.

Fordham, Peta. *The Robbers Tale: The Real Story of the Great Train Robbery*. London: Hodder & Stoughton, 1965.

Fraser, George M. *The Steel Bonnets*. New York: Alfred A. Knopf, 1972.

Gard, Wayne. *Sam Bass*. Boston: Houghton Mifflin, 1936.

Garza, Phyllis de la. *The Apache Kid*. Tucson, Ariz.: Westernlore Press, 1995.

Gatto, Steve. *Curly Bill: Tombstone's Most Famous Outlaw*. Lansing, Mich.: Protar House, 2003.

_____. *Johnny Ringo*. Lansing, Mich.: Protar House, 2002.

Hardin, John Wesley, Jo Stamps, and Roy Stamps. *The Letters of John Wesley Hardin*. Austin, Tex.: Eakin Press, 2001.

Hillerman, Tony. *The Great Taos Bank Robbery, and Other True Stories of the Southwest*. New York: Perennial, 2001.

Hogg, Thomas E. *Authentic History of Sam Bass and His Gang*. 1878. Reprint. Bandera, Tex.: Frontier Times, 1926.

Jersig, Shelby. *Black Jack Ketchum*. Clovis, N.Mex.: Jersig Printing, 2001.

Jones, Ian. *Ned Kelly: A Short Life*. Rev. ed. South Melbourne, Victoria, Australia: Lothian Books, 2003.

Kelly, Charles. *The Outlaw Trail: A History of Butch Cassidy and His Wild Bunch*. Lincoln: University of Nebraska Press, 1996.

Knight, James, and Jonathan Davis. *Bonnie and Clyde: A Twenty-First-Century Update*. Austin, Tex.: Eakin Press, 2003.

Knight, Stephen. *Robin Hood: A Mythic Biography*. Ithaca, N.Y.: Cornell University Press, 2003.

_____, ed. *Robin Hood: An Anthology of Scholarship and Criticism*. Rochester, N.Y.: D. S. Brewer, 1999.

Kooistra, Paul. *Criminals as Heroes: Structure, Power, and Identity*. Bowling Green, Ohio: Bowling Green State University Popular Press, 1989.

Lake, Stuart. *Wyatt Earp: Frontier Marshall*. 1931. Reprint. New York: Pocket Books, 1994.

Lewis, Jon E. *The Mammoth Book of the West: The Making of the American West*. New York: Carroll & Graf, 2001.

Lubet, Steven. *Murder in Tombstone: The Forgotten Trial of Wyatt Earp*. New Haven, Conn.: Yale University Press, 2004.

McCord, Jason. *Johnny Ringo: Unknown Destiny*. San Ramon, Calif.: Falcon Books, 2002.

Mackenzie, Colin. *Most Wanted Man: The Story of Ronald Biggs*. London: Panther, 1976.

McNab, Chris, ed. *Gunfighters: The Outlaws and Their Weapons*. San Diego, Calif.: Thunder Bay Press, 2005.

Marks, Paula M. *And Die in the West: The Story of the O.K. Corral Gunfight*. Norman: University of Oklahoma Press, 1996.

Meadows, Anne. *Digging up Butch and Sundance*. 3d ed. Lincoln, Nebr.: Bison Books, 2003.

Miller, Rick. *Bloody Bill Longley: A Biography*. Wolfe City, Tex.: Henington, 1996.

_____. *Sam Bass and Gang*. Austin, Tex.: State House Press, 1999.

Molony, John. *Ned Kelly*. Rev. ed. Melbourne, Australia: Melbourne University Press, 2002.

Morgan, Wendy. *Ned Kelly Reconstructed*. Cambridge, England: Cambridge University Press, 1994.

Murphy, Jan. *Outlaw Tales of Colorado: True Stories of Colorado's Notorious Robbers, Rustlers, and Bandits*. Guilford, Conn.: The Globe Pequot Press, 2006.

Murray, W. H. *Rob Roy MacGregor: His Life and Times*. Edinburgh: Canongate Books, 1998.

National Archives of Scotland. *The Real Rob Roy: A Guide to the Sources in the Scottish Record Office*. Edinburgh: Author, 1999.

O'Neal, Bill. *Encyclopedia of Western Gunfighters*. Reprint. Norman: University of Oklahoma Press, 1991.

Ontko, Gale. *Thunder over the Ochoco: And, The Juniper Trees Bore Fruit*. Bend, Oreg.: Maverick, 1999.

Owen, Richard, and James Owen. *Gangsters and Outlaws of the 1930's: Landmarks of the Public Enemy Era*. Shippensburg, Pa.: White Mane, 2003.

Patterson, Richard M. *Butch Cassidy: A Biography*. Lincoln, Nebr.: Bison Books, 1997.

Pointer, Larry. *In Search of Butch Cassidy*. Norman: University of Oklahoma Press, 1977.

Pollard, A. J. *Imagining Robin Hood*. New York: Routledge, 2004.

Prassel, Frank Richard. *The Great American Outlaw: A Legacy of Fact and Fiction*. Norman: University of Oklahoma Press, 1993.

Pryor, Alton. *Outlaws and Gunslingers: Tales of the West's Most Notorious Outlaws*. Roseville, Calif.: Stagecoach, 2001.

Reaney, James C., ed. *The Donnelly Documents: An Ontario Vendetta*. Toronto, Ont.: The Champlain Society, 2004.

Reasoner, James. *Draw: The Greatest Gunfights of the American West*. New York: Berkley, 2003.

Ridge, John Rollins (Yellow Bird). *The Life and Adventures of Joaquín Murieta: The Celebrated California Bandit*. 1854. Reprint. Norman: University of Oklahoma Press, 1977.

Sadler, John. *Border Fury: England and Scotland at War, 1296-1568*. New York: Longman, 2005.

Secrest, William B. *California Desperadoes: Stories of Early California Outlaws in Their Own Words*. Clovis, Calif.: Word Dancer Press, 2000.

Settle, William A. *Jesse James Was His Name: Or, Fact and Fiction Concerning the Careers of the Notorious James Brothers of Missouri*. Columbia: University of Missouri Press, 1966.

Sharpe, James. *Dick Turpin*. London: Profile Books, 2004.

Shirley, Glenn. *Belle Starr and Her Times*. Norman: University of Oklahoma Press, 1982.

Singman, Jeffrey L. *Robin Hood: The Shaping of a Legend*. Westport, Conn.: Greenwood Press, 1998.

Skovlin, Jon M. *Hank Vaughan, 1849-1893: A Hell-Raising Horse Trader of Bunchgrass Territory*. Cove, Oreg.: Reflections, 1996.

_____. *In Pursuit of the McCartys*. Cove, Oreg.: Reflections, 2001.

Smith, Robert B. *Daltons! The Raid on Coffeyville*. Norman: University of Oklahoma Press, 1996.

_____. *Last Hurrah of the James-Younger Gang*. Norman: University of Oklahoma Press, 2001.

Spraggs, Gillian. *Outlaws and Highwaymen: The Cult of the Robber in England*. London: Pimlico, 2001.

Starr, Henry. *Thrilling Events: Life of Henry Starr*. College Station, Tex.: Creative, 1982.

Steele, Phillip W., and Marie Barrow Scoma. *The Family Story of Bonnie and Clyde*. Gretna, La.: Pelican, 2000.

Stevenson, David. *The Hunt for Rob Roy: The Man and the Myths*. Edinburgh: John Donald, 2004.

Stiles, T. J. *Jesse James: Last Rebel of the Civil War*. New York: Alfred A. Knopf, 2002.

Tanner, Karen Holliday. *Doc Holliday: A Family Portrait*. Norman: University of Oklahoma Press, 2001.

Terfertiller, Casey. *Wyatt Earp: The Life Behind the Legend*. New York: John Wiley and Sons, 1997.

Thornton, Bruce. *Searching for Joaquín: Myth, Murieta and History of California*. San Francisco: Encounter Books, 2003.

Turner, Alford E., ed. *The Earps Talk*. College Station, Tex.: Creative, 1980.

Tuska, Jon. *Billy the Kid: His Life and Legend*. Reprint. Albuquerque: University of New Mexico Press, 1997.

Utley, Robert M. *Billy the Kid: A Short and Violent Life*. Lincoln: University of Nebraska Press, 1989.

Walters, Lorenzo D. *Tombstone's Yesterday: True Chronicles of Early Arizona*. Glorieta, N.Mex.: Rio Grande Press, 1928.

Wellman, Paul I. *A Dynasty of Western Outlaws*. Norman: University of Oklahoma Press, 1998.

Younger, Cole. *The Story of Cole Younger by Himself*. 1903. Reprint. St. Paul: Minnesota Historical Society, 2000.

PIRATES

Abbott, John S. C. *The Pioneers and Patriots of America: Captain William Kidd*. New York: Dodd Mead, 1874.

Bawlf, Samuel. *The Secret Voyage of Sir Francis Drake, 1577-1580*. New York: Penguin, 2004.

Benyowski, M. A. *Memoirs and Travels*. London: G. G. J. & J. Robinson, 1791.

Bonner, Willard Hallam. *Pirate Laureate: Life and Legends of Captain Kidd*. New Brunswick, N.J.: Rutgers University Press, 1947.

Botting, Douglas. *The Pirates*. Alexandria, Va.: Time-Life Books, 1978.

Bradford, Ernle. *The Sultan's Admiral: The Life of Barbarossa*. New York: Harcourt, Brace, 1968.

Breverton, Terry. *Admiral Sir Henry Morgan: King of the Buccaneers*. Gretna, La.: Pelican, 2005.

Brooks, Graham, ed. *Notable British Trials: Trial of Captain Kidd*. Edinburgh, Scotland: William Hodge, 1930.

Butler, Lindley S. *Pirates, Privateers, and Rebel Raiders of the Carolina Coast*. Chapel Hill: University of North Carolina Press, 2000.

Chambers, Anne. *Granuaile: The Life and Times of Grace O'Malley, c. 1530-1603*. Dublin, Ireland: Wolfhound Press, 1997.

Clifford, Barry. *Expedition Whydah*. New York: Cliff Street Books, 1999.

Cordingly, David, ed. *Pirates: Terror on the High Seas from the Caribbean to the South China Sea*. Atlanta, Ga.: Turner, 1996.

_____. *Under the Black Flag: The Romance and the Reality of Life Among the Pirates*. New York: Random House, 1995.

Cummins, John G. *Francis Drake: Lives of a Hero*. New York: St. Martin's Press, 1997.

Davis, Robert C. *Christian Slaves, Muslim Masters: White Slavery in the Mediterranean, the Barbary Coast, and Italy, 1500-1800*. New York: Palgrave Macmillan, 2004.

Davis, William C. *The Pirates Laffite: The Treacherous World of the Corsairs of the Gulf*. Orlando, Fla.: Harcourt, 2005.

Defoe, Daniel. *A General History of the Robberies and Murders of the Most Notorious Pyrates, by Captain*

Charles Johnson. 1725. Reprint. Edited by David Cordingly. Mineola, N.Y.: Dover, 1999.

Dow, George F., and John H. Edmonds. *The Pirates of the New England Coast, 1630-1730*. Introduction by Ernest H. Pentecost. Glorieta, N.Mex.: Rio Grande Press, 1993.

Druett, Joan. *She Captains: Heroines and Hellions of the Sea*. New York: Simon & Schuster, 2000.

Heers, Jacques. *The Barbary Corsairs: Warfare in the Mediterranean, 1480-1580*. Translated by Jonathan North. London: Greenhill Books, 2003.

Kelesey, Harry. *Sir Francis Drake: The Queen's Pirate*. New Haven, Conn.: Yale University Press, 1998.

Klausmann, Ulrike, Marion Meinzerin, and Gabriel Kuhn. *Women Pirates and the Politics of the Jolly Roger*. Montreal: Black Rose Books, 1997.

Konstam, Angus. *The History of Pirates*. Guilford, Conn.: The Lyons Press, 2002.

_____. *The Pirate Ship, 1660-1730*. London: Osprey, 2003.

Lee, Robert E. *Blackbeard the Pirate: A Reappraisal of His Life and Times*. Winston-Salem, N.C.: Blair, 1974.

Lewis, Jon E. *The Mammoth Book of Pirates: Over 25 True Tales of Devilry and Daring by the Most Infamous Pirates of All Time*. New York: Carroll & Graf, 2006.

Lorimer, Sara. *Booty: Girl Pirates on the High Seas*. San Francisco: Chronicle Books, 2002.

Marine Research Society. *The Pirates Own Book: Authentic Narratives of the Most Celebrated Sea Robbers*. 1924. Reprint. New York: Dover, 1993.

Meltzer, Milton. *Piracy and Plunder: A Murderous Business*. New York: Dutton Children's Books, 2001.

Pendered, Norman. *Stede Bonnet: Gentleman Pirate*. Manteo, N.C.: Times Printing, 1977.

Pennell, C. R., ed. *Bandits at Sea: A Pirates Reader*. New York: New York University Press, 2001.

Petrovich, Sandra Marie. *Henry Morgan's Raid on Panama: Geopolitics and Colonial Ramifications, 1669-1674*. Lewiston, N.Y.: Edwin Mellen Press, 2001.

Platt, Richard. *Eyewitness: Pirate*. New York: DK, 2000.

Pope, Dudley. *Harry Morgan's Way*. London: Secker & Warburg, 1977.

Preston, Diana, and Michael Preston. *A Pirate of Exquisite Mind: Explorer, Naturalist, and Buccaneer—The Life of William Dampier*. New York: Walker, 2004.

Rediker, Marcus. *Villains of All Nations: Atlantic Pirates in the Golden Age*. Boston: Beacon Press, 2004.

Remini, Robert. *The Battle of New Orleans*. New York: Viking, 1999.

Ritchie, Robert C. *Captain Kidd and the War Against the Pirates*. Cambridge, Mass.: Harvard University Press, 1986.

Rochon, Abbé Alexis. *A Voyage to Madagascar and the East Indies*. London: E. Jeffery, 1793.

Rogozinski, Jan. *A Brief History of the Caribbean from the Arawak and Carib to the Present*. Rev. ed. New York: Facts On File, 1999.

Seitz, Don C. *Under the Black Flag: Exploits of the Most Notorious Pirates*. Mineola, N.Y.: Dover, 2002.

Shipman, Joseph P. *William Dampier: Seaman-Scientist*. Lawrence: University of Kansas Libraries, 1962.

Weatherly, Myra. *Women Pirates: Eight Stories of Adventure*. Greensboro, N.C.: Morgan Reynolds, 1998.

Williams, Daniel E. *Pillars of Salt: An Anthology of Early American Criminal Narratives*. Madison, Wis.: Madison House, 1993.

Williams, Glyndr. *The Great South Sea: English Voyages and Encounters, 1570-1750*. New Haven, Conn.: Yale University Press, 1997.

Wren, Laura Lee. *Pirates and Privateers of the High Seas*. Berkeley Heights, N.J.: Enslow, 2003.

POLITICAL REBELS AND REVOLUTIONARIES

Anderson, Jon Lee. *Che Guevara: A Revolutionary Life*. New York: Grove Press, 1997.

Aust, Stefan. *The Baader-Meinhof Group: The Inside Story of a Phenomenon*. London: Butler and Tanner, 1985.

Avrich, Paul. *Sacco and Vanzetti: The Anarchist Background*. Princeton, N.J.: Princeton University Press, 1991.

Benjamin, Thomas. *La Revolución: Mexico's Great Revolution as Memory, Myth, and History*. Austin: University of Texas Press, 2000.

Bimba, Anthony. *The Molly Maguires*. New York: International, 1932.

Brissenden, P. F. *The I.W.W.* 1920. Reprint. New York: Russell & Russell, 1957.

Broehl, Wayne G., Jr. *The Molly Maguires*. Cambridge, Mass.: Harvard University Press, 1964.

Brunk, Samuel. *Emiliano Zapata: Revolution and Betrayal in Mexico*. Albuquerque: University of New Mexico Press, 1995.

Burke, William H. *Anthracite Lads: A True Story of the Fabled Molly Maguires*. Erie, Pa.: Erie County Historical Society, 2005.

Carlson, Peter. *Roughneck: The Life and Times of Big Bill Haywood*. New York: W. W. Norton, 1983.

Castandeda, Jorge G. *Compañero: The Life and Death of Che Guevara*. New York: Knopf, 1997.

Coltman, Leycester. *The Real Fidel Castro*. New Haven, Conn.: Yale University Press, 2003.

Conlin, Joseph R. *Big Bill Haywood and the Radical Union Movement*. Syracuse, N.Y.: Syracuse University Press, 1969.

Conner, Clifford D. *Jean Paul Marat: Scientist and Revolutionary*. Atlantic Highlands, N.J.: Humanities Press International, 1997.

Deutscher, Isaac. *The Prophet Unarmed*. New York: Verso, 2003.

Erickson, Carolly. *To the Scaffold: The Life of Marie Antoinette*. New York: Morrow, 1991.

Falk, Candace Serena. *Love, Anarchy, and Emma Goldman*. New York: Holt, Rinehart & Winston, 1984.

Frankfurter, Felix. *The Case of Sacco and Vanzetti: A Critical Analysis for Lawyers and Laymen*. Boston: Little, Brown, 1927.

Fraser, Antonia. *Faith and Treason: The Story of the Gunpowder Plot*. New York: Anchor, 1997.

_____. *Marie Antoinette: The Journey*. New York: Talese/Doubleday, 2001.

Feuerlicht, Roberta Strauss. *Justice Crucified: The Story of Sacco and Vanzetti*. New York: McGraw-Hill, 1977.

Gilbert, Helen. *Leon Trotsky: His Life and Ideas*. Seattle, Wash.: Red Letter Press, 2003.

Giles, Steve, and Maike Oergel. *Counter-Cultures in Germany and Central Europe: From Sturm und Drang to Baader-Meinhof*. New York: Peter Lang, 2004.

Goldman, Emma. *Living My Life*. 1931. Reprint. New York: Da Capo Press, 1970.

Goodrich, Thomas. *Black Flag: Guerrilla Warfare on the Western Border, 1861-1865*. Bloomington: Indiana University Press, 1995.

Gottschalk, Louis R. *Jean Paul Marat: A Study in Radicalism*. Chicago: University of Chicago Press, 1967.

Gregorovius, Ferdinand. *Lucretia Borgia, According to Original Documents and Correspondence of Her Day*. Translated by Leslie Garner. New York: B. Blom, 1968.

Guevara, Che. *Guerrilla Warfare*. 1961. Reprint. Lincoln: University of Nebraska Press, 1998.

_____. *The Motorcycle Diaries: A Latin American Journey*. Edited and translated by Alexandra Keeble. Rev. ed. New York: Ocean Press, 2003.

Hearst, Patty, with Alvin Moscow. *Patty Hearst: Her Own Story*. New York: Avon, 1998.

Higham, Charles. *American Swastika*. Garden City, N.Y.: Doubleday, 1985.

Hoffman, Abbie. *The Autobiography of Abbie Hoffman*. 2d ed. New York: Four Walls Eight Windows, 2000.

Jenkins, Philip. *Hoods and Shirts: The Extreme Right in Pennsylvania, 1925-1950*. Chapel Hill: University of North Carolina Press, 1997.

Kaarthikeyan, D. R., and Radhavinod Raju. *Triumph of Truth: The Rajiv Gandhi Assassination—The Investigation*. Chicago: New Dawn Press, 2004.

Katz, Friedrich. *The Life and Times of Pancho Villa*. Stanford, Calif.: Stanford University Press, 1998.

Kenny, Kevin. *Making Sense of the Molly Maguires*. New York: Oxford University Press, 1998.

Kenyon, J. P. *The Popish Plot*. London: Heinemann, 1972.

Knecht, Robert J. *The Valois: Kings of France, 1328-1589*. London: Hambledon, 2005.

Lane, Jane. *Titus Oates*. 1949. Reprint. Westport, Conn.: Greenwood Press, 1971.

Leslie, Edward E. *The Devil Knows How to Ride: The True Story of William Clarke Quantrill and His Confederate Raiders*. New York: Da Capo Press, 1998.

Lever, Evelyne. *Marie Antoinette: The Last Queen of France*. New York: Farrar, Straus and Giroux, 2000.

Lichtenstein, Nelson. *State of the Union: A Century of American Labor*. Princeton, N.J.: Princeton University Press, 2002.

Lukas, J. Anthony. *Big Trouble: A Murder in a Small Western Town Set Off a Struggle for the Soul of America*. New York: Simon & Schuster, 1997.

Machado, Manuel A., Jr. *Centaur of the North: Francisco Villa, the Mexican Revolution, and Northern Mexico*. Austin, Tex.: Eakin Press, 1988.

McLynn, Frank. *Villa and Zapata: A History of the Mexican Revolution*. New York: Carroll & Graf, 2001.

Martin, Jane A., and Jeremy Ross, eds. *Spies, Scouts, and Raiders: Irregular Operations*. Alexandria, Va.: Time-Life Books, 1985.

Morrison, Toni, ed. *To Die for the People: The Writings of Huey P. Newton*. 1972. Rev. ed. New York: Writers and Readers Press, 1999.

Newton, Huey P. *Revolutionary Suicide*. New York: Writers and Readers Press, 1995.

_____. *War Against the Panthers: A Study of Repression in America*. Reprint. New York: Harlem River Press, 2000.

Nicholls, Mark. *Investigating the Gunpowder Plot.* New York: Manchester University Press, 1991.

Nichols, Bruce. *Guerrilla Warfare in Civil War Missouri, 1862.* Jefferson, N.C.: McFarland, 2004.

Pinkerton, Allan. *The Molly Maguires and the Detectives.* New York: Dover, 1973.

Quirk, Robert E. *Fidel Castro.* New York: W. W. Norton, 1993.

Radzinsky, Edvard. *Stalin.* Moscow: Vagrius, 1997. Translated by H. T. Willetts. London: Sceptre, 1997.

Raskin, Jonah. *For the Hell of It: The Lives and Times of Abbie Hoffman.* Berkeley: University of California Press, 1996.

Richardson, John. *Paradise Poisoned: Learning About Conflict, Terrorism, and Development from Sri Lankha's Civil Wars.* Kandav, Sri Lanka: The International Center for Ethnic Studies, 2005.

Sandeson, David. *Che Guevara.* New York: Octopus, 1997.

Sayers, Michael, and Albert Kahn. *Sabotage! The Secret War Against America.* New York: Harper and Brothers, 1942.

Schapiro, Leonard B. *The Communist Party of the Soviet Union.* 2d ed. New York: Vintage, 1971.

Schultz, Duane. *Quantrill's War: The Life and Times of William Clarke Quantrill, 1837-1865.* New York: St. Martin's Press, 1996.

Seale, Bobby. *Seize the Time: The Story of the Black Panther Party and Huey P. Newton.* 1970. Rev. ed. Baltimore: Black Classic Press, 1997.

Shakur, Assata. *Assata: An Autobiography.* 1987. Reprint. Chicago: L. Hill Books, 2001.

Skierka, Volker. *Fidel Castro: A Biography.* Translated by Patrick Camiller. Cambridge, England.: Polity Press, 2004.

Somasundaram, Daya. *Scarred Minds: The Psychological Impact of War on Sri Lankan Tamils.* Thousand Oaks, Calif.: Sage, 1998.

Szulc, Tad. *Fidel: A Critical Portrait.* New York: Morrow, 1986.

Topp, Michael, ed. *The Sacco and Vanzetti Case: A Brief History with Documents.* New York: Macmillan, 2005.

Travers, James. *Gunpowder: The Players Behind the Plot.* London: National Archives, 2005.

Trotsky, Leon. *My Life: An Attempt at an Autobiography.* New York: Charles Scribner and Sons, 1930.

Tuck, Jim. *Pancho Villa and John Reed: Two Faces of Romantic Revolution.* Tucson: University of Arizona Press, 1984.

Vanzetti, Bartolomeo. *Background to the Plymouth Trial.* Chelsea, Mass.: Road to Freedom Press, 1927.

Varon, Jeremy. *Bringing the War Home: The Weather Underground, the Red Army Faction, and Revolutionary Violence in the Sixties and Seventies.* Berkeley: University of California Press, 2004.

Volkogonov, Dmitri. *Trotsky: The Eternal Revolutionary.* Translated and edited by Harold Shukman. New York: Free Press, 1996.

Zinn, Howard. *Emma.* Cambridge, Mass.: South End Press, 2002.

POLITICIANS

Ambrose, Stephen E. *Nixon.* 3 volumes. New York: Simon & Schuster, 1987-1991.

Andrew, Christopher. *The Sword and Shield.* New York: Basic Books, 1999.

Arnold, Edward J., ed. *The Development of the Radical Right in France, from Boulanger to Le Pen.* Basingstoke, England: Macmillan, 2000.

Baham, Roy, Jamelle Folsom, and E. Jimmy Key. *The Strawberry Pickers.* Nashville, Tenn.: Southern Arts, 2000.

Baker, Robert Gene, with Larry L. King. *Wheeling and Dealing: Confessions of a Capitol Hill Operator.* New York: Norton, 1978.

Bates, Anna Louise. *Weeder in the Garden of the Lord: Anthony Comstock's Life and Career.* Lanham, Md.: University Press of America, 1995.

Bates, Daisy. *The Long Shadow of Little Rock.* 1962. Reprint. Fayetteville: University of Arkansas Press, 1987.

Behr, Edward. *Kiss the Hand You Cannot Bite: The Rise and Fall of the Ceauşescus.* New York: Villard, 1991.

Beria, Sergio. *Beria, My Father: Inside Stalin's Kremlin.* Translated by Brian Pearce. London: Duckworth, 2001.

Bernstein, Carl, and Bob Woodward. *All the President's Men.* 1974. 2d ed. New York: Simon & Schuster, 1994.

Bix, Herbert P. *Hirohito and the Making of Modern Japan.* New York: HarperCollins, 2000.

Blight, James, and Peter Kornbluh. *Politics of Illusion: The Bay of Pigs Invasion Reexamined.* Boulder, Colo.: Lynne Rienner, 1998.

Boulard, Gary. *The Big Lie: Hale Boggs, Lucille May Grace, and Leander Perez in 1951.* Gretna, La.: Pelican, 2001.

Bradford, Sarah. *Lucrezia Borgia: Life, Love, and Death in Renaissance Italy.* London: Viking, 2004.

_____. *Phoenix: Cesare Borgia, His Life and Times*. London: Phoenix Press, 2001.

Bradley, Erwin S. *Simon Cameron, Lincoln's Secretary of War: A Political Biography*. Philadelphia: University of Pennsylvania Press, 1966.

Burrows, Edwin G., and Mike Wallace. *Gotham: A History of New York City to 1898*. New York: Oxford University Press, 1999.

Butow, Robert. *Tojo and the Coming of the War*. Princeton, N.J.: Princeton University Press, 1961.

Byrnes, Robert F. *Pobedonostsev: His Life and Thought*. Bloomington: Indiana University Press, 1968.

Callow, Alexander B., Jr. *The Tweed Ring*. Westport, Conn.: Greenwood Press, 1981.

_____, ed. *The City Boss in America: An Interpretive Reader*. New York: Oxford University Press, 1976.

Cameron, Maxwell A. *Democracy and Authoritarianism in Peru*. New York: St. Martin's Press, 1994.

Caro, Robert A. *Lyndon Johnson: Master of the Senate*. New York: Knopf, 2002.

Carter, Dan T. *The Politics of Rage: George Wallace, the Origins of the New Conservatism, and the Transformation of American Politics*. Baton Rouge: Louisiana State University Press, 2000.

Catton, Philip E. *Diem's Final Failure*. Lawrence: University Press of Kansas, 2002.

Chang, Jung, and John Halliday. *Mao: The Unknown Story*. New York: Alfred A. Knopf, 2005.

Cohn, Roy M., with Sidney Zion. *The Autobiography of Roy Cohn*. New York: Lyle Stuart, 1988.

Colson, Charles W. *Born Again*. Old Tappan, N.J.: Chosen Books, 1976.

Conaway, James. *Judge: The Life and Times of Leander Perez*. New York: Alfred A. Knopf, 1973.

Conquest, Robert. *The Great Terror: A Reassessment*. Rev. ed. New York: Oxford University Press, 1990.

Copsey, Nigel. *Contemporary British Fascism: The British National Party and the Search for Legitimacy*. London: Palgrave Macmillan, 2004.

Crippen, Lee F. *Simon Cameron: Antebellum Years*. New York: Da Capo Press, 1972.

Cullather, Nick. *Secret History: The CIA's Classified Account of Its Operations in Guatemala, 1952-1954*. Palo Alto, Calif.: Stanford University Press, 1999.

Davies, Peter. *The Extreme Right in France, 1789 to the Present*. New York: Routledge, 2002.

Davis, Margaret. *The Dark Side of Fortune: Triumph and Scandal in the Life of Oil Tycoon Edward L. Doheny*. Berkeley: University of California Press, 1998.

Dean, John W. *Blind Ambition: The White House Years*. New York: Simon & Schuster, 1976.

Deletant, Dennis. *Ceauşescu and the Securitate: Coercion and Dissent in Romania, 1965-1989*. Armonk, N.Y.: M. E. Sharpe, 1996.

Dorsett, Lyle W. *The Pendergast Machine*. New York: Oxford University Press, 1968.

Dudley, Steven. *Walking Ghosts: Murder and Guerrilla Politics in Colombia*. New York: Routledge, 2004.

Ehrlichman, John. *Witness to Power*. New York: Simon & Schuster, 1982.

Ellison, Katherine. *Imelda: Steel Butterfly of the Philippines*. New York: McGraw-Hill, 1988.

Fawthrop, Tom, and Helen Jarvis. *Getting Away with Genocide?* London: Pluto Press, 2004.

Fehrenbacher, Don Edward. *Slavery, Law, and Politics: The Dred Scott Case in Historical Perspective*. New York: Oxford University Press, 1981.

Fowler, Gene. *Beau James: The Life and Times of Jimmy Walker*. New York: Viking, 1949.

Fraser, Nicholas, and Marysa Navarro. *Evita: The Real Lives of Eva Perón*. London: André Deutsch, 2003.

Fried, Albert, ed. *McCarthyism, the Great American Red Scare: A Documentary History*. New York: Oxford University Press, 1996.

Garner, Paul. *Porfirio Díaz*. New York: Longman, 2001.

Gilbert, Helen. *Lyndon Larouche: Fascism Restyled for the New Millennium*. Seattle: Red Letter Press, 2003.

Gilbey, Emma. *The Lady: The Life and Times of Winnie Mandela*. London: Jonathan Cape, 1993.

Ginsborg, Paul. *Italy and Its Discontents: Family, Civil Society, State, 1980-2001*. New York: Palgrave Macmillan, 2003.

Grafton, Carl, and Anne Permaloff. *Big Mules and Branchheads: James E. Folsom and Political Power in Alabama*. Athens: University of Georgia Press, 1985.

Green, A. Wigfall. *The Man Bilbo*. Baton Rouge: Louisiana State University Press, 1963.

Guillermoprieto, Alma. *Looking for History: Dispatches from Latin America*. New York: Pantheon Books, 2001.

Hack, Richard. *Puppetmaster: The Secret Life of J. Edgar Hoover*. Beverly Hills, Calif.: New Millennium Press, 2004.

Haldeman, H. R. *The Ends of Power*. New York: Times Books, 1978.

Hass, Eric. *Dave Beck, Labor Merchant: The Case History of a Labor Leader*. New York: New York Labor News, 1957.

Haygood, Wil. *King of the Cats: The Life and Times of Adam Clayton Powell, Jr.* New York: Houghton Mifflin, 1993.

Healey, Thomas S. *The Two Deaths of George Wallace: The Question of Forgiveness.* Montgomery, Ala.: Black Belt Press, 1996.

Hemelrijk, Emily A. *Matrona Docta: Educated Women in the Roman Elite, from Cornelia to Julia Domna.* New York: Routledge, 1999.

Holli, Melvin G. *The American Mayor: The Best and the Worst Big-City Leaders.* University Park: Pennsylvania State University Press, 1999.

Huebner, Timothy S. *The Taney Court: Justices, Rulings, and Legacy.* Santa Barbara, Calif.: ABC-CLIO, 2003.

Jacobs, James B. *Mobsters, Unions, and Feds: The Mafia and the American Labor Movement.* New York: New York University Press, 2006.

Jeansonne, Glen. *Leander Perez: Boss of the Delta.* Baton Rouge: Louisiana State University Press, 1977.

Johnson, Ben F., III. *Arkansas in Modern America, 1930-1999.* Fayetteville: University of Arkansas Press, 2000.

Kahan, Stuart. *The Wolf of the Kremlin: First Biography of L. M. Kaganovich, the Soviet Union's Architect of Fear.* London: Robert Hale, 1989.

Kalman, Laura. *Abe Fortas: A Biography.* New Haven, Conn.: Yale University Press, 1990.

Karnow, Stanley. *Vietnam: A History.* 2d ed. New York: Viking Press, 1997.

Kilch, Kent. *Children of Ceaușescu.* New York: Umbrage Editions, 2002.

Kimura, Rei. *Alberto Fujimori of Peru: The President Who Dared to Dream.* New York: Beekman, 1998.

King, Dennis. *Lyndon Larouche and the New American Fascism.* New York: Doubleday, 1989.

Kleiner, Diana E. E., and Susan Matheson, eds. *I, Claudia: Women in Ancient Rome.* New Haven, Conn.: Yale University Art Gallery, 1996.

Knight, Amy. *Beria, Stalin's First Lieutenant.* Princeton, N.J.: Princeton University Press, 1993.

Koestler, Arthur. *Darkness at Noon.* Translated by Daphne Hardy. London: Jonathan Cape, 1940.

Kromova, C. *Dzerzhinsky: A Biography.* Moscow: Progress, 1988.

Kutler, Stanley I. *The Wars of Watergate: The Last Crisis of Richard Nixon.* New York: Alfred A. Knopf, 1990.

Larsen, Lawrence H., and Nancy J. Hulston. *Pendergast.* Columbia: University of Missouri Press, 1997.

Laybourn, Keith. *Fifty Key Figures in Twentieth Century British Politics.* London: Routledge, 2002.

Lee, Lilian. *The Last Princess of Manchuria.* New York: Morrow, 1992.

Leinwand, Gerald. *Mackerels in the Moonlight: Four Corrupt American Mayors.* Jefferson, N.C.: McFarland, 2004.

Lesher, Stephan. *George Wallace: American Populist.* Reading, Mass.: Addison-Wesley, 1994.

Levitas, Daniel. *The Terrorist Next Door: The Militia Movement and the Radical Right.* New York: St. Martin's Press, 2002.

Lewis, Walker. *Without Fear or Favor: A Biography of Chief Justice Roger Brooke Taney.* Boston: Houghton Mifflin, 1965.

Liddy, G. Gordon. *When I Was a Kid, This Was a Free Country.* Washington, D.C.: Regnery, 2002.

_____. *Will.* 3d ed. New York: St. Martin's Press, 1996.

Llewellyn, Peter. *Rome in the Dark Ages.* New York: Praeger, 1971.

Long, Huey Pierce. *Every Man a King: The Autobiography of Huey P. Long.* 1933. Reprint. Cambridge, Mass.: Da Capo Press, 1996.

McCallum, John. *Dave Beck.* Mercer Island, Wash.: Writing Works, 1978.

McCord, James W., Jr. *A Piece of Tape: The Watergate Story, Fact and Fiction.* Rockville, Md.: Washington Media Services, 1974.

Mallett, Michael Edward. *The Borgias; The Rise and Fall of a Renaissance Dynasty.* New York: Barnes and Noble, 1969.

Manley, John. *The Politics of Finance: The House Committee on Ways and Means.* Boston: Little, Brown, 1970.

May, Robert E. *Manifest Destiny's Underworld.* Chapel Hill: University of North Carolina Press, 2004.

Medvedev, Roy. *All Stalin's Men.* New York: Doubleday, 1984.

Meltzer, Milton. *Winnie Mandela: The Soul of South Africa.* New York: Viking Kestrel, 1988.

Min, Anchee. *Becoming Madame Mao.* Boston: Houghton Mifflin, 2000.

Montefiore, Simon Sebag. *Stalin: The Court of the Red Tsar.* New York: Alfred A. Knopf, 2003.

Moore, Ambrose Yoemans. *The Life of Schuyler Colfax.* Philadephia: T. B. Peterson & Brothers, 1868.

Morgan, Chester. *Redneck Liberal: Theodore G. Bilbo and the New Deal.* Baton Rouge: Louisiana State University Press, 1985.

Morgan, Iwan W. *Nixon*. New York: Oxford University Press, 2002.

Morgan, Philip. *Fascism in Europe: 1919-1945*. London: Routledge, 2002.

Morgan, Ted. *McCarthyism in Twentieth Century America*. New York: Random House, 1999.

Murphy, Bruce Allen. *Fortas: The Rise and Ruin of a Supreme Court Justice*. New York: W. Morrow, 1988.

Nixon, Richard. *RN: The Memoirs of Richard Nixon*. 1975. Reprint. New York: Simon & Schuster, 1990.

Noggle, Burl. *Teapot Dome: Oil and Politics in the 1920's*. Baton Rouge: Louisiana State University Press, 1962.

Olson, Keith W. *Watergate: The Presidential Scandal That Shook America*. Lawrence: University of Kansas Press, 2003.

Ortiz, Alicia Dujovne. *Eva Perón*. Translated by Shawn Field. New York: St. Martin's Griffin, 1997.

Payne, Stanley G. *A History of Fascism: 1914-1945*. London: UCL, 1995.

Perón, Eva. *Evita: In My Own Words*. Translated by Laura Dail. New York: New Press, 2005.

Perry, Laurens Ballard. *Juárez and Díaz: Machine Politics in Mexico*. De Kalb: Northern Illinois University Press, 1978.

Pipes, Richard. *Russia Under the Bolshevik Regime*. New York: Knopf, 1994.

Powell, Adam Clayton, Jr. *Adam by Adam: The Autobiography of Adam Clayton Powell, Jr.* New York: Dial Press, 1971.

Ranville, Michael. *To Strike at a King: The Turning Point in the McCarthy Witch Hunts*. Ann Arbor, Mich.: Momentum Books, 1997.

Rappaport, Helen. *Joseph Stalin: A Biographical Companion*. Santa Barbara, Calif.: ABC-CLIO, 1999.

Rayfield, Donald. *Stalin and His Hangmen: The Tyrant and Those Who Killed for Him*. New York: Random House, 2004.

Reddig, William M. *Tom's Town: Kansas City and the Pendergast Legend*. Columbia: University of Missouri Press, 1986.

Reed, Roy. *Faubus: The Life and Times of an American Prodigal*. Fayetteville: University of Arkansas Press, 1997.

Reeves, Richard. *President Nixon: Alone in the White House*. New York: Simon & Schuster, 2001.

Reeves, Thomas C. *The Life and Times of Joe McCarthy: A Biography*. Lanham, Md.: Madison Books, 1997.

Riasanovsky, Nicholas V. *A History of Russia*. 6th ed. New York: Oxford University Press, 2000.

Rogovin, Vadim Z. *1937: Stalin's Year of Terror*. Translated by Frederick S. Choate. Oak Park, Mich.: Mehring Books, 1998.

Rowe, Robert. *The Bobby Baker Story*. New York: Parallax, 1967.

Sabatini, Rafael. *The Life of Cesare Borgia of France*. Rockville, Md.: Wildside Press, 2003.

Safire, William. *Before the Fall: An Inside View of the Pre-Watergate White House*. Garden City, N.Y.: Doubleday, 1975.

Sampson, Anthony. *Mandela: The Authorized Biography*. New York: Knopf, 1999.

Schudson, Michael. *Watergate in American Memory: How We Remember, Forget, and Reconstruct the Past*. New York: Basic Books, 1992.

Service, Robert. *Stalin: A Biography*. Cambridge, Mass.: Harvard University Press, 2004.

Shawcross, William. *Sideshow: Nixon, Kissinger, and the Destruction of Cambodia*. 1979. Rev. ed. Boulder, Colo.: Cooper Square Press, 2002.

Simkins, Francis Butler. *Pitchfork Ben Tillman: South Carolinian*. 1944. Reprint. Columbia: University of South Carolina Press, 2002.

Sims, George E. *The Little Man's Big Friend: James E. Folsom in Alabama Politics, 1946-1958*. Tuscaloosa: University of Alabama Press, 1985.

Skirda, Alexandre. *Facing the Enemy: A History of Anarchist Organization from Proudhon to May, 1968*. Oakland, Calif.: AK Press, 2002.

Slaughter, Jane, and Robert Kern, eds. *European Women on the Left: Socialism, Feminism, and the Problems Faced by Political Women, 1880 to the Present*. Westport, Conn.: Greenwood Press, 1981.

Smith, Willard H. *Schuyler Colfax: The Changing Fortunes of a Political Idol*. Indianapolis: Indiana Historical Bureau, 1952.

Solomon, Noal. *When Leaders Were Bosses: An Inside Look at Political Machines and Politics*. Hicksville, N.Y.: Exposition Press, 1975.

Stalin, Joseph. *The Stalin-Kaganovich Correspondence: 1931-1936*. Edited by R. W. Davies et al. New Haven, Conn.: Yale University Press, 2003.

Stratton, David. *Tempest over Teapot Dome: The Story of Albert B. Fall*. Norman: University of Oklahoma Press, 1998.

Summer, Anthony. *Official and Confidential: The Secret Life of J. Edgar Hoover*. New York: Putnam, 1993.

Tate, Katherine. *Black Faces in the Mirror: African Americans and Their Representatives in the U.S. Congress*. Princeton, N.J.: Princeton University Press, 2002.

Taylor, J. M. *Eva Perón: The Myths of a Woman*. Chicago: University of Chicago Press, 1981.

Terrill, Ross. *Madame Mao: The White-Boned Demon*. Rev. ed. Stanford, Calif.: Stanford University Press, 2000.

Vaksberg, Arkady. *Stalin's Prosecutor: The Life of Andrei Vishinsky*. Translated by Jan Butler. New York: Grove Weidenfeld, 1990.

Warren, Robert Penn. *All the King's Men*. 1946. Reprint. San Diego: Harcourt, 2005.

Webb, Samuel L., and Margaret E. Armbrester, eds. *Alabama Governors: A Political History of the State*. Foreword by Albert P. Brewer. Tuscaloosa: University of Alabama Press, 2001.

White, Theodore H. *Breach of Faith: The Fall of Richard Nixon*. New York: Atheneum, 1975.

Wianda, Howard J., and Harvey F. Kline. *Latin American Politics and Development*. Boulder, Colo.: Westview Press, 2000.

Williams, T. Harry: *Huey Long*. 1969. Reprint. New York: Vintage Books, 1981.

Witke, Roxane. *Comrade Chiang Ch'ing*. New York: Little, Brown, 1977.

Zelizer, Julian E. *Taxing America: Wilbur D. Mills, Congress and the State, 1945-1975*. New York: Cambridge University Press, 1998.

POPES

Boase, T. S. R. *Boniface VIII*. London: Constable, 1933.

Chamberlain, E. R. *The Bad Popes*. New York: Dorset Press, 1986.

Cloulas, Ivan. *The Borgias*. Translated by Gilda Roberts. New York: Watts, 1998.

Eusebius. *The History of the Church*. New York: Penguin Books, 1989.

Ferrara, Orestes. *The Borgia Pope, Alexander the Sixth*. New York: Sheed, 1940.

Gouwens, Kenneth, and Sheryl E. Reiss, ed. *The Pontificate of Clement VII: History, Politics, Culture*. Burlington, Vt.: Ashgate, 2005.

Kelly, J. N. D. *The Oxford Dictionary of the Popes*. New York: Oxford University Press, 1986.

McBrien, Richard. *Lives of the Popes*. San Francisco: HarperCollins, 1997.

Masson, Georgina. *The Borgias*. New York: Penguin, 2001.

Menache, Sophia. *Clement V*. Cambridge, England: Cambridge University Press, 2003.

Paravicini-Bagliani, Agostino. *The Pope's Body*. Chicago: University of Chicago Press, 2000.

Partner, Peter. *The Lands of St. Peter*. Berkeley: University of California Press, 1972.

Rendina, Claudio. *The Popes: Histories and Secrets*. Santa Ana, Calif.: Seven Locks Press, 2002.

Tobin, Greg. *Selecting the Pope: Uncovering the Mysteries of Papal Selection*. New York: Barnes and Noble, 2003.

Ullmann, Walter. *The Origins of the Great Schism: A Study in Fourteenth-Century Ecclesiastical History*. 1948. Reprint. Hamden, Conn.: Archon Books, 1972.

Walsh, Michael, ed. *Lives of the Popes*. Gordon, Australia: Universal International, 1998.

Williams, Paul L. *The Vatican Exposed: Money, Murder, and the Mafia*. Amherst, N.Y.: Prometheus Books, 2003.

Wood, Charles T., ed. *Philip the Fair and Boniface VIII: State vs. Papacy*. New York: Krieger, 1976.

RACISTS AND HATEMONGERS

Abanes, Richard. *American Militias*. Downers Grove, Ill.: Intervarsity Press, 1996.

Abelmann, Nancy, and John Lie. *Blue Dreams: Korean Americans and the Los Angeles Riots*. Cambridge, Mass.: Harvard University Press, 1995.

Anti-Defamation League. *Poisoning the Web: Hatred Online*. New York: Author, 1999.

Barkun, Michael. *Religion and the Racist Right: The Origins of the Christian Identity Movement*. Chapel Hill: University of North Carolina Press, 1997.

Berlet, Chip, and Matthew M. Lyons. *Right-Wing Populism in America: Too Close for Comfort*. New York: Guilford Press, 2000.

Black, Jeremy, ed. *Culture and Society in Britain, 1660-1800*. Manchester, England: Manchester University Press, 1997.

Blee, Kathleen M. *Women and the Klan*. Berkeley: University of California Press, 1991.

Bock, Alan. *Ambush at Ruby Ridge*. New York: Berkley Books, 1996.

Bockris, Victor. *Warhol: The Biography*. New York: Da Capo Press, 2003.

Bredin, Jean-Denis. *The Affair: The Case of Alfred Dreyfus*. Translated by Jeffrey Mehlman. New York: George Brazilier, 1986.

Brennan, James F. *The Reflection of the Dreyfus Affair in the European Press, 1897-1899*. New York: Peter Lang, 1998.

Bridges, Tyler. *The Rise of David Duke*. Jackson: University Press of Mississippi, 1994.

Brinkley, Alan. *Voices of Protest: Huey Long, Father*

Coughlin, and the Great Depression. New York: Alfred A. Knopf, 1983.

Brodsky, Alexandra Fanny. *A Fragile Identity: Survival in Nazi-Occupied Belgium.* New York: Radcliffe Press, 1998.

Browning, Robert M. *Forrest: The Confederacy's Relentless Warrior.* Washington, D.C.: Brassey's, 2004.

Burns, Michael, ed. *France and the Dreyfus Affair: A Documentary History.* New York: St. Martin's Press, 1999.

Bushart, Howard L., John R. Craig, and Myra Barnes. *Soldiers of God: White Supremacists and Their Holy War for America.* New York: Kensington Books, 1998.

Cannon, Lou. *Official Negligence: How Rodney King and the Riots Changed Los Angeles and the LAPD.* Reprint. New York: Basic Books, 1999.

Carpenter, Ronald H. *Father Charles E. Coughlin: Surrogate Spokesman for the Disaffected.* Westport, Conn.: Greenwood Press, 1998.

Clark, Nancy L., and William H. Worger. *South Africa: The Rise and Fall of Apartheid.* New York: Pearson Longman, 2004.

Cohen-Almagor, Raphael. *The Boundary of Liberty and Tolerance: The Struggle Against Kahanism in Israel.* Gainesville: University Press of Florida, 1994.

DeLaughter, Bobby. *Never Too Late: A Prosecutor's Story of Justice in the Medgar Evers Case:* New York: Simon & Schuster, 2001.

Denoon, Donald, with Balam Nyeko and J. B. Webster. *Southern Africa Since 1800.* New York: Praeger, 1973.

Derfler, Leslie. *The Dreyfus Affair.* Westport, Conn.: Greenwood Press, 2002.

Dixon, Thomas, Jr. *The Clansman: An Historical Romance of the Ku Klux Klan.* 1905. Reprint. Lexington: University Press of Kentucky, 1970.

Dobratz, Betty A., and Stephanie Shanks-Meile. *The White Separatist Movement in the United States.* Baltimore: Johns Hopkins University Press, 1999.

Elon, Amos. *A Blood-Dimmed Tide: Dispatches from the Middle East.* London: Penguin, 2000.

Evans, Richard J. *Lying About Hitler: History, Holocaust, and the David Irving Trial.* New York: Basic Books, 2002.

Ezekiel, Raphael S. *The Racist Mind.* New York: Penguin Books, 1995.

Fehrenbacher, Don Edward. *Slavery, Law, and Politics: The Dred Scott Case in Historical Perspective.* New York: Oxford University Press, 1981.

Flynn, Kevin, and Gary Gerhardt. *The Silent Brotherhood: Inside America's Racist Underground.* New York: Free Press, 1989.

Forth, Christopher E. *The Dreyfus Affair and the Crisis of French Manhood.* Baltimore: Johns Hopkins University Press, 2004.

Fried, Albert, ed. *McCarthyism, the Great American Red Scare: A Documentary History.* New York: Oxford University Press, 1996.

Friedman, Robert J. *The False Prophet: Rabbi Meir Kahane, from FBI Informant to Knesset Member.* Chicago: Chicago Review Press, 1990.

Fuchs, Richard L. *An Unerring Fire: The Massacre at Fort Pillow.* Mechanicsburg, Pa.: Stackpole Books, 2002.

George, John, and Laird Wilcox. *American Extremists: Militias, Supremacists, Klansmen, Communists, and Others.* Amherst, N.Y.: Prometheus Books, 1996.

Gibson, Rachel K. *The Growth of Anti-Immigrant Parties in Western Europe.* Lewiston, N.Y.: Edwin Mellen Press, 2001.

Gilman, Susan. *Blood Talk: American Race Melodrama and the Culture of the Occult.* Chicago: University of Chicago Press, 2003.

Gobineau, Arthur, comte de. *The Inequality of Human Races.* Preface by George L. Mosse. New York: H. Fertig, 1999.

Goodrick-Clarke, Nicholas. *Black Sun: Aryan Cults, Esoteric Nazism, and the Politics of Identity.* New York: New York University Press, 2002.

_____. *Hitler's Priestess: Savitri Devi, the Hindu-Aryan Myth, and Neo-Nazism.* New York: New York University Press, 1998.

Green, A. Wigfall. *The Man Bilbo.* Baton Rouge: Louisiana State University Press, 1963.

Griffin, Robert S. *The Fame of a Dead Man's Deeds: An Up-Close Portrait of White Nationalist William Pierce.* Lavergne, Tenn.: Lightning Source, 2001.

Griffin, Roger. *The Nature of Fascism.* New York: St. Martin's Press, 1991.

Guttenplan, D. D. *The Holocaust on Trial.* New York: W. W. Norton, 2002.

Hamann, Brigitte. *Winifred Wagner: A Life at the Heart of Hitler's Bayreuth.* Translated by Alan Bance. London: Granta Books, 2005.

Herzog, Chaim. *Living History: A Memoir.* London: Weidenfeld and Nicolson, 1997.

Huebner, Timothy S. *The Taney Court: Justices, Rulings, and Legacy.* Santa Barbara, Calif.: ABC-CLIO, 2003.

Hurst, Jack. *Nathan Bedford Forrest: A Biography*. New York: A. A. Knopf, 1993.

Jeansonne, Glen. *Gerald L. K. Smith: Minister of Hate*. New Haven, Conn.: Yale University Press, 1988.

Kantrowitz, Stephen. *Ben Tillman and the Reconstruction of White Supremacy*. Chapel Hill: University of North Carolina Press, 2000.

Katz, David S. *The Jews in the History of England: 1485-1850*. New York: Oxford University Press, 1994.

Köhler, Joachim. *Wagner's Hitler: The Prophet and His Disciple*. Translated by Ronald Taylor. Malden, Mass.: Blackwell, 2000.

Koon, Stacey C., with Robert Deitz. *Presumed Guilty: The Tragedy of the Rodney King Affair*. Washington, D.C.: Regnery, 1992.

Kotler, Yair. *Heil Kahane*. New York: Adama Books, 1986.

Kuzenski, John C., Charles S. Bullock III, and Ronald Keith Gaddie. *David Duke and the Politics of Race in the South*. Nashville, Tenn.: Vanderbilt University Press, 1995.

Lacour-Gayet, Robert. *A History of South Africa*. Translated by Stephen Hardman. London: Cassell, 1977.

Landau, Elaine. *The White Power Movement: America's Racist Hate Groups*. Brookfield, Conn.: Millbrook Press, 1993.

Lang, Robert, ed. *The Birth of a Nation*. New Brunswick, N.J.: Rutgers University Press, 1994.

Langer, Elinor. *A Hundred Little Hitlers*. New York: Metropolitan, 2003.

Lee, Martin. *The Beast Reawakens*. Boston: Little, Brown, 1999.

Lewis, Walker. *Without Fear or Favor: A Biography of Chief Justice Roger Brooke Taney*. Boston: Houghton Mifflin, 1965.

Lindsey, Hal. *The Road to Holocaust*. New York: Bantam Books, 1989.

Lipstadt, Deborah E. *Denying the Holocaust: The Growing Assault on Truth and Memory*. New York: Free Press, 1993.

_____. *History on Trial: My Day in Court with David Irving*. New York: Ecco, 2005.

Macintyre, Ben. *Forgotten Fatherland: The Search for Elisabeth Nietzsche*. New York: HarperPerennial, 1993.

MacLean, Nancy. *Behind the Mask of Chivalry*. New York: Oxford University Press, 1994.

Mintz, Frank P. *The Liberty Lobby and the American Right: Race, Conspiracy, and Culture*. Westport, Conn.: Greenwood Press, 1985.

Morgan, Chester. *Redneck Liberal: Theodore G. Bilbo and the New Deal*. Baton Rouge: Louisiana State University Press, 1985.

Morris, W. *Ghosts of Medgar Evers: A Tale of Race, Murder, Mississippi, and Hollywood*. New York: Random House, 1998.

Peters, H. F. *Zarathustra's Sister: The Case of Elisabeth and Friedrich Nietzsche*. New York: Crown, 1977.

Phillips, John W. *Sign of the Cross: The Prosecutor's True Story of a Landmark Trial Against the Klan*. Louisville, Ky.: Westminster John Knox Press, 2000.

Ranville, Michael. *To Strike at a King: The Turning Point in the McCarthy Witch Hunts*. Ann Arbor, Mich.: Momentum Books, 1997.

Reeves, Thomas C. *The Life and Times of Joe McCarthy: A Biography*. Lanham, Md.: Madison Books, 1997.

Rubenstein, Richard. *Approaches to Auschwitz: The Holocaust and Its Legacy*. Atlanta: John Knox Press, 1987.

Savitri Devi. *The Lightning and the Sun*. Buffalo, N.Y.: Samisdat, 1958.

Shermer, Michael. *Denying History: Who Says the Holocaust Never Happened and Why Do They Say It?* Berkeley: University of California Press, 2002.

Simkins, Francis Butler. *Pitchfork Ben Tillman: South Carolinian*. 1944. Reprint. Columbia: University of South Carolina Press, 2002.

Simmons, Harvey G. *The French National Front: The Extremist Challenge to Democracy*. Boulder, Colo.: Westview Press, 1996.

Sparks, Allister. *The Mind of South Africa*. New York: Ballantine Books, 1990.

Strum, Philippa. *When the Nazis Came to Skokie: Freedom for Speech We Hate*. Lawrence: University of Kansas Press, 1999.

Summer, Anthony. *Official and Confidential: The Secret Life of J. Edgar Hoover*. New York: Putnam, 1993.

Swain, Carol M. *The New White Nationalism in America*. New York: Cambridge University Press, 2002.

Sykes, Alan. *The Radical Right in Britain*. London: Palgrave Macmillan, 2004.

Thompson, Leonard. *A History of South Africa*. New Haven, Conn.: Yale University Press, 1995.

Tyndall, John. *Eleventh Hour: A Call for British Rebirth*. London: Albion Press, 1988.

Wade, Wyn Craig. *The Fiery Cross*. New York: Simon & Schuster, 1987.

Wagner, Friedelind, with Page Cooper. *Heritage of Fire: The Story of Richard Wagner's Granddaughter*. New York: Harper, 1945.

Wagner, Nike. *The Wagners: The Dramas of a Musical Dynasty*. London: Weidenfeld & Nicolson, 1998.

Walker, Martin. *The National Front*. Glasgow, Scotland: Fontana/Collins, 1977.

Warren, Donald. *Radio Priest: Charles Coughlin, the Father of Hate Radio*. New York: Free Press, 1996.

Weaver, Randy, and Sara Weaver. *The Federal Siege at Ruby Ridge: In Our Own Words*. Marion, Mont.: Ruby Ridge, 1998.

Wilkie, C. *Dixie: A Personal Odyssey Through Events That Shaped the Modern South*. New York: Simon & Schuster, 2001.

Williams, Mary E. *The White Separatist Movement*. San Diego: Greenwood Press, 2002.

Wyeth, John A. *That Devil Forrest*. 1899. Reprint. Baton Rouge: Louisiana State University Press, 1989.

SCIENTISTS AND DOCTORS

Ameringer, Carl F. *State Medical Boards and the Politics of Public Protection*. Baltimore, Md.: The Johns Hopkins University Press, 1999.

Betzold, Michael. *Appointment with Dr. Death*. Troy, Mich.: Momentum Books, 1993.

Blass, Thomas. *The Man Who Shocked the World: The Life and Legacy of Stanley Milgram*. New York: Basic Books, 2004.

Galliher, John F., Wayne Brekhus, and David P. Keys. *Laud Humphreys: Prophet of Homosexuality and Sociology*. Madison: University of Wisconsin Press, 2004.

Henderson, Leigh A., and William J. Glass, eds. *LSD: Still with Us After All These Years*. San Francisco: Jossey-Bass, 1994.

Iserson, Kenneth V. *Demon Doctors: Physicians as Serial Killers*. Tucson, Ariz.: Galen Press, 2002.

Leary, Timothy. *Flashbacks: An Autobiography—A Personal and Cultural History of an Era*. New York: G. P. Putnam's Sons, 1990.

Lifton, Robert Jay. *The Nazi Doctors: Medical Killing and the Psychology of Genocide*. New York: Basic Books, 1986.

Loving, Carol. *My Son, My Sorrow: A Mother's Plea to Dr. Kevorkian*. East Rutherford, N.J.: New Horizon Press, 1998.

Milgram, Stanley. *Obedience to Authority: An Experimental View*. 1974. Reprint. New York: Harper-Collins, 2004.

Nicol, Neal, Harry Wylie, Cheeni Rao, and Jack Kevorkian. *Between the Dying and the Dead: Dr. Jack Kevorkian's Life and the Battle to Legalize Euthanasia*. Madison: University of Wisconsin Press, 2006.

Olsen, Gregg. *Starvation Heights*. New York: Warner Books, 1997.

Srebnick, Amy Gilman. *The Mysterious Death of Mary Rogers: Sex and Culture in Nineteenth Century New York*. New York: Oxford University Press, 1997.

Stevens, Jay. *Storming Heaven: LSD and the American Dream*. New York: The Atlantic Monthly Press, 1987.

Young, James Harvey. *The Medical Messiahs: A Social History of Health Quackery in Twentieth-Century America*. 1966. Reprint. Princeton, N.J.: Princeton University Press, 1992.

SERIAL KILLERS

Barfield, Velma. *Woman on Death Row*. Nashville: Oliver Nelson Books, 1985.

Beattie, Robert. *Nightmare in Wichita: The Hunt for the BTK Strangler*. New York: New American Library, 2005.

Begg, Paul. *Jack the Ripper: The Definitive History*. London: Longman, 2003.

Bledsoe, Jerry, and Velma Barfield. *Death Sentence: The True Story of Velma Barfield's Life, Crimes, and Execution*. New York: E. P. Dutton, 1998.

Burnside, Scott, and Alan Cairns. *Deadly Innocence*. New York: Warner Books, 1995.

Cahill, Tim. *Buried Dreams: Inside the Mind of a Serial Killer*. New York: Bantam Books, 1986.

Cannon, Angie. *Twenty-Three Days of Terror: The Compelling True Story of the Hunt and Capture of the Beltway Snipers*. New York: Pocket Books, 2003.

Chance, John Newton. *The Crimes at Rillington Place*. London: Hodder & Stoughton, 1961.

Clarkson, Wensley. *Death at Every Stop*. New York: St. Martin's Press, 1997.

Cornwell, Patricia. *Portrait of a Killer: Jack the Ripper, Case Closed*. New York: G. P. Putnam, 2002.

Curtis, L. Perry. *Jack the Ripper and the London Press*. New Haven, Conn.: Yale University Press, 2001.

Dahmer, Lionel. *Father's Story*. New York: William Morrow, 1994.

Davis, D. *The Milwaukee Murders: Nightmare in Apartment 213, the True Story*. New York: St. Martin's Press, 1991.

Eddowes, John. *The Two Killers of Rillington Place*. London: Little, Brown, 1994.

Egger, Steven A. *The Killers Among Us*. 2d ed. Upper Saddle River, N.J.: Pearson Education, 2002.

Fox, James Alan, and Jack Levin. *Extreme Killing: Understanding Serial and Mass Murder.* Thousand Oaks, Calif.: Sage, 2005.

Franke, David. *The Torture Doctor.* New York: Hawthorn Books, 1975.

Frasier, David K. *Murder Cases of the Twentieth Century: Biographies and Bibliographies of 280 Convicted or Accused Killers.* Jefferson, N.C.: McFarland, 1996.

Furneaux, Rupert. *The Two Stranglers of Rillington Place.* London: Panther, 1961.

Geary, Rick. *The Beast of Chicago: The Murderous Career of H. H. Holmes.* New York: NBM Comics, 2003.

Gordon, R. Michael. *Alias Jack the Ripper: Beyond the Usual Whitechapel Suspects.* Jefferson, N.C.: McFarland, 2001.

Grombach, John V. *The Great Liquidator.* New York: Doubleday, 1980.

Haining, Peter. *Sweeney Todd: The Real Story of the Demon Barber of Fleet Street.* London: Robson Books, 2003.

Harrington, Joseph, and Robert Burger. *Justice Denied.* New York: Plenum, 1999.

Hazel, Harry. *Sweeney Todd: Or, The Ruffian Barber.* New York: H. Long, 1865.

Henton, Darcy, and Greg Owens. *No Kill, No Thrill.* Calgary, Alta.: Red Deer Press, 2001.

Hickey, Eric W. *Serial Murderers and Their Victims.* 2d ed. Albany, N.Y.: Wadsworth, 1997.

Holmes, H. H. *Holmes' Own Story.* Philadelphia: Burk & McFetridge, 1895.

Holmes, Robert M., and Stephen T. Holmes, eds. *Contemporary Perspectives on Serial Murder.* Thousand Oaks, Calif.: Sage, 1998.

Horowitz, Sari, and Michael E. Ruane. *Sniper: Inside the Hunt for the Killers Who Terrorized the Nation.* New York: Ballantine Books, 2004.

Indiana, Gary. *Three Month Fever: The Andrew Cunanan Story.* New York: HarperCollins, 1999.

Iserson, Kenneth V. *Demon Doctors: Physicians as Serial Killers.* Tucson, Ariz.: Galen Press, 2002.

Jaeger, R. W., and M. W. Balousek. *Massacre in Milwaukee: The Macabre Case of Jeffrey Dahmer.* Oregon, Wis.: Waubesa Press, 1991.

Jesse, F. Tennyson, ed. *The Trials of Timothy John Evans and John Reginald Halliday Christie.* London: William Hodge, 1957.

Junger, Sebastien. *A Death in Belmont.* New York: W. W. Norton, 2006.

Kelleher, Michael D., and C. L. Kelleher. *Murder Most Rare: The Female Serial Killer.* London: Praeger, 1998.

Kelly, Susan. *The Boston Stranglers: The Public Conviction of Albert Desalvo and the True Story of Eleven Shocking Murders.* New York: Pinnacle Books, 2002.

Kennedy, Ludovic. *Ten Rillington Place.* London: Victor Gollancz, 1961.

Klausner, Lawrence D. *Son of Sam: Based on the Authorized Transcription of the Tapes, Official Documents, and Diaries of David Berkowitz.* New York: McGraw-Hill, 1981.

Krivich, Michail. *Comrade Chikatilo.* Fort Lee, N.J.: Barricade Books, 1993.

Larson, Erik. *The Devil in the White City: Murder, Magic, and Madness at the Fair That Changed America.* New York: Vintage, 2004.

Lasseter, Don. *Die for Me!* New York: Pinnacle Books, 2000.

Linedecker, Clifford L. *The Man Who Killed Boys: The John Wayne Gacy, Jr., Story.* New York: St. Martin's Press, 1993.

Lourie, Richard. *Hunting the Devil.* New York: HarperCollins, 1993.

McNally, Raymond T., and Radu Florescu. *In Search of Dracula.* Greenwich, Conn.: New York Graphic Society, 1972.

Maeder, Thomas. *The Unspeakable Crimes of Dr. Petiot.* 1980. Reprint. London: Penguin Books, 1992.

Martingale, Moira. *Cannibal Killers.* New York: Carroll & Graf, 1994.

Masters, B. *The Shrine of Jeffrey Dahmer.* London: Hodder and Stoughton, 1993.

Mendenhall, Harlan H. *Fall of the House of Gacy.* West Frankfort, Ill.: New Authors, 1998.

Michaud, Stephen, and Hugh Aynesworth. *Ted Bundy: Conversations with a Killer.* New York: Signet, 1989.

Moose, Charles A., and Charles Fleming. *Three Weeks in October: The Manhunt for the Serial Sniper.* New York: Signet, 2004.

Nelson, Polly. *Defending the Devil: My Story as Ted Bundy's Last Lawyer.* New York: W. Morrow, 1994.

Neville, Richard, and Julie Clarke. *The Life and Crimes of Charles Sobhraj.* Sydney: Jonathan Cape, 1997.

Newton, Michael. *The Encyclopedia of Serial Killers.* New York: Checkmark Books, 2000.

Norris, Joel. *Serial Killers.* New York: Doubleday Anchor, 1989.

O'Brien, Darcy. *Two of a Kind: The Hillside Stranglers.* New York: Carroll & Graf, 2003.

Orth, Maureen. *Vulgar Favors: Andrew Cunanan, Gianni Versace, and the Largest Failed Manhunt in U.S. History*. New York: Delacorte, 1999.

Penrose, Valentine. *The Bloody Countess: The Atrocities of Erzsébet Báthory*. London: Creation, 2000.

Pocs, Eva. *Between the Living and the Dead*. Budapest, Hungary: Central European University Press, 1999.

Pron, Nick. *Lethal Marriage: The Unspeakable Crimes of Paul Bernardo and Karla Homolka*. New York: Seal, 1995.

Rae, William. *Confessions of the Boston Strangler*. New York: Pyramid Books, 1967.

Reynolds, Martin. *Dead Ends: The Pursuit, Conviction, and Execution of Female Serial Killer Aileen Wuornos, the Damsel of Death*. New York: St. Martin's Press, 2004.

Rule, Ann. *The Stranger Beside Me*. 4th ed. New York: W. W. Norton, 2000.

Russell, Sue. *Lethal Intent*. New York: Kensington, 2002.

Schechter, Harold. *Depraved: The Shocking True Story of America's Most Fiendish Killer*. New York: Pocket, 1994.

_____. *The Serial Killer Files*. New York: Ballantine Books, 2003.

Schwartz, Ted. *The Hillside Strangler: A Murderer's Mind*. New York: Vivisphere, 2001.

Sherman, Casey. *A Rose for Mary: The Hunt for the Real Boston Strangler*. Urbana, Ill.: Northeastern University Press, 2003.

Shipley, Stacey L., and Bruce A. Arrigo. *The Female Homicide Offender: Serial Murder and the Case of Aileen Wuornos*. Upper Saddle River, N.J.: Prentice Hall, 2003.

Singular, Stephen. *Unholy Messenger: The Life and Crimes of the BTK Serial Killer*. New York: Simon & Schuster, 2006.

Smith, C. *The BTK Murders: Inside the Bind Torture Kill Case That Terrified America's Heartland*. New York: St. Martin's Press, 2006.

Smith, Dame Janet. *The Shipman Inquiry*. 6 vols. Manchester, England: Shipman Inquiry, 2002-2005.

Stewart, James B. *Blind Eye: The Terrifying Story of a Doctor Who Got Away with Murder*. New York: Touchstone Books/Simon & Schuster, 1999.

Sullivan, Terry, and Peter T. Maiken. *Killer Clown: The John Wayne Gacy Murders*. New York: Kensington, 2000.

Tatar, Marie. *Secrets Beyond the Door: The Story of Bluebeard and His Wives*. Princeton, N.J.: Princeton University Press, 2004.

Treplow, Kurt W. *Vlad III Dracula*. Oxford, England: Center for Romanian Studies, 2000.

Vronsky, Peter. *Serial Killers: The Method and Madness of Monsters*. Goleta, Calif.: Berkley Trade, 2004.

Walz, Robin. *Pulp Surrealism: Insolent Popular Culture in Early Twentieth Century Paris*. Berkeley: University of California Press, 2000.

Wertham, Frederic. *The Show of Violence*. New York: Doubleday, 1949.

Williams, Stephen. *Invisible Darkness*. Toronto, Ont.: Bantam, 1996.

Wilson, Colin. *The History of Murder*. New York: Carroll & Graf, 2000.

Woods, Paul Anthony. *Ed Gein: Psycho*. New York: St. Martin's Press, 1995.

Wuornos, Aileen, and Christopher Berry-Dee. *Monster: My True Story*. London: John Blake, 2004.

SEXUAL PREDATORS AND ACCUSED PREDATORS

Barrows, Sydney Biddle. *Getting a Little Work Done*. New York: HarperCollins, 2000.

_____. *Just Between Us Girls: Secrets About Men from the Mayflower Madam*. New York: St. Martin's Press, 1996.

Barrows, Sydney Biddle, with Ellis Weiner. *Mayflower Manners*. New York: Doubleday, 1991.

Berry, Jason. *Lead Us Not into Temptation: Catholic Priests and the Sexual Abuse of Children*. New York: Doubleday Press, 1992.

Bongie, Laurence L. *Sade: A Biographical Essay*. Chicago: University of Chicago Press, 1998.

Boston Globe. *Betrayal: The Crisis in the Catholic Church*. Boston: Little, Brown, 2002.

Burnside, Scott, and Alan Cairns. *Deadly Innocence*. New York: Warner Books, 1995.

Cahill, Tim. *Buried Dreams: Inside the Mind of a Serial Killer*. New York: Bantam Books, 1986.

Dahmer, Lionel. *Father's Story*. New York: William Morrow, 1994.

Davis, D. *The Milwaukee Murders: Nightmare in Apartment 213, the True Story*. New York: St. Martin's Press, 1991.

Dominguez, P. *Amy Fisher: Anatomy of a Scandal—The Myth, the Media, and the Truth Behind the Long Island Lolita Story*. Lincoln, Nebr.: Writers Club Press, 2001.

Dress, Christina, Tama-Lisa Johnson, and Mary Kay Letourneau. *Mass with Mary: The Prison Years*. Victoria, British Columbia: Trafford, 2004.

Du Plessix Gray, Francine. *At Home with the Marquis de Sade*. New York: Simon & Schuster, 1998.

Eberle, P., and S. Eberle. *The Abuse of Innocence: The McMartin Preschool Trial*. New York: Prometheus Books, 2003.

Fisher, Amy, and Robbie Woliver. *If I Knew Then*. New York: IUniverse, 2004.

Fleiss, Heidi. *Pandering*. Los Angeles: One Hour Entertainment, 2002.

_____. *The Player's Handbook: The Ultimate Guide on Dating and Relationships*. Los Angeles: One Hour Entertainment, 2004.

Harrington, Joseph, and Robert Burger. *Justice Denied*. New York: Plenum, 1999.

Harris, Frann. *Martensville: Truth or Justice? The Story of the Martensville Daycare Trials*. Toronto, Ont.: Dundrun Press, 2004.

Henton, Darcy, and Greg Owens. *No Kill, No Thrill*. Calgary, Alta.: Red Deer Press, 2001.

Hickey, Eric W. *Serial Murderers and Their Victims*. 2d ed. Albany, N.Y.: Wadsworth, 1997.

Holmes, Robert M., and Stephen T. Holmes, eds. *Contemporary Perspectives on Serial Murder*. Thousand Oaks, Calif.: Sage, 1998.

Jaeger, R. W., and M. W. Balousek. *Massacre in Milwaukee: The Macabre Case of Jeffrey Dahmer*. Oregon, Wis.: Waubesa Press, 1991.

Jenkins, Philip. *Pedophiles and Priests: Anatomy of a Contemporary Crisis*. New York: Oxford University Press, 1996.

Linedecker, Clifford L. *The Man Who Killed Boys: The John Wayne Gacy, Jr., Story*. New York: St. Martin's Press, 1993.

Martingale, Moira. *Cannibal Killers*. New York: Carroll & Graf, 1994.

Masters, B. *The Shrine of Jeffrey Dahmer*. London: Hodder and Stoughton, 1993.

Mendenhall, Harlan H. *Fall of the House of Gacy*. West Frankfort, Ill.: New Authors, 1998.

Nathan, D., and M. R. Snedeker. *Satan's Silence: Ritual Abuse and the Making of a Modern American Witch Hunt*. New York: Basic Books, 2001.

Olsen, Gregg. *If Loving You Is Wrong: The Shocking True Story of Mary Kay Letourneau*. New York: St. Martin's Press, 1999.

Philipps, John. *The Marquis de Sade: A Very Short Introduction*. New York: Oxford University Press, 2005.

Plante, Thomas G., ed. *Sin Against the Innocents: Sexual Abuse by Priests and the Role of the Catholic Church*. Westport, Conn.: Praeger, 2004.

Pron, Nick. *Lethal Marriage: The Unspeakable Crimes of Paul Bernardo and Karla Homolka*. New York: Seal, 1995.

Schechter, Harold. *The Serial Killer Files*. New York: Ballantine Books, 2003.

Shupe, Anson. *In the Name of All That's Holy: A Theory of Clergy Malfeasance*. Westport, Conn.: Praeger, 1995.

Sullivan, Terry, and Peter T. Maiken. *Killer Clown: The John Wayne Gacy Murders*. New York: Kensington, 2000.

Washburn, C. *Come into My Parlor: A Biography of the Aristocratic Everleigh Sisters of Chicago*. New York: Arno Press, 1974.

Wertham, Frederic. *The Show of Violence*. New York: Doubleday, 1949.

Williams, Stephen. *Invisible Darkness*. Toronto, Ont.: Bantam, 1996.

TERRORISTS

Aust, Stefan. *The Baader-Meinhof Group: The Inside Story of a Phenomenon*. London: Butler and Tanner, 1985.

Becker, Jililan. *Hitler's Children: The Story of the Baader-Meinhof Terrorist Gang*. New York: J. B. Lippincott, 1977.

Bennett, David H. *Party of Fear: From Nativist Movements to the New Right in American History*. New York: Vintage, 2001.

Bergen, Peter L. *Holy War, Inc.: Inside the Secret World of Osama bin Laden*. New York: Free Press, 2001.

Brisard, Jean-Charles, and Damien Martinez. *Zarqawi: The New Face of al-Qaeda*. New York: Other Press, 2005.

Burke, Jason. *Al Qaeda: The Real Story*. London: Penguin Books, 2004.

Calame, Russell, and Bernie Rhodes. *D. B. Cooper: The Real McCoy*. Salt Lake City: University of Utah Press, 1991.

Chase, Alton. *Harvard and the Unabomber: The Education of an American Terrorist*. New York: W. W. Norton, 2003.

Clarke, Richard. *Defeating the Jihadists: A Blueprint for Action*. New York: Foundation Press, 2004.

Comerford, R. V. *Fenians in Context: Irish Politics and Society, 1848-1882*. Dublin, Ireland: Wolfhound Press, 1985.

Corbin, Jane. *Al-Qaeda: In Search of the Terror Network That Threatens the World*. New York: Thunder's Mouth Press/Nation Books, 2002.

Daly, Sara A. *Aum Shinrikyo, al Qaeda, and the Kinshasa Reactor: Implications of Three Case Studies for Combating Nuclear Terrorism.* Santa Monica, Calif.: RAND, 2005.

Dennis, Anthony. *Osama Bin Laden: A Psychological and Political Portrait.* Lima, Ohio: Wyndham Press, 2002.

Dyer, Joel. *Harvest of Rage: Why Oklahoma City Is Only the Beginning.* Boulder, Colo.: Westview Press, 1998.

Farrell, William Regis. *Blood and Rage: The Story of the Japanese Red Army.* Lexington, Mass.: Lexington Books, 1990.

Follain, John. *Jackal: Finally, the Complete Story of the Legendary Terrorist Carlos the Jackal.* New York: Arcade, 1998.

Freeh, Louis J., with Howard Means. *My FBI: Bringing Down the Mafia, Investigating Bill Clinton, and Fighting the War on Terror.* New York: St. Martin's Press, 2005.

Gallagher, Aileen. *The Japanese Red Army.* New York: Rosen, 2003.

Gelernter, David. *Drawing Life: Surviving the Unabomber.* New York: Free Press, 1997.

Gerges, Fawaz A. *The Far Enemy: Why Jihad Went Global.* Cambridge, England: Cambridge University Press, 2005.

Giles, Steve, and Maike Oergel. *Counter-Cultures in Germany and Central Europe: From Sturm und Drang to Baader-Meinhof.* New York: Peter Lang, 2004.

Graysmith, Robert. *Unabomber: A Desire to Kill.* New York: Regnery, 1997.

Himmelsbach, Ralph P., and Thomas K. Worcester. *Norjak: The Investigation of D. B. Cooper.* West Linn, Oreg.: Norjak Project, 1986.

Jones, Stephen, and Peter Israel. *Others Unknown: Timothy McVeigh and the Oklahoma City Bombing Conspiracy.* New York: PublicAffairs, 2001.

Juergensmeyer, Mark. *Terror in the Mind of God: The Global Rise of Religious Violence.* Berkeley: University of California Press, 2000.

Kaczynski, Theodore. *The Unabomber Manifesto: Industrial Society and Its Future.* New York: Jolly Roger Press, 1995.

Katz, Samuel M. *Relentless Pursuit: The DSS and Their Manhunt for the al-Qaeda Terrorists.* New York: Forge, 2002.

Katzenstein, Peter J. *Defending the Japanese State: Structures, Norms, and the Political Responses to Terrorism and Violent Social Protest in the 1970's and 1980's.* Ithaca, N.Y.: Cornell University Press, 1991.

Kee, Robert. *The Green Flag: A History of Irish Nationalism.* London: Penguin Books, 2000.

Lance, Peter. *One Thousand Years for Revenge.* New York: Regan Books, 2003.

Landau, Elaine. *Osama bin Laden: A War Against the West.* Brookfield, Conn.: Twenty-First Century Books, 2002.

Lifton, Robert Jay. *Destroying the World to Save It: Aum Shinrikyo, Apocalyptic Violence, and the New Global Terrorism.* New York: Henry Holt, 1999.

McDermott, Terry. *Perfect Soldiers: The Hijackers—Who They Were, Why They Did It.* New York: HarperCollins, 2005.

Melman, Yossi. *The Master Terrorist: The True Story of Abu-Nidal.* New York: Adama Books, 1986.

Michel, Lou, and Dan Herbeck. *American Terrorist: Timothy McVeigh and the Oklahoma City Bombing.* New York: Regan Books, 2001.

Moussaoui, Abd Samad, and Florence Bouquillat. *Zacarias Moussaoui.* New York: Seven Stories Press, 2003.

Murakami, Haruki. *Underground: The Tokyo Gas Attack and the Japanese Psyche.* New York: Vintage International, 2001.

Mylroie, Laurie. *Study of Revenge.* Washington, D.C.: AEI Press, 2001.

Napoleoni, Loretta. *Insurgent Iraq: Al Zarqawi and the New Generation.* London: Constable and Robinson, 2005.

National Commission on Terrorist Attacks upon the United States. *The 9/11 Commission Report: Final Report of the National Commission on Terrorist Attacks upon the United States.* New York: W. W. Norton, 2004.

O'Broin, Leon. *Revolutionary Underground: The Story of the Irish Republican Brotherhood, 1858-1924.* Totowa, N.J.: Rowman and Littlefield, 1976.

Outman, James L. *Terrorism: Biographies.* Detroit: UXL, 2003.

Padilla, Lana, and Ron Delpit. *My Blood Betrayed: My Life with Terry Nichols and Timothy McVeigh.* New York: HarperCollins, 1995.

Reader, Ian. *Religious Violence in Contemporary Japan: The Case of Aum Shinrikyo.* Honolulu: University of Hawaii Press, 2000.

Reeve, Simon. *The New Jackals.* Boston: Northeastern University Press, 1999.

Robinson, Adam. *Bin Laden: Behind the Mask of the Terrorist.* New York: Arcade, 2001.

Scheuer, Michael. *Through Our Enemies' Eyes: Osama*

bin Laden, Radical Islam, and the Future of America. Washington, D.C.: Brassey's, 2002.

Schuster, Henry, with Charles Stone. *Hunting Eric Rudolph*. New York: Berkley Books, 2005.

Seale, Patrick. *Abu Nidal: A Gun for Hire*. New York: Random House, 1992.

Simons, Chaim. *Did or Did Not Dr. Baruch Goldstein Massacre Twenty-Nine Arabs?* Kiryat Arba, Israel: Chaim Simons, 2003.

Tosaw, Richard T. *D. B. Cooper: Dead or Alive?* Ceres, Calif.: Torsaw, 1984.

Townshend, Charles. *Political Violence in Ireland: Government and Resistance Since 1848*. Oxford, England: Clarendon Press, 1983.

Tu, Anthony T. *Chemical Terrorism: Horrors in the Tokyo Subway and Matsumoto City*. Fort Collins, Colo.: Alaken, 2002.

Varon, Jeremy. *Bringing the War Home: The Weather Underground, the Red Army Faction, and Revolutionary Violence in the Sixties and Seventies*. Berkeley: University of California Press, 2004.

Walls, Kathleen. *Man Hunt: The Eric Rudolph Story*. Saint Augustine, Fla.: Global Authors, 2003.

Waugh, Billy, and Tim Keown. *Hunting the Jackal: A Special Forces and CIA Ground Soldier's Fifty-Year Career Hunting America's Enemies*. New York: William Morrow, 2004.

Yallop, David. *Tracking the Jackal: The Search for the World's Most Wanted Man*. New York: Random House, 1993.

Zayyat, Montasser al-. *The Road to Al-Qaeda: The Story of Bin Laden's Right-Hand Man*. Sterling, Va.: Pluto Press, 2004.

THIEVES AND BANK ROBBERS

Ainsworth, William Harrison. *Jack Sheppard: A Romance*. London: Richard Bentley, 1839.

Beattie, J. M. *Policing and Punishment in London, 1660-1750: Urban Crime and the Limits of Terror*. New York: Oxford University Press, 2001.

Charrière, Henri. *Banco: The Further Adventures of Papillon*. New York: Morrow, 1973.

_____. *Papillon*. Translated by June P. Wilson and Walter B. Michaels. 1970. Reprint. New York: HarperCollins, 2001.

Defoe, Daniel. *The Life and Actions of Lewis Dominique Cartouch: Who Was Broke Alive upon the Wheel at Paris, Nov. 28, 1721*. London: Printed for J. Roberts, in Warwick-Lane, 1722.

Devi, Phoolan, with Marie-Thérèse Cuny and Paul Rambali. *The Bandit Queen of India: An Indian Woman's Amazing Journey from Peasant to International Legend*. Guilford, Conn.: Lyons Press, 2003.

Edwards, Samuel. *The Vidocq Dossier: The Story of the World's First Detective*. Boston: Houghton Mifflin, 1977.

Fielding, Henry. *Jonathan Wild the Great*. Edited by Peter Ackroyd. London: Hesperus Press, 2004.

Gibson, John S. *Deacon Brodie: Father to Jekyll and Hyde*. Edinburgh, Scotland: Paul Harris, 1977.

Hibbert, Christopher. *The Road to Tyburn: The Story of Jack Sheppard and the Eighteenth Century Underworld*. New York: Longmans, Green, 1957.

Johnson, J. A., Jr. *Thief: The Bizarre Story of Fugitive Financier Martin Frankel*. New York: Lebhar-Friedman Books, 2000.

McNally, Raymond T., and Radu R. Florescu. *In Search of Dr. Jekyll and Mr. Hyde*. Los Angeles: Renaissance Books, 2000.

Mell, Ezra Brett. *The Truth About the Bonnot Gang*. London: Coptic Press, 1968.

Morton, James. *The First Detective: The Life and Revolutionary Times of Eugène Vidocq, Criminal, Spy, and Private Eye*. London: Ebury Press, 2005.

Parry, Richard. *The Bonnot Gang: The Story of the French Illegalists*. London: Rebel Press, 1987.

Raghuram, Sunaad. *Veerappan: The Untold Story*. New York: Viking Books, 2001.

Reynolds, Quentin. *I, Willie Sutton*. 1953. Reprint. New York: Da Capo Press, 1993.

Schofield, Carey. *Mesrine: The Life and Death of a Supercrook*. New York: Penguin Books, 1980.

Serge, Victor. *Memoirs of a Revolutionary*. Translated by Peter Sedgwick. Iowa City: University of Iowa Press, 2002.

Sharma, Ravi. "The End of Veerappan." *Frontline* 21, no. 23 (November 6, 2004).

Sutton, Willie, with Edward Linn. *Where the Money Was*. New York: Broadway Books, 2004.

Swierczynski, Duane. *This Here's a Stick-Up: The Big Bad Book of American Bank Robbers*. New York: Alpha, 2002.

Varias, Alexander. *Paris and the Anarchists: Aesthetes and Subversives During the Fin-de-Siècle*. New York: St. Martin's Press, 1996.

Vidocq, Eugène François. *Memoirs of Vidocq: Master of Crime*. 1935. Reprint. Oakland, Calif.: AK Press, 2003.

TRAITORS AND SPIES

Alden, J. R. *General Charles Lee: Traitor or Patriot?* Baton Rouge: Louisiana State University Press, 1951.

Alexander, Martin S. *The Republic in Danger: General Maurice Gamelin and the Politics of French Defense, 1931-1940.* New York: Cambridge University Press, 2002.

Anders, Wladyslaw. *Russian Volunteers in Hitler's Army.* Bayside, N.Y.: Axis Europa, 1998.

Andrew, Christopher, and Vasili Mitrokhin. *The Mitrokhin Archive: The KGB in Europe and the West.* London: Gardners Books, 2000.

Andreyev, Catherine. *Vlasov and the Russian Liberation Movement.* Cambridge, England: Cambridge University Press, 1987.

Barth, Else M. *A Nazi Interior: Quisling's Hidden Philosophy.* New York: Peter Lang, 2004.

Ben-Yehuda, Nachman. *Betrayals and Treason.* Boulder, Colo.: Westview Press, 2001.

Bentley, Toni. *Sisters of Salome.* New Haven, Conn.: Yale University Press, 2002.

Black, J. B. *The Reign of Elizabeth.* 2d ed. New York: Oxford University Press, 1994.

Blitzer, Wolf. *Territory of Lies.* New York: Harper and Roe, 1989.

Boravik, Genrikh, and Phillip Knightley, eds. *The Philby Files: The Secret Life of Master Spy Kim Philby.* New York: Little, Brown, 1994.

Boyle, Andrew. *The Climate of Treason.* London: Hutchinson, 1979.

_____. *The Fourth Man: The Definitive Account of Kim Philby, Guy Burgess, and Donald Maclean and the Man Who Recruited Them to Spy for Russia.* New York: Dial Press, 1979.

Brandt, Clare. *The Man in the Mirror: A Life of Benedict Arnold.* New York: Random House, 1994.

Burrin, Philippe. *France Under the Germans: Collaboration and Compromise.* New York: New Press, 1998.

Cairncross, John. *The Enigma Spy.* London: Century, 1997.

Caravantes, Peggy. *Petticoat Spies: Six Women Spies of the Civil War.* Greensboro, N.C.: Morgan Reynolds, 2002.

Carter, Miranda. *Anthony Blunt: His Lives.* London: Pan, 2001.

Cecil, Robert. *A Divided Life: A Personal Portrait of the Spy Donald Maclean.* New York: Morrow, 1989.

Chambers, Whittaker. *Witness.* New York: Random House, 1952.

Cherkashin, Victor. *Spy Handler: Memoir of a KGB Officer.* New York: Basic Books, 2005.

Cole, J. A. *Lord Haw Haw and William Joyce: The Full Story.* New York: Farrar, Strauss, and Giroux, 1964.

Coulson, Thomas. *Mata Hari: Courtesan and Spy.* 1930. Reprint. Whitefish, Mont.: Kessinger, 2004.

Dahl, Hans Fredrik. *Quisling: A Study in Treachery.* New York: Cambridge University Press, 1999.

Davis, J. C. *Cromwell.* London: Arnold, 2001.

Deacon, Richard. *Kempei Tai: The Japanese Secret Service, Then and Now.* Tokyo: Tuttle, 1990.

Doherty, M. A. *Nazi Wireless Propaganda: Lord Haw-Haw and British Public Opinion in the Second World War.* Edinburgh: Edinburgh University Press, 2000.

Earley, Pete. *Confession of a Spy: The Real Story of Aldrich Ames.* New York: Putnam, 1997.

Edwards, John Carver. *Berlin Calling: American Broadcasters in Service to the Third Reich.* New York: Praeger, 1991.

Eggleston, Larry. *Women in the Civil War.* Jefferson, N.C.: McFarland & Company, 2003.

Feklisov, Alexander, Sergei Kostin, and Ronald Radosh. *The Man Behind the Rosenbergs.* New York: Enigma Books, 2004.

Feldman, Louis H. *Josephus's Interpretation of the Bible.* Berkeley: University of California Press, 1998.

Fleming, Thomas. *Duel: Alexander Hamilton, Aaron Burr, and the Future of America.* New York: Basic Books, 1999.

Flexner, James Thomas. *The Traitor and the Spy: Benedict Arnold and John André.* 1975. Reprint. Syracuse, N.Y.: Syracuse University Press, 1991.

French, Allen. *General Gage's Informers.* 1932. Reprint. Westport, Conn.: Greenwood Press, 1968.

Fuller, M. Williams. *Axis Sally: The Most Listened-To Woman of World War II.* Santa Barbara, Calif.: Paradise West, 2004.

Gannon, James. *Stealing Secrets, Telling Lies.* Washington, D.C.: Brassey's, 2001.

Green, Dominic. *The Double Life of Doctor Lopez.* London: Century, 2003.

Green, Thomas Marshall. *The Spanish Conspiracy.* 1891. Reprint. Gloucester, Mass.: P. Smith, 1967.

Hadas-Lebel, Mireille. *Flavius Josephus: Eyewitness to Rome's First Century Conquest of Judea.* New York: Macmillan, 1993.

Hall, J. W., ed. *The Trial of William Joyce.* London: W. Hodge, 1946.

Hamrick, S. J. *Deceiving the Deceivers: Kim Philby,*

Donald Maclean, and Guy Burgess. New Haven, Conn.: Yale University Press, 2004.

Havill, Adrian. *The Spy Who Stayed out in the Cold.* New York: St. Martin's Press, 2001.

Henderson, Bernard. *Pollard: The Spy's Story.* New York: Alpha Books, 1988.

Hiss, Alger. *In the Court of Public Opinion.* New York: Alfred A. Knopf, 1957.

Høidal, Oddvar K. *Quisling: A Study in Treason.* Oslo: Norwegian University Press, 1989.

Howe, Russell Warren. *Mata Hari: The True Story.* New York: Dodd, Mead, 1986.

Jackson, Julian. *France: The Dark Years, 1940-1944.* New York: Oxford University Press, 2003.

Joyce, William. *Twilight Over England.* Berlin: Internationaler Verlag, 1940.

Kennedy-Nolle, Sharon. Introduction to *Belle Boyd in Camp and Prison.* Baton Rouge: Louisiana State University Press, 1998.

Knightley, Phillip. *Philby: K.G.B. Masterspy.* London: Andre Deutsch, 1988.

Leonard, Elizabeth D. *All the Daring of the Soldier: Women of the Civil War Armies.* New York: W. W. Norton, 1999.

Levin, Carole. *The Reign of Elizabeth I.* New York: Palgrave, 2002.

Lewis, David Stephen. *Illusions of Grandeur.* Manchester, England: Manchester University Press, 1987.

Lindsey, Robert. *The Falcon and the Snowman: A True Story of Friendship and Espionage.* New York: Simon & Schuster, 1979.

_____. *The Flight of the Falcon.* New York: Simon & Schuster, 1983.

Lomask, Milton. *Aaron Burr.* 2 vols. New York: Farrar, Straus and Giroux, 1979, 1982.

Lottman, Herbert R. *Pétain: Hero or Traitor? The Untold Story.* New York: Morrow, 1985.

Markle, Donald E. *Spies and Spymasters of the Civil War.* New York: Hippocrene Books, 2004.

Martin, James Kirby. *Benedict Arnold, Revolutionary Hero: An American Warrior Reconsidered.* New York: New York University Press, 2000.

Martland, Peter. *Lord Haw Haw: The English Voice of Nazi Germany.* London: National Archives, 2003.

Mason, Steve, ed. *Understanding Josephus: Seven Perspectives.* Sheffield, England: Sheffield Academic Press, 1998.

Meeropol, Robert. *An Execution in the Family: One Son's Journey.* Gordonsville, Va.: St. Martin's Press, 2003.

Melton, Buckner F. *Aaron Burr: Conspiracy to Treason.* New York: John Wiley & Sons, 2002.

Melton, George E. *Darlan.* Westport, Conn.: Praeger, 1998.

Modin, Yuri, et al. *My Five Cambridge Friends: Blunt, MacLean, Philby, Burgess, and Cairncross, by Their KGB Controller.* New York: Farrar, Strauss and Giroux, 1994.

Montgomery, M. R. *Jefferson and the Gun-Men: How the West Was Almost Lost.* New York: Crown, 2000.

Mosley, Sir Oswald. *My Life.* London: Nelson, 1968.

Moss, Norman. *Klaus Fuchs: The Man Who Stole the Atom Bomb.* New York: St. Martin's Press, 1987.

Newton, Vern W. *The Cambridge Spies: The Untold Story of Maclean, Philby, and Burgess in America.* Lanham, Md.: Madison Books, 1991.

Nizer, Louis. *The Implosion Conspiracy.* Garden City, N.Y.: Doubleday, 1973.

Ostrovsky, Erika. *Eye of Dawn: The Rise and Fall of Mata Hari.* New York: Macmillan, 1978.

Owen, David. *Hidden Secrets: A Complete History of Espionage and the Technology Used to Support It.* Toronto, Ont.: Firefly Books, 2002.

Patterson, S. M. *Knight Errant of Liberty; The Triumph and Tragedy of General Charles Lee.* New York: Lantern Press, 1958.

Pfau, Ann Elizabeth. *Miss Yourlovin: Women in the Culture of American World War II Soldiers.* Rutgers, N.J.: Rutgers University Press, 2001.

Philby, Kim. *My Silent War.* New York: Grove Press, 1968.

Philby, Rufina, et al. *The Private Life of Kim Philby.* London: Warner, 2000.

Plutarch. *The Rise and Fall of Athens.* Translated by Ian Scott-Kilvert. London: Penguin Books, 1960.

Pomeroy, Sarah B., ed. *Women's History and Ancient History.* Chapel Hill: University of North Carolina Press, 1991.

Radosh, Ronald, and Joyce Milton. *The Rosenberg File: A Search for the Truth.* New York: Holt, Rinehart & Winston, 1983.

Rajak, Tessa. *Josephus.* Rev. ed. London: Duckworth, 2002.

Richelson, Jeffrey T. *The U.S. Intelligence Community.* Boulder, Colo.: Westview Press, 1999.

Rousso, Henri. *The Vichy Syndrome: History and Memory in France Since 1944.* Cambridge, Mass.: Harvard University Press, 2004.

Sale, Richard T. *Traitors: The Worst Acts of Treason in*

American History, from Benedict Arnold to Robert Hanssen. New York: Berkley, 2003.

Sallust. *The Jugurthine War: The Conspiracy of Catiline*. Translated by S. A. Handford. New York: Penguin Books, 1963.

Schiller, Lawrence. *Into the Mirror: The Life of Master Spy Robert P. Hanssen*. New York: HarperCollins, 2002.

Shaw, Mark. *Miscarriage of Justice: The Jonathan Pollard Story*. St. Paul, Minn.: Paragon House, 2001.

Shreve, Royal Ornan. *The Finished Scoundrel: General James Wilkinson, Sometime Commander-in-Chief of the Army of the United States, Who Made Intrigue a Trade and Treason a Profession*. Indianapolis: Bobbs-Merrill, 1933.

Sigaud, Louis A. *Belle Boyd: Confederate Spy*. Richmond, Va.: Dietz Press, 1944.

Skidelsky, Robert. *Oswald Mosley*. London: Macmillan, 1990.

Soley, Lawrence C. *Radio Warfare: OSS and CIA Subversive Propaganda*. New York: Praeger, 1989.

Stafford, David, and Rhodri Jeffreys-Jones. *American-British-Canadian Intelligence Relationships, 1939-2000*. London: Routledge, 2000.

Straight, Michael. *After Long Silence*. London: Collins, 1983.

Strik-Strikfeldt, Wilfried. *Against Stalin and Hitler: A Memoir of the Russian Liberation Movement, 1941-1945*. New York: Macmillan, 1970.

Swan, Patrick, ed. *Alger Hiss, Whittaker Chambers, and the Schism in the American Soul*. Wilmington, Del.: ISI Books, 2003.

Tanenhaus, Sam. *Whittaker Chambers: A Biography*. New York: Random House, 1997.

Thayer, T. *The Making of a Scapegoat: Washington and Lee at Monmouth*. Port Washington, N.Y.: Kennikat Press, 1976.

Vidal, Gore. *Burr*. New York: Random House, 1973.

Vise, David A. *The Bureau and the Mole: The Unmasking of Robert Philip Hanssen, the Most Dangerous Double Agent in FBI History*. New York: Atlantic Monthly Press, 2002.

Volkman, Ernest. *Espionage*. New York: J. Wiley and Sons, 1995.

Walker, Jeffrey B. *Devil Undone: The Life and Poetry of Benjamin Church, 1734-1778*. New York: Arno Press, 1982.

Weinstein, Allen. *Perjury: The Hiss-Chambers Case*. 2d ed. New York: Random House, 1997.

West, Nigel. *The Illegals: Double Lives of the Cold War's Most Secret Agents*. London: Hodder & Stoughton, 1994.

West, Rebecca. *The Meaning of Treason*. London: Macmillan, 1949.

Wheelan, Joseph. *Jefferson's Vendetta: The Pursuit of Aaron Burr and the Judiciary*. New York: Carroll & Graf, 2005.

Wheelwright, Julie. *The Fatal Lover: Mata Hari and the Myth of Women in Espionage*. West Sussex, England: Collins & Brown, 1992.

White, G. Edward. *Alger Hiss's Looking-Glass Wars: The Covert Life of a Soviet Spy*. New York: Oxford University Press, 2004.

Williams, Robert Chadwell. *Klaus Fuchs, Atom Spy*. Cambridge, Mass.: Harvard University Press, 1987.

Williamson, G. A. *The World of Josephus*. London: Secker and Warburg, 1964.

Wise, David. *Spy: The Inside Story of How the FBI's Robert Hanssen Betrayed America*. New York: Random House, 2002.

WAR CRIMINALS

Annussek, G. *Hitler's Raid to Save Mussolini*. New York: Da Capo Press, 2005.

Barnett, Correlli, ed. *Hitler's Generals*. New York: Grove Press, 2003.

Belknap, Michal R. *The Vietnam War on Trial: The My Lai Massacre and the Court Martial of Lieutenant William Calley*. Lawrence: University Press of Kansas, 2002.

Berenbaum, Michael. *The World Must Know: The History of the Holocaust as Told in the United States Holocaust Memorial Museum*. Boston: Little, Brown, 1993.

Bilton, Michael, and Kevin Sim. *Four Hours in My Lai*. New York: Penguin Books, 1993.

Bloch, Michael. *Ribbentrop*. London: Abacus, 2003.

Bormann, Martin. *The Bormann Letters*. New York: AMS Press, 1981.

Botwinick, Rita Steinhardt. *A History of the Holocaust: From Ideology to Annihilation*. Upper Saddle River, N.J.: Pearson Prentice Hall, 2004.

Braun, Eva. *The Diary of Eva Braun*. 1949. Reprint. Bristol, England: Spectrum International, 2000.

Breitman, Richard. *The Architect of Genocide: Himmler and the Final Solution*. New York: Alfred A. Knopf, 1991.

Butler, Rupert. *An Illustrated History of the Gestapo*. Osceola, Wis.: Motorbooks International, 1992.

Collett, Nigel. *The Butcher of Amritsar: General Reginald Dyer*. London: Hambledon & London, 2005.

Colvin, Ian Duncan. *The Life of General Dyer*. Edinburgh, Scotland: W. Blackwood & Sons, 1929.

Davidson, Eugene. *The Unmaking of Adolf Hitler*. Columbia: University of Missouri Press, 1996.

Dönitz, Karl. *Ten Years and Twenty Days*. Translated by R. H. Stevens. Annapolis, Md.: Naval Institute Press, 1990.

Edwards, Bernard. *Dönitz and the Wolf-Packs: U-Boats at War*. London: Brockhampton Press, 1999.

Evans, Richard J. *The Third Reich in Power*. New York: Penguin, 2005.

Fein, Helen. *Imperial Crime and Punishment: The Massacre at Jallianwala Bagh and British Judgment, 1919-1920*. Honolulu: University Press of Hawaii, 1977.

Giblin, James Cross. *The Life and Death of Adolf Hitler*. New York: Clarion, 2002.

Gilbert, G. M. *Nuremberg Diary*. New York: Da Capo Press, 1995.

Goldhagen, Daniel Jonah. *Hitler's Willing Executioners: Ordinary Germans and the Holocaust*. New York: Vintage Books, 1997.

Gun, Nerin E. *Eva Braun: Hitler's Mistress*. New York: Meredith Press, 1968.

Gutman, Roy. *Crimes of War*. W. W. Norton, 1999.

Harris, Whitney R. *Tyranny on Trial: The Trial of the Major German War Criminals*. Dallas: Southern Methodist University Press, 1999.

Hesseltine, William Best. *Civil War Prisons: A Study in War Psychology*. Columbus: University of Ohio Press, 1930.

Honig, Jan Willem. *Srebrenica: Record of a War Crime*. New York: Penguin Books, 1997.

Kater, Michael. *The Nazi Party: A Social Profile of Members and Leaders, 1919-1945*. Cambridge, Mass.: Harvard University Press, 1983.

Kilzer, Louis. *Hitler's Traitor*. Novato, Calif.: Presidio, 2000.

Knopp, Guido. *Hitler's Henchmen*. Translated by Angus McGeoch. Stroud, England: Sutton, 2000.

Lange, Jochen von. *The Secretary*. New York: Random House, 1979.

Lemmons, Russel. *Goebbels and Der Angriff*. Lexington: University Press of Kentucky, 1994.

Manvell, Roger, and Heinrich Fraenkel. *Hess: A Biography*. New York: Drake, 1973.

Marvel, William. *Andersonville: The Last Depot*. Chapel Hill: University of North Carolina Press, 1994.

Olson, James S., and Randy Roberts. *My Lai: A Brief History with Documents*. New York: Bedford/St. Martin's Press, 1998.

Overy, Richard. *Interrogations: The Nazi Elite in Allied Hands, 1945*. New York: Penguin Books, 2002.

Padfield, Peter. *Dönitz, the Last Führer: Portrait of a Nazi War Leader*. New York: Harper and Row, 1984.

_____. *Himmler, Reichsführer*. London: Macmillan, 1991.

Perisco, Joseph E. *Nuremberg: Infamy on Trial*. New York: Penguin, 1995.

Reed, Anthony. *The Devil's Disciples: Hitler's Inner Circle*. New York: W. W. Norton, 2003.

Rees, Laurence. *Horror in the East: Japan and the Atrocities of World War II*. Cambridge, Mass.: Da Capo Press, 2002.

Reuth, Ralf Georg. *Goebbels*. Translated by Krishna Winston. New York: Harcourt Brace, 1993.

Ribbentrop, Joachim von. *Documents on the Events Preceding the Outbreak of the War*. Honolulu: University Press of the Pacific, 2004.

Rosenbaum, Ron. *Explaining Hitler: The Search for the Origins of His Evil*. New York: Random House, 1998.

Schmittroth, Linda, and Mary Kay Rosteck. *People of the Holocaust*. Detroit: UXL, 1998.

Skorzeny, Otto. *My Commando Operations: The Memoirs of Hitler's Most Daring Commando*. Translated by David Johnson. Reprint. Atglen, Pa.: Schiffer, 1995.

_____. *Skorzeny's Special Missions*. New York: Greenhill Books, 1997.

Smelser, Ronald, and Rainer Zitelmann. *The Nazi Elite*. Translated by Mary Fischer. New York: New York University Press, 1993.

Smith, Bradley F. *Heinrich Himmler: A Nazi in the Making, 1900-1926*. Palo Alto, Calif.: Hoover Institution Press, 1971.

Snyder, Louis L. *Hitler's Elite: Shocking Profiles of the Reich's Most Notorious Henchmen*. New York: Berkley Books, 1989.

Tanaka, Yuki. *Hidden Horrors: Japanese War Crimes in World War II*. Boulder, Colo.: Westview Press, 1996.

Thomas, W. Hugh. *The Murder of Adolph Hitler: The Truth About the Bodies in the Berlin Bunker*. New York: St. Martin's Press, 1996.

Vizulis, Izidors. *The Molotov-Ribbentrop Pact of 1939*. New York: Praeger, 1990.

Waller, John H. *The Devil's Doctor: Felix Kersten and the Secret Plot to Turn Himmler Against Hitler*. New York: John Wiley and Sons, 2002.

Warlimont, Walter. *Inside Hitler's Headquarters*. New York: Presidio Press, 1991.

Weitz, John. *Hitler's Diplomat: Joachim von Ribbentrop*. London: Weidenfeld and Nicolson, 1992.

WHITE-COLLAR CRIMINALS

Ackerman, Kenneth D. *The Gold Ring: Jim Fisk, Jay Gould, and Black Friday, 1869*. New York: Dodd & Mead, 1988.

Ambrose, Stephen E. *Nothing Like It in the World: The Men Who Built the Transcontinental Railroad, 1863-1869*. New York: Simon & Schuster, 2000.

Ames, Charles Edgar. *Pioneering the Union Pacific: A Reappraisal of the Builders of the Railroad*. New York: Appleton-Century-Crofts, 1969.

Bain, David Haward. *Empire Express: Building the First Transcontinental Railroad*. New York: Viking, 1999.

Braithwaite, John, and Peter Drakes. *Global Business Regulation*. Cambridge, England: Cambridge University Press, 2000.

Davia, Howard R. *Fraud 101: Techniques and Strategies for Detection*. New York: John Wiley, 2000.

Eichenwald, Kurt. *Conspiracy of Fools: A True Story*. New York: Random House, 2005.

Fallon, Ivan, and James Strodes. *Dream Maker: The Rise and Fall of John Z. DeLorean*. New York: G. P. Putnam's Sons, 1983.

Fishman, Ted. *China, Inc*. New York: Scribner, 2005.

Fogel, Robert William. *The Union Pacific Railroad: A Case in Premature Enterprise*. Baltimore: The Johns Hopkins University Press, 1960.

Gilbert, Helen. *Lyndon Larouche: Fascism Restyled for the New Millennium*. Seattle: Red Letter Press, 2003.

Gordon, John Steele. *The Scarlet Woman of Wall Street: Jay Gould, Jim Fisk, Cornelius Vanderbilt, the Erie Railway Wars, and the Birth of Wall Street*. New York: Weidenfeld & Nicolson, 1988.

Grodinsky, Julius. *Jay Gould: His Business Career, 1867-1892*. Philadelphia: University of Pennsylvania Press, 1957.

Haddad, William. *Hard Driving: My Years with John DeLorean*. New York: Random House, 1985.

Hunt, Luke, and Karen Heinrich. *Barings Lost: Nick Leeson and the Collapse of Barings*. London: Butterworth-Heinemann, 1996.

King, Dennis. *Lyndon Larouche and the New American Fascism*. New York: Doubleday, 1989.

Klein, Maury. *The Life and Legend of Jay Gould*. Baltimore: The Johns Hopkins University Press, 1986.

Leeson, Nick, with Ivan Tyrell. *Back from the Brink: Coping with Stress*. London: Virgin Books, 2005.

Leeson, Nick, with Edward Whitley. *Rogue Trader*. London: Little, Brown, 1996.

Levin, Hillel. *Grand Delusions: The Cosmic Career of John DeLorean*. New York: Viking Press, 1983.

Levitas, Daniel. *The Terrorist Next Door: The Militia Movement and the Radical Right*. New York: St. Martin's Press, 2002.

McLean, Bethany, and Peter Elkind. *The Smartest Guys in the Room: The Amazing Rise and Scandalous Fall of Enron*. New York: Portfolio, 2003.

Mizell, Louis R. *Masters of Deception: The Worldwide White-Collar Crime Crisis and Ways to Protect Yourself*. New York: J. Wiley & Sons, 1997.

Renehan, Edward. *Dark Genius of Wall Street: The Misunderstood Life of Jay Gould, King of the Robber Barons*. New York: Basic Books, 2005.

Shover, Neal, and John Paul Wright, eds. *Crimes of Privilege: Readings in White-Collar Crime*. New York: Oxford University Press, 2001.

Skeel, David. *Icarus in the Boardroom: The Fundamental Flaws in Corporate America and Where They Came From*. New York: Oxford University Press, 2005.

Swanberg, W. A. *Jim Fisk: The Career of an Improbable Rascal*. New York: Charles Scribner's Sons, 1959.

Wells, Joseph T. *Frankensteins of Fraud: The Twentieth Century's Top Ten White-Collar Criminals*. Austin, Tex.: Obsidian, 2000.

WITCHES AND OCCULTISTS

Asbury, Herbert. *The French Quarter: An Informal History of the New Orleans Underworld*. 1936. Reprint. New York: Capricorn Books, 1968.

Baddeley, Gavin. *Lucifer Rising: A Book of Sin, Devil Worship, and Rock and Roll*. Medford, N.J.: Plexus, 2006.

Barton, Blanche. *The Church of Satan*. New York: Hell's Kitchen Productions, 1990.

_____. *The Secret Life of a Satanist*. Los Angeles: Feral House, 1992.

Briggs, Robin. *Witches and Neighbors: The Social and Cultural Context of European Witchcraft*. New York: Penguin, 1998.

Cohn, Norman. *Europe's Inner Demons: An Inquiry Inspired by the Great Witch-Hunt*. New York: Basic Books, 1975.

Crowley, Aleister, John Symonds, and Kenneth Grant. *The Confessions of Aleister Crowley: An Autobiography*. New York: Penguin, 1989.

Curran, Bob. *A Bewitched Land*. Dublin: The O'Brien Press, 2005.

Davidson, L. Sharon, and John O. Ward. *The Sorcery Trial of Alice Kyteler: A Contemporary Account*. Binghamton, N.Y.: Center for Medieval and Early Renaissance Studies, 1993.

Davies, Owen. *Cunning-Folk: Popular Magic in English History*. New York: Hambledon, 2003.

Demos, John. *Entertaining Satan: Witchcraft and the Culture of Early New England*. New York: Oxford University Press, 2004.

Farrar, Janet, and Stewart Farrar. *A Witches' Bible: The Complete Witches' Handbook*. Custer, Wash.: Phoenix, 1984.

Gardner, Gerald Brosseau. *Witchcraft Today*. 1954. Reprint. London: Magickal Chile, 1991.

Gibson, Marion, ed. *Early Modern Witches: Witchcraft Cases in Contemporary Writing*. London: Routledge, 2000.

Guiley, Rosemary Ellen. *The Encyclopedia of Witches and Witchcraft*. 2d ed. New York: Checkmark Books, 1999.

Harris, J. Henry. *Cornish Saints and Sinners*. 1906. Reprint. Kila, Mont.: Kessinger, 2003.

Heselton, Philip. *Wiccan Roots: Gerald Gardner and the Modern Witchcraft Revival*. London: Capall Bann, 2000.

Hill, Francis. *The Salem Witch Trials Reader*. Cambridge, Mass.: Da Capo Press, 2000.

Hutton, Ronald. *The Triumph of the Moon*. New York: Oxford University Press, 2001.

Jones, Kelvin I. *The Wise Woman: Her Lives, Charms, Spells, and Cures*. Corpusty, Norwich, England: Oakmagic, 2000.

Karlsen, Carol F. *The Devil in the Shape of a Woman: Witchcraft in Colonial New England*. New York: W. W. Norton, 1998.

Kellet, Arnold. *Mother Shipton, Witch and Prophetess*. Maidstone, Kent, England: George Mann Books, 2002.

Kieckhefer, Richard. *Magic in the Middle Ages*. 2d ed. New York: Cambridge University Press, 2000.

Klaits, Joseph. *Servants of Satan: The Age of the Witch Hunts*. Bloomington: Indiana University Press, 1985.

LaVey, Anton Szandor. *Satan Speaks!* Los Angeles: Feral House, 1998.

_____. *The Satanic Bible*. New York: HarperCollins, 1976.

Martinez, Raymond. *Mysterious Marie Laveau: Voodoo Queen and Folk Tales Along the Mississippi*. Jefferson, La.: Hope, 1956.

Nettle, Daniel, and Suzanne Romaine. *Vanishing Voices: The Extinction of the World's Languages*. New York: Oxford University Press, 2000.

O'Brien, Lora. *Irish Witchcraft from an Irish Witch*. Franklin Lakes, N.J.: The Career Press, 2005.

O'Dowd, Mary. *A History of Women in Ireland: 1500-1800*. Harlow, England: Pearson, 2005.

Regardie, Israel. *The Eye in the Triangle: An Interpretation of Aleister Crowley*. Phoenix, Ariz.: Falcon Press, 1982.

Rhys, John. *Celtic Folklore: Welsh and Manx*. 2 vols. 1901. Reprint. London: Wildwood House, 1980.

Rowley, William, Thomas Dekker, and John Ford. *The Witch of Edmonton*. Edited by Peter Corbin and Douglas Sedge. Manchester, England: Manchester University Press, 1999.

Semmens, Jason. *Witch of the West*. Plymouth, England: Jason Semmens, 2005.

Seymour, John D. *Irish Witchcraft and Demonology*. 1913. Reprint. London: Portman Books, 1989.

Sutin, Lawrence. *Do What Thou Wilt*. New York: St. Martin's Press, 2000.

Trenhaile, John. *Dolly Pentreath, and Other Humorous Cornish Tales*. 1854. Reprint. Newcastle upon Tyne, England: F. Graham, 1968.

Valiente, Doreen. *Witchcraft for Tomorrow*. New York: St. Martin's Press, 1978.

Wright, Thomas, ed. *Alice Kyteler: A Contemporary Narrative of the Proceedings Against Dame Alice Kyteler, Prosecuted for Sorcery by Richard de Ledrede, Bishop of Ossory, 1324*. London: Camden Society, 1843.

ELECTRONIC RESOURCES

The Web sites listed below were visited by the editors of Salem Press in May, 2006. Because URLs frequently change or are moved, the accuracy of these sites cannot be guaranteed; however, long-standing sites, such as those of university departments, national organizations, and government agencies, generally maintain links when sites move or upgrade their offerings.

Accused of Witchcraft
http://www.rootsweb.com/~nwa/witch.html

This page from *Notable Women Ancestors* provides links to biographies about the women who were accused of witchcraft during the 1692 witchcraft trials in Salem, Massachusetts.

Adolf Hitler and the Holocaust
http://www.auschwitz.dk/Hitler.htm

A thorough investigation into the life of Adolf Hitler and his actions that led to the Holocaust. The site also profiles other prominent Nazi members, includes photos from Hitler's early life, and provides details about many of the Jewish death camps.

American Experience: The Nuremberg Trials
http://www.pbs.org/wgbh/amex/nuremberg/index.html

A companion Web site to a 2006 episode of the Public Broadcasting Service (PBS) series *American Experience*. Brings together profiles of the judges, defendants, and the prosecution of the International Military Tribunal at Nuremberg; photographs from the trials; and an interactive time line which encompasses the trials and the events of World War II that preceded them.

The Cold Warriors
http://www.cnn.com/SPECIALS/cold.war/kbank/

A companion Web site to the Central News Network (CNN) 1998 series *Cold War*, which examined five decades of international tensions and conflicts. The site features an interactive "profile" database in which users can select the names of notable Cold War figures such as Joseph Stalin, Richard Nixon, Joseph McCarthy, or Fidel Castro in order to get their biographies. Also includes the text of historical declassified documents, interactive maps, and a time line of the Cold War.

Crime Library: Criminal Minds and Methods
http://www.crimelibrary.com/index.html

The Court TV cable television channel created this virtual encyclopedia of information about notorious criminals. It features a collection of more than six hundred articles, which are divided into five sections: Serial Killers, featuring information about sexual predators and mass murderers; Gangsters and Outlaws, focusing on the activities of mob bosses and crooked cops; Terrorists, Spies, and Assassins; Notorious Murder Cases; and the Criminal Mind, with articles about criminal profiling, forensic investigation, and scams and hoaxes. Although the focus is on modern-day crimes, the site also contains an expanding collection of materials about historically notorious characters dating back to the fifteenth century.

Crime Magazine: An Encyclopedia of Crime
http://crimemagazine.com/index.html

A collection of articles about crime and criminality. The site is divided into several sections about specific types of crime, including True Crime, Organized Crime, Celebrity Crime, and Serial Killers. It also features reviews of crime books and films.

Dictators of the Twentieth Century
http://www.cbv.ns.ca/dictator/default.html

This simple but informative site was created by political science students at Glace Bay High School in Nova Scotia, Canada. It contains an index of eighteen twentieth century dictators which provides access to brief biographies and Web links for each dictator. Pol Pot, Adolf Hitler, Joseph Stalin, Fidel Castro, and Idi Amin are among the dictators included.

Famous Trials
http://www.law.umkc.edu/faculty/projects/ftrials/ftrials.htm

Created by a faculty member of the University of Missouri-Kansas City School of Law, this site features descriptions of famous trials throughout history, including those of Big Bill Haywood, Lizzie Borden, Alger Hiss, Ethel and Julius Rosenberg, Charles Manson, and O. J. Simpson. Each case profile offers biographies of trial participants, related time lines and historical context, and court transcripts.

FBI History: Famous Cases
http://www.fbi.gov/libref/historic/famcases/famcases.htm

The official Web site of the Federal Bureau of Investigation (FBI) contains a page that provides access to monographs about the bureau's investigations of some of America's most notorious criminals. The cases are divided into five categories: Bank Robbery, Historical Ten Most Wanted, Organized Crime and Gangsters, Violent Crime, and Espionage. Al Capone, Willie Sutton, Baby Face Nelson, John Dillinger, and Aldrich Ames are among the criminals described in the monographs.

Genocide Under the Nazis

http://www.bbc.co.uk/history/war/genocide/

A companion Web site to the British Broadcasting Corporation (BBC) 2005 television series *Auschwitz: The Nazis and the "Final Solution."* It features a time line of acts of Nazi genocide between 1933 and 1945 and an interactive map of the Auschwitz concentration camp. Among the site's many articles is a discussion of the thoughts and actions of Rudolf Hess, the commandant of the Auschwitz death camp; an analysis of the Nazi regime's policy toward Jews; and an explanation of why the Nazis hated certain groups of people and how this hatred led to genocide and mass murder.

Hunting Bin Laden

http://www.pbs.org/wgbh/pages/frontline/shows/binladen/

A companion Web site to an episode of *Frontline,* the Public Broadcasting Service (PBS) documentary news program. It examines the life, mind, and motives of Osama Bin Laden, the man behind the September 11, 2001, terrorist attacks and other terrorist acts. Features a biography of Bin Laden, a chronology of his life, a report on his family, and his statements and fatwas against the United States.

Joseph Stalin: Biographical Profile

http://www.stel.ru/stalin/

Presents biographical details of Joseph Stalin's life and political career in chronological order. Users select a date and are able to read about important events in Stalin's life during that year. The site also has photographs and video files of Stalin.

Kansas Gunfighters

http://www.vlib.us/old_west/guns.html

This Web site provides links to biographies of many Kansas outlaws; some include detailed family tree histories. Descriptions of several well-known shoot-outs can be found here, including the O.K. Corral gunfight.

MurderInc.com

http://www.murderinc.com/

The site states that it intends "to bring a clear understanding of the history of organized crime, mainly during the early part of the twentieth century." It features a family tree of members of the Murder Incorporated crime organization, which then links to individual biographies of some of the mobsters. The site also links to other Web sites about the mob and organized crime.

The Overland Trail: Links to Personalities of the West

http://www.over-land.com/westpers4.html

This Web site contains a page of links providing biographical information about outlaws and gunslingers of the American West, including Butch Cassidy and the Sundance Kid, Billy the Kid, Wyatt Earp, John Wesley Hardin, and members of James Younger Gang.

Partners Against Hate

http://www.partnersagainsthate.org/

This site provides information about and counteraction strategies against hate crimes. Includes a hate crime database, in which users can search hate crime statistics and laws by state, and educational resources for parents, teachers, and community members.

Pirates!

http://www.piratesinfo.com/main.php

Presents a history of piracy, descriptions of various types of piracy, and information about pirate ships and pirate life. It also includes a section with brief biographies of famous pirates, including Henry Morgan, Edward "Blackbeard" Teach, Anne Bonny, Bartholomew Roberts, William Kidd, and Mary Read.

Public Enemy #1: The Legendary Outlaw John Dillinger

http://www.pbs.org/wgbh/amex/dillinger/index.html

The site accompanies a 2001 episode of the Public Broadcasting Service (PBS) series *American Experience* about John Dillinger. Users can read a transcript of the program, view 1930's newsreel footage of Dillinger, and chart Dillinger's midwestern crime spree during the final year of his life. The site also contains information about, and photographs of, Depression-era gangsters, some of Dillinger's fan mail, a time line of Dillinger's life, and suggested books and Web sites for further information.

The Rick A. Ross Institute for the Study of Destructive Cults, Controversial Groups, and Movements

http://www.rickross.com/

The Rick A. Ross Institute is a New Jersey-based not-for-profit organization that has organized this database of materials about cults, hate groups, and other controversial movements. Users can access the group's extensive archive by using the Information Database, an alphabetical listing of cults and movements, which links to information about each organization. Among the cults included in the site are the Branch Davidians, the Jewish Defense League, and Heaven's Gate.

Southern Poverty Law Center

http://www.splcenter.org/index.jsp

Since its founding in 1971, the Montgomery, Alabama-based Southern Poverty Law Center has taken legal action against racism by white supremacists and other hate groups in the United States. The group also monitors the activities of American-based hate groups, publishing its findings in its magazine, *The Intelligence Report*. The center's Web site contains a virtual version of the magazine, featuring its news reports about neo-Nazis, the Ku Klux Klan, skinheads, and other hatemongers. In addition to the magazine, the site contains a map showing the location of various hate groups throughout the United States, as well as Hate Watch, a collection of news reports of recent incidents involving racist organizations and hate groups.

Terrorism Knowledge Base

http://www.tkb.org/Home.jsp

Described as a resource for "analysis on global terrorist incidents, terrorism-related court cases, and terrorist groups and leaders," the site gives detailed information into such groups as Germany's June 2nd Movement, the Abu Nidal Organization, the Aryan Nations, the Shining Path, and the World Islamic Jihad.

Time Magazine 100: The Most Important People of the Century

http://www.time.com/time/time100/index_2000_time100.html

While primarily a celebration of notable figures who made a positive impact during the twentieth century, *Time* magazine's Web site also provides links to thorough biographies of such notorious figures as Adolf Hitler, Mao Zedong, Ho Chi Minh, and Ayatollah Khomeini.

Traitors in American History

http://americanhistory.about.com/od/traitors/

Created by About.com, this site features links to information about several traitors, including Aldrich Ames, Benedict Arnold, and Julius and Ethel Rosenberg.

Women Criminals

http://womenshistory.about.com/od/criminals/

Part of About.com, this page provides links to biographies of several notorious female criminals, including Lizzie Borden, Ma Barker, Salome, and Mary Surratt.

—*Rebecca Kuzins*

Great Lives from History

Indexes

CATEGORY INDEX

LIST OF CATEGORIES

Geographical Index

PERSONAGES INDEX

TAKOMA PARK MD LIBRARY

3 9803 10037283 0

39803100372830

R   071213
364.1092   Notorious lives
NOTORIO
V: 3   TAKOMA PARK MD

DISCARDED